Dordogne
Berry-Limousin

S. Sauvignier/MICHELIN

... by the Auvézère
Poppies and day's eyes and the green émail
Rose over us; and we knew that stream,
And our two horses had traced the valleys;
Knew the low flooded lands squared out with poplars,
In the young days when the deep sky befriended.

Ezra Pound (1885-1972)
Near Périgord

Travel Publications

MICHELIN TYRE PLC
38 Clarendon Road – WATFORD Herts WD1 1 SX – U.K.
Tel. (01923) 415 000
www.michelin-travel.com

Manufacture française des pneumatiques Michelin
Société en commandite par actions au capital de 2 000 000 000 de francs
Place des Carmes-Déchaux – 63000 Clermont-Ferrand (France)
R.C.S. Clermont-Fd B 855 200 507

Typesetting: NORD COMPO, Villeneuve d'Ascq
Printing and binding : I.M.E., Baume-les-Dames

Cover Design: Agence Carré Noir à Paris 17ᵉ

THE GREEN GUIDE:
The Spirit of Discovery

The exhilaration of new horizons, the fun of seeing the world, the excitement of discovery: this is what we seek to share with you. To help you make the most of your travel experience, we offer first-hand knowledge and turn a discerning eye on places to visit.

This wealth of information gives you the expertise to plan your own enriching adventure. With THE GREEN GUIDE showing you the way, you can explore new destinations with confidence or rediscover old ones.

Leisure time spent with THE GREEN GUIDE is also a time for refreshing your spirit and enjoying yourself.

So turn the page and open a window on the world. Join THE GREEN GUIDE in the spirit of discovery.

Contents

St-Céré: Artful half-timbering

J. Damase/MICHELIN

Joseph's Dream: window in Bourges Cathedral

S. Sauvignier/MICHELIN

Practical information

Trip in a gabare near La Roche-Gageac

Ripe red strawberries from Périgord

Maps
and plans

COMPANION PUBLICATIONS

Regional and detailed maps

To make the most of your journey, travel with Michelin maps at a scale of 1:200 000: Regional maps nos 233, 234, 235, 238 and 239 and the detailed maps nos 64, 65, 68, 69, 72, 73, 75, 76 and 79.

Maps of France

And remember to travel with the latest edition of the **map of France no 989**, which gives an overall view of the region of Provence, and the main access roads which connect it to the rest of France. The entire country is mapped at A 1:1 000 000 scale and clearly shows the main road network. Convenient Atlas formats (spiral, hard cover and "mini") are also available.

Internet

Michelin is pleased to offer a route-planning service on the Internet: **www. michelin-travel. com.** Choose the shortest route, a route without tolls, or the Michelin recommended route to your destination; you can also access information about hotels and restaurants from The Red Guide, and tourists sites from The Green Guide.

There are a number of useful maps and plans in the guide, listed on the following page.

Bon voyage!

Thematic maps

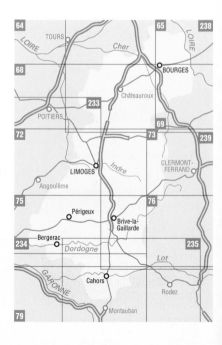

Using this guide

● The summary maps on the following pages are designed to assist you in planning your trip: the **Map of principal sights** identifies major sights and attractions, the **Touring programmes** propose regional driving itineraries and the **Places to stay map** points out pleasant holiday spots.

● We recommend that you read the **Introduction** before setting out on your trip. The background information it contains on history, the arts and traditional culture will prove most instructive and make your visit more meaningful.

● The main towns and attractions are presented in alphabetical order in the **Sights** section. In order to ensure quick, easy identification, original place names have been used throughout the guide. The clock symbol ⊙, placed after monuments or other sights, refers to the **Admission times and charges** section at the end of the guide, in which the names appear in the same order as in the Sights section.

● The **Practical information** section offers useful information for planning your trip, seeking accommodation, indulging in outdoor activities and more; opening hours and admission prices for monuments, museums and other tourist attractions; festival and carnival dates; suggestions for thematic tours on scenic railways and through nature reserves, and more.

● The **Index** lists attractions, famous people and events, and other subjects covered in the guide.

Let us hear from you. We are interested in your reaction to our guide, in any ideas you have to offer or good addresses you would like to share. Send your comments to Michelin Travel Publications, 38 Clarendon Road, Watford, Herts WD 1 1SX, U.K. or by e-mail to The Green Guide-uk@uk.michelin.com.

J. Vertut

Key

Tourism

⊘	Admission Times and Charges listed at the end of the guide
◉ ⇒	Sightseeing route with departure point indicated
♠ ♦ ♠ ♦	Ecclesiastical building
⬚ ⌣	Synagogue – Mosque
▭	Building (with main entrance)
■	Statue, small building
♱	Wayside cross
◎	Fountain
●–●–■	Fortified walls – Tower – Gate

►►	Visit if time permits
AZ B	Map co-ordinates locating sights
🛈	Tourist information
⊨ ⁂	Historic house, castle – Ruins
∪ ☼	Dam – Factory or power station
☆ ∩	Fort – Cave
⋔	Prehistoric site
▼ Ⱳ	Viewing table – View
▲	Miscellaneous sight

Recreation

🏇	Racecourse
⛸	Skating rink
≋ ▦	Outdoor, indoor swimming pool
⛵	Marina, moorings
⌂	Mountain refuge hut
□–■–■–□	Overhead cable-car
🚂	Tourist or steam railway

🚶	Waymarked footpath
♦	Outdoor leisure park/centre
🎢	Theme/Amusement park
⚥	Wildlife/Safari park, zoo
⊛	Gardens, park, arboretum
◒	Aviary, bird sanctuary

Additional symbols

═══ ══	Motorway (unclassified)
❶ ❶	Junction: complete, limited
⊨══	Pedestrian street
⌶ ⌶ ⌶ ⌶	Unsuitable for traffic, street subject to restrictions
⋯⋯ ⋯⋯	Steps – Footpath
🚆 🚌	Railway – Coach station
□⊢⊢⊢⊢□	Funicular – Rack-railway
—•— ⊙	Tram – Metro, Underground
Bert (R.)...	Main shopping street

⊠ ⊚	Post office – Telephone centre
⊠	Covered market
⁺✕⁺	Barracks
△	Swing bridge
∪ ✕	Quarry – Mine
Ⓑ Ⓕ	Ferry (river and lake crossings)
⛴	Ferry services: Passengers and cars
⛵	Foot passengers only
③	Access route number common to MICHELIN maps and town plans

Abbreviations and special symbols

A	Agricultural office (Chambre d'agriculture)		**P**	Local authority offices (Préfecture, sous-préfecture)
C	Chamber of commerce (Chambre de commerce)		**POL.**	Police station (Police)
H	Town hall (Hôtel de ville)		🛡	Police station (Gendarmerie)
J	Law courts (Palais de justice)		**T**	Theatre (Théâtre)
M	Museum (Musée)		**U**	University (Université)
			❸	Hotel

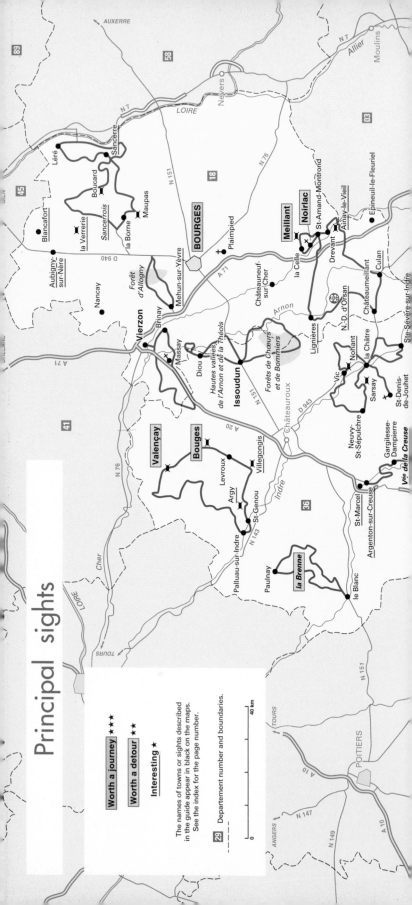

Principal sights

Worth a journey ★★★

Worth a detour ★★

Interesting ★

The names of towns or sights described
in the guide appear in black on the maps.
See the index for the page number.

29 Departement number and boundaries.

0   40 km

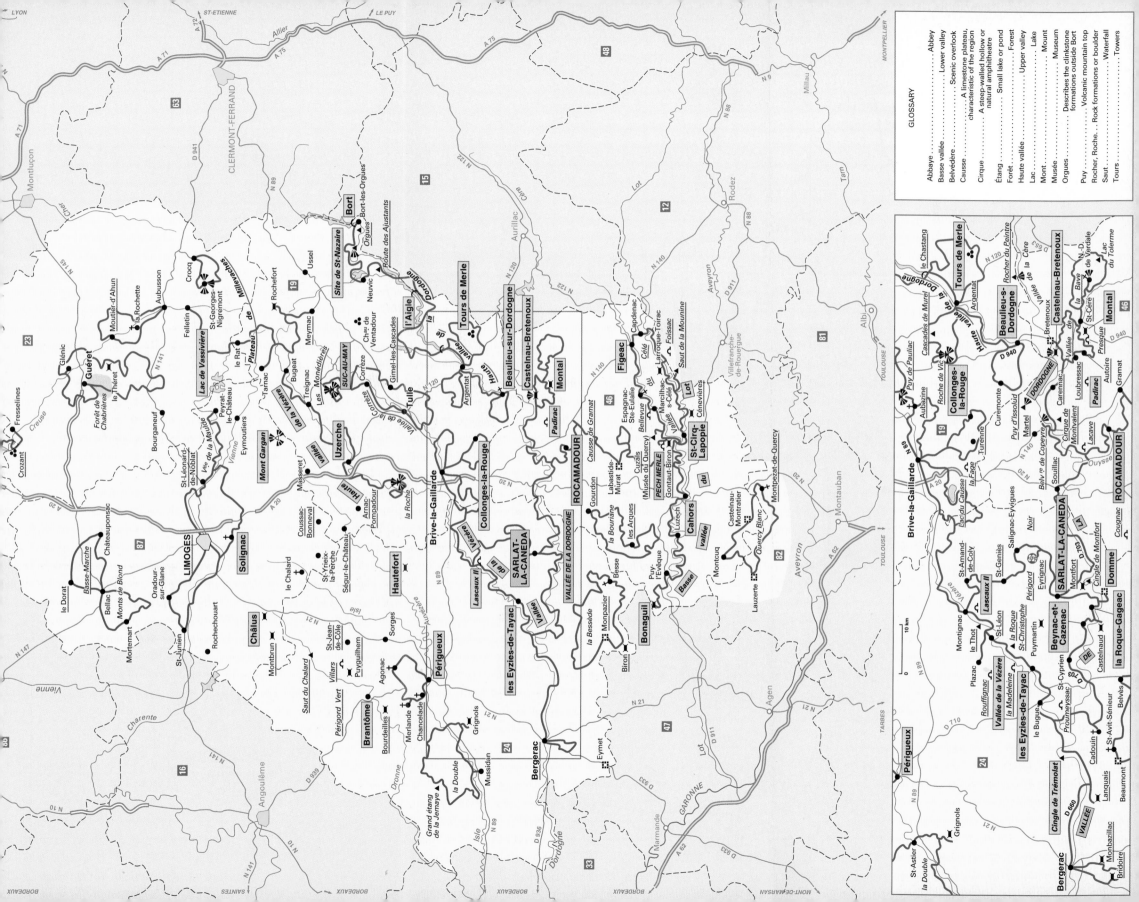

Touring programmes

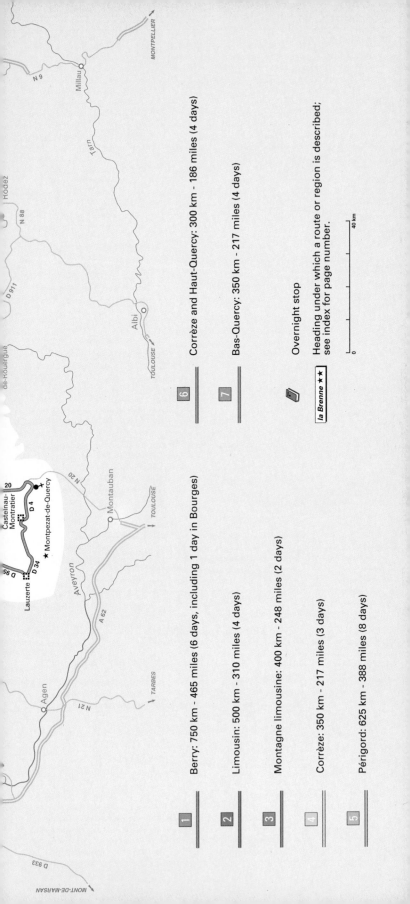

1 Berry: 750 km - 465 miles (6 days, including 1 day in Bourges)

2 Limousin: 500 km - 310 miles (4 days)

3 Montagne limousine: 400 km - 248 miles (2 days)

4 Corrèze: 350 km - 217 miles (3 days)

5 Périgord: 625 km - 388 miles (8 days)

6 Corrèze and Haut-Quercy: 300 km - 186 miles (4 days)

7 Bas-Quercy: 350 km - 217 miles (4 days)

Overnight stop

la Brenne ★★ Heading under which a route or region is described; see index for page number.

0 — 40 km

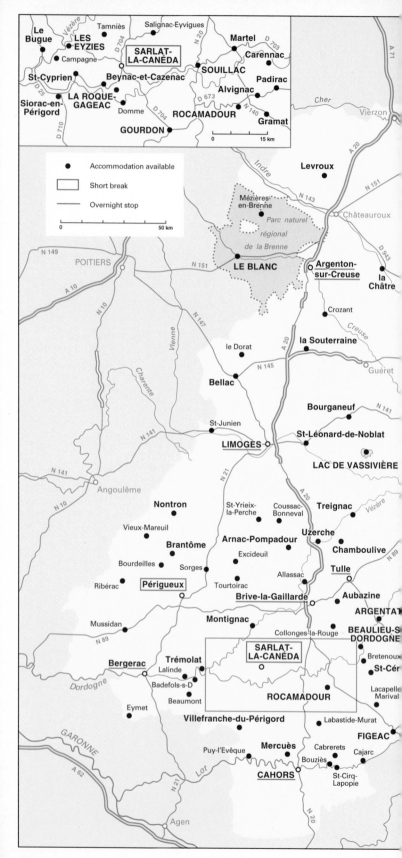

Inset map (Sarlat-la-Canéda area):

Le Bugue
Tamniès
Salignac-Eyvigues
LES EYZIES
Martel
Campagne
SARLAT-LA-CANÉDA
Carennac
SOUILLAC
St-Cyprien
Beynac-et-Cazenac
Padirac
Alvignac
LA ROQUE-GAGEAC
Siorac-en-Périgord
Domme
ROCAMADOUR
Gramat
GOURDON

0   15 km

Vézère
D 704
D 20
D 703
Cher
Vierzon
D 673
N 140
D 710
D 25

Legend:
● Accommodation available
▢ Short break
─ Overnight stop

0   50 km

Main map:

Levroux
Mézières-en-Brenne
Châteauroux
Parc naturel régional de la Brenne
POITIERS
LE BLANC
Argenton-sur-Creuse
la Châtre
Crozant
la Souterraine
le Dorat
Creuse
Guéret
Bellac
Bourganeuf
St-Junien
St-Léonard-de-Noblat
LIMOGES
LAC DE VASSIVIÈRE
Angoulême
Nontron
St-Yrieix-la-Perche
Coussac-Bonneval
Treignac
Vieux-Mareuil
Brantôme
Arnac-Pompadour
Uzerche
Chamboulive
Bourdeilles
Excideuil
Sorges
Allassac
Tulle
Ribérac
Périgueux
Tourtoirac
Brive-la-Gaillarde
Aubazine
ARGENTAT
Mussidan
Montignac
Collonges-la-Rouge
BEAULIEU-SUR-DORDOGNE
Bergerac
Trémolat
SARLAT-LA-CANÉDA
Bretenoux
Lalinde
St-Céré
Badefols-s-D
Lacapelle-Marival
Beaumont
ROCAMADOUR
Eymet
Villefranche-du-Périgord
Labastide-Murat
FIGEAC
Puy-l'Evêque
Mercuès
Cabrerets
Cajarc
Bouziès
CAHORS
St-Cirq-Lapopie
Agen

Indre
N 143
N 151
N 149
A 10
N 10
N 151
N 147
Vienne
N 145
A 20
N 141
Charente
N 141
N 21
Vézère
A 20
N 89
GARONNE
Dordogne
Lot
A 62
N 20
N 89

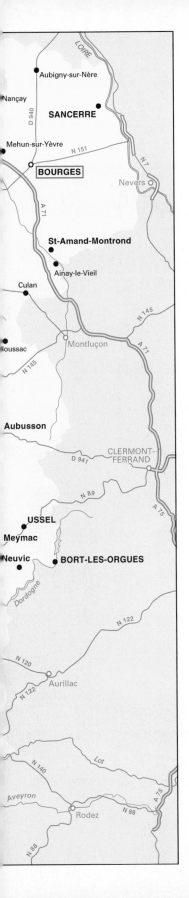

LOCAL WORDS
AND SPECIAL TERMS

Arcvôlt: a covered passage in the towns and villages of Quercy

Barri or **barry**: a settlement outside the town walls

Bastide: fortified town of the 13C

Bolet: porch=staircase characteristic of houses in Quercy

Boride: dry=stone hut

Cabecou: small goat cheese

Caselle: dry-stone hut

Causse: limestone plateau

Caveur: truffle hunter

Chabrol: soup with wine added

Chartreuse: 17-18C noble or bourgeois house with one storey

Cingle: meander (from the Latin word *cingula* meaning belt), loop or bend found in the Lot and Dordogne Valleys

Cloup: depression in the *causse*

Cluzeau: shelter dug into the cliff

Cornière or **couvert**: arcaded gallery

Gariotte: dry-stone shelter

Igue: wells or natural chasms in limestone countryside formed by the dissolving action of water or the caving-in of the roof of a cave; known as *edzes* or *eidges* in Périgord

Jarrissade (or **garrissade**): typical *causse* vegetation consisting of clumps of stunted oak trees and extensive open spaces

Lauzes: limestone slabs used as roofing material

Pech or **puy**: small hill topped with limestone cliffs

Ribeyre: a valley in Quercy

Segala: arid plateau with acidic soil which supports the cultivation only of rye (*seigle*); opposite to ground suited to the cultivation of wheat (*fromental*)

Soleilho: open space under the eaves of houses in Quercy, used for drying laundry, storing wood etc

Sotch: large hollow (enlarged *cloup*)

11

Introduction

Landscapes

ADMINISTRATIVE DIVISIONS

The *Région* (there are 22 in France) is the largest administrative division, followed by the *département* (96, exclusive of overseas territories), which is divided into *arrondissements*; each of these is further split into *cantons* and finally *communes* which are run by an elected mayor. There are 36 394 mayoralties in France.

Berry (formerly *Berri*) is the name historically and popularly applied to the area south of the Paris basin, comprising the *départements* of Cher and Indre *(Région Centre)*. This old county, later a duchy, came under the crown in the 13C.

Limousin is the name of an administrative *Région* which includes three *départements:* Corrèze, Creuse, Haute-Vienne. Long an Anglo-Norman fief, it was united to the French throne by Henry IV, and later administered by appointed *Intendants*.

Dordogne is a *département*, part of the larger *Région* of Aquitaine. The French *départements* were created in 1790, and generally given the name of the main river within the territory, hence, "Dordogne". Before that time, the same area was known as **Périgord** (named after the Petrocorii who lived there at the time of the Gauls), a free county dating back to the 11C, which fell into the possession of the Albret family. Henry IV, its last feudal lord, brought it under the authority of the French crown. Many French people still use the old appellation to refer to this popular holiday destination, especially when evoking its culinary delights.

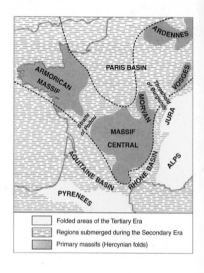

Folded areas of the Tertiary Era

Regions submerged during the Secondary Era

Primary massifs (Hercynian folds)

FORMATION OF THE LAND

Primary Era – This began about 600 million years ago. It was towards the end of this era that an upheaval of the earth's crust took place. This upheaval or folding movement, known as the "Hercynian fold", the V-shaped appearance of which is shown by dotted lines on the map, resulted in the emergence of a number of high mountains, notably the Massif Central, formed by crystalline rocks which were slowly worn down by erosion.

Secondary Era – This began about 260 million years ago. Towards the middle of this era, there was a slow folding of the Hercynian base and the seas then flooded the area. Sedimentary deposits, mainly calcareous, from the sea, accumulated on the edge of the Massif Central, forming the Quercy causses (limestone plateaux) during the Jurassic period and then the beds of Cretaceous limestone of the Périgord region. The same types of formations are also found in Champagne Berrichonne, Boischaut and Sancerre.

Tertiary Era – This began about 65 million years ago. During this period siderolithic deposits (clay and gravel, rich in iron) originating from the Massif Central covered some parts of Quercy, such as the Bouriane region, whereas clay-rich sands accumulated to the west of Périgord, creating the heathlands dotted with lakes (Brenne, Sologne, Double and Landais regions).

Quaternary Era – This began about 2 million years ago. It was during this period that human evolution went forward. The effects of erosion had by now given the region its present appearance. Rivers emanating from the catchment area of the Massif Central had created the Vézère, Dordogne and Lot valleys.

The countryside today – Regions which are totally different in character lie side by side in the area between Berry and the plains of Agenais. This region of contrasting countrysides is one of great natural beauty: the wide horizons of Berry succeeded by the green mountain country of Limousin; the limestone plateaux of Quercy stretching out in stark silhouette; the wooded plateaux of Périgord divided by picturesque valleys and rich orchard country.

The works of local inhabitants from the earliest prehistoric shelter to the most modern dam also merit the attention of a visitor. Rich in prehistoric sites, the area has many visible traces of the earliest settlers. The religious buildings ranging from charming churches to the solid sanctuaries of Limousin and the hundreds of fortresses, castles, manors and mansions in a variety of architectural styles are witness to the rich historical past of the region. Further to this are thoughts of savoury cuisine and local wines, adding enticement to a tour.

BERRY

This province is one of the oldest agricultural regions in France. Its unity is a result of shared heritage, rather than geography. The geological position of Berry forms the contact zone between the Paris Basin and the Massif Central. Berry consists of a vast low-lying plateau, rising in the northeast to the Sancerre Hills (the Humbligny Beacon 434m/1 424 ft) and tilting westwards in a series of steps towards the Brenne depression. In the south the countryside is more undulating with many isolated hills and escarpments. The Cher and Indre rivers belong to the Loire drainage system whereas the Creuse is a tributary of the Vienne.

Northern Berry – The **Pays Fort** and **Sancerrois** are transitional areas bordering the Loire country. The former with its marl and clay soils slopes towards the Sologne whereas the latter's vine-covered, chalk slopes rise above the river banks. This once-forested landscape has been remodelled as *bocage* (wooded farmland). The Allogny Forest, the last important outpost of the primitive forest cover, overlooks the vast orchards of St-Martin-d'Auxigny.

Northern Boischaut is an area of rich grazing lands.

Southern Berry – **Champagne Berrichonne** is a plateau region with limestone soil which extends between the Loire in the east and the Indre in the west; scattered woods and forests cover much of it. Manure and rich fertilisers have made this light, sandy soil into excellent farm land. In addition to grain crops, Normandy dairy cows and sheep are kept inside and fed on beetroot pulp; bee-keeping is an important economic activity around Châteauroux. Away to the east, the **Vale of Germigny** is a long depression, formerly marshland, which runs along the foot of the escarpments crowned by the Meillant Wood. The grazing pastures have become the territory of the Charolais cattle.

Boischaut – This district lies between the Cher and the Creuse and its clay soils overlap the neighbouring Marche province. This is an area of small farms concentrating on livestock rearing, in particular the Charolais breed and sheep.
The countryside, criss-crossed with many rivers, farms and gardens, is much the same as when described by the novelist George Sand *(see NOHANT)*.

Brenne – This is a vast depression with sand and clay soils where pools and marshes abound, amid heather, pine trees and broom. Once the exclusive haven of hunters and fishers, the Brenne is now a nature park, which welcomes tourists interested in observing the exceptional flora and fauna *(see the illustration under La BRENNE)*.

LIMOUSIN

This vast region of crystalline rocks forms the western bastion of the Massif Central. The area takes its name from the Lemovices, the large tribe which occupied the country at the time of the Gauls. The individuality of the region is emphasised by its wet winter climate and the verdant countryside. Limousin has been aptly described by Jérôme and Jean Tharaud in their novel *La Maîtresse Servante*: "Before us unrolled a green and ever changing countryside, silent and impenetrable, cut by thick hedges, filled with dark shadows and watered by running brooks. No rivers, only streams; no lakes, only pools; no ravines, only valleys."

La Montagne – This vast series of plateaux, at altitudes no higher than 977m/3 205ft, has been levelled by erosion. The "Mountain" is the source of many rivers and streams which filter out over the rest of the region. The weather on these highlands is rugged, the rains heavy, the winds strong and snow has been known to lie on the ground for four months at a time. Farms are few and far between and stony wastes and moors are more common than ploughed land, particularly on the Millevaches Plateau *(see Plateau des MILLEVACHES)* and in the Monédières Massif *(see Les MONÉDIÈRES)*. Passing through this eerily quiet landscape, the traveller gazes upon sheep, moors, an occasional meadow, woodlands of beech and pine.

The Plateaux of Haut-Limousin – The northwest plateaux form an undulating area – **Ambazac** and **Blond Hills** – with alternating escarpments and deeply incised valleys. The *bocage* is a patchwork of woods and fields. Trees thrive with the wet climate; oak and beech on the uplands and chestnut trees lower down. Quickset hedges surround fields and meadows. The pastures enriched by manure and artificial fertilisers make good cattle grazing country. Further north, the drier less wooded **Marche** area is a marshland between the Massif Central and the Loire country. The **Haute-Marche**, drained by the Creuse, is an area of stock rearing whereas arable farming prevails in the **Basse-Marche**, around Bellac.
To the west the **Confolentais** is the name given to these foothills of the Massif Central, green and forested, crossed by the river Vienne.

The Plateaux of Bas-Limousin – This area, where the influence of Périgord and Quercy may already be seen, is characterised by a greater luminosity, milder climate and fertile basins. The **Xaintrie** is an area alternating with pine and silver birch woods. This granite plateau is deeply incised by the Dordogne, the Maronne and numerous other rivers.
The depression of the **Brive Basin** straddles lower Limousin and the northernmost part of Périgord. The **Nontronnais** is also partly in Limousin, and largely resembles it: grassy fields, chestnut trees, heather and gorse, isolated farm houses.

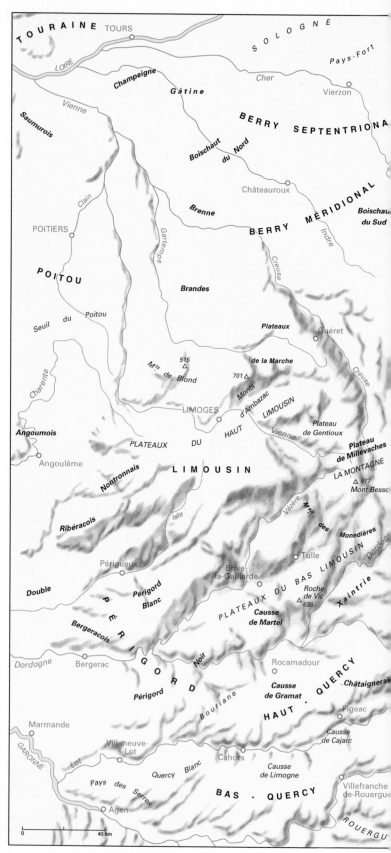

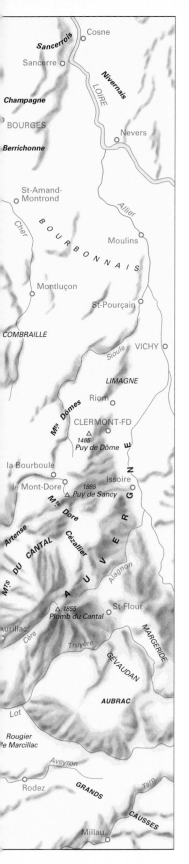

Brive Basin – The depression of the Brive Basin is a sunken zone between the crystalline escarpments of the Uzerche plateau and the limestone ridges of the Quercy *causses*. It is an area made of sandstone and schist, drained by the rivers Vézère and Corrèze. In the green valleys segmented by screens of poplars, the gentle slopes facing the sun are given over to orchards. Today Brive is an important centre for canning fruits and vegetables.

South of Brive, the **Corrèze causse** is covered with large holdings which are used for sheep rearing, truffle oak plantations and gaggles of geese.

PERIGORD

Périgord Vert – Between the Nontronnais and Excideuil is Périgord Vert (*vert = green*), made up of fragments of the old massif, small basins scoured out of the soft Lias marl and a few limestone tables. Its landscape of woodlands, well-tended farms and patches of bright sunflowers echoes the neighbouring Limousin. The handful of towns scattered across this lush borderland provide the link between light industry and the marketing of farm products.

Périgord Blanc – "White" Périgord is thus named because of the frequent outcrops of chalky limestone, which bleach the light in this open landscape. Contrasting colours are provided by pastures where dairy cattle and calves (for veal) take their leisure, especially around Ribérac, and fields for cereal crops. Numerous agricultural markets are held in the local towns.

Central Périgord – The countryside of hills and slopes around Périgueux consists of meadows interspersed with coppices of oak and chestnut trees. This region is drained by the rivers Beauronne, Vern and Dronne, and the river valley bottoms are covered with pasture and arable land; the large Isle valley is scattered with small industrial towns and the alluvial soil is used as pasture, or for growing maize (corn), tobacco or walnuts. South of Périgeux around Vergt and Rouffignac, the siderolithic deposits (rich in iron) which cover the limestone have proven to be an ideal soil for strawberries, which are exported to all parts of France.

Northeast, Central Périgord meets the **Périgord Causse**. This block of Jurassic limestone, scored by the Isle, Auvézère and Loue valleys, exhibits sparse vegetation. At the foot of the characteristic stunted oaks, the most aromatic truffles hide away from all but the most skilled seekers.

Double and Landais regions – Lying in the west between the rivers Dronne and Isle the **Double** is an area of forests where tall oak and chestnut trees predominate. The clay soil favours the formation of ponds. The **Landais** lying to the south of the Isle is a less rugged region where fruit trees flourish. The chestnut gives way to the maritime pine and meadows become more abundant.

Bergerac region – The region around Bergerac is divided into several sections, all of which share a mild climate favourable to southern crops. The Dordogne valley, very wide at this point, is divided into plots of land where tobacco, maize (corn), sunflowers and cereals flourish in the rich alluvial deposits.

West of Bergerac, arboriculture predominates. The slopes are covered with the vineyards of Bergerac and Monbazillac.

Bergerac holds an important position in the tobacco and wine industries.

Périgord Noir – Cut across by the Vézère and Dordogne valleys this area owes its name (*noir* = black) to the great density of trees growing in the sandy soil covering the limestone areas, and also to the predominence of the holm oak with its dark, dense foliage, particularly in the area around Sarlat. The alluvial soil of the valleys, whose river courses are lined with screens of poplars or willows, supports a variety of crops: wheat, maize (corn), tobacco and walnuts. The lively and prosperous markets sell excellent nuts, mushrooms, truffles and *foie gras*. In the limestone areas resurgent springs, grottoes with concretions, caves and shelters with sculpted or painted walls all attract tourists. Along the river Dordogne landscapes are gentle and harmonious, as seen from the viewpoints of the Domme Barre and Beynac and Castelnaud castles. The former capital of Périgord Noir, Sarlat-la-Canéda, with its *lauze* roofs and medieval atmosphere, is a lively tourist centre *(see photograph introducing Practical information, at the end of the guide)*.

South of the Dordogne – Vast stretches of gently undulating molassic hillside, with limestone outcrops forming terraces here and there, extend beyond the wine-producing slopes of Monbazillac. Small farms interspersed with woodlands are planted with cereal crops, vineyards (AOC Bergerac) and plum trees. Towards the east, making the transition with the Bouriane region in Quercy, is the thick forest of **Bessède**, which flourishes on the millstone or siderolithic sands, hardly disturbed at all by the foundation of bastides and abbeys during the Middle Ages.

QUERCY

Quercy corresponds to the region which stretches from the Massif Central to the plains of Aquitaine and was occupied by the Cadurques who made Cahors their capital. The region has a strong historical unity. In the Middle Ages Quercy belonged to the province of Guyenne. Under the *Ancien Régime* two regions were recognised, the Haut-Quercy, centred on Cahors and seat of the main administrative departments and Bas-Quercy, depending on Montauban. During the Revolution they were reunited under the Lot *département*. However in 1808 Napoleon separated them again, creating the *département* of Tarn-et-Garonne which covers most of Bas-Quercy, and parts of Rouergue, Gascony and Languedoc.

The Causses – This dry land with no drainage is cut across by dry valleys (known locally as *combes*). Flocks of sheep graze on the sparse grass of the pastures which are sub-divided by dry stone dikes. Stunted oaks and maple are the only trees. In the valleys there are temporary pastures, vineyards and other crops.

The **Martel Causse** is a vast arid plain covered in stones, which is crossed by a relatively fertile zone. The many dry stone dikes were built by shepherds as they cleared stones from the ground to allow sheep to graze and marked out boundaries. It takes its name from Martel, a large agricultural town where sheep skins are sold.

The **Gramat Causse**, a great limestone plateau, at an average altitude of 350m/1 150 ft offers many natural phenomena *(see Gouffre de PADIRAC)* and unusual landscapes. Magnificent canyons break the monotonous but grand horizons: in the north lie the Ouysse and Alzou Canyons (the spectacular village of Rocamadour clings to the cliff face); in the south the much longer Célé Canyon. Between the narrow gashes of the Alzou and the Célé lies the waterless **Braunhie**. This arid region is riddled with caves and ravines. The towns of Gramat and Labastide-Murat have suffered from the rural exodus.

The **Carjac Causse**, a low lying plateau, is hemmed in by the banks of the Célé and Lot rivers, whose meanders are richly cultivated.

The **Limogne Causse** with its drier climate has a very different appearance. Bordered by the valley of the Lot, the plateau is dotted with dolmens and megaliths which appear amid the clumps of white truffle oaks, the juniper shrubs and the fields of lavender. Here and there are to be found the curious shepherd's shelters built of flat stones with strange conical roofs, known as *garriottes*, *cazelles*, or *bories (see photograph of Cabanes de Breuil, under SARLAT, Excursions)*. There are few big towns, although Limogne-en-Quercy and Lalbenque remain the busiest centres of the truffle market.

The valleys – Cutting deeply into the hard limestone, the rivers have carved out their valleys, shaping meanders which enlarge as the valley broadens, to the point that they become ever widening *cingles* – loops in the river's course.

These valleys of the Dordogne, Célé and Lot have been inhabited since prehistoric times. In the Roman era, settlers lived in fortified *oppidums;* castles and châteaux bear witness to the role of these valleys in the region's later history. Today, they are richly covered with crops, vineyards and orchards, and people live in towns such as Souillac (Dordogne valley), Figeac (Célé) and Cahors (Lot).

Landscape of the lower Lot valley

Haut-Quercy – Limestone plateaux or causses with an average altitude of 300m/1 000 ft form the greater part of Haut-Quercy. The fertile areas known as **Limargue** and **Terrefort**, are spread out in flat basins and over vast plains; the soils of the region favour the production of a variety of crops including greengage plums and strawberries (between Carennac and St-Céré), grapes, walnut and tobacco. The eastern part of Haut-Quercy also embraces the **Châtaigneraie**, an area with a cold, damp climate and poor soils. This plateau at an altitude of 700m/2 300 ft tilts to the east and is cut by deep gorges. The widely cultivated chestnut tree has given the area its name; cereal crops are grown on the lowering hilltops and cattle raised on small farms. The **Bouriane** is blanketed in heath, coppices and woods, bearing more resemblance to Périgord than Quercy. Here, maritime pines are tapped for resin, timber, chestnuts and walnuts are harvested, and livestock raised and sold. The capital of this area is Gourdon.

Quercy Blanc – Southwest of the Lot Valley and Cahors, the Jurassic limestone disappears under the tertiary limestone creating unusual landscapes, *planhès*, vast undulating white areas which have given the region the name Quercy Blanc. These plateaux are cut into narrow ridges, *serres*, by the rivers. The crests of the *serres* are levelled off into plains which are covered with sheep-grazing grazing pastures and oak forests and, when the soil becomes argillaceous, rich crops. Between the *serres*, the valleys are fertile corridors, spreading between the sandstone as they get closer to the Garonne. Pastures lined with poplars produce abundant crops of fruit, cereals and tobacco and support vineyards as well. The towns of Montcuq, Lauzerte, Castelnau-Montratier, Montpezat-de-Quercy are all situated on *puechs*, rocky hilltops; they have lively market days.

FLORA AND FAUNA IN BERRY-LIMOUSIN

Water

The region has a dense network of rivers and streams. In Limousin, the rivers tumble through picturesque valleys, whereas in Berry they flow more peacefully. With a few exceptions (near urban areas), the waters are pure and clean, harbouring many species of fish. The region is covered in natural ponds and wetlands as well as man-made lakes, abundant in flora and fauna.

La Brenne – This nature park represents the regional commitment to the preservation of wetlands and their ecosystems, and to the development of "green" tourism. The hundreds of ponds and the diversity of habitats make it an ideal refuge for many species, including a host of migrating birds. *(See La BRENNE for further details and illustrations of local wildlife.)*

Wetlands in perspective – The terrestrial ecosystems characterised by the presence most or all of the time of sluggishly moving water or saturated soil, have been making headlines in recent years, as their importance in maintaining ecological balance has been highlighted. The protection of these often fragile areas has led to a better understanding of their morphology.

I. Wet meadows – The outer ring of the pond system, these meadows of variable size are often gay with wildflowers in the springtime. The flora is diverse and in La Brenne includes as many as 50 species: marsh violets, gentian, orchids, etc.

II. Swamps – The waterlogged banks of the many ponds are invaded by willows which form groves extending from the water's edge to firmer ground. The trees provide nesting for green-winged teal; the branches dipping in the water protect paddling ducks; the grey heron and the black-crowned night-heron gather beneath them. The muddy banks are teeming with mollusks which attract waders: black-tailed godwits, curlews, crested lapwings, snipe. Partially submerged plant life includes perennial herbs, quillwort, clovers and ferns.

III. Marshes – Plant life in the mineral-rich soil is dominated by grasses in many forms: sedge, reeds, cattails, bulrushes. Impenetrable, considered undesirable for fish hatcheries, these grassy areas are essential to the survival of certain rare species. Waders such as bitterns and other members of the heron family build their nests in these protected zones, alongside marsh harriers, and other perching birds which alight on reeds and rushes (millerbirds, swamp sparrows, reed-buntings).

IV. Ponds – Floating plants make good nests for crested grebes; black and striped terns glide over the water. Many species of duck are found: mallard, pintail (wide, spatula-shaped bills), canvas-backs, grey ducks, and more; osprey stop to rest on their migratory flight.

European pond turtles are shy little creatures, living off water lilies and sunbathing by the reeds. Insects are everywhere, as many as 600 to 1000 species can be identified. Snakes, frogs, toads and newts and some rare mammals have been spotted, including a remarkable sighting of the European mink, at the Ricot pond (Chérine reserve) in 1982.

In the **lakes and rivers** of Limousin, an abundance of fish makes for popular sport: the Creuse is a favourite for trout, while the Gartempe is known for carp. In the racing, oxygen-rich waters of rivers, trout, grayling and other fish from the salmon family swim. In still waters, look for freshwater fishes (carps, barbels, tenches, breams, goldfishes, chubs, dace, shiners). Some of the fish grow to considerable size, such as varieties of pike and perch. *For more details on fishing and other water sports, see Practical information, at the end of this guide.*

Moors and forests

Moorland, peatland – The Brenne is poor in pastureland, and has been gradually abandoned by its rural population, so that the few tilled fields have mostly given way to idle, uncultivated land. The humid ground is covered with besom heather, a tall bushy plant with greenish-white flowers. On drier ground, gorse, Scotch broom and bracken grow beneath a few isolated trees. Birds of prey circle overhead: kingfishers, harriers, hawks. Wildlife rustles in the undergrowth: hare, boar, deer, badger, genet. In Limousin, the high plateaux with their vast granite depressions (Millevaches, Gentioux) have highly acidic soil, where sphagnum moss flourishes, and parts of the countryside have developed into peat bogs. Near Meymac, a protected bog, *la tourbière du Longéroux*, harbours the source of the Vézère.

Peat is made by the slow decomposition of organic materials (especially sphagnum) in cold, acidic water. The process takes centuries. In Longéroux, where the average thickness of the peat is 2m/6.5ft, the analysis of fossilised pollen shows that the deposits began forming 8000 years ago. The bog's inhabitants include lizards, snakes, toads, frogs, newts, and the birds who prey on them, as well as the elusive otter, whose presence can often only be deduced by its spoor.

The granite hills around the site are drier, covered with common heather and fuzzy broom and scattered bilberry bushes. But indigenous deciduous trees (birch, ash) have been disappearing as uncontrolled growth runs amok.

The Forest – In the 19C, State forests began operating a coppice-with-standards system: selected stems are retained, as standards, at each felling to form an unevenly-aged canopy which is harvested selectively. The forest is managed so that part of the growth is natural, and part of seedling origin, together forming a composite forest. The Indre *département*, one of the first to use this method, has become a leading producer of oakwood for panelling. The **Châteauroux forest** (5 204ha/13 000 acres) and the **Bommiers Forest** (4 470ha/11 000 acres) are remarkable examples of successful forestry: The dark, low-acid soil has produced a seedling forest of English oak, growing alongside plantations of hornbeam and ash, with ferns growing low to the ground. Boar, deer, martens, skunks, squirrels and wild cats wander the reserve, and the bird population includes wood pigeons and woodpeckers.

Beech

Spruce

To the north, the acidic, wet soil of the Boischaut is home to birch (Gâtine forest); oak and beech are found in the Marche, while pubescent oak grow on the limestone plateaux in the southwest of Indre. On the highest plateaux of Limousin, conifers have multiplied: spruce, larch, and pines have replaced meadows of heather or fields of grain crops.

To the south, and on the borders of Périgord, deciduous hardwood forests prevail on the sunny slopes. Chestnut trees, which are native to the region, are cultivated for their nuts.

A walk in the woods will tempt those who love **mushrooms** to keep their eyes down and carry a long stick. King bolete *(Boletus edulis)*, bay bolete *(Boletus badius)*, chanterelle *(cantharellus cibarius)*, yellow morel *(Morchella esculenta)* are just a few of the species a careful hunter can uncover. Beware of "toadstools", poisonous varieties which may have toxic, or even fatal effects on gatherers. In the French countryside, many pharmacists are able to identify edible mushrooms, so have your basket checked before firing up the stove.

Fields and bocage

The northernmost area covered in this guide, the **Champagne Berrichonne** is an open land of large, tilled fields. The grain crops attract many birds. Yet just south of this area, in the **Boischaut-Sud** and parts of **La Brenne**, a very different, more secretive landscape offers itself to the traveller. Here the timeworn marks of man on nature are like the lines etched in a country farmer's face. The landscape known as *bocage* is one of hedges and hedgerows, groves of trees, small plots of land and protected pastures.

The labyrinth is further outlined by *chemins creux*, pathways which feel like tunnels, laid out between high banks topped with vegetation. It seems as though one could wander unobserved into a previous century by following such a country lane. Then the past rationality of this landscape would be revealed: the deep lanes prevented erosion (although they are now too narrow for tractors, and overgrown); prickly bushes held tight in climbing vines kept the animals safely enclosed; trees provided wood for cooking and making tools; the leaves of elm trees could be used as fodder. *(See ST-AMAND-MONTROND for itineraries through this region.)*

Chestnut

CAVES AND CHASMS IN DORDOGNE

Although dispersed throughout the region, the arid *causse* slices through the otherwise luxuriant landscape of Périgord. In Quercy, the limestone plateaux roll away to the far horizon, stony, grey and deserted. The dryness of the soil is due to the calcereous nature of the rock which absorbs rain like a sponge.

Water infiltration – Rainwater containing carbonic acid dissolves the carbonate of lime found in the limestone. Depressions form; these are **cloups**, which are usually circular in shape and small in size. When the cloups increase in size, they form large, closed depressions known as **sotches**. Where rainwater infiltrates the countless fissures in the plateau more deeply, the hollowing out and dissolution of the calcereous layer produces wells or natural chasms which are called **igues**.

Underground rivers and resurgent springs – Infiltrating waters eventually reach the impermeable layers (marl) of the earth and there become rivers, sometimes flowing for miles. The waters merge in stronger streams, widen their beds, tumble over falls. In zones where the impermeable marl comes close to the surface of a hillside, the water bubbles up to the surface, sometimes powerfully, in the form of a **resurgent spring**. The circulation of water underground through chasms and galleries follows an unpredictable course, for the cracks in the rock continually affect the underground drainage. There are many dry river beds underground, where waters have sought out deeper domains.

When water flows slowly, as at Padirac, small lakes are formed by natural dams called **gours**. The walls holding back the waters, often shaped like a fanciful festoon, are built up by the deposit of lime carbonate. Dissolution of limestone continues above the water level; blocks of stone fall from the roof, causing domes to form. As the dome pushes upwards and its roof grows thin, it may cave in,

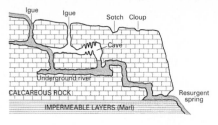

Development of a resurgent spring

opening the chasm to the surface above. The **Gouffre de Padirac** is such a dome; the top of its "ceiling" is only a few feet beneath the surface of the earth.

Cave formations – As it circulates underground, water deposits the lime it carries, building up concretions of fantastic shapes, which seem to defy the laws of gravity. Seeping waters deposit calcite (carbonate of lime) to form pendants, pyramids, draperies, and of course, stalactites, stalagmites and eccentrics.

Stalactites are formed on the roof by water dripping down. The concretion builds up slowly as drops deposit calcite on the surface before falling.

Cave with concretions:
① Stalactites – ② Stalagmites
③ Pilar in formation –
④ Completed pillar

Stalagmites are a sort of mirror image, rising up from the floor below dripping water, and eventually meeting the stalactite above to form a pillar. Such concretions form very slowly: the rate of growth in temperate climates is about 1cm/half an inch every 100 years.

Eccentrics are very delicate protuberances, formed by crystallisation, which seldom exceed 20cm/8in long. They emerge at odd angles, as slender spikes or in the shape of small translucent fans.

From prehistory to modern exploration – The caves and grottoes of Dordogne, providing a natural shelter, were initially inhabited by animals and then by people, who abandoned these abodes about 10 000 years ago.

At the end of the 19C, the methodical and scientific exploration of the underground world led to the discovery of a certain number of caves and their conversion into tourist attractions. But despite significant research, many mysteries still lie beneath the surface of the earth.

The economy

The regional economy has long depended on the agricultural activities, as the scarcity of mineral wealth and raw materials did not allow the establishment of major industrial centres as in northern and eastern France. More recently, investment in a wider range of sectors, inlcuding high technology, tourism, and the development of high-quality culinary and craft products have expanded the region's potential. Communication infrastructures have improved, making the countryside less isolated. And of course, the region's trademark productions still stimulate sales and growth: porcelain (Limoges), foie gras, truffles. For information on regional wines, consult *Food and wine* (at the end of this Introduction) and *Practical information* (at the end of this guide).

AGRICULTURE

Berry

Agriculture has long been the mainstay of the regional economy, although improved road networks have enabled industrial development. Mechanisation and the use of fertilisers also brought about a revolution in **Champagne Berrichonne**, which has become France's second-largest grain-producing region. But there are few processing plants to handle the harvest, and this impedes growth. In the Indre *département*, another handicap is the ageing of the farming population (60% of the working farmers are over the age of 55).

Limousin

Small farms have decreased in number over the years, as elsewhere, while larger more modern establishements have taken their place. In the north, fields are planted with grain crops, whereas the southern areas specialise in orchards, mostly apple.

Périgord-Quercy

The Dordogne *département* is ranked number one producer of **strawberries** (with Lot-et-Garonne) in France, with almost 20 000 tonnes picked annually. Travellers may notice long silvery ribbons of plastic in the fields in the spring. These protect the plants from bad weather and enable them to flower and grow in a controlled environment. The fruit ripens under these sheets before it is picked and packed off to large markets in the Paris region or the north of France, where the Périgord strawberry is particularly appreciated.

Walnuts are another local speciality, harvested in large quantities (5-7 000 tonnes per year), although on the decline. There are still many varieties on the market: Marbot walnuts ripen early and are often sold fresh; Grandjean are produced around Sarlat and Gourdon, accounting for most of the green walnuts; Corne is a small nut of good quality; Franquette is the name of a variety which has recently become popular.

Conditions in Périgord and Quercy, and in all of southwest France are favourable to the growing of **tobacco**. It is a hardy plant, imported from America in the 16C and initially used for medicinal purposes *(see BERGERAC, Musée du Tabac)*. The traditional dark tobacco that long gave French cigarettes their strong, disctinctive flavour and scent now grows side-by-side with lighter varieties such as Virginia tobacco, which have increased in popularity. There are about 3 000 planters in the region, mostly in family-run operations. The Dordogne *département*, with 1 300 planters, produces 15% of all French tobacco, making it the leader.

No discussion of the fruits of the earth in Périgord would be complete without a word about the strange and rare fungus: the **truffle**. It grows secretly underground, at the base of a tree, where it must be sniffed out by specially trained pigs or dogs and their savvy masters. Exchanged on the market for fabulous sums which seem incongruous with their lumpy, dusty appearance, these subterranean delights are not as plentiful as in days of yore: hundreds of tonnes were collected a century ago, while the Dordogne now produces only four tonnes annually. Oak trees have been planted in likely ground in the hope of encouraging renewed growth of the "black diamonds" *(for more details, visit the Maison de la Truffe in Sorges, see BRANTÔME, Excursions)*.

Stock raising

Each province directs its stock raising according to the natural fertility of its soil – rich pastureland provides cattle fodder, the more arid plateaux are suitable for sheep rearing.

The Sheep of Berry and Quercy – Sheep rearing was the only way of earning a living long ago when a lack of money and materials were major obstacles to the improvement of the Berry plains.

The Berry breed is declining in numbers and is being replaced by the English Southdowns or the Charmois breed. Sought after for their meat they are now reared inside in sheepfolds and no longer roam the open pasturelands. Goat herds are also increasing with the production of cheese as the main by-product.

The Causses are an important sheep-rearing centre (with about 300 000 head). The plateau sheep or Gramat species is known as the "spectacled" breed, for they have white fleece and black rings around their eyes. These hardy, prolific animals bear fine wool, but are especially prized for their meat (very little fat). A strict selection is made for ewe-lambs and young rams.

The Limousin breed – Limousin beef-cattle with their short withers and distinctive russet hides were already widely known in the 17 and 18C. Improved by culling and better feeding, the breed now produces some of the finest meat in the world. To supply market requirements, Limousin farmers have turned to the production of young calves for white veal.

Natural features make Limousin a leader in the production and export of both the breed and the meat. The indigenous meadowland has been complemented by specially sown pastures where grass grows more profusely.

Other crafts and industries

The presence of metallic oxides in the Limousin underground needed for the production of enamelware favoured the establishment of an **enamelling industry** in Limoges.

After three centuries of decline, the craft in the last fifty years has regained its reputation which is now as high as it was in the days of such master-enamellers as the Nardon Pénicauds, the Limosins and the Nouailhers.

The discovery at the end of the 18C, of important deposits of kaolin near St-Yrieix, is the basis of the **china industry**. The first factories were scattered in the southern area of Haute-Vienne, the wood needed for the kilns otherwise being liable to city tolls on entry into Limoges. By the end of the 19C, due to improvements in the production processes, porcelain had become a major industry in the city.

Another traditional manufacturing activity is centred around Aubusson, famous for its **tapestries**.

The **leather industry** and its many offshoots developed thanks to abundant water supplies, tanning resins from the forests and hides obtained from large-scale stock raising. In the early 19C, some fifty tanneries were established in the region. Today shoes are made at Limoges and St-Amand-Montrond, and St-Junien is famous for its gloves. While this industry seems to be past its heyday, the forest holds promise for the development of the **paper industry**, which is on the upswing.

On the **high-tech** end, the area around Limoges has seen a steady increase in new business due to the synergy created by the existence of top-level national institutes (industrial ceramics, engineering, biotechnology, optical and microwave communication, etc) and leading industries such as Ariane Espace and Airbus Industrie. Many smaller businesses have started up and some have become international players.

Prospection of the old Limousin granite massifs led to the discovery of the first **uranium** deposit near Crouzille in 1948, which became the largest western European processing centre. These mines are closed now, but a **gold** mine is still in operation in Bourneix, the last of its kind in France.

Limousin cattle

Prehistory in Dordogne

The Quarternary Era is relatively young, since it began only about two million years ago. Nevertheless, it is during this short period that human evolution has taken place.There is no definitive evidence of life having existed on the earth in the Pre-Cambrian Age; reptiles, fish and tailless amphibians appeared in the course of the Primary Era, mammals and birds during the Secondary Era. The primates, the most ancient ancestors of man, appeared at the end of the Tertiary Era and were followed in the Quarternary Era by ever more advanced species.

The slow pace of human progress during the Paleolithic Age stuns the imagination: it took people nearly two million years to learn to polish stone. But then the few thousand years that followed saw in the Middle and Far East the development of brilliant civilizations, which reached their climax in the construction of the pyramids in Egypt. A few centuries later a new step was taken with the discovery of bronze and later still, in approximately 900BC, of iron.

The researchers – The study of prehistory is a science essentially French in origin, begining in the early 19C. Until that time only the occasional allusion by a Greek or Latin author, a study by the Italian scholar Mercati (1541-93) in the 16C and a paper by Jussieu, published in 1723, gave any hint of the existence of ancient civilizations. In spite of the scepticism of most learned men – led by Cuvier (1769-1832) – the researchers pursued their investigations in Périgord, Lozère and in the Somme valley. To Boucher de Perthes (1788-1868) falls the honour of having **prehistory** (the science of human society before the invention of writing) recognised. His discoveries at St-Acheul and Abbeville were the starting-point for an important series of studies. Among the eminent pioneers who laid the foundations on which modern archeology is based are:

Édouard Lartet (1801-71), who undertook many excavations in the Vézère valley and established a preliminary classification for the various eras of prehistory; Gabriel de Mortillet (1821-98), who took up and completed the classification adding the names Chellean, Mousterian, Aurignacian, Solutrean and Magdalenian to correspond with the

UPPER PALAEOLITHIC

INDUSTRIES	PERIODS AND CULTURES (in 100s of years BC)	PRINCIPAL SITES NEAR LES EYZIES open to the public
Bone and ivory craftsmanship at its peak: harpoons with single and double rows of barbs	M A G D A L E N I A N — 100	**Rouffignac** Paintings and engravings (100 engravings of mammoths)
Point Harpoon		**Les Combarelles** Over 100 figures visible of horses, bison, reindeer
Age of the reindeer		
Needles with eyes	— 150	**Abri du Cap-Blanc** Carved frieze of horses
Greatest achievements of stone cutting industry		**Font-de-Gaume**
Evolution of bone and ivory craftsmanship: tools and ornaments	SOLUTREAN	Paintings and engravings of mammoths and bisons
	— 200	Black relief of a horse: Font-de-Gaume
Female figure: engravings and carving	AURIGNACIAN PERIGORDIAN	**Lascaux** Paintings in the Bulls' Hall (Facsimile in Lascaux II)
Scraper on the end of a blade	— 250	**La Grèze** Engraving of a bison with "turned profile"
Finely knapped and extremely sharp flint blades		**Abri du Poisson** Sculpture of salmon
Beginnings of bone and ivory craftsmanship		
Points	— 300	
Bifaces and scrapers produced by knapping Use of ochre	— 350	

places where the most prolific or most characteristic deposits were found: Chelles in Seine-et-Marne, Le Moustier in Dordogne, Aurignac in Haute-Garonne, Solutré in Saône- et-Loire and La Madeleine in Dordogne.

Excavations can only be performed by specialists with knowledge of the geological stratigraphy, the physics and chemistry of rock formations, the nature and form of stones and gravels, and of how to analyse fossilised wood, coal and bone fragments. In the rock shelters and cave mouths, prehistorians have discovered hearths (accumulations of charcoal and kitchen debris), tools, weapons, stone and bone furnishings and bone fragments. The vestiges are collected in layers; during excavations each of these different layers is uncovered and the civilization or period is then reconstructed.

Prehistory in Périgord – Périgord has been inhabited since Paleolithic times. The names Tayacian (Les Eyzies-de-Tayac), Micoquean (La Micoque), Mousterian (Le Moustier), Perigordian and Magdalenian (La Madeleine) are evidence of the importance of these prehistoric sites. Nearly 200 deposits have been discovered, of which more than half are in the Vézère Valley near Les Eyzies-de-Tayac.

Evolution in the Paleolithic Age – Our most distant ancestors (some three million years ago) were the early hominids (i.e. the family of man) of East Africa, who, unlike their instinctive predecessors, were rational thinkers. They evolved into *Homo habilis* followed by *Homo erectus*, characterised by his upright walking (Java man or *Pithecanthropus erectus*, discovered by E Dubois in 1891, with a cranial capacity halfway in size between the most highly developed ape and the least developed man; and Peking man or *Sinanthropus*, identified by D Black in 1927), who made rough-hewn tools, tools for chopping from split pebbles and heavy bifaced implements.

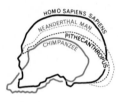

Neanderthal man appeared c150 000 years ago. In 1856, in the Düssel valley (also known as the Neander valley, east of Düsseldorf, Germany) portions of a human skeleton were discovered with the following characteristics: cranial capacity approximately 1500cu cm/91.5cu in, elongated cranium (dolichocephalus), sharply receding forehead, prominently developed jawbones and small stature (1.60m/5ft 3in).

Skeletons with similar characteristics were found in France at La Chapelle-aux-Saints (Corrèze) in 1908, at Le Moustier (Dordogne) in 1909, at La Ferrassie (Dordogne) in 1909 and 1911, and at Le Régourdou (Dordogne) in 1957. The Neanderthal group completely disappeared without descendants 35 000 years ago; at the same time the first burial sites started to appear.

Homo sapiens was flourishing in France about 40 000 years ago. Their essential characteristics – perfect upright stance, raised forehead, slightly projecting eyebrows – showed them to be highly developed and comparable to people today (*sapiens* = intelligent). Several races have been traced as belonging to this same family. Cro-Magnon individuals must to have been quite similar in appearance, in fact, to the present *Homo sapiens*.

Cro-Magnon man (skeletons found in the rock shelters of Cro-Magnon in Dordogne and Solutré in Saône-et-Loire) was tall – about 1.80m/5ft 11in – with long, robust limbs denoting considerable muscular strength; the skull was dolichocephalic in shape. These people lived from the Upper Paleolithic to the Neolithic Age.

Chancelade man (skeleton discovered in 1889 at Chancelade, near Périgueux) appeared in the Magdalenian Period; these people had a large cranium of dolichocephalic form, a long, wide face, pronounced cheek-bones and a height of not more than 1.55m/5ft 1in.

CULTURE AND ART IN THE PALEOLITHIC AGE

The oldest skeletons, belonging to Neanderthals, found in Périgord and Quercy, date from the Mousterian Culture (Middle Paleolithic).

Later, during the Ice Age, tribes are thought to have come from eastern Europe and settled in the Vézère and Beune Valleys. Bordering these valleys were cliffs and slopes pitted with caves and shelters offering many natural advantages which flat country could not offer: protection from the cold, nearby springs and rivers abundant in fish and narrow ravines used for intercepting game as it passed through. There were, however, several dwelling huts found in the Isle Valley, upstream from Périgueux.

The Paleolithic Age (*paleos* = ancient, *lithos* = stones) covers the period in which people knew only how to chip flints. An intermediate age, the Mesolithic (*mesos* = middle), separates it from the Neolithic Age (*neos* = new), when they learnt to polish stone. The first group were predators (hunting, fishing and gathering), whereas the last group were farmers and breeders. Skill in flint knapping evolved very slowly and, therefore, the Paleolithic Age is subdivided into three periods: the Lower, Middle and Upper.

Lower Paleolithic

This began about two million years ago. People living in this period in Périgord knew how to use fire and hunted big game. The earth suffered three successive ice ages known as the Günz, the Mindel and the Riss Ice Ages (after the tributary valleys of the Danube where they were studied). Between each ice age, France and Britain had a tropical climate.

Flint knapping began with a cut made by striking two stones violently one against the other, or by striking one against a rock which served as an anvil.

Grotte de Rouffignac – Mammoth
and ibex (line drawings)

Abri du Cap-Blanc –
Horses (relief sculptures)

Fond de Gaume –
Polychrome bison (painted)

Pech-Merle – Hand stencil
(colour blown over hand pressed
against the rock)

Abri du Poisson –
Salmon carved into the ceiling

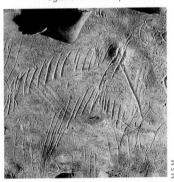
Grotte de Rouffignac –
Horse head (engraving)

Prehistoric art

Grotte de Lascaux –
The "dead man",
bird-spear,
and disembowelled
bison (painting)

27

Middle Paleolithic

This began about 150 000 years ago. With Neanderthal society appeared better finished and more specialised tools. Mousterian industry used both bifaced implements and flakes. New methods enabled triangular points to be produced, also scrapers, probably used for working skins, and flints adapted to take a wooden handle and serve as hunting clubs (bear skulls pierced by such weapons have been found).

During the Mousterian Culture some cave entrances were used as dwelling places, others were used as burial places. More sophisticated weapons were developed and used to hunt big game and animal skins provided protection from the cold.

Upper Paleolithic

This began about 35 000 years ago. Cro-Magnon and Chancelade individuals replaced Neanderthals. There was a constant improvement in the production of tools; the life style was made easier with the perfecting of new hunting methods, resulting in more leisure time and therefore, artistic expression.

Perigordian and Aurignacian Cultures — These two cultures, following the Mousterian and Levalloisian Cultures and preceding the Solutrean Culture, were contemporary but parallel.

The **Aurignacian** stone industry produced large blades, stone flake tools, burins (a sort of chisel) and points made from antlers (early ones have a split base). Cave decoration, applied to blocks of limestone (La Ferrassie near Le Bugue) and at times in tiny caves, consisted of engraved animals, painted or partially carved, or female figures.

At the end of the Perigordian Culture, Gravettians made burins and points; these people decorated their shelter walls (Le Poisson, Laussel) and carved "Venus" figurines, small female statues with exaggerated curves evoking fertility.

The burial places contain some ornaments and jewellery: shells and bead necklaces.The first examples of wall decoration appear as hands placed flat against the rock and outlined in black or red; these are to be found at Font-de-Gaume and at Le Pech Merle. The animals are only rudimentarily sketched. By the end of this period, people had truly discovered their artistic nature, as the sculptures at Le Poisson (Fish) Shelter and the engravings and paintings found at Font-de-Gaume and Lascaux show. La Grève Cave with its engraved bison in "turned profile" dates from between the late Perigordian and the early Solutrean.

Solutrean Culture — Very well represented in the Dordogne, this period is distinguished by exquisite low reliefs carved out of limestone slabs (such as the Devil's Oven, found near Bourdeilles and now exhibited in the National Museum of Prehistory at Les Eyzies). The stone-cutting industry also underwent a brilliant period during the Solutrean Culture. Flint blades, following a method of splitting under pressure, became much slimmer, forming blades in the shape of laurel or willow leaves. Shouldered points were used as weapons, after they had been fitted with wooden shafts. It was during this period that the first needles with eyes appeared.

Magdalenian Culture — It was in this period that bone and ivory craftsmanship reached its peak. The existence of herds of reindeer, which is accounted for by the very cold climate that occurred at the end of the Würm Glacial Period, encouraged carvers to work with bone and antler, producing perforated batons, sometimes engraved, which were used as armatures for points and harpoon heads; projectile tips, sometimes engraved, used as spears; and decorated flattened points.

This is also the period when cave wall art, depicting essentially animal subjects, reached its peak. To protect themselves from the cold, people of the Magdalenian culture lived in the shelter of overhanging rocks or at the mouths of caves; inside, these caves were underground sanctuaries, at times quite some distance from the cave entrance.

They used the shelter (as at the Cap-Blanc Shelter) and sanctuary walls to express their artistic or religious emotions by low-relief carving, engraving and painting. This period introduced a very sophisticated style compared to the more rudimentary outline drawings of the Perigordian and Aurignacian Cultures. However, due to the juxtaposition or superimposition of the figures drawn and deterioration (only a few Magdalenian caves are open to the public due to the difficulty in preserving these works of art), the study of these paintings is not easy.

After Lascaux, during the Middle and Upper Magdalenian, numerous cave-sanctuaries appeared. Portable art, manifested through smaller objects, is another form of expression developed in the shelters. Animals are much less stylised and increasingly realistic, in the details of their anatomy and their movements as well as the faithful and detailed rendering of their physical aspects: coat, tail, eyes, ears, hoofs, antlers, tusks.

Nonetheless, the style is more ornamental. The perspective of the animals in profile, non-existent in the beginning, was pursued and even distorted during Lascaux's last period. New graphic techniques appeared: stencilling, areas left intentionally without colour, polychrome colours etc. Towards the end of the Magdalenian Culture, art became more schematic and human figures made their appearance. This great animal art then disappeared from France and Spain, as the herds of reindeer migrated northwards in search of the lichen which was disappearing during the climatic warming at the end of the Würm Glacial Period.

History

HISTORICAL TABLE AND NOTES

Prehistory As early as the Middle Paleolithic Age, the region is inhabited.

Gauls and Romans

BC	Périgord is inhabited by Petrocorii and Quercy by Caduici.
6-5C	The Bituriges Cubi people settle in Berry.
59-51	Conquest of Gaul by Caesar. The last Gaulish resistance to Caesar is at Uxellodunum, which historians believe to be in Quercy.
16	Emperor Augustus creates the province of Aquitaine. The capital of the land of the Petrocorii is Vesunna (Périgueux) and of that of the Caduici, Divona Cadurcorum (Cahors).
AD **1-3C**	Pax Romana. For three centuries towns develop (several public buildings built). In the country around the towns new crops are introduced by the Romans: walnut, chestnut and cherry trees and above all vineyards.
late 3C	Berry and Limousin are incorporated into primitive Aquitaine; Bourges is its capital.
235-284	Alemanni and Franks invade the region. In 276 several towns are razed. Vesunna defends itself behind fortifications hastily built from the stones taken from Roman public buildings.
313	Edict of Milan. Emperor Constantine grants Christians the freedom of worship.
476	End of the Roman Empire.

Merovingians and Carolingians

486-507	Clovis, king of the Franks, conquers Gaul and Aquitaine.
8C	Quercy and Périgord become counties under the kingdom of Aquitaine.
800	Charlemagne crowned Emperor of the West in Rome.
9C	The Dordogne and Isle valleys and Périgueux are laid waste by Vikings.
10C	The four baronies of Périgord – Mareuil, Bourdeilles, Beynac and Biron – are formed as well as the overlordships of Ans, Auberoche, Gurson, etc. The Périgord County passes to the house of Talleyrand. Powerful families rule Quercy.
c950	Beginning of the Pilgrimage to St James' shrine in Santiago de Compostela.
12C	Many influential abbeys founded in the region (Noirlac, Chancelade, Cadouin, Rocamadour, etc). Construction started on the cathedral in Bourges.

Wars between England and France

1152	Eleanor of Aquitaine marries Henry Plantagenet, bringing as dowry all southwest France *(see below)*. In 1154 Henry Plantagenet becomes King Henry II.
1190	Quercy is ceded to the English with the exception of the abbeys of Figeac and Souillac.
1191	Richard the Lion Heart dies at Châlus.
early 13C	Albigensian Crusade. Simon de Montfort raids Quercy and Périgord.
1234	Louis IX purchases Berry from the count of Champagne.
1259	By the Treaty of Paris, Saint Louis cedes Périgord and Quercy to the English. The treaty puts an end to the constant fighting and enables the people of the region to live in peace until the Hundred Years War.
1273	Construction started on the cathedral in Limoges.
1324	Bourges Cathedral consecrated.

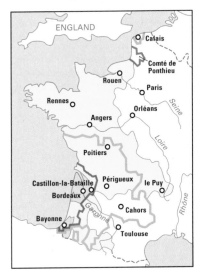

Lands held by the English

in 1253

at the beginning of
the Hundred Years War (1338)

after the Treaty of Brétigny (1360)

after the reconquests by Charles V and
Du Guesclin (1380)

1337	French king Philip VI declares the English-held duchy of Guyenne confiscated.
1340	Edward III of England proclaims himself king of France.
1345	Beginning of the Hundred Years War in Aquitaine.
1346	Edward III defeats the French at Crécy.
1355-1370	Edward the Black Prince begins his campaign, ravaging Berry and Limousin. Edward defeats and captures King Jean II (Battle of Poitiers 1356).
1360	The Treaty of Brétigny cedes Aquitaine to the English as part of the ransom for Jean II's liberty.
1369	Quercy and Périgord are won back by the king of France (Charles V). Du Guesclin, Constable of France, is active in the liberation of Périgord. During the period that follows the lords of the north of Périgord owe allegiance to the king of France; the lords of the south of Périgord to the English. Many regularly swap sides in unabashed support of their own interests.
1415	Henry V defeats the French at Azincourt.
1420	Henry V of England recognised as king of France under the Treaty of Troyes. France divided into three parts controlled by Henry V (Normandy, Guyenne, Paris area), Philip the Good, duke of Burgundy (also Paris area, Burgundy) and the Dauphin (Central France and Languedoc).
1444	Truce of Tours (Charles VII and Henry V); the English retain Maine, the Bordelais region, parts of Artois and Picardy and most of Normandy.
1449	The French begin a campaign in Guyenne, but the people of the region are hostile to the French from years of loyalty to the English crown; Bergerac falls in 1450, Bordeaux in 1451.
1453	Defeat of John Talbot, Earl of Shrewsbury, at the Battle of Castillon, which marks the end of the Hundred Years War.
1463	University of Bourges founded.
2nd half of 15-early 16C	During this period of peace towns and castles are rebuilt.
1558	England loses Calais to the French.

Wars of Religion

1562	Massacre of Protestants at Cahors.
1572	St Bartholomew's Day Massacre (20 000 Huguenots die).
1570-90	War is declared; Bergerac and Ste-Foy-la-Grande are Huguenot bastions while Périgueux and Cahors support the Catholic League. Vivans, the Huguenot leader, scours Périgord; Périgueux falls in 1575 and Domme in 1588.
1580	Cahors taken by Henri de Navarre (Henri IV).
1589	Henri IV accedes to the throne and converts to Catholicism in 1593; is crowned in 1594. Under Henri IV, the county of Périgord becomes part of the royal domain.
1594-95	Croquant peasant revolt.
1598	Edict of Nantes grants Huguenots freedom of worship and places of refuge.
1607	The Viscounty of Limoges comes under the French crown.
1610	Henri IV assassinated; Louis XIII's reign begins.
1637	Croquants revolt against Louis XIII's government and Richelieu's taxes.
1643-1715	Louis XIV's reign.
1685	Revocation of Edict of Nantes. Huguenots flee France.

18 to 20C

1743-57	Tourny, administrator of the Treasury of Bordeaux, instigates a number of town planning projects in the southwest (Allées de Tourny in Périgueux).
1763	Peace of Paris ends French and Indian War (1754-63); it marks the end of France's colonial empire in America.
1768	Kaolin discovered in St-Yrieix-la-Perche.
1789	Storming of the Bastille and beginning of the French Revolution.
1790	Creation of Dordogne *département*.
1792	Proclamation of French Republic after Battle of Valmy.
1812-14	Périgord is a Bonapartist fief; several of Napoleon's generals and marshals are natives of the region: Murat, Fournier-Sarlovèze, Daumesnil.
1868	Phylloxera destroys the vineyards of Cahors and Bergerac, causing a rural exodus.
	Discovery of Cro-Magnon cave skeletons.

1914-18	First World War.
1940	Discovery of Lascaux Cave.
1942-1944	French Resistance movement intensifies in Limousin during the Second World War.
1944	Massacres at Tulle and Oradour-sur-Glane.
20C	Marked by a continued rural exodus; the depopulated regions live essentially from agriculture and tourism.
1963	The first Maison de la Culture opens in Bourges, an initiative of André Malraux.
1964	The Région Limousin is created.
1977	Le Printemps de Bourges music festival holds its first concerts.
1989	The Brenne nature park is established. A new motorway is inaugurated, from Paris to the centre of France, via Bourges.

THREE LIVES

Exceptional individuals mark exceptional times, and the three figures whose brief biographies are given here spark the imagination and bring the history of the region to life, giving it a human dimension.

Eleanor of Aquitaine, an extraordinary destiny

Eleanor of Aquitaine

In 1122, a daughter was born to William X, duke of Aquitaine and count of Poitiers; she became heiress to one of the largest domains in France (bigger than the king's). In 1137, Eleanor wed Louis VII, who succeeded his father to the throne just one month later. The young queen of France was beautiful and influential, though some historians have criticised her juvenile frivolity. Eleanor accompanied her husband on the Second Crusade, where her capricious enthusiasms fired Louis' jealousy, and the marriage was annulled in 1152, shortly after their return to France. Thanks to feudal customs, she regained possession of Aquitaine, and two months later married Henry Plantagenet, count of Anjou and duke of Normandy. When her second husband became king of England (1154), as Henry II, England, Normandy and the west of France were united under one crown. In addition to her two daughters from her first marriage, Eleanor became the mother of eight more children, including Richard the Lion Heart, John Lackland, Eleanor, (who married the king of Castille) and Joan (who married the king of Sicily and later the count of Toulouse). No wonder some have called her the "grandmother of Europe"!

Eleanor was both a political and cultural force to be reckoned with. She turned the court at Poitiers into a centre of courtly life and manners, celebrated by the troubadours; she also promoted the historical legends of Brittany, romantic songs in the Celtic tradition. She supported her sons in a failed revolt against their father; afterwards, Henry had her kept guarded under close watch in England until his death. Released at last, she became an invaluable advisor to her son Richard, keeping the kingdom intact and administering it during his long absences. She was 80 years old when she set off across the Pyrennees to fetch her granddaughter Blanche of Castille for marriage to the son of the French king, hoping thus to cement peace between the Plantagenets and the Capetians. Her influence was felt even after her death: following the loss of Normandy (1204), her ancestral lands, and not the old Norman territories, remained loyal to England.

She died in 1204 in the monastery at Fontevrault where she had retired. The nuns of Fontevrault described this exceptional queen as "beautiful and just, imposing and modest, humble and elegant".

Jean de Berry, politician and patron of the arts

In the 14C, there were about 350 000 people settled in Berry, which was plunged in the turmoil of the Hundred Years War, following the Black Prince's raids. The region had strategic importance as a potential base for the conquest of Poitou and Aquitaine. King John the Good raised Berry and Auvergne to the rank of duchies, and granted them to his third son; thus Jean de Berry came into control of at least one-third of the territory of France in 1360.

The young duke, after a period spent in captivity in England, was in urgent need of funds. He taxed his lands heavily for the defense of the kingdom, and also spent lavishly on the arts. His military career was marked by a triumphant march on Limoges, which brought the local bourgeoisie and clergy into the Valois camp, but also led to terrible English reprisals. Pursuing his campaign with Du Guesclin and the duke of Anjou, he took control of Poitou in 1373.

Meanwhile, his brother, by then King Charles V, passed away, and his nephew, the young Charles VI, took the throne. As a member of the regency council from 1380-88, Berry shared royal powers while Charles was too young to rule. He thus gained control of Languedoc. In conflict with the royal family, Berry also struggled against the peasants' revolt (1381-84) which resulted from his oppressive fiscal policies and opulent lifestyle. The king finally announced his determination to rule alone, but soon earned the surname "Charles the Mad", beset by fits of insanity. Still avid for power, and always ready to take advantage, Berry handled negotiations between the conflicting factions of John the Fearless, duke of Burgundy, and his own brother Louis, duc d'Orléans, and even promised the English to deliver the province of Guyenne (1412). The end result of his scheming was the siege of the city of Bourges by royal troops. Berry capitulated, and died four years later, at the age of 76.

Throughout his life, he showered his fortune on the arts and artists, building palaces and fine residences in his cities; at his death there was not enough in the coffers to pay for his funeral. History has recognised his importance as a supporter of the arts, and the treasures he commissioned remain as his monument: paintings, tapestries, jewellery and illuminated manuscripts, including the world-famous *Très riches heures du duc de Berry*.

Jacques Cœur, wheeling and dealing in the 15C

Born the son of a furrier in Bourges, Cœur's life is exemplary of the spirit of enterprise and the rise of the merchant classes in the period of prosperity that began as the Hundred Years War finally ebbed. His generation was perhaps the first in Europe to aspire to honours, noble rank, wealth and property, without being born into the aristocracy. If he may be said to represent the rise of the merchant class, his downfall signifies how difficult it was for such social changes to take root.

Gifted with an uncanny flair for business opportunities, Cœur gained the confidence of Charles VII, and became his *argentier* – managing the royal funds like a modern-day investment tycoon. His power and fortune grew simultaneously as he became a member of the king's council, the tax collector for Languedoc and the inspector general of the salt tax. He diversified his affairs, stocking all kinds of merchandise – cloth, spices, jewels, armour, wheat, salt – from around the world in his vast stores in Tours. He had a large staff of salesmen, shipowners (he himself owned seven ships) and negotiators, as well as 40 manor houses and a beautiful palace in Bourges, one of the finest examples of lay Gothic architecture in Europe. Cœur set up individual companies for each branch of trade, and sought political support from all quarters. His prosperity was held up by a delicately spun web of bills of exchange, credit, and fiscal receipts issued by the king. A creditor for many of France's aristocrats and the king himself, Cœur was the object of intense jealousy.

His skyrocketing career plummeted to the depths on 31 July, 1451, when he was arrested on trumped-up charges of having poisoned Agnès Sorel, the king's mistress. His enemies came forth with more accusations: currency fraud, trading arms with the infidels, returning a Christian slave to a Muslim master, running ships with slave crews, and abuse of power. Found guilty on all counts except the poisoning, he was sentenced to banishment, and Cœur was also ordered to relinquish all of his goods and property, and pay an impossibly high fine for his release.

Meanwhile, French troops, paid with the confiscated funds, won the final battle of the Hundred Years War. And the fate of Cœur, financial adventurer and proto-bourgeois? Friends helped him escape from prison; he took refuge in Italy before setting out on a naval expedition organised by the Pope against the Turks. He is believed to have died on the Aegean island of Chios in 1456. The following year, King Louis XI, to make amends for his father's treatment of Cœur, returned his unsold property to his sons and revived some of his old companies.

PIX

Jacques Cœur

Literary life

THE COURTS OF LOVE

In the 12C appeared an original type of lyric poetry which developed and flowered in the feudal courts where idle but educated nobles and their ladies enjoyed singing, music and poetry. **Troubadours** were inventors (*tobar* is the occitan word for "find") of musical airs – melodies for verses in the Oc language. Under the protection and encouragement of their lords, they created new poetic forms; love poems (songs and romances) in which lyrical homage to the lady of the castle illustrated the theme of courtly love; songs of war and satirical ballads. The courts of love each had several troubadours who would vie in wit with one another on a set subject. **Bernard de Ventadour, Bertrand de Born**, author of the political and moralist *Sirventès*, Bertrand de Gourdon, Aimeric de Sarlat, Girault de Borneil, native of Excideuil, and Arnaut de Ribérac were the most famous of these troubadours. **Dormunda de Cahors** is the only woman poet of this time whose name has managed to come down to us. The social influence of the poets themselves was unprecedented in the history of poetry, and their work strongly influenced all European poetry that followed.

HUMANISTS

After the Hundred Years War, during the 15C, intellectual life continued, centring on new universities – Cahors was founded in 1331 by Jacques Duèze, who became Pope John XXII. In the early 16C, printing houses were established in Périgueux, Cahors and Bergerac. But it was the Renaissance, and the intellectual movement known as humanism, which restored respect for classical languages and poetic forms. A native of Cahors, **Clément Marot** (1496-1544), one of the great poets of the French Renaissance, excelled in composing epigrams and sonnets. His brilliant life at court, where he rose from his initial station of valet to that of official court poet, was often interrupted by prison sentences, due to his penchant for the Reformation. In Limoges, **Jean Dorat** (1508-1588) was a scholar of Greek and a poet in Latin, a teacher who inspired Ronsard and other French writers. He also influenced **Olivier de Magny** (1529-65), from Cahors and **Etienne de la Boétie** (1530-63), a native of Sarlat who was a friend of the essayist Montaigne, and denounced tyranny in his *Discourse on Voluntary Subjection and Against One*. In addition, there was Pierre de Bourdeille (1535-1614), who wrote under the pseudonym of **Brantôme** (name of the abbey of which he was abbot), a talented chronicler, who described the lives of great captains and soldiers as well as giving accounts of life in the French courts. **Jean Tarde** (1561-1636), born in La Roque-Gageac, was one of the most learned men of his time; a historian, cartographer, astronomer and mathematician.

AGE OF ENLIGHTENMENT

In Limousin, historians **Étienne Baluze** (1630-1718) and **Jean-François Marmontel** (1723-1799) gained fame for works on the Middle Ages and as the king's historian, respectively. On the banks of the Dordogne, **Fénelon** (1631-1715) worked on *Télémaque*, a tract for the edification of his student the duke of Burgundy, dauphin of France. Philosophers **Joseph Joubert** (1754-1824) and **Maine de Biran** (1766-1824) wrote sensitive, precise treatises which heralded the movement of spiritualistic philosophy.

ROMANTIC AND CONTEMPORARY AUTHORS

Probably the most famous writer to emerge from Berry was **George Sand** (1804-1878). Born Aurore Dupin in Paris, she spent her youth in the countryside, and her many works are strongly imprinted with images of the region. **Eugène Le Roy** (1836-1907) is likewise the novelist of Périgord; his *Jacquou le Croquant*, set in l'Herm castle, describes the peasant uprising which ravaged the region in a very vivid style. Success came after death to **Alain-Fournier** (1886-1914), based on his sole novel, *Le Grand Meaulnes*, inspired by the school in his town of Épineuil-le-Fleuriel. The playwright **Jean Giraudoux** (1882-1944) has been influential on an international scale, and is also appreciated for his novels.

Jean Giraudoux

ABC of architecture

Religious architecture

CADOUIN – Ground plan of the abbey church (1119-1154)

This ground plan is characteristic of the Aquitaine school of ecclesiastical architecture with aisles flanking the nave and chancel on both sides, forming a Latin cross with short arms.

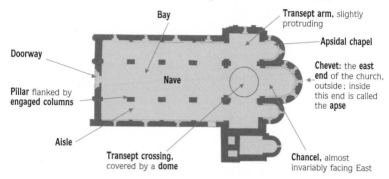

Bay

Transept arm, slightly protruding

Doorway

Apsidal chapel

Chevet: the east end of the church, outside; inside this end is called the apse

Pillar flanked by engaged columns

Nave

Aisle

Transept crossing, covered by a dome

Chancel, almost invariably facing East

CARSAC-AILLAC – Vaulting in Saint-Caprais (12-16C)

Stellar vault (16C) covering the nave

Ridge-rib or lierne: a transverse rib set at a 45° angle to the main diagonal rib

Cell: a compartment formed by the ribs of a vault

Pendant bracket: sculpted in the form of a bust

Arch band: a narrow elongated surface forming or connected to the arch

Key-stone

Tierceron or secondary rib: emanates from a main springer or central boss and leads to the ridge-rib

Rib arch or wall rib: the side arch of a vault, also called an arc formeret

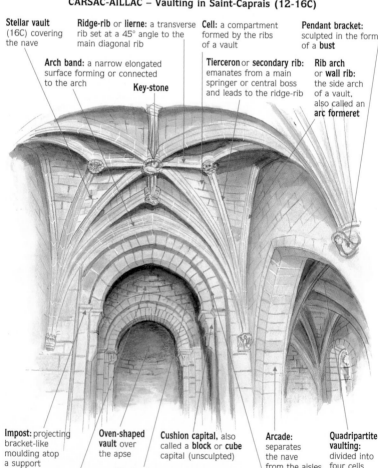

Impost: projecting bracket-like moulding atop a support (no capital)

Chancel entrance covered by a dome on pendentives

Oven-shaped vault over the apse

Pendentive: concave spandrel leading from the angle of two walls, a means for supporting a circular dome over a square or polygonal compartment

Cushion capital, also called a block or cube capital (unsculpted)

Arcade: separates the nave from the aisles

Pointed arch with a double row of arch stones

Quadripartite vaulting: divided into four cells by the ribs

R. Corbel

ST-LÉONARD-DE-NOBLAT – Church belltower (12C)

Belltower with 4 storeys of square design surmounted by 2 receding storeys on a octagonal plan; characteristic of Romanesque gabled belfries in Limousin.

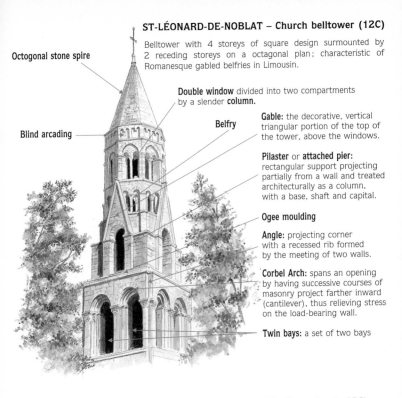

Octogonal stone spire

Blind arcading

Double window divided into two compartments by a slender **column.**

Belfry

Gable: the decorative, vertical triangular portion of the top of the tower, above the windows.

Pilaster or **attached pier:** rectangular support projecting partially from a wall and treated architecturally as a column, with a base, shaft and capital.

Ogee moulding

Angle: projecting corner with a recessed rib formed by the meeting of two walls.

Corbel Arch: spans an opening by having successive courses of masonry project farther inward (cantilever), thus relieving stress on the load-bearing wall.

Twin bays: a set of two bays

BEAULIEU-SUR-DORDOGNE – East end (chevet) of St-Pierre (early 12C)

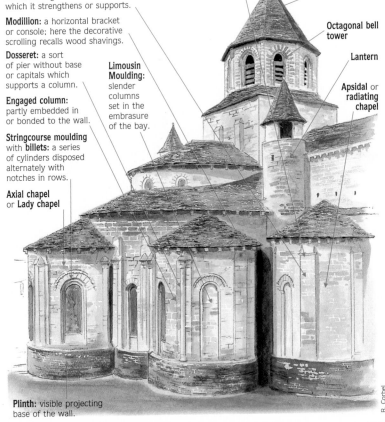

Buttress: exterior mass of masonry set at an angle or bonded into a wall which it strengthens or supports.

Modillion: a horizontal bracket or console; here the decorative scrolling recalls wood shavings.

Dosseret: a sort of pier without base or capitals which supports a column.

Engaged column: partly embedded in or bonded to the wall.

Stringcourse moulding with **billets:** a series of cylinders disposed alternately with notches in rows.

Axial chapel or **Lady chapel**

Talus wall: the sloping face of the buttress.

Limousin Moulding: slender columns set in the embrasure of the bay.

Polygonal roof

Octagonal bell tower

Lantern

Apsidal or **radiating chapel**

Plinth: visible projecting base of the wall.

R. Corbel

35

Military and Civil Architecture

Château de MONTBRUN (12C and 15C)

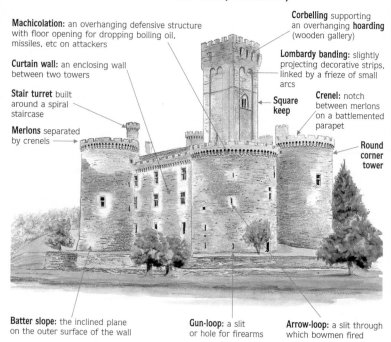

Machicolation: an overhanging defensive structure with floor opening for dropping boiling oil, missiles, etc on attackers

Curtain wall: an enclosing wall between two towers

Stair turret built around a spiral staircase

Merlons separated by crenels

Corbelling supporting an overhanging **hoarding** (wooden gallery)

Lombardy banding: slightly projecting decorative strips, linked by a frieze of small arcs

Square keep

Crenel: notch between merlons on a battlemented parapet

Round corner tower

Batter slope: the inclined plane on the outer surface of the wall

Gun-loop: a slit or hole for firearms

Arrow-loop: a slit through which bowmen fired

Château de MEILLANT – Western side (early 14C)

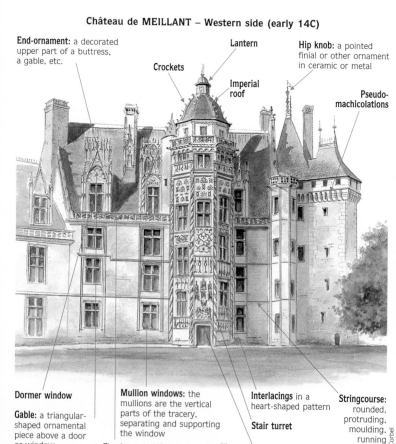

End-ornament: a decorated upper part of a buttress, a gable, etc.

Crockets

Lantern

Imperial roof

Hip knob: a pointed finial or other ornament in ceramic or metal

Pseudo-machicolations

Dormer window

Gable: a triangular-shaped ornamental piece above a door or window

Mullion windows: the mullions are the vertical parts of the tracery, separating and supporting the window

Flamboyant-style open-work **railing**

Interlacings in a heart-shaped pattern

Stair turret

Flattened arch

Stringcourse: rounded, protruding, moulding, running horizontally

R. Corbel

Architecture of the bastides

DOMME – Porte des Tours (late 13C)

In the 13C, the new towns known as bastides, often fortified, became common in Périgord and Quercy. This was the most important defensive gateway in the ramparts of Domme.

Crown of the tower, raised and fitted with loop-holes in the 14C

Two **circular towers**

Gable-wall

Curtain wall: an enclosing wall between two towers or bastions

Bartizan: a small overhanging turret with lookout holes and defensive loops

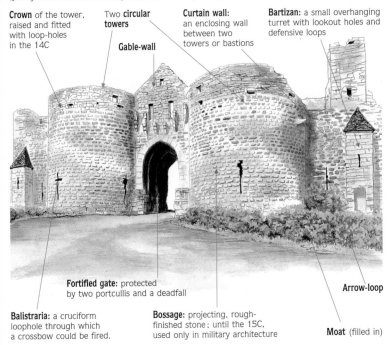

Fortified gate: protected by two portcullis and a deadfall

Arrow-loop

Balistraria: a cruciform loophole through which a crossbow could be fired.

Bossage: projecting, rough-finished stone; until the 15C, used only in military architecture

Moat (filled in)

MONPAZIER – Central square in the bastide (late 13C and 14C)

The most typical and best preserved of the Périgord bastides, it is designed around a central rectangular area, bordered by a covered market on the southern side.

The church in a bastide is generally placed near the central square

Spire: the pitch on the lower section is different

Covered market (timber)

Bays: in groups of two, three, four, etc.

Andron: (regional term) narrow passage for fire protection, used as a sewer

Arcade or **cornière**

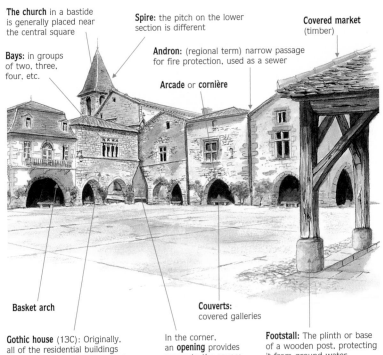

Basket arch

Gothic house (13C): Originally, all of the residential buildings in the bastide were the same size

In the corner, an **opening** provides access to the square

Couverts: covered galleries

Footstall: The plinth or base of a wooden post, protecting it from ground water

R. Corbel

Public building and civil engineering

FIGEAC – Hôtel de la monnaie (late 13C)

Probably a marketplace for money-changers, the "Oustal de lo Monédo" is representative of the urban architecture of Haut Quercy built during the Gothic period.

Relieving or **discharging arch:** an arch built over a lintel to relieve or distribute the weight of the load-bearing walls

Oculus: a circular bay

Solelho: (regional term) open attic space used for drying laundry or storing wood, etc.

Chimney stack: (the part of a chimney which projects above a roof) the "gothic" stack is one of the distinctive features of Figeac's architecture

Quatrefoil: a circular design made up of four converging arcs

Double window divided into two compartements by a slender column

Cornice

Mezzanine: small square windows light the upper part of a high-ceilinged room

Arcade of Gothic arches: this is typically found in commercial buildings in Quercy

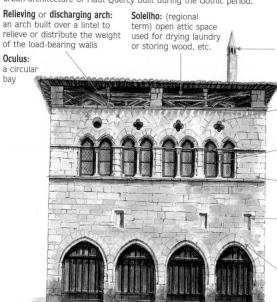

CAHORS – Pont Valentré (14C)

A remarkable example of Medieval military art, this fortified bridge has such an imposing air that it was never attacked.

Rectangular tower (length greater than width)

Mantelet: a movable cover protecting a crenel

Square tower

Cut-water: the angular edge reinforcing the pier, facing upstream

Bartizan

Trefoil arch

Chatelet controlling the bridgehead

Straight-stair: a steep stairway built against a fortification

Deck

Abutment: end support of mansonry that relieves the thrust of the arches

Arch

Crenelation

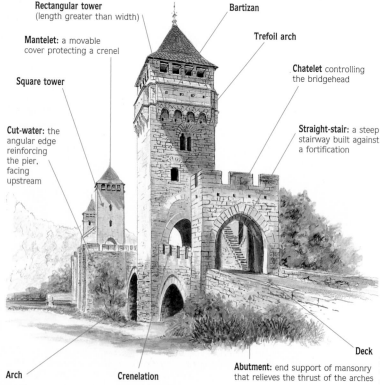

R. Corbel

Art and architecture

The Vézère Valley, the prehistoric sites of Les Eyzies and the caves of Quercy contain some of the finest known examples of prehistoric art, the earliest manifestations of art in France. Since that time, art and architecture have evolved in close connection with the region's turbulent history. The significant periods of construction took place in periods of peace: the Pax Romana, the 12C (many monasteries date from that century) and the period spanning the end of the 14C to the 16C. During times of war – the Hundred Years War, the Wars of Religion – the people's main concern was their protection, hence the fortifications of their towns, castles and churches.

GALLO-ROMAN ART

Of the buildings constructed by the Gauls and the Romans only a few have withstood the test of time. Remnants of the period of the Gauls do survive however. Excavations undertaken at **Drevant**, near St-Amand-Montrond, have established that on the site of a small Gaulish market town developed a large Gallo-Roman centre. The theatre, baths and a vast walled area which may have been a forum or a temple of Gallo-Roman times, have been uncovered.

At **Limoges** an amphitheatre was built on the northwest outskirts of the old town; it was razed to the ground in the 16C and its ruins are now hidden beneath the Orsay Gardens.

Traces have been discovered at Périgueux of the ancient **Vesunna**, capital of the Petrocorii. The finds include the Vesunna Tower, the arena and the perimeter wall. The Puy d'Issolud near Vayrac is believed to be the site of the **Uxellodunum** encampment – this was the last bastion of the Gauls in their resistance to the all-conquering Caesar. At Luzech, also, there are traces of the Impernal encampment which commanded a bend in the river Lot and, near the Vers valley, the ruins of the Murcens encampment.

ROMANESQUE ART

Religious architecture

In Berry – Though characteristics of the Poitou School may frequently be seen, most Romanesque churches in Berry have a precise plan with certain features peculiar to the area: the chancel generally consists of two bays flanked by aisles which communicate with the choir through arches resting on columns adorned with historiated capitals; the apse is semicircular; the transept has a dome on squinches above the crossing and barrel vaulting above the arms; the nave is wider than the transept crossing and communicates with the arms of the transept by narrow passages known as **Berrichon passages**.

The abbey churches are based on the Benedictine design, for the Order of St-Benedict spread throughout Berry and built abbeys at Fontgombault, Chezal-Benoît and at Châteaumeillant where the Church of St-Genès has an unusual arrangement of the chevet with six parallel apsidal chapels. Noirlac was created by the Cistercians, Plaimpied and Puy-Ferrand by the Augustinian Canons Regular. One church alone in the Bourges diocese is designed quite differently: it is the basilica of Neuvy-St-Sépulcre which was built in the form of a rotunda and was inspired by the Church of the Holy Sepulchre in Jerusalem.

The Limousin School – The Limousin School combines many of the characteristics of its neighbours: the Auvergne School, whose chief feature is that the vaulting above the nave is buttressed by the semi-barrel vaulting of the aisles or the galleries (Beaulieu-sur-Dordogne); the Poitou School, whose influence can be seen in the Collegiate Church of St-Pierre in Le Dorat – blind nave with broken-barrel vaulting and aisles with groined vaulting; and the Périgord School – the domes on the church at Solignac.

Nevertheless, certain elements can be considered as purely Limousin. Firstly, the use of granite, which is found throughout the region and whose colour, while usually grey, sometimes verges on a golden tone.

Secondly, in the peculiar design of some belfries: the octagonal spire which crowns them is joined to the square tiers that form the base of the tower by one or two octagonal storeys; the gables that stand on the topmost of the square tiers are not only ornamental but play a part in the overall construction since they divide and balance the weight of the upper octagonal tiers; the best examples of this style are the **belfries** at St-Léonard *(see detailed illustration on page 35)*, Collonges, Uzerche and Brantôme (in Périgord). The belfry at St-Junien was probably planned to follow this pattern as the beginning of a steeply sloping gable can be seen above the second square tier.

Finally the façades present a more or less uniform style: massive belfry-porches adorned with blind arcades of various sizes and forms (Le Dorat, St-Junien); doorways with recessed elongated arcades on either side (St-Junien); a first storey flanked by bell turrets which are pierced at Le Dorat and encircled by a corbelled gallery at St-Junien and lastly doorways with twin doors framed by recessed covings, which in some cases are scalloped thus showing the influence of Islamic art («Mozarabic" style).

In Dordogne – The plain, almost severe appearance of the many Romanesque churches was enhanced with the use of fine golden sandstone with warm overtones. The exteriors are starling for the extreme simplicity of their decoration: the doorways without tympana were embellished with recessed orders, carved with rounded mouldings and festoons in a saw-tooth pattern. Inside, the churches are plain as well; apsidal chapels open off the chancel, which is usually flat. Only a few churches were built with side aisles, generally the nave stands alone.

The originality of the **Périgord Romanesque** style is in its vaulting – the **dome.** Some specialists believe that this shows eastern influence, others that it is a French invention. The dome offers several advantages over cradle vaulting, which requires powerful buttresses. The dome on pendentives allows the support of the weight of the vault to be divided between the side walls and the transverse arches of the nave. Often set over the transept crossing, the domes also vault the nave when they follow one right after another (St-Étienne-de-la-Cité, Périgueux) in a series. The nave is thus divided into several square bays vaulted with a dome on pendentives. The pendentives serve as a transition from a square base to the circular dome. The St-Front cathedral in Périgueux *(see illustration under PÉRIGUEUX)* is unique, with its five domes over a Greek-cross plan. Yet some of the numerous Romanesque churches illustrate different designs: in St-Privat-des-Prés and Cadouin the nave has aisles with rounded and pointed barrel-vaulting. Some façades are adorned with rows of arcades; this reflects the influence of the Saintonge and Angoumois regions.

Neighbouring **Quercy** has a slightly different Romanesque style, characterised by richer sculptural embellishment (influence of the Moissac and Languedoc schools). Inspired by Byzantine art, illuminations and Antiquity, some of the carved doorways and tympana in this region are stunning: Cahors, Carennac, Martel, Collonges-La-Rouge (the last on the border of Limousin).

Civil and military architecture

Berry-Limousin – The Fortresses of Turenne, Merle and Ventadour, Châlus, Montbrun *(see detailed illustration page 00)* and Chalusset all existed in Limousin in the 13C. The ruins of Crozant overlooking the valley of the Creuse evoke what was once the powerful stronghold of the counts of Marche.

Numerous castles were built in Berry during the Middle Ages: on Henry II's accession to the throne of England in 1154 the English controlled Aquitaine and threatened neighbouring Berry. The local lords therefore improved the fortification of their castles to resist the enemy. Culan castle, taken by Philip Augustus in 1188, was rebuilt in the 13C but retained its severity of appearance emphasised by its three round towers topped by a wooden hoarding. Ainay-le-Vieil is protected by its perimeter wall with nine towers. Meillant still possesses its seven haughty feudal towers.

Dordogne – There are few traces left of the civil architecture of the Romanesque period. The feudal fortresses erected in the 10 and 11C were greatly altered in later centuries and can scarcely be said to have withstood the warfare and destruction of the times. The only remaining buildings of this period are the square keeps, last refuge of the defensive system. Castelnau-Bretenoux in Quercy, with its strongly fortified keep, is a good example of feudal construction built on a hilltop site.

In Périgord, parts of the castles of Biron and Beynac, Bourdeilles, Commarque and Castelnaud date back to the Romanesque period.

Decorative arts

The Abbey of St-Martial in Limoges, with its many dependent priories, was the principal centre in Limousin from which enamel craftsmen and gold and silversmiths developed their art. From the 10C the monks produced shrines, episcopal rings and statues in gold and silver. The skill of the Limousin gold and silversmiths and their proven technique no doubt opened the way, later, for **enamelwork**.

Using methods practised from the 6C onwards by Byzantine enamellers, the Limousin workshops at first undertook *cloisonné* ware (in which the colours are kept apart by thin outline plates). But in the 12C they turned entirely to *champlevé* enamelware (in which a thick sheet of copper is hollowed out in certain areas and the cavities are filled in with enamel). Towards the end of the Romanesque period colours became more subtle and often the cavities were filled with two or even four colours, placed one on top of the other. The folds of garments were rendered by the use of a highlight – white, light blue or yellow – around areas of dark blue and green.

Most of the work was inspired by the art of the illuminators, by manuscripts, ivories and Byzantine and Oriental silks. From the beginning of the 12C, small enamelled figures were represented on a background of smooth gilded copper. From 1170 onwards this background was chiselled with decorative foliage motifs. Fantastic fauna are mingled with religious symbols. The compositions, although often naive, show a very strong artistic sense. Of the many objects *(see illustration page 00)* produced in this way the most remarkable are the reliquary shrines of Ambazac, Gimel and Bellac. The municipal museums of Limoges and Guéret contain rich collections of enamelwork.

Limoges enamelwork

Thomas Becket shrine,
circa 1200, champlevé on copper

La sibylle Agrippa,
Léonard Limousin, circa 1535,
enamel painted on copper

Triptych
of the Nativity,
Grands Fronts Master craftsman, early
16C, enamel
painted on copper

Festin de Didon et Enée,
(Ewer representing
Didon and Aeneas)
mid-16C, enamel
painted on copper

Vase, Henriette Marty,
1930, translucent enamel on a
copper base, with silver sheath

The Drunkard, Léon Jouhaud, 1912,
enamel painted on copper

Noces de printemps,
Alain Duban, Lea Sham's, 1994,
enamel on copper, partially sheathed
in silver, nickel silver, bean motif

F. Magnoux/Musée municipal de l'Évêché, Limoges

GOTHIC ART

Religious architecture

The essential elements of Gothic art – quadripartite vaulting based on diagonal ribs and the systematic use of the pointed arch – underwent various regional modifications. Diagonal ribs revolutionised construction. The architect became master of the thrust and balance of a building; through the use of pointed arches, piers and flying buttresses, architects freed the inner space so that a church could be lofty and light, illuminated by stained-glass windows.

Berry – The most important Gothic building in the region, recognised world-wide as an architectural masterpiece, inscribed on UNESCO's World Heritage List, is the **Bourges Cathedral**. It bears no resemblance to any of the other great cathedrals of France; its high nave covered with sexpartite vaulting, its double side aisles which extend round the chancel and the absence of a transept make it unique.

Limousin – The simultaneous influences of the Languedoc School (southern Gothic) and the schools of northern France were in play in the region. The passion for building in the 13 and 14C is illustrated in the **Cathedral of St-Étienne** and the Churches of St-Pierre-du-Queyroix and St-Michel-des-Lions at Limoges, in the nave of the Church of St-Martin at Brive, the collegiate Church at St-Yrieix, and the belfry-porch of Tulle Cathedral.

Dordogne – **Sarlat Cathedral** is an example of the influence of both southern and northern Gothic styles: the nave has wide side aisles and soaring flying buttresses typical of the north, whereas the side chapel shows southern influence. Another commonly found aspect of the Languedoc school is the nave's shape, almost as wide as it is high, with side chapels but no aisles (Gourdon, Martel, Montpezat-du-Quercy, St-Cirq-Lapopie).

In Berry, Limousin and Dordogne, many **monasteries** were built during this period, although few have emerged intact from the ravages of time. In Cadouin and Cahors, there are still cloisters built in the Flamboyant style, and in Périgueux the cloisters were built between the 12-16C.

During the 13-14C, **fortified churches** were built in the region in response to unrest, in particular during the Hundred Years War. These sanctuaries provided villagers with a safe place of refuge from marauders. These churches and abbeys were like fortified castles in appearance, too, with crenellations, watchpaths, and sometimes even protective moats.

Sculpture and painting

Berry – Art in stained glass reached its climax in Bourges with the completion in the 13C of a remarkable series of windows.

About the middle of the 14C, Berry became, under the guidance of duke Jean de Berry, a great intellectual and artistic centre. In the cathedral at Bourges, the stained-glass window known as the *Grand Housteau* was a gift from the duke.

The duke assembled excellent artists but most of the masterpieces executed in the studios and workshops in Bourges have unfortunately disappeared: only a few fragments of Berry's tomb remain in the cathedral crypt (originally placed in the Sainte-Chapelle in Bourges, since demolished). The greater part of the statuary, however, dates from this period and has survived. At Issoudun, in the chapel of the former Hôtel-Dieu, there is a fine carved Tree of Jesse.

Limousin – At Limoges, the Cathedral of St-Étienne contains in the ambulatory around the chancel two tombs executed in the purest 14C style. The village of Reygade in Corrèze possesses an Entombment dating from the 15C resembling the one at Carennac. The church at Eymoutiers is ornamented with interesting stained glass dating from the 15C. Limousin enamelwork which flourished in the Romanesque period was transformed in the 15C with the appearance of painted enamels produced under the direction of such famous master-craftsmen as Monvaerni and Nardon Pénicaud.

Dordogne – From the second half of the 13C and up until the 15C, several remarkable works were produced: the tomb of St Stephen at Aubazine, a magnificent shrine carved in limestone in the second half of the 13C; the Entombment (15C) at Carennac; the tomb of the Cardaillacs at Espagnac-Ste-Eulalie; the recumbent figures of Cardinal Pierre des Prés and his nephew Jean in the church at Montpezat-du-Quercy.

Frescoes, mural painting done with water-based paint on fresh plaster (a technique which allows the colours to sink in), were used to decorate many chapels and churches. The west dome of Cahors cathedral is entirely covered with 14C frescoes. Naive 14C and 15C polychrome statuary and certain frescoes give a good idea of how peasants and nobility dressed at the time. In Rocamadour, chapels are painted inside and the façades are decorated as well.

Civil and military architecture

Berry and Limousin – There are a few Gothic residences left in the region, but the most noteworthy example is the **Palais Jacques Cœur** in Bourges, which is one of the finest Gothic palaces in all of Europe. Built on the vestiges of a Gallo-Roman wall, the edifice joins massive and forbidding towers to a lively, sculpted façade. Inside, the architecture seems to hint at the approaching Renaissance in its graceful lines and fanciful motifs.

Dordogne – Many of the **castles** in Périgord and Quercy were constructed during the Gothic period, as the architectural details reveal (Bourdeilles, Beynac-et-Cazenac, Castelnaud, Castelnau-Bretenoux). Bonaguil is in a class of its own, for although it was built at the end of the 15C and in the early part of the 16C, it has all the features of a medieval fortress.

In **towns** an important burst of construction occurred after the Hundred Years War. This building boom hit Sarlat, Périgueux and Bergerac as well as Cahors, Figeac, Gourdon and Martel. The façades of town houses are decorated with large pointed arches on the ground floor – where small shops were set up – flattened arches or rose windows on the upper floors, and the whole was ornamented with turrets. Among the finest examples of this period, note the Hôtel de la Raymondie in Martel, the Hôtel de la Monnaie in Figeac (see detailed illustration on page 38), the Hôtel Plamon in Sarlat and the famous Pont Valentré

Bourges – Octogonal tower, Hôtel des Échevins

in Cahors (see detailed illustration on page 38, photograph under CAHORS).

The bastides – These new, more or less fortified towns (in the *Oc* language: *bastidas*) appeared in the 13C and in the 14C their fortified aspect was further developed (see detailed illustrations on page 37).

The founders – The principal founders were Alphonse de Poitiers (1249-71) – count of Toulouse and brother to Saint Louis – and, from 1272 on, the seneschal lords under Philip the Bold, Philip the Fair and King Edward I of England, also duke of Aquitaine.

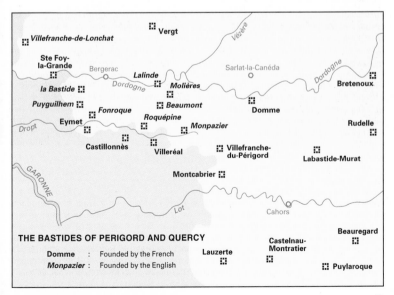

THE BASTIDES OF PERIGORD AND QUERCY

Domme : Founded by the French
Monpazier : Founded by the English

Development – Their construction satisfied economic, military and political needs. The founders took advantage of the growth of the population and encouraged people to settle on their land, rationalising its use and cultivation. In return, they were granted a charter, guaranteed protection, exempted from military service and given the right to inherit. The bailiff represented the king, dispensed justice and collected taxes, whereas the consuls, elected by the people, administered the town; towns flourished under this system. After the Albigensian Crusade when the count of Toulouse, Raymond VII, built about 40 bastides, and with the outbreak of hostilities between the French and the English over Périgord, Quercy and the Agenais, the political and military advantages of the bastides were confirmed. Alphonse de Poitiers had built Eymet, Catillonès and Villeréal along the Dropt river as well as Villefranche-du-Périgord and Ste-Foye-la-Grande. The king of England responded with the construction of Beaumont, Molières, Lalinde and Monpazier, while in 1281 Philip the Bold founded Domme.

All of the bastides, French and English, were built to the same plan – a square or rectangle – and yet they differed because of the terrain and the type of site, the potential for population growth, or the defensive plan. Furthermore, the bastide was at times built around a pre-existing building such as a fortified church (Beaumont) or a castle. The design of Monpazier is most characteristic: it is on a quadrilateral plan with straight streets crossed at right angles by alleys known as **carreyrous**; narrow spaces, **androne**, stand between the houses and serve as fire breaks, drains or even latrines. In the centre of town, the main square is surrounded by covered arcades, **couverts** (also known as **cornières**). The covered market, **halle**, also stands in this square. The church and the cemetery stand nearby; the outer walls are punctuated with towers and gateways. The best preserved bastides are today found in Monpazier, Domme and Eymet.

THE RENAISSANCE

At the beginning of the 16C the artistic movement in France was revitalised by the influence of Italy. King François I and the aristocracy were moved by the desire to copy Italian architecture and sculpture and introduced new styles by employing Italian artists. In the space of a century, hundreds of châteaux were built or restored, as financial resources boomed with the end of the Hundred Years War. Other factors encouraging this artistic movement in the region included improved returns on farm estates (thanks to the development of share-cropping); increased freedom of trade; the mining of iron ore; low labour costs and the advent of ready credit.

Château de Monbazillac

Architecture

Berry – At least half of the châteaux in Berry were rebuilt in the years between 1430 and 1550, and most of the urban centres were transformed. Yet it took a long time for the Italian influence to be felt in Berry where Gothic art was so strongly implanted. Generally, the Italian styles were interpreted, rather than copied. In Bourges, which was ravaged by fire in 1487, the most notable examples of Renaissance architecture are the Hôtels Lallemant and Cujas and the Hôtel des Échevins. In the countryside, defensive castles became more comfortable residences such as Ainay-le-Vieil, Meillant, la Verrerie and Villegongis.

Limousin – In Limoges, the Renaissance influence can be seen on the monumental entrance to the cathedral, Saint John's doorway. In Tulle, the Loyac manor house dates from the 16C. The châteaux which were built or transformed in what is considered a transitional style include Rochechouart, Coussac-Bonneval, Pompadour, and Sédières.

Dordogne – The new style flourished in Montal and Puyguilhem, which look very much like the châteaux of the Loire Valley. Most of the other 16C châteaux incorporate significant defensive features besides the windows, dormers, chimneys and other purely Renaissance elements; such is the case in Monbazillac. In Cénevières, Bourdeilles, Lanquais, Les Bories and Rouffignac (church), buildings were partially transformed; the Biron château is graced by a marvellous Renaissance chapel.

Civil architecture was also influenced by the Italian style: Roaldès Mansion in Cahors, Cayla House (or Consul's House) in Périgueux, Hôtel de Maleville in Sarlat, and Hôtel Labenche in Brive.

Sculpture and other arts

Berry-Limousin – In the Marche tapestry making progressed rapidly: throughout the 16C the Aubusson, Bourganeuf and Felletin workshops profited form the part played in contemporary furnishings by tapestries and hangings which came to be considered indispensable.

Aubusson and Felletin continued to take pride in making tapestries and even as late as the Revolution produced *verdures* or "greeneries" in which plants and fantastic animals appeared against a background of foliage.

Sculpture may be seen at Limoges in the magnificent rood screen erected between 1533 and 1535 and the tomb of Jean de Langeac.

Limousin enamelwork, after the exceptional developments of the 12 to 14C, found new favour in the 16C with the families of the Pénicauds, the Nouailhers and the Limosins whose founder, Léonard Limosin, reached new artistic heights through the use of innovative techniques.

In Bourges, the art of making stained-glass windows revived with the work of the artist Lescuyer.

Dordogne – The inner court of the Montal château is an outstanding example of the Italian style, with its busts in high relief, superb works of art which are realistic and refined. Inside, the remarkable staircase rivals those of the Loire valley châteaux. In the chapel at Biron, the recumbent figures of the Gontaut-Birons are decorated with figures influenced by the Italian Quattrocento (15C).

FROM THE 17C TO THE 20C

Art, copying the styles of Paris and Versailles, lost all its regional character in the 17C.

In Berry, François le Vau, brother of the architect who designed the Louvre, Vaux and Versailles, planned Lignières Château in the style of the *Grand Siècle*: the frontons are supported by pilasters, the main buildings are reflected in sheets of water beyond which extend the French-style gardens.

Hautefort Château, on the borders of Limousin and Périgord – ravaged by fire in 1968 and since completely restored – is a very good example of classical architecture in its planning and unity of design. Rastignac Château was built at the end of the 18C: the purity of its lines and harmony of its proportions place it among the most interesting buildings of that period.

Moutier d'Ahun – Missal stand

S. Sauvignier/MICHELIN

In architecture, the 19C was largely devoted to the restoration and renovation of old buildings. Painting and tapestry, however, saw many innovations. Auguste Renoir and Suzanne Valadon were both from the region of Limousin, although both left the province at a young age. Corot, on the other hand, was born in Paris and came to the region often to paint. His student Berthe Morisot, a native of Bourges, was influenced by Renoir and Manet. Claude Monet was inspired by the ruins at Crozant, and painted thirty versions of the site in 1889. Ingres and Bourdelle, both from Montauban, are the most eminent representatives of Quercy from this period.

Tapestry arts were revived in the 20C thanks to the new ideas and techniques introduced by Lurçat, Dufy, Marc Saint-Saëns, Gromaire and the Association of Tapestry Cartoon-Painters. Modern art has found a place in the many regional and municipal museums as well as the Vassivière centre, devoted exclusively to contemporary art.

Traditional rural architecture

BERRY

Limestone, sandstone and cob are the traditional building materials of the Berry countryside, yet there are distinctive differences in styles from one area to another. For example, in **Champagne Berrichonne**, large farm buildings are set around a courtyard. The low roof is covered in flat brown tiles (or slate closer to the Loire). Inside, the floor is tiled also; a big common room is heated by a stone chimney. The **Pays Fort** farms are more modest, with walls of cob (clay and straw). Thatched roofs have gradually been replaced by tile; the eaves extend amply to protect the walls from wet weather. Around **Sancerre**, farms have a long façade of white limestone, topped with a roof with dormer windows. The living area is often flanked by a barn or stable. Other types of houses are found near the Sologne region and in la Brenne, but some of the characteristics shared by all are the ceramic finials, weathercocks or other ornaments placed on the ridge of the roof or at the apex of a gable, and plain interior furnishings.

LIMOUSIN

Most of the houses in the countryside date from the 19C, and are made of local granite. In the area known as **la Montagne**, the low-built dwellings are attached to the barn and stable. The double-sloped roofs used to be predominently thatch, but have been mostly replaced by slate. Many houses have lean-to additions next to the garden or orchard, and in the past each farm had its own well or spring.

In the **Xaintrie**, the barn-dwellings are often built into a hillside, the rough cast walls are biscuit-coloured. In the southern-most areas, half-timbering appears, along with upper storeys, wooden terraces protected by overhanging *lauze* roofs.

The granite houses of **la Haute-Marche** are usually built with a door and a small window on the ground floor, two small windows on the floor above, and an attic used for storing grain on top.

Limousin house

In the **Bas-Pays Corrézien**, the ground floor is used for storage, whereas the dwelling rooms are located above. The blocky, sandstone houses are covered with a four-sloped roof; an outer stairway links the two storeys by way of a landing and the cellar entrance is at the bottom of the steps.

Higher up on the **plateau**, the boxy buildings in blue or ochre granite have little windows and round-tiled roofs. In addition to the stables, where the hay is stored above the animals, many farms have a special room for drying chestnuts, or a dovecot; all are equipped with a well.

DORDOGNE

The most typical house in the **Périgord Noir** is a sturdy, block-like construction in golden limestone topped with a steeply pitched roof covered with flat brown tiles or *lauzes*. The *lauzes* are neither slate nor layered schist tiles, but small limestone slabs. Set horizontally, their weight is such (500kg per m²/about 102lb per sq ft) that they require a strong, steeply pitched timberwork roof to distribute the weight. Some towers or dovecots adjoin the houses of the more affluent residents.

In the **Périgord Blanc**, low houses in grey or white limestone are lit through windows topped with bull's-eyes *(œils-de-bœuf)*. The flat roof covered with Roman-style terracotta tiles already reflects the more southern style.

In the **Double**, a forest region, the houses were traditionally built of cob and half-timbering.

In the vineyards of **Bergerac**, the wine-growers' houses are, naturally, organised around the activities of pressing grapes and making wine; generally they form a U-shape or else have two adjoining courtyards. The tumble-down cottages in the surrounding vines are dwellings for *bordiers*, labourers.

The houses of **Quercy** are built in blocks of white limestone mortared in lime, displaying a range of shapes, additions, towers and windows. The lower level is partly below ground and called the *cave*. The stable, shed and store rooms were traditionally located there. The floor above that was reserved for the living quarters; the two levels are connected by an outside staircase above a terrace protected by a porch, which is supported by stone or wood columns.

Quercy house

Dovecots

There are numerous dovecots in the area, many of them quite elegant. Some are small towers attached to the main building, others stand alone, either resting on a porch or supported by columns. Before the French Revolution, the right to keep pigeons was generally reserved for large landowners, but Quercy and Périgord (where the right could be purchased for a fee) were exceptions. Dovecots were built mainly for collecting pigeon droppings. The value of these droppings is evident in the fact that when property was divided up after a death, the dung was shared out between the heirs in the same way as the livestock. Not only was it excellent manure, but it was also prized by bakers (for the aroma it gave the bread) and by pharmacists (as a relief for goitre, among other things). The appearance of chemical fertilisers after 1850 led to a decline in production.

The oldest types of free-standing dovecots were arcaded (so-called hanging dovecots), built on small columns to protect them from the damp *(see illustration)*. The stubby capitals *(capels)* created overhangs to deter would-be predators from climbing up the columns.

A dovecot

Dry-stone huts

Here and there, isolated in a field or, more rarely, grouped together *(see Cabanes de Breuil under SARLAT, Excursions)*, stand small constructions built entirely of dry stones, with conical roofs of stones supported by joggles (notches in each new layer are fitted into notches of the layer below to stop the roof from slipping, and the whole roof is fixed at the top by a sort of keystone). They are known as *gariottes*, *caselles* or *bories*, but it is not known precisely what their function used to be nor exactly when they were built. Today's farmers may speculate about the mysterious origins of these surprisingly solid huts; meanwhile, they are happy to use them as tool sheds and storage space and proudly show them off to visitors.

Folklore and traditions

The regions of Berry, Limousin and Dordogne are the hearthstones of age-old rural civilisations. Old-fashioned costumes and ancient crafts have been preserved and are promoted in the many regional festivals *(see the Calendar of events at the end of this guide)*. Legends, superstitions and folktales have continued to flourish alongside religious practices where the lives and legends of the saints play an important role. Alchemists, sorcerers, werewolves; wild and baneful beasts such as the toad, the owl, the wolf have long marked the local imagination.

Local accents trace the boundaries of the different regions as clearly as a line drawn on a map. Regional *patois* (provincial dialects) are seldom heard nowadays, although interest in preserving the traditions of the *langue d'Oc* is reviving.

LANTERNS OF THE DEAD

The earliest recorded reference to "lanterns of the dead" is found in a 12C text by Pierre le Vénérable, abbot of Cluny, *De Miraculis*. The legend recounts that a young novice from Charlieu Abbey (Loire) received a visit from his uncle Achard, the monastery's former prior, who had been dead for some years. The wraith led the youth to the cemetery where, wrapped in a glowing light which seemed to ring them in concentric circles, a group of holy persons gathered. "In the middle of the cemetery, a stone edifice rose up; on the top, there was a small compartment for holding a lamp which, nightly and in honour of the faithful resting there, lights this sacred place. Steps lead to a platform where two or three people can stand or sit down." This definition is very similar to one given in a study written in 1882 by a local abbot and scholar. Mostly built between the 11C and the 13C, in cemeteries near Romanesque churches, many of the lanterns were destroyed, moved or converted to other uses in later years.

These structures, dubbed "lanterns of the dead" in the 19C, seem to be the expression of ancient ideals.

Felletin   St-Genou   Coussac

The form, with the height equal to six or eight times the diameter, complies with ancient Roman canon. The vertical design is symbolic of prestige, but also designates security, and indeed no reference to mourning or suffering seems apparent in the decoration or the exultant skyward movement. Experts still question the use made of the stone dais: perhaps a movable altar was placed upon it, perhaps it was used to indicate the East, the direction of the Holy City of Jerusalem, thus serving to define the alignment of the graves in the cemetery. People have long believed that the spirits of those who have passed away seek out the light which death has extinguished for them. While the early Christian church condemned the practice of lighting candles on tombs, the symbol of the eternal flame soon came to be totally assimilated.

THE LIMOUSIN OSTENSIONS

Every seven years the Haute-Vienne and Creuse *départements* honour their saints: St. Martial the Limousin, St Valérie, the "good St Eligius" founder of the monastery at Solignac, St Stephen of Muret and many others; also the hermits who lived in the Limousin and Marche forests and St Junien, St Victurnien, and St Leonard, founders of monasteries scattered in the valleys. The Virgin Mary is sometimes included under such invocations as Our Lady of the Relics (Aixe-sur-Vienne).

The *ostensions* or solemn exhibition of relics to the faithful date back to the 10C. One of the earliest of these festivals was held at Limoges when a terrible epidemic of ergotism, also known as Saint Anthony's fire, was raging. To combat the malady, the relics of St. Martial were brought out. A visitation – whether in the form of a plague or an illustrious personage – became an occasion for holding these ceremonies which later came to be repeated at regular intervals.

Each town has a traditional ceremony of its own, sponsoring religious festivals which also call on local folklore. The blessing of the banner which is solemnly hoisted to the belfry pinnacle marks the opening of the *ostension*. Once the festival has been opened on the Sunday after Easter, the relics are presented to the faithful for veneration in their shrines or reliquaries, which are, in some cases, masterpieces of the gold and silversmith's art. Picturesque processions march through bunting and flower-decked streets in towns and villages, ac-

companied by fanfares, drums and banners and escorted by guards of honour, occasionally in surprising costume, representatives of different craft guilds and other groups in rich finery. Neighbouring parishes, sometimes in great numbers, join in these manifestations; in Le Dorat, fifty parishes join forces for the closing ceremonies.

The next *ostensions* will be held in 2002.

THE FÉLIBRÉE

Every year in July a different town in Périgord hosts the Félibrée, a meeting of a society of poets and writers set up in the late 19C with the aim of preserving the Provençal language. The chosen town is decorated with thousands of multi-coloured paper flowers around the windows and doors and brightening up the trees and shrubs to form triumphal arches. The people of Périgord flock from all corners of the *département* decked out in traditional costume: lace head-dresses, embroidered shawls and long skirts for the women, huge black felt hats, full white shirts and black velvet waistcoats for the men.

The queen of the Félibrée, surrounded by a member of the Félibrige society committee and the guardians of the local traditions, receives the keys of the town and makes a speech in the local dialect. The assembled gathering flies off in procession to Mass, accompanied by the sound of hurdy-gurdies, before sitting down to a sumptuous feast. Traditionally, the meal begins with *chabrol*, a soup of wine and clear stock typical of the southwest, which is served in dishes made especially for the occasion, bearing the year and the name of the host town. Everyone present keeps these soup dishes as a souvenir and they are displayed proudly in homes or even in regional museums (Mussidan).

Hurdy-gurdy man

Food and wine

BERRY

Cookery in Berry makes use of farm products and is plain and simple. While vegetable, salt pork or bread soup blended with a little cream is the principal regional dish, the true Berry speciality is *poulet en barbouille* – "chicken on the chin". This is chicken set alight with brandy, cut in pieces and cooked in a sauce of blood blended with cream, an egg yolk and the chopped liver. Look forward to dishes in wine or cream sauce: stuffed rabbit, eggs in wine, ox-tongue *au gratin*, kidneys, calf's liver, game and fish, often garnished with fresh mushrooms. Try pumpkin pâté, *truffiat* – potatoes covered in pastry – and for dessert, plum flan, *sanciaux* (honey fritters) and *millats* (stewed black cherries), to complete the traditional local fare.

Wines from Berry are good quality, and especially appreciated by those who enjoy a clean, fresh flavour. Sancerre wines are a well-known *appellation*, mostly white, although red and rosé do exist. There are many small growers scattered in villages round about, and some of the best wine is produced in Bué, Chavignol, Ménétréol and Fontenay. Drink it young to appreciate its spiciness. A good companion for local dishes and cheeses is Menetou-Salon, a choice wine produced locally on a limited scale and not easily found elsewhere. Grown in the same chalky soil as Sancerre, many find it to be fuller and rounder than its neighbours.

LIMOUSIN

Cookery is in the region in hearty; the traditional soup course is *bréjaude*, a pork rind and cabbage soup garnished with rye bread.

S. Sauvignier/MICHELIN

Chestnuts

Pâtés with truffles or wrapped in pastry, which are sometimes garnished with a mixed veal and pork stuffing, and especially the *pâté de foies gras* from Brive-la-Gaillarde, are deservedly famous.

Of course, the region is renown for its tasty beef, but other local fare is delicious too, for example, *Lièvre en chabessal*, hare stuffed with veal, fresh pork, ham and seasoned with salt, pepper, spices and condiments. Cabbage turns up with partridge, braised with chestnuts, or in heart-warming *potées* – country-style boiled dinner. Chestnuts, *châtaignes*, which for a long time were a staple of the farmer's diet, garnish turkey and goose, black pudding, veal or pork stew and are served whipped into a *purée* with venison.

Perhaps the dish most closely associated with Limousin is *clafoutis*, a creamy flan in pastry dotted with succulent, ruby red cherries.

PÉRIGORD-QUERCY

Cookery in the Dorgogne (which the French invariably refer to as "Périgord" when speaking of culinary delights) ranks high among the marvels of France. For centuries, the region has been synonymous with such delectable delicacies as truffles, *foie gras* and *confits*. Sit down to a traditional meal, and you may never want to eat any other way again: for a starter, *tourain blanchi* – a white soup made from garlic, goose fat and eggs, sometimes with sorrel or tomato added; next comes the *foie gras* or *pâté de foie* (a general term for liver pâté); third course, a farm-fresh omelette made with wild *cèpes* (mushrooms) or truffles delicately sliced. For the main course, tuck into a *confit d'oie aux pommes sarladaises* (goose preserved in its own fat, fried until brown, with potatoes fried in goose fat and garlic, garnished with mushrooms). A salad is refreshing then, in a light walnut oil dressing, followed by the cheese plate. Indulge in a sweet slice of walnut cake or a freshly-baked plum pie for dessert.

La truffe is the elegant name of a knobby, black fungus which weighs about 100grams/3.5oz, and imbues all it touches with its unique aroma. A truffle must be fresh, or very carefully preserved, to give full satisfaction. Their rarity and price make them a gourmet luxury. *(Also see Périgord-Quercy, Agriculture, above.)* It is found in delicate black specks in foie gras, pâté, poultry dishes, *ballotines* (white turkey meat and liver moulded in aspic) and *galantines* (cold cuts); it is sliced thinly into salads and omelettes. A truffle wrapped and cooked whole over an open fire – *à la cendre* – is a supreme extravagance.

Foie gras is certainly the pride of Périgord. Once their feathers have grown in (about 1 month), ducks and geese are put outdoors. To prepare for force-feeding, they are nourished with grains and alfalfa, which help expand the digestive system. After three months in the open air, the birds are placed in individual cages for 15-18 days. Progressively overfed, they are given ground meal then whole corn with a funnel-like feeding device known as the *gaveuse*. A

Foie gras

Nouail/IMAGES PHOTOTHÈQUE

duck thus absorbs 10-15kg/22-33lb, a goose up to 20kg/44lb of corn, tripling or even quadrupling the weight of its liver to achieve an ideal weight: 450-500 grams (about one pound) for a duck; 800-900 grams (nearly two pounds)for a goose.

Preparation – Foies gras can be preserved with excellent results, and are labelled according to content; read the label or menu carefully to know what you are getting. **Foie gras entier** is sliced from a whole liver, the nerve fibres removed, seasoned and sterilised (*mi-cuit* livers must be kept refrigerated and eaten fresh). A **bloc de foie gras** is reconstituted, made from bits of liver chopped and mixed at high speed and emulsified with water. Other forms of foie gras are *parfait* (75% liver), *mousse*, *pâté*, *médaillon* and *galantine* (50% liver).

Savouring foie gras – Foie gras should be served chilled (allow 50grams/2oz per person), and cut with a knife rinsed in hot water. Enjoy a glass of cool, sweet Monbazillac wine with your foie gras.

Confits are traditionally the base of regional cooking. *Confit* was first used as a method of preserving various parts of the goose, before the advent of the freezer. Now regarded as a gourmet dish, it is still prepared using traditional methods. The pieces of goose are cooked in their own fat for three hours and then preserved in large earthenware pots *(tupins)*. This procedure is also used to preserve duck, turkey and pork (pork *confit* is called *enchaud*). Goose grease is used instead of butter in local cooking, for example, in frying up the delicious *pommes de terre sarladaises*.

Stuffings and sauces flavourful, enriched with liver and truffles, are used frequently to garnish poultry, game, suckling pigs and in a favourite regional dish – *cou d'oie farci* – stuffed goose neck.

The most commonly used sauces are the *rouilleuse*, which is used to give colour and to accompany poultry fricassee, and *sauce Périgueux*, a Madeira sauce made from a base of chicken stock, to which fresh truffles are added.

Wines from the region have been well-known and sought-after since the Middle Ages. **Cahors** wine was transported by barges *(gabares)* to Bordeaux and from there by ship to the capitals of Europe. A deep red colour, with a robust flavour to match, Cahors accompanies hearty foods including game, roast meats and strong cheese. The bouquet only achieves subtlety and loses its rather harsh presence on the tongue after ageing two to three years in the cask and another dozen in the bottle.

The vineyards of **Bergerac** are largely planted with Sauvignon grapes, producing white and red wines. Among the whites, **Monbazillac** holds pride of place. Golden, smooth, with a heady aroma, this syrupy wine is served as an aperitif, with foie gras or with dessert. Like other sweet, highly alcoholic wines (notably Sauternes), Monbazillac depends on the effects of the "noble mold" *(Botrytis cinerea)*, a highly beneficent mold which forms on the skins of the ripening grapes, bringing about a concentration of sugar and flavour and a vast improvement in the quality of the resulting wine (it imparts no moldy taste whatsoever). The process has been employed since the Renaissance. The grapes are harvested in several batches as they reach the desired state. Monbazillac develops its full flavour after two to three years and will keep for up to 30 years.

Dry white wines such as Montravel and Bergerac, vigorous and fruity, go well with seafood and fish; sweeter wines like Côtes de Bergerac, Côtes de Montravel, Rosette and Saussignac are good as aperitif wines or with white meats.

The red Bergerac wines are firm, with a fruity bouquet, and can be enjoyed soon after bottling. **Pécharmant** is fuller-bodied, more complex, and must be left to mature peacefully before its charms can be appreciated.

Château de Castelnaud

Sights

ARGENTAT★

Population 3 189
Michelin map 75 fold 10 or 239 fold 27

The old houses of Argentat rise in the centre of the picturesque plateaux to the Bas-Limousin at the outlet of the upper valley of the Dordogne.

In the 16C and 17C, the town prospered from activities related to carrying wood for barrel-making down to Bergerac aboard gabare barges. During these propitious days, elegant houses, distinguished by turrets and pepper pots, were built in the town centre and along the riverside.

It is easy to cross town on the N 120 bypass, going over a new bridge over the Dordogne, downstream from the old stone one.

★**The site** – You discover the full beauty of Argentat when approaching from the south. From the bridge across the Dordogne, a panoramic scene of the left bank unfolds: the houses crowd together, their wooden balconies jutting out over the river. Straight on, the busy main street divides the town into two distinct neighbourhoods. You see a curious mixture of the **lauze** (roughly hewn slabs of stone of either schist or lava) and slate roofs, with here and there a turret, a gable or pepper-pot tower.

Argentat – View of the town

The best way to approach the town is to leave your car in rue Eymard-Ledamp *(parking behind the school)*. A bit farther on, to the right, a path leads to the river and the cobblestones of **quai Lestourgie**. Innumerable barges have tied up here since it was built in 1844. Beyond the bridge, continue along the riverside promenade as far as rue des Contamines, passing by the typical narrow streets. Continue up towards the centre by place Delmas and the old houses (Eyrial Manor, the Filliol house). From St-Pierre's, go down the stairs towards rue Ste-Claire, to the *Hôtel* where the Vicomtes de Turenne lived in style. Cross rue Henri IV to rue Goudous; the date of construction has been chiselled into the lintels above venerable dwellings. Past the chapel dedicated to Jeanne d'Arc, rue Ledamp leads back to the car park.

Barrage d'Argentat – This is one of five dams with a hydro-electric power station on the upper Dordogne. It was built 2km/1mi upstream from Argentat to utilise the waters of the Le Chastang Reservoir to best advantage. It rises to a maximum height of 35m/15ft and is 190m/23ft long, along the crest. Four sluices can empty 4 000m³/8000 gallons a second. This power station has five hollow piles, three of which are equipped with hydro-electric generators. Four of the dams use equipment similar to that found in the Rance Tidal Power Station (Brittany), in an experimental endeavour.

St-Martial-Entraygues – *6km/3.6mi northeast on D 18*
Near the church, a trail leads to **Roc Castel**, a viewpoint over the river and the dam.

EXCURSIONS

☐1 La Xaintrie *Round trip of 60km/37mi – 2hr*

Leave Argentat to the southeast on N 120.

At La Broquerie, within sight of the Hautefage dam, the road crosses the river and rises rapidly, making many turns above the rocky and wooded ravines. In Sexcles take D 136 to the left, climbing amid wooded slopes, up to the plateau from where there are fine views of the Maronne valley and the mountains of Auvergne. The road then skirts the foot of the **château du Rieux** (13C and 16C) before passing trough St-Bonnet-les-Tours, and clings to the side of the ravine. Then take D 13 on the left; as the road winds down the hillside, the Merle Towers pop into view from one perspective and another, until you reach the river Maronne.

★★Tours de Merle – *See Tours de MERLE.*

To reach St-Privat D 13 crosses **Xaintrie** – a corruption of the word Saint-Trie. It consists of a granite plateau deeply cut by the gorges of the Dordogne, the Maronne and the Cère, where moorland and scrubland alternate with pine and silver birch woods. The contrast between the open plateau and the enclosed valleys adds to the enjoyment of the excursion.

Moulin de Malesse ⊙ – This 12C mill has been artfully restored and furnished with items such as millstones for wheat and walnuts, a huge oil press (one of the oldest in France); the mill wheels have been reconstructed.

In la Maisonneuve, turn right on D 75, a scenic route to Servières-le-Château.

St-Privat – The 13C and 16C church has a powerful square tower.

Servières-le-Château – This former stronghold, owned successively by the Turenne and the Noailles families, rises in a picturesque **setting★** overlooking the deep gorges of the Glane. With its stone *lauze* roofs, Servières stands encircled by jagged rocks and pine trees.
Beyond the town, there is a view downhill over the Chastang dam and reservoir. A trail leads to a belevedere overlook.

★Barrage de Chastang (Dam) – *See Haute Vallée de la DORDOGNE.*

Glény – The chapel, all that remains of the former church, has an attractive chevet and a bell gable (a high wall pierced with openings).
Just before you reach the Argentat Dam you will see the elegant outline of the **Château du Gibanel** which stands reflected in the reservoir.

☐2 Vallée de la Souvigne

Leave Argentat travelling northwest

The road rises up the wooded hills of the Souvigne valley.

St-Chamant – The church doorway, preceded by the belfry-porch with its wooden gallery, is interesting. Note the doorway capitals and the tympanum with its double register of carvings showing above the Twelve Apostles, Christ in benediction with an angel on either side.

Calvaire d'Espargilière – *15min round trip on foot.* The view from the monument extends over meadows to the wooded hillsides of the surrounding valleys.

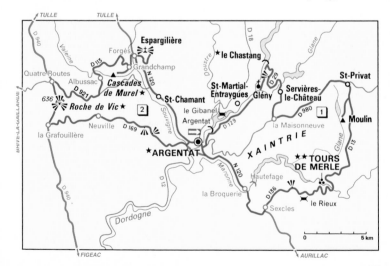

★Cascades de Murel – *Take D 113ᴱ from Grandchamp.*
Walk along the bank of the Valeine with its clear waters to reach the waterfall which is situated in a delightful setting of greenery and rocks.

Return to Grandchamp. Take D 113 left, which flanks the hillside and provides fine views of the Souvigne valley. On leaving Albussac follow D 87 before turning right on N 121. This road crosses pretty little valleys interspersed with chestnut woods before reaching the moorland plateau.

★Roche de Vic – *15min round trip on foot.* Altitude 636m/2087ft.
This bare-flanked hill is crowned with granite blocks supporting a small chapel and a statue of the Virgin Mary, clearly visible from D 940. The **panorama★** from this viewpoint widens over the Lower Limousin (*orientation table*). The hills roll northward to meet the Mondédières range, and south to the limestone plateaux known as the Causse de Quercy.

D 940 carries you across a valley region of woodlands and meadows.

Just beyond Neuville (5km/3mi) there is a view, on the right, of the Dordogne valley and shortly afterwards, on the left, of a wooded ravine.

ARGENTON-SUR-CREUSE★

Population 5 193
Michelin map 68 folds 17 and 18 or 238 fold 39
Local map see Vallée de la CREUSE

Argenton, today, is a pleasant little town with its picturesque old houses spread along the river banks of the Creuse; it replaces the Gallo-Roman city of Argentomagus which lay 2km/1mi to the north on the hill of St-Marcel. In the 19C, the town begin to specialise in the garment industry in particular whitewear, and the manufacture of household linens.

SIGHTS

Begin your visit on rue Charles-Brillaud, by the tourist office on place de la République.

Musée de la Chemiserie ⊘ (**M**) – Stuffed shirts, the shirt off your back, shirttails, shirtsleeves ... here is a museum devoted solely to that sartorial item which keeps our topsides covered. It is located in the building which housed the first industrial shirt manufactory, started up by Charles Brillaud in 1860. The region has long been associated with textile processing, and today concentrates on top-of-the-line men's shirts (Cardin, Dior, Gaultier, etc).

The history of these indispensable garments from the Middle Ages through the present day includes the raiment of stars such as Richard Burton, Charlie Chaplin and Frank Sinatra, as well as the world's largest shirt (3918 pieces of fabric and 25km/15mi of thread). Fashion hounds can try on virtual tops in a simulation booth.

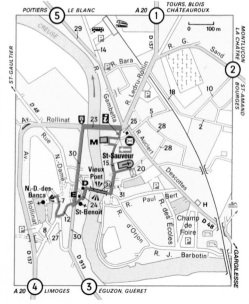

ARGENTON-SUR-CREUSE

D Maison ancienne
E Ancien collège
M Musée de la Chemiserie

Église St-Sauveur – The foundations probably date from the settlement of the lower town (13C). Before the church stands a belfry-porch surmounted by a pierced stone spire (50m/164ft). The nave rebuilt in the 19C has groined vaulting with emblazoned keystones.

Farther on, to the left, down impasse de Villers, a 17-18C manor (Hôtel de Scévole) is now a centre for forensic medicine.

Vieux Pont – The old bridge (17C, but rebuilt in the 19C) provides a good **view**★ of the river Creuse, the old quarter and the upper part of the town. Looking left you see a fine stretch of the Creuse, with twin overflows to provide water for the mills; houses with balconies, balustrades and wooden galleries and with slate roofs, overlooking the river and others built along the cliff which is densely overgrown. The great gilded statue of Notre-Dame of Argenton dominates the Chapel of Notre-Dame des Bancs, on the right with the stone spire of St-Sauveur, and in the far distance the belfry of the Church of St-Marcel.

Beyond the bridge is an **old house** (**D**) with a small Renaissance door.

Turn left on rue Raspail. On the right, you will see the **ancien collège** (**E**), now a regional archaeological centre, built in the Renaissance style (late 15C), crowned with a bell turret and a sculptured doorway. The building is also known locally as "the old prison", for it served that purpose in 1782.

Chapelle St-Benoît – This former Gothic collegiate chapel (15-16C) was restored and consecrated anew in 1873: the belfry was added in 1965. Outside there is a fine doorway with wreathed columns; on the left stands a statue (1485) of the Virgin and Child. Opposite the chapel, the pretty rue de la Coursière leads uphill and affords a view of the town and site.

Chapelle Notre-Dame des Bancs ⊙ – This pilgrimage chapel is dominated by an enormous gilded statue of the Virgin Mary. All that remains of a fortress dismantled in 1632, it was erected in the 15C on the site of the ruins of a 2C sanctuary built by St. Ursinus, first bishop of Berry. The small statue that stands above the high altar is venerated under the name of Good Lady of Argenton (Bonne Dame d'Argenton) and it is said she protected the town from the plague in 1632. The sanctuary got a new lease on life in the late 19C, with a complete restoration. The monumental, gilded Virgin was unveiled in 1899: it weighs about 3 tons and measures 6.5m/21ft.

From the terrace you get a complete **view**★ of the town: the eye travels from the picturesque quays to the houses adorned with gables and turrets, roofs of slate or brown tiles, dwells briefly on the belfries of St-Sauveur's Church and St-Benoît's Chapel and follows the line of the valley of the Creuse as it circles the town in a hilly setting.

EXCURSIONS

★**St-Marcel** – *2km/1mi to the north. See ST-MARCEL.*

▶ ▶ **Le Pont-Chrétien-Chabenet** (15C château serving as Town Hall; covered bridge); **Tendu** (13C church; Prunget and Mazières keeps, 15C château de la Rocherolle); **Château de Courbat** (Town Hall).

ARNAC-POMPADOUR★

Population 444
Michelin map 75 fold 8 or 239 fold 25

These two towns in Corrèze, 2km/1mi apart, today form a single administrative area *(commune).*

ARNAC

Church – Consecrated in 1082, it initially belonged to the St-Martial Abbey in Limoges. The current church was built in the 12C; the severe lines and sheer size are striking.

There is an unusual juxtaposition of Romanesque and Gothic forms. The doorway, characteristic of the regional style, is decorated with capitals, medallions and pointed, hanging ornaments at the apexes of the vaults. Three statues are set into the façade above: left to right, St Martial, the Virgin, St Pardoux – the two saints are patrons of the Limousin region.

Inside the nave, the keystones bear the arms of Pompadour; the transept is Romanesque. Interesting historiated capitals adorn the columns in the nave, including scenes of the Annunciation, Daniel in the Lion's Den.

Château de Pompadour

POMPADOUR

The château and title of Pompadour were proffered by King Louis XV to his *favorite* in 1745. In 1761, the stud farm stables became the cradle of the Anglo-Arabian breed in France. Celebrated races and various competitive events are held here regularly in the summer.

Château ⊘ – Currently accommodating the officers of the equestrian establishment, this imposing 15C construction stands proudly on well-groomed grounds. Round towers and square pavilions are connected by curtain walls whose high towers rest upon the projecting parapet pierced with machicolations. The terrace in front is protected by moats and low towers.

Haras (National Stud Farm) ⊘ – The Puy-Marmont stallion farm, in the park, is home to some fifty steeds, pure-bred Arabians, and especially Anglo-Arabians, revered in France and abroad as studs and recreational mounts. The stables also house other handsome and rare breeds, including quarter horses from the French regions of Ardennes, Brittany, Franche-Comté, and rugged Percherons.

EXCURSIONS

Jumenterie nationale de Beyssac ⊘ – *4km/2.4mi southeast via D 7 and D 7[63].* The verdant Domaine de la Rivière, 88ha/217 acres in all, was created in the 18C on the site of a ruined 15C castle (only the towers and a Gothic chapel remain), and became a national establishment for raising mares in the 19C. About forty state-owned mares live there, and others join them periodically for covering and births. In the months of May and June, the proud mothers can be seen gambolling in the fields with their colts.
The riding centre also owns a dozen stallions.

Chartreuse de Glandier ⊘ – *9km/5.4mi southeast on D 7 and D 148.* In the heart of the Loyre valley, a Carthusian monastery was established in the 13C. Destroyed during the Revolution, the order repurchased it in 1860 and built it up again over 10 years.
Now the buildings serve as a medical centre, with an exhibit area devoted to the history of the place (including a scale model of the site). One of the **monk's pavilions** has been reconstructed and its two storeys show a workshop (ground floor), a chamber and the library on the floor above.

The Practical information section at the end of the guide lists:
  – information on travel, motoring, accommodation, recreation
  – local or national organisations providing additional information;
  – calendar of events
  – admission times and charges for the sights described in the guide.

Les ARQUES★

Population 160
Michelin map 79 fold 7 or 235 fold 10 – 6km/3.5mi south of Cazals
Local map see BOURIANE

In this tranquil Bouriane village are two interesting churches both of which have undergone extensive restoration.

Ossip Zadkine – Russian by birth and French by adoption, the sculptor Zadkine (1890-1967) arrived in Paris in 1909. He was first influenced by Cubism, a style which he subsequently abandoned.

In 1934 he bought a house in Les Arques where he realised his most important works (Diana, Pietà, Christ); their monumental expression and well-constructed forms give them a widespread and long-lasting appeal.

Pieta by Ossip Zadkine (St-Laurent's crypt)

Musée Zadkine ⊙ – Three rooms display examples of the artist's work: lithographs, tapestries, bronzes (Musical Trio, 1928) and monumental wood sculptures (Diana). There is an audio-visual presentation of an interview with Zadkine.

★**Église St-Laurent** – Located in the centre of the village, this church is all that is left of a priory-deanery founded in the 11C by Marcilhac Abbey. When the nave was restored in the 19C, it was narrowed and shortened; yet the apse and apsidal chapels have kept the purity of the Romanesque style. Certain archaisms have been preserved such as the oculus in the south arm of the transept, a characteristic of the Carolingean style, and the tori at the base of the columns supporting the transverse arches. The most original part of the interior is the shape of the arches: round horseshoe-shaped arches onto which open the apsidal chapels and rampant arches which adorn the passageway between the apse and apsidal chapels.

Two moving works by Zadkine enhance the church's interior: the monumental **Christ★** (on the back of the façade) and the **Pietà★** (in the crypt).

Chapelle St-André-des-Arques ⊙ – *Go down towards the Masse river, cross D 45.* Set in a clearing, this church presents a remarkable series of **frescoes★** from the late 15C, discovered in 1954 by Zadkine.

The chancel window is framed by the Annunciation and on either side by the apostles with either the instruments of their punishment – St Andrew and the X-shaped cross and St Matthew and the halberd – or the instruments with which they are symbolised in art: St Peter with his keys, St James with his pilgrim's staff and St Thomas with his architect's set square. On the vault, spangled with red stars, is Christ in Majesty seated on a rainbow-shaped throne with one hand held up in blessing and the other holding the globe. He is surrounded by the symbols of the four Evangelists. On the pillars of the apse, which are holding up a triumphal arch, are St Christopher and, on the other side, the Infant Jesus waiting for Christopher to help him cross the river.

The key on the inside cover explains the abbreviations and symbols used in the text or on the maps.

AUBAZINE★

Population 788
Michelin map 75 fold 9 or 239 fold 26
Local map under BRIVE-LA-GAILLARDE: Excursions

Aubazine is pleasantly situated between the rivers Corrèze and Coiroux, on a promontory set back from the main roads.

A Dual Monastery – During the first few months of the 12C a group of men and women, united by a common desire to lead a life of fasting and prayer, gathered together in the forest of Aubazine to join the hermit St Stephen who had come from the nearby Xaintrie district in the Corrèze valley. Having adopted the rule of St Benedict, this small community built a monastery at Aubazine, and then a convent only 600m/656yds away from this in the Coiroux valley. In 1147, although the existence of a community of women proved to be a severe handicap, St Stephen nevertheless gained admittance for his communities into the Cistercian Order. This distinction of a dual monastery was preserved until the Revolution. The founder had decreed that the women take vows of complete enclosure, so they were totally dependent, both spiritually and materially, on the monastery. This no doubt gave rise to the local joke that anyone with a daughter at Coiroux gained a son-in-law at Aubazine.

The Monastery – The **abbey★** was built in the second half of the 12C and dedicated to the Blessed Virgin, as were most Cistercian churches. In the 18C it was truncated, losing six of its nine bays, so it is easy to imagine how large the original must have been. The west façade was built during that period.

The **belltower★** crowning the transept crossing is of a very original design; the transition from a square shape to an octagonal one is made by a system of stone tiers, which form a geometrically regulated surface, a technical achievement unique to that time.

Inside, the central nave has a barrel-vault and the huge square of the transept is topped with an elegant dome on pendentives. Three radiating chapels, with flat apses, open from each side of the choir which itself ends in a five-sided apse. The stained-glass windows in grisaille are the only ones to have been permitted in a Cistercian Church.

Furnishings★ – In the south arm of the transept there is the remarkable **tomb of St Stephen★** made from limestone between 1250 and 1260, probably by artists from a studio in the Paris area. The face of the recumbent figure has been disfigured by the faithful flock (who believed that the dust they obtained by scraping at the stone held miraculous powers). A blind arcade cuts across the height of the alcove in which the figure lies, and the canopy above has two sloping sides which are decorated with scenes in relief. On the side that can be seen, the Virgin holding the Child Jesus greets St Stephen and his communities on earth. Opposite the tomb, the Coiroux **Entombment** is on display. This piece of stonework was originally polychrome and is of an exceptional quality; it was rediscovered in 1985 during the excavation of the convent. In the first chapel in the north arm of the transept a 15C stone Pietà, with traces of polychrome, has a striking expression of immense spirituality.

At the foot of the great staircase which led to the dormitory there is the oldest **liturgical cupboard★** in France. Made in the 12C from oak beams, it is decorated with blind arcades on its sides.

The choir stalls date from the 18C, when the abbey was chosen as the noviciate for the whole of western Aquitaine. On the misericords of the stalls, now dispersed around the building, there are some very expressive carved figures.

Bâtiments conventuels ⊙ – The convent is home to a community of Catholic nuns. Visitors are admitted to the small library, the chapter-house with its groined vaulting resting on two columns, the nuns' common room, the kitchen and the large fish-breeding pond, fed by the "nuns' canal". This was built in the 12C, starting from a capture on the river Coiroux, partly hollowed out of the rock itself and partly cantilevered above a sheer drop of over 50m/164ft, and it is a technical work of art of an exceptional standard. It is possible to follow the whole of its course *(see route indicated to the right along the course of the Coiroux river; distance: 1.5km/1mi).*

Convent – *600m/656yds from the market town; to get there take the road towards Palazinges.*

All that remains standing of the convent, which was abandoned in 1791, is the church walls. However, recent excavation work has unearthed the irrigation system for drinking water and, beneath the embankment of the modern road, the arched doorway by which the monks and nuns communicated. This is designed like a lock chamber; one of the communities had the key to the outside door and the other the key to the inside door.

EXCURSION

Puy de Pauliac – *Take D 48 along the Coiroux Gorges and bear left on a smaller road to the summit.*

A path *(15min round trip on foot)* through heather and chestnut trees leads up to the top (520m/1 760ft) from where there is a wide **view★** *(viewing table)* southeast onto Vic Rock and northwards onto Monédières Massif.

Continue along D 48 to the **Coiroux Tourist Centre** (Centre Touristique du Coiroux) where facilities (swimming, sailing, windsurfing and golf) have been set up around a lake.

Population 388
Michelin map 75 fold 3 or 233 folds 40, 41

Overlooking the Dronne valley and its green grazing, Aubeterre is a small, old town of narrow, steep streets, built at the foot of its castle. The town rises up the slopes of an amphitheatre set into the white chalk cliffs which gave the town its name (*alba terra* in Latin: white land).

The town is centred around place Travieux, and the bust in honour of Ludovic Travieux, born in Aubeterre, who founded the League for the Defence of the Rights of Man. From here, you can either climb up towards the church of St Jacques, or walk down towards the monolithic church.

CHURCHES

★★**Église monolithe** ⊘ – Dedicated to St John, this monolithic church is a rare example of a building hewn from a single block of rock. A corridor bordered with niches leads to a vast cavity cut into the rock; the inner surface is bare and rough. A baptismal font from the 5C or 6C, sculpted in the shape of a Greek cross, testifies to the presence of a primitive church and evokes the practice of baptism by total immersion. The crypt must have hosted followers of Mithras, a god worshipped by members of a mystery cult which was one of early Christianity's most serious rivals. Mithraism excluded women, and was popular among Roman soldiers in Gaul. One of the seven rites of initiation they performed was slaying a bull (as Mithras killed the cosmic bull of creation, representing the conquest of evil and death).

The present church was probably started in the 12C to house relics brought back from the Holy Sepulchre in Jerusalem by the crusaders Pierre II de Castillon, who owned the castle here. Under the Revolution, the church was used as a saltpetre works, and later as the local cemetery (until 1865). The 20m/65ft high nave,

Aubeterre-sur-Dronne – Monolithic church

running parallel to the cliffs, is composed of three bays. It is flanked by a single aisle where a small spring venerated by early pilgrims still filters. The apse surrounds a monolithic Romanesque monument, carved from a block left in place when the church was hollowed out. In it, a shrine holds the relics of the Holy Sepulchre.

At the other end of the nave is a primitive 6C chapel; transformed into a necropolis in the 12C after work on the church was completed. Excavations have revealed a series of tombs hollowed out of the rock.

In the higher part of the nave, a gallery above the ambulatory overlooks this place of primitive worship.

There used to be a castle above the church which was linked to the gallery by a small staircase. The lords of the castle could easily spy on the crowd and attend the service.

Église St-Jacques – This church was formerly the Benedictine Abbey of St-Sauveur, which later became the home church for a chapter of canons. The Romanesque façade, punctuated by arcades, is decorated with finely sculpted geometric motifs based on Arabic designs. Left of the central doorway, a carved frieze depicts the Labours of the Months.

Below the church, the tower's battlements protect the chapter house.

AUBIGNY-SUR-NÈRE★

Population 5 803

Michelin map 65 fold 11 or 238 folds 18, 19

On the borders of Berry and the Sologne, Aubigny is on the river Nère which here flows partly underground. The town is small but busy, holding annual fairs, producing electric motors and precision instruments, drawing crowds for events at the modern sports facilities.

The Stuart City – In 1423 Charles VII gave Aubigny to a Scotsman, John Stuart, his ally against the English. He was succeeded by Béraud Stuart, who effected a reconciliation between Louis XI and his cousin, the future Louis XII, and then by Robert Stuart, known as the Marshal of Aubigny, who fought in Italy under François I.

Craftsmen from Scotland settled here, working as glass-makers, or using white wool from Sologne to ply the weaver's trade.

SIGHTS

★**Old houses** – A number of early-16C half-timbered houses have survived. The oaks used in their construction were given by Robert Stuart from the nearby forest of Ivoy. There are several along rue du Prieuré and its continuation, rue des Dames, charming and busy streets hung with shop signs from the town hall to the church, as well as in rue du Charbon and place Adrien-Arnoux. No 10 rue du Pont-Aux-Foulons is the only house to have survived the fire of 1512. In rue du Bourg-Coutant stands the **Maison du Bailli★** with its carved beams, and almost opposite, at the corner of rue de l'Église, the pretty **Maison François I**.

Église St-Martin ⊘ – The church is built in Gothic style, marking the arrival of Ile-de-France influences in Berry. At the entrance of the chancel two 17C painted statues represent a charming Virgin and Child and a dramatic Christ Reviled, while in the chancel a 16C stained glass window depicts the life of St Martin. In the third chapel to the right there is an admirable 17C wood *Pietà*.

Ancien château des Stuarts ⊘ – This 16C building was the work of Robert Stuart; altered by Louise de Kéroualle, duchess of Portsmouth, it now serves as Aubigny's town hall. The entrance gatehouse, dating from the time of Robert Stuart, is flanked with attractive brick bartizans; the keystone of the vault is emblazoned with the Stuart coat of arms. Pass into the charming irregular courtyard with its mullioned windows and round or polygonal turreted staircases. One of the rooms of the château presents a small museum devoted to the life and work of **Marguerite Audoux** (1863-1937), the local writer whose novel about a shepherdess *Marie-Claire* is based on her own childhood and gave rise to the popular French magazine of the same name.. In summer, the château hosts both the Festival of Mural Poetry and the Sologne Art Exhibition.

Parc de la duchesse de Portsmouth – These gardens, still called the Grands Jardins, were laid out in the 17C and adorned with clipped hedges, arbours and fine trees. They are named after Charles II's favourite, the Duchess of Portsmouth, who lived at Château de la Verrerie *(see below)*.

Ramparts – The line of the old town wall, built originally by Philippe-Auguste, is marked by the streets enclosing the town centre and the two round towers overlooking the Mall.

EXCURSION

★ Château de la Verrerie ⊙ – *11km/7mi southeast on D 89.*
The château stands in an isolated but beautiful **setting★** near the forest of Ivoy beside a lake formed by a broad stretch of the Nère. It is thought to have inspired Alain-Fournier for one of the episodes in his novel *Le Grand Meaulnes.*
The château originally consisted of four ranges of buildings round a courtyard; the oldest part was built by Charles VII who gave it to John Stuart at the same time as Aubigny-sur-Nère. At the end of the 15C Béraud Stuart built a château (house and chapel) which was completed during the Renaissance by his nephew Robert, Maréchal d'Aubigny. In 1670 the château reverted to the crown; in 1673 Louis XIV gave it to the Duchess of Portsmouth, the favourite mistress of Charles II of England.
The graceful **Renaissance gallery★** was erected by Robert Stuart in 1525, the date when the frescoes were painted in the 15C chapel; the tabernacle in carved wood dates from the Renaissance. The 19C wing added behind the Renaissance gallery contains some fine furniture from the Renaissance to the Louis XVI period; two 18C Beauvais tapestries hang in the dining room; the Renaissance cupboard in the salon contains four remarkable 15C alabaster **weeping figures★** from the tomb of Jean de Berry.
The boudoir displays a collection of 19C dolls together with their furniture as well as the library of **Melchior de Vogüé** (1829-1916), a member of the Académie Française, a diplomat and archeologist who directed excavations in Palestine and Syria.

AUBUSSON

Population 5 097
Michelin map 73 fold 1 or 239 fold 4

Aubusson, built in the upper valley of the Creuse, still manufactures the tapestries and carpets that have won it renown over the last five centuries. A College of Decorative Arts opened in 1884 offers courses aimed at keeping up this tradition. The Jean Lurçat Cultural Centre has recently been set up to promote this craft.

TAPESTRIES

A time-honoured craft – It would appear that tapestry weaving was imported from Flanders in the 14C by Marie de Hainault who became countess of Marche and it was only in the 15C that the tapestry weavers of Aubusson won wide fame. The Lady and the Unicorn, a 15C masterpiece now in the Cluny Museum in Paris, is believed to have been woven by the craftsmen of Aubusson. Their fame peaked in the 16C and 17C with *verdures* (flower and foliage designs in shades of green) as well as sacred, mythological and historical themes, and Colbert granted them the title of royal tapestry-makers.
With the departure abroad of many of the weavers, particularly to Germany, in 1685 at the Revocation of the Edict of Nantes, the industry faced ruin. It recovered only at the beginning of the 18C, thanks to the work of certain painters of that time: Watteau, Lancret and Boucher. The 19C was a period of decline between the aftermath of the Revolution and competition from wallpaper. Nowadays the town takes pride in several factories weaving by methods that have been well tried for over a hundred years. The great speciality of Aubusson is *basse-lisse* (low-warp) tapestry using horizontal looms; the same technique predominates at Beauvais and Gobelins.

A fresh start – At the beginning of the 20C inspiration was flagging. Although technically perfect the tapestries were mere copies of paintings in a variety of colours.
In the 1930s a fresh impetus was given thanks to a collector, Madame Cuttoli, who commissioned designs from the greatest contemporary painters. From 1939 **Jean Lurçat** (1892-1966) in collaboration with Gromaire, played a decisive part in the rebirth of the art of tapestry weaving. A new generation of cartoon designers emerged with Prassinos, Tourlière, Saint-Saëns, Picart-le-Doux, Dom Robert and Wogensky among others. Aubusson did not neglect traditional themes, and showed renewed creative originality and gained further international renown.

Tapestry techniques – There are two main stages in the production of a tapestry. First, the colours and shapes of the pattern are painted on the **cartoon** or preliminary design, by a specialised artist, and traced onto a reference model. The colours in the design are assigned numbers; each artist has a special set assigned to his or her creations. Then the second stage, weaving, can begin.
The **warp** threads, linen, wool, or cotton, are stretched on a frame to allow the interweaving of the **weft** threads, wrapped around a **shuttle**. The threads are gathered in bunches, which are separated by a rounded rod into bundles of odd and even-numbered threads. Sets of parallel cords or wires with their mounting, **heddles**, compose the harness which guides the warp threads in the loom.

AUBUSSON

On a low-warp loom the warp threads are stretched horizontally between two rollers (the technique commonly used in Aubusson); the high-warp loom is vertical. The heddles on the low-warp loom are arranged underneath the warp threads and controlled by treadles. By pressing down with the foot alternately on the treadles, the weaver can lower first one and then the other series of warp threads, allowing the shuttles to pass under and over them.

The fabric thus created is pressed tight, or beaten in, against the previous rows of weft by a metal batten; the reed, a comb-like wooden device, keeps the warp threads evenly spaced. The weaving is done upside down, so a mirror is used to check the work as it advances. It takes about one month to produce one square metre.

"**Savonnerie**" carpets are made on a high-warp loom using knotting techniques.

DISCOVERING TAPESTRY

Centre culturel et artistique Jean Lurçat – This austere, functional building on the banks of the river Creuse (avenue des Lissiers) was built in 1981 and has since been devoted to the art of tapestry weaving. There is a theatre *(la Scène nationale)*, a gallery for large temporary exhibitions, a library and a reference section as well as a demonstration workshop.

Aubusson – Jean Lurçat tapestry

★ **Musée départemental de la tapisserie** ⊘ – The collection embraces all types of tapestries and carpets from the 17C, 18C and 19C. The 20C is illustrated by various works, on display alternately, by contemporary artists including Lurçat, Gromaire, Saint-Saëns, Picart le Doux, Tourlière and Julien. The modern works demonstrate the brilliance of the period of renewal inspired by Lurçat. A tour of the museum concludes with an exhibit on the history and technique of this art.

Yearly exhibits are planned around themes linked to tapestry and textile arts; at certain times, demonstrations of the different production phases are given.

École Nationale d'Art Décoratif d'Aubusson ⊘ – This school offers a course leading to a nationally recognised diploma in textile design, and frequently puts on, public exhibits.

Forum de la tapisserie ⊘ (**H**) – The exhibit in the Hôtel de Ville (town hall) comprises tapestries and carpets worked to traditional and modern designs. In the nearby shops on Grande-Rue, many private galleries display local work.

Manufacture de Tapis et de Tapisseries St-Jean ⊘ – The workshops in the former royal manufactory work on commissions only.

The tour begins with a look at different styles and techniques. Note the artists' signature marks on the right-hand side of modern works, and the manufacturer's mark on the left. An identifying mark (**bolduc**) is also found on the back.

A tapestry begins to see the light of day in the design workshop. The artist creates a scale design (1:10), and once the client approves, the cartoon is painted lifesize. Yarns are selected from the storage room accordingly and the different shades sorted out.

The **savonnerie** workshop is a spectacular place. Carpets are made by specialised weavers on high-warp looms *(see photograph in the Practical information section)*. A linen warp 36m²/387sq ft large requires 2 weeks to set up, and 4 weavers need 11 weeks to complete it.

Other carpets (**ras**), with a rougher finished feel, are woven on a low-warp loom, with a cotton warp. The weavers work on one section at a time.

AUBUSSON

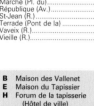

B	Maison des Vallenet
E	Maison du Tapissier
H	Forum de la tapisserie (Hôtel de ville)

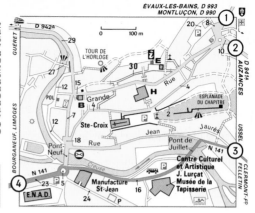

The restoration workshop handles carpets which have been damaged over time. After finding the right colours and materials, the tapesters rebuild the warp and weft.

Maison du Tapissier ⊘ (**E**) – In this lovely 16C house which once belonged to the Corneille family of weavers, pieces of local furniture and other objects evoke life in Aubusson in times past. On the upper floor, an old-fashioned workshop displays a low-warp loom, reels, wheels for preparing shuttles and bobbin stands, as well as several tapestries, cartoons and embroidered pieces.

ADDITIONAL SIGHTS

Old Town – It stretches on both sides of the Grande-Rue. Go along **rue Vieille** (**30**) which is reserved for pedestrians and where the old houses have been completely renovated and turned into art galleries, craft and antique shops. The attractive place de la Libération contains a 16C turreted house known as the **Maison des Vallenet** (**B**) and a fountain dating from 1718, adorned with heraldic devices.
There is a pleasant view from the old bridge, Pont de la Terrade, an interesting 16C construction with pointed cutwaters, of the houses rising in terraces on the left bank of the Creuse at the foot of some impressive sized rocks.

Warp, weft, weave

The word textile (from the Latin *texere*, "to weave") originally meant a fabric made from woven fibres. The earliest known samples of yarn and fabric were found near Robenhausen, Switzerland, and are estimated to be about 7000 years old. Excavations and research by archeologists and historians have revealed that tapestry weaving techniques were known and used by the Hebrews, Greeks, Romans, Chinese, and Incas, among other ancient peoples.

The hand loom in many variations was for centuries the basic weaving instrument; foot-powered looms with several sets of heddles appeared in Europe during the 13C. During the 16C and early 17C, Brussels became the capital of European tapestry production, and the fame of Flemish weavers spread. Some of them are known to have immigrated to the region of Aubusson, and in particular to the town of Felletin, considered to be the cradle of this art in France.

For the next two centuries, the French royal factories founded by Louis XIV at Gobelins (1662), Beauvais (1664), and Aubusson (1665) dominated European production with tapestry series designed by great painters. When Beauvais was amalgamated with Gobelins in 1940, Aubusson became the major centre for tapestry design and production. An exciting new era began when Jean Lurçat (1892-1966) settled there for the purpose of reinventing the tapestry industry at the request of the French Ministry of National Education, and founded the Association of Tapestry Cartoon-Painters (1945), stimulating a revival of tapestry as a modern and original artistic expression (rather than designs copied from paintings).

May the warp be the white light of morning,
May the weft be the red light of evening,
May the fringes be the falling rain,
May the border be the standing rainbow.
Thus weave for us a garment of brightness.

Tewa Pueblo Indian poem

Église Ste-Croix – This sturdy church was built in the 13C and largely redone in the 19C. Only one of the four tapestries which once adorned its walls remains.

View – From the terrace near the church, a steep path climbs to the summit of the hill and the Esplanade du Chapitre where the ruins of the castle of the counts of Aubusson still stand.

The adventurous walker may continue up a more difficult trail towards the Marchedieu farm, where a wide **panorama** enfolds the five valleys which cradle the town.

HAUTE VALLÉE DE LA CREUSE

Round trip of 90km/ 54mi – 4hr

From Aubusson, take D 942ᴬ towards Guéret.

Église de Chénérailles – Built in the 13C, it contains a handsome **haut-relief★** in the third bay on the right, which dates from the early 14C and was placed there in memory of Barthélémy de la Place, the church's founder. Sculpted in hard white limestone, this finely wrought, expressive "tombstone" has a lower section representing the funeral scene, a middle part showing the Virgin and Child in the company of St Aignan and St Barthélemy, and finally an upper panel illustrating the Crucifixion. The Virgin is a rendering of the 13C polychrome stone statue in the side chapel. The woodwork, stalls and gilded altar date from the 17C.

Château de Villemonteix ◷ – From the road, this 15C feudal stronghold sets a suggestive scene.

The entrance yard is preceded by two corner towers (the one on the right was converted into a dovecote in the 17C). Strategically located, it was previously protected by a moat and drawbridge.

In the middle of the austere façade, a square, recessed tower surrounds a spiral stairway. The watchpath, supported by corbels and two gargoyles, has a watchtower at each end. On the western side, two more towers fill out the defensive structure, safeguarding the rear of the central building.

Inside, the evolution from fortress to residential manor is apparent. On the ground floor: kitchen, salon (Berry porcelain and faience) and reception room, with 18C furnishings and woodwork, giving onto a small Gothic chapel. A granite stairway in the tower leads to the upper floors. In the main room hang three 17C Aubusson tapestries relating the tale of Achilles. The other rooms are occupied by various groups of period furniture.

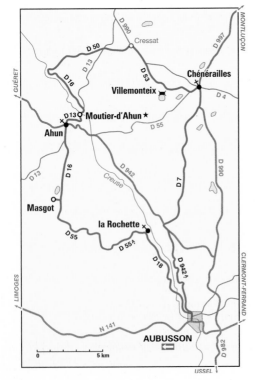

Leaving the château, turn left and go back to D 53, towards Cressat.

★Moutier-d'Ahun – *See MOUTIER-D'AHUN.*

Take D 13.

Ahun – Looking over the river Creuse, this small town was once the brilliant *Acitodunum*, a major city on the map of the Roman Empire, and probably one of the first places to be evangelised by St Martial.

Église St-Sylvain – On the outside, between the arched bays of the chevet, the capitals atop the columns are carved with animals and palmettos. Inside, the remarkable **woodwork★** panels and columns date from the 17C; a statue shows St Sylvain holding a book and a palm frond. A gilded wood rood screen, a 12C Baptismal font hewn in granite and a 15C polychrome stone *Pietà* complete the church furnishings.

The **crypt** (*use the stairway outside the church*) covers the area below the chevet and the far end of the chancel. There are two semi-circular rooms: one has three naves with vaulted ceilings supported by monolithic pillars; the second is pre-Romanesque and shelters a reliquary-tomb.

Take D 13 towards Pontarion.

Village de Masgot – This hilltop village is peopled with odd, immobile characters, crouching on walls, perched in leafy gardens. They are the work of François Michaud (1810-1890), a stone mason who brought a new dimension to the traditional local craft and the granite quarried here.

A **museum** ⊘ has been opened in his home; in the summer, aspiring artists can take chisel to stone as well as taking inspiration from the many traces of dextrous hands (the buildings themselves are works of art) from generations past.

Chapelle de la Rochette – Built in 1569 in Romanesque style and since restored, the chapel has a belfry topped with wooden shingles. The **site** is appealing; the sound of the river running through rolling meadows a melodious accompaniment.

C. Boisvieux

Masgot – Nude
by François Michaud

BEAULIEU-SUR-DORDOGNE★★

Population 1 263
Michelin map 75 north of fold 19 or 239 north of fold 39

Built on the right bank of the Dordogne, Beaulieu is famous for the fine Romanesque church there, once part of a Benedictine abbey.

Foundation and growth of the Abbey – Raoul, archbishop of Bourges, visited this part of the country in 855 and, enchanted by the beauty of this particular site which he christened *bellus locus – beau lieu* (beautiful place) – decided to found a community there. The monastery grew to significance despite the warlike struggles for control waged by the lords of Turenne and Castelnau. The abbots became the equals of city merchants and, as their special privileges increased, became virtually independent.

The Benedictine reform – The monks gradually came to interpret the order's rule of discipline more and more liberally. When the Wars of Religion (1562-1598) raged, they deserted their monastery. In 1663 the Abbot of La Tour d'Auvergne called on the austere Benedictine Congregation of Maurists to undertake the necessary reforms and to repair the buildings. The community prospered thereafter, until the Revolution took hold, and drove them out again.

★★ÉGLISE ST-PIERRE

The influence of both the Limousin and the Southwest are apparent in the architecture of this abbey church, built mostly in the 12C.

Exterior – The sandstone building is typical of Benedictine establishments which served as places of pilgrimage. The choir, transept and eastern bay of the nave were the first to be completed, from about 1100 to 1140. In the middle of the 12C, works were continued from the southern end of the nave to the northern parallel walls. The project was finished in the 13C, with the western bay of the nave and the façade.

The **south doorway** was carved in 1125 and is one of the great masterpieces of early Romanesque sculpture. The craftsmen who made it came from Toulouse and worked on the carvings at Moissac, Collonges, Souillac and Carrennac.

The doorway is preceded by an open porch; the sculpture is remarkable for both composition and execution. The theme on the tympanum is the Last Judgement.

(1) In the centre, Christ in Majesty dominates all by his height and extends his arm in welcome to the chosen.

(2) On either side two angels sound trumpets, while above, four angels (3) hold the instruments of the Passion – the Cross, the Nails and the Crown of Thorns. The Apostles are grouped left and right (4) and above them (5) the dead rise from their graves. Monsters line the upper part of the lintel (6). The lower part (7), as at Moissac, is decorated with rosettes from which emerge chimera, serpents and monsters. (8) Three prophets in clinging robes stand against the pier.

Two rounded arcades supported on small columns stand on either side before the door; they are badly mutilated but behind them can be seen, on the left, (9) Daniel in the lion's den and, on the right, (10) the Temptation of Christ.

Chevet – The style and proportions of the graceful eastern end of the church are highlighted by the window mouldings typical of the Limousin region, and cornices with sculpted modillions. The apse is crowned with chapels; above them rise the fine octagonal tower which covers the transept crossing. The sobriety of the upper levels of the façade add to the overall elegance; the dome is set within a square enclosure between two small spires.

The central belfry has one octagonal story with eight arched apertures in the local style. As you walk around the outside of the chevet, note the vestiges of the cloisters where they once extended from the northern side of the church (sacristy).

Western façade – There is no tympanum above the wide doorway. The tower rising up to the right was added in the 14C during the Hundred Years War. Raised higher in 1556, it served as the town belfry.

Interior – The sanctuary was designed for pilgrimages and, like others so-dedicated, planned out to facilitate the movement of crowds, as evidenced in the wide aisles.

Architecture – The nave has cradle vaulting, no windows on the wide side aisles which extend beyond the arms of the transept into an ambulatory with radial chapels. The tall, asymmetrical dome on pendentives rises above the transept from recessed columns. Dark galleries open off the nave through twin bays whose arches stand on two small squat columns. The same arrangement is to be found in the transept and the chancel which has oven vaulting and is lit by five rounded bays.

Decoration – The decorative aspect is rather rustic compared to the intricate beauty of the southern doorway. There are but a few sculpted capitals, at the entrance to the ambulatory and the transept chapels: they are embellished with garlands and caryatids.

The other capitals bear geometrical designs typical of the Quercy region. In the northern arm of the transept, above the door to the stairway, an unsophisticated lintel carving represents two lions and a tree. The fourth bay on the same side has a similar carving above the old door to the cloisters, showing a person sitting between two bushes and two lions.

Trésor ⊙ – Kept safely in a special cupboard in the left wing of the transept, the treasury holds a remarkable 12C seated **Virgin**★ in silver-plated wood, a 10C silver reliquary, a chased enamel shrine (chest) from the 13C, two 14C reliquary pieces and other pieces in vermilion and pewter.

Beaulieu-sur-Dordogne – La chapelle des Pénitents

ADDITIONAL SIGHTS

★**Old town** – Winding closely around the church, a maze of narrow streets and old houses: note the 16C tower, with its decorative shell motif, on rue Ste-Catherine, and the Renaissance building known as "Adam and Eve's house" on place de la Bridolle, with its ornamentation of statues and medallions.

Chapelle des Pénitents ⊘ – Downstream, the banks of the Dordogne are especially lively in the summertime. A lovely Romanesque chapel is reflected in the waters; the belfry is in the form of an extended gable rising above the main entrance, with four arches open to the sky. This 12C building, restored, now serves as a museum of local history.

BEAUMONT

Population 1 166
Michelin map 75 fold 15 or 235 fold 5

Beaumont was built as a bastide in 1272 by the Seneschal of Guyenne in the name of Edward I, king of England, and today retains only traces of the fortifications but still has many houses with angle irons.

Église St-Front – Built after 1272 in the Early Gothic style and squared-off by four huge towers connected by a rampart walk, this church was the last place of refuge for the inhabitants of the town during periods of siege. The asymmetry of the towers on the main façade reflects their different functions; the lower was a belltower until 1789, and the higher a crenellated keep armed with machicolations. The towers frame a doorway, which has five archivolts and is supported by clustered columns, and a **gallery**★ with a beautifully decorated balustrade and an illuminated frieze underneath it. The elegant south porch has a trefoil arcade dominated by a lancet dais. It is protected by a brattice. Major restoration work during the last century has significantly altered the church's originally military character.

Interior – In the belltower to the left, the enormous arch-stone (weighing 450kg/992lb!) of the chancel vault can be seen. It is decorated with carved figures of faces, including that of the church's patron, St Front. In the same side aisle towards the middle of the nave there is the chapel of St Joseph, almost certainly the remainder of a much older church. Notice in between two tombs the little *piscina* in which the priests used to perform their ritual ablutions.

Rampart ruins – A good view of the curtain walls, the 13C fortified Luzier Gate (Porte de Luzier) and the impressive outline of the church can be seen by going westwards, beyond the line of ramparts.

EXCURSION

Château de Bannes – *5km/3mi northwest on D 660 and then up a road on the left.* Perched on a rocky spur, the château was built at the end of the 15C by the bishop of Sarlat, Armand de Gontaud-Biron. What is so incongruous in this château is that the military features – machicolated towers – are tempered by the carved doorway and richly decorated dormer windows surmounted by finials and pinnacles in the Early Renaissance style.

BELLAC

Population 4 924
Michelin map 72 fold 7 or 233 fold 22

Bellac rises up on a spur overlooking the valley of the Vincou which flows into the Gartempe – a picturesque setting in green and undulating countryside on the borders of the Limousin plateaux and the Poitou plains.

Giraudoux's native soil – Châteauroux may claim the glory of having educated Jean Giraudoux at its lycée, but it was in Bellac that he was born, in 1882 (d 1944). The countryside he knew as a child is depicted in an early work of poetic fiction, *Suzanne et le Pacifique*. He describes Bellac with the following words: "a countryside of streams and hills, a patchwork of fields and chestnut woods for it was a land with a long history, it was the region of Limousin."

Author of five novels, numerous short stories and influential political and literary essays, Giraudoux is best known for his 15 plays. He created a new type of drama for the theatre, containing irony, poetry and magic. *Siegfried et le Limousin, Amphytrion 38, Intermezzo, Tiger at the Gates, Electra, Ondine* and *The Madwoman of Chaillot* (the last published and produced posthumously) have been performed to appreciative audiences around the world. His style is sparkling, full of twists and innovations.

As a young man, he travelled widely in Europe and North America, and spent a year (1906-07) as an instructor at Harvard. Returning to France, he served in the First World War, was twice wounded, and became the first writer ever to be awarded the wartime Legion of Honour. In 1939-40, he was Commissioner of Information in Daladier's short-lived government.

Every year in July, a performance festival (theatre, music, dance) commemorates this talented native son. (*See Practical information at the end of this guide.*)

SIGHTS

The setting – Leave the car on place de la République near the town hall, a 16C mansion, and go up rue Lafayette. From a terrace about 100m/100yd up the street, you get a good view of the church, the river flowing rapidly between rocky banks, the old stone bridge and the viaduct.

Église Notre-Dame – The church is built on a terrace overlooking the Vincou and shows a strange juxtaposition of the Romanesque and Gothic styles. A great square belfry surmounts the two naves, one 12C and Romanesque, the other 14C and Gothic. The two naves lead to the chancel which ends in a flat chevet. The southern doorway is adorned with small, serpentine capitals.

★**Shrine** – To the left of the entrance, in a chest set in the wall, there is a beautiful 12C shrine (the oldest in Limousin), embellished with *cabochons* and medallions of *champlevé* enamel. Among the figurative decorations on the sacred receptacle are the symbols of the four Evangelists around the figure of Christ.

Mementoes of Giraudoux

A **monument** (**D**) commemorating the author, by the sculptor Chauvenet, was erected in 1951 in the town hall garden, beneath the magnificent trees there. On either side of his portrait, cameos of six heroines from his works: Ondine, Alcmène, Judith and Bella, Isabelle, Suzanne.

Giraudoux's childhood home ⊙ – The author's admirers will find a treasure trove of documents concerning the author and his family: letters, photographs, set models and posters for his plays. In his room, the library includes a priceless collection of his books and manuscripts.

★LA BASSE MARCHE *Round trip of 55km/33mi – 2hr30min*

Leave Bellac travelling east on D 1 towards Châteauponsac.

Rancon – In the Gartempe valley, this peaceful hamlet is built into the hillside. The 12C "Lantern of the Dead" is surmounted by a cross with five foils (cusps).

The 13C **church** in the transitional Romanesque-Gothic style, fortified in the 14C, was formerly part of the town's defensive perimeter. Note the machicolations on the chevet and the openings for the archers; the belfry, a 16C square tower ends in an onion-shaped dome covered with shingles. In the chancel is a fine 13C wooden Christ.

Châteauponsac – The oldest part of this small town hems in the **church**, dating largely from the 12C, though the pointed vaulting was added in the narrow nave and aisles in the 15C. The tall transept is crowned with a dome on pendentives.

Châteauponsac – Musée René-Baubérot

J. D. Sudres/DIAF

The chancel has fine round columns with carved capitals. Also of interest are the stone pulpit dating from 1642, a great 18C lectern and 16-17C painted wooded statues.

Go around the church and walk to the promontory for a **view of the Gartempe**. From there the valley can be seen sloping steeply on the left bank. The Sous-le-Moutier quarter is in the foreground, with its busy pattern of old houses and terrace gardens.

Musée René-Baubérot ⊘ – In a former Benedictine priory near the church, there is a fine collection of minerals and fossils in the prehistoric section, as well as a quartz **polishing tool**. In the archeological section, there are Gallo-Roman chests, funerary urns, pottery and other items, mostly found in the area, and in the section devoted to traditions and folklore, there is a fine recreation of a **Limousin home setting** and exhibits on local history and crafts.

Magnac-Laval – This town is famous for a procession to St Maximus which wends its way through more than 50km/30mi of the countryside on Whit Monday (Pentecost). The pilgrims wearing garlands of flowers round their necks leave after midnight mass and return the following day after sunset.
The 12C **church** has a flat chevet and a hexagonal belfry; it contains the relics of St Maximus.

★**Le Dorat** – *See Le DORAT.*
Return to Bellac on D 675, travelling through the Gartempe valley.

Consult the Index to find an individual town or sight.

BELVÈS

Population 1 663
Michelin map 75 fold 16 or 235 fold 5

Perched as it is on a limestone promontory on the site of a Gallo-Roman castrum, Belvès has a marvellous position overlooking the Nauze valley. Approach from the southeast on D 52 or the south on D 710 to get a charming view of the whole town with its old turreted houses, belltowers and terraces arranged as gardens and covered with greenery.
Plaques attached to the major monuments make these easy to identify.

Place d'Armes – The belltower and the 15C covered market *(halle)* with stone and wooden supports have been preserved. In a small window on one of the pillars, the pillory chain can still be seen. All around the square, the façades are embellished with pretty wrought-iron balconies. Take the covered passage to the right of the Archbishop's House.

Rue Rubigan – This attractive little street leads to the Maison des Consuls (Consuls' House).. The Tour de l'Auditeur (Auditor's Tower), which may date from as early as the 13C, was once part of a magnificent house.

Rue des Filhols – On the right there is the lovely Renaissance façade of the Hôtel Bontemps. Cross the place d'Armes once again.

Rue Jacques Manchotte – Stop and admire the half-timbered house at no 40; its roughcast walls are decorated with herringbone pattern brickwork. Several alleyways leading off to the left have pretty old houses along them. The road opens into Croix-des-Frères square, in which the most noticeable feature is the belltower of the old Dominican monastery, capped with an octagonal turret. This building now houses the tourist office.
In another outlying district of the town are the remains of the medieval fortress; the 12C castle keep and the Gothic church of Notre Dame de Montcuq, which used to be a Benedictine priory.

FORTIFIED TOWNS OF BESSÈDE FOREST: THE BASTIDES
Round trip of 105 km/65mi leaving from Belvès – allow a whole day

The small town of Belvès is surrounded by the forbidding forest of Bessède, which is an extension eastwards of the Belvès forest country (Pays au Bois), antechamber of the Bouriane region. A thick layer of clay covers most of the limestone plateau, and this results in acidic soils which are hardly ideal for cultivation. The area was not really inhabited until after a number of bastides *(see the Introduction for more information on these fortified towns)* had been built there. Trees now far outnumber any other occupants of the area, and the forest is an important natural resource, as witnessed by the many sawmills along the route. The forest also yields quantities of chestnuts and wild mushrooms in the autumn.

Montferrand-du-Périgord
– Take D 53 southwest from Belvès, then turn right onto D 26.

The main feature of this pretty terraced village above the Couze is the semi-ruined château with its 12C keep.

The covered market with its beautiful columns, the old houses and the dove-cotes all contribute to the charm of the scene.

In the cemetery above the village, the Romanesque chapel is decorated with a lovely collection of mural frescoes dating from between the 12C and the 15C.

Ste-Croix
– This village has a charming Romanesque church surrounded by the half-ruined buildings of what used to be a priory. This 12C church has a clear, uncluttered outline. The nave is covered in round tiles, in contrast to the apse and side chapel

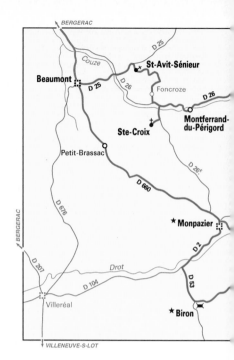

which are covered in *lauzes* – the small limestone slabs typical of the region. A gabled belfry adorns the top of the façade.

St-Avit-Sénieur
– This small village is humbled by the massive church and monastery buildings, vestiges of a former Benedictine abbey constructed in the 11C in honour of Avitus Senior, a soldier in the service of the Visogoth king Alaric II who later became a hermit. The fortifications on the church date from the 14C. Among the monastic vestiges, the dormitory has been transformed into a regional **Museum of geology and archeology** ⊙.

The route along D 25 as far as Beaumont goes past many attractive manor-farmhouses.

Beaumont
– *See Beaumont.*

At the top of the area known as **Petit Brassac** (5 km/3mi south of Beaumont on D 660) opposite a signpost advertising guest rooms (*chambres d'hôte*) is a splendid dovecot supported on pillars of wood and brickwork.

★Monpazier
– *See Monpazier.*

★Château de Biron
– *See Château de Biron.*

Villefranche-du-Périgord
– *See Besse: Excursion.*

Besse
– *See Besse.*

After leaving Besse, the road enters a thick forest of pines and chestnut trees, one of the most sombre parts of the Périgord. Just before St-Pompon this gives way to a coppice of scattered oak trees with stones here and there on the ground. There is some cultivation, of maize and tobacco in particular, confined to the dry valleys.

St-Pompon
– This old village contains many houses typical of the Périgord region. There are pretty dormer windows surmounted with shell ornamentation and framed with spiral scrolls. A **fortified doorway★** is all that remains of a fortress built here by the English in the 15C, forgotten behind a pile of wood and brickwork. On leaving the village in the direction of Prats-du-Périgord, a footpath goes along an unusual Cyclopean wall and then climbs the Gillous hill, leading to a "Gallic fort" (300m/328 yd), a cairn which has been said to be a megalithic burial place.

Prats-du-Périgord
– The Romanesque **church★**, fortified in the 15C, has an unusual appearance, with its nave being framed by the tall apse and the graceful belfry wall.

Orliac
– This tiny village, buried in the hollow of a valley which is otherwise occupied by a pine forest, has a fortified church, where the nave served as a protective keep, and the Renaissance doorway is the only decorative touch. Notice the typical positioning of the rain water stone on one of the houses.

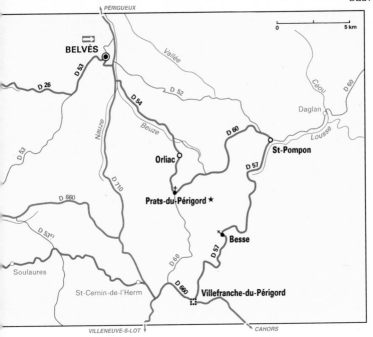

BERGERAC★

Population 26 899
Michelin map 75 folds 14 and 15 or 234 folds 4 and 8 or 235 fold 5
Local maps below and under DORDOGNE VALLEY

Spread out on both banks of the Dordogne where the river tends to be calmer and the valley widens and forms an alluvial plain, Bergerac is surrounded by prestigious vineyards and fields of tobacco, cereals and maize.

In the heart of this town, which evokes all the charm of the southern towns, the restoration of the old quarter brought about the renovation of 15C and 16C houses.

An intellectual and commercial crossroads – The town's expansion began as early as the 12C. Benefiting from the town's situation as a port and bridging point, the local middle class developed rapidly, profiting from successful trade between the central provinces of Auvergne and Limousin and Bordeaux on the coast. In the 16C, this Navarre fief became one of the bastions of Protestantism. The city flourished. The town's printing presses published pamphlets which circulated throughout the Protestant world. In August 1577 the Peace of Bergerac was signed between the king of Navarre and the representatives of King Henri III; this was a preliminary to the Edict of Nantes (1598). But in 1620, Louis XIII's army took over the town and destroyed the ramparts. After the Revocation of the Edict of Nantes (1685), the Jesuits and Recollects tried to win back their Protestant disciples. A certain number of Bergerac citizens, faithful to their Calvinist beliefs, emigrated to Holland, a country where they had maintained commercial contacts.

Bergerac was the capital of Périgord until the Revolution, when the regional capital was transferred to Périgueux, which also became Préfecture of the *département*.

In the 19C, wine growing and shipping prospered until the onslaught of phylloxera and the arrival of the railway respectively.

Bergerac today – Essentially an agricultural centre, Bergerac is the capital of tobacco in France, and as a result the Experimental Institute of Tobacco and the Tobacco Planters Centre of Advanced and Refresher Training are located here.

In addition the 11 000ha/27 170 acres of vineyards surrounding the town produce wine with an *appellation d'origine contrôlée* (which means it is of an officially recognised vintage) including: Bergerac, Côtes de Bergerac, Monbazillac, Montravel and Pécharmant. The Regional Wine Council, which establishes the appellation of the wines, is located in the Recollects' Cloisters *(see Old Bergerac below)*.

The main industrial enterprise of the town is the powder factory producing nitrocellulose for use in such industries as film-making, paint, varnish and plastics.

Famous citizens – Oddly enough, the "Cyrano" of Edmond Rostand's play was inspired by the 17C philosopher Cyrano de Bergerac whose name had nothing to do with the Périgord town. Not discouraged in the slightest, the townspeople took it upon themselves to "adopt" this wayward son and erect a statue in his honour in place de la Myrpe. The philosopher Maine de Biran, on the other hand, was a native son of Bergerac; he was born here in 1766.

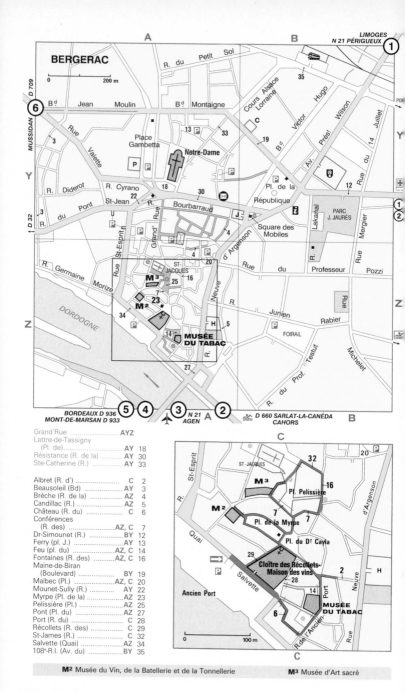

BERGERAC

M² Musée du Vin, de la Batellerie et de la Tonnellerie   M³ Musée d'Art sacré

★★OLD BERGERAC *30min walk (4hr including the museums)*

Ancien port (C) – Try to imagine the *gabares* of yore mooring here to drop off goods and wood, which came from the upper valley, and load on the barrels of wine bound for England and Holland via Bordeaux. Today visitors can board tour boats ⊘ for a view of the town.

Leaning against the house, at the bottom of rue du Port, is an interesting metre bar, which gauges the Dordogne's floods.

Cloître des Récollets ⊘ (C) – Located between place du Docteur-Cayla and the quays, the old Recollects' monastery houses the Regional Wine Council. The brick and stone building was built between the 12C and 17C. The interior courtyard has a 16C Renaissance gallery beside an 18C gallery. In the southeast corner is the monks' small oven. Go down the steps into the vaulted wine cellar where the meetings of the Bergerac wine society, Conférence des Consuls de la Vinée, are held. There is an audio-visual presentation on the Bergerac vineyards.

There is a fine view of the Monbazillac vineyards from the sumptuously decorated great hall on the first floor.

The wine-testing laboratory is in the eastern part of the building. In the wine-tasting room (open to visitors), all the Bergerac wines are tasted annually to determine whether they are worthy of the *appellation d'origine contrôlée* – the "A.O.C." mark on the label.

Rue du Château (C 6) – An unusual balustraded balcony overhangs a sharp bend in the street.

★★**Musée du Tabac** ⊘ (C) – The museum is located in the **Maison Peyrarède★**, also known as the French Kings' House, an elegant building built in 1603 and ornamented with a corbelled turret. This remarkable and beautifully presented collection traces the history and evolution of tobacco through the centuries.

On the **first floor** the origin and evolution of the plant is described. Until the 15C tobacco was used only by the American Indians, who believed it possessed medicinal properties. On display are tobacco pouches, calumets or **peace pipes** and Indian pipes. After the discovery of the New World, tobacco was introduced to Europe. Jean Nicot brought it into France in c1560; he sent snuff to Catherine de' Medici to cure her migraines.

Use of tobacco was controversial from the very start: Pope Urbain VIII ordered the excommunication of nicotine fiends and Louis XIII forbade its sale (before hitting on the idea of taxing it). In those days, tobacco was sold as a carrot-shaped lump which was grated into powder. The familiar diamond-shaped orange sign, *Tabac*, which hangs outside of shops licensed to sell tobacco products, is still called a *carotte* today. At the end of the 18C snuff was sold directly in powder form, which was preserved in large hand-painted **porcelain jars**. Each smoker carried his own snuffbox. Exhibited alongside the jars are a number of these **snuffboxes**, some of which were decorated with portraits of Louis XVIII, Napoleon or Charles X.

The next step in the art of smoking was the pipe. The pipe had been in use in Holland since the early 17C, but its use was considered vulgar and common. Officers of the First Empire started the fashion and were quickly followed by the Romantics, including George Sand. There are 19C **satirical engravings** depicting the art of consuming tobacco. In the display cabinets, **pipes** in porcelain, meerschaum and wood have been decorated with comic subject matters and portraits of famous people.

Finally in the mid-19C, the cigarette arrived on the scene and with it its accessories, including the elegant ivory **cigarette holders**.

On the **second floor** works of art depicting tobacco and smokers are displayed. *Two Smokers* from the 17C northern French School, *Three Smokers* by Meissonier and the charming *Interior of the Tobacconist's Shop* by David II Teniers, known as Teniers the Younger, are among the works exhibited.

Nearby is a pedestal table made by the Mexican Indians. It is fascinating to see how many cigar bands have been used to make the table's marquetry.

A section is devoted to the cultivation of tobacco (planting, harvesting, drying, etc) with special reference to the Bergerac region.

Musée d'Histoire Urbaine ⊘ – In a house adjoining the Peyrarède Mansion there is a display of various objects – maps, documents, architectural remains, furnishings – evoking Bergerac's history.

Also worth noting are old town plans and glazed earthenware (faïence), made in Bergerac in the 18C.

Rue d'Albret (C 2) – At the end of this street to the right is the town hall, the former convent of the Sisters of Faith.

On the left, on the corner of place du Feu, is a vast building with pointed arched doorways.

Bergerac – Old town

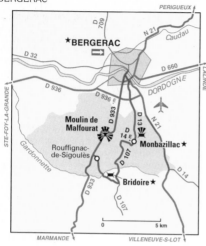

Place du Docteur-Cayla and Place de la Myrpe (C) – This large, charming shaded square is lined with half-timbered houses. In the middle of place de la Myrpe stands the statue of Cyrano de Bergerac swathed in his cape.

★ **Musée du Vin, de la Batellerie et de la Tonnellerie** ⊘ (C M²) – Located in a lovely brick and half-timbered house at the end of place de la Myrpe, this museum is divided into three sections.

On the first floor, the importance of barrel-making to the Bergerac economy is explained. The coopers had to submit to strict control standards of barrel capacity, type of wood used and so on.

The section on wine shows the evolution of the Bergerac vineyards over the centuries and the type of houses the wine-growers lived in.

The second floor concerns the river boats. There are models of the various kinds of river boats, gabares, flat-bottomed boats sometimes with sails, which transported the different kinds of goods on the Dordogne river. They did not go above Bergerac, which was the port where the goods were transhipped. Photos show the bustling port of Bergerac in the 19C, as well as scenes of fishing with cast-nets strong enough to bring in enormous catches during the spawning season of fish such as salmon or shad.

Place Pélissière (C) – This large square was opened up after the demolition of some run-down houses. Spread on different levels around a fountain it is over-looked by the église St-Jacques ⊘, the church once a centre for pilgrims on their way to Santiago de Compostela; near it is the Museum of Sacred Art.

Musée d'Art Sacré ⊘ (C M³) – Displayed in the small mission station are religious works of art: paintings, sculptures and sacred vases of different styles. Note the Lauzerte stone, an unusual archaic statue discovered in a chapel in Lauzerte (in the Tarn-et-Garonne *département*).

Rue St-James (C 32) – There are 15C, 16C and 17C half-timbered houses with mullioned windows all along this street.

Rue des Fontaines (C 16) – The Vieille Auberge at the corner of rue Gaudra has well-preserved moulded arcades, 14C capitals, and pointed arched windows.

Rue des Conférences (C 7) – The name of this street calls to mind the conferences held before the Peace of Bergerac. It is bordered by half-timbered houses. Cross place de la Myrpe and place du Docteur-Cayla and take rue des Récollets to the old port (and car park).

ADDITIONAL SIGHT

Église Notre-Dame (AY) – Built in the Gothic style this 19C church has a slender belltower. There are two fine paintings in the east chapel: an Adoration of the Magi attributed to Pordenone, a Venetian painter and student of Giorgione, and more especially an Adoration of the Shepherds attributed to the Milanese, Ferrari, student of Leonardo da Vinci. In the west chapel is an immense Aubusson tapestry portraying the Bergerac coat of arms.

VIGNOBLE DE MONBAZILLAC

Round trip of 27km/16.5mi – about 1hr30min. Leave Bergerac southwards on D 13.

This road crosses a market-garden area and then the meadowlands of the Dordogne's wide alluvial plain before reaching the first slopes of the hill on which the vineyards are situated *(the vineyard area is marked in green on the local map below)*.

The famous vineyard of Monbazillac has a reputation that goes back hundreds of years. There is a story that in the Middle Ages, when pilgrims from Bergerac were visiting Rome, the pope asked, "And where is Bergerac?" "Near Monbazillac", replied their chamberlain.

The white wine of Monbazillac is a sweet wine and is served with foie gras as well as with dessert. The bunches are picked when affected with the "noble mold" (*Botrytis cinerea*), which concentrates the juice and heightens sweetness by dehydration – a guarantee of quality.

Bergerac vineyards

★**Monbazillac Château** – *See Château de MONBAZILLAC.*

The road winds its way through carefully cultivated vineyards.

★**Château de Bridoire** – This Protestant fortress was partly destroyed by Montluc in 1568 and rebuilt under Henri IV. It was restored in the 19C and 20C. The castle is made up of two large main buildings set at right angles flanked by round towers facing an inside courtyard which is closed by a crescent-shaped curtain wall. Its grey stone, its roof of brown tiles and massive round machicolated towers are reminiscent of the Château de Monbazillac.

The road goes through **Rouffignac-de-Sigoulès**, a wine growers' village, where many of the houses have been roofed with round tiles.

Take D 933 to the right which runs alongside the vineyards. A road climbs up to Malfourat Mill.

Moulin de Malfourat – Viewing table. The mill, now without its sails, stands on top of a hillock. From the bar terrace there is a **panorama**★ of the Monbazillac vineyard and Bergerac and the Dordogne Plain to the north.

D 933 is picturesque as it drops down through the vineyards to Bergerac.

VALLÉE DU CAUDAU *38km/23.5mi. Allow 1hr*

Leave Bergerac by ① on the town plan, N 21

Lamonzie-Montastruc – Perched on a rock to the left of the road is Château de Montastruc, a handsome building in the classical style. Its main building is 16C, flanked by 15C circular corner towers, while another façade is 18C.

Continue along D 21 then at Clermont-de-Beauregard take a path to the left.

Château de la Gaubertie – Built in the 15C, this castle was completely restored in the early 20C. The large main building, its façade overlooking the Caudau valley, is flanked by a square tower on one side and a round corbelled tower on the other side. A machicolated rampart walk runs right around the castle. The 17C chapel stands not far from the castle.

At Clermont-de-Beauregard, take a small road along the Caudau valley towards St-Laurent-des-Bâtons.

Château de St-Maurice – The castle is partly hidden by the trees in its grounds, but its 14C and 15C buildings crowned with machicolations are nonetheless an attractive sight.

Go through St-Armand-de-Vergt, which has a pretty Romanesque church.

Lac de Neuf Font is a recreational lake with swimming beaches and pedal boat rental.

Vergt – This large agricultural town has become one of the main strawberry centres. The sandy soil of the region is perfect for the cultivation of this fruit. At certain times during the year, big plastic sheets are spread over the strawberries to protect them.

BESSE

Population 171
Michelin map 75 fold 17 or 235 fold 10

Standing in the centre of the forest that covers much of Quercy between the Lot and the Dordogne is the little village of Besse. Its interesting Romanesque church roofed with lauzes makes an attractive picture with the 16C and 17C château.

Besse – Detail of the church doorway

Église – An ogive doorway and a double flight of stairs lead into the remarkable carved **doorway**★ in the west front, dating most probably from the 11C. Such features are rare in the architecture of the Périgord region, and this particular example is exceptional. The sculptures on the archivolt depict the Redemption, including images of Adam and Eve before and after the Original Sin, St Michael slaying the dragon and Isaiah being purified by a glowing coal. The arch moulding is surmounted by a triangular pediment with lozenge patterning, supported by two free-standing columns and six illuminated corbels which, together with the capitals and parts of the door, depict Sin and Damnation; monsters devouring human souls, headless contortionists etc.

EXCURSION

Villefranche-du-Périgord – *8km/5mi to the south on D 57*
This bastide was founded in 1261 by Alphonse de Poitiers. An enormous covered market with heavy pillars and part of the covered arcades are still to be seen.
In the main street the **Maison du Chataignier, Marrons et Champignons** ⊘ is devoted to exhibits on the chestnut tree, chestnut and mushrooms (lovers of the delectable fungus will enjoy the "Mushroom Nature Trail").

BEYNAC-et-CAZENAC★★

Population 489
Michelin map 75 fold 17 or 235 fold 6 – Local map see DORDOGNE VALLEY

The Château de Beynac stands on a remarkable **site**★★, rising from the top of a rock; it overlooks the beautiful Dordogne valley winding between hills crowned with castles. The village tucked at the foot of the cliff by the river is where the poet Paul Éluard chose to end his days.

A formidable stronghold – In the Middle Ages Beynac, Biron, Bourdeilles and Mareuil were the four baronies of Périgord. When the Capetians and the Plantagenets were at war, the castle, which had been captured by Richard the Lion Heart, was used as a base by the sinister **Mercadier**, master-at-arms, whose bands of men pillaged the countryside on behalf of the king of England. In 1214, during the Albigensian Crusade, Simon de Montfort seized the castle and demolished it. The castle was later rebuilt, as we see it today, by a lord of Beynac.
During the Hundred Years War, the Dordogne marked the front between the English and the French, and there were constant skirmishes and raids between Beynac under the English in 1360, then the French in 1368, and Castelnaud under the English *(see Château de CASTELNAUD)*. Once peace had returned, Beynac Castle was left once more to watch over the village.

★**Château** ⊘ – *Access by car: take D 703 on leaving the village to the west (3km/2mi) or on foot via the village.*
The castle is in the form of an irregular quadrilateral extended on the south side to form a bastion. The austere crenellated keep dates from the 13C. A double curtain wall protected the castle from attack from the plateau; on all the other

sides there is a sheer drop of 150m/492ft to the Dordogne. The main building, dating from the 13C and 14C, is extended by the 15C seigneurial manor-house to which a bartizan was added in the 16C.

Interior – The great Hall of State, where once the nobles of Périgord used to assemble, has fine broken barrel vaulting; the oratory is decorated with Gothic frescoes, naïve in style, with lively draughtsmanship depicting the Last Supper, a Christ of Pity at the foot of His Cross (as He appeared to St Gregory according to the medieval legend), and members of the Beynac family.

From the watchpath and the south bastion, which overlook the Dordogne and are reached by the main staircase (17C), there is a wonderful **panorama**★★ of the valley and from left to right, of the "threshold" to Domme and the castles of Marqueyssac, Castelnaud and Fayrac.

Wayside cross – This *calvaire* stands on the cliff edge 150m/492ft to the east of the castle. A **panorama**★★ as wide as the one from the castle watchpath can be seen from this point.

★**Village** – A steeply sloping footpath known locally as the **Caminal del Panieraire**★ (basket makers' path) leads from the bottom of the village, through rows of houses dating from the 15C to the 17C, to the castle and the church. All along the climb the architectural décor exudes elegance and the prosperity of - Renaissance Beynac. There are gabled doorways, façades decorated with coats-of-arms or discs, ornate dormer windows, and small, beautifully laid out squares. From the car park, visitors can board old-fashioned *gabares* for a **river tour** ⊙.

Beynac – Caminal del Panieraires

Musée de la protohistoire ⊙ – Objects (originals and facsimiles) relative to the theme of the earliest human activities introduce the civilisation (2000/1000BC) and techniques of the region's first farmers and iron workers.

Beyond the pointed-arched gateway in the village's curtain wall, the footpath continues to the church, the former castle chapel, remodelled in the 15C.

Parc archéologique ⊙ – This includes about ten reconstitutions based on the discoveries of archeological research, mainly living quarters from the end of the Neolithic period, a fortified gateway and an oven made of Gallic earthenware. The display is further enhanced by demonstrations of flint-stone carving, the making and firing of earthenware and so forth.

Cazenac – 3km/2mi west. This hamlet possesses a 15C Gothic church from which there is a lovely view of the valley.

Château de BIRON★

Michelin map 75 fold 16 or 235 fold 9

From its perch at the top of a *puy*, Biron Castle commands an impressive view, the massive bulk of its towers and walls towering over the borders of the Périgord and Agenais regions.

From the Capitol to the Tarpeian Rock – Among the many celebrated men of the Biron family, Charles de Gontaut met with a particularly memorable fate.

Friend of Henri IV and one of his first lieutenants, he was appointed first Admiral and then Marshal of France. In 1598 the Barony of Biron was created and conferred as a dukedom on Charles de Gontaut who was next promoted to Lieutenant-General of the French Army and then Governor of Burgundy. Even these honours did not satisfy him and, in league with the Duke of Savoy and the Spanish Governor of the state of Milan, he laid a plot which would have led to the breaking up of the kingdom of France. Biron, his treason exposed, was pardoned. But the mercy of Henri IV did nothing to halt his ambitions. Once more he plotted against his lord. Once again he was exposed and was taken before the king, who agreed to pardon him if he would confess his crime. The proud Biron refused. He was beheaded in the courtyard of the Bastille prison on 31 July 1602.

From medieval fortress to the present building – This castle is made up of buildings of very different styles, the work of fourteen generations of Gontaut-Birons, who owned the castle from the 12C to 20C.

As early as the 11C a medieval fortress existed here. Razed by Simon de Montfort in the 13C, the castle was reconstructed. During the Hundred Years War, the castle changed hands constantly between the English and the French, getting badly damaged in the process.

In the late 15C and during the 16C, Pons de Gontaut-Biron, former chamberlain of Charles VIII, decided to transform his castle into a lovely Renaissance château like those he had seen in the Loire valley. He altered the buildings east of the main courtyard and had the Renaissance chapel and colonnaded arcade built. It was planned that a great staircase would lead from this arcade down to the bottom of the slope. Work was interrupted, however, and not resumed until the 18C.

This mass of buildings and the 10 000m² /107 600sq ft of roof have made it exceedingly difficult for individual owners to maintain the castle. The Dordogne département bought it in 1978 and began a massive restoration programme. It also set up an art centre, which organises exhibitions every summer.

TOUR ⊙

Outer courtyard – Surrounding the castle's living quarters on three sides, the outer courtyard includes the caretaker's lodge, chapel, the receiving house and the bakery. The guards' tower, now the **conciergerie**, is an elegant building in which crenellations, a watchpath and Renaissance decoration are in felicitous juxtaposition.

The **chapel** was built in the Renaissance style in the 16C. A pierced balustrade runs round the base of the roof. The lower chamber once served as a parish church for the village; the upper chamber or seigneurial chapel, which opens directly onto the courtyard has remarkable pointed vaulting. It shelters **two tombs with recumbent figures**, the sculptures showing the influence of the Italian Quattrocento (15C) period. The recumbent figure of Armand de Gontaut-Biron, bishop of Sarlat, is decorated with three seated figures of the virtues, while the recumbent figure of his brother Pons (d 1524) is carved in low relief and recounts the life of Christ in a macabre frieze. Both figures were damaged during the Revolution. The chapel also contained a Pietà and an Entombment, two remarkable works of art, which are now in the Metropolitan Museum of Art in New York City.

From the terrace between the chapel and the receiving house, an imposing building with a turret, there is a bird's-eye view of the town.

The *salette* was used for storing provisions preserved with salt.

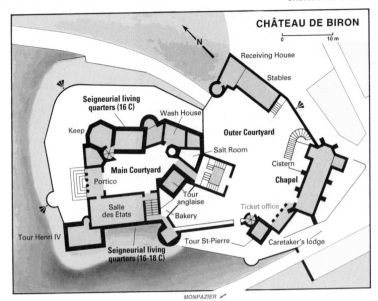

CHÂTEAU DE BIRON

MONPAZIER

La cour d'honneur (main courtyard) – Access is by a staircase (1) and a pointed vaulted corridor (2). Opening onto this inner main courtyard (cour d'honneur) is a portico. On the right, the 16C seigneurial living quarters, with Renaissance windows, contain elegant restored galleries now used for art exhibitions. On the left, the 16C to 18C main building has an elegant remodelled staircase (3), which goes up to the Great Hall of State, the timber work roof of which is in the form of a ship's keel and has just been rebuilt.

In the basement, the kitchen, the former garrison's refectory, is a vast room (22 x 9m/72 x 30ft) with pointed barrel vaulting. The large 13C polygonal keep was redesigned in the 15C and made part of the other buildings.

From the castle terraces, the **view**★ extends over the rolling countryside and the Birons' other fief, the bastide of Monpazier.

BLANCAFORT★

Population 991
Michelin map 65 north of fold 11 or 238 fold 19

In the centre of this fetching hamlet, the church has an unusual belfry-porch.

★**Château** ⊘ – The 15C château is built of red brick and has a plain façade. The 17C courtyard is flanked by two pavilions. The visit includes the library with its Regency panelling and the dining room with its walls covered in Flemish leather, painted, gilded and embossed; fine display of pewter. The park provides a pleasant walk among the scroll-like flower beds laid out in the French style near the château or along woodland paths beside the river.

EXCURSION

Take D 8 towards Concressault at the Domaine de la Jonchère; follow the sign-posted route.

Fire burn and cauldron bubble

Ethnologists have an explanation for the prevalence of witchery and the supernatural in Berry. The flat landscape is often swathed in mist, and solitary trees, burned by lightning or twisted by the wind, create dark and menacing silhouettes in the lonely countryside.

Ask one of the *Compagnons de vin de Bué*, a local wine-growers association, and you may get a different answer. The members call themselves *birettes* and dress in appropriate costumes for festive occasions. A local *birette d'honneur*, (who also serves as *sommelier* in a fine restaurant), has a word of advice: it is best to seek out spirits in the wee hours, for in the daylight you can see right through them.

BLANCAFORT

Musée de la Sorcellerie

Domaine de la Jonchère – Musée de la Sorcellerie

Musée de la Sorcellerie ⊙ – This Witchcraft Museum is set up in a 19C barn in the north of the Berry, a region known for its strong connections with sorcery. Around twenty scenes, some involving video animation and special effects (courtesy of the resident sorceress?), and many explanatory panels delve into the mysterious world of superstition, myth, legend and no doubt a dash of realty. The first floor, decorated and furnished in the Sologne tradition, evokes the tales of witchcraft that the locals used to tell each other during the long winter evenings, conjuring up *birettes*, local spirits, headless and handless, with a predilection for haunting Berry.

Château de BONAGUIL★★

Michelin map 79 fold 6 or 235 fold 9
Local map under LOT VALLEY: Meanders of the Lower Reaches

This majestic fortress, standing on the borders of Périgord Noir and Quercy, is one of the most perfect examples of military architecture from the late 15C and 16C. Its uniqueness is that, although it appears to be a typical medieval defensive stronghold, its design was adapted to the use of firearms. Such weapons were fairly common in Europe by the mid-14C, but not until the 15C did the invention of a mechanical firing mechanism make firearms accurate enough to have a significant impact on the conduct of warfare.

A strange character – It was a strange quirk of character that made **Bérenger de Roquefeuil** enjoy proclaiming himself the "noble, magnificent and most powerful lord of the baronies of Roquefeuil, Blanquefort, Castelnau, Combret, Roquefère, Count of Naut". He belonged to one of the oldest families of Languedoc and was a brutal and vindictive man who, in his determination to be obeyed, did not hesitate to use force. But extortion and other outrages he perpetrated incited revolt. In order to crush this, Bérenger transformed Bonaguil Castle, which had been built in the 13C, into an impregnable fortress from which he would be able to observe and quell any signs of an uprising without delay. It took him nearly 40 years to build his fortified eagle's eyrie, which looked an anachronism when compared with the châteaux being erected by his contemporaries for a life of ease at Montal, Assier and along the Loire. However, his castle was never attacked and was intact until the eve of the Revolution. Although demolished during the Revolution in the prevailing urge to destroy all signs of the old feudal system, this colossus, notwithstanding its mutilations, still evokes the absolute power it once represented.

S. Sauvignier/MICHELIN

Château de Bonaguil

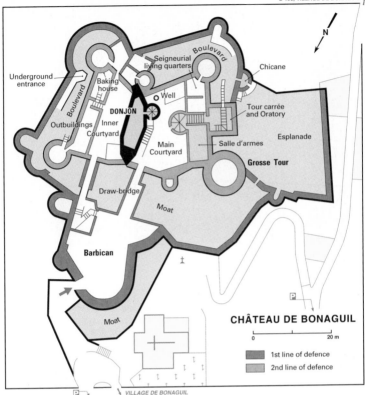

TOUR ⊙

To reach the **castle stronghold**, the visitor passes through the barbican. This was an enormous bastion on its own with an independent garrison, powder store, armouries and escape routes. The barbican formed part of the 350m/380yd long first line of defence; its bastions, thanks to the embrasures, permitted cross-firing. The second line of defence consisted of five towers of which one, known as the Grosse Tour, is among the strongest round towers ever to have been built in France. The tower is 35m/115ft high and is crowned with corbels; the upper storeys served as living quarters, the lower contained weapons, such as muskets, culverins and harquebuses, etc.

The keep overlooked both lines of defence; it served, with its cant walls, not only as a watch tower but also as a command-post. Shaped like a vessel with its prow, the most vulnerable point, turned towards the north, it was the last bastion of the defence. Inside, a room houses arms and objects found during the excavation of the moats.

With a well sunk through the rock, outbuildings (baking house) where provisions could be stored, monumental chimneys and drainage systems, dry internal ditches, and vaulted tunnels which enabled the troops to move about quickly, the castle garrison of about a hundred men could easily withstand a siege provided they were not betrayed or starved out.

BORT-LES-ORGUES

Population 4 950
Michelin map 76 fold 2 or 239 fold 29

The town of Bort, on a lovely site in the Dordogne valley, is known for its huge dam and for the cliffs looming above it. The cliffs are known as *les orgues*, because the formation, seen from below, resembles the pipes of a massive organ.

Tourism has boosted the local economy, the dam has brought jobs in the hydroelectric power field, the town produces regional specialities and leather goods.

★★Barrage de Bort (Bort Dam) – *There are car parks on either side of the dam, on D 979 and D 922.*

From the roadway atop the dam (390m/1280ft long), the upstream view is over the vast reservoir it creates, criss-crossed by the wakes of **pleasure cruisers** ⊙; downstream, the main power plant and the spillway.

Bort-les-Orgues – Dam

The Aubazine **overlook** just up the road on D 979 is a good vantage point for seeing the whole lake, covering 1 400ha/3 459 acres. A **tour** ⊙ starts at the base of the dam (between the small village of Les Granges and the Bort Tannery).

The Bort dam is a key player in the hydroelectric power system established along the river Dordogne and its tributaries. The powerhouse at its base is equipped with two sets of 115 000kW turbines, and another (10 700kW) is located in the Rhue plant, on the roadway level.

Église – The church dates from the 12-15C. The plain architecture provides a frame for a 15C statue of St Anne, modern stained glass windows, a bronze Christ sculpted by Chavignier. Outside, near the east end, traces of fortifications are still apparent. Next door, the former priory was built in the 17C.

★ORGUES DE BORT

Leave Bort via D 127 south, near the cemetery.

The view to the left is the Rhue valley.

Just beyond the last houses in Chantery, take a stairway to the right, which leads directly to the stone columns.

The "organ pipes" are fine-grained stone composed primarily of phonolite rock, known also as "clinkstone" or "soundstone".

Go back to D 127, continue for 2km/1mi until the right turn-off marked "point de vue des Orgues", and drive a short distance to the car park and picnic area on the plateau (alt. 679m/2228ft). From the parking area, there is a 15min walk there and back to the scenic overlook. Another path goes further along the cliff top for the more adventurous.

There is a wide **panoramic view**★★ over the Dordogne valley, the Cantal region and the Mont Dore range. To the southwest, Lake Madic lies on the former course of the Dordogne. A rock formation known as the *Tête d'Homme* (man's head) offers a perilous perch for a superior 360° view.

Go back to your car and take up D 127 again for 500m/0.5mi. A path on the left climbs to a rocky outcropping (15min round trip on foot).

The panorama embraces the Puy de Sancy and the mountains of Cantal, the river Dordogne and its tributaries, the Monédières range and the Plateau des Mille Vaches.

At the Bort gap (*col du puy de Bort*), the roadway runs along a ledge on the flank of the hillside. From D 979, as you travel towards Bort, keep an eye out for the pretty Pierefitte château on the right, and more views of the lake and dam.

The length of time given in this guide
– for touring allows time to enjoy the views and the scenery
– for sightseeing is the average time required for a visit.

Château de BOUGES★★

Michelin map 68 fold 8 – 9.5km/6mi northeast of Levroux

Set in the heart of Berry-Champagne this château built in the 18C in the Italian style on the site of a former stronghold, closely resembles the Petit Trianon at Versailles by the arrangement of its pediments and façades.

TOUR ⊙

The outbuildings are vast edifices with tall mansard roofs and include fine stables with a **harness room** containing an important collection of saddles, harnesses and riding boots. In the wing set at right angles, there are several horse drawn carriages dating from the beginning of the century.

The château contains an interesting collection of 18C **furniture★**, particularly sofas and chairs (many of the pieces bear the marks of famous cabinet makers), which was patiently assembled by the previous owners. Note in particular the small Louis XV salon, the games room with its fine furniture, the drawing-room with its marble chimney piece and astronomical clock, and the charming Louis XVI bedroom.

French style gardens and a 80ha/198 acre **park★** planted with a variety of fine trees and with a pond bring the visit to an end.

Inside the château

BOURDEILLES★

Population 811
Michelin map 75 fold 5 or 233 north of fold 42

The impressive castle of Bourdeilles, with the village clustered at its foot, makes a delightful picture as it stands on the rocks that rise up sheer above the Dronne river. It was here that the famous chronicler, Brantôme, was born in 1540.

A coveted spot – In 1259 Saint Louis ceded Périgord and Bourdeilles, his most important barony, to the English. This incredible desertion made the country rise in revolt and divided the Bourdeille family: the elder branch supported the Plantagenets, and the Maumonts, the younger branch, the Capetians. A while later, after plots and lawsuits, Géraud de Maumont, Counsellor to King Philip the Fair, who urged him on, seized the castle of his forebears. He turned it into a fortress. Then, to show his strength in Périgord, Philip the Fair exchanged land in Auvergne for Bourdeilles and, during a period of peace, set up a strong garrison within the fief of his enemies, the English.

The Renaissance touch – Credit for the plans for the 16C château must go to Jacquette de Montbron, wife of André de Bourdeille and sister-in-law to Pierre de Brantôme, with her active and informed interest in geometry and architecture.

Building was started in haste at the promise of a visit by Catherine de' Medici, but was abandoned when the visit was cancelled. The Renaissance element, nevertheless, is an interesting illustration of the architecture of that period and adds a lighter note to the group of 13C buildings.

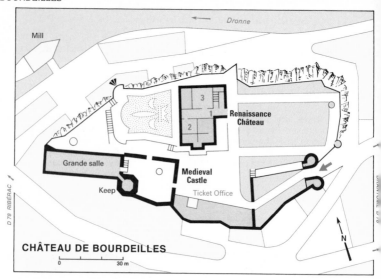

CHÂTEAU DE BOURDEILLES

0   30 m

N

★CHÂTEAU ⊘

Cross the first fortified curtain wall, pass under the watchpath to get inside the second wall and enter the outer courtyard, in which there is a fine cedar. Continue to the esplanade, on which the two castles were built, one in the 13C, the other in the 16C.

Medieval castle – The 13C castle, built by Géraud de Maumont on older foundations and hence given the name *Château neuf* ("new"), is an austere building surrounded by a quadrangular curtain wall. Inside the main building, exhibitions are held in a great hall. This is surmounted by an octagonal keep dating from the early 14C topped with machicolations; its walls are 2.4m/7ft thick. From the upper platform of the keep there is a good overall **view** of the castle and a sweeping, bird's-eye view of the river Dronne.

Renaissance château – Sober and elegant in appearance, the château consists of a rectangular main building with a wing at right angles to it. It houses remarkable **furnishings★★** collected by two patrons who donated their collection to the Dordogne *département*.

On the ground floor, a gallery (1) houses 15C and 16C wooden chests, an interesting Limoges granite salt mill and a splendid 16C carved panel of the German School portraying the Passing of the Virgin. In an adjoining room (2) note the recumbent figure of Jean de Chabannes and a replica of the Holy Sepulchre, which came from Montgé Priory (16C Burgundy School). The hall of armour (3), with its fine old tiling, contains metal chests in which gunpowder was kept, and a magnificent Renaissance table.

Emperor Charles V's bedroom

On the first floor visit the dining hall with its 16C carved **chimney piece**★★ decorated with palm leaves and the Gothic room preceding the "**salon doré**"★. This sumptuously decorated room was built to accommodate Catherine de' Medici; it has a painted ceiling, woodwork and monumental chimney pieces by Ambroise Le Noble of the Fontainebleau School. Note the magnificent tapestry, based on a cartoon by Laurent Guyot, showing François I and his falconers.

In three rooms on the second floor there is a bright 15C **Catalan primitive painting** of St Bartholomew exorcising a demon from an Armenian princess, cabinets with secret drawers, a 16C canopied bed, armchairs in Cordoba leather, a fine 17C octagonal table and especially the heavily carved and gilded bedroom of Emperor Charles V.

From the rampart walk to the far (east) end of the promontory overhanging the river Dronne, there is a lovely **view**★   of the castle and its setting; a Gothic bridge with cutwaters, a very attractive 17C seigneurial mill in the shape of a boat roofed with round tiles and the green waters of the river lapping at the rocks below.

VALLÉE DU BOULOU *Round trip 22km/14mi- 1hr15min*

Leave Bourdeilles northwards on D 106^{E2} towards Brantôme. Pass the rock formation known as la Forge du Diable (the Devil's Forge), and take a small road on the left.

St-Julien-de-Bourdeilles – In this modest hamlet is a small Gothic church with two lovely statues in polychrome wood and parts of a 17C altarpiece.

Boulouneix – A Romanesque chapel with a domed belltower stands in the middle of a cemetery. In the chancel, 17C mural paintings represent Mary Magdalene and St Jerome. The façade with two storeys of arcades is of Saintonge influence.

About 100m/109yd after the church, bear left towards Au Bernard.

The road descends through the woods (hornbeam and filbert) to the marshy Boulou valley. Several prehistoric sites have been discovered in the region.

Paussac-et-St-Vivien – Several 16C houses and an interesting fortified church are of interest in this village.

The church's defensive areas, built above the three domes covering the nave and chancel, can still be seen. The south wall is decorated with arcades. Inside, note the capitals decorated in low relief with naïve carvings, a large Christ in polychrome wood and a Louis XV-style pulpit.

Take the C 2 towards Brantôme; at Les Guichards turn right towards Les Chauses, leaving the road to Puy-Fromage on the left.

From the road you will soon see Bourdeilles and its tall keep.

BOURGES★★★

Population conurbation 94731
Michelin map 69 fold 1 or 238 fold 31

From whichever direction you approach the city you see, soaring above the Berry-Champagne countryside, the Cathedral, classified by the UNESCO as a World Heritage Monument. From afar it foretells the rich medieval past that the tourist will discover in the heart of this old city built on the slopes of the hill whose base is washed by the waters of the Yèvre and the Auron and a network of rivers and marshes. Bourges has kept dazzling souvenirs of its hours of glory and its incomparable artistic treasures will appeal to the art lover. As the commercial and industrial centre of Berry, the city has become the regional capital.

HISTORICAL NOTES

"One of the loveliest towns in Gaul" – *Avaricum*, "town of abundant water", made its mark in history in 52 BC, during the tumultuous Gallic wars. The Bituriges, a powerful Celtic people (whose name is the origin of the word "Berry"), took part in the resistance to Roman occupation. The celebrated warrior Vercingétorix had adopted a scorched-earth policy, destroying town and field before the invading army's advance. When he arrived in Bourges, the denizens begged him to leave their dwellings intact, and assured him that the town could never be taken, thanks to its strategic location atop a hill surrounded by rivers and marshland. Exception was made, Caesar's legions attacked, and the town, despite its bravest efforts, fell. Caesar estimated the population at 40000: all were massacred. After a few days rest, the sated soldiers of the Roman empire moved on, leaving the shell of the looted, desolate city behind them. Caesar reported that the town was "one of the loveliest in Gaul"; archeological research has revealed that it was a busy iron craft and trade centre, but little is known of how it appeared before its defeat.

Bourges under Roman rule – Avaricum set about healing its wounds and once again rose to prominence as a capital city and trade centre. Prosperous and attractive, the town spread to the surrounding hillsides, monuments were erected. Recent digs have uncovered a 2C fountain and a monumental gateway which extended over 75m/80yd at the foot of the hill; they probably bordered a commercial avenue. The town boasted a vast amphitheatre; a river port with harbour and wharves; necropolises on the outskirts. In the 3C, St Ursinus established Christianity there while Avaricum, like other towns in the Empire, was gradually surrounded by a fortified wall. As many as 50 towers were built into it, and four gateways opened up to the surrounding countryside. The ramparts, still clearly visible in places, had a strong influence on the shape and face of the city, including the Cathedral. At the end of the 12C, a new wall extended the defensive structures of Bourges.

A patron of the Arts: Jean de Berry – The young Duke Jean de Berry, third son of King John the Good of France, made Bourges the capital of his duchy and a centre of the arts of utmost importance. From 1360 to 1416 the Duke, an inspired lover of the arts, spent a fortune as, with mad prodigality, he commissioned work from painters, illuminators such as Paul de Limbourg, the author of the *Très Riches Heures* (The Rich Hours), now to be seen in the Chantilly Museum, gold and silversmiths, potters, master glassworkers, sculptors such as André Beauneveu and architects.

"A vaillans cœurs, riens impossible" – "To a valiant heart, nothing is impossible" was the motto of **Jacques Cœur**, Master of the Mint to King Charles VII of France at a time when that kingdom was largely occupied by the English.
This man of humble origin, son of a furrier, had an extraordinary life: amazingly gifted in commerce and trade, he soon made a colossal fortune. He armed merchantmen with the idea of seizing the markets of the eastern Mediterranean from the traders of Genoa and Venice; he set up counting-houses in Marseilles and Montpellier, and bought houses and land; from being the man in charge of the finances of Bourges, he became, in 1427, counsellor to Charles VII and principal emissary for the kingdom's expansion of trade; finally he built a magnificent palace at Bourges, though he was to see little of it. Hated by many courtiers who were jealous of his political and diplomatic offices, the honours he had bestowed upon him and the king's favour, he fell into disgrace, a victim of his own advancement. He was arrested in 1451 and condemned to perpetual banishment, confiscation of all his properly and a heavy fine.
But this was not the end for Jacques Cœur: he escaped from Beaucaire Prison, sought refuge in Rome and was given command by the pope of a fleet of ships. It was while he was on the Ninth Crusade to liberate the Christian islands in the Greek archipelago, that he died in 1456 in Chios.

The University, cradle of new ideas – The town of Bourges owes the foundation of its university in 1463 to Louis XI, who was born in Bourges Palace. Its influence spread far beyond the duchy for over a century. The law school under such masters as Alciat (1529-1533) and Cujas (1559-1566) attracted many students some even from abroad. It was thus that German students coming from Heidelberg brought with them the new doctrines of Luther; Calvin, at that time a student at Bourges, learnt these

BOURGES

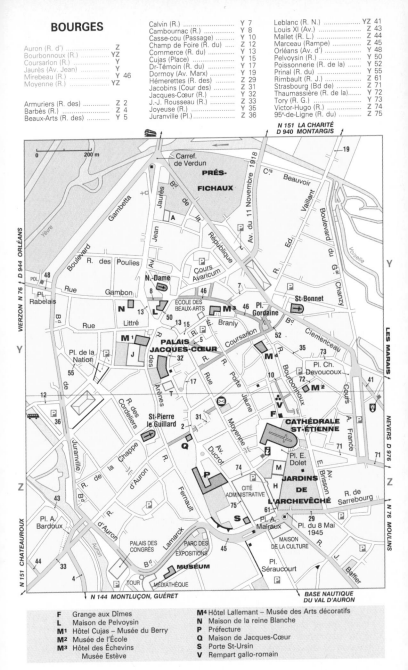

new theories and began to form the outlines of the principles he was later to publish in his *Institutes of the Christian Religion*. His ideas on reforming the Church found many adherents and, in spite of persecution, soon gained support in Bourges and throughout Berry.

The duchy was thus divided and became a battlefield during the period of the Wars of Religion; the prosperity of the city, which had been much reduced by a terrible fire in 1487 which destroyed two-thirds of the town, came to an end.

Sleep and reawakening – By the mid-17C, Berry was in a sort of stupor which lasted two more centuries. Off the main routes, it was by-passed while towns like Tours and Orleans, on the river Loire, underwent economic expansion. The bourgeoisie were not drawn into industry and trade, as elsewhere, but lived lives circumscribed by regional politics and religion. As convents and churches proliferated, and the aristocracy grew poorer, Bourges gained a deplorable reputation as a lacklustre backwater.

The construction of the Berry canal (1819-1842), the railway and the establishment of the armaments industry in Bourges under the Second Empire breathed new economic life into the region.

Since the end of the Second World War, Bourges has expanded rapidly. Many industries have arrived, creating thousands of jobs; trade fairs flourish; the university has specialised in high technology; the army has set up training centres – all contributing to the lively dynamics of the town today.

City of Music – The cultural influence of Bourges is far greater than its small size might suggest. The capital of Berry is home to an unparalleled *Maison de la Culture*, a national music academy, an experimental music centre and a fine arts school reputed for mastery of earthenware techniques. The musical festival **le Printemps de Bourges** is a yearly event drawing crowds of young fans of popular music, while music lovers of other tastes appreciate the great organ concerts in the Cathedral or the **Synthèse** electro-acoustical music festival.

★★★CATHÉDRALE ST-ÉTIENNE (Z)

The vigour of the architecture, the harmony of proportion and the richness of the decoration make one marvel before this cathedral.

Construction – The original 4C place of worship is supposed to have been rebuilt in the 9C, yet no traces of the seminal buildings remain. However, part of the edifice erected in the early 11C still stands, that is the small crypt.

The significant initiative came from **Henri de Sully** (archbishop from 1183 to 1199). The master architect he engaged (his name is unknown) certainly came from northern France, where Gothic architecture was rising triumphant in Soissons, Sens, Chartres and Paris. Indeed, the construction of Notre Dame had been undertaken by Archbishop Maurice de Sully, Henri's brother.

Construction took place in two stages. From 1195 to 1215, the chevet and the chancel were built. The lower church had to be built outside the fortifications standing at that time, for lack of space within. In the same way, the radiating chapels of the apse were attached almost as an afterthought. Viewed from the side (facing the south entrance, standing in the car park), the chevet gives a curious impression of being suspended in space. Only as you walk back towards the eastern end of the cathedral, where a flight of steps runs along the wall, does the lower church come into view.

Additions and Restorations – The southern tower was consolidated during the 14C by a construction linked to the tower by a reinforced arcade known as the *pilier butant* – the buttress pile. It is clearly visible from the car park facing the southern entrance, and its singularity (for it is not echoed on the other side of the main entrance) is apparent when standing in front of the façade. Once this had been built it was possible to install the great window above the central door. The chapels between the buttresses were built in the 15C.

Misfortune came with the 16C; in 1506 the north tower collapsed and had to be entirely rebuilt; in 1562 a Protestant army pillaged the cathedral and destroyed the magnificent statues that adorned the west face; two hundred years later the canons decided to remove the rood screen and the eighteen stained glass windows in the chancel. Last century restoration was undertaken but much of it was unfortunate as balustrades, bell towers and pinnacles were added to the building.

Exterior –The doorways of the west face are aligned by the pedestal formed by the fifteen steps up to the cathedral. Dignity and strength seem to emanate from this grouping of steps and doors framed by the two towers of unequal height. On the right, the so-called "Deaf Tower" (*Tour Sourde* – because no bell was hung), never completed, is architecturally more sober in style than the flamboyantly decorated "Butter Tower" on the left (*Tour de Beurre* – perhaps an allusion to the exemptions purchased by the faithful who preferred to continue to enjoy butter and cream during Lent, which helped to pay for the tower's construction).

Five doorways beneath individual gables stand in a line beneath the great stained glass window, known as the *grand housteau* – the great western gable. The asymmetry of the doorways gives an impression of originality and great variety.

A frieze of 62 bas-reliefs (1) runs between two lines of niches from left to right and depicts the life of Christ: the Annunciation, the Nativity, the Adoration of the Magi, the Flight into Egypt, scenes from the Passion and episodes from the book of Genesis.

The five doorways of the west face, from right to left, are as follows:

St Ursinus' Doorway – The story of St. Ursinus, the first bishop of Bourges, and of St. Justus is depicted on the tympanum (2). The two saints, having received their mission from the Pope St. Clement, leave for Berry; St. Justus dies on the way; St. Ursinus preaches at Bourges and consecrates a church there; he converts and baptises Léocade, the governor of Aquitaine, and his son. Figures of angels, father-confessors and prophets adorn the covings (3); against the pier (4) stands a modern statue of the saint.

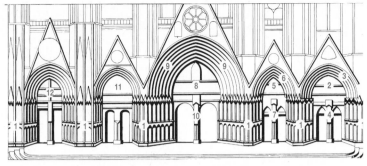

Cathédrale St-Étienne – Doorways on the western façade

St. Stephen's Doorway – The tympanum (5) is devoted to episodes in the life and the martyrdom of St. Stephen, patron of the cathedral. Angels and prophets are to be seen in the covings (6); a modern statue of St. Stephen stands before the pier (7).

Central Doorway – Its theme is the Last Judgement. Great vitality and realism make the doorway one of the masterpieces of 13C Gothic sculpture. The lower part of the tympanum (8) depicts the Resurrection: the naked dead raise their tombstones and turn to look towards heaven; above them, the Archangel Michael with his scales proceeds to judgement, weighing souls: on his right, the chosen fly to the bosom of Abraham who symbolises heaven, on his left the damned are hurled into the burning cauldron of hell.

The upper part of the tympanum represents Christ surrounded by angels bearing the instruments of the Passion; to the left and right the Virgin and St. John ask for this blessing on their knees while above Him two angels hold the sun and the moon to mark the passage of time. Cherubim, angels, saints, martyrs, patriarchs and prophets are to be seen in the covings (9), a modern figure of Christ stands before the pier (10).

The Virgin's Doorway – The doorway had to be partly rebuilt after the collapse of the north tower in the 16C. The Death, the Assumption and the Coronation of the Virgin are depicted on the tympanum (11).

St. Guillaume's Doorway – On the tympanum (12) are episodes in the life of the saint who was archbishop of Bourges at the beginning of the 13C; he is shown receiving offerings for the building of the cathedral, protecting the unfortunate, performing miraculous cures and exorcising a man while the devil flees, disguised as a wolf.

Go round the cathedral by the north.

The north face is embellished by a 12C doorway which was incorporated in the present cathedral. The lintel is adorned with a frieze of flowers and foliage. On the tympanum are scenes from the life of the Virgin.

The chevet is original in having little turrets above the radial chapels. The outline is harmonious and the double flying buttresses built above it add to its grace.

The south face is also adorned with a 12C doorway. Christ appears in majesty on the tympanum, surrounded by the symbols of the Evangelists; angels and the prophets and kings of the Old Testament crowd the covings. Biblical scenes decorate the capitals at the top of the statue-columns; before the pier stands a fine 13C Christ. The right panel of the door was given to the cathedral by Jacques Cœur and bears his monogram.

Go round the south tower and enter the cathedral by the Virgin's Doorway.

Interior – St. Stephen's Cathedral, which is 124m/407ft long, 41m/135ft wide and 37m/121ft high to the top of the inner vaulting, is one of the largest Gothic cathedrals in France (Gloucester Cathedral is 420ft long and 144ft wide). There are no transepts and this gives the nave with its four side aisles a feeling of greater majesty; the five aisles correspond to the five doorways.

The columns of the nave rise in a single thrust to a height of 17m/56ft and they are encircled by groups of smaller columns, some of which reach the vaulting. To extend the perspective the architect slightly increased the distance between the pillars in the chancel.

The building is original in having double side aisles of different height with windows on two levels; the five bands of light and shade thus created within the cathedral considerably enhance the architectural effect *(see cross section)*.

A double ambulatory continues the line of the twin aisles. Five small radial chapels, each semicircular in shape, open on to the apse.

Bourges – Central doorway of the cathedral

The furnishings of the cathedral were dispersed during the Revolution, and the only original pieces remaining are the praying figures of the Duc de Berry and his second wife, Jeanne de Boulogne (in the Chapelle de la Vièrge; the heads, cut off during the Revolution, have been restored based on drawings by Holbein); the statues of the Aubespine family (Chapelle Jacques Coeur); two paintings, *The Adoration of the Shepherds* (Chapelle des Le Roy) and *John the Baptist* (Chapelle Jean-Baptiste) by Jean Boucher; the astronomical clock (southwest corner) made in 1424 and the Great Organ (1663).

★★★**The windows** – Although they have incurred some damage over the years, the collection of stained glass windows in the cathedral is one of the most remarkable in France, dating from the 12-17C. Apart from their striking colours, they illustrate the powerful narratives of Christianity in medieval France.

The five apsidal chapels and the windows between them are adorned with windows shaped to fit the architecture, and medallion windows, most of which were made between 1215 and 1225. The themes draw a parallel between the Old and New Testaments, Christ's parables, and teachings from the lives of the saints and prophets; probably reflecting the influence of St Guillaume, archbishop of Bourges (1199-1209).

Bourges – Joseph's dream

Some of the works were donated by trade guilds (note the distinguishing medallions representing carpenters, barrel-makers and wheelwrights at the bottom of the window relating the story of St Joseph). These are generally attributed to the three workshops under the hands of the masters whose names have not come down to us.

First the **master of the "Last Judgement" and the "New Alliance"**, employs a style both exuberant and majestic, apparent in the bodies and clothing draped over them. The use of white, which enhances the elegance of posture and the careful composition, are associated with the "style 1200", originating in Champagne and northern France.

The "Good Samaritan" master is also supposed to be the artist responsible for the execution of the intermediate windows representing the Passion and the Apocalypse, the windows of St Mary the Egyptian, St Nicholas and the martyrdom of Saint Stephen (radial chapels). The style leads to believe that the artist was from the town of Angers; the fanciful compositions include a variety of extravagant details.

The master of the "St Stephen reliquaries" illustrates some of the typical traits of Gothic representational art: over-long bodies on spindly legs, disproportionate heads, faces seeming to express displeasure, yet these windows are lively and evocative. The artist carried the message across through spontaneous gesture, unencumbered attitudes, the decorative effects of costume, and the objects and animals of the bestiary surround the medieval characters.

Entering the chancel by the outer south aisle you see:

1) Window on the life of Joseph: among the scenes depicted are Joseph's dream – first medallion at the bottom; Joseph in Egypt – second medallion; Pharaoh's dream and Joseph being recognised by his brothers – top medallion.

2) Chapel of St. Francis of Sales: episodes are shown in the lives of, left, St. James the Apostle, centre, John the Baptist and right, John the Evangelist.

3) St. Thomas' window: Thomas, a skilful architect, is shown summoned before Gondophares, king of India. The apostolate and martyrdom of St. Thomas.

4) Window of the Apocalypse: Christ sits on a rainbow in the central medallion surrounded by twenty-four old men.

5) Chapel of St. Philomena: the life and martyrdom of the chief three deacons of the early church, St. Lawrence, St. Stephen and St. Vincent.

6) Window of the Passion of Our Lord.

7) Window on the Last Judgement.

8) The Lady Chapel: the window is of 16C glass, the statues at the entrance are of Duke Jean de Berry and his wife Jeanne de Boulogne.

9) Window depicting Abraham, Isaac, Moses, David and Jonah (has been removed).

10) Window of the Prodigal Son.

11) Chapel of Our Lady of Lourdes: the figures of St. Denis, St. Peter, St. Paul and St. Martin can be seen.

12) Window of the Good Samaritan.

13) Window giving the story of St. Stephen's relics.

14) Chapel of Sainte-Croix (Holy Cross): scenes depicted show St. Mary of Egypt, St. Nicholas and Mary Magdalene.

15) Window on the wicked rich man: the story of Lazarus whom the wicked Dives refused to help. Above, Lazarus is shown in triumph.

★**Astronomical Clock** – Designed by mathematician and astronomer Jean Fusoris in 1424, this magnificent clock (6.2m/20ft high) is set in a square frame, surmounted

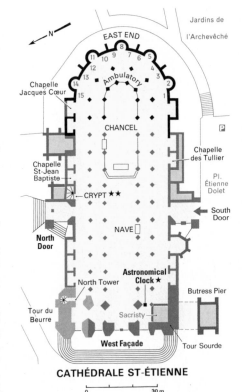

CATHÉDRALE ST-ÉTIENNE

0   30 m

From 1195 to 1215	From 1225 to 1260
14C	15C
16C	

by a concave roof and a bell. The decorative elements were designed by Jean Grangier, and the paint has recently been restored to its original brightness.

The most remarkable aspect of this timepiece is the ingenious outfitting of the lower face, which relates astronomical data. An informed clock-watcher can get seven precise readings from the dial, six of them with one single hand. The outer dial (revolving once every 24 hours) gives the time in relation to the position of the sun. The inner ring (one revolution per month) represents the lunar cycle and indicates the number of days since the last full moon as well as the current phase of the moon. The central face (one full revolution per year) bears the 12 signs of the zodiac divided into days, thus giving the date. This disk also supports an opaque panel representing the night and a panel of golden rays symbolising the day. A sun figure moves up and down, marking its position in relation to the horizon, according to the solstices. The 12 daytime spaces indicate the current hour.

The original mechanism, a complex set of gears and cogs, is on exhibit to the right of the clock (inside, the works are a facsimile).

★★Crypt – A long sloping gallery leads down to the vast late 12C crypt known as the Underground Church of the Church of St-Guillaume. Twelve large windows light the sanctuary. Six massive pillars (diameter 2.10m/7ft) flanked by columns with crocheted capitals support the vaulted ceiling on diagonal ribs which, in turn, supports the Cathedral above. The sturdy ribs set in five-sided formations shape counter-balanced curvatures (the same feature is seen in the ambulatory of the chancel). The marks on the floor were left there by the original building crew.

In the crypt, note the recumbent white marble figure of the Duke of Berry, the only vestige of a grandiose mausoleum erected between 1422 and 1438, sculpted by Jean de Cambrai. The tomb once stood in the Sainte-Chapelle at Bourges, destroyed in 1757. The 14C windows of the prophets are from the same chapel. Fragments saved when the rood screen was destroyed in the 17C are on view. Set against the Gallo-Roman outer wall, a 16C *Entombment* consists of ten statues under a canopy. Behind the sculpture, stairs lead to a little cradle-vaulted gallery, the only remains of the 11C sanctuary.

Bourges – Palais Jacques-Cœur

Ascent of the North Tower ⊘ – The attempt to complete the northern tower at the end of the 15C met with catastrophe on 31 December 1506, which had an impact on the entire northwest corner.

Reconstruction lasted until 1540, carried out under the direction of architect Guillaume de Pelvoysin, who introduced new decorative elements in the Renaissance style. A spiral stair leads to the top, where an excellent **view**★★ rewards those who venture up.

★**Jardins de l'Archevêché** (Z) – Le Nôtre is credited with the designing of these gardens in the 17C; they were extended during the 18C. From the garden's beautiful flowerbeds and shaded alleys, there is a good view of St. Stephen's Cathedral, particularly of the great nave and chevet.

Tithe Barn (Grange aux Dîmes) (Z F) – Opposite the cathedral's north doorway at the corner of rue Molière, this massive building with its buttresses and stairway designed as a half-timbered balcony, was used to store the dues paid to the church.

★★PALAIS JACQUES CŒUR ⊘ (Y)

The architectural elegance, the richness and variety of decoration, make this one of the most beautiful and sumptuous secular buildings of the Gothic age. This splendid mansion was commissioned in 1443 for Charles VII's famous Master of the Mint, and was intended no doubt, as the place to which he would retire. It was completed in less than ten years; the cost was 100 000 gold *écus*.

Jacques Cœur fell into disgrace in 1451 and so never enjoyed his completed palace. In 1457 it was restored to his heirs and from then on knew many changes of fortune. In 1679 it belonged to Colbert (statesman: 1619-1683); soon afterwards it was acquired by the city of Bourges. Since 1925, when it was bought by the State, it has been completely restored.

Exterior – Jacques Cœur's Palace consists of four main buildings round a central court. Whereas the west face, which may be seen from the rue des Arènes, looks like the exterior of a fortress with massive towers and bare walls rising above the remains of the Gallo-Roman perimeter, the east face draws attention through the delicacy and richness of its decoration. This appears, in one instance, as a motif of hearts and shells – emblems from Jacques Cœur's coat of arms – adorning the mullioned windows of the top floor and the balustrade at the base of the eaves.

On either side of a balcony (1) note the amusing figures of a man and a woman, the master and mistress of the house.

To the left of this wing, at the base of the octagonal staircase tower (2), Jacques Cœur's motto may be seen inscribed: *A vaillans cœurs, riens impossible* (To a valiant heart, nothing is impossible). As you enter the central court there is a striking difference to be seen between the sober appearance of the galleries – no doubt kept for business by the Master of the Mint –

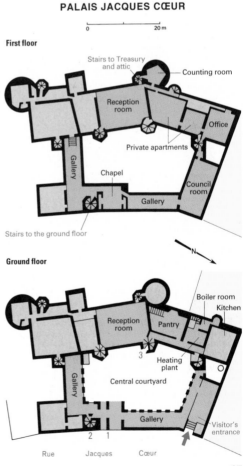

PALAIS JACQUES CŒUR

0   20 m

First floor

Stairs to Treasury and attic
Counting room
Reception room
Office
Private apartments
Gallery
Chapel
Council room
Gallery
Stairs to the ground floor

N

Ground floor

Boiler room
Kitchen
Reception room
Pantry
Heating plant
Gallery
Central courtyard
Gallery
Visitor's entrance

Rue   Jacques   Cœur

and the rich decoration of the main living quarters containing the banqueting and ceremonial halls and the private apartments. Three staircase towers divide the façade. The central tower (3), which is hexagonal, is carved with exotic trees such as palms, oranges and dates, reminiscent of Jacques Cœur's distant travels, and bears another of the master's well known mottoes: *Dire, Faire, Taire* (Speak, Act, Be Silent).

Interior – A tour of the palace gives an idea of the luxury to which a wealthy burgher with a taste for beautiful things and practical sense could aspire. The taste for luxury produced the magnificence of the dining hall with its monumental chimney piece where a 15C tapestry with a thistle motif now hangs; the practical sense comes out in the installation of running water, a boiler-room and bathroom and the planning of staircases and corridors so that those wishing to take a bath could do so without going outside to adjoining buildings. The same practical and good sense made him install a pigeon loft beneath the eaves for the homing pigeons which kept him in close touch with his counting-houses. A gallery with wooden cradle vaulting in the shape of an inverted boat keel leads to the chapel. This has a remarkable painted ceiling: on a blue ground strewn with stars, angels bear streamers on which, in Gothic lettering, are passages from the *Gloria* and the *Song of Songs*. Two oratory chapels, which could be heated, are contained within the thickness of the north and south walls on either side of the altar and were probably used by Jacques Cœur and his wife.

In one of the private apartments a fine monochrome stained glass depicting a gallery is noteworthy. Interesting architectural details may be seen in different parts of the buildings: armorial bearings, high and low reliefs and bosses such as those in the room known as The Treasury which has a heavy iron door closed with a secret lock. One of the bosses shows a scene from the romance of *Tristan and Iseult*: Queen Iseult goes to find Tristan in the garden; King Mark, forewarned of the meeting, hides in a tree, but Tristan seeing the reflection of the king's face in a pool, is careful to speak only commonplaces to Iseult.

AROUND TOWN

Shops – The central pedestrian zone is the most enjoyable place to have a gander at local shop windows, with plenty of opportunity to stop for a drink on a terrace. The local pace is restful and unhurried. Near the Palais Jacques Cœur, take rue Coursarion and rue Mirebeau; near the Cathedral, rue Bourbonnoux and rue Moyenne.

Sweets – *La Forestine* is a local speciality, created by Georges Forest in 1878, a sugary, colourful bon-bon filled with chocolate praline. The original recipe is still venerated at the Maison des Forestines, 3 place Cujas.

Shows – Bourges is a musical capital. In addition to the popular Printemps festival, the **Palais des Congrès** welcomes all kinds of artists; at **Germinal**, fans can hear jazz and rock; the **Maison de la Culture** presents a classical programme (and dramatic arts).

Society – Mingle with the crowd in the centre of town:
Place Gourdaine: restaurants, sidewalk cafés, theatres.
Avenue Jean Jaurès: Pubs and bars.
Rue Moyenne: sidewalk seating for people-watchers at the **Cujas** (corner of rue des Beaux-Arts); jazz is hot at the **Pub des Jacobins** (across from the Post Office); karaoke party at the **Victor Hugo** brasserie.
Rue Prima/Halle aux Blés: **Palais de la Bière** serves up frothy cold ones, while the **Eden** is equipped for would-be pop stars (karaoke).

ADDITIONAL SIGHTS

★**Hôtel Cujas (Y M¹)** – This elegant building was designed in about 1515 by Guillaume Pelvoysin for Durando Salvi, a rich Florentine merchant who had settled in Bourges. The famous jurist Cujas bought the mansion and finally died there in 1590. Since 1877 it has been owned by the city which uses it to house the Berry Museum.

Musée du Berry (Berry Museum) ⊘ – This quiet, unpretentious museum gives a good general picture of life in Berry over many centuries, through the display of all sorts of every day and ceremonial objects.

On the ground floor are **archeological collections**★ dating from prehistory to the end of the Gallo-Roman period, including building materials, utensils, toilet articles, accessories, jewellery, coins, models and diagrams of roads, theatres and amphitheatres, houses.

Bourges – Place Gordaine

The last gallery is a striking display of 200 steles (funerary stones, laid out as in a cemetery) vividly evoking the life of long-gone inhabitants, the prominent and the obscure. The religious inscriptions reveal how pagan beliefs slowly came to merge with spreading Christianity.

The rural life of Berry in the 18C and 19C is illustrated on the first floor in an exhibit which includes solid wood furniture worn smooth by time – a patina no amount of money or elbow grease could obtain today – and local costumes, pottery and other household objects. There are some amusing items displayed here without much explanation, lending the rooms an air of grandma's attic, arousing a delightful curiosity.

★ **Prés-Fischaux Gardens** (Y) – A beautiful garden has been laid out on marshland between the river and the close of St. Ambroise Abbey where the Protestants used to gather in the 16C to sing.

The designer has kept the avenue of plane trees and added a rose garden, French style flower-beds and ponds, to make a setting of pleasing perspectives through arches of clipped yew trees.

★ **Hôtel Lallemant** (Y M⁴) – This magnificent Renaissance mansion has retained the name of Jean Lallemant, the rich cloth merchant who had it built; it was altered in the 17C and has been converted into a museum of decorative art. The site on which the mansion was built straddled the Roman wall of the town and certain parts of the house are on different levels.

Musée des Arts décoratifs ⊙ – A sloping ramp, covered with cradle vaulting and used to lead horses in and out of the building, goes through to the **main courtyard** which is on two levels. The large main building shows the styles of different architectural periods: the mullioned windows and arcades are 15C, the doors to the corridors and the window-frames of the bays above the passageway are 16C and the entablature and round frontons bearing the arms of the Dorsannes who once owned the mansion, are 17C. Right round the courtyard at first floor level, is a kind of frieze of terracotta medallions portraying the heads of prominent personages of Antiquity. An Italian-style loggia, formerly used for summer dining, has 17C frescoes representing hunting scenes and a polychrome bas-relief dedicated to St Christopher. On the top floor, one room houses a notable **collection of miniatures**★; toys, master craft pieces, models and various small-scale fancies, all perfectly executed and together providing an unusual and thorough summary of the history of furniture from Louis XV to Art Nouveau.

Also included in the museum's collection, displayed in elegant rooms with covered ceilings: enamels, porcelains and ivories; 17C French and Flemish tapestries; paintings, 16-18C furniture (several marquetry pieces: chests, Louis XIV bureaux and a large encrusted ebony cabinet decorated about 1650).

The **chapel** has a curious coffered ceiling decorated with the symbols of alchemy, philosophy and heraldry, including the coat of arms of the Lallemant family. The symbols of the Evangelists painted in the four corners of the ceiling have contributed to make the decoration of the oratory one of the enigmas of 16C French art.

Antique toys and games are on exhibit in the final room, devoted to the 19C.

Musée de l'École ⊘ (Y **M²**) – Built in 1857 as an asylum and later used as a nursery school, today the school museum recalls the age of Jules Ferry, the French statesman credited with the establishment of free, compulsory, secular education (law of 1882): school children's smocks and wooden shoes, tables and ink wells, abacus, blackboard and desk.

Bourges classique – Built in the 17-18C and transformed for administrative use, many classical-style buildings embellish the centre of Bourges. The peace following the Wars of Religion allowed authorities to restore mansions, convents and abbeys. **Jean le Juge** (1589-1650) was the major architect of the period, which saw the construction of the Hôtel des Échevins and the Bureau des Finances (18, rue Jacques Cœur).

Under the reign of Louis XIV, the pace kept up with the grandiose project of Phélypeux de la Vrillière, archbishop of Bourges from 1677 to 1694. **Pierre Bullet** (1639-1716), who had just made a name for himself from the design of the Porte St Martin in Paris, was the architect behind the plans. The visitor can still see the signs of this collaboration in the oldest wing of the Town Hall, and the Grand Séminaire.

While the 18C was less spectacular, it gave Bourges the municipal library (26 av. de Branly) and the **Hôtel de la Préfecture** (Z **P**), enlarged and restored in the 19C. On that site once stood the palace of Duc Jean de Berry; today only a few archeologists are apt to get a glimpse of any part of its long-vanished splendour.

Old Houses (Y) – The whole town centre comes under a preservation and renovation scheme which aims at restoring the half-timbered houses (many date from the 15C and 16C) to their former glory. The results are particularly noticeable in the lively pedestrian area from rue Mirebeau to rue Coursalon via **place Gordaine**.

Maison de Pelvoysin (Y **L**) – An interesting group of old, half-timbered houses stand at the corner of Pelvoysin and Cambournac streets. Next to these is the house of Pelvoysin, the cathedral architect. It is built of stone and now houses the savings bank. The street was so narrow when it was being built, that the architect designed the front to stand at an angle to the street thus giving the house an appearance of greater width and dignity. Inside there is a fine chimney piece. The courtyard can best be seen from rue Cambournac.

Maison de la Reine Blanche (Y **N**) – Standing at nos 17-19 rue Gambon this is the most interesting of the old houses because of the richness of its decoration. On the ground floor the capitals beneath the brackets are ornamented with religious scenes; from left to right these are: St. Martin sharing his cloak, the Saviour, the Annunciation and the Visitation. On the first floor every column is decorated with two small dancers, some of which have been damaged. Each window on the ground floor has an arcade with sculptured crotchets and finials in relief above it.

Birthplace of Jacques Cœur (Z **Q**) – A half-timbered, corbelled house, standing at the corner of rue d'Auron and rue des Armuriers, bears an inscription describing it as the house in which Jacques Cœur was born (c 1395-1456). In fact it was built early in the 16C on the site of a house which came to Jacques Cœur through his marriage.

Gallo-Roman ramparts (YZ **V**) – Visible in several places, the ramparts are clearly distinguished along the **Promenade des Remparts** behind and below the Cathedral (also accessible from rue Bourbonnoux). Ingeniously integrated into the fabric of the contemporary town (what a delightful place it must be to live!), the dressed stone wall dates back to the 3C, when it was erected for protection against barbarian invasions. Some of the façades lining this leafy walkway date from the Middle Ages.

Le Printemps de Bourges

Created in April 1977, this musical event initially aimed at bringing together musicians overlooked by the Hit Parade and underplayed on the radio. The first year, 15000 people flocked to hear such non-conformist French artists as Béranger, Font and Val, Lavilliers. Two years later, ever more popular, the festival was extended to one week and welcomed other musical genres (rock, folk, jazz). Most of the spectators are young (75% between ages 15 and 25), and now number more than 100000. Shows take place in a dozen different halls, and the street life is certainly as big an attraction as what goes on inside. Over the decades, some of the groups and individual artists who have won acclaim at Bourges: Téléphone, Charles Trenet, Claude Nougaro, Murray Head, Touré Kunda, Patricia Kass, Johnny Hallyday, Véronique Sanson, Joe Cocker, Miles Davis, Nina Simone, The Cure, U2, Frank Zappa, Khaled, Rita Mitsouko. Some of the latest trends have included world music, rap and techno, and in its 20th year, the spring festival remains fresh and exciting ... Play on!

Church of St-Pierre-le-Guillard (Z) – *Closed for restoration*. According to legend, funds for building the church were provided by the Jew, Zacharie Guillard, whose mule knelt before the Holy Sacrament as it was being carried by S. Antony of Padua through Bourges in about 1225.

A massive belfry-porch leads to the nave flanked by side aisles to which chapels were added in the 15C. The sexpartite vaulting rests on crocheted capitals above slim columns. The two-storey nave is of a somewhat primitive Gothic design.

★**Hôtel des Échevins** (Y M³) – Formerly the Town Hall, this building now houses the musée Estève. There is a striking difference in architectural style between the two parts of the building:
– the living quarters at the far end of the courtyard date from 1488 and were built in the Renaissance style. A fine **octagonal tower**★ juts out from the façade and, rising to a height of three storeys, contains a circular staircase which gives access to each floor. This tower is richly decorated with arches embellished with foliated crotchets in a variety of leaf motifs which include thistle, oak, cabbage and tapering maple.
– the gallery on the left was built between 1629 and 1633 by the architect Jean le Juge in the classical style: open arcades with hanging keystones separated by Corinthian pilasters; cross windows alternating with niches, and alternating styles of pediments set above each. *See photograph page 43.*

★★**Musée Estève** ☉ – Since 1987, this museum has been home to a unique collection of 130 works in oil and on paper.

Born in Culan in 1904, **Maurice Estève** had no formal training as an artist. His work reveals a stunning evolution in technique, while themes from his native Berry are repeated over time: the home (curtains, window, table, other household objects), his grandmother, the natural environment.

In Paris, Estève worked under difficult conditions, but was able to absorb the influence of surrealism and later, Cézanne. Until 1947, his work shifted between the figurative (*La Toilette Verte*, 1934) and the abstract (*Embarquement pour Cythère*, 1929), before settling on the latter course. Most of his paintings (*Skibet*, 1979, is one of the best examples) are a subtle combination or a juxtaposition of masses of colour. Freed through abstraction of references to a single subject, enlivened by a sumptuous palette, Estève's works solicit the imagination and fascinate the viewer. Oil paintings, tapestries and water-colours are placed on rotating exhibit over three-month cycles in the well-restored rooms, illustrating the artist's itinerary from 1919 to 1989.

Maurice Estève – Skibet, 1979

Church of Notre-Dame (Y) – The church was almost entirely gutted by the fire of 1487 which destroyed two-thirds of the town. The church was known as St-Pierre-le-Marché before being dedicated to Our Lady. When it was rebuilt many modifications were made to the original plan including the addition of side aisles and the square tower which rises at the north end of the west face. The church is therefore a mixture of styles: the nave has ogive vaulting with emblazoned keystones, the south door is Renaissance and adorned with a statue of the Virgin Mary. In the south aisle, opposite the door, a white marble baptismal font adorned with lilies bears an inscription from the *Romance of the Rose*, the French medieval poem which inspired Chaucer (and which he translated in part).

Église St-Bonnet ⓥ (Y) – The church stands on the site of a building which burned down in the fire of 1487. Construction began in 1510, using plans by the architect Pelvoysin. To save expense, soft local stone of inferior quality was used; capitals were not added to the columns; the largest pillars are set directly under the ribs of the vaulting, creating a unity of space within. The 20C addition of two bays to the western part and a neo-Flamboyant façade have effected the 16C simplicity.

Inside, the most remarkable features are the stained glass windows by Jean Lescuyer in three chapels (one shows the Holy Women in regional Berry headdress); a 15C stone altarpiece representing the Apostles (St Jean chapel); a work by the local painter Jean Boucher from the late 16C.

Next to the church, on place St-Bonnet, the present-day rectory was formerly the home of the Abbesses of St-Laurent (1674).

Porte St-Ursinus (Z **S**) – Near the administrative centre (*préfecture*), rue du 95ᵉ-de-Ligne, stands the only vestige of a Romanesque collegiate church, whose community was founded in the 6C, and which was destroyed in 1799. This gateway (late 11C-early 12C) was moved in the beginning of the 19C. The tympanum, with its two arch stones, is intriguing. Signed *Girardus fecit istas portus* ("Gerard made this door"), it is embellished with non-religious scenes. On the upper portion, fables (*The Ass Schoolmaster, the Wolf and the Stork, The Fox Plays Dead*); in the middle, a lively hunting scene, perhaps inspired by an older work of art; on the bottom, a series of little people at work, illustrating the labours of the different months of the year – one of the first such depictions to be made in France. A delicate pattern of foliage covers the lintels and piers.

The visitor should continue down the street to the right, the Maison de la Culture; from the stairs leading up to it, there is a good view over the Cathedral and gardens. The esplanade (now a parking area) was created in the 17C.

★**Musée d'Histoire Naturelle** ⓥ (Z) – The natural history museum was created in 1927 and renovated in 1989. It is entertaining and educational, with an emphasis on the regional environment as well as the work of local naturalists and scientists.

★**Les Marais** – *Southeast of boulevard G-Clemenceau, take rue Charlet then turn left, cross the bridge and follow the Chemin de Prébendes.*

A pleasant walkway wanders through the wetlands and canals formed by the river Voiselle, a small tributary of the Yèvre, winding among the many garden plots held by the residents of Bourges. Between rows of poplars and willows, each garden reveals something of the personality of its tender: orderly tomato and bean plants, regal purple iris, rows and rows of strawberries, or perhaps a few bright marigolds set around an inviting hammock. In the distance, the Cathedral raises a benevolent spire above it all, as if keeping an eye on the greenery and the folks who care for it.

EXCURSION

Ancienne abbaye de Plaimpied – *12km/7mi south.*
The church is all that remains of a large abbey founded by Richard II, archbishop of Bourges. Construction began in the late 11C and went on for 100 years. Additions and renovations were made up until the 18C. The sculpted capitals are of particular interest.

La BOURIANE

Michelin map 79 folds 6 and 7 or 235 folds 9, 10 and 14

The region known as La Bouriane extends from Gourdon to the Lot Valley and west of N 20. It is a region where the limestone formation disappears under a bed of sideritic sand (iron carbonate bearing), which is a lovely red and ochre colour. This rather infertile soil nevertheless allows the cultivation of chestnut, pine and walnut trees. There are vineyards on the more exposed slopes.

A great number of rivers carve through the plateau creating a hilly, wooded countryside scattered with farms.

ROUND TRIP FROM GOURDON 94km/58mi – 3hr

★**Gourdon** – *See Gourdon.*
Leave Gourdon southwest on D 673.

Salviac – The Gothic church has some lovely 14C stained-glass windows depicting scenes from the life of St Eutrope.

Cazals – This old bastide built by English kings is designed around a large central square. A moat was dug around the castle mound.

Château de Montcléra –
The fortified entrance gate dates from the 15C. Behind it is a square keep and residential quarters flanked by round, machicolated towers.

After 3 km/1.8mi, turn off D 673 to the left, on a small road which leads to D 660.

Goujounac – There used to be a Romanesque priory around the church, but there are now only a few vestiges of this. On the south wall of the church, the Romanesque tympanum, depicting Christ in Glory giving the sign of God's blessing surrounded by the symbols of the four Evangelists, is the work of a Quercy artist who was probably influenced by the tympanum at Beaulieu-sur-Dordogne.

After crossing over the Masse, take D 45 to the left towards Cazals, then D 172 on the right.

Lherm – This little village of white limestone houses with steeply-pitched roofs covered with small brown tiles is dominated by a belltower, a turret and several dovecotes. In a small isolated, wooded valley, the church, once a priory, has a Romanesque apse and a plain barrel-vaulted nave of ashlar-stone. The chancel contains a profusely decorated altarpiece of gold and carvings against a blue background, a rather grandiose, local interpretation of the Baroque style. The building was altered in the 16C; there is a fine Renaissance-style door.

Leave Lherm travelling south on D 37.

Les Junies – The 15C castle flanked by round towers is decorated with elegant Renaissance windows.

Set apart from the village, the 14C church, an austere building, is of massive proportions. It was part of a priory, which was attached to the Dominican order in 1345, and had been founded by one of the local lords, Gaucelin des Junies, Cardinal of Albano.

Turn right on D 660.

Église St-André-des-Arques – *See Les ARQUES.*

★Les Arques – *See Les ARQUES.*

Leave Les Arques travelling northward. In Gindou, turn right on D 25.

Rampoux – There is an interesting 12C Romanesque church here, made of red and white stone, which used to be a Benedictine priory. Inside, the 15C frescoes illustrate the Life of Christ in naïve style.

In Lavercantière, continue eastward on D 25. After crossing the railway, turn left on a small road which leads to D 12.

Beyond Concorès, this scenic route wends its way along part of the Céou valley before turning back to Gourdon by way of the river Bléou.

BRANTÔME★★

Population 2 080
Michelin map 75 fold 5 or 233 south of fold 31

Brantôme lies in the charming valley of the Dronne. Its old abbey and picturesque **setting**★ make it one of the most delightful places in Périgord.

The chronicler Brantôme – The literary fame of Pierre de Bourdeille, better known as Brantôme, brought renown to the abbey of which he was commendatory abbot.
Born the third son of the baron of Bourdeilles in 1540, Brantôme spent the first years of his life at the court of Marguerite of Valois, queen of Navarre, since both his mother and maternal grandmother were members of the royal household. In 1549 he went to Paris to continue his education, which he completed in 1555 at the University of Poitiers. He began life as a soldier of fortune and courtier, went to Scotland with Mary Stuart, travelled to Spain, Portugal, Italy and the British Isles and even to Africa. Wild adventures brought him into contact with the great and famous in an era rich in scandal.
After fighting at Jarnac in 1569, he withdrew to his abbey and began his famous chronicles. The Huguenots twice threatened to destroy the abbey during the Wars of Religion, he thereby had to use all his diplomatic skill with Coligny, one of the leaders of the Protestants, to save it from being pillaged. He left the abbey to return to court as chamberlain to Charles IX. In 1584 a fall from his horse crippled him, he then left the restless and impetuous Valois court to retreat to the peace of his monastery and finish his chronicles.
Brantôme's posthumous fame lies in his *Les vies des hommes illustres et grands capitaines* ("Lives of Illustrious Men and Great Leaders") and *Les vies des dames galantes* ("Lives of Court Mistresses") in which morality and historical facts are sometimes confused. He was a lively, witty and sometimes cynical historian, who personally knew great writers of his time, such as the poet Ronsard; he could tell a good tale well, with many a spicy detail; his style was simple and has served as a model to many writers.

SIGHTS

★★ **Banks of the river Dronne** – To get a complete picture of this romantic spot amble along the banks of the Dronne; the old houses with their flower-covered balconies and trellises and the lovely gardens near the abbey are reflected in the tranquil mirror of water. The charm lies in the harmony, serenity and calm of the scene and the softness of the light.
A 16C elbow bridge with asymmetrical arches, a Renaissance house with mullioned windows and the abbey, clinging to the limestone cliffs, make an attractive sight.
Boat tours ⊙ are available.

Ancienne abbaye – Brantôme Abbey, which was founded by Charlemagne in 769, under the Benedictine rule, to house the relics of St Sicaire, attracted a multitude of pilgrims. Sacked by the Normans, it was rebuilt in the 11C by Abbé Guillaume.

Brantôme – The banks of the Dronne

In the 16C, it became a commandery headed by Pierre de Mareuil as abbot (he had constructed the most interesting of the buildings); later his nephew, Pierre de Bourdeille, became the administrator.

The present buildings are those built in the 18C by Bertin, administrator of Périgord.

Église abbatiale (Abbey church) – Angevin vaulting, a compromise between cross-ribbed vaulting and a dome, replaced the two original domes in the 15C. The nave is plain and elegant; a bay in the form of a cross and three depressed-arched windows below it illuminate the flat east end.

The baptistery is adorned with a 14C low relief in stone of the Baptism of Christ. Another low relief, this time dating from the 13C and showing the Massacre of the Innocents, may be seen underneath the porch above the font, which rests on a fine Romanesque capital.

Near the main doorway go into one of the cloistral galleries from where it is possible to get a glimpse of the former chapter-house; its palm tree vaulting is supported by a central column.

★★**Clocher (belfry)** ◷ – The belltower was built apart from the church upon a sharp rock towering 12m/39ft high, beneath which are vast caves. It was erected in the 11C and is the oldest gabled Romanesque belltower in Limousin. It was made of four storeys, each stepped back and slightly smaller than the one below, and topped with a stone pyramid. The ground floor is roofed with an archaic dome where the evolution from the square to the ellipse is obtained from triangular ribs held up by marble columns, an architectural element most likely recovered from a Merovingian construction. The three other storeys are opened by round arched bays supported on columns with simply decorated capitals.

Convent Buildings – These now house the town hall and the **Fernand-Desmoulin Museum** ◷ which displays prehistoric art and works by local painters. There are temporary exhibitions held in what used to be the monks' dormitory.

Troglodyte tour ◷ ("Du Creusé au Construit") – The hermits who had converted the "fountain of the rock", originally a place of pagan worship, to Christianity were succeeded by monks, who initially occupied the caves in the rock face. Later on they continued to use the caves as outbuildings, or as refuges when the abbey buildings came under attack (in the 11C, 12C, 14C and 17C). The tour circuit shows the monks' calefactory and the lavacrum, the remains of the abbey mill and the troglodyte dovecote. The "fountain of the rock", dedicated to St Sicaire, is still believed to have life-giving properties and the power to cure infant diseases in particular. The awesome atmosphere of the **Cave of the Last Judgement**, decorated with an epigrammatic Triumph of Death and an Italianate Crucifixion sculpted in the 15C, is an indication of the sort of spirituality that pervaded in the monastic community of Brantôme for a thousand years.

The final cave contains a breeding ground for young trout, which are eventually used to restock the river Dronne.

Musée rêve et miniatures ◷ – This museum displays a plentiful collection of miniature houses filled with diminutive furnishings in silver, china and glass, with all the details just right. The scale of the models is 1:12. Among the many exhibit cases, a series of several, describes the evolution of style from the Middle Ages through Art Deco. Another series, a proven child-pleaser, arrays imaginary habitats where animals are the denizens.

EXCURSIONS

Thiviers – This busy little town is known for its markets and fairs. The Château de Vaucocourt, much restored, raises its gothico-Renaissance towers around the corner from the church. The **Maison de l'oie et du canard** ◷, to the right of the tourist office, has an exhibit devoted to foie gras; Thiviers is one of the capitals of its production.

★**Grottes de Villars** ◷ – A winding corridor gives way to the caverns and concretions. Among the most remarkable formations: yellow and ochre draperies, two small rimstone pools, and very finely-wrought stalactites hanging from the ceiling. The first chambers are stunning for the brightness of the white concretions composed of almost pure calcite. Prehistoric paintings done in manganese oxide probably date from the same period as the paintings at Lascaux (17 000 years old). The calcite flows which cover up sections of them help to authenticate their age.

★**Château de Puyguilhem** ◷ – This 16C château is typical of those built in and around the Loire valley in the days of François I. The towers, balustrades, sculpted chimneys and mullioned windows create a graceful exterior impression. Inside, visitors admire the **chimney pieces★**; panels representing six of the Labours of Hercules; massive beams hewn of chestnut.

Château de Puyguilhem

Sorges – This pleasant village has a century-old reputation for producing truffles, and a museum to honour them. The **Maison de la Truffe** ⊙ in the tourist office tells you everything you ever wanted to know about this rare, delectable fungus, and directs you to a walking tour outside of town, where, if you are very lucky, you just might find one yourself.

La BRENNE★★
Michelin map 68 folds 6, 7, 16 and 17 or 238 folds 26, 38

The northern limit of La Brenne is drawn by the river Claise, the eastern limit by the Lancosme forest; to the west and south, the Creuse valley borders it. The region's main feature is its 7 500ha/18 533 acres of lakes and ponds.
At the end of 1889, the **Parc naturel régional de la Brenne** (regional nature park) was created, covering 1 660 km²/640sq mi and involving 47 different local governments and 32 000 inhabitants. Visitors interested in the tourist and cultural activities here can get information at the **Maison du Parc** *(see Practical information at the end of this guide)*.

Land of a thousand waters – La Brenne is a land of legends: it has inspired painters and poets; fairies, elves and sorcerers as well. The name recalls Geoffroy de Brenne, lord of Mézières in the 13C. Once neglected woodlands and moors, the area was cleared out by monks (from St-Cyran, Méobecq and Fontgombault) who engineered the ponds for the purposes of cultivating fish to enjoy on meatless fast days. Later, in the 19C, the region was further improved, removing the risk of malaria; roads were laid and swampy lands drained, opening the land to agriculture. Today the area is a patchwork of mixed uses.
The ponds and lakes mark the landscape and symbolise the close ties linking man and nature in this region, in addition to providing a rich ecosystem and a lovely setting. The waters are also a major factor in the local economy, for 10 000 tonnes of fish (carp, roach, tench, pike, bass and eel) are drawn out annually. Every year, a sluice gate is opened to drain the waters.

Fauna and flora – The natural environment welcomes wildlife, in particular numerous species of birds. A good observation point is the **Réserve naturelle de Chérine** ⊙.

TOUR STARTING FROM LE BLANC *80km/50mi – 2hr30min*

Le Blanc – This busy burg is a commercial centre for the area, attracting fairs and markets, drawing regional inhabitants to its shops and cinemas. The upper town is a picturesque labyrinth of old houses, while the lower town gathers around St-Génitour, the church dedicated to the 4C martyr and *cephalophore* saint (which is to say he was decapitated, but nonetheless picked up his severed head and walked to the church, where he was buried) reputed for curing diseases of the eye.

Fauna of La Brenne

② Purple heron

① Marsh harrier

③ Whiskered tern

⑤ Crested grebe

④ European pond turtle

⑥ Pintail duck

⑦ Gray heron

⑧ Cormorant

⑨ Northern lapwing

① ② ③ ④ ⑤ ⑥ ⑦ d'après photos J. F. Hellio, N. Van Ingen, in Brenne, Terre sauvage. Éditions La Pommeraie ⑧ d'après photo Ermie/JACANA, Paris

Leave Le Blanc to the north-east on D 975, then turn left after crossing the railway.

Étang de la Mer Rouge – The "Red Sea" pond is believed to have been given its name by a former owner, Aimery Sénébaud, on his return from the Holy Land, where he had been imprisoned beside the Red Sea. It is the biggest lake in La Brenne, and has a surface area of 180ha/445 acres. It provides a natural refuge for migrating waterfowl *(see Introduction page 19).* The church of Notre Dame de la Mer Rouge, rebuilt in 1854, stands on a headland to the south and is the site of a yearly pilgrimage. The statue of the Virgin, miraculously found in the hollow of an oak tree by Aimery in the 13C, was stolen and later replaced by a copy which is kept in the church in Rosnay, and is brought out for the pilgrimage. As access to the chapel is difficult,

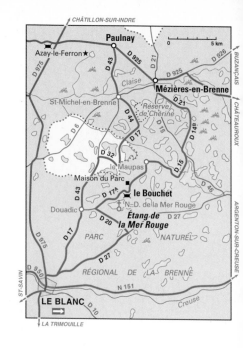

the ceremonies are held at Croix de l'Hermitage in the forest near the lake. *Continue along D 17ª.*

Château du Bouchet ⊘ – This impressive medieval fortress, occupied by the English during the Hundred Years War, was restored in both the 15C and 17C. For 300 years it belonged to the Rochechouart-Mortemart family and for a while served as the residence of the Marquise de Montespan who was born a Rochechouart-Mortemart and was the daughter and sister of the lords of Le Bouchet. You may walk round the outside of the castle and visit the keep, terrace and part of the ground floor. From the keep and the terrace there is a view of the Brenne countryside and the Mer Rouge pond.

Mézières-en-Brenne – The most important town in Brenne is built on the banks of the Claise whose course is marked by a line of poplars. The **church** belfry, flanked by two stone turrets, has a porch ornamented with sculpture, much of which was badly broken at the time of the Revolution. Go in by the south aisle. The nave has wooden vaulting with painted uprights and crossbeams. A Renaissance chapel was added to the south aisle by Nicolas of Anjou between 1543 and 1559. The stained glass windows date from the 14C and 16C. Some were restored in the 19C.

Maison de la Pisciculture de Brenne ⊘ – Established in one˚of the last vestiges of the 11C stronghold, the exhibits inside this nature museum are related to fish and fishing in the region. In addition to aquariums, displays recount the history of the village and provide information on techniques for catching local fish.

Paulnay – The **church** dating from the 12C and 13C has an interesting Romanesque **doorway★**. Three rows of finely sculptured covings are supported on elegant capitals. Other capitals adorn the arcades surrounding the doorway. Inside the oven-vaulted chancel and the narrow bay are decorated with lovely ochre-coloured frescoes. The modern Stations of the Cross carved in wood and painted are the work of a monk from Fontgombault abbey.

BRIVE-LA-GAILLARDE

Population 49714
Michelin map 75 fold 8 or 239 fold 26

Brive, which owes its nickname *La Gaillarde* – the bold – to the courage displayed by its citizens on the many occasions when it was besieged, is an active town in the Corrèze alluvial plain. It is in the middle of the rich Brive basin, where market gardening and orchards prosper.

Brive, located at the crossroads of Bas-Limousin (Lower Limousin), Périgord and the Quercy *causses* (limestone plateaux), is an important railway junction and is seeking to become the economic capital of the region.

Its main industries concern the canning of food, especially fruit and vegetables picked in the area.

A popular book fair has taken place annually in the Georges Brassens hall since 1982. Prizes are awarded mainly to books on tourism.

The plan of Brive is an excellent example of concentric urban expansion, with the old quarter and St Martin's Collegiate Church as its centre.

The "King of Brive" – The assassination of Chilgéric in 584 plunged Merovingian France into anarchy. A meeting of towns and villages at Brive proclaimed Gondowald, grandson of Clovis, king. Following Frankish custom, he was raised up on a shield and carried three times round the fortress. However the reign of the "King of Brive" was but brief; he was assassinated almost immediately, and for good measure his assassins also razed the basilica of St Martin to the ground.

A brilliant career – Guillaume Dubois (1656-1723), the son of an apothecary from Brive, took the Orders and became tutor to Philip of Orléans. He became prime minister when Philip was appointed regent during the minority of Louis XV. Offices and honours were heaped upon him; he became Archbishop of Cambrai and then a cardinal. He made an alliance with England, which thus ensured a long period of peace in France.

A glorious soldier – Guillaume-Marie-Anne Brune enlisted in the army in 1791 and rose to become a general commanding the army in Italy in 1798. Following victories in Holland and Italy he was appointed ambassador to Constantinople. Elected Maréchal de France in 1804, he was banished by Napoleon soon afterwards for his "republican attitude". He became the symbol of the Revolution and died, a victim of a Royalist mob, in 1815 at Avignon.

OLD TOWN

The old town located in the heart of the city, bounded by a first ring of boulevards, has been successfully restored. The buildings, old and new, create a harmonious ensemble of warm beige sandstone and bluish tinted rooftops.

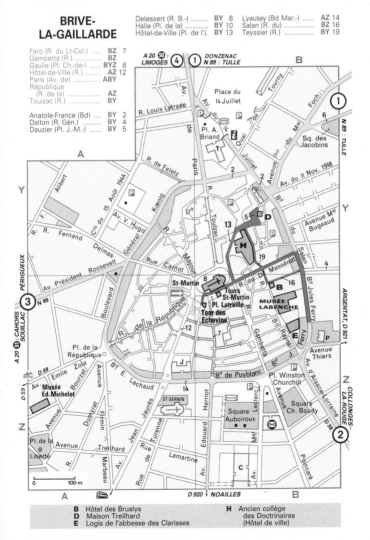

BRIVE-LA-GAILLARDE

Delessert (R. B.-)	BY 6	Lyautey (Bd Mar.-)	AZ 14
Halle (Pl. de la)	BY 10	Salan (R. du)	BZ 16
Hôtel-de-Ville (Pl. de l')	BY 13	Teyssier (R.)	BY 19

Faro (R. du Lt-Col.) ..... BZ 7
Gambetta (R.) .... BZ
Gaulle (Pl. Ch.-de-) ..... BYZ 8
Hôtel-de-Ville (R.) .... AZ 12
Paris (Av. de) .... ABY
République
  (R. de la) .... AZ
Toulzac (R.) .... BY

Anatole-France (Bd) .... BY 2
Dalton (R. Gén.) .... BY 4
Dauzier (Pl. J.-M.-) ...... BY 5

B Hôtel des Bruslys
D Maison Treilhard
E Logis de l'abbesse des Clarisses

H Ancien collège des Doctrinaires (Hôtel de ville)

Collégiale St-Martin

(BZ) – In this church, only the transept, apse and a few of the capitals are Romanesque, the traces of a 12C monastic community. Inside, over the transept crossing, is an octagonal dome on flat pendentives, characteristic of the Limousin style. The nave and side aisles are 14C. The chancel was faithfully rebuilt by Cardinal Dubois in the 18C; note the 12C baptismal font, decorated with the symbols of the Evangelists. From the outside admire the historiated capitals and modillioned cornice of the apsidal chapels.

Archeological Crypt – Vestiges of previous churches have been uncovered beneath the chancel, including the primitive construction dating from the 5C over the tomb of St Martin the Spaniard, who brought the Gospel to the town but was massacred by its inhabitants.

Brive – Tour des Échevins

Tour des Échevins (BZ) – In the narrow rue des Échevins stands a town house with a fine corbelled Renaissance tower pierced by mullioned windows.

Place Latreille – This square was once the spiritual and commercial heart of the city and is still surrounded by old houses. The house known as Tours St-Martin dates from the 15C and 16C.

Positioned at the corner of rue Raynal and rue du Salan is the 18C Hôtel des Bruslys (BZ **B**).

Turn right into Boulevard Jules-Ferry.

★**Musée Labenche d'art et d'histoire** ⊘ (BZ) – Built in 1540 by Jean II de Calvimont, lord of Labenche and the king's keeper of the seals for the Bas-Limousin, this town house (Hôtel de Labenche) is a magnificent example of Renaissance architecture in Toulouse style and is the most remarkable secular building in town. From the inside courtyard the two main buildings can be seen set at right angles, above which are large arches. The roseate hue of the stone enhances the beauty of the building's decorative elements: mullioned windows adorned with festoons and slender columns and surmounted by busts of men and women set in niches.

Inside, it has been converted into a museum. The Roman-style **main staircase** with brackets carved as busts of warriors and ladies exudes the same exuberance as the outside.

Mortlake tapestry

Museum – The Counts of Cosinac room is decorated with a marvellous collection of **tapestries**, known as the Mortlake tapestries, made in the 17C using the widely renowned techniques of English high-warp tapestry. In the Cardinal Dubois room, there is the tomb of the pilgrim to Santiago di Compostela and a wonderful 11C silver and bronze **eucharistic dove** hanging above the altar, in which the sacred Host used to be kept. One of the main attributes of this museum is the successful reconstruction of the various series of excavations.

Logis de l'Abbesse des Clarisses (Residence of the Mother Superior of the Order of St Clare) **(BZ E)** – This Louis XIII building is distinguished by its dormer windows with semi-circular pediments decorated with keel-shaped spheres.

Ancien collège des doctrinaires (BY H) – This college was maintained by the Brothers of Christian Doctrine, who were as much open-minded humanists as men of faith, and its prosperity increased up until the Revolution.
Today these 17C buildings house the town hall. The façade on rue Teyssier is of fine classical arrangement and the wall decorated with a colonnade overlooks an inner courtyard.

Place de l'Hôtel de Ville (BY 13) – On this large square, modern buildings (Crédit Agricole bank) and old turreted mansions form a harmonious architectural unit.
The 16C **Maison Treilhard (D)** consists of two main buildings joined by a round tower, decorated by a turret.

ADDITIONAL SIGHT

Musée de la Résistance et de la Déportation Edmond-Michelet ⊙ **(AZ)** – The museum traces the history of the Resistance movement and deportation with paintings, photographs, posters and original documents relating to the camps, especially Dachau, where Edmond Michelet, former minister under General De Gaulle, was interned.

EXCURSIONS

★**Les Terres de Monsieur de Turenne** *Round trip of 55km/34mi– 4hr*

This trip crosses the central area of the old viscounty of Turenne, which was not united with the French crown until 1738 *(see TURENNE)*. After Turenne, the wooded hills of the Limoges region give way to the first limestone plateaux of the Quercy region.
Leave Brive-La-Gaillarde travelling southwest on D 38 towards Meyssac.

Château de Lacoste – This former stronghold, built of local sandstone, has a main building flanked by three 13C towers. It was completed in the 15C with an elegant turret and a polygonal staircase.
At Noailhac you enter the region of red sandstone, which is used to build the lovely warm-coloured villages of the area. Soon Collonges-la-Rouge, perhaps the best known, can be seen against a backdrop of greenery.

★★**Collonges-la-Rouge** – *See Collonges-la-Rouge.*

Meyssac – Meyssac is in the centre of hilly countryside where walnut and poplar trees, vineyards and orchards prosper. Like Collonges-la-Rouge, the town is built of red sandstone.
The **church** is an unusual mixture of architectural elements: a Gothic interior, a belfry-porch fortified by hoarding and a limestone doorway in the Romanesque Limousin style, adorned with small capitals decorated with animals and foliage.

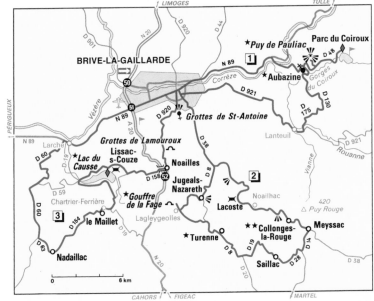

Near the church, the **18C covered market**, which has a timberwork roof resting on alternating pillars and columns, is set in the middle of a square surrounded by elegant town houses, some of which have towers.

The picturesque nature of this village is confirmed by some of the houses, which are half-timbered with overhanging storeys and porch roofs.

The red earth, known as Collonges clay, is also used in pottery manufacture, which has developed in Meyssac.

Leave Meyssac on D 14 south, towards Martel. After 2km/1mi, turn right on D 28.

Saillac – The village nestles among walnut trees and fields of maize. Inside the small Romanesque church is a doorway, preceded by a narthex, with a remarkable **tympanum★** in polychrome stone, relatively rare in the 12C. On the tympanum there is a representation of the Adoration of the Magi: the upper register depicts the Virgin Mary and Infant Jesus surrounded by Saint Joseph and the three kings; the lower register shows a winged leopard and an angel overcoming Leviathan. The tympanum is held up by a pier, composed of twisted columns adorned with foliage and hunting scenes, which probably came from a pagan monument.

In the chancel, topped by a dome on pendentives, are elegant historiated capitals.

Leave Saillac travelling northwest to reach D 19, then turn south to D 8.

★Turenne – *See Turenne.*

Continue along D 8. After 3km/1.8mi, turn left towards Lagleygeolle.

★Gouffre de La Fage (Chasm) ⊘ – The underground galleries form two separate groups, which can be visited successively. A staircase leads into the chasm, which was created by the collapse of the roof section. The first group of chambers, to the left, contains fine draperies in the form of jellyfish in beautiful rich colours. In the Organ Hall (Salle des Orgues), the concretions are played like a xylophone.

The second group, with many stalagmites and stalactites, also has a forest of needle-like forms hanging from the roof. In the last chamber excavations are underway to uncover bones from prehistoric times.

The cave is occupied by a very large colony of bats, including six different species.

Gouffre de la Fage – "Bat Cave"

Return to Lagleygeolle, and take the left turn that will bring you to D 73.

Jugeals-Nazareth – The village of Nazareth was founded by Raymond I of Turenne on his return from the First Crusade. He built a leper-house which he entrusted to the care of the Knights Templars. Beneath the town hall there are several vaulted chambers, each equipped with a well and closed off with a railing, in which the lepers used to stay.

As you leave town to the north on D 8, a scenic overlook comes into view on the right. At the Monplaisir crossroads, D 38 goes back to Brive-la-Gaillarde.

La Causse Corrézien *Round trip of 45km/29mi – 3hr*

Leave Brive on D 920 south, towards Cahors.

The road rises up above the Brive basin.

Grottes de St-Antoine – These caves, hollowed out of sandstone, were used as a retreat by St Antony of Padua while he was living at Brive. They form an open-air sanctuary. Franciscans still provide hospitality for today's pilgrims. Follow the Stations of the Cross to the top of a hill to get a good view of Brive.

Take the small signposted road to the left.

Grottes de Lamouroux – This picturesque group of caves arranged in five tiers was used by man in times of danger.

Noailles – Noailles, lying in a pleasant setting of green hills, is overlooked by its castle and church perched on a hill.

The **church** ⊘, topped with a Limousin style bell gable, has a Romanesque apse and chancel with realistic historiated capitals (cripples on crutches) on slender columns.

In the pointed-vaulted nave are memorial plates of the De Noailles family. There is a painting by Watteau's teacher Claude Gillot *(Instruments of the Crucifixion)*.

The Renaissance **château**, seat of the De Noailles family, is decorated with pinnacle windows, which have pediments ornamented with angels bearing the De Noailles coat of arms.

Leave Noailles on D 158 west.

The road climbs towards the lake and Corrèze Causse, an area of white limestone and with here and there a dip filled with red clay and covered with juniper bushes and stunted oak trees.

Lissac-sur-Couze – Set back from the lake, this elegant manor, flanked by battlemented turrets, was a military tower in the 13C and 14C. The church beside it has a bell gable.

★**Lac du Causse** – Also called Chasteaux Lake, this superb stretch of water (90ha/222 acres), set in lush green countryside in the lovely Couze valley, is a **recreational centre** ⊘ (swimming, sailing, water-skiing, windsurfing, sculling etc).

Leave Lissac on D 59 southwest.

The itinerary runs along the lake shore, revealing its extent and beauty.

Le Maillet – The limestone walls of the houses in this hamlet are constructed in a traditional way using "house martin" mortar, that is lumps of clay pressed into cracks. The vivid red of the clay gives a lot of character to the scene.

Continue along D 154.

Nadaillac – This charming country village is famous for its high-quality truffles. Some of the medieval houses have typical *lauzes*-covered roofs . The fortified church is entered through a deep-set doorway preceded by a vaulted passageway. The pre-chancel is covered by a dome on pendentives.

Leave Nadaillac on D 63.

Further on, scenic road D 63 weaves in and out of the *départements* of Dordogne and Corrèze at their borders. In Larche, take N 89 back to Brive.

Le BUGUE

Population 2 764

Michelin map 75 fold 16 or 235 fold 1

This active commercial centre, where locally grown products are marketed, is situated at the gateway of the Périgord Noir, on the north bank of the Vézère, near its confluence with the Dordogne.

MUSEUMS

Aquarium du Périgord Noir ⊘ – This has been designed to make visitors feel as if they were moving under water, like divers. The open-topped aquariums have natural lighting and open onto large windows. They contain fresh water fish, crustaceans and invertebrates from various parts of Europe. Of particularly impressive dimensions are the gleaning catfish, originating from the centre and east of the continent (some of the larger specimens are over 1.5m/5ft long), white and silver grass carp and sturgeons. There is a separate display on the breeding cycle of the salmon.

Musée de la paléontologie ⊘ – Four exhibit rooms house the collection of over 3 000 items, grouped together in families: ammonites, trilobites, gastropods, rudistae, and so forth.

Maison de la vie sauvage ⊘ – The focus of the museum is birds, including a collection of stuffed and mounted specimens, their habits and habitats in Europe. The displays address aspects such as the how and why of feathers, beaks, and song: techniques for flying, hunting and fishing. Migratory routes and their many dangers are described.

One section is devoted to the evolution of reptiles into birds, and another to mammals found in France.

Village du Bournat ⊘ – This is a reconstitution of a regional village-farm at the turn of the last century. In each of the buildings, figures stage the joys and chores of the past: harvest supper, a wedding celebration, washerwomen at work. Bakers and smithies perpetuate their traditional tradecraft, also highlighted by the collection of farm tools and machinery.

CAVES AND CASTLES

Caverne de Bara-Bahau ⊘ – Just west of Bugue, the cave, which is about 100m/300ft long, ends in a chamber blocked by a rock fall. On the roof of the chamber, amid the protrusions in the rock face, may be seen drawings made with sharpened flints and fingers (Magdalenian Culture) and by scratching with bears' claws (Mousterian Culture). The finger drawings were discovered in 1951 by the Casterets and depict horses, aurochs, bison, bears and deer.

★Gouffre de Proumeyssac ⊘ – *3km/2mi to the south via D 31ᴱ*
A tunnel drilled into a hill, overlooking the Vézère, leads to a platform built half-way up the chasm. This platform offers a view of this underground dome which is decorated, particularly at the base of the walls, with fine yellow and white con-cretions. Water seeps through abundantly, adding to the stalactites which, in some places, are very numerous and form draperies, pure coloured stalagmites and fan-tastic shapes such as the eccentrics and triangular crystallisations that are building up from the floor of the caves. Various objects subjected to encrustation with lime which lie scattered over the floor of the cave do not really fit in with the splendid natural décor.

The minute basket suspended in mid-air was until 1952 the only way of getting into the chasm. The 52m/171ft descent in complete darkness at the mercy of the fluctuations in temperament of the mule which was working the winch must have been an unforgettable experience for the three tourists allowed down each time with their guide. In the little museum by the entrance, a display of photographs, records this pioneering phase of visiting the chasm.

The use of construction materials which contrast in tone, ranging from yellow to purple-red, gives a very attractive, patchwork appearance to the church of Audrix and some of the farms surrounding it.

Grotte de St-Cirq ⊘ – *6km/3.6mi northeast on D 31*
In a small cave underneath an overhanging rock engravings from the Magdalenian Period, representing horses, bison and ibex, have been discovered. However, the cave is best known for the painting of the Man of St-Cirq (at times inappropriately called the Sorcerer of St-Cirq), one of the most remarkable representations of a human figure found in a prehistoric cave.
A small museum exhibits fossils and prehistoric tools.

Campagne – At the opening of a small valley stands a small Romanesque church preceded by a belfry.
The castle of the lords of Campagne, built in the 15C, was restored in the 19C. The towers with crenellations and machicolations which flank the living quarters and the neo-Gothic elements give the castle the appearance of an English manor-house. The last marquis de Campagne gave the castle to the state in 1970.

CADOUIN★

Population 378
Michelin map 75 fold 16 or 235 fold 5 – Local map see Vallée de la DORDOGNE

The Abbey of Cadouin, founded in a narrow valley near the Bessède forest in 1115 by Robert d'Arbrissel, was taken over soon after by the Cistercians and was extremely prosperous during the Middle Ages.
The church and cloisters, restored after the Revolution, constitute an interesting archi-tectural group around which has grown a small village, with an old covered market. On 14 October 1890, the cinematographer **Louis Delluc**, seminal film critic and founder of cinema clubs, was born here in a house on the market square.

The Holy Shroud of Cadouin – The first written mention of the Holy Shroud appeared in 1214 in an act decreed by Simon de Montfort. This linen cloth adorned with bands of embroidery had been brought from Antioch by a priest from Périgord and was believed to be the cloth that had been wrapped around Christ's head.
The shroud became an object of deep veneration and attracted large pilgrimages, bringing great renown to Cadouin. It is said that Richard the Lion Heart, St Louis and Charles V came to kneel before it in reverence. Charles VII had it brought to Paris and Louis XI to Poitiers. When the abbey was threatened by the English during the Hundred Years War – the Romanesque cloisters and many of the outbuildings were destroyed – the Holy Shroud was first entrusted to the care of the monks at Toulouse and then later to those at Aubazine. It was only returned to Cadouin, at the end of the 15C, after endless lawsuits and the intervention of the Pope and Louis XI. Restora-tion was undertaken and new buildings were built, but they in turn were damaged during the Wars of Religion.

Tradition vs. science – In 1934, two experts attributed the Holy Shroud of Cadouin to the 11C, as the embroidered bands bore Kufic inscriptions citing an emir and a caliph who had ruled in Egypt in 1094 and 1101. The bishop of Périgueux therefore had the pilgrimage to Cadouin discontinued.
In 1982 two researchers from the C.N.R.S. went over the study from the beginning and added further details to the 1934 conclusions: only the embroidered bands, char-acteristic of the art work produced during the Fatimid dynasty, date from the late 11C; after all, it was quite unlikely that an Egyptian craftsman in the late 11C would have embroidered a cloth that was said to have been wrapped around Christ's head 1 000 years before.

ABBEY

★ Church – The building, completed in 1154, presents a massive, powerful west front divided horizontally into three sections, where the influence of the Saintonge style is evident: the middle section, opened by three round-arched windows which light the church's interior, divides upper and lower arcaded sections. Tall buttresses running vertically cut the façade into three, showing the church's interior plan quite precisely: one nave with side aisles.

This austere architectural plan *(illustration page 34)*, where decoration is limited virtually to the play of light on the stone, emphasises the ornamental effect brought about by the gold colour of the Molières stone. The finely proportioned building broke away from Cistercian architecture with

Cloisters

Lasfargue/IMAGES PHOTOTHÈQUE

its interior plan: a chancel with an apse between two apsidal chapels, a dome at the transept crossing capped by a pyramidal belltower roofed with chestnut shingles, and a more elaborate interior decoration (windows surrounded by mouldings, capitals with foliage and stylised animals and, in the two arms of the transept, elegant capitals decorated with interlacing and palm fronds). Nonetheless, the harmonious proportions and the grandeur of the construction emanate a spirituality entirely in keeping with Cistercian sanctuaries.

★★ Cloisters ⊙ – Thanks to the generosity of Louis XI, the cloisters were built at the end of the 15C in the Flamboyant Gothic style. The work, in fact, continued to the middle of the 16C, as the Renaissance capitals of some of the columns bear witness. Despite the damage suffered during the Wars of Religion and the Revolution, the cloisters were saved and restored in the 19C, owing to the enthusiastic attention they were given by historians and archeologists alike.

At each corner there is a fine door: the royal door is adorned with the arms of France and Brittany as both Charles VIII and Louis XII had been married to Anne of Brittany, the benefactress of Cadouin. The pendants are carved into people and lively little scenes. In the north gallery, facing the reader's lectern, the abbot's throne can be seen emblazoned with the abbey arms: the many scenes illustrated in low relief on either side end in a large fresco of the Annunciation. Four small columns cast in the form of towers are decorated with themes from the Old and New Testaments (Samson and Delilah, Job, etc).

The chapter-house and two other rooms have been set up as a **Musée du Suaire (Shroud Museum)** ⊙, where the restored relic is on display, forming the centrepiece of an exhibition to mark the eight centuries of pilgrimage and religious fervour that it provoked.

Musée du Vélocipède ⊙ – France's biggest bicycle museum occupies an outbuilding of the convent with a display of about one hundred models. Huge "pennyfarthings", distinguished by the large front wheel and very small rear wheel, other old bicycles and tricycles represent the finest hours of technology and inventions in this field since the middle of the 19C. There are the pedals invented by the Michaux brothers, brake rod systems, the chainless bicycle produced by the Acatène company, the first tyres with inner tubes and the "hammock saddle". The beginnings of competitive cycling are represented by the model from the Paris-Brest return race of 1891 and a bicycle from the first ever Tour de France in 1903. The British postman's quadricycle bears witness to the long-standing relationship between the bicycle and the postal service. The two World Wars are also recorded by the folding "Gérard" bicycle used by French soldiers in the First World War and the towing tricycle that came to symbolise the exodus of 1940.

EXCURSION

Molières – *4km/2.4mi west via D 25 and D 27*
This unfinished English *bastide (see page 43)* has a Gothic church with a façade flanked by a tall two-storey square defensive tower.

CAHORS★★

Population 19735
Michelin map 79 fold 8 or 235 fold 14
Local maps see Causse de GRAMAT and Basse Vallée du LOT

Cahors, enclosed by a meander in the Lot river and overlooked by rocky hills, was a flourishing commercial and university city in the Middle Ages and still retains precious vestiges of its past. The city, which for centuries occupied only the eastern section of the peninsula, has slowly spread to cover the entire tongue of land and has now reached the neighbouring hills. **Boulevard Gambetta (BYZ)**, a typical southern town promenade lined with plane trees, cafés and shops, is the great north-south thoroughfare of the city; its busy,

bustling atmosphere reflects the fact that Cahors is an important commercial centre. As *Préfecture* of the Lot *département*, the city has expanded its administrative and public services, which employ many local residents.

As a tourist centre, the former capital of Quercy is an excellent starting point for tours of the Célé and Lot valleys; wine-lovers can also begin a tour of the vineyards here *(see Practical information, Regional wines, at the end of this guide)*. Boat trips ◷ on the Lot are also available.

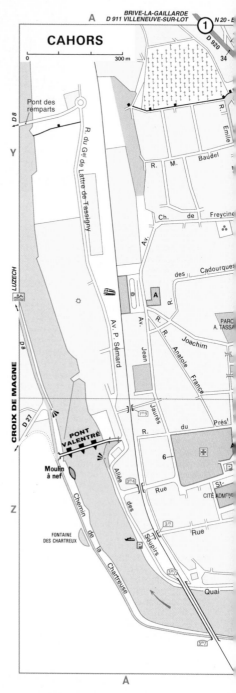

The sacred spring – A spring, discovered by Carthusian monks, led to the founding of Divona Cadurcorum, later known as Cadurca and later still as Cahors. First the Gauls and then the Romans worshipped the spring with a devotion which was confirmed by the discovery in 1991 of about a thousand coins dating from the beginning of Christianity, which had been thrown into the fountain as offerings. The town grew rapidly in size: a forum, a theatre, temples, baths and ramparts were built. This spring still supplies the town with drinking water.

The golden age – In the 13C Cahors became one of the great towns of France and experienced considerable economic prosperity due in no small part to the arrival of Lombard merchants and bankers. The Lombards were brilliant businessmen and bankers, but also operated somewhat less reputedly as usurers.

The Templars, in turn, came to Cahors; gold fever spread to the townspeople and Cahors became the leading banking city of Europe. Money was lent to the pope and to kings, and Cahors' counting houses were internationally widespread. The word *cahorsin*, which was what the people of Cahors were called, became synonymous with the word usurer.

The loyal city and the ungrateful king – At the beginning of the Hundred Years War, the English seized all the towns in Quercy. Cahors alone remained impregnable, in spite of the Black Death which killed half the population.

*Use **Michelin** Maps with **Michelin** Guides.*

In 1360, under the Treaty of Brétigny, Cahors was ceded to the English. By 1450, when the English left Quercy, Cahors was a ruined city.

Cahors and the Reformation – After several decades of peace, Cahors was able to regain some of its past prosperity; unfortunately in 1540 the Reformation reached the city and rapidly caused dissension among the population. In 1560 the Protestants were massacred.

Twenty years later the town was besieged by the Huguenots, led by Henri de Navarre.

The assault lasted three days and ended in the ransacking of the city.

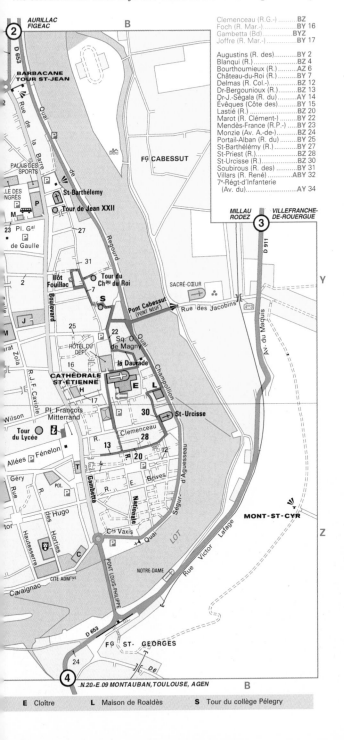

E   Cloître   L   Maison de Roaldès   S   Tour du collège Pélegry

Gambetta's childhood – Léon Gambetta has a special place among the famous men of Cahors, who included Pope John XXII (1316-34), founder of the successful university in Cahors in 1332 (which was combined with that of Toulouse in the 18C), and the poets Clément Marot (1496-1544) and Olivier de Magny (1529-61).

Born the son of a grocer in 1838 – his father was of Genoese extraction and his mother the daughter of a chemist from Molières – young Gambetta played truant from school, dreamed of wild adventures and hoped to sail the seven seas.

However, after a short spell at boarding school, he suddenly developed a passion for learning, reading and translating Greek and Latin on sight and winning prizes.

One day the young student went to watch a case at the Assize Court and became fascinated with the drama of the courtroom: the die had been cast, Gambetta gave up all ideas of going to sea and became a barrister.

In 1856 Gambetta left Cahors for Paris to enrol in the Faculty of Law. His outstanding career as a lawyer and statesman had begun. This ardent patriot, member of the Legislative Assembly, played an active part in the downfall of Napoleon III, in the proclamation of the Third Republic on 4 September 1870, and in the forming of a provisional government (he became Minister of the Interior).

Gambetta escaped from Paris, under enemy siege, in a balloon in October 1870, floating over the German lines and landing in Tours where he was able (in his capacity as War Minister) to organise the country's defence against the Prussian Army; an armistice was signed in 1871.

He became head of the Republican Union, then president of the Chamber of Deputies in 1879 and prime minister from November 1881 until January 1882. He died at the age of 44 on December 31, 1882.

There is scarcely a town or city in France which has not paid homage to this republican statesman by naming a street or square after him.

★★PONT VALENTRÉ ⊘ (AZ)

An illustration of the bridge and a description of its main architectural features can be found on page 38.

The Valentré Bridge is a remarkable example of French medieval military architecture. The three towers, with machicolations and crenellated parapets, and the pointed cutwaters breaking the line of the seven pointed arches, give it a bold and proud appearance.

The best view of the Valentré Bridge and its towers, which rise 40m/130ft above the river, is from a little way upstream on the north bank of the Lot.

A legend in which the Devil plays an important part, although he loses in the end, is linked to the construction work which began in 1308 and went on for more than fifty years. The architect was in despair at the slow progress of the bridge and agreed to sign a pact by which the Devil would bring all the materials neces-

Cahors – Pont Valentré

S. Sauvignier/MICHELIN

sary to the site and the architect, in exchange, would hand over his soul on successful execution of all his requests. The bridge grew quickly and work neared completion. The architect did not relish the idea of eternal torment, however, and had the bright idea of asking the Devil to bring him water in a sieve. After a few vain attempts the Devil confessed himself beaten but, in revenge, he broke off the topmost stone of the central tower, which has been known ever since as Devil's Tower. Every time the stone was replaced, it fell off. When the bridge was restored last century, the architect had the stone firmly fixed and on the corner he had carved the little figure of a devil trying to dislodge it.

The original appearance of Valentré Bridge was considerably modified in 1879 when the bridge was restored; the barbican, which reinforced the defences from the town side, was replaced by the present-day gate.

The bridge was originally an isolated fortress commanding the river; the central tower served as an observation post, the outer towers were closed by gates and portcullises. A guard house and outwork on the south bank of the Lot provided additional protection. The fortress defied the English during the Hundred Years War, and Henri de Navarre at the time of the siege of Cahors (1580); it has never even been attacked.

A restored **millboat (moulin à nef)** ⊘ has been moored near the bridge. From its position in the very middle of the river, it used the force of the current to drive a millwheel in its keel to crush the grain. Boats like this used to provoke arguments with sailors of other boats, as they impeded navigation; one such small craft was once deliberately capsized by a larger vessel in the middle of the night.

★CATHÉDRALE ST-ÉTIENNE AND SURROUNDINGS

★Cathédrale St-Etienne (St. Stephen's) (BY) – The clergy built this church as a fortress to provide a place of safety in troubled times, as well as to bolster prestige. At the end of the 11C, Bishop Géraud of Cardaillac began to build a church on the site of a former 6C church. Much of Bishop Géraud's church remains standing to this day. The trefoiled south door dates from 1119. The north door is 12C, the restoration work on the original east end dates from the 13C. The west front was built early in the 14C, and the paintings inside the domes and in the chancel were completed at the same time. The Flamboyant-style cloisters and some of the outbuildings were commissioned at the beginning of the 16C by Bishop Antoine de Luzech.

Exterior – The west front is made of three adjoining towers. The central one has a belfry above it and opens with double doors. On the first floor, the rose window is surrounded by blind arcades. In spite of windows with twin bays completing the decoration, the appearance of the façade remains austere and military.

★★ North Doorway – This Romanesque door was once part of the west front; it was transferred to the north side of the cathedral before the present façade was built. The tympanum depicts the Ascension. It was carved in about 1135 and from its style and technique belongs to the Languedoc School.

A mandorla (almond-shaped glory) is the centrepiece of the composition; the haloed figure of Christ (1) stands with the right hand upraised and the left clasping a closed book. On either side an angel (2) explains the miracle to the Apostles who are seen below in the trefoiled blind arcades (3); beneath the central arch is the Virgin Mary (4) raising her hand to point to her Son. Above Christ, four cherubim (5) fly out from the clouds to greet Him and take His halo. On either side of Christ 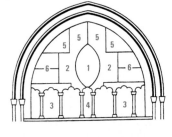 and the angels the sculptor has depicted scenes from the life of St Stephen (6): his sermon, his arrest by the Jews, his stoning, and the vision of the hand of God appearing in the sky to protect the martyr.

The cathedral's apse, with its two balustrades on the upper register, gives an overwhelming impression of power without interfering with the building's overall harmony.

Interior – Enter by the west door and cross the narthex which is slightly raised; the nave is roofed with two huge domes on pendentives. There is a striking contrast between the nave, in pale-coloured stone, and the chancel, adorned with stained glass and paintings. The frescoes of the first dome were uncovered in 1872; these show the stoning of St Stephen in the central medallion, the saint's executioners around the frieze and eight giant-sized figures of prophets in the niches.

The chancel and the apse have Gothic vaulting. Among the radiating chapels, which were added in the 15C, is the Chapel of St Antony, which opens onto the chancel through a beautiful Flamboyant door.

★Cloisters (BY E) – Dating from 1509, these Renaissance cloisters were built after those of Carennac and Cadouin, with which they have a number of stylistic similarities. Access to the cloisters is through a door on the right of the chancel. They are still rich in carved ornamentation in spite of considerable damage. The galleries are roofed with stellar vaulting; of the decorated pendants, only one remains above the northwest door, showing Jesus surrounded by angels. The jambs are decorated with niches which used to contain statues. Near the chancel door is a spiral staircase, and on the northwest corner pillar a graceful carving of the Virgin of the Annunciation, wrapped in a fine cloak, her hair falling to her shoulders.

In the **Chapelle St-Gausbert** ⊘ a fresco of the Last Judgement and 16C paintings on the ceiling have been discovered.

The chapel also contains ecclesiastical objects: church vestments, statues and portraits of 93 bishops of Cahors from the 3C to the 19C.

Enter the inner court of the former arch-deaconry of St John through the door in the northeast corner of the cloisters. Note the lovely Renaissance decoration.

Rue Nationale (BZ) – This was the main thoroughfare of the active Badernes Quarter. At no 116, the panels of a lovely **17C door** are decorated with fruit and foliage.

Across the way, the narrow **rue St-Priest** (BZ **28**) has kept its medieval appearance.

Rue du Docteur-Bergounioux (BZ **13**) – At no 40 a 16C town-house has an interesting Renaissance façade opened by windows influenced by the Italian Renaissance style.

Rue Lastié (BZ **20**) – At no 35 note the Rayonnant-style windows.

On place St-Priest a wooden staircase (Louis XIII style) can be seen; it served two buildings. At no 117, a 16C house has kept its small shop on the ground floor above which are twin bays on the first floor.

At the far end of the street, the pretty brick houses have been recently restored.

Rue St-Urcisse (BZ **30**) – The late 12C St-Urcisse Church is entered through a 14C doorway. Inside, the two chancel pillars are decorated with elegant historiated capitals.

In this street there are several half-timbered houses with *soleilhos*, open attics, in which laundry was hung out to dry.

Maison de Roaldès ⊘ (BY L) – The mansion is also known as Henri IV's Mansion because it is said that the king of Navarre stayed there during the siege of Cahors in 1580.

The house dates from the end of the 15C and was restored in 1912. In the 17C it became the property of the Roaldès, a well-known Quercy family.

The half-timbered south side is surmounted by a balcony and topped with a massive round tower.

The north side, overlooking the square, has mullioned doors and windows and different ornamental motifs – Quercy roses, flaming suns, lopped off trees – used by the Quercy School of the early 16C.

Inside, a spiral staircase gives access to the rooms, which are furnished with interesting pieces of furniture and, more especially, lovely carved chimneys where the decorative motifs – the briar rose, the heraldic "tree raguly" (row of sawn-off branches) – of the Quercy School have been used.

Pont Cabessut (BY) – From the bridge there is a good **view★** of the upper part of the city, the Soubirous district. The towers bristling in the distance are: Tower of the Hanged Men or St John's Tower, the belltower of St-Bartholomew, John XXII's Tower, Royal Castle Tower and the Pélegry College Tower.

Tour du Collège Pélegry (BY S) – The College was founded in 1368 and at first took in thirteen poor university students; until the 18C, it was one of the town's most important establishments. The fine hexagonal tower above the main building was constructed in the 15C.

Tour du Château du Roi (BY) – Near Pélegry College stands what is today the prison and was once the governor's residence. Of the two towers and two main buildings erected in the 14C, the remaining massive tower is known as "château du roi".

Îlot Fouillac (BY) – This area, once insalubrious, has undergone an extensive programme of redevelopment. By getting rid of the most run-down buildings, a square has been cleared. Its sides are decorated with **murals**, and it is brightened by a particularly interesting **musical fountain**.

La Daurade (BY) – This varied set of old residences around the Olivier-de-Magny square includes the Dolive house (17C), the Heretié house (14C to 16C) and the so-called Hangman's House (Maison du Bourreau), with windows decorated with small columns (13C).

ADDITIONAL SIGHTS

★**Barbican and Tour St-Jean** (BY) – The ramparts, constructed in the 14C, completely cut the isthmus formed by the meander of the Lot river off from the surrounding countryside. Remains of these fortifications can still be seen and include a massive tower at the west end, which sheltered the powder magazine, and the old gateway of St-Michel, which now serves as entrance to the cemetery. It is on the east side, however, where the N 20 enters the town, that the two most impressive fortified buildings remain: the barbican and St John's Tower. The barbican is an elegant guard house which defended the Barre Gateway; St John's Tower or the Tower of the Hanged Men (Tour des Pendus), was built on a rock overlooking the Lot river.

Église St-Barthélémy ⊙ (BY) – This church was built in the highest part of the old town and was known until the 13C as St-Etienne de Soubiroux, "Sancti Stephani de superioribus" (St Stephen of the Upper Quarter), in contrast to the cathedral built in the lower part of the town. The church was rebuilt to its present design in several stages. It now contains a rectangular belfry-porch with three lines of bays of depressed arches one above the other. The belfry, the base of which dates from the 14C, has no spire, and it is built almost entirely of brick.

The nave, with its ogive vaulting, was designed in the Languedoc style. In the chapel nearest the entrance, on the left, a marble slab and bust call to mind that John XXII was baptised in this church.

The cloisonné enamels on the cover of the modern baptismal font depict the main events in the life of this famous Cahors citizen.

The terrace near the church affords a good view of the Cabessut suburb and the Lot valley.

Tour de Jean XXII (BY) – This tower is all that remains of the palace of Pierre Duèze, brother of John XXII. It is 34m/112ft high and was originally covered in tiles. Twin windows pierce the walls on five storeys.

Tour du Lycée (BZ) – From the Lycée Gambetta building, which was once a Jesuit college, rises a graceful 17C octagonal tower built of rose-coloured brick.

EXCURSIONS

★**Mont St-Cyr Viewpoint** (BZ) – *7km/4mi via the Louis-Philippe Bridge south of the plan and D 6 which you leave after 1.5km/1mi to reach the mount, keeping to the left.*

From the top (viewing table) there is a good **view**★ of Cahors; the contrast between the old and the new quarters of the town, which are separated by Boulevard Gambetta, Cahors' main artery, is striking. In the background the distinctive shape of Valentré Bridge can be seen.

★**La Croix de Magne Viewpoint** – *5km/3mi. From the western end of the Valentré Bridge, turn right and then left immediately; take the first left after the agricultural school, and left again at the top of the rise.*

Around the cross, a **view**★ extends in all directions over the plateau, to the river Lot, Cahors and the Valentré Bridge.

► ► **Château de Roussilon** – *9km/5.4mi north on N 20*
Château de Cieurac – *10km/6mi south via D 6*

CARENNAC★

Population 370
Michelin map 75 fold 19 or 235 northeast of fold 38
Local map see Basse Vallée du LOT

One of the most attractive sights to be found along the Dordogne is the village of Carennac, where the picturesque houses of the Quercy, with their brown tile roofs, and the manor-houses, flanked with turrets, cluster round the old priory where Fénelon once lived.

Fénelon at Carennac – The priory-deanery at Carennac, which was founded in the 10C and attached to the famous abbey at Cluny in the following century, owes its fame to the length of time spent there by François de Salignac de la Mothe-Fénelon before he became archbishop of Cambrai. While he was still a student at Cahors, Fénelon used to enjoy spending his holidays at the house of his uncle, senior prior of Carennac. In 1681 Fénelon's uncle died and was succeeded by the young abbot, who remained at the priory for 15 years. Fénelon was greatly revered at Carennac; he enjoyed describing the ceremonies and general rejoicing that greeted his arrival by boat and his installation as commendatory prior. Tradition has it that Fénelon wrote *Télémaque* while living at Carennac. The description of the adventures of Ulysses' son was at first only a literary exercise, but was subsequently turned into a tract for the edification of the duke of Burgundy, Louis XIV's grandson, when Fénelon was appointed his tutor. The Île Barrade, in the Dordogne, was renamed Calypso's Island, and visitors will still be shown a tower in the village which is called Telemachus' Tower in which, it is maintained, Fénelon wrote his masterpiece.

THE VILLAGE

This charming village, where some of the houses date from the 16C, has barely changed since Fénelon's day, although the deanery and its outbuildings suffered considerable damage at the time of the Revolution. The deanery was suppressed by order of the Royal Council in 1788, and put up for auction and sold in 1791. Of the old ramparts there remains only a fortified gateway, and of the buildings, only the castle and the priory tower are left. Go through the fortified gateway.

Château – Next to St-Pierre's church *(see below)*, the main building of this 16C edifice is flanked by corner turrets and a gallery built above the church's Gothic chapels. The severe façade looks over the Dordogne and Calypso Island. Recently restored, the three storeys of the château house a discovery area devoted to the river Dordogne where it passes through the Lot.

Maison de la Dordogne Quercynoise ⊘ – The theme of this historical museum is "People and the River". A **scale model** is enlivened by lights and sounds which create a picture of the Dordogne valley from Biards to Souillac. The other rooms also use audio-visual programmes to explore various subjects: flora and fauna, regional arts, the history of navigation, prehistoric times (3-D projection). From the gallery, there is a charming **view** over the nave of the church.

Église St-Pierre – In front of this Romanesque church dedicated to St Peter, stands a porch with a beautiful 12C carved **doorway★**. It is well preserved and from its style would appear to belong to the same school as the tympana of Beaulieu, Moissac, Collonges and Cahors. In a mandorla (almond-shaped glory) in the centre of the composition, is Christ in Majesty. His right hand is raised in blessing. He is surrounded by the symbols of the four Evangelists. On either side are the Apostles on two superimposed registers, and there are two prostrate angels on the upper register. The tympanum is framed with a foliated scroll in the Oriental style. Its base is decorated with a frieze of small animals. The continuation of the animals was pursued on a protruding band which doubled the doorway arch, of which a dog and bear can still be seen on the left.

Inside, the interesting archaic capitals in the nave are decorated with fantastic animals, foliage and historiated scenes.

Cloisters ⊘ – The restored cloisters consist of a Romanesque gallery adjoining the church and three Flamboyant galleries. Stairs lead to the terrace.

The chapter-house, which opens onto the cloisters, shelters a remarkable **Entombment★** (15C). Christ lies on a shroud carried by two disciples: Joseph of Arimathea and Nicodemus. Behind these figures, two holy women accompany the Virgin and the Apostle John; on the right, Mary Magdalene is wiping away a tear. The faces seem quite rustic in character.

Carennac – Northern entrance to the town

CASTELNAU-BRETENOUX CASTLE★★

Michelin map 75 fold 19 or 239 fold 39
Local maps see Vallée de la DORDOGNE and ST-CÉRÉ: Excursions

On the northern border of Quercy stands Castelnau-Bretenoux Castle with the village of Prudhomat tucked beneath it. The great mass of the castle's red stone ramparts and the towers rise up from a spur overlooking the confluence of the Cère and the Dordogne. The scale on which the castle defence system was built makes it one of the finest examples of medieval military architecture.

Seen from the countryside more than three miles round, the castle, as Pierre Loti wrote, "is the beacon... the thing you cannot help looking at all the time from wherever you are. It's a cock's comb of blood-red stone rising from a tangle of trees, this ruin poised like a crown on a pedestal dressed with a beautiful greenery of chestnut and oak trees".

Turenne's egg – From the 11C onwards the barons of Castelnau were the strongest in Quercy; they paid homage only to the counts of Toulouse and proudly styled themselves the Second Barons of Christendom. In 1184 Raymond de Toulouse gave the suzerainty of Castelnau to the viscount of Turenne. The baron of Castelnau refused to accept the insult and paid homage instead to Philip Augustus, king of France. Bitter warfare broke out between Turenne and Castelnau; King Louis VIII intervened and decided in favour of Turenne. Whether he liked it or not the baron had to accept the verdict. The fief, however, was only symbolic: Castelnau had to present his overlord with... an egg. Every year, with great pomp and ceremony a yoke of four oxen bore a freshly laid egg to Turenne.

Château fort ⊙ – Round the strong keep built in the 13C, there grew up during the Hundred Years War a huge fortress with a fortified curtain wall. The castle was abandoned in the 18C and suffered depredations at the time of the Revolution. It caught fire in 1851 but was skilfully restored between 1896 and 1932.

Château de Castelnau – Bretenoux

The ground plan is that of an irregular triangle flanked by three round towers and three other towers partially projecting from each side. Three parallel curtain walls still defend the approaches, but the former ramparts have been replaced by an avenue of trees.

From along the ramparts there is a far-reaching **view★** of the Cère and Dordogne valleys to the north; of Turenne Castle set against the horizon to the northwest; of the Montvalent Amphitheatre to the west; and of Loubressac Castle and the Autoire valley to the southwest and south.

A tall square tower and the seigneurial residence, a rectangular building still known as the *auditoire* (auditorium), suggest the vast scale of this fortress; the garrison numbered 1 500 men and 100 horses.

Interior – In addition to the lapidary depository, containing the Romanesque capitals of Ste-Croix-du-Mont in Gironde, many other rooms should be visited on account of their decoration and furnishings done by the former proprietor, a singer of comic opera, Jean Moulierat, who bought the castle in 1896.

The former chamber of the Quercy Estates General is lit by large windows: the pewter hall and the *Grand Salon* contain Aubusson and Beauvais tapestries: the oratory has stained-glass windows dating from the 15C and two 15C Spanish altarpieces.

Collégiale St-Louis – The church was built by the lords of Castelnau in red ferriferous stone, at the foot of the castle. A few canons' residences can be seen nearby.

Enter the church. The lords' chapel has lovely quadripartite vaulting, the pendant of which is emblazoned with the Castelnau coat of arms. The furnishings include 15C stalls, a 17C rood screen and 18C altars; one of which is surmounted by a multicoloured wood Virgin with bird (15C), quite naïve in style. The chancel houses two 15C works of art in polychrome stone; a Virgin in Majesty and a depiction of the Baptism of Christ.

EXCURSION

Gorges de la Cère – The river Cère meets the Dordogne downstream of Bretenoux, where the Château de Castelnau rises on the headland. On its way, it wanders through the wilds *(no road travels along side)*, and can be admired from the **Rocher du Peintre★**.

Château de CASTELNAUD★

Michelin map 75 fold 17 or 235 west of fold 6
Local map see Vallée de la DORDOGNE

The impressive ruins of Castelnaud Castle stand on a wonderful **site★★** commanding the valleys of the Céou and the Dordogne. Right opposite stands Beynac Castle (*see BEYNAC-ET-CAZENAC*), Castelnaud's implacable rival throughout the conflicts of the Middle Ages.

An eventful history – In 1214 Simon de Montfort (c1165-1218, father of the English statesman and soldier) took possession of the castle, whose occupants had taken the side of the Cathars. In 1259 Saint Louis ceded the castle to the king of England who held it for several years.

During the Hundred Years War the castle constantly changed hands between the French and the English. When at last peace was declared the castle was in terrible condition. During the whole of the second half of the 15C the castle was under reconstruction. Only the keep and curtain wall have kept their 13C appearance. In the 16C the castle was once again transformed in various ways, and the artillery tower was added.

After the Revolution it was abandoned and later used as a stone-pit.

In 1969 a major restoration program was undertaken which has enabled most of the buildings to be rebuilt.

Castle ⊘ – The castle is a typical example of a medieval fortress with its powerful machicolated keep, curtain wall, living quarters and inner bailey. Nonetheless, certain parts of the castle – artillery tower, loopholes – which were added later

Château de Castelnaud

reflect the evolution of weapons in siege warfare. In the artillery tower, reconstructed scenes demonstrate artillerymen in action. A primitive cannon, stone balls, and a number of other weapons complete the display. The main part of the building contains the **Middle Ages Siege Warfare Museum**.

There are two audio-visual presentations: one explains the history of the castle and the other a history of fortifications and siege warfare tactics in the Middle Ages. The barbican, the bailey and the reconstruction of siege apparatus, including a 12C mangonel, or ballista, and other stone-casting devices and a 15C mortar are in the castle grounds.

From the ward the view extends southwards over the Céou valley. From the east end of the terrace there is an exceptional **panorama**★★★ of one of the most lovely views of the Dordogne valley: in the foreground the patchwork of fields with screens of poplars encircled by a wide loop in the river; further off Beynac with its castle, Marqueyssac Castle and, at the foot of the cliffs, La Roque-Gageac and in the far distance a line of wooded and rocky hills skirting the Dordogne valley. In the summer, the history of the castle is the subject of a nocturnal pageant *(see the section on Practical Information: Festivals)*.

Vallée du CÉLÉ★

Michelin map 79 folds 9 and 10 or 235 folds 10, 11 and 14

The Célé, which owes its name to its fast-flowing waters (*celer*, the root of the English word "celerity", signifies "swift"), is a delightful Quercy river which has cut a steep-sided valley through the *causse*. The Célé valley, in addition to passing through beautiful countryside, contains important prehistoric sites and archeological remains.

Le Val Paradis – The Célé rises in the chestnut woods that grow on the granite soil of Cantal; it enters Quercy and makes directly for the Lot river, but within 5km/3mi its course is blocked by Capdenac Hill. The Célé gets round its obstacle by turning westwards and cutting through 40km/25mi of limestone. This has resulted in a series of picturesque defiles, where the river can be seen winding along, still undermining the bases of the steep and many-hued rock walls.

Adding to the beauty of the valley are the old mills built beside the river, and the archaic villages that stand perched on cliff ledges or half-hidden in the greenery; it is not surprising that the former priory at Espagnac has been graced with the name "Vale of Paradise".

The "Hébrardie"' – Throughout the Middle Ages the greater part of the Célé valley was under the control of the Hébrard family of St-Sulpice, so that it virtually constituted a feudal benefice. The period of influence of the Hébrards was known locally as the "Hébrardie". The family, which lived at St-Sulpice, enlarged or rebuilt the priories of Espagnac and Marcilhac and protected the local inhabitants, particularly at the time of the Hundred Years War. This great family numbered not only soldiers among its members; one of them was appointed seneschal of Quercy and others included such eminent ecclesiastics as Aymeric, bishop of Coïmbra in Portugal and Anthony, bishop of Cahors.

FROM CONDUCHÉ TO FIGEAC

65km/40mi – about half a day

D 41 starts at Conduché, where the Célé flows into the Lot, and goes up the valley. The road is squeezed between the river bed and the cliff face, which rises on one side like a wall and at times even overhangs the road below. Many crops grow in the valley with maize tending to replace tobacco. A characteristic line of poplars marks the course of the river.

Cabrerets – Cabrerets, set in a rocky amphitheatre, occupies a commanding position at the confluence of the Sagne and Célé rivers.

There is a good overall **view★** of Cabrerets and its setting from the left bank of the Célé, which is reached by crossing the bridge. Opposite stand the ruins of the Devil's Castle (Château du Diable), or Castle of the English, clinging to the formidable Rochecourbe cliff. This eagle's eyrie, a typical cliff-top castle, served as a base from which the English could pillage the countryside during the Hundred Years War.

On the far left is the impressive mass of the 14C and 15C Gontaut-Biron Castle overlooking the valley. A big corner tower flanks the buildings that surround an inner courtyard. One of the façade's mullioned windows opens onto a terrace with ornamental balustrades which juts out 25m/82ft above the road.

D 13 then D 198 lead up the valley of the Sagne to Pech Merle Cave.

★★★**Grottes de Pech Merle (Cave)** – *See Grottes de Pech Merle.*

Shortly after Cabrerets the cliff road crosses the face of high stone cliffs.

Fontaine de la Pescalerie – This is one of the most attractive sights of the Célé valley; a beautiful waterfall pours out of the rock wall close to the road. It marks the surfacing of an underground river that has cut its way through the Gramat Causse. Beside the waterfall stands an ivy-covered mill, half-hidden by trees.

By the exit to a tunnel, spectacular overhanging rock formations frame the **Liauzu sailing centre**.

⋆**Cuzals – Musée de plein air de Quercy (Quercy Open-Air Museum)** ⊘ – *To do justice to this lively exhibition area, visitors should allow at least half a day.*

All the aspects of life in the Quercy region, from before the Revolution until the Second World War, are illustrated in the park, covering 50ha/124 acres. Visitors are offered an authentic, scientific approach to the area's cultural heritage.

Furniture, machinery, a rather unsettling dentist's surgery dating from 1900, milliner's and baker's shops, and of course examples of Quercy architecture, regional crop specialities and a collection of pieces of improbable-looking agricultural equipment are on display. In the summer, people from local communities gather together to operate the exhibits; including the thresher, the mill, the bread oven; teams of tireless oxen take children for rides.

Sauliac-sur-Célé – This old village clings to an awe-inspiring cliff of coloured rock. In the cliff face can be seen the openings to the fortified caves used in time of war as refuges by the local inhabitants. The more agile climbed up by way of ladders; invalids and animals were hoisted up in great baskets.

Beyond Sauliac the valley widens out. Crops and pasture land grow well on the alluvial soil of the valley bottom, and several round dry-stone shelters can be seen.

Marcilhac-sur-Célé – *See MARCILHAC-SUR-CÉLÉ.*

⋆**Grottes de Bellevue (Cave)** – *See MARCILHAC-SUR-CÉLÉ.*

Between Marcilhac-sur-Célé and Brengues the contrast intensifies between the rocks with their sparse vegetation and the valley, which is densely cultivated with maize, sunflowers, vineyards and tobacco plantations.

St-Sulpice – The houses and gardens of this old village lie within the shadow of an overhanging cliff. The approach is guarded by a 12C castle which was rebuilt in the 14C and 15C. It is still the property of the Hébrard family of St-Sulpice.

Brengues – This small village is in a pleasant setting, perched on a ledge overlooked by a vertiginous bluff.

As far as Boussac, the valley at times opens out and at others closes in; farmhouses stand here and there, their nearby cylindrical dovecotes topped with local *lauze* roofing slate.

Espagnac-Ste-Eulalie – In this delightful village built in the picturesque setting of a series of cliffs, the houses with their turrets and pointed roofs are grouped round the former priory known as "Notre-Dame du Val-Paradis". The **Ancien Prieuré Notre-Dame** was founded in the 12C; during the Hundred Years War the convent suffered considerably; the cloisters were destroyed and the church was partly demolished. It was rebuilt in the 15C, however, and the community carried on until the Revolution. The buildings are now occupied by a rural centre and holiday rentals *(gîtes communaux)*, managed by the local authorities.

The present Flamboyant-style **church** ⊙ has replaced the 13C building (only the walls of the nave, a doorway and ruined bays remain). Inside, the three tombs with recumbent figures placed in funerary niches are those of Aymeric Hébrard de St-Sulpice (d 1295) and of a knight, Hugues de Cardaillac-Brengues (buried here in 1342) and his wife, Bernarde de Trian.

Above Boussac the cliffs finally disappear, giving way to wooded hillsides, while the Célé spreads out over a wide alluvial bed.

Ceint d'Eau – This 15-16C castle, flanked by massive machicolated towers, rises above D 13 and overlooks the generous width of the Célé valley.

★★ Figeac – See Figeac.

Château de CÉNEVIÈRES★

Michelin map 79 fold 9 or 235 fold 15 (7km/4mi east of St-Cirq-Lapopie)
Local map see Basse Vallée du LOT

This imposing castle perches on a sheer rock face overlooking the Lot valley from a height of more than 70m/230ft. As early as the 7C the dukes of Aquitaine had a stronghold built here. In the 13C the lords of Gourdon had the keep built. During the Renaissance, Flottard de Gourdon, who had participated in the campaigns in Italy with François I, completely rearranged the castle. His son, Antoine de Gourdon, converted to Protestantism and participated alongside Henri IV in the siege of Cahors in 1580. He pillaged the cathedral in Cahors and loaded the high altar and altar of the Holy Shroud onto boats returning to Cénevières Castle. The boat carrying the high altar sank in a chasm along the way. Before his death Antoine built a small Protestant church, which is in the outer bailey. He died childless, his widow remarried at La Tour du Pin and a new lineage took over Cénevières.

The château was pillaged during the French Revolution, but escaped arson.

TOUR ⊙

The outside of the castle boasts a 13C keep and 15C wings joined by a 16C Renaissance gallery. The gallery is held up by Tuscan columns and above it are dormer windows. The moat, once crossed by a drawbridge, is now filled in. Inside, the ground floor includes the vaulted salt room and kitchen. The keep has a trap door, which permits a glimpse of the three floors below: cellar, prison and dungeons.

On the first floor the great drawing room with a lovely Renaissance painted ceiling contains 15C and 16C Flemish tapestries and the shrine of the Holy Shroud brought back from Cahors. The small alchemy room is decorated with fascinating 16C naive frescoes illustrating Greek mythology. The alchemist's oven has a representation of the philosopher's stone.

Finally, from the terrace there are commanding views of the Lot valley and the "hanging village" of Calvignac, perched on the hillside.

Château de Cénevières

CHÂLUS

Michelin map 72 fold 16 or 233 fold 32

The old city of Châlus, dominated by its keep, recalls the memory of **Richard the Lion Heart's** tragic death. On every side are the solid granite masses, densely wooded, of the Châlus Hills, last buttresses of the Massif Central.

A Fatal Siege – The tale is told of how in 1199 a serf belonging to Adhemar V, viscount of Limoges, discovered a fabulous treasure trove of "ninepins and large balls, all in solid gold" (these items now figure in the arms of Châlus together with a long bow). The viscount of Limoges hid the treasure in his castle at Châlus. Nevertheless rumours of the find reached Richard the Lion Heart, king of England and lord of Western France. Richard demanded his share of the booty as overlord, and when his vassal refused to give it up, laid siege to Châlus. When he was directing the attack on the castle from far enough away, he thought, to be beyond the range of enemy arrows, he was struck on the shoulder by a quarrel from a prototype of a new cross-bow, a medieval "secret weapon". Richard refused to dress the wound which turned black, the poison went to his heart and the end came. So died, at forty-two, one of the greatest men of the Middle Ages.

The castle defenders paid dearly for the death of the king: all were hanged except the sharp-eyed archer – he was flayed alive.

★★CHÂTEAU ⊘

The remains of the castle known as **Châlus-Chabrol**, stand on rising ground in the upper part of the village.

Donjon – This cylindrical keep (25m/82ft high and 10m/33ft in diameter), an excellent illustration of feudal military architecture, dates from the 11C. Originally, it had four levels, but the highest one, crowned by machicolations, fell in 1870. A metal stairway leads up and in: the only entrance to the keep is 6m/20ft above ground.

A very narrow passage opens on to a vaulted room (8.5m/18ft high); an opening set in the floor provides a view of the lower room, used for storage. The knights and soldiers were quartered on the upper floors, reached by a stairway safely ensconced in the

Richard the Lion Heart

thick walls. The view from the top platform stretches far, to the Tadoire valley, Puyconnieux and the fields of Limousin.

The keep's thick, smooth walls of gneiss stone, rising vertically, were a good protection against attack by battering ram, axe and fire.

A short distance from the keep are vestiges of the **chapel** where King Richard's remains were brought. At the time, the chapel was Romanesque; in the 15C a side chapel was added (one arch still stands).

Main building – The entrance is located in the 17C wing built by the Countess of Bermondet, who had the old foundations demolished without blinking an eye. Today it houses a small museum devoted to the regional craft performed by *feuillardiers*, hoopwood makers who used chestnut to make the circular strips used for holding together barrel staves *(see Practical information, Thematic itineraries)*. Another room has been devoted to the history of the castle and Richard's life; next door, the salon Bourbon is the only furnished room here. Perhaps the most spectacular part of the tour is the exhibit on the discovery of architectural remains from the 11C and 13C.

The main building opens onto a 13C room which contains a Romanesque column squeezed into a wall erected at a later date. In the next room, you can see the other side of it, as well as two Romanesque windows. The walls are hung with the coats of arms of the castle's different owners.

A little corridor leads to the oldest section, dating from the 11C. Beyond an escape shaft tucked into a nook in the fortifications, an eight-sided room forms the base of a corner tower; note the vaulted ceiling and the loopholes. A spiral stairway climbs to the top, where the view is panoramic.

Beside this tower room, a smaller room dissimulates another shaft, 16m/52ft high, and the entrance (walled off) to the watchpath. The lower level, once open to the air, was the ground floor. Note the 11C chimney, the pointed arch of a doorway giving on a vestigial stairway and primitive wall; outside, at the end of the shaft, twin doors under an arch.

EXCURSIONS TO OTHER CHÂTEAUX IN THE AREA

★**Montbrun** – This imposing castle *(illustration page 36)* stands deep in a valley, where it reflects in the waters of a pond surrounded by lawns and trees. Edified in the 12C, it once defended the borders of the ducal realm of Aquitaine, and still boasts a moat, high walls and an impregnable square keep surmounted by machicolations. *Closed to visitors.*

► ► **Château des Cars** ⊘: Mostly in ruins (13C – 16C); lapidary museum
Château de Lastours ⊘: Ruins of a 12C keep, 13-16C buildings restored
Château de Brie ⊘: This fortified house was built around 1500; Louis XVI furnishings, granite stairway.

Abbaye de CHANCELADE★

Michelin map 75 fold 5 or 233 fold 42 (7km/4mi northwest of Périgueux)

The abbey appears as a peaceful haven tucked at the foot of the green slopes overlooking the Beauronne. Founded in the 12C by a monk who adopted the rule of St Augustine, the abbey was protected by the bishops of Périgueux and later answered directly to the Holy See. It therefore prospered and was accorded considerable privileges: asylum, safety and franchises. From the 14C the abbey's fortunes declined; the English captured it, sent the monks away and installed a garrison. Du Guesclin freed it, but not for long as the English recaptured it and held it until the mid-15C. During the Wars of Religion, the abbey buildings were partly destroyed by the Protestants from Périgueux.

In 1623 Alain de Solminihac, the new abbot, undertook the reformation and restoration of Chancelade. He was so successful that he was named bishop of Cahors by Louis XIII. The abbey was able to function calmly until the Revolution, when it became national property.

Church – The Romanesque doorway has recessed orders with nailhead moulding and is surmounted by an elegant arcade, showing Saintonge influence, underlined by a modillioned cornice. The square, Romanesque belltower is made up of three tiers of arcades, some rounded, others pointed.

Inside, few elements are left of the original 12C church: the nave was re-vaulted with pointed vaulting and the east end was demolished. The 17C stalls, in walnut, still have "misericords" (a small projection on the bottom of a hinged seat that gives support to the standing worshipper when the seat is turned up) carved with motifs of palm leaves, roses, shells, etc.

Conventual Buildings ⊘ – These include the abbot's lodgings and the outbuildings around the courtyard and garden, which comprise the 15C pointed barrel-vaulted laundry room (now an exhibition hall), stables, workshops and a fortified mill. Adjoining the courtyard is the garden. The north façade (called Bourdeilles' lodgings) is flanked by two turrets, one of which is opened by a finely decorated door (late 15C). To the east is an elegant building which used to be the abbot's residence, built at the beginning of the 17C, with a terrace surrounded by pavilions.

Chapelle St-Jean – This small, charming parish church was consecrated in 1147. Its façade is opened by an unusually small semicircular doorway with three barely perceptible pointed-recessed arches, surmounted by a bay framed with slender columns, and above that, a low relief of a lamb carrying a cross (the Benedictine Pax). There is a fine rounded apse with buttress-columns.

EXCURSION

Prieuré de Merlande – *8km/5mi northwest on D 1*
The road between Chancelade and Merlande rises through a wood of chestnut and oak trees. In a deserted clearing in Feytaud forest stand a small fortified chapel and a prior's house, as solitary reminders of the Merlande Priory founded here in the 12C by the monks of Chancelade. Both have been restored. The chapel appears to be a fortress-like structure with its 4-sided plan and the little fort protecting its east end. It is a Romanesque building with two bays; the first has a transverse arch and pointed-barrel vaulting replacing the original dome, the second is roofed with an attractive dome on pendentives. The chancel, the oldest part, is slightly above the level of the nave and preceded by a rounded triumphal arch. It has barrel vaulting and a flat east end and is bordered by a series of blind arcades adorned with finely carved archaic **capitals**★; tangled-up monsters and lions devouring palm-leaf scrolls make up a bizarre but striking fauna.

La CHÂTRE

Michelin map 68 fold 19 or 238 fold 41

La Châtre is built on a hill overlooking the Indre valley, in the centre of the area known locally as the "Vallée Noire" (black valley) beloved by George Sand *(see NOHANT)*. It is a dark green countryside of wooded farmland that the "good woman of Nohant" described in so many of her novels. Only the old castle keep recalls the fact that the town had a military origin and was a Roman encampment (*castrum*, which became "Châtre" over time).

SIGHTS

Donjon – "The prison at La Châtre, an old feudal fortress in the control of provincial lords, was then nothing more than a huge square tower, blackened by the centuries and standing straight upon the rock on the side of a narrow ravine where the river Indre flows amid luxuriant green ..." (George Sand, *Les Maupras*). Built in the 15C by Guillaume III de Chauvigny, used as a prison from 1743 to 1934, it now houses the **Musée George-Sand et de la Vallée Noire** ⊙. In a modern building, 3 000 stuffed and mounted birds, collected from the late 18C and early 19C, are on display. This ornithological museum includes species now extinct or threatened, as well as birds of prey and sea birds. The upper floor is devoted to George Sand and her guests at Nohant, including portraits, letters, first editions, novels and mementoes of her personal friends. Exhibits on the other floors evoke the folklore and art of the "Black Valley".

Walk through town – The **Église St-Germain** is a contemporary church. The porch and tower fell down in 1896, carrying the 12C nave with them. Inside, the pillars and Romanesque capitals have been remade. A 14C *Pietà*, from the Carmelite convent is in the Lady chapel on the left of the chancel; the painting, *Pentecost*, is by Jean Boucher.

Around the church, and towards the river, the **old town** invites strolling. There are many interesting old houses and the view from the old humpbacked bridges is charming. At the river's edge, former tanneries with their typical sheltered porches are quiet today, and the water runs clear beneath them.

① GEORGE SAND TOUR *75km/46mi – 3hr*

This tour wanders through the countryside that served as backdrop for Sand's novel set in rural Berry. "The moon began to scatter diamonds on the black moss... the white stems of birch trees stood as shrouded ghosts... the fire reflected in the pool..." While the exact location of the *Haunted Pool* may be in debate, and the mill at Angibault may have lost some of its cachet, readers of her pastoral novels *(The Country Waif, Fanchon the Cricket)* will recognise that their settings have changed but little in the past century. Still "vivid and sombre in colour ...the melancholy far distant views".

Lys-St-Georges – Doorway

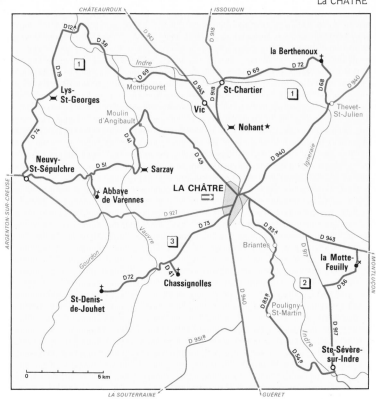

Leave La Châtre northeast travelling on D 940 towards Lignières.

La Berthenoux – The church ⊘ is a vast 12C edifice surmounted by a powerful belfry crowning a fine dome resting on squinches. The capitals in the transept are adorned with carved figures, animals, and foliage.

St-Chartier – The interesting small church and château (restored in the 19C) can be admired as you go through the **park** ⊘.

Château de Nohant – *See NOHANT.*

Vic – *See VIC.*

D 69 and D 38 wind along the green Indre valley.

A forest clearing off D 38 was probably the site of the marsh known as the haunted pool *(La Mare au Diable)*, the title of one of Sand's most well-read novels.

Lys-St-George – The **château**, whose towers rise straight up out of the moat, combines the architectural severity of a medieval fortress with the charm of the Renaissance. From the terrace *(visitors are allowed up to the postern but not across the moat)*, you will see the 15C façade and the Gourdon valley.

Neuvy-St-Sépulchre – This small town gets its name from the basilica modelled on the Holy Sepulchre in Jerusalem. It consists of a rectangular structure joined more or less happily to a circular one. The first was completed in 1049. The vast **rotunda★** on the other round side is 22m/72ft across; the upper part was restored by Violet-le-Duc in the 19C.

Abbaye de Varennes ⊘ – The abbey, founded in 1148 is not far from the road, at the bottom of a dale. The 13C buildings are open to the public. The church dates from the 12C, and is remarkable for the purity of its Cistercian architecture. George Sand wrote of the abbey in her novel *Les Beaux Messieurs de Bois-Doré* (1857).

Château de Sarzay ⊘ – A proud feudal domain where the tall round towers have tiled roofs, Blanchemont Castle in George Sand's novel *The Angibault Miller* is based on Sarzay.

Beyond the now idle mill which stands on the Vauvre (a tributary of the Indre), take D 49 back to La Châtre.

② HAUTE VALLÉE DE L'INDRE
Round trip about 25km /16mi – 1hr15min

Leave La Châtre travelling southeast on D 83ᴬ towards Briantes.

Ste-Sévère-sur-Indre – The ruins of the keep look down on the fertile valley of the Indre. In the place du Marché, there is an old 17C covered market and a 15C fortified gateway. Nearby houses sport old towers.
It is pleasant to stroll through the **château grounds**. The main building dates from the 18C. Vestiges of the 12C keep remain; it was once held by the English, and overtaken by Du Guesclin in 1372. From the terrace, there is a nice view of the surroundings and the river valley.

La Motte-Feuilly – In the **church** is the damaged tomb of Charlotte d'Albret, wife of Cesare Borgia. The 15C castle keep, like that of Briantes, is described by George Sand in her novel *Les Beaux Messieurs de Bois-Doré*.

③ BETWEEN COUARD AND GOURDON *15km/10mi – 30min*

Leave La Châtre by D 83ᴬ southwest towards le Magny.

Chassignoles – The **church** is crowned by a large belfry-tower. A small Renaissance door with an emblazoned pediment opens into the north transept.

St-Denis-de-Jouhet – The Gothic church has a shingle-covered steeple.

Michelin Maps, Red Guides and Green Guides are complementary publications.

COLLONGES-LA-ROUGE★★
Michelin map 75 fold 9 or 239 fold 26 – Local map see BRIVE-LA-GAILLARDE

Cars are not allowed in the village during the summer. Use the car park by the old station.
Collonges "the Red", built of red sandstone, is set with its small manor-houses, old houses and Romanesque church in a countryside characteristic of the Quercy region, with juniper bushes, walnut plantations and vineyards all around. A historic atmosphere pervades the streets of this lovely old town.
The village grew up in the 8C around its church and priory, a dependency of the powerful Charroux Abbey in the Poitou region. In the 13C, Collonges was a part of the viscounty of Turenne and thus received franchises and liberties. Much later on, in the 16C, Collonges was the place chosen by prominent denizens of the viscounty for their holidays. For their pleasure, they erected charming manors and mansions flanked with towers and turrets, which give the town its unique image.
The old centre displays a harmonious use of traditional materials, and a fluent interplay of proportions, creating an architectural symphony.

TOUR

Start near the old station (ancienne gare).

Maison de la Sirène ⊙ – This 16C corbelled house, with a porch and beautiful lauze roof, is adorned with a mermaid holding a comb in one hand and a mirror in the other. The interior has been reconstructed as the inside of a Collonges house of olden days.
Further along, the pointed gateway arch (Porte du Prieuré) marks the entrance of the former Benedictine priory, which was destroyed during the Revolution.

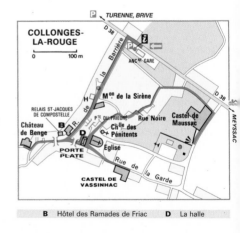

B Hôtel des Ramades de Friac   **D** La halle

Hôtel des Ramade de Friac (B) – The hôtel, crowned by two turrets, was once the town house of the powerful Ramade de Friac family.
Go past the Relais de St-Jacques-de-Compostelle – the name recalls that Collonges was a pilgrims' stopping place along the famous route to Santiago de Compostela – and through a covered passageway and soon afterwards in an alley, on the right, there is an old turreted house.

Collonges-la-Rouge – Church

Château de Benge – Set against a backdrop of poplars and walnuts is this proud towered and turreted manor-house with its lovely Renaissance window. The lords of Benge were top of the league of the famous Collonges vineyards, until these were decimated by phylloxera.

Porte Plate – This "flat" gateway, so named because it has lost its towers, was part of the town walls protecting the church, cloisters and priory buildings.

Halle aux grains (**D**) – Its massive framework is supported by strong pillars, the covered market served as a central granary store and shelters the communal oven.

Church – The church, which dates from the 11C and 12C, was fortified during the Wars of Religion in the 16C. It was at this time that the great square keep was strengthened by a defence chamber communicating with the watchpath, and that the tympanum was placed in the new gable out of harm's way. It was restored to its original place in 1923.

★ **Tympanum** – Carved in the white limestone of Turenne, the 12C tympanum stands out among all the red sandstone. It depicts the Ascension (or perhaps the second coming of Christ) and was apparently carved by sculptors of the Toulouse School. The upper register shows the figure of Christ surrounded by angels, holding the Gospels in one hand, the other raised in benediction. The lower register shows the saddened Virgin surrounded by the eleven Apostles. The whole tympanum is outlined by a pointed arch ornamented with a fine border of carved animals.

★ **Belltower** – The 12C belltower is in the Limousin style: two lower square tiers pierced with round-arched bays are surmounted by two octagonal tiers flanked by gables. The belfry is built onto the transept crossing.

Interior – In the 12C, the church had a cruciform plan around the transept crossing. The dome above the transept crossing rests on 11C pillars. Modifications were made in the 14C and 15C, when side chapels were added as well as a second nave in the Flamboyant style.

★ **Castel de Vassinhac** – This elegant manor house was owned by Gédéor de Vassinhac, lord of Collonges, captain-governor of the viscounty of Turenne. Built in 1583, the manor-house bristles with large towers and turrets with pepper-pot roofs. Despite a large number of mullioned windows, its defensive role is obvious from its many loopholes and castellated turrets.

Ancienne Chapelle des Pénitents – The chapel was built in the 13C and modified by the Maussac family at the time of the Counter-Reformation.

Rue Noire – This street cuts through the oldest part of Collonges, where old houses can be seen set back one from the other, ornamented with turrets and towers and adorned with wisteria and climbing vines.

Castel de Maussac – This building is embellished with a turret and a porch roof above the main door. A castellated turret projects from the square tower, which is overlooked by a dormer window.

Before the Revolution this manor-house was the refuge for the last member of the Maussac family, who emigrated to Italy where he became the chaplain to Napoleon's sister, princess Pauline Borghese.

Continue further south along the street to enjoy a pretty **view**★ of Collonges, Vassinhac Manor-house and the belltower.

Vallée de la CORRÈZE★

Michelin map 75 folds 8, 9 or 239 folds 26, 27

Surging forth to the west of Meymac, at an altitude of nearly 900m/2 952ft, the river Corrèze crosses the Monédières range and digs a deep valley in the granite. It is the main artery of the *département* which bears its name, and passes through Tulle and Brive before joining forces with the Vézère.

THE UPPER VALLEY *Round trip of 110km/68mi – 4hr*

Tulle – *see TULLE.*
Continue on N 89 towards Brive.

Cornil – A 4-storey square tower above the village, all that remains of the castle, rises next to the Romanesque church. There is a scenic overlook of the bend in the river.

In the village, take D 48ᴱ.

Parc du Coiroux – This park has been developed around a large lake with swimming beaches and sailing, golf and tennis facilities.

Outside Coiroux, turn left on D 48.

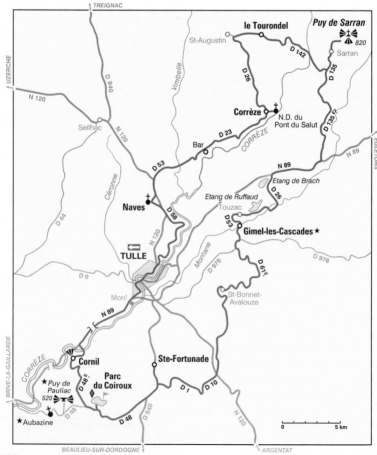

Ste-Fortunade – Near a much-restored 15C castle stands a small Romanesque church containing on the left at the entrance to the south chapel, the **reliquary-head★** of Ste Fortunade. This is a delightful 15C work in bronze.

Follow D 940 for 1km/0.5mi, then turn left on D 1.

★Gimel-les-Cascades – *See GIMEL-LES-CASCADES.*

Take D 53 towards Touzac.

The road runs alongside the southern shore of the **Étang de Ruffaud**. This lovely stretch of water with bathing beaches lies in a romantic setting.
The **Étang de Brach**, 3.5km/2mi further on, has boating facilities.

Continue on D 26 to la Gare-de-Corrèze, then take N 89 right towards Égletons.

Puy de Sarran – A narrow, bumpy road, lined with conifers, climbs steeply over 1.5km/1mi to reach the summit at 820m/2 690ft. The wayside crosses form an impressive calvary, dominating the surrounding mounts, bare of vegetation.

From the village of Sarran, take D 135 for 1km/0.5mi, then turn left on D 142 towards St-Augustin.

Le Tourondel – This charming little village has an attractive château and a communal bread oven. The oven is in a thatched-roof shelter, where other items once used by local farmers are on display.

At the end of D 142, turn left on D 26.

Corrèze – In this old hamlet the granite houses are topped with slate roofs; the cluster around the massive 15C church, next to the Magot gateway, last vestige of the fortifications which once surrounded the village.

A short distance away, the site of the **chapelle Notre-Dame du Pont du Salut** is a pleasant detour. The little chapel nestles between the rocks and the river, which is crossed here by an old bridge.

Take D 23 towards Bar.

The winding road tumbles over woods and fields. The village of **Bar** sits on a promontory overlooking the river valleys of the Vimbelle and the Corrèze.

Naves – The 15C church, flanked by a fortified turret, contains a huge **reredos★** is sculpted wood. The vertical imagery is centred around Christ; horizontally, the carvings detail the founding of the church (St Peter in chains).

Carry on along D 58, which joins up with N 120 for a short distance before branching off to the left towards the river.

The road swerves down to the water's edge, and follows its course as far as Tulle.

THE LOWER VALLEY *20km/10mi – 1hr30min*

Parc du Coiroux – *See the Upper Valley, above.*

Take D 48 south, travelling through the Gorges du Coiroux towards Aubazine.

★Puy de Pauliac – *30min round trip on foot.* Altitude 520m/1 706ft.
The footpath makes its way through heather and chestnut trees, leading upwards to reveal a splendid **view★**. An **orientation table** helps to identify the Roche de Vic to the southeast and to the north, the Monnédières range.

Continue on D 48.

★Aubazine – *See AUBAZINE.*

N 89 takes you Brive.

Brive-la-Gaillarde – *See BRIVE-LA-GAILLARDE.*

COUSSAC-BONNEVAL★

Michelin map 72 folds 17, 18 or 239 fold 13

The castellated towers of Bonneval Castle rise on a height overlooking the village of Coussac in a typically Limousin countryside where fields divided by small streams alternate with hedges and chestnut coppices. It is the native hearth of the Bonneval family.

Achmet-Pasha – Claude-Alexandre was born in Bonneval Castle in 1675 and at an early age showed his desire to be a fighting man. He fought in the Italian Campaigns (1701-1706) then offered his services to the Austrian Emperor, becoming a general in the army. After a personal quarrel he again became a soldier of fortune, this time in the lands of the Ottoman Empire. He offered his talents to the Turkish ruler, reorganised the Turkish Army and led it in decisive victories against the Austrians. He was by this time a general in the artillery and took the title of Achmet-Pasha, "Pasha of the three tails", an honour which gave him precedence over ordinary pashas. But in spite of all his efforts he was never able to return to France and died in Constantinople at the age of 72.

Coussac-Bonneval – Le château

SIGHTS

★Château ⊘ – The castle was built in the middle of the 14C and the inside was altered in the 18C and 19C. The plan is square with an inner courtyard: the corner towers are crowned with machicolations and topped with pepper-pot roofs; the keep and the Devil's Tower (Tour du Diable) adjoin another tower.

Inside the castle there are furnishings dating from the period of the Renaissance to the Directory (16C to the end of 18C). Remarkable tapestries and Louis XVI woodwork, portraits, engravings and contemporary documents recall the life of Bonneval-Pasha.

★Lanterne des Morts – This imposing "lantern of the dead" *(see Introduction, Folk-lore and traditions)* dates from the 12C and was restored in the 14C. It once marked the cemetery entrance. The small door was used to insert a lamp, which was then raised up to the top of the structure, where light could shine through the openings. The light served several purposes: symbolically, it paid homage to the dead and reminded the living of their fate; in the dark medieval night, it guided lost travellers.

Church – A small 12C building, renovated in the 15C, in which there are remains of a fresco (right arm of the transept), a 16C polychrome, wooden bas-relief, a *Pietà* and a painting by Lebrun, *God the Father* (17C).

Vallée de la CREUSE★
Michelin map 68 fold 18 or 238 folds 39,40

The Creuse, with the granite slopes of the Massif Central behind it, has cut a picturesque course between Fresselines and Argenton. The variation of agricultural and wild landscapes, the grandiose ruins that mark the river banks, the artistic and literary associations of the area add to the enjoyment of a stay in the valley.

The Creuse nearly always flows at the bottom of a ravine, hence its name (*creuser* means to dig or hollow out). It derives from a great many streams that rise on the Millevaches Plateau 900m/2 952ft up; the river, thus formed, flows through a succession of rocky gorges and narrow basins, describing a great circular sweep as its waters flow past the old cities of Felletin, Aubusson and Moutier-d'Ahun. At Fresselines the main stream is joined by the waters of the Petite Creuse and begins the major part of its journey. For miles the river flows through the reservoir behind the Éguzon Dam, before being confined once more by a series of gorges until it reaches Argenton. Below the town the valley of the Creuse widens out and the river, now full and calm after its 240km/150mi journey, flows into the Vienne.

Prehistoric settlements – The valley has been occupied for a long time indeed: the earliest traces of human settlement are a million years old (Lavaud hunting camp at Éguzon-Chantôme, *see ST-MARCEL*). The site was clearly a stop on trade routes linking prehistoric peoples, as evidenced by the presence of flints from the area around Grand-Pressigny (in Indre-et-Loire) and the Metal Age construction of rudimentary ramparts atop rocky spurs (Crozant, Le Pin). A favourable climate (compared to the surrounding plateaux) made it a refuge for many animal species and a place of passage for herds of horses and reindeer, a fact well-exploited by Magdalenian hunters.

Painters – The rocks on the valley slopes, the attractive villages, the romantic ruins perched high above the river have long attracted artists. Crozant and Gargilesse were the favourite spots of a whole colony of painters, including Théodore Rousseau and Claude Monet, among many others.

Writers – To **George Sand** above all must go the credit for making the Creuse known. The valley was the setting for many of her novels: "The Creuse in April is perhaps the most beautiful river in the world", she wrote in *Laura*; in *Promenades autour d'un village* she even found the beauties of mountain scenery in the hills beside the Creuse: "It is true that the beauty is not obvious and of small proportions, but there are great sweeps and views and the graceful and subtle folds in the landscape are infinitely satisfying..." Maurice Rollinat the poet and Gabriel Nigond the local writer, have sung of the Creuse with its manors and melancholy heaths coloured by the broom and heather in flower.

FROM ARGENTON TO FRESSELINES
75km/45mi – 3hr

★**Argenton-sur-Creuse** – See *ARGENTON-SUR-CREUSE*.
Leave Argenton by ③, D 913.
Once outside the town, the road follows the course of the Creuse valley through an undulating region where farms stand alone surrounded by crops and meadows.

Ceaulmont – The name of this town derives from its high-perched location. The ruins of the **château de la Prune-au-Pot** ⊙ are open to visitors; Henri IV stayed there during the siege of Argenton (1589). To the right of the road, in a meadow, a lovely little Romanesque church on the edge of a spur. Go round it from the south side to enjoy a fine **view**★ of a loop made by the Creuse and in the distance of the Marche and Combraille plateaus.

Le Menoux – This village looking down on the river (scenic view from the Balicave hill) was once famous for its wines. Note the wine-growers houses and cellar entrances. The 19C church has been decorated by the Bolivian painter G. Carasco.
Follow a small road which slopes down to the Creuse and cross the river on the first bridge you come to going in the direction of Le Menoux.
Follow the road as it winds uphill and bear right on a narrow road which runs close to the swift waters of the Creuse and leads to the small Roche-Bat-l'Aigue dam.

La Roche-Bat-l'Aigle – A small dam, falls and a stretch of water are enclosed between rocks and high wooded slopes.
Turn back and go as far as Badecon-le-Pin.
As you come out of Les Chocats you get a good **view**★ of Le Pin meander, a wide bend made by the Creuse in an amphitheatre of rocks and hills. In the foreground and within the bend is a checkerboard of fields and meadows outlined with quickset hedges. On the opposite side of the river, above a high promontory stands the Romanesque Church of Ceaulmont.
After **Le Pin** (12-13C church), the road drops down into the Creuse Gorges, follows the bright Gargilesse valley and finally reaches Gargilesse-Dampierre.

Gargilesse-Dampierre – This is one of the most attractive villages in the valley, with its pleasant leafy setting, picturesque streets and old houses, church and, not least of all for its literary and artistic resonance.

Meander of the River Creuse

George Sand *(see NOHANT)* lived there and chose it as the background for several of her novels and accounts of rural legends and life. Claude Monet and Théodore Rousseau were among the several painters of their time who stayed in Gargilesse, attracted by the natural beauty of the place.

Church ⊙ – The Romanesque church (11-12C) stands within the walls of a medieval castle rebuilt in the 18C. The old keep and a door flanked by two towers are still standing. The church is well-proportioned and has interesting historiated capitals portraying the Twenty-four Old Men of the Apocalypse. The transept crossing is surmounted by a dome.

The crypt is enormous and decorated with 12-15C **frescoes**: *The Instruments of the Passion*, *St Gregory Celebrating Mass* and *The Apparition of Christ*, *Crucifixion*, *The Assumption*, *The Resurrection of the Dead*, *The Visitation* and *The Three Kings*. A 12C *Virgin and Child* stands in the main chapel.

George Sand's Retreat, "Aligra" ⊙ – Mementoes of the novelist, her son Maurice and her grand-daughter Aurore are on display in this little house.

Châteaubrun – The massive towers of Châteaubrun, a fortress built in a picturesque setting overlooking the valley in the 12C by Hugues de Lusignan, inspired George Sand to describe this wild country in two of her novels, *Le Péché de Monsieur Antoine* and *Les Maupras*.

Cross the river Creuse at Pont-des-Piles.

Éguzon – Éguzon was formerly a fortified town. On rue Athanase-Bassinet, daily life and traditional crafts of the region are recalled in the **musée de la vallée de la Creuse** ⊙.

Lac de Chambon – In a beautiful setting this great stretch of water contained by the Éguzon Dam makes a good water sports centre.

Go back to Pont-de-Piles, cross the Creuse and take D 45ᴬ to the right.

After the power station, there is a belvedere above the Éguzon Dam.

Barrage d'Éguzon (Éguzon Dam) – The dam came into service in 1926 and was one of the earliest of the really large dams to be built in Europe. It is 60m/197ft high and 300m/984ft long at the crest; the reservoir goes back (15km/9mi) to the confluence of the Sédelle and the Creuse, where the two stretches of water reach out on either side of the ruins of Crozant Castle.

From a belvedere above the dam, reached from D 45ᴬ on the right bank, there is a good view of the dam in its **setting★**, the reservoir receding into a landscape of hills and rocks and, downstream, of the valley of the Creuse.

The Creuse emerges from Chambon Lake and continues beside the road in the long climb to Crozant.

★ **Ruines de Crozant** (ruins) – *See Ruines de CROZANT.*

Fresselines – Maurice Rollinat, the poet, worked and died in this town. A rocky path leads from the church to the confluence of the two Creuse rivers *(30min round trip on foot)*, in picturesque surroundings.

Use the Map of principal sights to plan a special itinerary.

CROCQ

Michelin map 73 northeast of fold 11 or 239 fold 17

This little medieval stronghold, its cobbled streets intact but its fortifications long since fallen, is located on a high point, surrounded by woodlands, meadows and lakes.

Formerly under the feudal wing of Auvergne, Crocq made up one side of a defensive triangle, with Auzanac to the northeast and Herment to the southeast, which controlled the Clermont-Limoges road. Facing the stronghold of St-Georges-Nigremont *(see below)* on high ground, Crocq was the leading line of defence against attacks from the Limousin region.

The town gave its name to the peasant-rebels known as "**croquants**".

Chapelle Notre-Dame-de-la-Visitation – Founded at the end of the 12C, this small Romanesque edifice was thoroughly remodelled in the 15C and 16C, and restored in the 19C. It is surmounted by a belfry gable and a lantern of the dead, removed to the top of the building.

Inside, there is a remarkable **triptych**★ painted on wood, installed on the northern wall in 1995. This work, designed around 1530, relates the life of Saint Eligius in seven panels. An interesting feature on the representation of the Last Supper is the fork pictured on the back (whereas this utensil was not in common use before the 17C).

Castle towers ⊘ – Connected by a curtain wall, these towers are the only vestiges of the defensive castle built in the second half of the 12C, which fell in 1356 under assault by the troops of Edward, the Black Prince. Recently restored, the towers have been fitted with stairs making it possible to reach the **orientation table** in the eastern tower. The table indicates the sites in the vast **panorama**★: la Combraille to the north, the Dôme range and the Puy de Dôme to the east, the Dore range and the Sancy peak to the southeast, the Millevaches plateau to the southwest.

★THE SOUTHERN FRANC-ALLEU REGION
Round trip of 45km/27mi – 2hr30min

The name of this region recalls the Hundred Years War, which devastated it; in 1426, as compensation, an exemption from duties *(alleu)* was granted.

Crocq – *See above.*

Leave Crocq on D 966. Drive past the stadium, then turn left towards Dimpoux and park the car at Laval.

A pleasant lane bordered by beech and pine leads to a heath carpeted in fern. After 1km/0.5mi, in a little copse stands the **Urbe dolmen**.

You can return to Laval by continuing down the lane, which shortly leads back to the road.

There is a good view of Crocq as you head back to D 966.

At the crossroads, turn left on D 966.

Crocq – View of the town

S. Sauvignier/MICHELIN

137

After 2km/1mi through the heart of the Urbe forest, look for a little road on the right which leads to the **Montel-Guillaume church**, with its curious polychrome statues.

Return to D 966 and turn right (1km/0.5mi) on D 29.

At St-Agnant-près-de-Crocq, follow D 31 as it winds around ponds and lakes (Étang de la Motte is especially inviting). Nearby, the 15C **château de Theil** *(not open to the public)* is well sheltered behind its wall.

At Magnat-l'Étrange, turn northward on D 90.

St-Georges-Nigremont – Where the Limousin hills (the region known as "la Montagne") meet the Millevaches plateau, St-Georges-Nigremont holds the summit of a mount (referred to as *Nigers Mons* in Latin texts) which faced a Gaulish *oppidium*. This hillside fort served as an important religious and administrative centre under the Merovingian and Carolingian dynasties. From the terrace near the church, a wide **panorama** *(orientation table)* extends northeast to Crocq and beyond to the Combraille hills; to the southeast, the hills of Auvergne are visible.

Continue along D 90 then turn right on D 10. At Pontcharraud, take D 21 southeast for 7km/4.2mi, then turn left on D 28.

The road leads back to Crocq by way of the hamlet of Naberon, once home to a Knights of Malta commandery.

Ruines de CROZANT★

Michelin map 68 fold 18 or 239 fold 40 – Local map see Vallée de la CREUSE

The massive Crozant fortress, known as "the key to the Limousin", rises, still impressive though in ruins, from a rocky promontory commanding the confluence of the Creuse and the Sédelle. The most spectacular view of Crozant, the castle ruins and the Creuse valley with the river cutting its way through the ravines, is the one you come to suddenly as you approach from the east along D 30.

The stronghold, which was most likely founded in the 6C, was one of the most powerful and largest in the centre of France during the Middle Ages. A document dated from around the year 1000 mentions a certain Gérald de Crozant, lord of Bridiers. At that time, the castle was merely a wooden construction. In the 13C, the comte de la Marche, Hughes X de Lusignan, husband of Isabelle d'Angoulême, reinforced it and the building began to take on the appearance of a fortress. It measured 450m/490yd in length; the ramparts were more than half a mile round with ten towers to defend them, six facing the Creuse, four the Sédelle.

Strong in his position, Hughes X revolted against Blanche de Castille and then Saint Louis. Crozant eventually fell to the royal troops, while the Count and his father-in-law and ally Henry III of England were defeated at Saintes in 1242. The French king took possession of the castle for eight years, ordering Hughes X to bear the expenses of upkeep and protection. Several thousand men could be garrisoned in the citadel which, a century later, was to resist the attacks of Edward the Black Prince.

In 1436, the castle changed hands, from the Bourbons to the Armagnacs. Charles VII had it repaired, but Louis XI confiscated it along with the rest of the county, in order to hand it back to the Bourbons. After the treason of Constable Charles de Bourbon (one of the most highly-placed officials in the kingdom), the county was definitively confiscated. The Wars of Religion and an earthquake in 1606 brought calamity and destruction; by 1640, when Louis XIII sold the property to Henri de St-Germain, it was a ruin.

RUINES DE CROZANT

0   100 m

No longer exists

N

Sédelle

CREUSE

Tour Colin

Tour du Renard

Place d'Armes

Tour de l'Eau

Isabelle d'Angoulême keep

12C keep

Gateway

Hotel

D 30

CROZANT   ST-PLANTAIRE

VITRAT, LAC DE CHAMBON

TOUR ⊘

In its heyday, visitors to the castle passed through the Charles VII gate to enter the first courtyard. The square keep, in the second courtyard, was the 12C castle; 13m/42ft on each side, it had no abutments.

Modified in the 13C and 15C, it had three upper storeys and served as the seigniorial abode. It was surrounded by a curtain wall. A steep ramp leads to the third courtyard, the twin-walled section built by Hughes X.

The platform built on the rocky spur is 18m by 120m/20yd by 165yd; it was used as a parade ground.

The base of the massive tower built by Isabelle d'Angoulême in the 13C stands on a rise 5m/16ft high. The line of towers continued to the end of the point, where the ground floor of the Tour Colin is intact.

MOTOR BOAT TRIP ⊘

Excursions are offered on Éguzon Lake *(see Times and Charges, CROZANT, at the end of this guide).*

CULAN★

Michelin map 69 fold 11 or 238 fold 42 – Local map see ST-AMAND-DE-MONTROND

The powerful medieval fortress of Culan stands four square with its massive round towers looking straight down into the gorges of the river Arnon.

The best view of the castle **site★** is from D 943 coming from Montluçon where the bridge crosses the river; the stark façade, relieved only by its many mullioned windows, rises out of a tangled undergrowth and clings to the rock commanding both the ravine and the road.

Château ⊘ – Captured by Philip Augustus in 1188, it was reconstructed in the 13C and considerably altered during the 15C. At that time, 300m/984ft of wall surrounded the 3000m²/323000sq ft area. Admiral Culant, faithful partisan of Joan of Arc, welcomed her to his home in 1429; Louis XI was a guest in 1465. The castle was later bought by Sully who subsequently sold it to the prince of Condé; in the 17C it passed into the hands of Michel Le Tellier, father of the Minister Louvois.

Interior – The rooms reflect different periods of the castle's history: Admiral Culant's room (Gothic chest sculpted in folds); the archives room (war chest with seven locks); four guard rooms where you can admire the wooden galleries and the three-layered, star-shaped timber frame; a diorama explaining the revolt known as *la Fronde* and the siege of the castle; the red salon (18C Aubusson

Culan – Le château

tapestry); the George Sand room; Sully's Intendants' room (massive chimney).

After the tour, go to the end of the terrace where there is a good view of the Arnon valley.

Church – One doorway and the crypt of the former chapel are Romanesque; the rest of the building dates from the 15C.

Tourists should not go sightseeing in a church during a service.

DOMME★★

Population 1 030

Michelin map 75 fold 17 or 235 fold 6 – Local map see Vallée de la DORDOGNE

Domme, the "Acropolis of the Dordogne", is remarkably situated on a rocky crag overlooking the Dordogne valley.

Captain Vivans's exploit – While the struggles of the Reformation were inflaming France, Domme kept up resistance against the Huguenots who were overrunning Périgord. Yet, in 1588, the famous Protestant Captain **Geoffroi de Vivans** captured the town by cunning. One night he and 30 of his men climbed along the rocks of the cliff face known as *la Barre*, a place so precipitous that it had not been thought necessary to protect it, and entered the sleeping town. Vivans and his men created an infernal racket and during the ensuing confusion opened the tower doors to their waiting army. The inhabitants were too sleepy to resist, and Vivans thereupon became master of the town for the next four years. He installed a garrison, burned down both the church and the Augustine priory and established the Protestant faith. However, noting the increasing success of the Catholics in Périgord, he determined to sell the bastide to his rivals on 10 January 1592. The unwary purchasers found nothing but ruins.

★★★PANORAMA

From the promontory, the view embraces the Dordogne valley from the Montfort meander in the east, to Beynac in the west.

Flowing east to west from the undulating countryside of Périgord Noir, the Dordogne river widens at the foot of Domme, in a fertile valley scattered with villages and farms, and continues its way below the cliffs of La Roque-Gageac and Beynac.

Changing with the time of day – hazy in the early morning mist, bright blue between lines of green poplars in the noonday sun, a silver ribbon in the evening light – the Dordogne winds its way through the carefully cultivated fields (maize, tobacco, cereals) against a backdrop of wooded hills. Of all the creative artists who have come here seeking inspiration, the writer Henry Miller was perhaps the most affected, describing the area as the nearest thing to Paradise on earth.

Belvédère de la Barre – The esplanade at the end of the Grand'Rue offers a panorama of the valley below. The bust represents **Jacques de Maleville** (1741-1824) one of the authors of the French *Code Civil* (also known as the "Napoleonic code").

Promenade des Falaises –Take this cliffside walk along the promontory eastwards, passing below the gardens. The view is more extensive than at the Barre Viewpoint.

Jardin public du Jubilé – These attractive gardens *(orientation table)*, are situated at the tip of the promontory, on the site of the entrenched camp installed here in 1214 by Simon de Montfort. He had just beaten the Cathars and razed their fortress **Domme-Vieille**, leaving but a few ruins standing. To visit these, leave the gardens and go past the old Roy mill.

★THE BASTIDE

Founded by Philip the Bold in 1283, this bastide is far from presenting the perfect rectangular plan of the bastide as such – it is more in the form of a trapezium. The surrounding fortifications have been adapted to the terrain; inside the fortified town, the streets follow a geometric plan, as far as possible.

Domme – Gable with scroll

Ph. Saillans/ZAPA

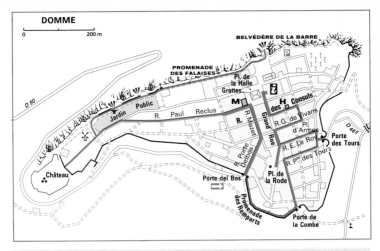

| **H** Hôtel de ville | **M** Musée d'Art et de Traditions populaires |

The bastide played an important role in the Hundred Years War. Its pivotal position made it the ideal headquarters for the Périgord-Quercy seneschalsy (a feudal estate). After the Wars of Religion, the Domme area entered a period of relative wealth, thanks to the quality of its vines, river trade on the Dordogne and the quarrying of millstone.

Promenade des Remparts – When you come to the **Porte del Bos** gateway, which has a pointed arch and was once closed with a portcullis, bear left to walk inside the ramparts. Opposite the **Porte de la Combe**, turn left towards the town where there are many fine houses to be seen. The beauty of the gold stone and the flat brown tiles is often enhanced by the addition of elegant wrought-iron balconies and brightened by climbing vines and flower-decked terraces. Go through the late 13C **Porte des Tours** ⊘, the most impressive and best preserved of the town's gateways. On the side of place des Armes, the wall is rectilinear but on the outside, the gateway is flanked by two massive semicircular rusticated towers, which were once defended by a brattice, of which one can still see the machicolations. The towers were built by Philip the Fair and originally served as guard rooms. Between 1307 and 1318 Knights Templars were imprisoned there and left their mark with graffiti.

There is an illustration of the Porte des Tours in the Introduction, under the heading ABC of architecture.

Rue Eugène-le-Roy – During the period he spent in a house along this street, Eugène le Roy wrote two of his masters-works: *L'ennemi de la mort* ("The Enemy of Death") and *Le moulin du Frau* ("Frau Mill").

Place de la Rode – This is the place where the condemned were broken on the wheel. The **Maison du batteur de monnaie** (Money Minter's house) is decorated with fine Gothic apertures.

Grand'Rue – This shopping street is lined with shops displaying many of the culinary specialities of Périgord.

Rue Geoffroy-de-Vivans – The house on the corner of the Grand'Rue has a lovely Renaissance window.

Rue des Consuls – The Hôtel de Ville (**H**) (town hall) is located in a 13C building, which was once the Seneschal law courts.

Place de la Halle – In this large square stands an elegant 17C covered market *(halle)*. Facing it is the 16C **Maison des Gouverneurs** (Governors' House) flanked by an elegant turret. It now houses the tourist information centre.

ADDITIONAL SIGHTS

Caves ⊘ – *The entrance is in the covered market.*
These caves served as refuge for the townspeople of Domme during the Hundred Years War and the Wars of Religion.
So far about 450m/490yd of galleries have been cleared for the public to visit; the chambers are generally small and are sometimes separated by low passages. The ceilings in certain chambers are embellished with slender white stalactites. There are also places where stalactites and stalagmites join to form columns or pillars. The "Salle Rouge" contains some eccentrics.

Bison and rhinoceros bones, discovered when the caves were being prepared for tourists, are displayed precisely as they were found.

Musée d'Art et de Traditions populaires ⊘ (**M**) – In an old house on place de la Halle, this museum presents a retrospective of every day life in Domme: displays of typical furnishings, clothing, farm tools. Amid the archives and photographs documenting the town's past, note the royal missives according special privileges and exemptions to the inhabitants of Domme.

Le DORAT★

Population 2 203
Michelin map 72 fold 7 or 233 fold 22

As the seat of the principal seneschalsy, or governorship of Basse-Marche from the 16C to the Revolution, Le Dorat prides itself on possessing one of the most remarkable buildings in Limousin, the Collegiate Church of St. Peter. The Porte Bergère, complete with its machicolations, is all that remains of the fortifications built about 1420.

Every seven years the Le Dorat *ostensions* give rise to unique ceremonies in which guards of honour take part – sappers and drummers in the uniforms of the First Empire (1804-1814).

Stock breeders take advantage of the region's natural pastureland; herds and flocks, fairs and markets flourish.

★★COLLÉGIALE ST-PIERRE

In about 1100, on the site of a monastery built in the 10C and probably destroyed in the 11C, construction began simultaneously at the east and west ends of a church which after fifty years of work bore the appearance we see today. A "collegiate" church is a church other than a cathedral that has a chapter of canons, or a church under the pastorate of more than one minister.

Exterior – The collegiate church, which is built in fine grey granite, is striking in size and pleasing in proportion. The façade is surmounted by a squat belfry supported by two bell-turrets and opens with a wide, multifoil doorway showing a Mozarabic influence which was perhaps inspired by the pilgrims who had journeyed to Santiago de Compostela. The doorway's festooned covings bring a gay and original touch, lightening the stark façade.

An elegant octagonal belfry on three tiers of unequal height surmounted by a soaring spire topped with a 13C copper gilt angel, rises above the transept.

From below the place de l'Église at a former churchyard where the roads from Guéret and Bellac meet, there is a good overall view of the chevet, the arrangement in tiers of the apse, the apsidal chapels and the stone belfries. The central apsidal chapel supports a semicircular tower which formed part of the 15C town's defence system. Two rectangular abutments shore up each apsidiole; each of the bays has a single Limousin-style arch.

At the entrance, in the axis of the nave, the large granite baptismal font is pre-Romanesque, embellished on both sides with fancy-tailed lions.

Interior – From the first bay which has a dome above, and is twelve steps above the level of the rest of the nave, one is struck immediately by the majesty of the building. The four bays following are broken barrel vaults on joists. Narrow aisles provide support for the central arching. The transept crossing, above which rises a tall dome on pendentives, is lit by Romanesque windows.

The arcades in the chancel rest on foliated capitals; two chapels hold shrines to Saint Israel and Saint Theobald.

Crypt ⊘ – The crypt is reached from the south arm of the transept. It extends the length of the chancel and resembles it in plan and proportion. This fine 11C sanctuary, dedicated to St. Anne, has columns whose primitive capitals are roughly hewn, one however is sculpted. The apsidal chapel contains fragments of 13C statues.

Sacristy – This exhibits a multicoloured statue of St. Anne and a *Pietà* dating from the 15C and a 13C reliquary cross with two crosspieces, which belonged to the treasure of the collegiate church.

Panorama – At the place de la Libération, the former rampart is now a belvedere which overlooks the public garden, Santillana del Mar, and gives a good view of the hills of Limousin beyond.

Consult the Map of places to stay at the beginning of the guide to choose a suitable location.

Vallée de la DORDOGNE★★★

Michelin maps 75 folds 9, 10, 15 to 19
or 235 folds 5, 6 and 239 folds 27, 28, 29, 37 to 39

The Dordogne is one of the longest rivers in France and is said to be the most beautiful. The variety and beauty of the countryside through which the river flows and the architectural glories that mark its banks make the valley a first-class tourist attraction.

A lovely journey – The Dordogne begins where the Dore and the Dogne meet at the foot of the Sancy, the highest peak in the Massif Central. Swift flowing and speckled with foam, it crosses the Mont-Dore and Bourboule basins and soon leaves the volcanic rocks of Auvergne for the granite of Limousin. Between Bort and Argentat, where the river once flowed between narrow ravines, there is now a series of reservoirs and great dams. The river calms down for a short while after Beaulieu as it crosses the rich plain, where it is joined by the Cère river, which rises in Cantal. From this point the Dordogne is a truly majestic river, though it remains nonetheless swift and temperamental. The *causses* (limestone plateaux) of Quercy bar its way and so in true Herculean style it cuts a path through the Montvalent Amphitheatre. Having reached the Périgord plateaux beyond Souillac, the river begins to flow past great castles, washing the base of the rocks on which they perch. Starting at Limeuil, where the river is joined by the Vézère, the valley widens out and, after crossing some rapids, reaches Bergerac and then the Guyenne plains with their vineyards. At the Ambès Spit, the Dordogne completes its 500km/310mi journey; joins the Garonne, which it almost equals in size, and the two flow on together as the Gironde.

The capricious Dordogne – The Dordogne flows swiftly through both the mountains and the plains, but its volume is far from constant. Winter and spring rain storms and the melting of the snows on the Millevaches Plateau and the mountains of Auvergne bring floods almost every year which are sudden, violent and at times devastating. Dam construction and other civil engineering projects – Bort, Marèges, L'Aigle, Le Chastang, Argentat – in the upper valley now control the ebb and flow.

The days of the gabares – For a long time there was river traffic on the Dordogne. Until the last century a world of sailors and craft lived on the river in spite of the dangers and the river's uneven flow. The boatmen used flat-bottomed boats known as *gabares* or *argentats*, after the town with the largest boat-building yards. These big barges, sailing downstream, carried passengers and cargo, especially oak for cooperage in Bordeaux; sailing upstream they loaded salt at Libourne and continued their journey up to Souillac where it was sold. The journey was full of the unexpected and the *gabariers* had to be skilled to get their boats through. When they arrived, the boats were broken up and sold for timber. Today river traffic plies solely on the lower Dordogne; upstream the only boats to be seen are those of anglers or canoeists.

Water-power – Considerable economic importance has accrued to the river Dordogne with the harnessing of the current. The construction of dams and their dependent artificial lakes as well as roads to the new hydro-electric stations has transformed the upper valley and has turned what was once an unknown and barely accessible area into a tourist region.

The harnessing of the upper Dordogne for hydro-electric power was favoured by the volume of the river, usually abundant, and by the impermeability of the granite rocks through which it has eroded a deep channel.

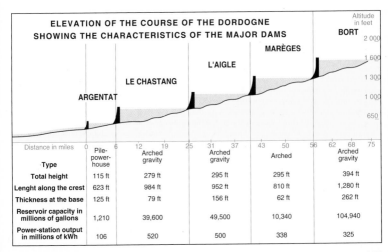

	ARGENTAT	LE CHASTANG	L'AIGLE	MARÈGES	BORT
Distance in miles	0 6	12 19	25 31 37	43 50 56	62 68 75
Type	Pile-power-house	Arched gravity	Arched gravity	Arched	Arched gravity
Total height	115 ft	279 ft	295 ft	295 ft	394 ft
Lenght along the crest	623 ft	984 ft	952 ft	810 ft	1,280 ft
Thickness at the base	125 ft	79 ft	156 ft	62 ft	262 ft
Reservoir capacity in millions of gallons	1,210	39,600	49,500	10,340	104,940
Power-station output in millions of kWh	106	520	500	338	325

ELEVATION OF THE COURSE OF THE DORDOGNE
SHOWING THE CHARACTERISTICS OF THE MAJOR DAMS

Altitude in feet: 2 000, 1 600, 1 300, 1 000, 650

Vallée de la DORDOGNE

The great dams at Bort, Marèges, L'Aigle, Le Chastang and Argentat provide the energy for large power stations. Similar projects have been carried out on the Dordogne's principal tributaries, the Rhue, the Diège, the Triouzoune, the Danstre, the Maronne, and the Cère, in all there are some twenty-three undertakings within the basin of the upper Dordogne; they are capable of producing on average 2900 million kWh a year or over 4 % of the electric power produced by all hydro-electric stations in France.

★★THE GREAT DAMS

From Bort-les-Orgues to Spontour *93km/58mi – 4hr*

Here the Dordogne used to flow through narrow gorges. The dams and reservoir lakes which now succeed one another down the valley, forming a gigantic water stairway 100km/60mi long, have altered the appearance of the countryside, however they often fit remarkably well into the beautiful settings. All the same try to avoid the seasons when the waters are low and the lower, erosion-worn slopes are visible.

Bort-les-Orgues – *See BORT-LES-ORGUES.*

Leave Bort-les-Orgues on D 979 to the northwest.

2km/1mi from Bort, a belvedere stands to the right of the road (car park).

From here there is a **view** of the dam, its lake and Val castle.

★★Saint-Nazaire Site – *30min round trip on foot.* After parking the car, bear right along the ridge on the slope and later follow a path to the *Calvaire* (Stations of the Cross). Pass a statue of St. Nazarius and make for the end of the promontory across the heather. A Calvary has been erected on the point from which there is a magnificent **view★★** of the Dordogne and Diège gorges. Return to car park.

Along the bottom of the valley stretches the lake controlled by the Marèges Dam.

Return to St-Julien and there turn left to take first D 127 and then 2km/1mi farther on D 20, again on the left. D 20 crosses the Diège, climbs wooded slopes and, as far as Roche-les-Peyroux provides views of the river.

After Liginiac take D 42ᴱ on your left then D 42.

From a terrace there is a bird's-eye view of the gorges and Marèges Dam below. The road continues to drop in hairpin bends (500 m/547yd further) – a belvedere affords a second view – down to the power station.

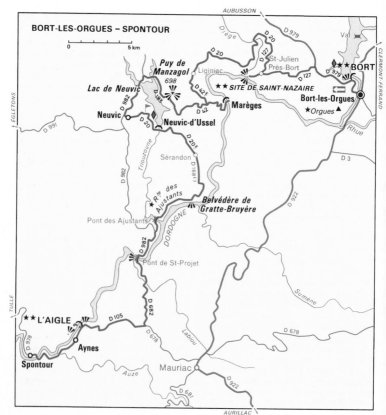

Marèges Dam – The dam is impressive. The steep road ends at the power station.

Puy de Mazagol – *2km/1mi. 800m/900yds from the junction of D 42 and D 20, a road on the right, D 183, leads to the summit from where there is a vast panorama of the Neuvic-d'Ussel Dam and the Massif Central (viewing table).*

Neuvic Lake – *D 183 and then D 982 on the left skirt the beautiful lake into which flow the waters of the Triouzoune, a tributary of the Dordogne from the north, contained by the Neuvic d'Ussel dam.*

Neuvic – This attractive village, built on the hillside has a beach with a sailing school and a centre for water skiing.

Neuvic-d'Ussel Dam – This undertaking, which is of the arched dam type, is 27m/89ft high and 145m/476ft long. The reservoir with a capacity of 5 000 million gallons pumps water to a power station 5km/3mi away, situated south of Sérandon in the valley of the Dordogne (annual output of about 45 million kWh).
After Charlane the **Ajustants Tourist Road★** *(Route Touristique des Ajustants)* follows the Dordogne valley with its rock-strewn and wooded slopes.

Gratte-Bruyère Belvedere – To the left below the road. This is a magnificent point from which to see the Sumène flowing into the Dordogne.
The road has been cut out of the side of the rock.
Cross the reinforced concrete Pont des Ajustants (bridge) to reach D 982 which you follow to the left.

At first the road looks down on the L'Aigle reservoir from high up but affords only intermittent views of it. D 982 crosses to the fare bank of the river by the graceful Pont de St-Projet (suspension bridge) which provides a good view of the reservoir, and then goes up the narrow wooded Labiou valley.
Take D 678 on the right and then turn right again to reach D 105, which, after Chalvignac, provides beautiful views of the L'Aigle reservoir with its intended shoreline.

★★L'Aigle Dam – *Leave the car opposite the L'Aigle Dam and go on foot up D 16 to the belvedere built below the dam (the path lies between two road tunnels).*
From the belvedere there is a good view of the dam as a whole and the valley below it.
The dam impresses by its size and the boldness of concept. Two "ski-jump" flood control gates can let through 880 000 gallons a second.
Return to the left bank and D 105 which is now laid out as a corniche road and provides views from different angles of the L'Aigle Dam.

Aynes – The granite houses with their slate roofs are grouped round the chapel.

Spontour – From the bridge, admire the village where you can still enjoy a taste of the past by boarding a traditional **gabare** ⊘ for a trip on the river.

From Spontour to Beaulieu *85km/53mi – 3hr*

There is no road beyond Spontour that runs beside the river and a long detour has to be made before you rejoin the Dordogne at the Le Chastang Dam.
For a few miles after Spontour D 978 runs beside the river as it bends in an enclosed part of the valley. This good winding road then climbs up to the plateau. Branching off D 978, D 13, affords good views, between La Chapeloune and Bassignac-le-Haut and particularly from the suspension bridge, of the Le Chastang reservoir.

Marcillac-la-Croisille – This small village on the granite plateau grew at the point where Roman roads met. It is situated near La Vallette Lake and Meyrignac with its recreation facilities.

★Barrage du Chastang (Dam) ⊘ – This great dam is 85m/280ft high and 300m/985ft along the crest. Less than a mile beyond the dam a narrow winding path (signposted) leads off to the right of D 29 and brings you to a belvedere on the left bank of the Dordogne. From this point downstream, you get a new view of the dam and the reservoir. The power station of this dam is the valley's greatest producer of electricity.

Servières-le-Château – *See ARGENTAT, Excursions.*
Return to the dam and take D 129 towards Argentat.

After a right-hand bend you get a good view of the whole undertaking. The road, sometimes bordered by tall rocks, continues along the left bank of the river.

Glény – *See ARGENTAT, Excursions.*
After Glény and short ly before the Argentat Dam you see the small **Le Gibanel Castle,** its elegant silhouette reflected in the waters of the Argentat reservoir.

★Argentat – *See ARGENTAT.*

★★Beaulieu-sur-Dordogne – *See BEAULIEU-SUR-DORDOGNE.*

Vallée de la DORDOGNE

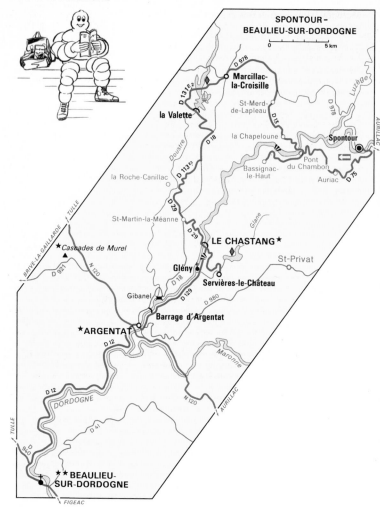

★★THE QUERCY STRETCH OF THE DORDOGNE

From Bretenoux to Souillac *56km/35 miles – 3hr*

Bretenoux – In its leafy riverside setting, this former bastide, founded in 1277 by a powerful lord of Castelnau, has kept its grid plan, its central square, covered arcades and parts of the ramparts.

After visiting the picturesque place des Consuls with its 15C turreted town house, go through a covered alley to the old manor at the corner of the pretty rue du Manoir de Cère. Turn right and right again returning via the charming quay along the Cère. Having collected the waters of the Cère, the river passes within sight of the impressive mass of Castelnau-Bretenoux Castle.

★★Château de Castelnau-Bretenoux – *See Château de CASTELNAU-BRETENOUX.*

Downstream from Castelnau, the Bave tributary joins the Dordogne, which divides into several streams flowing in a wide valley bounded to the south by abrupt cliffs.

★Carennac – *See CARENNAC.*

Beyond Carennac, the Dordogne cuts a channel between the Martel and Gramat *causses* before entering the beautiful area of the Montvalent Amphitheatre.

Floirac – A 14C keep is all that remains of the old fortifications.

★Cirque de Montvalent – The road is very picturesque, running for the most part beside the river, though sometimes running along a ledge above it. There are attractive views of the valley and the *causse* cliffs from every bend.

Cross the Dordogne, take D 140 towards Martel and then turn right on D 32 to the Copeyre Viewpoint.

★Belvédère de Copeyre – There is a good **view★** of the Dordogne and the Montvalent Amphitheatre from a rock beside the D 32 on which there is a wayside cross.

At the foot of the cliffs, the Dordogne can be seen flowing in a wide arc through pastures divided by lines of poplars; on the left, to one side of the river, is the Puy d'Issolud and on the right, to the other side, the village of Floirac.

Turn back and follow the north bank of the Dordogne.

Gluges – This village (with old houses) lies in a beautiful **setting★** beside the river at the foot of the cliffs.

The road then winds upwards around a tall overhanging ochre-coloured cliff, hidden in places by a thick carpet of ivy. At times the road carves a route out of the cliff.

Gluges

Creysse – The charming village of Creysse with pleasant, narrow streets, brown-tiled roofs, houses bedecked with climbing vines and flights of steps leading to their doors, lies at the foot of the rocky spur, on which stands a pre-Romanesque church, the former castle chapel, with its curious twin apses. The church and the remains of the nearby castle are reached by a stony alleyway, which climbs sharply to a terrace. It is from a little square shaded by plane trees, near the war memorial, that you get the best overall view of the village.

After Creysse the road follows the willow-bordered bank as far as St-Sozy and then crosses the river over the bridge at Meyronne.

Meyronne – From the bridge over the Dordogne, there is a pretty **view★** of the river and the village – former home of the bishops of Tulle – with its charming Quercy houses built attractively into the cliffs.

The road subsequently follows the course of the Dordogne through beautiful countryside of rocks and cliffs, then crosses the Ouysse river near Lacave.

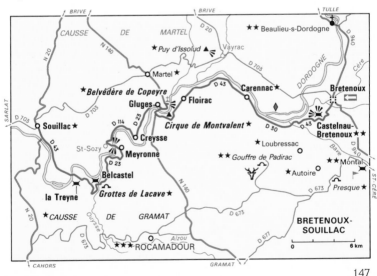

★**Grottes de Lacave** ⊙ – Near the valley of the Dordogne as it makes a deep cut through the Gramat Causse, a series of caves was discovered in 1902 by Armand Viré, a student of the geographer and speleologist E. A. Martel, at the foot of the cliffs beside the river.

The galleries open to visitors are a mile long *(complete tour, on foot)* and divide into two groups: concretions and stalactites prevail in the first; in the second, underground rivers run in between natural rimstone dams (gours) and flood out into placid lakes.

Château de Belcastel – A vertical cliff dropping down to the confluence of the Ouysse and the Dordogne is crowned by a castle standing proudly in a remarkable **setting**★. Only the eastern part of the main wing and the chapel date from the Middle Ages; most of the other buildings were reconstructed later.

Château de la Treyne ⊙ – The château *(photograph p 83)* stands perched on a cliff, which on one side overlooks the east bank of the Dordogne and on the other side a vast park. Burned by the Catholics during the Wars of Religion, the château was rebuilt in the 17C; only the square tower is 14C.

The buildings are now a hotel. The park (French gardens) and chapel (where exhibitions are held) are open to the public.

The road then crosses the Dordogne, to run along the north bank to Souillac.

★**Souillac** – See SOUILLAC.

★★★THE PÉRIGORD STRETCH OF THE DORDOGNE

From Souillac to Sarlat *32km/20mi – 1hr30 min*

★**Souillac** – See SOUILLAC.

The countryside of Quercy is only very slightly different from that of Périgord Noir, through which the Dordogne flows below Souillac. The river is calmer and its meanders, separated only by narrow rock channels, form a series of rich basins. Mountain peaks crowned with dark trees ring the horizon.

The road crosses the well cultivated alluvial plains surrounded by wooded hills and follows the river bordered with poplars – a typical Périgord valley scene.

Carlux – Overlooking the valley from its commanding position, the village still has some old houses and a small covered market. A rare Gothic chimney, jutting out from a gabled wall, adds a touch of the unexpected to the scene. Two towers and an imposing curtain wall are all that remains of the large castle, which once belonged to the viscounty of Turenne. From the castle terrace, there is a lovely view of the valley and the cliffs, which were used as the castle foundations.

The crossing of the Dordogne is guarded by the **Château de Rouffillac**; its attractive outline can be seen rising out of the green oak trees.

Château de Fénelon ⊙ – François de Salignac de Lamothe-Fénelon, later to become the duke of Burgundy's mentor and author of *Télémaque (See Introduction, Literary life, and CARENNAC)*, was born here on 6 August 1651 and spent his early childhood within these walls. His family had been feudal lords since the 14C and remained so until 1780.

Built near Ste-Mondane village, on a hill overlooking the Dordogne and the Bouriane forest, Fénelon castle underwent substantial alterations in the 17C, although its foundations actually date back to the 15C and 16C. Its triply-fortified walls give it the appearance of being a very powerful fortress. The residential buildings and towers are still covered with *lauze* slate roofs. A beautiful staircase with two bends gives access into the main courtyard. Inside, the Fénelon bedroom, the chapel, the kitchen hollowed out of the rock and a collection of medieval military miscellany are all open to visitors.

Carsac-Aillac – The modest but delightful church of Carsac, built in lovely golden stone, stands in a country setting not far from the Dordogne.

The porch in the façade has five recessed arches resting on small columns. The massive Romanesque belltower and the apse are roofed with *lauzes*.

The nave and the lower aisles had stellar vaulting decorated with elegant discs or bosses added to them in the 16C *(illustration page 34)*. A small dome on pendentives rises above the transept crossing. The chancel ends in a Romanesque apse with oven vaulting and is adorned with interesting archaic oriental-style capitals. Gothic chapels are situated on either side of the nave and at the entrance to the chancel.

There are strikingly modern **stained-glass windows**; the **Stations of the Cross** are the work of the artist Zack. Unpretentious and austere in design, the work includes texts from the writings of Paul Claudel (diplomat and author: 1868-1955).

There is an illustration of the church vaults in the Introduction: ABC of architecture.

★**Montfort Meander and** ★**château de Monfort** – Occupying an advantageous site on the Dordogne river, Montfort has given its name to one of Périgord's most famous meanders. The bend in the river, known in French as the *Cingle de Montfort (along D 703 – car park)*, offers a lovely **view**★ encircling the Tursac peninsula and its walnut tree plantations; the château clings to its promontory. The castle stands in a grandiose **setting**★, which aroused the envy of those who wished to rule Périgord; its history consisted of a long series of sieges and battles. Seized by the formidable Simon de Montfort in 1214 and razed to the ground, it was rebuilt and then later destroyed three times – during the Hundred Years War (1337-1453), under Louis XI (1461-83), and again by order of Henri IV (1562-1610). The renovation work carried out in the 19C gives it the whimsical look of a stage setting for light opera.

★★★**Sarlat** – *See SARLAT-LA-CANÉDA.*

From Sarlat to St-Cyprien 60km/37mi – 4hr

This trip is the most attractive in Périgord. Great rocks rise up at every step, golden in colour and crowned with old castles and picturesque villages.

★★★**Sarlat** – *See SARLAT-LA-CANÉDA.*

Soon after Vitrac, Domme comes into view on its rocky promontory on the left.

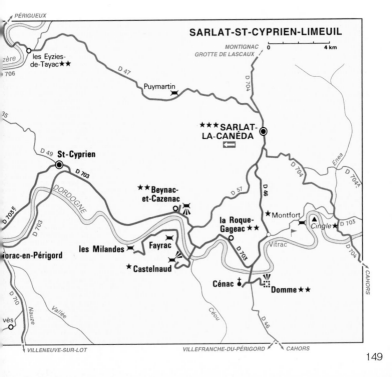

Cénac – The only remaining evidence of the large priory built in Cénac in the 11C is the small **Romanesque church** ○, which stands outside the village. Even the church did not escape the Wars of Religion, and only the east end escaped the depredations of the Protestants serving under Captain Vivans in 1589. The short nave and transept were rebuilt in the 19C.

Go into the churchyard to get an overall view of the east end with its fine stone roof and its column-buttresses topped with foliated capitals. A cornice, decorated with modillions bearing small carved figures, runs round the base of the roof of the apsidal chapels.

Inside, in the chancel and the apse, there is a series of interesting historiated capitals, which date from 1130. The realistic and diverse animal art enlivens these capitals; the scenes depicted include Daniel in the Lions' Den and Jonah and the Whale.

★★**Domme** – *See DOMME.*

This is the most beautiful part of the whole valley; in between lines of poplars the Dordogne spreads its course to flow calmly through a mosaic of farmland and meadows. A succession of increasingly spellbinding settings for towns and castles unfolds.

★★**La Roque-Gageac** – *See La ROQUE-GAGEAC.*

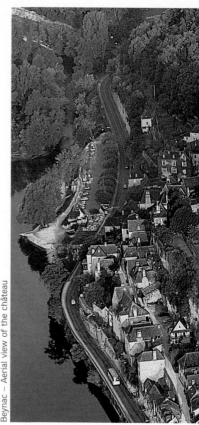

Beynac – Aerial view of the château

★**Château de Castelnaud** – *See Château de CASTELNAUD.*

A short stretch of road between Castelnaud and Les Milandes Castle passes below Fayrac Castle.

Château de Fayrac – A double curtain wall surrounds the interior courtyard, which is reached by two drawbridges. The 16C buildings bristling with pepper-pot roofs form a complex yet harmonious unit in spite of the 19C restorations (note the pseudo-keep). The castle is tucked amid the greenery on the south bank of the Dordogne opposite Beynac-et-Cazenac.

Les Milandes ○ – Built in 1489 by François de Caumont, the estate remained the property of this family until the Revolution and was eventually purchased by the well-known American singer, Josephine Baker or *La Perle Noire* as she was known in her

---

Josephine Baker
1906, St Louis, Missouri – 1975, Paris, France

An early symbol of the beauty and vitality of artistic expression in the American black community, Josephine Baker was also an honoured hero of the Second World War, winning the Croix de Guerre for her work as a member of the Free French forces and the Résistance. She began her theatrical career in her early teens, eventually earning a place as a chorus girl in the revue *Shuffle Along*, which brought her to New York City. Still a very young woman, she stirred sensation in Paris with her *danse sauvage*, playing on colonial fantasies and high-octane sexuality, while learning much about the world, her art, and herself. She got star billing for her performance at the Folies-Bergère, clad in the famous banana skirt. Baker became a French citizen in 1937. When war broke out, she used her special position as a European entertainer (albeit one who had caused much scandal in cities more conservative than libertine Paris) to carry secret messages and to help spirit friends out of France to safety. She retired at age fifty, but, short of funds and determined to continue building her dream and her family at Les Milandes, she returned to the stage within a few years, and worked tirelessly up until the day of her death.

J.-D. Sudres/SCOPE

Paris cabaret heyday in the Twenties and Thirties. It was here that she sought to create a "world village", gathering together and adopting children of different races, religions and nationalities and bringing them up to promote mutual understanding. The story of her exciting and singular life is recounted in a series of rooms, some with furnishings in place at the time she bought the house, some with the star's furnishings, others displaying enlargements of poignant photographs of Josephine and her rainbow tribe. Accompanying the visitor everywhere, are songs she recorded between the two world wars and towards the end of her career. A short film captures some of her fine stepping for posterity.

An unrelated addition to the tourist attraction is the collection of birds of prey, and the demonstrations given regulary by falconers on the grounds.

★★ **Beynac-et-Cazenac** – *See BEYNAC-ET-CAZENAC.*

Beyond Beynac, the valley does not widen out much before St-Cyprien.

St-Cyprien – St-Cyprien clings to the side of a hill near the north bank of the Dordogne, in a setting of hills and woodlands characteristic of the Périgord Noir. It is dominated by the massive outline of its **church**, the old houses of the village clustered close around. The big church was built in the 12C and restored in the Gothic period; the belfry keep is Romanesque. Inside, the enormous main body of the church has pointed vaulting. A wealth of 17C furnishings include altarpieces, a pulpit, stalls, an organ loft and a wrought-iron balustrade.

From St-Cyprien to Limeuil *34km/21mi – 1hr30min*

St-Cyprien – *See above.*

Below St-Cyprien, the Dordogne runs through an area where meadows and arable fields spread out to the cliffs and wooded slopes, marking the edge of the valley.

Siorac-en-Périgord – This small village, sought after for its beach, has a 17C castle and a small Romanesque church.

Drive through **Coux-et-Bigaroque**, to see an old farrier's sling used for shoeing oxen.

Urval – This village set in a small valley nestles in the shadow of its massive 12C church. The walls of the rectangular chancel are covered with blind arcades held up by archaic capitals. The grey marble column has been taken from an earlier construction.

Next to the church is the medieval **communal oven**★ (still in use) in which the baron allowed villagers to bake their bread for a nominal fee.
Take the small road, southwest of Urval, to Cadouin.

★**Cadouin** – *See CADOUIN.*

From Cadouin, D 25 continues northeast to Le Buisson through rolling hills covered with underbrush and chestnut trees.

Chapelle St-Martin – Henry II Plantagenet funded the construction of this chapel as penance for the murder of Thomas Becket, archbishop of Canterbury. It was completed after his death at the request of his son, Richard the Lion Heart. His name and the date of consecration of the chapel, 1194, are inscribed on the **foundation stone** set in the left wall of the nave (it is rare to find churches with their foundation stone). The transept crossing is topped with a rustic dome.

Limeuil – Walk up the main street. Built on a steep promontory, this old village, arranged in tiers overlooking the confluence of the Dordogne and Vézère rivers, occupies a picturesque **site**★. Its two bridges, unusually set at right angles and spanning each of the rivers, mark the confluence. Traces of its past as a fortress town can be seen on climbing up the ancient narrow streets to the site of the old castle and church. Limeuil's role as "arsenal and watchtower" established itself quite early on, thanks mainly to its strategic position, which aroused desire and envy in those who saw it. At one point the militant peasants known as *Croquants* gained control of the town during an uprising. Limeuil was also for many centuries a port and "safe haven" for heavy barges.

From Limeuil to Bergerac *53km/33mi – 2hr30min*

Limeuil – *See above.*

Soon after the confluence of the Dordogne and the Vézère, the very picturesque road overlooks the Dordogne at Roches Blanches *(viewpoint)* across from Sors Plain.

Trémolat – Built on a meander in the Dordogne, this charming village was made famous by the shooting of Claude Chabrol's film *The Butcher*. It has a 12C Romanesque church which represents a condensed version of all the religious architectural features of the Périgord region.
In it, heavy fortifications are combined with a vaulting system which sets off the dome favourably. The massive belltower-keep and the high walls with buttresses pierced by narrow loop-holes make it every inch a fortress. The huge defensive chamber covering the whole of the interior was a refuge for the entire village.
Inside, the unusual nave is vaulted with a row of **three domes** resting on pendentives. A fourth, more graceful dome sits atop the transept crossing.
In the churchyard, the **Chapelle St-Hilaire** is a small Romanesque chapel reached by a lovely doorway, above which runs a modillioned cornice.
When you get to Trémolat head north on the road to the Trémolat Meander: "Route du Cingle de Trémolat".

Trémolat meander

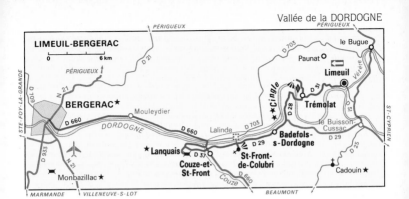

Vallée de la DORDOGNE

★★ Cingle de Trémolat (Trémolat Meander) — At the foot of a semicircle of high, bare, white cliffs highlighted by clumps of greenery, the river coils in a large loop, spanned by bridges of golden stone and reflecting lines of poplars. Beyond the wonderful stretch of water, which is often used for rowing regattas, on the convex bank lies a vast mosaic of arable fields and meadows; far away on the horizon, one can see the hills of Bergerac, Issigeac and Monpazier.

Return to Trémolat and cross the south bank of the Dordogne.

The valley is dotted with tobacco-drying sheds.

Badefols-sur-Dordogne — The village occupies a pleasant site beside the Dordogne. The country church stands close to the foot of the castle ruins perched on the cliff. This fortress served as the hide-out for the local thieves and robbers who used to ransack the *gabares* as they sailed downstream.

Chapelle St-Front-de-Colubri — Built in the 12C on top of a cliff overlooking the Dordogne, this chapel sheltered sailors who were venturing along the Saut de la Gratusse rapids. This passage was the most difficult of the river's middle section; specialised pilots were needed to guide sailors through it until the mid-19C, when the Lalinde canal was dug, enabling them to bypass it.

There is a marvellous **view★** of the valley and the rapids up-river.

Couze-et-St-Front — Located at the mouth of the small Couze valley, this active little town has specialised since the 16C in the manufacture of Dutch paper, which was sold as far away as Russia. It was the most important paper making centre in Aquitaine, and, at its peak, 13 mills were functioning. Only two mills remain from those prosperous times; at the **Larroque Mill** ⊙ one can see the making of filigreed paper using traditional methods.

Several old mills can be seen one after the other along the banks of the river Couze, along D 66 (south) over a distance of about 1km/0.6mi. On the top floor of these are large, window-like openings with wooden shutters; this was where the finished paper was unloaded.

★ Château de Lanquais ⊙ — The 14C and 15C main building, with all the defensive characteristics of a **fortified castle**, had a **Renaissance building** added to it during the Wars of Religion. In the courtyard, the elegant **façades★** are divided into vertical registers. Inside, two finely carved **chimneys★** are worth noting, as is the collection of flints.

Turn back, take D 37 on the left and cross the Dordogne once again.

The D 660 follows the wide alluvial valley down to Bergerac.

★ Bergerac — *See BERGERAC.*

La DOUBLE

Michelin map 75 folds 3, 4 and 5 or 233 folds 41 and 42

During the Tertiary Era waterways came down from the Massif Central spreading deposits of clay and sand which formed, notably, the Sologne, Brenne and Double regions.

The Double, in the west of the Périgord between the rivers Dronne to the north and Isle to the south, has a wild landscape of forest, sprinkled with lakes and dotted with half-timbered and clay houses.

Once a poor, desolate area; rife with fever, thieves and wolves, the landscape was transformed under the Second Empire (1852-70), when roads were built, lakes drained, soils improved and maritime pines planted. These pines, together with oak and chestnut trees, now constitute the major part of the forest cover.

The people of the Double region have always bred fish, draining the networks of lakes and reedy channels (these elongated ponds are called *nauves* in the local parlance) every other year to gather the fish for sale or consumption. More than half of the area is now overrun by the forest; the wood is used for timber and the area is a paradise for hunters. The rest of the land is devoted to medium-sized farms which concentrate on dairy farming and fattening up livestock.

FOREST, LAKES AND HALF-TIMBERED HOUSES
Round trip 80km/50mi from St-Astier – allow half a day

St-Astier – Lying on the banks of the river Isle, the old town centre contains a few remaining Renaissance houses. It is overlooked by the church, supported by massive buttresses, and a magnificent **belltower** adorned with two tiers of blind arcades. The cement works near the river Isle give the appearance of an industrial town.

D 43 carries the traveller out of St-Astier on steeply climbing hairpin-bends to reveal beautiful views of the town; then it plunges into the forest.

St-Aquilin – The church, built in a transitional Romanesque Gothic style, ends in a chancel with a flat east end.

Château du Bellet – The fine tiled roofs and massive round towers of this castle, built on the side of a hill, come into view on the right.
Nearby, the lake of Garennes has facilities for swimming and other recreation.

Château de la Martinie – This enormous 15C and Renaissance building, with a balustrade above the carriage gateway, has been converted into a farm.

Segonzac – The Romanesque church (11-12C) was altered and enlarged in the 16C. The **apse** is remarkable for its ribbed half-dome and the capitals with enormous, richly sculpted abaci on its blind arcades.

Return to D 43.

The road along the crest offers fine views of the Dronne valley and Ribérac area, the undulating countryside swathed in fields of grain, dotted with green groves.

Siorac-de-Ribérac – Overlooking a small valley, the fortified Romanesque **church** has a single nave roofed at the end with a dome.

Turn left on D 13, then right on D 44 towards St-Aulaye.

Creyssac – Surrounded by the waters of a small lake, the tall square dovecot and the hen houses tucked alongside it make a pleasant sight.

200m/220yd further on take the left fork towards Grand Étang de la Jemaye.

Grand Étang de la Jemaye – In the middle of Jemaye Forest, the lake has been set up as a water sports centre with a beach and facilities for fishing, windsurfing and a splashing good time.

St-André-de-Double – The small church with a lopsided tower-façade is built in local speckled sandstone.

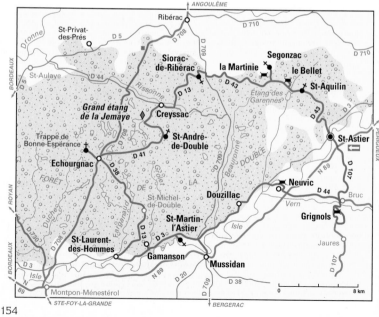

La Double – Grand étang de la Jemaye

Echourgnac – Not far from this village *(along D 38)* stands a **Trappist Monastery** (Trappe de Bonne-Espérance). The monastery was founded in 1868 by Trappist monks from Port-du-Salut in Normandy. They set up a model cheese-making farm, collecting milk from the neighbouring farms. Their "Trappe" cheese is very similar to Port Salut. The monks had to leave the monastery in 1910 and were replaced in 1923 by Trappist nuns, who continued the cheese-making industry.

Towards the south, D 38 takes a route through the forest, skirting a network of long narrow ponds. Local farms, visible in the clearings, are developing kiwi fruit orchards.

St-Laurent-des-Hommes – Opposite the Gothic church, the 17C half-timbered house with a decorated balcony is widely held to be the "prettiest house in the Double region".

Return towards St-Astier on D 3.

Gamanson – Set back slightly from the road, this hamlet constitutes the richest collection of traditional half-timbered and clay-walled houses of the Double region.

St-Martin-l'Astier – The unusual outline of the Romanesque **church** in the middle of the cemetery is right at the extremes of most Double architecture. The great octagonal belltower, its corners reinforced with buttressed columns, houses on ground level a **chancel**, also octagonal, which is covered by a dome supported on eight engaged columns. It is connected to a simple timber-frame nave by an opening in one of the panels of a narrow doorway. The nave leads to the outside through a porch with five arch mouldings.

Mussidan – This old Huguenot city on the banks of the river Isle was laid to siege on several occasions during the Wars of Religion. The siege in 1569, which was particularly bloody, inspired one of Montaigne's famous Essays *(L'heure des Parlements dangereuse)*.

Musée des Arts et Traditions Populaires du Périgord André-Voulgre ⊘ – Displayed in the lovely Périgord mansion where Doctor Voulgre lived, this collection is rich and varied; it includes furniture, objects and tools collected by the doctor during his lifetime.

A handsomely furnished 19C bourgeois interior – kitchen, dining room, drawing room, bedrooms – has been reproduced in several of the museum's rooms.

Workshops (cooper's shop, sabot maker, blacksmith) have also been re-

155

La DOUBLE

constituted. A collection of agricultural machinery and tools is set up in the barn: a 1927 steam engine, a still, a tractor (1920) built with the tracks of tanks used in World War I, and a reaper-binder.

In a large exhibition hall, brass, pewter, glazed earthenware (faïence) and stuffed and mounted animals are displayed.

Return to D 709 travelling towards Ribérac, then turn right on D 3 at St-Front-de-Pradoux.

Douzillac – A memorial has been built in honour of Corporal Louis Maine, one of the very few survivors of the memorable battle fought by the French Foreign Legion in Mexico in 1863.

Continue along D 3. After Neuvic-gare (station), turn right on D 44, which crosses the river Isle.

Château de Neuvic ⊘ – From D 44, go round the church and turn left at the cross. A walkway lined with trees leads to this handsome building on the left back of the river Isle; it is currently in use as a medical training centre.

ÉPINEUIL-LE-FLEURIEL

Population 478
Michelin map 69 fold 11 or 238 fold 43

Located on the edge of the region known as the Bourbonnais, Épineuil was the childhood home of author Alain-Fournier (1891-1898). Readers of his most famous work *Le Grand Meaulnes* will recognise the fictional Sainte-Agathe, where the story was set.

The novel (written in 1913, translated as *The Wanderer* in early editions and later as *The Lost Domain*), about the transition from the innocence of childhood to the excitement of adolescence, blends memory, dream, and reality. His work inspired many 20C writers dissatisfied with Realism and Naturalism, including Simone de Beauvoir, who said that his book had greatly influenced her. A consummate coming-of-age tale, *Meaulnes* portrays both the fresh intensity of youthful friendship, and a

Épineuil-le-Fleuriel – Alain-Fournier classroom

tingling sense of the imminent tragedy of adult love. He also paints a vibrant picture of rural France at the beginning of the 19C: ancient barns, rough and frosty roads, the wood stove in the schoolroom corner.

L'École du Grand Meaulnes ⊘ – The universe of the author, and of the young heroes of *Le Grand Meaulnes* is recreated here in the schoolhouse (a guided tour, in French, makes use of headphones), the town hall, and the schoolmaster's apartments. In one room, exhibits trace the author's life. Alain-Fournier is also remembered as a poet and a journalist. The author was killed in the First World War.

EYMET

Michelin map 75 fold 14 or 234 fold 8

On the border of the Bergerac and Agen regions, Eymet is a small Périgord town famous for its gourmet food factories which preserve goose and duck liver *(foie gras)*, *galantines* and *ballottines*, local specialities on view in the window of any shop selling cold-cuts worthy of the name *charcuterie*.

The bastide – Founded in 1271 by Alphonse de Poitiers, the bastide was ruled by several seigneurial families – even though it was granted a charter guaranteeing privileges and liberties – who were alternately in allegiance with the king of France and the king of England. Consequently, it had an eventful history during the Hundred Years War and the Wars of Religion. The ramparts were razed under Louis XIII.

Place Centrale – The arcaded square is lined with old half-timbered or stone houses, some of which have mullioned windows. In its centre is a 17C fountain.

Donjon (Keep) – This 14C tower is all that remains of the castle.
A small **museum** ⊘ has been set up inside and displays regional art and folklore (clothes, tools etc.) as well as prehistoric objects.

Les EYZIES-DE-TAYAC★★

Michelin map 75 folds 16 and 17 or 235 fold 1

The village of Les Eyzies occupies a grandiose setting of steep cliffs crowned with evergreen oaks and junipers, at the confluence of the Vézère and Beune rivers. The popular-lined Vézère river winds between meadows and farmland, sometimes narrowing to flow between sheer, vertical walls of rock 50 to 80m/164 to 262ft high. Shelters cut out of the limestone base served as dwelling places for prehistoric people; caves located higher up on the cliff face were used as sanctuaries. The discovery within the last 100 years of many such dwellings within a limited radius of Les Eyzies has earned the town the title "European capital of prehistory".

On the outskirts of town, on the road to Tursac, stands the old ironworks which bring to mind the town's and region's industrial past (from the Middle Ages to the Second Empire of 1852-70). Although the present buildings (warehouse and workers' accommodations) date from the 18C, the forge's origin goes back to the 16C, when its main livelihood came from supplying iron to the merchants of Bordeaux.

THE CAPITAL OF PREHISTORY

The lower Vézère in prehistory – During the Second Ice Age and at the time when the volcanoes of Auvergne were active, in the wake of the animals they hunted for food, prehistoric people abandoned the northern plains, where the Acheulean and Abbevillian civilisations had already evolved, and headed for the warmer areas of the south. The bed of the lower Vézère was then some 90 feet above its present level, and the river attracted the migrants because of its thick forests, its easily accessible natural caves and overhanging rocks, which could be hollowed out into shelters more easily than the cracked and crumbly limestone of the Dordogne valley.

People inhabited these cave dwellings for tens of thousands of years and left in them traces of their daily tasks and passage such as bones, ashes from their fires, tools, weapons, utensils and ornaments. As their civilisation evolved, so did animal species: after elephants and cave bears came bison, aurochs, mammoths and, later still, muskoxen, reindeer, ibex, stags and horses.

When the climate grew warmer and rainfall became more abundant at the end of the Magdalenian Period, our forebearers abandoned their rock shelters for the hillsides facing the sun.

The archeologists' paradise – Methodical study of the deposits in the Les Eyzies region has considerably increased our knowledge of prehistory (see Introduction, Prehistory). The Dordogne département has greatly contributed to the study of prehistory with more than 200 deposits discovered there, of which more than half are in the lower Vézère valley. In 1863 work began at the Laugerie and La Madeleine Deposits; the discovery of objects such as flints, carved bones and ivory, tombs (in which the skeletons had been coloured with ochre) greatly encouraged early research workers. In 1868 workmen levelling soil unearthed the skeletons of the Cro-Magnon shelter. Soon afterwards, more thorough research in Le Moustier and La Madeleine caves enabled two great periods of the Paleolithic Age to be defined: the periods were named after the cave deposits – Mousterian and Magdalenian. Discoveries followed thicker and faster as Les Eyzies proved to be one of the richest prehistoric sites in the world with its deposits: La Micoque, Upper Laugerie, Lower Laugerie, La Ferrassie (south of Savignac-de-Miremont), Laussel and the Pataud Shelter; with its shelters and caves containing hidden carvings and drawings: Le Cap Blanc, Le Poisson, La Mouthe, Les Combarelles, Bernifal and Commarque; caves containing polychrome wall paintings in Font-de-Gaume and Lascaux. The study of the engravings on bone, ivory and stone, as well as wall carvings and paintings has made it possible to begin to imagine the beliefs, rituals, way of life and artistic evolution of our Paleolithic ancestors.

SIGHTS

Les Eyzies

★**Musée National de la Préhistoire (National Museum of Prehistory)** ⊘ – The museum is in the old castle of the barons of Beynac. The 13C fortress, restored in the 16C, clings to the cliff half-way up, beneath a rocky outcrop, overlooking the village. From the terrace, there is a good view of Les Eyzies and the valleys of Vézère and Beune. Part of the rich collection of prehistoric objects and works of art discovered locally over the last eighty years is on display in two buildings, in connection with castings of tombs and equipment which have contributed to the fame of other important prehistoric sites. This display is completed by diagrams showing the chronology of prehistoric eras, sections of the earth's strata and photographs.

A gallery on the first floor is devoted to different stone-chipping techniques and a synthesis of prehistory. Prehistoric art is represented by wall paintings and rock carvings as well as domestic objects.

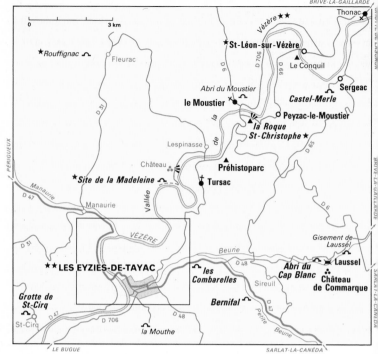

The second floor contains objects from all the prehistoric periods combined. The Breuil Gallery displays castings of prehistoric works of art from other museums. One gallery has assembled an impressive collection of carved limestone slabs dating from between 30 000 and 15 000 years BC and representing animals, female silhouettes and so on. Nearby ornaments made in stone, teeth or bone and weapons (spears, pierced bone implements, harpoons) are exhibited alongside castings of female figurines found in Europe.

On the top floor in a large gallery is a display explaining the evolution of flint knapping as far as 2.5 million years ago.

In another building the Magdalenian tomb of a woman from St-Germain-la-Rivière, complete with its skeleton and a skeleton from Roc de Marsal, has been reconstructed.

Abri de Cro-Magnon (Cro-Magnon Shelter) – This cave was discovered in 1868 and it revealed, in addition to flints and carved bones of the Aurignacian and Gravettian Cultures, three adult skeletons which were studied by Paul Broca, the surgeon and anthropologist who founded the School of Anthropology in France. The discoveries made in this cave were of prime importance for prehistoric studies, since they enabled the characteristics of Cro-Magnon individuals to be defined.

★**Grotte de Font-de-Gaume** ⊙ – *Leave the car by the road to St-Cyprien opposite a cliff-spur. A path takes you up 400m/440yd to the cave entrance.*

The cave runs back in the form of a passage 120m/130yd long with chambers and other ramifications leading off it. The cave has been public knowledge for some time, and since the 18C, visitors have regrettably left their mark, not recognising the importance of the wall paintings. Detailed examination and study of the paintings date them as belonging to the Magdalenian Period. Beyond a narrow passage, known as the Rubicon, are many multi-coloured paintings, often superimposed on one another; all the drawings of horses, bison, mammoths, reindeer and other deer indicate great artistic skill and, after Lascaux, form the finest group of polychrome paintings in France. The frieze of bison, painted in brown on a white calcite background, is remarkable *(see illustration in Introduction, Prehistoric art)*.

Abri Pataud (Pataud Shelter) ⊘ – A museum on site shows objects and bones discovered during excavation work, and a video recording introduces visitors to the tour of the Pataud shelter. This is in fact a cavity 90m by 15m/295ft by 49ft, in which a 9m/30ft deep mound conceals the remains of civilisations dating from the beginning of the Upper Paleolithic Era (Aurignacian, Gravettian and Solutrean) between 35 000 and 20 000 years BC. In two large stratigraphic sections, bones, flints and the remains of fireplaces can be seen in place, as well as a carved Venus in the most recent Gravettian layer. A three-minute film projected onto the rock face portrays a deer-hunters' camp from 25 000 years ago.

Rocher de la Peine – This great rock, worn jagged by erosion, partially overhangs the road. A Magdalenian deposit was discovered within it.

Église de Tayac ⊘ – The warm, gold-coloured stone enhances this 12C fortified church. Two towers roofed with *lauzes* frame the main body of the church. The tower above the doorway serves as the belltower.
The doorway is intriguing; the first scalloped arch gives it an Eastern air while the two outermost columns, with Corinthian capitals of white marble, show Gallo-Roman influence.
Inside, the arrangement of the three naves, divided by large arcades resting on piers, and the timberwork ceiling are features rarely found in the Périgord.

Along the D 47

Musée de la Spéléologie (Museum of Speleology) ⊘ – The museum is installed in the rock fortress of Tayac, which overlooks the Vézère valley. The four chambers, cut out of the living rock, contain a selection of items pertaining to speleology: caving equipment, exhibits describing the geological formations and plant and animal life in local caves as well as several models.

Abri du Poisson (The Fish Shelter) ⊘ – A 1.05m/3.3ft long fish has been carved on the roof of a small hollow *(see illustration in Introduction, Prehistoric art)*. It is a species of salmon which was very common in the Vézère until quite recently. It dates from the Gravettian Period (about 20 000 years BC), and, with the Laussel Venus, it is the oldest cave sculpture yet discovered.

★★**Grotte du Grand Roc (Grand Roc Cave)** ⊘ – There is a good **view**★ of the Vézère valley from the stairs leading up to the cave and the platform at its mouth. The length (40m/45yd) of tunnel enables one to see, within chambers that are generally small in size, an extraordinary display of stalactites, stalagmites and eccentrics resembling coral formations, as well as a wonderful variety of pendants and crystals.

Les Eyzies – Aerial view

Gisement de Laugerie Haute (Upper Laugerie Deposit) ◯ – Scientific excavations going on for over a century in a picturesque spot at the foot of high cliffs have revealed examples of the work and art of prehistoric people at different stages of civilisation. The excavations begun in 1863 were subsequently conducted in phases: 1911, 1921, 1936-39 and more recently as well. The work has demonstrated the importance of this area, inhabited continuously from the middle of the Perigordian to the middle of the Magdalenian Period; that is to say, during the 25 000 years of the Upper Paleolithic Age.

The establishment of a time line startles the imagination, clearly illustrating the painfully slow progress of the human race through these millennia. Two skeletons have been discovered beneath masses of fallen earth in the western part of the deposits. Note the drip stones or channels cut in the rock in the Middle Ages to prevent water from running along the walls and entering the dwellings.

Habitats Préhistoriques de Laugerie Basse (Lower Laugerie Deposit) ◯ – Prehistoric bones, stone tools and other artefacts were discovered in this deposit, downstream from the Upper Laugerie Deposit. They are in various museums and private collections, but an exhibition centre here contains reproductions of the best of them.

Gisement de la Micoque (La Micoque Deposit) – This deposit revealed many items belonging to periods known as the Tayacian and Micoquian Ages, which fall between the end of the Acheulean and the beginning of the Mousterian Ages. The finds are exhibited at Les Eyzies National Museum of Prehistory.

Along the Vézère River

The sights are described from north to south.

Castel-Merle – *See Vallée de la VÉZÈRE.*

Le Moustier – This village, at the foot of a hill, contains a famous prehistoric shelter (**Abri du Moustier**). The prehistoric finds made here include a human skeleton and many flint implements. A culture in the Middle Paleolithic Age was named Mousterian after the finds.

An interesting 17C carved confessional can be seen in the village church.

★**La Roque St-Christophe** (St Christopher's Rock) ◯ – For more than 900m/0.5mi, this long and majestic cliff rises vertically (80m/262ft) above the Vézère valley. It is like a huge hive with about 100 caves hollowed out of the rock on five tiers. Excavations are underway along its foot, proving that the cliff dwellings were inhabited from the Upper Paleolithic Age onwards.

In the 10C the cliff terraces served as the foundation for a fortress which was used against the Vikings and during the Hundred Years War, and then subsequently destroyed during the Wars of Religion, at the end of 16C. The many holes for posts, the drainage channels and water tanks, the fireplaces, the stairways and passages hollowed out of the rock all show that St Christopher's Rock was the site of continued, lively human activity. From the Pas du Miroir, it was once possible to see one's reflection in the Vézère, for the river at one time flowed at the foot (30m/99ft below) of the cliff.

From the terrace, admire the **view**★ of the green Vézère valley, the river flowing along a straight course.

Tursac Préhistoparc – In a small cliff-lined valley, carpeted with undergrowth, a discovery trail reveals about twenty reconstituted scenes of Neanderthal and Cro-Magnon daily life: mammoth hunting, cutting-up of reindeer, cave painting, burial customs etc.

Tursac church is dominated by a huge, forbidding bell-tower. There is a series of domes, characteristic of the Romanesque Périgord style, covering the church.

The road once more scales the cliff, giving good views of Tursac village and the Vézère valley.

Tursac Préhistoparc

Beune Valley

Grotte des Combarelles ◯ – A winding passage 250m/275yd long has many markings on its walls for the last 130m/140yd of its length, some of which are superimposed one upon another. The drawings include nearly 300 animals: horses, bison, bears, reindeer and mammoths can be seen at rest or in full gallop.

This cave was discovered in 1901 at about the same time as Font-de-Gaume Cave and demonstrated the importance of Magdalenian art at a time when some scholars were still sceptical about the worth of prehistoric studies.

A second passage with similar cave drawings shows traces of domestic settlement and the tools of Magdalenian inhabitants.

Grotte de Bernifal ⊙ – *10min on foot*
Cave paintings and delicate carvings from the Magdalenian period are spread over about 100m/330ft. They include mammoths, donkey-like figures and shapes suggesting dwellings.

Abri du Cap-Blanc (Cap-Blanc Shelter) ⊙ – Excavation of a small Magdalenian deposit in 1909 led to the discovery of **carvings★** in high relief on the walls of the rock shelter *(see illustration in Introduction, Prehistoric art)*. Two bison and in particular a frieze of horses were carved in such a way as to use to full advantage the relief and contour of the rock itself. A human grave was discovered at the foot of the frieze.

Château de Commarque – The impressive castle ruins on the south bank of the Beune river stand opposite Château de Laussel. Commarque was built as a stronghold in the 12C and 13C and for a long time it belonged to the Beynac family. As a result of treachery, it fell into English hands, but was later retaken by the lord of Périgord, who then returned it to the baron of Beynac. Considerable parts of the fortifications are still standing. The keep, crowned with machicolations, the chapel and the various living quarters are set amid a mass of greenery, a romantic scene.

Château de Laussel – This 15-16C château (redesigned in the 19C) is perched on a cliff which drops precipitously into the Beune valley. The building is small but elegant.

A few hundred yards further along the valley a large prehistoric deposit **(Gisement de Laussel)** was discovered, which contained several human-like forms in low relief and a Venus with the horn of plenty from the Gravettian Culture; this is now exhibited in the Aquitaine Museum in Bordeaux.

FIGEAC★★

Population 9 549
Michelin map 79 fold 10 or 235 fold 11
Local maps see Vallée du CÉLÉ and Basse Vallée du LOT

Sprawled along the north bank of the Célé, Figeac's development began at the point where the Auvergne meets Upper Quercy. A commercial town, it had a prestigious past as is shown in the architecture of its tall sandstone town houses.

The small city's main industrial concern is Ratier, a company which specialises in aeronautical construction.

From abbots to king – Figeac began developing in the 9C around a monastery, which itself began expanding in the 11C and 12C.

The abbot was the town's lord and governed it with the aid of seven consuls. All administrative services were located inside the monastery. Because Figeac was on the pilgrimage route running from Le Puy and Conques and on to Santiago de Compostela, crowds of pilgrims and travellers flocked through it.

Benefiting from the town's geographical situation between Auvergne, Quercy and Rouergue, local craftsmen and shopkeepers were prosperous.

In 1302, following a disagreement between the abbot and the consuls, Philip the Fair took control of the town, represented by a provost. He won back the inhabitants' favour by allowing them the rare privilege of minting money.

The Hundred Years War and the Wars of Religion had an adverse effect on the town's development. From 1598 to 1622 Figeac was a safe stronghold for the Calvinists, until Richelieu broke their fortifications up.

Jean-François Champollion – Champollion, the outstanding Orientalist, whose brilliance enabled Egyptology to make such great strides, was born at Figeac in December 1790. At the beginning of the 19C, Ancient Egyptian civilisation was still a mystery, since the meaning of hieroglyphics (the word means "sacred carving") had not yet been deciphered.

By the time Champollion was 14, he had a command of Greek, Latin, Hebrew, Arabic, Chaldean and Syrian. After his studies in Paris, he lectured in history, at the youthful age of 19, at Grenoble University.

He set himself the task of deciphering a polished basalt tablet, showing three different inscriptions (Egyptian hieroglyphics, demotic – simplified Egyptian script which appeared around 650 BC – and Greek), which had been discovered in 1799 by members of Napoleon's expedition to Egypt near Rosetta in the northwest Nile delta, from which it derives its name – the Rosetta Stone.

FIGEAC

However he was not able to carry out his research on the stone itself, which had been seized by the English while at war with France (it is now in the British Museum, London), but had to make do with copies. Drawing on the work of a predecessor, the English physicist Thomas Young (1773-1829), who had succeeded in identifying genders and proper nouns, Champollion gradually unravelled the mystery of hieroglyphics.

He was harassed for his Bonapartist views during the Restoration, and for several years progress with his work was slow; then in 1822, by illustrating that hieroglyphics are "a complex system of writing which is at once figurative, symbolic and phonetic", he hit upon the essential discovery that, while the Egyptians used their signs as letters for proper names, these same signs could be used to represent ideas, words and syllables the rest of the time.

Champollion left for Egypt to put his theory to the test and deciphered many texts while he was there.

In 1826, he founded the Egyptology Museum at the Louvre Palace, Paris, and became its first curator. In 1831, he was appointed professor of Archeology at the Collège de France, however he gave only three lecture courses before dying a year later, worn out by all his hard work.

★OLD FIGEAC 1hr30min

The old quarter, surrounded by boulevards which trace the line of the former moats, has kept its medieval town plan with its narrow, twisting alleys.

The buildings, built in elegant beige sandstone, exemplify the architecture of the 13C, 14C and 15C. Generally the ground floor was opened by large pointed arches and the first floor had a gallery of arcaded bays. Underneath the flat tiled roof was

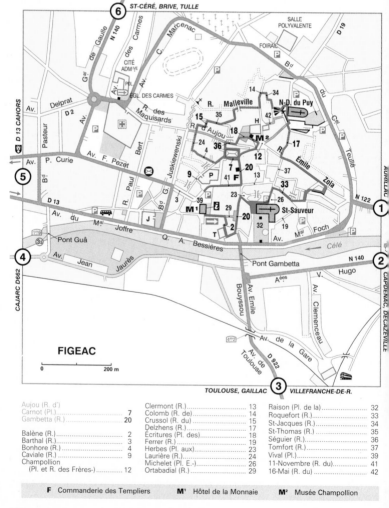

F Commanderie des Templiers   **M¹** Hôtel de la Monnaie   **M²** Musée Champollion

the *soleilho*, an open attic, which was used to dry laundry, store wood, grow plants etc. Its openings were separated by columns or pillars in wood or stone, sometimes even brick, which held the roof up.

★ **Hôtel de la Monnaie (Mint) (M¹)** – *Tourist information centre*
This late 13C building, restored in the early 20C, exemplifies Figeac's secular architecture with its *soleilho*, pointed arches on the ground floor and the depressed arched windows placed either singly, paired or grouped in the façade *(illustration page 38)*. It is interesting to compare the façade, overlooking the square, which was rebuilt with the elements of the former consul's house of the same period, with the other plainer façades. The octagonal stone chimney was characteristic of Figeac construction at one time, but very few examples remain.
The name *Oustal dé lo Mounédo* owes its name to the Royal Mint created in Figeac by Philip the Fair. It has since been established that the stamping workshop was located in another building and that this handsome edifice was the place where money was exchanged.
The Mint contains a **museum** ⊙ which includes sculpture from religious and secular buildings (the door of the Hôtel de Sully), sarcophagi, grain measurements, old coins and town seals originating from the period when the town had its seven consuls.
Take rue Orthabadial and turn right on rue Balène.

Rue Balène (2) – At no 7 stands the 14C Balène Castle (Château de Balène), which houses the community hall. Its medieval fortress-like façade is lightened by an ogive doorway and chapel windows with decorated tracery. Exhibitions are held in ogive vaulted rooms.
At no 1, the 15C Hôtel d'Auglanat, which housed one of the king's provosts, is decorated with a lovely basket-arched doorway and castellated turret.

Rue Gambetta (20) – This is the old town's main street. The houses at nos 25 and 28 are half-timbered, with decorative brickwork, and have been beautifully restored.
Continue via rue Gambetta and place aux Herbes to place Edmond-Michelet.

St-Sauveur – This used to be an abbey church, the oldest parts of which date from the 11C. It has kept its original cross plan: a high nave with 14C chapels off the aisles. The nave is unusual for the lack of symmetry between its north and south sides. The south side includes: in the lowest section, rounded arcades; in the middle section, a tribune with twinned bays within a larger arch; and in the upper section, 14C clerestory windows.
On the north side, rebuilt in the 17C (as was the vaulting), the tribune was destroyed during the Wars of Religion.
The chancel, surrounded by the ambulatory, was rebuilt in the 18C. Four Romanesque capitals, remnants of the earlier doorway, support the baptismal font.

★ **Notre-Dame-de-Pitié** – This former chapter-house became a place of worship after the departure of the Protestants in 1623. A sumptuous carved and painted **wooden décor★** was added to it, apparently the work of the Delclaux, a family of master painters from Figeac. To the right of the altar there is a striking panel depicting the infant Jesus asleep on the cross, dreaming of his future Passion.
Between the church and the Célé river is the place de la Raison, on the site of the community buildings which were destroyed in the Revolution. The main feature of this square is the obelisk dedicated to Champollion.

Rue du Roquefort (33) – The house with the bartizan on a carved corbel belonged to Galiot de Genouillac, Grand Master of the Artillery of François I.

Rue É.-Zola – The oldest street in the town still has ogival arcades and an interesting sequence of Renaissance doorways from nos 35-37.

Rue Delzhens (17) – At no 3, the Provost's House (Hôtel du Viguier) has a square keep and a watch turret. Restoration is currently underway to convert it into a hotel.

Église Notre-Dame-du-Puy – The church is on a hill which gives a good view of the town and its surroundings. The Protestants used it as a fortress, strengthening the façade with a watch room.
This Romanesque building underwent many alterations between the 14C and the 17C; it has an enormous altarpiece carved in walnut dating from the end of the 17C, which frames two pictures representing the Assumption and the Coronation of the Virgin.
Go back down the hill along ruelle St-Jacques, a narrow lane.

Rue Malleville – This road is blocked by a covered passageway painted with the coat of arms of the Hôtel de la Porte.

Rue St-Thomas (35) – This also passes under a covered passageway, featuring corbelled galleries under the eaves *(soleilhos)*.

Rue du Crussol (15) – The courtyard of the 16C Hôtel de Crussol, now a terrace-bar, is decorated with two superimposed balconies.

Take rue Laurière then rue Bonhore to get to place Carnot. At the far end of rue Caviale, opposite no 35 (l'Hôtel d'Ay-de-Lostanges), is the **Maison du Roi**, so-called because Louis XI is supposed to have stayed there in 1463.

Place Carnot (7) – Formerly place Basse, this was headquarters to the wheat exchange, which was closed down in 1888. In the north-west corner, with a small side turret, is the house of Pierre de Cisteron, Louis XIV's armourer.

From place Carnot, after crossing the narrow, medieval-looking rue Séguier (36), go through a porch to get to place des Écritures.

★**Place des Écritures (18)** – Surrounded by medieval buildings, this square has an enormous (14m by 7m/46ft by 23ft) replica of the Rosetta Stone underfoot. This was sculpted in black granite from Zimbabwe by the American conceptual

Place des Écritures, Figeac

artist Joseph Kossuth. Unveiled in 1991, this significant contemporary work of art is more clearly understood from the hanging gardens overlooking the square. The French translation of the inscriptions is carved on a glass plaque kept in a small neighbouring courtyard. An archway gives access to the Champollion Museum.

★**Musée Champollion** ⊙ (**M²**) – A collection of documents in Champollion's birthplace traces the life history of this local hero, while original objects or reproductions evoke the use of Egyptian writing and the rites and customs of Ancient Egypt. On the first floor the Salle de l'Écriture displays in particular a casting of the Rosetta Stone, the original being in the British Museum in London, also carved steles, a large statuette in black granite of the architect Djehouty (15 BC) and a scribe's palette (an essential writing tool which was included in the mortuary equipment). On the second floor, striking exhibits include a mummy and various sarcophagi from the Thebes necropolis, canopic burial jars, one of which still contains the deceased person's entrails, an offertory table carved with images of food (it was believed that such images would be transformed into solid objects) and two pieces of porcelain; a mummy's costume decoration and the splendid bust of a worker, in a vivid blue underlain with black.

Place Champollion (12) – The 14C infirmary of the Knights Templars has beautiful Gothic windows on the second floor.

Return along rue Gambetta.

Commandery of the Knights Templars ⊙ (**F**) – *No 41 rue Gambetta*
Around 1187 the Order of the Knights Templars, which was expanding rapidly, came to establish itself at Figeac. It built this commandery, and the Gothic façade certainly brightens up rue Gambetta. In the 15C, another building closed off the elegant courtyard. A remarkable 15C wooden staircase leads to the first floor where the guard room, the chapter-house and the chapel are to be found. The latter are connected by oratory hatches. On the second floor a restored wooden balcony links the monks' dormitory with the commander's residence in which there is also a private chapel. The watchtower at the top of the building has had a 15C timber frame added to it.

EXCURSIONS

Domaine du Surgié ⊙ – This large leisure centre (14ha/35 acres) is situated northeast of Figeac, on the banks of the Célé river.

Aiguilles de Figeac – These two octagonal-shaped obelisks to the south and west of the town measure (base included) respectively 14.50m/47ft and 11.50m/38ft. It is believed that there were four "needles" and that they marked the boundaries of the land over which the Benedictine abbey had jurisdiction.
One of the needles – **Aiguille du Cingle**, (the "meander needle"), also known as Aiguille du Pressoir – can also be seen from D 922, south of Figeac.

Cardaillac – *11km/7mi northwest of town. Leave Figeac by ⑥ travelling westward on N 140 and then take D 15 to the right.*
This town is the home territory of the Cardaillacs, one of the most powerful Quercy families.
The section with the fort stands on a rocky spur above the town. Of this triangular-shaped fortification, dating from the 12C, there remain two square towers: the Clock or Baron's Tower and Sagnes Tower. Only the latter is open to visitors. The two tall rooms with their vaulted ceilings are reached by a spiral staircase. From the platform there is a lovely view of the Drauzou valley and the surrounding countryside.

Musée Éclaté ⊙ – This museum consists of several different sites scattered *(éclaté)* around the village in a determined effort to integrate evidence of the past firmly into the modern life of the village. Exhibits represent the village school, local crafts and the rural way of life. A study of the manufacture of wine-growers' baskets, once a speciality of Cardaillac, is given pride of place.

Grottes de FOISSAC★

Michelin map 79 fold 10 or 235 folds 11 and 15
13km/8mi south of Figeac

Discovered in 1959, Foissac Caves have a total of 8km/5mi of galleries. An underground stream, which drains the caves, is a tributary of the Lot, joining it near Balaguier.

TOUR ⊙

During the visit note the gleaming white stalactites and the lovely rock formations in the Obelisk Chamber (Salle de l'Obélisque); and the reflections, the stalagmites and ivory tower-like formations in the Michel Roques Gallery. In one gallery, known as the "Cave-in Gallery" *(Salle de l'Éboulement)*, there is a roof covered with round mushroom-like formations, thus proving that the stalactites were in the gallery well before earthquakes changed the aspect of the cave. These bulbous stalactites known as "the onions" *(Oignons)* are also worth noting.
These caves were inhabited during the Copper Age (2700-1900 BC), when they were used as quarries, caves and a cemetery, as evidenced throughout: the "hearth", copper utensils and large rounded pieces of pottery. Also visible are human skeletons, some of which are accompanied by offerings suggesting some sort of ritual burial, and the imprint of a child's foot, fixed here in the clay 4000 years ago.

EXCURSION

Château de Larroque-Toirac ⊙ – This 12C fortress belonged to the Cardaillac family, partisans of Quércy in the Hundred Years War. It went back and forth between English and French hands, until finally it was burned to the ground at the end of the 14C, later to be resurrected from the ruins by Louis XI. Within, there are Romanesque and Gothic elements to be admired, as well as furnishings from Louis XIII (early 17C) through the Directoire style (late 18C).

For a quiet place to stay
*Consult the annual **Michelin Red Guide France**, which offers a selection*
of pleasant and quiet hotels in a convenient location.

GIMEL-LES-CASCADES★

Population 566
Michelin map 75 fold 9 or 239 fold 27

Gimel stands in a remarkable **setting**★, one of the most picturesque of the Bas-Limousin, near Tulle and the Corrèze valley. The Montane flows over the tumbling rocks of a wild ravine and hurls itself down waterfalls 140m/460ft high.

★★The Cascades ⊙ – *1hr round trip on foot (requires stamina)*
Follow the marked pathway through the Vuillier Park (the entrance is located just beyond the bridge, downhill from the church).

The walk to the falls provides the opportunity to have a good look at them. The *Grande Cascade* (also known as the *Grand Saut*) tumbles down 45m/145ft; the next falls, *la Redole*, is 27m/90ft high. The two cascades one above the other are an impressive sight. The third one, with its amusing name of *Queue de Cheval* ("Pony Tail"), appears suddenly, spouting from a little rocky promontory; it plunges 60m/200ft into the deep ravine of "Hell's Swallow Hole" *(le Gouffre du l'Inferno)*.

Church – The most interesting furnishings are the 18C pulpit, a 15C Pietà, and the Treasure.

★Trésor – The **Shrine of St Stephen★★**, a decorative chest from the late 12C, is embellished with Limoges enamels, the figures are in relief, with eyes of precious stones. The iconography represents the stoning of St Stephen, three angels with wings unfurled, Peter, Matthew, Mark and Andrew. The silver-gilt reliquary bust is a 14C homage to St Dumaines, a soldier from Clovis' army who retreated to the Montane Ravines as a hermit; note the 14C champlevé enamel pyx (receptacle for the Eucharist) and a 13C gilded copper monstrance (vessel in which the consecrated host is exposed for veneration).

EXCURSION

▶ ▶ **Château de Sédières**
ⓥ – This elegant Renaissance château stands in a pleasant setting near a waterfall.

"Pony Tail" Falls

GOURDON★

Population 4 851
Michelin map 75 fold 18 or 235 fold 6

Gourdon is the capital of the green undulating countryside called Bouriane. The town, situated on the borders of Quercy and Périgord, is arranged in tiers up the flank of a rocky hillock, upon which the local lord's castle once stood. Follow the circular route of avenues which have replaced the old ramparts for pleasant views of the hills and valleys of Bouriane.

SIGHTS

★Rue du Majou – The fortified gateway, Porte du Majou, and, on the left, the chapel of Notre-Dame-du-Majou lead to the street of the same name. This picturesque and narrow street was once the high street; all along it there are old houses with overhanging storeys and ground floors with large pointed arches. Just after no. 24, there is a good view, to the right, of the old-fashioned rue Zig-Zag. No. 17, Anglars Mansion, has pretty mullioned windows.

Hôtel de Ville (Town Hall) (H) – This former 13C consulate, enlarged in the 17C, has covered arcades which are used as a covered market.

Église St-Pierre – The church (dedicated to St Peter) was begun in the early 14C and used to be a dependency of Le Vigan Abbey *(see Excursions below)*. The chancel is supported by massive buttresses. The door in the west face is decorated

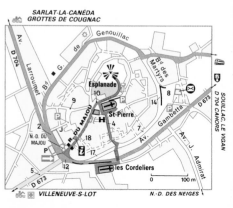

with elegant archivolts and is framed by two tall asymmetrical towers. The large rose window is protected by a line of machicolations, a reminder of former fortifications. The vast nave has pointed vaulting; 17C wood panels, carved, painted and gilded, decorate the chancel and the south transept.

Go round the left of the church outside and go up the staircase and then the ramp, which leads to the esplanade where the castle once stood.

Esplanade – A panorama★unfolds from the terrace *(viewing table)*: beyond the town and its roofs, which can be seen in tiers below the massive roof of the church (St-Pierre) in the foreground, one can see the churchyard, a forest of cypress trees, then the plateaux stretching out around the valleys of the Dordogne and the Céou.

Return to place de l'Hôtel de Ville and go round the outside of the church starting from the right.

There are some old houses opposite the east end, including one with a lovely early-17C doorway. Opposite the south door of the church take rue Cardinal-Farinié which goes downhill and contains old houses with mullioned windows and side turrets. This will bring you back to place de la Libération.

Église des Cordeliers ⊙ – The church which used to be part of the Franciscan monastery is worth a visit, despite being slightly marred by a massive belfry porch which was added in the 19C. The slender lines of the nave, restored in 1971, are characteristic of early Gothic; the fine seven-sided apse is lit by 19C stained-glass windows. At the entrance, in the middle of the nave, stands a remarkable **baptismal font**★. On the outside Christ the King and the twelve Apostles (14C) are depicted on the thirteen trefoiled blind arcades.

EXCURSIONS

★**Grottes de Cougnac** – *3km/2mi north on D 70*
These caves are fascinating for two reasons: their natural rock formations and their Paleolithic paintings similar to those of Pech-Merle.

Tour ⊙ – The caves, consisting of two chasms about 200m/300yd apart, spread their network of galleries beneath a limestone plateau.
The first cave consists of three small chambers; closely packed and sometimes extremely delicate stalactites hang in profusion.
The second cave is bigger and has two remarkable chambers: the **Pillar Chamber**★ (Salle des Colonnes) is made particularly striking by the perspectives offered by columns reaching from floor to ceiling, and the **Hall of Prehistoric Paintings** (Salle des Peintures Préhistoriques) contains designs in ochre and black featuring deer, mammoths and human figures.

Chapelle de Notre-Dame-des-Neiges ⊙ – *1.5km/1mi to the southeast*
Set in the small valley of the Bléou, this 14C chapel, a pilgrimage centre which was restored in the 17C, has a 17C altarpiece. A "miraculous spring" flows through the chancel.

Le Vigan – *5km/3mi east on D 673*
A Gothic **church** ⊙, all that remains of an abbey founded in the 11C, became a regular chapter for canons in the 14C. The church's east end is overlooked by a tower rising from the transept crossing. There is fine pointed vaulting over the nave and the spectacular east end, in which defensive turrets are tucked in between the apsidal chapels.

Musée Henri-Giron ⊙ – *Follow signs to Les Prades.*
The museum's collection includes about forty of this Belgian painter's works. His style reflects a classic heritage and Flemish influence, all the while integrating remarkably modern subjects, including some unsettling interpretations of feminine forms.

Causse de GRAMAT★

Michelin map 75 folds 18, 19 and 79 folds 8 and 9 or 235 folds 6, 7, 10 and 14

The Gramat Causse, which stretches from the Dordogne valley in the north to the Lot and Célé valleys in the south, is the largest – and wildest – *causse* in Quercy. It is a vast limestone plateau which lies at an average altitude of 350m/1 148ft and contains a variety of natural phenomena and unusual landscapes.

Autumn is the time to cross the *causse*, when the trees are donning their seasonal colours and shedding a golden light on the grey stones and rocks, with the maples adding a splash of deep red.

OUTING ON THE CAUSSE

Route from Cahors to Souillac – 140km/87mi – allow one day

★★**Cahors** – *See CAHORS.*
The road (D 653) runs along the north bank of the Lot, past **Laroque-des-Arcs** and **Notre-Dame-de-Vêles Chapel** *(see Basse Vallée du LOT)*, and then climbs the charming Vers valley, which in some places widens out into meadowland and in others cuts between tall grey cliffs.

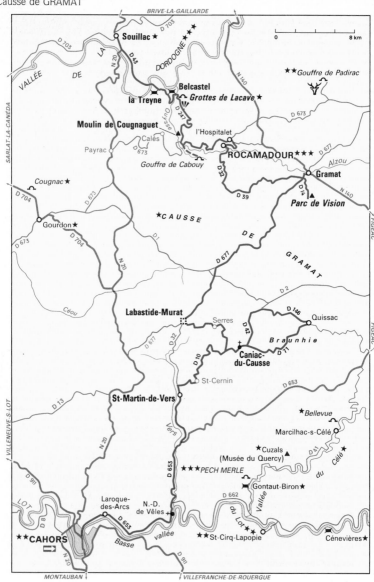

St-Martin-de-Vers – In this small village the houses with brown-tiled roofs cluster round the old priory church and its asymmetrical belltower.

Take D 10 and D 71 to arrive at the Braunhie "desert", the most arid part of the plateau.

Here, dry-stone walls seem to stretch forever into the distance, and the scrubby vegetation includes oaks, maples and stunted walnut trees, or stony heath with junipers and thorn bushes.

To get the most out of this region, continue along D 71 to Quissac, and then back to Caniac-du-Causse on D 146 and D 42.

Old sheep and goat tracks have been cleared and now offer tempting opportunities to stroll around and discover the various nooks and crannies caused by water infiltrating the limestone *(see Introduction: Caves and Chasms)*. Besides attractive farmhouses, the village of Quissac has conserved its *travail à bœufs*, a farrier's sling used for shoeing oxen, at one time common throughout the communities of the plateau.

Caniac-du-Causse – Beneath the church, the crypt was built by the monks of Marcilhac-sur-Célé in the 12C to shelter the relic of St Namphaise, an officer in the army of Charlemagne who became a hermit and whom the inhabitants of Braunhie held in great esteem. He was supposed to have hewn the so-called "St Namphaise's lakes" out of the rocks himself; the sight of these underlines the aridity of the area. This diminutive crypt has an unusual vault and an attractive central colonnade.

Labastide-Murat – *See LABASTIDE-MURAT.*

Beyond Labastide-Murat, D 677 crosses the east side of the *causse* and then wends its way down to Gramat.

Just before the Gramat railway station turn right and take D 14 for 1km/0.5 mile.

Parc animalier de Gramat ⊘ – This nature park extends over 38ha/94 acres. It was acquired by the local authorities so that animals and plants could be observed in their natural environment.

A botanical park is home to trees and shrubs from the *causse* (durmast oak, dogwood, ash etc).

The animal park contains mainly European species living in semi-captivity in their natural habitat. Some of these animals – wild oxen, Przewalski's horses, ibexes, bison – are species which existed during prehistoric times.

A collection of farmyard animals includes a variety of domestic fowl, pigs etc.

Follow the signposted itinerary over 3km/2mi for an enjoyable and informative outing.

Take D 677 which leads to Gramat.

Gramat – Capital of the *causse* that bears its name, Gramat is also a busy commercial centre attracting agricultural fairs.

It is the ideal starting point for visits to Padirac, Rocamadour and the area that lies between the Lot and the Dordogne.

It was here that the French **Centre de formation des maîtres de chien de la Gendarmerie** (Police Dog Handler Training Centre) was established in 1945.

Causse de Gramat – Sheep at pasture

Roulland/IMAGES TOULOUSE

Return to D 677 and almost immediately take D 39 to the right; at the point where it joins D 32, turn right.

The D 32 reaches the edge of the plateau from where there are lovely **views** of Rocamadour, before it crosses Alzou Canyon. Enter Rocamadour by the narrow ogive gateways.

★★★ **Rocamadour** – *See ROCAMADOUR.*

L'Hospitalet – *See ROCAMADOUR: L'HOSPITALET.*

At L'Hospitalet join D 673 towards Calès.

The pleasant road drops down through the deep Alzou and Ouysse valleys. The GR 6 rambling trail below, a wide, well-maintained track, makes an easy walk *(1hr round trip)* along the meanders of the river as far as the yawning **Cabourg chasm**, resurgence of the river Ouysse.

Moulin de Cougnaguet ⊘ – The rounded arches of this fortified mill span a derivation of the Ouysse in a cool, lush and charming **setting**. The mill was built in the 15C at the foot of a sheer cliff, on the site of a mill to which the water rights were granted in 1279. In the Middle Ages grain and flour, both highly sought-after commodities, needed to be particularly well-defended, as is illustrated by the impressive defence system here. The opening of the sluice gates hurled assailants to a watery fate. The mill has four millstones; one of which is still in working order.

Continue along the small road which climbs up to D 247 and turn left.

There are splendid **views**★ along this road of the Dordogne valley and of Belcastel Castle at its most attractive.

★**Grottes de Lacave** ⊘ – *See Vallée de la DORDOGNE.*

Take D 43 on the left, and follow it past the foot of Belcastel Castle.

Belcastel Castle – *See Vallée de la DORDOGNE.*

Château de la Treyne – *See Vallée de la DORDOGNE.*

Beyond Château de là Treyne the road cuts across a bend in the Dordogne before reaching Souillac.

★**Souillac** – *See SOUILLAC.*

GUÉRET

Population 14706
Michelin map 72 fold 9 or 239 fold 3

Guéret grew up near the Creuse valley, on a plateau which stretches to the Chabrières forest. The town developed around a monastery founded there in the 8C by a count from Limoges, in a place known as Garactus, at the foot of a hill called Grandcheix. In the 13C, Guéret became the capital of the county of La Marche, and has been an administrative centre ever since.

Musée de la Sénatorerie ⊘ (Z M¹) – The museum is in a fine 18C classical building surrounded by a large flower garden. On the ground floor there is a collection of local archeological finds and sculpture from the 19C and early 20C (accompanied by a collection of dolls); also a collection of stuffed and mounted animals. In the armoury, swords and scimitars are displayed side by side with pistols and blunderbusses.

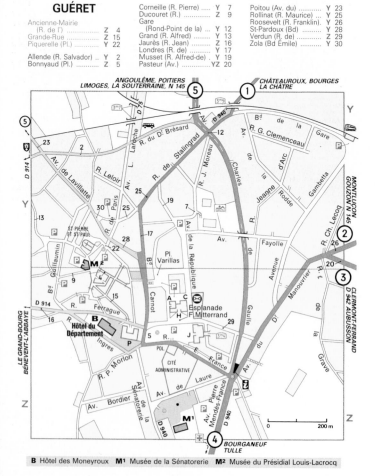

B Hôtel des Moneyroux   **M¹** Musée de la Sénatorerie   **M²** Musée du Présidial Louis-Lacrocq

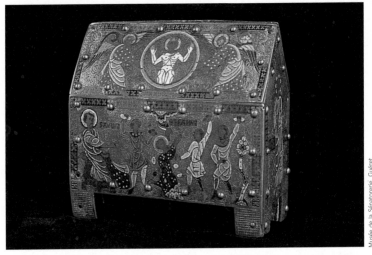

Guéret – Musée de la Sénatorerie, Malval shrine

A section on "civilisation and spirituality" includes images of Egyptian, Greek, Roman and Indian gods (the Buddhas are of special interest).

The walls of the stairway leading to the upper floor have been hung with very fine 17C Aubusson tapestries which make their best impression when viewed from the top landing. Other tapestries are displayed in the rooms on this floor.

Two of the galleries stand out for the interest and value of their exhibits.

★**Salle du Trésor d'orfèvrerie**: a magnificent collection of Limousin *champlevé* enamel work from the 12C to the 15C. Note in particular a processional cross, pyxes (to hold the host) and the collection of shrines (chests and boxes). The vivid colours of the enamels harmonise with the gilding and polished stones. Scenes depicted include the Crucifixion (early 13C), the Adoration of the Magi (late 13C), the Stoning of St Stephen (late 12C) and the Martyrdom of St Thomas Becket (late 12C).

Several of the enamel pieces (15-18C) can be attributed to great masters of the art, namely Limosin, Laudin and Nouailher. The contents of this gallery are completed by 18C and 19C religious objects and a 13C embossed shrine.

Salle de céramique: it contains china from Nevers, Moustiers, Rouen, Strasbourg and Delft as well as some Italian "majolica" earthenware and glassware. In the next room there are 140 Chinese pieces: from the Han to Song dynasties (2 BC-13C); the Yuan and Ming dynasties (13C-17C); Kang-Hi and Kien-Long dynasties (17C-18C).

The sculpture gallery displays 15-18C works.

In the painting section, there are pictures by French, Flemish and Dutch artists as well as more recent works by Guillaumin, Suzanne Valadon, and Marinto, among others.

The museum's collection includes 19-20C drawings.

The basement rooms house monumental sculptures of Gaulish deities and Gallo-Roman funerary steles.

Musée du Présidial Louis-Lacrocq ⊘ (Y M²) – This little museum provides a well-designed learning experience. The subjects illustrated make up an excellent introduction to life and history in the Creuse region. On the ground floor, geological formations and the uses people have made of the land are shown. There are displays on gold, for centuries a profitable resource in Limousin, pewter and different types of granite. One room is devoted to painting (rotating exhibit), particularly from the Crozant School. Fauna and flora are given space on the upper floor, as is the ethnological department, with its various furnishings and costumes. In the last room, life on the farm is evoked through the display of tools.

Hôtel des Moneyroux (Z B) – This late Gothic style building, contemporary with the Palais Jacques Cœur in Bourges *(see BOURGES)*, consists of two buildings joined by a corner turret.

The right wing was built after 1447 by Antoine Alard, lord of Moneyroux and treasurer of the counts of Marche; his successor, Pierre Billon, had the other wing built at the beginning of the 16C. The façade is pierced by many mullioned windows and is topped by dormer windows ornamented with finials and pinnacles.

★THE EASTERN PART OF THE HAUTE MARCHE
Round trip 140km/84mi – 5hr

Leave Guéret travelling south on D 940, towards Bourganeuf.

Forêt de Chabrières – The forest is dense with pines, oaks, beeches and birch; bracken forms a thick carpet underfoot. Several walks are marked. A stonemason's workshop along the roadside indicates the importance of this craft in the past.

Sardent – 2km/1mi outside of the village, the St-Pardoux chapel rises up on the right. The site is lovely, and popular with pilgrims who come for the virtues attributed to the water; other visitors, simply seeking a calm and pleasant environment, will enjoy the site and the little town further on.

Pontarion – Settled along the banks of the Taurion, the salient feature of the hamlet is the 15C **château**, its corner towers and battlements. The south façade faces the river and can be admired from the water's edge.
The **church** (13C) has a characteristic Limousin doorway, decorated with a frieze. Inside, the tombstones honour stonemasons.

After crossing the river Taurion, turn left on D 13.

Nécropole des Sagnes – A path leads through the woods to this Gallo-Roman site used for funeral ceremonies. The burial grounds contained incinerated remains in 300 tombs, some in the form of funerary urns.
From the car park, take another path 1km/0.6mi farther on, and walk under the oak trees to the site known as the **Pierre aux Neuf Gradins** *("Nine Steps Rock"). The site is both mysterious and lovely.*

Continue along D 13 as far as Soubrebost.

Pont Peri – A footpath leads to this Roman bridge spanning the Gosne. In the picturesque setting, admire the vaulting arch formed by massive hewn stones.
Continue along D 43 to St-Georges-la-Pouge.

Sous-Parsat – This charming little village is enlivened by many balconies and window boxes. The small church has some surprising **frescoes**, the work of Gabriel Chabrat. Two main colour themes play off each other: yellow (symbolising joy) and blue (dream). The energetic composition is a whirl of form and hue. The artist has used the walls to illustrate different Bible scenes with a personal interpretation. Genesis is found at the end of the chancel, facing a flamboyant Apocalypse. Light filters through the windows, also designed by Chabrat, accentuating the unique ambience of the place.

Continue on D 45 as far as Mareille.

Maisonnisses – Nearby the source of the river Gartemps, the village was once a headquarters for the Knights Templar; the château surrounded by a moat. Only the church has survived, and within a **recumbent figure★** discovered in 1830 and replaced in its wall-niche tomb in 1955. It probably represents a 13C Knight.
Take D 50 to St-Yriex-les-Bois.

Château du Théret – This handsome 15C construction comes into view as you round a bend, at the end of a bumpy access way. On the left, a pretty Renaissance fountain is the first of many waterworks which grace the château's landscape. Beyond the moat and front porch, in the main courtyard stands an Italian-style granite fountain. The main façade of the rectangular building is castellated; a square tower projects in asymmetry on the left-hand side, with a spiral stairway inside, and a convex roof topped with a bell. The back wall is framed by two corner towers, pierced with narrow windows and loopholes. Two wings extend the central section: the southern

Sous-Parsat – Frescoes in the church

S. Sauvignier/MICHELIN

part was added in the 16C, and the northern side (reception) in the 17C. Legend has it that the Grand Condé (a rebellious military leader involved in the complicated intrigues of the 1648-1653 civil wars known as *La Fronde*) slept in the "Prince's Bed Chamber".

Leave the château and take D 17 to the left towards Saunière.

Ste-Feyre – The town is dominated by the château, erected in the 18C.

The **church**, built in the 13C and fortified in the 14C, has an elegant Limousin-style doorway on the western façade. The single nave has four bays; the last of these forms the chancel. It is shored up on the southern side (16C) and has three chapels on the northern side (15C). In one of these chapels, note the polychrome stone statuary also dating from the 15C: Saint Anne, the Virgin and Child.

Take D 3 towards St-Laurent.

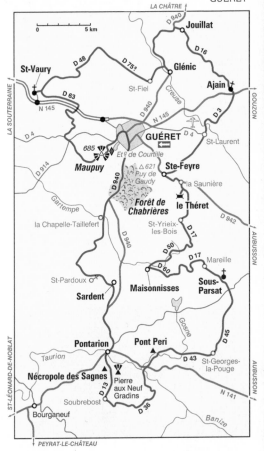

Ajain – The **church** (13C) was fortified with a watch path atop the battlements, and buttressed watch towers. In the nave with its diagonal rib vaulting, a cornice runs the length of the walls above expressive grimacing faces (mascarons).

Continue along D 3 towards Châtelus-Malvaleix for 1km/0.5mi, then turn left on D 16.

Jouillat – The local **church** (12-13C) has a single nave which ends in an apse with five arcades (sculpted capitals). A 13C fresco representing Christ decorates the chancel vaulting.

Outside, on the southern side, a Carolingian tomb is embellished by a pattern of squares and rosettes, and a crouching lion in granite.

The château is an attractive 15C building, square and flanked by corner towers.

Take D 940 towards Guéret.

Glénic – This village is perched on a promontory above the Creuse. The Romanesque **church** was fortified during the Hundred Years War. The east end is protected by towers; the other corners have corbelled turrets; the fourth bay and the chancel are elevated. In the 15C, the nave was lengthened and diagonal ribbed vaulting added. Beyond the 12C doorway, surmounted by a niche with a Romanesque statue of the Virgin, a 14C fresco faces the entrance, illustrating the fall of Adam and Eve.

Go towards D 940, then cross the Creuse and turn right; travel as far as St-Fiel, passing under the viaduct.

St-Vaury – The **church** ⊘ contains, at the back of the altar, a bas-relief cut in limestone, depicting scenes from the Passion. There are also two small 13C enamelled reliquaries.

At the crossroads next to the cemetery, take D 63.

Le Maupuy – A rocky plateau 685m/2247ft high, its summit, together with its neighbour the Puy de Gaudy (621m/2037ft), forms a natural barrier protecting Guéret. The view from the top provides surprising contrasts in landscape all around.

At the bottom of the hill, turn left. This scenic route winds back to Guéret through the woods and along the Courtille Lake (recreational facilities).

Château de HAUTEFORT★★

Michelin map 75 fold 7 or 233 fold 44

Hautefort Château dates from the 17C and has been the property of the Bastard family since 1929. Its proud outline dominates the skyline, reminiscent more of the royal palaces of the Loire Valley than of the fortresses of Périgord. The château was badly damaged by fire on the night of 30-31 August 1968. Restoration was begun in 1969 and was executed with great care, adhering closely to the design of the original building.

Bertrand the Troubadour – The first castle of Hautefort was built by the Limousin family of Las Tours. In the 12C it passed by marriage to the house of De Born, of whom Bertrand, the very same mentioned by Dante in the Divine Comedy, is the most well-known member. **Bertrand de Born**, the famous troubadour who was much admired in the courts of love, became a warrior-knight when the need arose to defend the family castle against his brother Constantine. With the support of Henry Short Coat, he succeeded in having Henry II acknowledge his rights in 1185 in spite of all Constantine's efforts, which were supported by Richard the Lion Heart. However, in 1186 Constantine returned to Hautefort and razed the castle to the ground. Renouncing everything, Bertrand withdrew to take monastic orders.

Marie de Hautefort – Marie, also known as Aurore, daughter of the first marquis of Hautefort, lady-in-waiting to Anne of Austria, is said to have possessed great beauty and an impeccable reputation. She is best remembered for the deep admiration and platonic love she inspired in Louis XIII (1610-43). In 1646 she married the duke of Halluin. She reigned over literary circles and *Salons des Précieuses* (Society drawing rooms) until her death in 1691 at 75 years of age.

Château de Hautefort

TOUR ⏱ 1hr

The strategic position of the Hautefort site on a hill in the middle of an immense amphitheatre was certainly exploited very early on: in the 9C the viscounts of Limoges are known to have built a stronghold here. During the Middle Ages several castles succeeded one another, leaving some traces (the courtyard's west corner tower). The defensive position of the castle was strengthened in the 16C (barbican flanked by two crenellated bartizans and equipped with a drawbridge) during the tumultuous years of the Wars of Religion.

Complete reconstruction of the castle was instigated by Jacques-François de Hautefort (c1630). This lasted some forty years; the plans are attributed to the architect Rambourgt, who kept the former living quarters but made considerable alterations elsewhere. The pavilions set at opposite ends were not completed until the 18C. The harmonious combination of architectural styles – Renaissance and classical – contributes to the building's original and elegant appearance.

Walk – Go round the perimeter of the beautiful park (40ha/99 acres) to the terraces, planted with flowers and cypress trees, which overlook the village and offer views of the park.

To reach the entrance to the château go to the end of the esplanade and cross the drawbridge over the moat, which is now decorated with flowers and boxwood. The main courtyard is a vast square open on one side to the village, which nestles at the foot of the castle walls, while on the other three sides it is surrounded by the living quarters. To the south are two round towers topped with domes and lantern turrets.

Interior – The extensive restoration has recreated several rooms in their original finery and has repaired the great staircase, very badly damaged in the 1968 fire. The gallery houses two marble busts of the 16C and 18C (Seneca and Marcus Aurelius, respectively) and two vases in Toro stone; the doors are exact replicas of the originals.

The tapestry gallery includes three 16C Flemish wall-hangings and another from Brussels, which depicts scenes from the Old Testament. The dining room contains 17C paintings and the state room's walls are covered with Cordoban leather.

Inside the southeast tower is a 17C chapel containing 16C paintings on leather and the altar from Charles X's coronation.

The southwest tower has beautiful chestnut **timberwork**★★, the work of the Compagnons du Tour de France guild. It also contains the museum of Eugène Le Roy (1836-1907), who was born at Hautefort, in the château itself, and wrote the adventure novel *Jacquou le Croquant*. Another room contains objects saved from the fire.

ISSOUDUN

Population 13 859
Michelin map 68 fold 9

Issoudun goes back to Gaulish times (*Uxellodunum* comes from a Celtic term meaning a high, thus fortified, site) and later, during the Middle Ages, was the stake in many a battle, the most famous being that between Philip Augustus and Richard the Lion Heart. The town was besieged several times, as well as set on fire.

The town keeps alive the memory of the journey to the castle abbey made by Louis XI, who had a special devotion to Our Lady. Every year on 8 September in the Basilica of Notre-Dame-du-Sacré-Cœur the traditional pilgrimage is celebrated.

Balzac et Issoudun – Honoré de Balzac (1799-1850) stayed at Frapesie Castel, near Issoudun, where wrote most of *César Birotteau* and also collected the information he needed to write *La Rabouilleuse (The Black Sheep)*. Issoudun has retained the peculiar street names which appear in Balzac's works: La rue du Boucher Gris (Drunken Butcher Street), La rue à Chercher (Hard to Find Street).

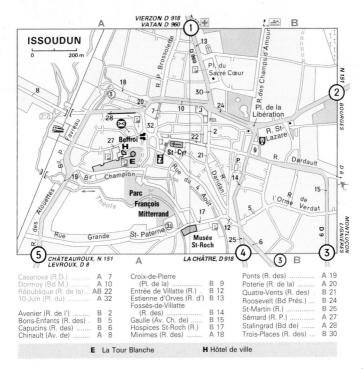

Casanova (R.D.)	A 7	Croix-de-Pierre		Ponts (R. des)	A 19
Dormoy (Bd M.)	A 10	(Pl. de la)	B 9	Poterie (R. de la)	A 20
République (R. de la)	AB 22	Entrée de Villatte (R.)	B 12	Quatre-Vents (R. des)	B 21
10-Juin (Pl. du)	A 32	Estienne d'Orves (R. d')	B 13	Roosevelt (Bd Prés.)	B 24
		Fossés-de-Villatte		St-Martin (R.)	B 25
Avenier (R. de l')	B 2	(R. des)	B 14	Sémard (R. P.)	A 27
Bons-Enfants (R. des)	B 5	Gaulle (Av. Ch. de)	B 15	Stalingrad (Bd de)	A 28
Capucins (R. des)	B 6	Hospices St-Roch (R.)	B 17	Trois-Places (R. des)	B 30
Chinault (Av. de)	A 8	Minimes (R. des)	A 18		

E La Tour Blanche   **H** Hôtel de ville

SIGHTS

Église St-Cyr (A) – There is a very fine 14-15C **stained glass window** in the chevet. It is divided into five vertical sections and in addition to depicting the Crucifixion contains medallions illustrating scenes from the lives of St Cyran and St Julitta. The choir and the Rosary Chapel contain fine sculptured stalls. Above the west door is a Descent from the Cross painted by Boucher of Bourges in 1625.

Beffroi (A) – The belfry, flanked by two round towers of unequal size, once served as a gateway through the castle wall to the town. Dismantled during the Wars of Religion, it was restored in the Renaissance style and used as a prison until 1914.

La Tour Blanche (A E) – The tower was built at the end of the 12C by Richard the Lion Heart. The inside is octagonal, the outside nearly circular; it is 33m/108ft high and the walls are 4m/13ft thick. To visit, apply to the caretaker at the Town Hall.
The three floors in the tower may be reached by the staircase of 145 steps. On the way you will see the fine ogive vaulted ceiling of the main hall. From the top platform there is a view over the town and the country that lies between the valleys of the Indre and the Cher.

Hôtel de Ville (A H) – The façade of the Town Hall dates from 1731; it is attached to a modern building and fronted by a courtyard designed by Marin Kasimir. This work, known as **La place des miroirs**, is made of eight glassed-in spaces surrounded by steps and waterworks. The artist created anthropomorphic symbols to compose the eight letters of the town's name. If you can't find the "I", it's because you are "I" – in the artist's scheme, the viewer represents this letter.
A footpath leads to the Tour Blanche, across a garden set out along the former ramparts, and offering a wide view of the Théols valley.

Issoudun – La place des miroirs

Parc François-Mitterrand (A) – This pleasant park is easily reached from all parts of town; the greenery stretches across both sides of the river.

Musée de l'Hospice St-Roch ⊘ (AB) – The museum is housed in the former hospital (Hôtel-Dieu) which is built on piles over the river Théols in a picturesque setting. Saint Roch (Rock in English, San Rocco in Italian) is legendary for healing victims of the plague in the 14C. Stricken himself, he was succoured by a dog, and is often pictured with one in paintings and statuary.

Salles des Malades (ward rooms) – There are two sickrooms, one for women *(salle des femmes)*, which displays furniture having belonged to the hospital, including a 1646 harpsichord, various surgical instruments and two 17C paintings. The men's ward *(salle des hommes* – access from the chapel) has been transformed into a lapidary museum. The exhibits explore the history of Issoudun and the region through funerary items from the Iron Age, Gallo-Roman architectural items, sculptures from the Notre-Dame d'Issoudun Abbey and swords and daggers from the late 18C and early 19C (notice the sword with rooster-head hilt).

Chapelle – Built around 1500, the chapel is connected to the men's ward by a door with a wooden shutter which could be opened during Mass, so that the patients could attend the service. The most outstanding items are two large carvings of the **Tree of Jesse★**; they were made at the end of the 15C and repre-sent the genealogical tree of Christ, showing the ancestors of the Virgin and figures of the prophets, kings and knights. The details in the robes and the expressive faces are remarkable; carved in local stone which hardens as it is exposed to the air, the statures were originally painted, as was the rest of the chapel. There are also interesting painted enamel plaques from Limoges including one by Léonard Limosan (16C) and many old statuettes (15-16C Madonnas).

★**Apothicairie** – The pharmacy is set up in a 17C wing, facing a garden where med-icinal herbs are cultivated. The small rooms on the ground floor display mementoes of celebrities who were born or lived in Issoudun. On the upper floor, go through the rooms decorated with Aubusson tapestries and remarkable furnishings formerly used by the hospital officials, then through the kitchen to view a valuable pharma-ceutical collection: 17-18C pharmacy (furniture, glassware and 400 Nevers porcelain jars), rare painted boxes and other unusual items, including a 80kg/176lb mortar and pestle dating from the 15C, used to make powders, elixirs and ointments.

EXCURSIONS

① Forêts de Chœurs et de Bommiers
Round trip of 50km/30mi – 3hr

Located in the *départements* of Indre and Cher, this lovely forest covers more than 7 500ha/18 525 acres; 75% of the trees are oaks.

Issoudun – *See ISSOUDUN.*

Leave Issoudun travelling eastward on D 8 towards St-Ambroix. In St-Hilaire, take D 48ᴱ.
Bordered by woods, the route goes along the picturesque Arnon valley. Above the river bank rise the vestiges of the **Prée Abbey**, founded in the 12C.

Moulin de Nouan ⊘ – An unusual site in this region, this windmill mainly served to back up the many watermills, which are often stilled in summer when rivers and streams are low. Built in 1819, the mill was recently restored and its sails turn again on festive occasions.
A lonely sentinel stands on the edge of the wood: the **Tour de la Croisette** ⊘. Built on the mound of a vanished feudal castle (vestiges of the moat remain), the tower now houses an exhibit on local fauna.
Return to the road, turning right on D 9.

Mareuil-sur-Arnon – Snug among the copses, this village was one of the metal-lurgical centres of the upper Arnon valley. All that remains of the old forge is a tall brick chimney alongside the lake which supplied water to the works. South-west of the town of Mareuil, this lake now serves as a **recreation centre**.
Outside of Mareuil, take D 18 to the right.

Abbaye de Chezal-Benoît – Founded in 1093 by the monk André de Vallombreuse, this former Benedictine monastery, now a psychiatric hospital, has kept the 12C nave of the church and the community buildings.
The façade is embellished by the foliage designs on the Romanesque capitals, and fluted pilasters (a rarity in Berry). The interior is pure Romanesque style: the blind nave is indirectly lit by the side windows. The foliated, spiral scrolls on the capitals are the precursor of the Gothic-style crocket (leafy projections). The modification of the supporting structure and the evolution of the sculpted décor show that construction was still taking place in the second half of the 12C.
Leave Chezal travelling southwest on D 65ᴱ.

Travel along the southern edge of the Choeurs forest, where many forest roads and trails lead to the central point known as the Croix Blanche.
At Pruniers, turn right on D 925.

Église St-Pierre de Bommiers – This 12C church is representative of the lower Berry by the clearly Benedictine plan (note the unusual *secretaria*, vaulted niches used as a sacristy, linking the chancel to the apsidal chapels in the transept). The capitals, also 12C, create an admirable ensemble: Christ handing over the Keys to Saint Peter and the Law to Saint Paul; the lively silhouettes seem to stretch out, the facial expressions underlined by lead set deep in the eyes. Other capitals bear a mixed arrangement of flowers, people and imaginary animals. The 48 magnifi-cent **stalls★** (1511-1515) are from the chapel and the Minimes convent in Bommiers. Above the entranceway, the wooden Madonna dates from the 15C.
Take D 925 towards Lignières. 1km/0.5mi before Pruniers, turn left on D 68.

The road back to Issoudun crosses the Bommiers forest as far as **St-Aubin**, where the church shelters a 15C sculptural ensemble: Saint Anne, The Virgin and the Infant Jesus. After crossing the Cousseron, the road crosses the ancient Roman road known as the **Levée de César**, which linked Argentonmagus *(see St-MARCEL)* to Bourges.

② Upper Arnon and Théols Valleys

Round trip of 45km/27mi – 2hr

Issoudun – *See ISSOUDUN.*

Leave Issoudun travelling northeast on N 151 towards Bourges.

Chârost – The origins of this hamlet go back to the Bronze Age. In Antiquity and the Middle Ages, Chârost enjoyed prosperity, as witnessed in the remains of its feudal castle, the defensive wall (northern gateway to the city) and especially its church.

Église St-Michel – This abbey church is a vast Romanesque edifice (12C), built of ferrous limestone. A wide nave, the timber framework dating from the 19C, leads to a hemispherical sanctuary: the transept and apsidal chapels have vanished. Note the high, narrow arch joining the chancel to the nave (northern side), typical of churches in the Berry. The capitals in the chancel are enlivened with human and animal figures.
Outside, above the entrances, a large cross with an intertwining motif supports the Pascal Lamb.
Go round the building and into the cemetery. From there, observe the apse and the wealth of carved ornamentation, as well as the marks left by the former arms of the transept and the apse (among the admirable capitals, look for the harpy – half woman, half bird – bearing a wheel).

Leave Chârost westward on D 2.

Diou – This well-groomed village on the banks of the Théols is a pleasant stopover. Near the pretty church of St-Clément (13C), a lawn rolls down to the water's edge, where a mill straddles the river, with a dovecot alongside.

Leave Diou travelling north on D 918 towards Mehun.

Château de la Ferté – *Not open to visitors.* Built in 1659, this lovely manor is reflected in the waters of the Théols.

Carry along until you cross the river Arnon, then take the road on the left which leads onto D 18 at Lazenay.

Reuilly – This village is known for its wines *(Appellation d'Origine Contrôlée)*, grown in vineyards spreading over the *départements* of Indre and Cher. Along the banks of the Théols and the Auron, 132ha/326 acres from Lury to Diou (Preuilly alone is isolated to the east) produce mostly white wine from Sauvignon grapes.

LABASTIDE-MURAT

Population 610

Michelin map 75 fold 18 or 235 fold 10 – Local map see Causse de GRAMAT

Labastide-Murat, which stands at one of the highest points on the Gramat Causse, was originally called Labastide-Fortunière, but changed its name to Murat in honour of the most famous of its sons.
The modest house in which Joachim Murat was born, on the southwest of the town, as well as the château that he had built for his brother André, preserve the memory of one of the French Empire's (1804-14) most valiant soldiers.

The miraculous destiny of Joachim Murat – Murat was born in 1767, the son of an innkeeper. He was destined for the Church, but at twenty-one decided instead to be a soldier. The campaigns in Italy and Egypt enabled him to gain rapid promotion under Napoleon, whose brother-in-law he became by marrying the First Consul's sister, Caroline; he was promoted to Marshal of the Empire, Grand Duke of Berg and of Cleves and King of Naples. The phenomenal bravery he displayed on all the battlefields of Europe and his influence over his troops, at whose head he unhesitatingly charged into battle, made him a legendary hero.
His glory faded with that of his master, whom he abandoned in the dark days of the Empire. His miserable end in 1815 was in keeping with the diversity in his life: after the Bourbons had returned to Naples, he tried to reclaim his kingdom, but was taken prisoner and shot.

Musée Murat ⊙ – The museum is in the house where Murat was born. The 18C kitchen, the inn's saloon and a large genealogical tree on which 10 European countries and several royal families are represented are on display to visitors. On the first floor there are mementoes of the King of Naples and of his mother.

EXCURSIONS

► ► **Soulomès** – Gothic church;
Vaillac – Feudal castle.

Grottes de LASCAUX

Michelin map 75 fold 7 or 233 fold 44 – Local map see Vallée de la VÉZÈRE

Lascaux Cave ranks as number one among the prehistoric sites of Europe by dint of the number and quality of its paintings.

The cave was discovered 12 September 1940 by four young boys looking for their dog, which had fallen down a hole. With a makeshift lamp, they discovered an extraordinary fresco of polychrome paintings on the walls of the gallery they were in. The teacher at Montignac was immediately told of the discovery, and he just as quickly notified Abbé Breuil. The abbot arrived and examined the paintings with meticulous care, baptising the cave the "Sistine Chapel of Périgord".

In 1948 the cave was officially opened to the public. Over fifteen years, more than a million people came to admire the famous Lascaux paintings. But, unfortunately, in spite of all the precautions taken (weak lighting, air conditioning, airlock), the carbon dioxide and the humidity resulted in two damaging effects: the "green" effect (the growth of moss and algae) and the "white" effect (less visible but much more serious as it leads to a build-up of deposits of white calcite).

In 1963, in order to preserve such a treasure, it was decided to close the cave to the public (a limited number of researchers are allowed in every year). Ten years later, to relieve public disappointment, a project was put forward to build a replica; Lascaux II was opened in 1983, under the care of the Dordogne Tourist Administration.

An exceptional group of paintings – The cave, carved out of Périgord Noir limestone, is a relatively small cavity, 150m/492ft long. It is made up of four galleries, the walls of which are covered with more than 1 500 representations, either engraved or painted. These works were created between 17 000 and 15 000 years ago, during the Magdalenian Culture.

At that time the cave was open to the outside air. Some time after the cave artists had decorated the cave, the entrance collapsed and a flow of clay tightly closed off the cave.

The airtight entrance and the impermeable ceiling are the reasons for the lack of concretions and the perfect preservation of the paintings fixed and authenticated by a thin layer of natural calcite.

The cave includes the Bulls' Hall, which extends into the Axial Gallery *(see Lascaux II)*; these two areas hold 90% of the cave paintings.

To the right of the Bulls' Hall a passage leads to the Apse, which extends into the Nave and the Feline Gallery. To the right of the apse the Well Gallery opens up; its lower section is decorated with a simplified scene of a wounded bison and a falling man *(see the photograph in the Introduction, Prehistoric art)*, one of the rare representations of a human figure. This collection of paintings is truly unique in the history of prehistoric art, in regard to the state of preservation, the number of works created over a long time span, and the precision of execution.

A wide range of fauna is depicted on the cave walls; the artists used the wall contours to give relief to the subject matter. There are reproductions of the animals hunted during the early Magdalenian Period: aurochs, horses, reindeer, bison, ibexes, bears and woolly rhinoceroses appear side by side or superimposed, forming part of extraordinary compositions.

The seemingly disorganised paintings (drawings superimposed onto previous drawings) or figures apparently illustrated with a sense of hierarchy leave researchers perplexed, and the absence of all landscape (ground, plants, small animals) suggest the paintings are more a ritual form of expression than a narrative. The geometric signs and enigmatic drawings accompanying the fauna (lines, points, cross-hatching, ovals) raise the question of the possible existence of a sanctuary.

The Lascaux style – There is a definite Lascaux style: lively animals with small, elongated heads, swollen stomachs and short legs, and fur illustrated by dabs of coloured pigment. The horns, antlers and hoofs are often drawn in three-quarter view - at times even full face – while the animal itself is drawn in profile; this procedure is known as the "turned profile".

★★ Lascaux II ⊙ – Located some 200m/219 yd from the original cave, the facsimile reconstitutes two galleries from the upper part of the cave; the Bulls' Hall and the Axial Gallery, which contain the majority of the cave paintings at Lascaux. "Airlock" antechambers retrace the cave's history in explanatory exhibits. The recreation of the unique atmosphere of the original cave has been made possible purely by real technological prowess and rigid scientific discipline. A detailed description of how the facsimile was made can be found at Le Thot Centre of Research and Prehistoric Art *(see Le THOT, ESPACE CRO-MAGNON)*, a worthwhile follow-up visit to Lascaux. As early as 1966, The National Geographic Institute *(Institut Géographique National – IGN)* had accomplished a precise photographic survey of Lascaux using three-dimensional scenes of the cave and stereo images. This survey enabled a shell to be constructed in reinforced concrete – similar to the process used in shipbuilding. Once the cave walls were reproduced, the painter Monique Peytral copied the cave paintings using slides and the results from numerous surveys she had made. She used the same methods and materials (pigments, tools etc) as the cave artists.

C.N.M.H.S. Paris © SPADEM

The Great Black Bull, Grotte de Lascaux

The two small rooms reproducing the original airlock display the history of Lascaux Cave, items discovered in the cave's archeological strata (tallow lamps, coloured powders, flints used by the engravers); a model of the scaffolding used; a copy of a panel of bison; an explanation of the dating methods used; and displays on flint and bone knapping.

In the **Bulls' Hall**, the paintings are on the calcite-covered upper part of the wall and the vaulting, so that the animals seem to be running along the natural rim as if along the horizon line. The graphic composition here is wonderful. The second animal, the only imaginary animal figure painted at Lascaux, has been nicknamed the "unicorn" because of the odd-looking horns above a bear-like muzzle, on a body not unlike that of a rhinoceros. Among the other animals represented there are some magnificent black bulls, one of which is 5m/16.5ft long, red bison, small horses and deer.

The **Axial Gallery** contains a vault and walls covered with horses, cows, ibexes, bison and a large deer. A charming frieze of long-haired ponies (dubbed "Chinese horses" by the first chroniclers because of their resemblance to figures from ancient Chinese vases), a great black bull and a large red pony, seeming to sniff at a branch, bear witness to a very developed style of art.

Régourdou – *1km/0.5mi east*

On this **prehistoric site** ⊘ discovered in 1954 numerous objects and bones were brought to light, including a skeleton, "Régourdou man", 70 000 years old and now displayed in the Périgord Museum in Périgueux. All these discoveries are representative of the Mousterian industry. In the cave, now open to the air, near the burial ground of the Régourdou man, a pile of bear bones was found, which some specialists have interpreted as evidence of a bear burial ground.

A small museum contains bones (a cast of the Régourdou man's jawbone) and tools.

LEVROUX

Population 3 045
Michelin map 68 fold 8 or 238 fold 28

Set between the wooded landscape of the Boischaut and the rich farmlands of the area known as Champagne Berrichonne, Levroux is in the heartland of tradition. In addition to producing especially savoury goat cheeses, it is also home to tawing (a form of leather processing using alum and salt) and parchment enterprises.

The land is steeped in history. The area has been inhabited since prehistoric times; the settlement of Levroux appeared at the end of the Celtic period. It was certainly one of the *oppida* burned to the ground by Vercingétorix as Caesar's armies approached in 52 BC. Once the *Pax Romana* was established, Levroux grew quickly, spreading from the towers on the hill to the area where the city now stands. The historical interest of this sector is such that the district of Levroux has become one vast archeological site. Besides the Gallo-Roman theatre, several villas have been discovered and are now being carefully unearthed.

Christianity had a difficult time making its way here: first introduced by a priest named Sylvain, it was later promoted by Saint Martin himself, who was run out of town. Later, he returned to destroy a richly-decorated pagan temple, and thus inspired the people to convert.

In the Middle Ages, the town grew around the feudal château of the princes of Châteauroux and the church of St-Sylvain, the site of pilgrimages. During the Hundred Years War, local residents took refuge behind a fortified wall (one of the gates remains). There are several well-preserved 15C and 16C buildings in Levroux.

SIGHTS

★**Collégiale St-Sylvain** – In the early 11C, Eudes de Déols founded a collegiate church (home to a chapter of clergymen sharing authority) in Levroux and made a special land grant to the canons. Thus, part of the town took on a separate status and became a place of refuge and asylum for fugitives and serfs.

The church was built in two stages beginning in the late 12C. The complex nature of the layout is due to the incorporation of pre-existing buildings, including the foundations of a large Roman temple. The crypt, the apse and the large bell tower came before the vaulting in the nave and the construction of the porch, undertaken around 1263. A few changes were made in the 16C (crypt entrances closed off, addition of chapels) and the 19C.

The east end of the church is a heptagonal apse flanked by a square belltower. The southern doorway is embellished with 21 different figures, including a devilish face with a beard and horns. The main doorway bears a much-damaged tympanum; the sculpted imagery represents the Resurrection of the Dead and the Last Judgement. Inside, the nave and side aisles are impressive for their soaring height. The chancel was built in transitional Romanesque-Gothic style; note the keystone in the sanctuary, showing Christ bestowing blessings. The vaulted apse is supported by ribs and statuary columns.

Maison de bois (Maison St-Jacques) – This wooden house was built between 1536 and 1547. Located in a street which leads to the façade of St-Sylvain, it is decorated with angelic carvings and the blazons of François I and Henri de Valois (later to become Henri II), as well as grotesque figures in the angles. A leper with scaly skin *(see photograph)* is probably a reminder of the miracle of Saint Martin, said to have cured a local dignitary of the disease. The house was once used as a hospice for pilgrims on their way to Santiago de Compostela.

Colline des Tours – *Access from the intersection of D 956 and D 2 by a steeply rising path.*
Atop this hill, an ancient fortified burg has left vestiges which include ramparts in a characteristic Gaulish style: the dry stone construction was reinforced with cross-beams.

Levroux – Leper on the Maison de bois

S. Sauvignier/MICHELIN

The ruins of the 14C château built by Bertrand de La Tour d'Auvergne paint a lonely picture. Two round towers guard the old entranceway and the main building (Gothic doorway); there is a good **view** of Levroux from this site.

Musée du Cuir et du Parchemin ⊙ – In the Tourist Office, this small temporary museum is devoted to the techniques of dressing hides by the dry process known as tawing, and to the manufacture of parchment.

CHÂTEAUX

Around Levroux, several interesting châteaux are found in the areas known as the Boischaut and Champagne Berrichonne.

★★**Château de Bouges** – *See Château de BOUGES.*

★★**Château de Valençay** – *See Château de VALENÇAY.*

Palluau-sur-Indre – Perched on a rocky crest above the Indre valley, set in a lovely park, the living quarters of the château are in the Gothic style (13C), protected by two defensive towers. The 12C keep is known as the "Tour de Philippe Auguste", in memory of the sovereign's visit in 1188. From the terrace, the view extends over the valley.

★**Château d'Argy** ⊙ – Restored by the association Club du Vieux Manoir, the château and the 17C fortified farm buildings now serve as a training centre for the Club, focusing on the theme "architecture and environment".

Fortified in the 12C, this impressive château, renovated in the 16C by Charles de Brillac, companion-at-arms to Louis XII, is set in a 40ha/99 acre park. The square, 15C keep is an excellent example of military architecture, with its trefoil machicolations and guard towers. A watch path connects the keep and the Brillac tower, where the upper levels have retained chimney pieces embellished with seigniorial monograms. The moat was filled in during the French Revolution. Under the Second Empire, the southwestern section was rebuilt and the towers fitted with windows.

In the courtyard, the Louis XII-style gallery, carefully restored, contrasts with the severity of the outer walls: the flowery ornamentation of the brackets, the slender columns rising to pinnacles and the superposition of the galleries belie Italian influence. Nearby, a mill and a building housing a museum devoted to rural traditions *(Traditions paysannes)* date from the 19C. In the barn, an exhibit of furnishings from the National Archives displays monumental items from the time of Napoléon III designed to store maps. The cast iron stairway is also worthy of note.

★**Château de Villegongis** – This lovely Renaissance château looks much as it did in 1575, when construction was completed. The park is open to the public year round, and visitors can admire the white limestone building framed by two round towers, reflected in the waters of the moat.

Villegongis – Le château

Édition Lescuyer, Lyon

Join us in our constant task of keeping up-to-date.
Please send us your comments and suggestions.

Michelin Travel Publications
38 Clarendon Road
WATFORD – Herts WD1 1SX
Fax: 01923 415250 or
TheGreenGuide-uk@uk.michelin.com

LIMOGES★

Population 170065
Michelin map 72 fold 17 or 239 fold 13

A ford across the Vienne and two stepped plateaux that could be put to defensive use are the reason for Limoges' existence. In the Gallo-Roman period when the town was known as Augustoritum, it spread out in an amphitheatre along the right bank of the river. In the Middle Ages two separate and rival townships developed: the *Cité* grouped round its cathedral built on a low shelf overlooking the Vienne, and the *Château*, the busy commercial town on the opposite slope in the shadow of the powerful abbey of St-Martial.

The town today spreads out widely north of the Vienne; its industrial rise is largely due to its porcelain and enamel works and shoe factories. Limoges also boasts a university (and hence plays an important cultural role in the region) and is the administrative capital of Limousin.

HISTORICAL NOTES

Limoges in Gallo-Roman days – Limoges appears to have entered history in the last decade of the 1C BC.

The presence of the Roman military road, Agrippa's Way, the existence of a natural crossing point of the river Vienne, and the southeastern exposure of the hillside most appropriate for settlement certainly contributed to the birth of the Augustoritum.

This new town occupied 80ha/198 acres, over a well-ordered grid plan based on two central, perpendicular roads. The town quickly acquired a number of significant structures such as the stone bridge (later to become the Pont St-Martial), a forum, a theatre, baths, aqueducts, an amphitheatre, a temple, a triumphal arch, and so on. The forum was located on the site of the current town hall, between the rue des Récollets and the rue Timbaud. Below, the baths welcomed visitors (place des Jacobins, archeological excavation from 1967 to 1978) in three immense heated rooms, an exercise room, and assorted outbuildings. The amphitheatre (now the site of the Orsay garden), built on a rise on the outskirts, was 137m x 116m (449ft x 380ft), making it one of the largest in Gaul. Despite the many facilities offered, Augustoritum was thinly populated: never more than 6000 inhabitants. Archeological research has shown gaps in the ancient urban fabric, which indicate that the town was not fully built up.

At the end of the 3C, the barbarian invasions squeezed the town in upon itself, as people gathered around the St-Étienne hilltop and settled behind ramparts, thus forming the core of the *Cité*. The cathedral may have been erected on the site of a former temple to Jupiter. The necropolis, outside the town walls, received the remains of Saint Martial, and thus gave rise to the part of town known as the *Château*.

The Limousin Apostle – In about the year 250AD, Martial came to convert the people of Limousin to Christianity. The country was hostile and the missionary, pursued by the priests of the god Mercury, owed his safety to the protection granted him by a brave woman. The zealous Martial soon converted his hostess' daughter, Valerie, who broke off her engagement with the Roman Governor Stephen. Valerie was condemned to death. The brilliance of her faith as she faced her execution left Stephen so moved that, in turn, he too was converted.

Sometime later Martial burst into a theatre, interrupted a bawdy scene and preached the Word of God. The actors seized him and, in front of the crowd, beat him before dragging him off to jail. A supernatural light began to glow within the prison and the people, crying out that a miracle had occurred, delivered Martial from captivity. He went immediately to the temple where he broke the false gods and consecrated the church to St. Stephen. From that time onwards Limousin became the "land of the saints".

The memory of St. Martial was perpetuated by building within the city itself, an abbey in which the saint's relics could be kept. The monastery soon became an important pilgrimage centre and a staging point on one of the routes to Santiago de Compostela. It was destroyed in 1791 *(see below, Le Château)*.

A traitor among the Consuls – During the Hundred Years War, Limoges suffered not only the assaults of the English, but had to defend itself against the treasonous Viscount Jean de Laigle, a power-hungry local lord.

In August 1425, Laigle took a fateful step: without sufficient military force to bring the town to heel, he sought out an inside accomplice. In return for 10000 *écus*, Gautier Pradeau, provost marshal in charge of defending the town, agreed to arrange for the arena gate to be opened on the morning of the 27th. In hopes of pulling the wool over the Consuls' eyes, the Viscount sent emissaries on a mission of peace the day before his planned attack; he asked for armed assistance to drive out the English. The Consuls were suspicious of his motives and kept a close watch on events. Thus when Laigle and his English allies attacked at the appointed time, they were defeated by vigilant soldiers. While the battle raged, a priest happened on a suspect document and carried it to the Consuls. Indeed, it was a letter in Gautier's hand, addressed to the treacherous Viscount.

The traitor Gautier confessed, his worldly goods were confiscated by the authorities and he was sentenced to death. The execution took place on place des Bancs: Gautier's head was stuck upon a pike, his body carved into four bits and displayed at the four corners of the city. His entrails were buried on the site of his infamy, the spot where the letter which betrayed him was found. Laigle retreated and Limoges remained free.

Famous Citizens of Limoges – Many of the sons of Limoges have gained fame. Among the artists are **Leonard Limosin** (1505-1576) "enameller and painter in ordinary to the king's royal chamber", who won favour with four monarchs. By his skill in engraving, painting and decoration he became one of the leaders of the great school of enamel artists of the 16C whose fame, through the Laudin dynasty, lasted until the 18C. The painter **Auguste Renoir** (1841-1919), one of the masters of the Impressionist School, worked for some time at the beginning of his career as a painter of porcelain.

Among statesmen, **Pierre Vergniaud** (1753-1793) was the most famous orator of the Girondin Group in the Convention; there was also **Sadi Carnot** (1737-1894) who became president of the Republic.

ENAMEL WORK AND PORCELAIN

Enamels – Enamels are made from glass with a lead base in colours which have count-less vivid variations of tone owing to metal oxides being added when they are compounded *(illustration page 40)*. The glass and colours are formed into hard, thin wafers which are powdered before being spread with a spatula over a flat backing of gold, silver or copper. Successive firings give the enamel the appearance of solid crystal. Enamel work has been known from ancient times but it was not until the 12C that Limoges acquired exceptional skill in its manufacture.

Cloisonné and champlevé enamels (in which the colours are kept apart by thin outline plates and in which the colours are fitted into hollows made in the surface, respec-tively) came into their own in the Middle Ages.

Lead silicates and rare metal oxides such as gold, silver, uranium, cobalt, manganese, tungsten and copper are all found in the locality due to the presence of Primary Era faults. Most of the enamel workshops have public visiting hours; many of them are located around place Wilson (**CY**).

Porcelain – Among the industries for which Limoges is famous, porcelain, a late 18C undertaking, has been outstandingly successful.

Soft-paste porcelain – Before the discovery of a local source of kaolin, fine white clay, several types of translucent pottery were produced using techniques which differed from those prevalent in China. The basic ingredients of soft porcelain, translucent and lead glazed, are sand, sodium, alum, gypsum and sea salt, mixed with a whitener of chalk and limestone. Fired at low temperatures, this type of chinaware was widely produced by 18C European potters.

Hard-paste porcelain – Often called "true" porcelain, its composition includes kaolin, feldspar and quartz. **Kaolin** is the most important ingredient. Its name comes from the hillside of Kao-ling in China where it was first discovered. **Feldspar** gives porcelain its translucence, while kaolin makes it pure white and **quartz** prevents shrinking. Other minerals are also active in the firing process.

Enormous cylinders churn and mix the ingredients with flint stone, which serves to make the mixture smooth. A flow of water carries the powder to tanks where it is stirred incessantly. The water and powder create a liquid mixture known as **slip**. This can either be reduced to a powder form or processed into a paste which is kneaded and rolled to remove the air bubbles, then cast into the required shape. Complex subjects are created by pouring liquid slip into several moulds; the pieces are assembled when the paste has hardened.

R.M.N.

Portrait of Anne de Montmorency

Once these preparations are finished, the pieces have thick edges which must be refined. A preliminary firing is carried out, in a kiln at 980-1000°C/1796-1832°F. This process, known as **biscuit** or **bisque**, lasts 10 to 12 hours, and serves to remove the water and carbon dioxide from the porcelain. The baked models are whiter, stronger and will ring slightly when tapped. Porous, they can absorb glazes. Each approved piece is marked with the manufacturer's symbol, and plunged in an enamel bath.

Before the next firing, the bisque pieces are placed in special cases which protect them from each other and from any smoke in the kiln. The gas oven is heated to 1400°C/2552°F. During this phase, the items diminish in size by about 14%. Any faults or defects become apparent when the pieces are removed from this firing, and rejects are set aside.

Different techniques are then used for decoration. Hand-painted porcelain requires the work of skilled artists who are able to produce an original design, make copies of famous works, or mark an entire service with a monogram which is reproduced with remarkable precision and exactitude on each item. Painted decoration is usually applied over a fired glaze (and the item is fired again at a much lower temperature), with the exception of the stable and reliable cobalt blue, which can be layered and baked to obtain a rich, deep colour. Gold and silver encrustations are achieved by depositing precious metal (22 carats for gold) in a design scratched on the surface. Motifs can also be put on using a stamp or transfer decals, less noble procedures. The pieces are generally fired after decoration in a kiln heated to 800°C/1472°F.

In Europe, porcelain was imported from China until the late 17C, when soft-paste methods came into use. Kaolin of remarkable purity was discovered at Saint-Yrieix in 1768. After encouraging experiments had been carried out at the Royal Factory at Sèvres, Turgot, who was then general intendant of Limousin, set up a porcelain works in 1771. This was under the patronage of the count of Artois and marked the beginning, for Limousin ceramics, of an era of prosperity which was hardly interrupted even by the troubled years of the Revolution. After 1815 the industry became concentrated round Limoges which, because of its position on the Vienne, could land the wood for the kilns from lumber rafts floated down river.

Nowadays, more than 50% of all the porcelain made in France comes from Limoges, a world famous manufacturing centre.

Production is chiefly of tableware, though the tradition of luxury articles continues, their high quality and finish denoting the great care with which the old standards are maintained.

LA CITÉ

★**Cathédrale St-Étienne (DZ)** – St. Stephen's Cathedral is the most outstanding building in Limoges and the only one in all Limousin to be built completely in the Gothic style. It bears such resemblance in its design to the Cathedrals of Clermont-Ferrand and Narbonne that it is thought all three must have been planned by the same architect, Jean Deschamps.

St. Stephen's was successor to a Romanesque church of which only a part of the crypt and the lower storeys of the belfry remain. The Gothic cathedral was begun in 1273; the chancel was completed at the beginning of the next century, and the first two bays of the nave had been constructed by the end of the 15C. Jean de Langeac undertook the completion of the cathedral in 1537, but died in 1541; Monsignor Dusquesnay completed the church between 1876 and 1888.

Cathedral – St-John doorway

Exterior – The **St. John Doorway** ´ is really the cathedral's main entrance. It is of very fine-grained granite and was constructed between 1516 and 1530 when the Flamboyant style was at its peak. Two pierced galleries divide the façade into three tiers. A statue of Christ stands at the pier; the entire tympanum is adorned with a background of blind arcades filled in with richly coloured mosaics. An elongated gable frames the archivolt and rises to the base of the large rose window. The two Renaissance wooden doors are carved to show scenes from the lives of St. Martial and St. Stephen.

There is a good overall view of the chevet from rue Porte-Panet on the east side. The belfry is square and just over 60m/203ft high. The lower three storeys are Romanesque, but the lowest has been submerged in stonework added to support the tower. The next four storeys are Gothic, of which the three uppermost are octagonal, a design often found in Limousin architecture. The spire that crowned this tower was struck by lightning and destroyed in 1571. The belfry stood apart from the nave until last century when a modern narthex and three bays were added.

Interior – The porch contains several memorial stones. The nave gives an impression of unity of style even though it took 600 years to build. The boldness and elegance of line of the roof vaulting are wonderful; the triforium is constructed to act as a base for the tall windows.

The rood screen★ (at the end of the nave under the organ-loft), built for Jean de Langeac by artists from Touraine between 1533 and 1534, once separated the chancel from the nave. This limestone screen is topped by a gallery with pendants decorated with statues of the Six Virtues, the work of Jean Arnaud. A large bay opens up the back wall. The niches on either side of the door are framed by columns and pilasters. The ensemble is decorated in a rich Italian style. The bas-reliefs at the base depict mythological scenes – note Hercules' labours.

The three **tombs★** that stand round the chancel are of considerable decorative interest. Walking round the chancel from the south you will see consecutively:

– The tomb of Raynaud de la Porte (14C), bishop of Limoges and later archbishop of Bourges and cardinal. He asked that he might be buried in the cathedral he had helped to build.

– The tomb of Jean de Langeac. This mausoleum built in 1544, is an example of the Renaissance style at its most delicate. Fourteen carved panels depict scenes in the life of St. John as described in the Book of Revelation. It is in effect an adaptation of the little Passion by Dürer, translated to stone with exceptional spirit and feeling for movement.

– The tomb of Bernard Brun who was, in turn, bishop of Le Puy, Noyon and Auxerre. This monument, in the pure 14C French style, is adorned with four low relief panels: the upper panels show, on one side, the Coronation of the Virgin, on the other, Jesus Christ, the Virgin and St. John; the lower panels, the martyrdom of St. Valerie and the Crucifixion.

F. Magnoux/Musée de l'Évêché, Limoges

Musée de l'Évêché – Toy box

★Musée de l'Évêché ☉ (**DZ M¹**) – The museum is housed in the former archbishop's palace. This elegant 18C building in grey granite near the cathedral was designed by two Limousin architects, the brothers Brousseaud.

Ground floor – This level encompasses nine rooms and a chapel. The museum has some 300 **Limousin enamels★** dating from the 12C to the late 18C. The Middle Ages was an especially rich period for this type of art, well-represented in the museum's display cases.

Cloisonné enamels use an early technique where thin strips of metal are soldered to a metal base to outline the design. Although this process works well for gold, it is less effective for copper and soon came to be replaced by **champlevé**.

In the museum, notable examples of the second technique include the Thomas Becket shrine dating from around 1200 and a plaque illustrating the Visitation from 1770-1775. These works were executed on a thick copper plate where the lines of the design were cut away from the surface, and the enamel applied to the recesses so created. By putting on one or many coats, artists create compositions on dark backgrounds; golden hues on black or blue, opaque and translucent polychromes where the colours are highlighted by gold or silver bits glittering between layers of enamel. The parts of the copper surface which were not cut away were usually gilded after enamelling. The works were embellished using techniques found in fine gold and silversmithing: cabochon cutting (convex, highly polished but unfaceted surfaces), filigree, floral motifs on metal leaf. The nail heads have been carefully worked into expressive human faces. Plaques, shrines, medallions and various religious items illustrate the copious production of workshops in Limoges in the late 12C and early 13C. By the 14C, the art was no longer at its peak.

A century later, **painted enamels** made their appearance; the design is painted on the enamel covering the copper plate. This tradition is alive in Limoges today, where artists have taken up the 16C methods. Each colour is fired separately, at temperatures ranging from 1100 to 800°C (1980 to 1470°F), decreasingly, so that colours are not altered.

In the series of painted enamels are two plaques by Monvaerni (late 15C), a **Nativity triptych** (1515-1520), the **altarpiece from Mesnil-sous-Jumièges** (1525-1530), a rare example of this type of item to have survived, a monumental statue representing the death struggle of the legendary Trojan priest **Laocoön** by Pierre Courteys (c1560), works by Léonard Limosin, and pieces from the 17C and 18C by the Laudins, including the **twelve Caesars medallions**.

The two rooms in the **Egyptology** section present a particularly rich collection of terracotta figurines and bronze statuettes; a life-size model of part of the vestibule of the tomb of Nakht, the pharaoh's Intendant in Thebes (18th dynasty).

The collection of **French painting** (three rooms) includes 17-18C works (*Bataille de Constantin* by Charles Le Brun), landscapes of Limoges and the area by Courtot, and canvasses by Renoir *(Portrait de Mademoiselle Laporte)*, Guillaumin, Pascin and Suzanne, Valadon.

Just before the bishops chapel, with its dignified and sober air, two rooms display contemporary enamel work. Limoges is still an international centre of enamel art, as witnessed in the *Biennale International de l'Art de l'Émail*, a major exhibition.

Cellars – The fine vaulted cellars which were formerly the bishop's palace kitchens complete with chimneys, ovens and well, make a good setting for the ancient and medieval exhibits of the **lapidary museum**. These include Iron Age funerary items from Glandon, stone lions, funerary chests, gravestones and statues, characteristic of local Gallo-Roman works in granite. The Middle Ages are represented by a collection of sarcophagi, a 9C mosaic from the tomb of Saint Martial, Romanesque and Gothic capitals, bas-reliefs and various fragments from the 13C through the 16C.

Upper level – A granite staircase embellished by an attractive cast iron rail leads to the upper level, devoted entirely to local archeology.

Scale models illustrate the evolution of the city from its founding up to medieval times. The first room, facing the stairway, holds a rare **fresco** (early 2C), discovered on the site of a villa which once stood on rue Vigne-de-Fer. Restored with care, it gives a hint of the beautiful decor found inside a luxurious residence: yellow and ochre traces on a red and black background, animal motifs (deer, cats, eagles). In the corridor are other fragments of frescos in the same style. The other rooms display household items, public monuments, items related to the network of city streets (in Roman times, Limoges was famous for its urban plan), and to archeological excavations, in particular the site known as the "old hospital".

Musée de la Résistance ⊘ (**DZ M²**) – During the Second World War, Limoges was hard hit by the numerous deportations and massacres in the region *(see ORADOUR-SUR-GLANE and TULLE)*. In the series of rooms which make up the museum, posters, maps, documents and photos are among the items on exhibit, evoking the dark days of the war. Courageous women and men of Haute Vienne were some of the first in France to band together in the Resistance movement to combat the barbarism of Nazism.

★**Jardins de l'Évêché (Bishop's Palace Gardens)** (**DZ**) – These pleasant gardens rise in terraces above the Vienne and provide a good view of the cathedral and the palace. There is also a botanical garden.

Limoges – Jardins de l'Évêché

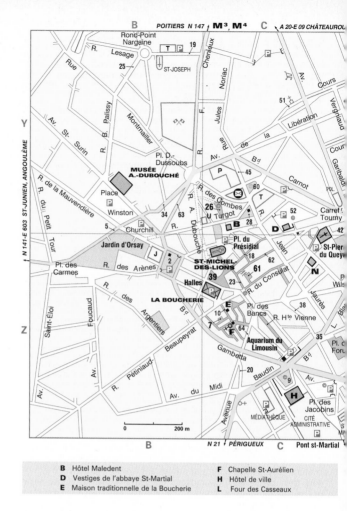

B	Hôtel Maledent	**F**	Chapelle St-Aurélien
D	Vestiges de l'abbaye St-Martial	**H**	Hôtel de ville
E	Maison traditionnelle de la Boucherie	**L**	Four des Casseaux

Haute Cité – Northwest of the Cathedral, rue des Allois (**DZ 4**) and rue Haute-Cité (**DZ 30**) are lined with old half-timbered houses and arcades.

Quartier de l'Abbesaille – From the east end of the Cathedral, a labyrinth of streets winds down to the river Vienne.
Rue de la Règle (**DZ 53**) is bordered by old houses once used by the clergy. It continues on into rue du Rajat (**DZ 48**), which leads to quai Louis-Goujaud, offering a view of the St-Étienne bridge. Rue du Pont-St-Étienne climbs upwards (**DZ 43**). Rue Porte-Panet (**DZ 44**) leads back to the Cathedral.

Pont St-Étienne (**DZ**) – Built in 1210 to provide access to the Cité, the hump-back span is made up of eight pointed arches. There is a nice view of the Puy St-Étienne and the Cathedral.

LE CHÂTEAU

The neighbourhood known as "Le Château" rose up long ago around the St-Martial abbey and the château. Today it serves as Limoges' downtown, busy with shops and activity.

Église St-Pierre-du-Queyroix (**CYZ**) – The flamboyant façade dates from 1534. The 13C bell tower is well-proportioned; it served as a model for the towers of two other churches in Limoges, St-Michel and St-Étienne.
Inside, the church forms an irregular rectangle of surprising width; from the 12C, it has preserved its enormous cylindrical pillars with flattened capitals embellished with palmettos. To the right of the choir, the brightly coloured window was created in 1510 by Jean Pénicaud and has since been restored; it shows Death and the Crowning of the Virgin.
Notice the wooden Christ (14C), very expressive, on the wall behind the main altar and, at the end of the second aisle, a 17C gilded wooden altar screen decorated with paintings. The church possesses a collection of reliquaries.

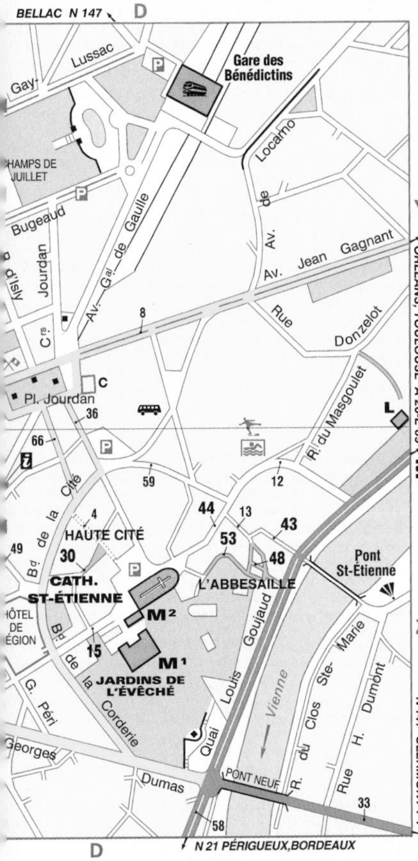

Gare des Bénédictins

ORLEANS, TOULOUSE A 20-E 09

Pl. Jourdan

HAUTE CITÉ

CATH. ST-ÉTIENNE

L'ABBESSAILLE

Pont St-Étienne

JARDINS DE L'ÉVÊCHÉ

PONT NEUF

N 21 PÉRIGUEUX, BORDEAUX

N 141 CLERMONT-F¹

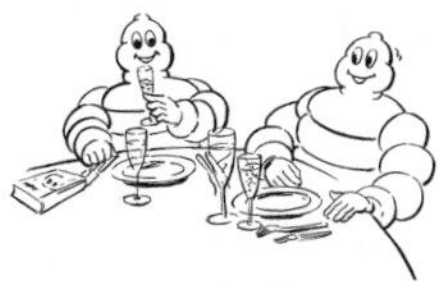

M¹	Musée de l'Évêché	M⁴	Musée des Distilleries Limougeaudes
M²	Musée de la Résistance	M⁵	Musée de l'Automobile
M³	Espace F.R.A.C.	N	Pavillon du Verdurier

Remains of the Abbey of St-Martial ⊘ (CY D) – Once located outside the city walls, place de la République stands over the site of a Gallo-Roman necropolis where St. Martial was buried. His tomb was highly venerated and a chapel was built above it in the 6C. The chapel's keepers adopted the Benedictine rule in 848, and the abbey grew, becoming affiliated with Cluny in 1063. During the Middle Ages, it was the site of intensive religious, cultural and artistic activity. Between the 9C and the 12C, the scriptorium produced such masterpieces as the so-called *manuscrit de la Seconde Bible*, now in the French National Library. Yet thereafter the abbey declined and its buildings were destroyed during the Revolution.

Three churches rose around Saint Martial's tomb: the Basilique du Sauveur, St Pierre and St Benoît.

The Église du Sauveur (Church of Our Saviour), to the south, was built in the 9C and expanded in the 11C, when it reached 102m/335ft, and served as an important way station for pilgrims on the road to Compostela. Rue St-Martial runs along the former axis of the building. The northern arm of the transept provided access to St-Pierre-du-Sépulcre, the "lower church". On the far western end, in the axis of the nave, a stairway led to the tomb. The Chapelle St Benoît, rebuilt in the 13C, was joined to the northern end of St Pierre.

Crypts – The current stairway was put in the 13C, with the Chapelle de l'Ange, to improve the flow of pilgrims. Martial and his two companions (Alpinien and Austriclinien) were laid to rest in the two big tombs measuring more than 2.80m/9ft long, still on view. In the 9C, Martial's remains were exhumed and placed in a gold reliquary on the main altar in the new basilica. The bird mosaic was also created at this time. In the opposite corner stood the tomb of Saint Valérie; according to legend, she was beheaded by her fiancé, Governor Étienne.

The second room or "sanctuary" contains the enormous granite tomb known by the name of Tève-le-Duc, dating from the 4C. To the south, excavations have revealed a 2C Gallo-Roman construction with a mantle of stone masonry and brickwork.

Beyond, there is a large room which lies underneath and shores up the churches of St Pierre and St Benoît, installed on the Gallo-Roman ruins and on the site of an early Christian cemetery. The numerous tombs are made of granite or lead, with brick bases; children's tombs were made of terra cotta plaques. The cemetery was also used in Merovingian and Medieval times.

On place de la République, markings on the ground illustrate the size of the former abbey church.

Place du Présidial (CZ) – The north doorway of the church of St-Michel-les-Lions opens on to this square where the 17-18C royal administrative buildings remain standing. Note at the corner of rue Haute-de-la-Comédie, the former **hôtel Maledent** (**CY B**) which dates back to 1639. Admire the pretty **place Fontaine-des-Barres** (16C) below (**CY 26**).

*★**Église St-Michel-des-Lions** (CZ) – Construction began in 1364 and continued during the 15C when the north doorway was built, and the 16C when a west bay was added. The plan is rectangular, characteristic of churches used for public gatherings more generally.

Outside near the belfry door on the south side can be seen the two lions carved in granite which have given the church its name. It is believed that in the Middle Ages these lions served to mark limits of jurisdiction of the abbots of St-Martial and the viscounts of Limoges. The upper octagonal tiers of the tower are braced by four walled turrets; a tall spire, topped with a pierced copper ball, rising to a height of 68m/223ft. The north doorway is delicately ornamented.

Three parts of equal height resting on slender columns (some are offset on the outside) make up the interior. On either side of the chancel, at the end of the aisles, lovely 15C windows show the life of the Virgin Mary and that of John the Baptist. Behind the high altar, a monumental altar of carved stone supports a 19C gilded wooden reliquary shrine which contains relics of St. Martial including the saint's head.

To the right of the first bay, a wall-niche contains a 13C reliquary in gilded silver and cut crystal.

AROUND TOWN

Shopping – Most of the shops are found in the "Château" neighbourhood, and in particular on the pedestrian streets around rue Clocher or the main avenues (rue Jean-Jaurès, boulevard Louis-Blanc, boulevard Gambetta). If you need something in a hurry, try the shopping centre St-Martial on avenue Garibaldi or the Forum des Bénédictins (avenue de Locarno).

Enamels and Porcelain – Many shops line boulevard Louis-Blanc (the Morel Michel boutique sells ends-of-series and other bargains), place des Jacobins (more bargains at the Cygne Bleu) and rue de la Boucherie (Art et Feu specialises in enamels). The big discount establishments are just outside of town (10-minute drive) on the road to Toulouse and Périgueux.

Regional dishes – Surrounded by cattle country, Limoges' restaurants offer excellent beef dishes: l'Abattoir (avenue de l'Abattoir); le Boeuf à la Mode (rue François-Chénieux); Les Petits Ventres (rue de la Boucherie).

One-of-a-kind – In the midst of the market (les Halles), two lively and unpretentious restaurants make the most of the fresh products at hand to offer simple meals and snacks, starting off early in the morning. At noon, dining is family-style, at long tables where workers and business men rub elbows and break bread. Join them at Chez Bernard and Chez Colette.

Al fresco – On a summer evening, enjoy a terrace café on place de la République (Le Boeuf Rouge, Café de France, Le Central, Pomme Cannelle), or place Fontaine-des-Barres (Le Chalet, La Marmite).

Exotic – Rue Charles-Michels welcomes food from afar: Le Pékin (Chinese), Achirama (Indian), Le San Marco (Italian), Le Salam (Moroccan), Le Yucatan (Mexican).

Coffee break – Classic: Le Paris (cours Jourdan), Le Trianon (boulevard Georges-Périn). Fashionable: Café de la Plage (rue Haute-Cité), Park Avenue (cours Jourdan). Hip: Café des Anciennes Majorettes de la Baule (rue Haute-Vienne), Café des Artistes (place Stalingrad).

Show time – Movie houses are concentrated around place Jourdan and place Denis-Dussoubs. The Théâtre Municipal (rue Jean Jaurès) programmes ballet, opera, and variety shows. Contemporary and classic drama is performed at La Limousine (rue des Coopérateurs) and L'Expression 7 (rue de la Réforme).

★**Cour du Temple** (CZ **61**) – Rue du Consulat, lined with 18C buildings, is linked to rue du Temple by a narrow passage (at no 22), which opens on to 16C half-timbered houses and arcaded galleries, known as the "temple courtyard". Rue du Temple leads from here down to rue Jean-Jaurès and place de la République.

Les Halles (CZ) – Built at the end of the 19C, the covered market stands on **place de la Motte**, probably named for the *motte*, or hillock, where the viscounts' castle once stood. A decorative porcelain frieze depicts market produce.

★VILLAGE DE LA BOUCHERIE

In the 13C, butcher shops were predominant along this stretch of the ancient Gallo-Roman way where tradesmen cut up and sold meat up until the time of the French Revolution.

The streets are liveliest in the summer months, and the neighbourhood is undergoing renewal which has worked to keep the charm of the 14C and 15C houses and quaint squares.

Rue de la Boucherie (CZ **10**) – This picturesque street is lined with half-timbered houses, some of which still have the accoutrements of the 80 butchers' shops which once operated there. The last Sunday in October, a regional festival known as the *Frairie des petits ventres (see Calendar of Events in Practical Information)* brings back the memory of bygone activities.

La Boucherie by night

Maison Traditionelle de la Boucherie ⊙ (CZ **E**) – The butcher's stall at no 36 is now devoted to preserving the heritage of the meat trade in Limoges. In the kitchen (also a shop), visitors can admire the butcher's block and its accessories, a 19C icebox and a hearth where tripe was simmered to perfection. The back room was used for slaughtering and as a stable. Upstairs are the furnished rooms where about 25 lived at a time (family, apprentices and employees) and an attic space used for salting meat and drying skins. Exhibits relate the activities of the trade guild and a few culinary clues for carnivores.

Place de la Barreyrrett (CZ **7**) – The name of this square comes from the fence *(barrière)* around the holding pen for animals awaiting slaughter. The pens disappeared when the municipal slaughterhouse was opened in 1832.

Chapelle St-Aurélien (CZ **F**) – A 14C monolithic cross marks the entrance to this unusual little building dating from 1475. Founded to hold the relics of Saint Aurélien, the chapel was sold at an auction in 1795 and secretly purchased by the butchers' guild *(see box)* which still maintains it today. The ex-votos and gilded wooden statues inside sparkle in the light from votive candles.

★MUSÉE NATIONAL ADRIEN-DUBOUCHÉ ⊙ (BY)

The museum was founded in 1867, became a national museum in 1881 and is named after the director Adrien Dubouché, who provided it with the foundation of its collections (4 000 items). Now the collection includes 11 000 items, dating from the pottery of ancient times to porcelain from factories in production at Limoges today, showing the evolution of chinaware in France and throughout the world.

Ground floor – This floor has recently been renovated. To the left of the vestibule and its bronze statue (1898 of Adrien Dubouché), eight display cases are given over to fine earthenware, popular in the 19C, and to clay pieces formed from slip (*Vase aux musiciennes* by Aube). A collection of pieces by **Théodore Deck** (1823-1891) recalls his important role in ceramic arts in the 19C. Stoneware comes next, from 15C Germany to 19C France, with fa-

Musée Adrien-Dubouché –
Porcelain from the comte d'Artois manufactory

mous names including Delaherche, Decoeur, Chaplet, Moreau-Nélaton. Pottery pieces in the collection date from Ancient Greece and Rome and carry through to the 19C. The last room provides explanations of the manufacturing techniques of the four major families of ceramics (pottery, earthenware, stoneware and porcelain) using illustrations, machines (for applying colour lithography), kiln models and an audio-visual presentation. 19C porcelain is in the right-hand aisle. One thousand two hundred pieces of Limoges porcelain amply demonstrate the reason for the world-wide renown of porcelain manufactured here since 1771. Notice the enormous service in a rice grain pattern from the Pouyat company, the unusual series of dishes from the First World War and the Art Deco collection. Visitors can compare Limoges porcelain with items produced at the same time elsewhere in France or in other countries.

Salon d'honneur – This room houses Chinese porcelain. *(Currently in renovation, may not be open to the public.)* Tang earthenware, Song porcelain, Yuan blue and white ware, 17C and 18C white China, and coloured ware known as *famille verte and famille rose* complete this collection of precious items from the Far East.

First floor – The history of ceramic manufacture, from its origins in the Middle East to Medieval times, is traced in the **right wing**. Ceramics arrived in Europe through Spain, reaching Italy by the end of the Middle Ages, where new techniques and artistic effects developed rapidly. During the second half of the 16C, the craft spread throughout Europe: in France in Nevers (blues), Lyon, and Rouen; in Spain in Talavera and Alcora; in the Netherlands in **Delft**, where the production sought to rival chinaware imported by the East Indian Trading Company; and in Germany. In France, the 17C and 18C were high points for ceramic design and manufacturing. Each size-able city had a production centre, distinguished by unique patterns and colours as well as the quality of the ceramics: **Moustiers** (Provence) invented the first polychrome motifs, while "china" was made in many different places, including Limoges.

The **left wing** contains the collection of 18C porcelain. The **soft-paste porcelain** technique (which does not use kaolin) was perfected in the 17C. First produced in Rouen, major manufacturing took off in Saint-Cloud as of 1677. Several centres in the Paris region became well-known for their wares: Chantilly, Mennecy, Vincennes and **Sèvres**, where the Royal Manufactory was established in 1753-1759. For the rest of Europe, there are some remarkable items from Tournai (Belgium), Marienberg (Switzerland), Chelsea (England), Naples and Madrid.

The first hard-paste porcelains manufactured in Europe were made in the Meissen factory in Saxony in 1710, when Bötttger and Tschirnhaus discovered a source of kaolin white china clay. The factory produced "chinoiserie" motifs on

---

1000 Year-Old Guild

Since 930, *Messieurs les Bouchers de Limoges* have administered a trade guild in the former rue Torte (now rue de la Boucherie). When the relics of Saint Aurélien (the bishop who succeeded Saint Martial) were discovered in 1315, the butchers of the city obtained the right to adopt the saint as their patron. They created a brotherhood which, in 1475, built the Chapelle St-Aurélien to receive the relics in a shrine. In the 16C, six families in the guild took control of the brotherhood (today, members are still elected by a secret ballot for a seven-year term). Since the time of Henri IV, the brotherhood has had the privilege of offering the keys to the city to visiting dignitaries. At the dawn of the 21C, the millenary tradition persists.

Little Lexicon for Limoges

True porcelain (hard-paste): resonant when struck, translucent, made from ground feldspathic rock and the special white clay known as kaolin. Also called "china", because that is where it was first made.

Artificial porcelain (soft-paste): made using clay and ground glass, it has a softer body and can be cut with a file, while true porcelain cannot. Dirt accumulated on an unglazed base can only be removed with difficulty; on true porcelain it comes off easily.

Bone china: developed by Josiah Spode the Second, contains calcined bones in a hard-paste formula, which makes it chip-resistant. Especially popular in England and the United States.

Earthenware: Opaque and porous, the most common type of pottery is made from clay baked at low temperatures.

Stoneware: fired at high temperatures until it is vitrified (glasslike and non-porous), it does not require a glaze; lead, salt and feldspathic glazes are used for decorative effects. Stoneware also originated in China, and came to Europe in the 17C, but by the early 19C its popularity had been superseded by porcelain.

Faience: Tin-glazed earthenware made in France, Germany, Spain or Scandinavia. In Italy, it is called Faenza majolica (the town of Faenza, the origin of the name, was a major production centre in the Renaissance). Manufactured in the Netherlands or England, it is referred to as "delft", after the Dutch city famous for its production.

Creamware: Fine white English lead-glazed earthenware (also produced briefly in France), more durable and less expensive to produce than faience. Wedgwood and Leeds are the best-known manufacturers.

---

tableware and later branched out into figurines and statuary. Kaolin was found near Limoges in 1768, enabling the development of hard-paste production in Sèvres, Paris, Lille, Bordeaux, Orléans and Valenciennes.

Four display cases in this wing summarise the history of glass from the Renaissance to the early 20C.

Virtual Limoges...

To find out more about exhibits, recent acquisitions, and special events, go to the web site of the association of friends of Limoges' museums: www.amimusees.fr/limoges. A site devoted to medieval illuminated manuscripts and sculpture, "Les Splendeurs de St Martial de Limoges", is found at www.culture.fr/limoges. To consult a catalogue of porcelain tableware, visit www.manufacture-royale.com.

ADDITIONAL SIGHTS

A ring of circular boulevards has taken the place of the old ramparts which isolated the centre from the outskirts.

Jardin d'Orsay (BZ) – Located behind the court house *(palais de justice)*, this public garden was created in the 18C on the site of the Gallo-Roman arena, filled in to accommodate the garden; some vestiges are still visible.

Aquarium du Limousin ⊘ (CZ) – Set up on place Haute-Vienne on the site of an old reservoir, the aquarium has made use of the vaulted architecture to welcome European freshwater fish, tropical species, piranhas and more.

Pont St-Martial (CZ) – On the foundations of the Roman bridge which stood until 1182 (razed by Henry II Plantagenet), a new bridge to the château was built in 1215.

Musée des Distillerie Limougeaudes ⊘ (CY M⁴) – *Not on the map. From place Denis-Dussoubs, take rue François-Chenieux; turn left on avenue G.-et V.-Lemoine, continue on place Sadi-Carnot.*

The distillery museum, at 52 rue de Belfort, is steeped in local traditions as well as the fragrance of the sweet liqueurs produced here. Tools and alembics, bottles and posters are among the items on display. Chestnut liqueur *(Feuillardier)* and other house specialities are on sale.

★① **FROM VIENNE TO BRIANCE** *Round trip of 90km/54mi – 2.5hr*

Leave Limoges on N 21 towards Périgeux.

This road is picturesque and goes up the valley of the Briance, winding its way through meadows. At Pont-Rompu hamlet, there is a view on the right of a picturesque old bridge with pointed cutwaters on which passed the ancient Roman way from Limoges to Bordeaux.

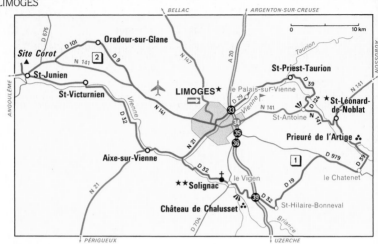

★Solignac – See SOLIGNAC.

Follow D 32 to Le Vigen. Its Romanesque church has a severe two-storied wall-belfry. Continue on D 32 which affords a good view of Chalusset Castle.

Château de Chalusset – The impressive ruins of Chalusset Castle are a perfect example of mediaeval military architecture in their plan and position on a rock promontory, which juts forward to the point where the Briance and Ligoure rivers meet. The castle was built in the 12C and in 1577 it fell into the hands of the Huguenots who used it as a base for their battles against Limoges. The troops of Limoges took the notorious castle by force and dismantled it.

Only traces remain of the three outer walls, the square towers, the keep and the ramparts, but these traces, in spite of the overgrowth and the accumulation of earth and stones are still impressive in scale.

Return to D 32 and bear right until you come to St-Hilaire-Bonneval where you turn left; take D 19 to join D 979. Turn right and drive to Le Chatenet.

Ancien Prieuré de l'Artige (Priory) – See ST-LÉONARD-DE-NOBLAT.

★St-Léonard-de-Noblat – See ST-LÉONARD-DE-NOBLAT.

D 941 crosses the Vienne and follows the river valley before it rises up to a plateau. At St-Antoine, take D 124 for a panoramic view of the Ambazac hills, then turn left on D 39, a lovely country road.

St-Priest-Taurion – This town rests peacefully at the fork of the rivers Taurion and Vienne, in a green valley cut across with dams.

After la Palais, take D 29 along the valley back to Limoges.

② LA VALLÉE TÉNÉBREUSE *Round trip of 80km/45mi – 3hr*

Leave Limoges travelling westward on N 141 towards Angoulême.

Oradour-sur-Glane – See ORADOUR-SUR-GLANE.

St-Junien – See ST-JUNIEN.

Site Corot – See ST-JUNIEN.

St-Victurnien – The altar screen in the church has a 14C decorative painting illustrating the Passion and the Resurrection. Also worthy of note are the 13C enamel shrine, the 14C polychrome Virgin and Child, and, in the cemetery *(road to Oradour)*, a lantern of the dead.

The winding road follows the river and rises up above the valley, revealing beautiful views.

Aixe-sur-Vienne – Every seven years, during the *Ostensions (see Introduction)*, 20 reliquaries are carried in a procession by representatives of the different trades, lit by torches as they return at night.

*The main shopping streets are printed in red
at the top of the street lists accompanying town plans.*

Basse Vallée du LOT

Michelin map 79 folds 5 to 10 or 235 folds 9 to 11 and 14 and 15

The river Lot is at its most beautiful where it cuts across the Quercy *causses*. The river flows at the foot of rocks thickly wooded with chestnut trees and promontories on which old villages are perched; elsewhere the waters flow in great loops around picturesque towns and cities.

From the Cévennes Mountains to the Agenais region – The Lot is a tributary of the Garonne. It rises in the Cévennes on the slopes of Le Goulet Mountain at an altitude of 1400m/4600ft and flows right across the southern part of the Massif Central. It follows the winding course of an uninterrupted series of meanders or loops, *cingles*, circling tongues of land, some only a couple of hundred yards across. As it flows between the tall limestone cliffs of the Quercy causses, its thousand curves provide a never-ending variety of magnificent views. The valley is attractive both in its wilder, unspoiled sections and its brighter, cultivated ones. The Lot leaves Quercy before Libos and, after flowing a further 480km/300mi, enters the Garonne in the Agenais Plain.

Scenes from the past – Before the advent of railway, the Lot was an important navigational route. The river was initially adapted by Colbert and was later equipped with dams and even canals to cut across the promontories of the wider bends, as at Luzech. A whole fleet of barges, known as *sapines* or *gabares*, used to travel down the Lot to Bordeaux, carrying cheeses from Auvergne, coal from Decazeville and wine from Cahors.

The Lot vineyards – The slopes of the valley of the Olt – the Occitan name for the Lot, which is still found in such place names as St-Vincent-Rive-d'Olt and Balaguier-d'Olt – have long been famous for their vineyards. Quercy wines, with their high alcoholic content, have played a great part in making Cahors and the Olt valley famous. In 1C AD the Roman Emperor Domitian punished Cahors for revolting by destroying its vineyards; after two centuries of teetotalism, Probus revoked the ban on wine. Despite the boycott by Bordeaux, through which the wine was shipped, wines from the Lot valley were preferred by the English for many centuries. Eleanor of Aquitaine brought Quercy to the king of England as part of her dowry; in 1287 letters patent were granted by the king in favour of these wines. The wine was exported to Poland, to Russia – where only the wine of Cahors could entice the Tsar Peter the Great from vodka – and even to Italy. Legend has it that popes insisted on serving this wine at mass.

Two men of Quercy, the poet Clément Marot , and Galiot de Genouillac, gave the wine to François I to taste, and the king's palate delighted in its velvet smoothness. Later, vines from the Lot were transported at great cost to Fontainebleau to create the Royal Vine Arbour.

★★CLIFFS AND PROMONTORIES

From Figeac to Cahors *115km/71.5mi – allow 1 day*

As it crosses Quercy, the Lot flows at the foot of slopes, or often sheer cliffs. Leaving Rouergue, the river hurls itself against the spur on which the old town of Capdenac stands, and then forces its way between the cliff walls of the causses. Sometimes the cliffs enclose the river, and from their tops, there are lovely views of the valley.

★★ Figeac – *See FIGEAC.*

Leave Figeac southeast.

Capdenac – Capdenac-le-Haut, perched on a promontory and enclosed by a meander in the Lot river, occupies a remarkable **site★**. This small town, which still looks much the way it did centuries ago, overlooks Capdenac-Gare, a busy railway junction which has developed in the valley.

The **ramparts** are vestiges of the 13C and 14C outer walls and the citadel as well as the Northern Gate (Comtale), the village entrance, and the Southern Gate (Vijane). The **keep**, a powerful square tower flanked by turrets (13-14C), houses the tourist information centre and a small **museum** ⊙ which recounts Capdenac's history.

Take D 86, along the south bank of the river, which makes a wide bend in the centre of an alluvial plain, rich farmland.

Beyond St-Julien-d'Empare, this picturesque road offers a good view of the Capdenac amphitheatre. After Pont-de-la-Madeleine the road runs beside the Lot through rocky countryside with dense undergrowth. Shortly after Balaguier-d'Olt comes St-Pierre-Toirac.

St-Pierre-Toirac – This small village, on the north bank of the Lot, contains an interesting **church**, its architecture dating from the 11C and 14C. The Romanesque apse alone belies the fortified appearance of this building which served as a defence point with its massive crenellated keep and upper floor.

The short nave has cradle vaulting and primitive style capitals. The chancel has trefoil arches, and saw-toothed arches surround the stained-glass windows of the apse. Recently discovered Merovingian sarcophagi have been placed behind the church.

Larroque-Toirac Castle – *See Grottes de FOISSAC.*

Many delightful villages are to be seen on the north bank which is overshadowed by high rocks and vertical cliffs.

As the valley walls open out, the Lot itself widens out into a great expanse of water with rows of poplars, and cultivated tobacco and cereals growing along its banks.

Montbrun – The village of Montbrun rises in tiers on a rocky promontory encircled by steep cliffs. It looks down on the Lot and faces the Saut de La Mounine *(see below)*. Towering above the village are the ruins of a fortress that belonged to one of Pope John XXII's brothers, and then to the powerful Cardaillac family *(see CHÂLUS).*

Cajarc – The town was brought into the public eye when President Pompidou had a house here. Near the church, the Hébrardie Mansion with Gothic windows is all that remains standing of a 13C castle. Inaugurated in 1989, the **Maison des Arts Georges Pompidou** organises retrospective exhibits of the works of contemporary European artists: Hartung, Bissière and Soulages have been featured, ranking Cajarc among the foremost centres of contemporary art in the region.

There is a very nice reservoir on the Lot here.

Cross the river at Cajarc and follow D 127 up the south bank as far as Saut de La Mounine. The road overhangs the Lot to start with, then immediately after Saujac rises and winds round to overlook a wooded gorge, before reaching the top of the causse.

★★**Saut de la Mounine** – There is a good **view**★ of the valley from the top of this cliff. The end of the spur overlooks a wide bend in the river as it encircles a mosaic of fields. Over on the left, on the far bank, stands Montbrun Castle.

The curious name, Saut de la Mounine – the little monkey's leap, comes from a rather strange legend. The lord of Montbrun decided to punish his daughter for her love of another lord's son and ordered her to be hurled from the top of the cliff; a hermit, appalled at this cruel idea, disguised a small blind monkey (*mounine* in the Oc language) in women's clothes and hurled it into the air. When he saw the object falling the father immediately regretted his brutal action; on seeing his daughter alive and well he was so overjoyed that he forgave her.

Return on D 127 to the river's north bank. From here the road climbs rapidly and passes near a little chapel ("la Capellette") built in the 12C and 13C. The apse is all that remains. From this spot there is a sweeping view of the valley.

Calvignac – This old village, where a few traces of its fortress may still be seen, is perched on a spur on the river's south bank.

Staying on the same bank take D 8 which leads to Cénevières.

★**Cénevières Castle** – *See Château de CÉNEVIÈRES.*

From Tour-de-Faure admire St-Cirq-Lapopie in its remarkable setting on the river's south bank.

★★**St-Cirq-Lapopie** – *See ST-CIRQ-LAPOPIE.*

Beyond St-Cirq-Lapopie, D 40, which is built into the cliff, has been designed as a tourist route. There is a good **view**★ of the confluence of the Lot and the Célé from a small viewpoint, the **belvédère du Bancourel**. From the same spot a wide bend of the Lot can be seen curving between white and yellow cliffs; magnificent poplars and fields enhance the beauty of the landscape.

Bouziès – On the bank opposite the village, the **Défilé des Anglais** ("Englishmen's Gorge") is the most famous of the "fortified gullies" constructed during the Hundred Years War in cave-like openings which could only be accessed by a rope-ladder.

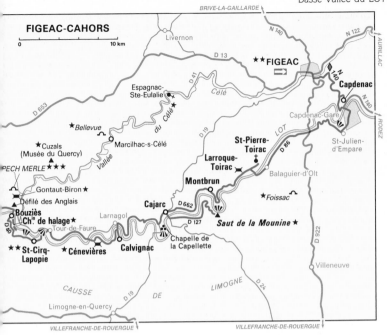

★**Towpath** along the Lot *(Chemin de halage)* – Take the GR 36 trail off to the right of the car park by the moorings.

After about 500m/547yd, the spectacular towpath comes into view, carved out of the rock because here, the cliff juts out over the river. In sections such as this, the barges coming up the Lot with their cargoes of salt, dried fish, spices or plaster could not be towed by the usual teams of horses or oxen, but had to be pulled along by strong fellows with a reputation for bad tempers and miserable lives. This pathway is now a marvellous walk. At the top of the first lock there is a 15m/9ft long bas-relief, the work of contemporary artist D. Monnier, decorating the limestone wall with fish and shellfish.

Immediately after Bouziès, cross the Lot and take D 662 again. This runs close beside the river in an attractive, sometimes wooded, cliff setting. In several places the road has been cut out of the rock face itself. After Vers the valley broadens out, cliffs give way to wooded hills, and the alluvial soil is put to farming.

Notre-Dame-de-Vêles – This small pilgrimage chapel was built in the 12C and has a lovely square belltower and a Romanesque apse.

Bouziès – Towpath with a bas-relief by Monnier

197

Laroque-des-Arcs – This village's name is a reminder of the aqueduct which crossed the Francoulès valley and supplied water to Cahors. A 3-tiered bridge bore the aqueduct which transported water over 20km/12mi from Vers to Divona (ancient Cahors). The consuls of Cahors had it demolished in 1370. An old tower perched on a rock beside the Lot enabled guards to watch the river traffic and exact tolls.

★★Cahors – *See CAHORS.*

THE MEANDERS OF THE LOT'S LOWER REACHES

From Cahors to Bonaguil *61km/38mi – about 4hr*

From Cahors to Puy-l'Évêque, the Lot winds in a series of meanders – *cingles* – through Quercy *causses*; beyond this, it flows into a flatter region and the valley broadens out.

★★Cahors – *See CAHORS.*

Leave Cahors travelling northwest.

Mercuès – Once the property of the count-bishops of Cahors, the château is now a hotel. It occupies a remarkable site overlooking the north bank of the Lot. In 1212 the château was a fortified castle, it was then enlarged in the 14C, besieged several times during the Hundred Years War and the Wars of Religion, altered in the 15C and converted in the 16C into a château with terraces and gardens. It was not restored completely until last century. There is an outstanding **view★** of the valley from the château.

West of Mercuès the road leaves the valley for a short distance to cross a flourishing countryside of vineyards and orchards; then the road returns to the river, following it closely.

Luzech – *See LUZECH.*

Follow the south bank for the best views of the valley.

Albas – This village has narrow streets lined with old houses.

Anglars-Juillac – A Crucifixion adorns the church's Renaissance doorway.

Bélaye – Once the fief of the bishops of Cahors, Bélaye stands on top of a hill. An extensive **view★** of the Lot valley unfolds from the top of the spur and from the upper square of this little village.

Grézels – Overlooking the village is the **feudal castle of La Coste** ⊙, which has been razed and rebuilt on several occasions. The bishops of Cahors possessed a fief which extended over the Lot valley from Cahors to Puy-l'Évêque, and Grézels marked the limits of their territory; therefore, a stronghold was built to defend the entrance to their fief.

During the Hundred Years War, it was transformed into a fortress. It was severely damaged during the different wars, then restored in the 14C and 16C. After the Revolution it was abandoned.

The curtain wall and crenellated corner towers are the oldest parts of the castle.

Basse vallée du Lot – Albas

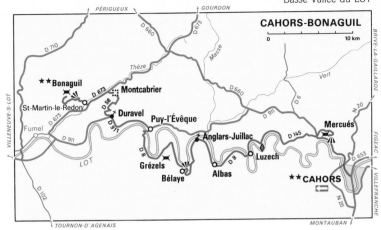

CAHORS-BONAGUIL

Puy-l'Évêque – This small town, which took its present name (*évêque* – bishop) when it came under the lordship of the bishops of Cahors, occupies one of the most picturesque sites in the valley downstream from Cahors; from the far side of the bridge into town, admire the old houses in golden stone.

The **church** ⊙ was built on the northeast side of the town, at the furthest point in the defence system of which it was itself a part. In front of the church stands a massive belfry porch flanked by a turret and buttresses. The nave was built in the 14C and 15C and ends in a polygonal apse. In the churchyard there are many old tombs, and on the left of the church stands a wayside cross ornamented with archaic-style sculpture. The **keep**, all that remains of the Episcopal castle, dates back to the 13C.

The terraces and hillsides are covered with vines, and the wide alluvial valley is carpeted with fields.

Duravel – The 11C church has historiated capitals decorating the chancel. There is an archaic crypt supported by columns with rough-hewn capitals. The bodies of Saints Hilarion, Poémon and Agathon lie buried at the back of the apse.

The *ostension*, or solemn exhibition of relics to the faithful, is held every five years.

Montcabrier – The bastide was founded in 1297 by Guy de Cabrier, who gave it his name. It was granted a charter of franchises by Philip the Fair. Overlooking the square, several old houses (including the 16C house of the king's court) are laid out in the regular pattern of the original plan. The church, partly rebuilt in the 14C, has a Flamboyant doorway (restored) surrounded by a fine open-bayed belltower. Inside, a plain 14C statue of St Louis, the parish's patron saint, is surrounded by ex-votos. This statue was the object of a local pilgrimage.

St-Martin-le-Redon – This charming village is known for the St-Martial mineral spring, reputed to cure skin ailments.

Shortly after St.Martin-le-Redon there is a lovely **view**★ of the fantastic outline of Bonaguil Castle , surrounded by woods.

★★Château de Bonaguil – *See Château de BONAGUIL.*

LUZECH

Michelin map 79 fold 7 or 235 north of fold 14

Luzech has grown up on the narrowest part of a tongue of land almost completely encircled by a loop in the Lot river. The isthmus at this point is some 100m (just over 100yd) wide. The town is crowned by the old castle keep. To the north lies the Roman city of Impernal and to the south the Pistoule Promontory, washed by the waters of the river as it sweeps round the bend. A reservoir has been formed by the construction of a dam upstream from the peninsula, and a water sports centre has been set up there (**boat tours** ⊙).

Impernal Hill – A natural defensive position, this rise has been inhabited since prehistoric times; Gauls, recognising its potential, transformed the plateau into a powerful stronghold. A citadel (the square keep can still be seen) was built below it in the Middle Ages. In 1118, Richard the Lion Heart was master of the citadel. Luzech became the seat of one of the four baronies of Quercy and was much sought as a prize by the English in the Hundred Years War. Nevertheless, the town resisted all attacks and became an important central stronghold. During the Wars of Religion, it remained a faithful bastion of Catholicism under the bishops of Cahors.

Excavations of the Impernal site have revealed walls and traces of buildings dating from the Roman and Gaulish periods.

★Viewpoint – From the top of Impernal Hill, the view encompasses Luzech clustered at its foot, as well as Pistoule Promontory, slicing through the wide alluvial plain like a ship's prow, and the Lot winding between rich and fertile crops.

Old town – In the old district known as the *faubourg du Barry*, picturesque alleyways link rue du Barry-del-Valat with the quays.
Around place des Consuls, on the other side of place du Canal, several examples of medieval architecture are still to be seen: Penitents' Chapel (12C), Capsol Gateway with its brick pointed arch and Consuls' House with its elegant paired windows.

Musée archéologique Armand-Viré ⊘ – Established in the fine vaulted cellar of the old Consuls' House, the museum retraces the history (from the Paleolithic Age to the Gallo-Roman times) of the site of Luzech. The items displayed (excavated from the Impernal site and the cave found on the hillside) include the exceptional **scale model of the Column of Trajan★**, and an unusual Gallo-Roman hinged spoon, of bronze and iron.

Keep – *Entrance via place des Consuls.*
The entrance used to be through the small pointed-arched doorway opening onto the first floor. From the terrace of the 13C keep there is a bird's-eye view onto the brown-tiled roofs of the town, tucked amid meadows and crops with a row of hills along the horizon.

Notre-Dame-de-l'Ile – The chapel, set in a calm landscape of vineyards and orchards against a backdrop of hills along the course of the Lot, stands at the furthest point of the isthmus. This Flamboyant Gothic sanctuary is a pilgrimage centre, which dates back to the 13C.

EXCURSION

Cambayrac – *8km/5mi south on D 23*
The hamlet possesses an odd-looking church identifiable from afar by a wall belfry with a shape reminiscent of a French policeman's hat. Inside, the Romanesque apse and the side chapels were recovered in the 17C with an unusual marble and stucco décor in the classical style.

Site de la MADELEINE★

Michelin map 75 fold 16 or 235 fold 1 – Local map see LES-EYZIES-DE-TAYAC

The location of La Madeleine Site *(access via Tursac and the bridge to l'Espinasse)* stands out very clearly, from the point where the wooded plateau meets the Vézère's alluvial plain below.

The terrain is formed by the river's narrowest and most distinctly shaped meander (80m/88yd at its source expanding to 2.2km/1mi). On the rock above stand the remains of a medieval castle, dating from the mid-15C.
Midway up the hill, and protected by a rock overhang, lies an old **troglodyte village** ⊘, which was probably occupied from the end of the 10C (Viking invasions) to the 19C. The village consists of some 20 dwellings carved out of the rock near a spring

Erskine/IMAGES TOULOUSE

Site de la Madeleine – Cliff dwellings

and protected by a narrow fortified entrance; about 100 people could live there, both during troubled times and times of peace. A chapel consecrated to St Mary Magdalene, which was enlarged and had ogive vaulting added to it in the 15C, gave the site its name.

At the foot of the cliff, beneath the village, lies the **prehistoric deposit** which established the characteristics of the Magdalenian Culture, which predominated during the last 60 centuries of the Upper Paleolithic Age (15000 to 9000 BC). The richness and quality of the items discovered by Lartet and Christy in 1863 (for example the ivory plaque of an engraved mammoth) enabled Mortillet, six years later, to propose a classification of the diverse epochs of prehistory based on the products (bone, flint) of human industry *(see Introduction, Prehistory)*. The majority of the objects are exhibited in the museums at Les Eyzies and St-Germain-en-Laye, west of Paris.

MARCILHAC-SUR-CÉLÉ

Population 196

Michelin map 79 fold 9 or 235 fold 11 – Local map see Vallée du CÉLÉ

Marcilhac is built in the centre of an amphitheatre of cliffs in the enchanting Célé valley. Interesting old houses surround the ruins of a Benedictine abbey.

The legal jungle – In the 11C the modest sanctuary of Rocamadour was under the care of Marcilhac Abbey, which let it fall into ruins. Noticing this negligence some monks from Tulle installed themselves in the sanctuary. However, in 1166 the discovery of the body of St Amadour turned the sanctuary into a rich and famous pilgrimage centre. Marcilhac recalled its rights and expelled the Tulle monks. Soon afterwards the abbot of Tulle threw out the Marcilhac monks and again occupied Rocamadour. Lawsuits were filed fast and furiously. The case was acrimonious, and the bishop of Cahors, the papal legate, the archbishop of Bourges, even the pope himself, were all called on to give judgement, but avoided reaching a decision; finally, after 100 years of squabbling, Marcilhac accepted an indemnity of 3000 sols and relinquished its claim to Rocamadour.

Marcilhac Abbey flourished until the 14C, but during the Hundred Years War it was virtually destroyed by marauding bands of Englishmen and French mercenary troops. After the Reformation, the abbey, a ghost of its former self, fell into the hands of the Hébrards of St-Sulpice; the monks had to give up the monastic way of life and be put up in local people's homes. The abbey church was secularised in 1764.

SIGHTS

Abbey – The ensemble is made up of two very distinct parts.

Romanesque part – The west porch and the first three bays of the nave are open to the sky. They are flanked by a tall square tower, which was probably fortified in the 14C. A round-arched door on the south side is topped with sculpture forming a tympanum and depicting the Last Judgement: Christ in Majesty, with figures on either side, thought to be representing the sun and moon, appears above two thick-set angels with open wings, St Peter and St Paul. These carvings are archaic in style, obviously reflecting the décor of gold and silverwork, and would appear to date from the 10C. Go through this doorway and enter the church to the right.

Gothic part – This part of the church, closed to the west from the fourth bay on, dates from the 15C and is built in the Flamboyant style. The chancel has stellar vaulting and is encircled by an ambulatory. A baroque pew decorated with the Hébrard family crest has a fabulous *miserere* (a hinged shelf which supports someone standing) carved with the head of an angel. A chapel on the left of the chancel has 15C frescoes: Christ giving Blessing with the twelve Apostles; under each Apostle is his name and a phrase which characterises him. The coat of arms in the centre of each triad is that of the Hébrards of St-Sulpice.

On leaving the church, turn right (from the second Romanesque bay) onto the path to the chapter-house, which has very delicate Romanesque capitals alternately made of grey-blue limestone and rose-coloured stalagmite stone. Go towards an esplanade shaded by plane trees; a round tower marks the site of the abbot's house. By the banks of the Célé (right), the line of the rampart wall is interrupted by a postern.

★Grotte de Bellevue ⊘ – *1.5km/1mi northwest*

The route leading up to the cave is a corniche road overlooking the Célé valley and giving fine glimpses of the village and abbey. After following a series of four steeply climbing hairpin bends, branch off to the left in the direction of the hamlet of Pailhès. *The car park is further along on the left.*

This cave was opened to the public two years after it was discovered in 1964. The cave contains a remarkable variety of concretions: stalactites, stalagmites, frozen falls, columns of different widths and vast flows of white calcite striped with ochre or dark red. Its large chamber is wonderful; the many eccentrics seem to flower like coral, forming different shapes in every direction.

The particularly delicate stalagmites resemble slim church candles. The regularity of **Hercules' Column**, reaching from the floor to the ceiling, is striking. It is 4m/13ft high with a circumference of 3.50m/11ft. Its upper part is made up of a disc at an angle of 45° to the top of the column.

MARTEL★

Population 1 462 Michelin map 75 fold 18 or 235 fold 2

Martel, built on the Upper Quercy *causse* to which it has given its name *(Causse de Martel)* is known as the "town of the seven towers". It still contains many medieval buildings. Today fine foods are part of its reputation: it is a central market for walnuts, and small industries process and preserve local gourmet products.

The three hammers – After stopping the Saracens at Poitiers in 732, Charles Martel chased them into Aquitaine. Several years later he struck again and wiped them out. To commemorate this victory over the infidels and to give thanks to God, Charles Martel had a church built on the spot; soon a town grew up around the church. It was given the name of Martel in memory of its founder and took as its crest three hammers, which were the favourite weapons of the saviour of Christianity.

Martel and the Viscounty of Turenne – The founding of Martel by the conqueror of the infidels is probably based more on fiction than on fact. However, it is known that the viscounts of Turenne made Martel an important urban community as early as the 12C. In 1219, Viscount Raymond IV granted a charter establishing Martel as a free town – exempt from the king's taxes, and with permission to mint money. However the town stayed faithful to the king. Very quickly Martel established a town council and consulate and thus became the seat of the royal bailiwick and of the seneschalship. It established a court of appeal which handled all the region's judicial matters; more than fifty magistrates, judges and lawyers were employed. It reached its peak at the end of the 13C and beginning of the 14C. Like the rest of the region, the town suffered during the Hundred Years War – batted backwards and forwards between English and French rule – and during the Wars of Religion – pillaged by the Huguenots. In 1738, when the rights of Turenne were sold to the king *(see TURENNE)*, Martel lost its privileges and became a mere castellany.

The rebellious son – At the end of the 12C, Martel was the scene of a tragic series of events which brought into conflict Henry Plantagenet, king of England and lord of all Western France, his wife Eleanor of Aquitaine and their four sons. The royal household was a royal hell. Henry could no longer stand the sight of Eleanor, and shut her up in a tower. The sons thereupon took up arms against their father, and the eldest, Henry Short Coat, pillaged the viscounty of Turenne and Quercy. To punish him, Henry Plantagenet gave his lands to his third son, Richard the Lion Heart, and stopped the allowance paid to his eldest son. Henry Short Coat found himself penniless, surrounded and in an altogether desperate situation: to pay his foot-soldiers he plundered the treasure houses of the provincial abbeys. He took from Rocamadour the shrine and the precious stones of St Amadour, whose body was profaned, and he sold Roland's famous sword Durandal. But as he was leaving Rocamadour after this sacrilegious act, the bell miraculously began to toll: it was a sign from God.

Henry fled to Martel and arrived there with a fever; he felt death to be upon him and was stricken with remorse. He confessed his crimes while Henry II was sent for, to come and forgive his son on his death bed; Henry II was at the siege of Limoges and sent a messenger with his pardon. The messenger found Henry Short Coat lying in agony on a bed of cinders, a heavy wooden cross upon his chest. Shortly afterwards he died, a last farewell to his mother Eleanor on his lips.

TOUR

Former perimeter walls – Wide avenues, the Fossé des Cordeliers and the Boulevard du Capitani, have been built on the site of the old ramparts (12-13C). The machicolated **Tournemire Tower** (**B**), which used to be the prison tower, and the Souillac and Brive Gateways (found at the end of Route de Souillac and rue de Brive; not on the town plan) hark back to the time when Martel was a fortified town, well protected by double perimeter walls. The second perimeter wall, built in the 18C, enclosed the suburbs.

Leave the car in the car park along the north wall. Pass between the post office and the Tournemire Tower to enter the old town.

Rue du Four-Bas – There are still some old houses along this street, which is spanned by an archway.

Église St-Maur – This Gothic church (13-16C) has some interesting defensive features; huge buttresses converted into defence towers, machicolations protecting the flat east end and a 48m/157ft high belltower which looks more like a keep. Beneath the porch is a fine historiated Romanesque *tympanum* depicting the Last Judgement. It shows Christ seated, His head adorned with a cruciform halo, His arms stretched wide to show His wounds; two angels hold the instruments of the Passion while two others sound the trumpets of the Resurrection. The width of the nave is striking. The chancel with its stellar vaulting is lit by a large 16C *stained-glass window* showing God the Father, the four Evangelists and scenes from the Passion.

Rue Droite – There are old town houses all along this road, one of which, **Hôtel Vergnes-de-Ferron** (**D**), is adorned with a lovely Renaissance door.

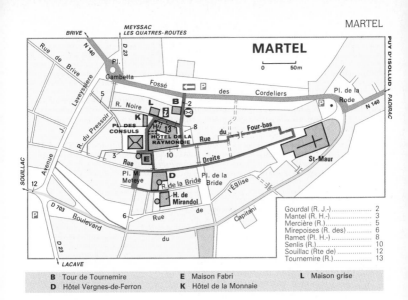

B Tour de Tournemire   **E** Maison Fabri   **L** Maison grise

D Hôtel Vergnes-de-Ferron   **K** Hôtel de la Monnaie

Hôtel de Mirandol – This town house features a great square tower with an adjoining round turret.

★★**Place des Consuls** – In the centre of the square is the 18C **covered market**. The timbering is supported on great stone pillars. On one side the old town measures can be seen.

★**Hôtel de la Raymondie** – Once the fortress of the Turenne viscounts, built around 1280, this building was converted into a Gothic mansion in the 14C. It is topped with corner turrets, and its most striking feature is a belfry. The **façade**★ overlooking the rue de Senlis has remarkable apertures: a row of ogive arches on the ground floor is surmounted by seven quatrefoil rose windows. The main entrance on place des Consuls is decorated with the town's coat of arms, a shield with three hammers. Having been law courts for a while, the mansion now houses the town hall.

In the first floor rooms note the two carved wooden chimney pieces and the Renaissance low relief. In the keep's upper room a small **museum** ⊘ contains items found at the Puy d'Issolud excavations (*see below*).

Maison Fabri (**E**) – The tower, called after Henry Short Coat since he died here in 1183, has windows with frontons decorated with balls at the intersections of their cornices on all five floors.

Rue Tournemire (**13**) – This attractive little street leads off to the left of the Hôtel de la Raymondie. The 13C **Hôtel de la Monnaie** (**K**) with intersecting turrets used to mint coins (écus and deniers) for the Turenne viscounty. The 16C **Maison Grise** (**L**) is decorated with a carved bust and a heraldic shield with three hammers.

EXCURSION

★**Puy d'Issolud** – *14km/9mi. Leave Martel to the east.*

The plateau near Vayrac, of which the highest point is Puy d'Issolud with an altitude of 311m/1020ft, is bordered by steep cliffs overlooking little tributaries flowing into the Dordogne.

Puy d'Issolud was surrounded, at the time of the Gauls, by such solid earthworks and dry-stone defences that it was one of the most redoubtable *oppida* of Quercy, and is said to have been the former Uxellodunum, site of the last Gaulish resistance to Caesar after Alésia, led by Drapes and Lucterius of the Caduici. Some historians place Uxellodunum at Capdenac or Luzech, but archeological research suggests that it is more likely to be the Puy d'Issolud.

The battle, led by the Roman legionaries, was waged with unbelievable ferocity and, after a spring had been diverted through underground caverns, causing those defending Uxellodunum to believe that their gods had deserted them by cutting off their water supply, ended in another defeat for the Gauls. Caesar, angered at the resistance put up by the besieged Gauls, is said to have ordered that each prisoner's right hand be cut off.

Items discovered during excavations are on display in the museum of the Hôtel de la Raymondie in Martel (*see above*).

From the plateau there is an extensive, albeit piecemeal **view**★ of the Dordogne.

The towns and sights described in this guide
are indicated in black lettering on the local maps and town plans.

MASSERET

Population 669
Michelin map 72 fold 18 or 239 fold 14

Masseret village stands in a part of the Limousin countryside which is mostly woodland. The N 20 runs right through the village.

In the centre of Masseret stands a modern tower with a viewing table as its top (104 steps). There is a beautiful circular **panorama★**: to the north can be seen the Ambazac Hills, to the east the Millevaches Plateau, the Monédières Massif and on a clear day the Mountains of Auvergne.

The Romanesque **church**, largely restored in the 16C, has a shrine dedicated to Saint Valérie dating from the 13C.

LE MONT GARGAN *39km/23mi – 1hr*

Leave Masseret travelling westward on D 20ᴱ9, towards Meuzac.

St-Germain-les-Belles – This building dating from the 14C is a fine example of a **fortified church** ⊙. The façade and chevet are protected by machicolations. Inside, to the right of the chancel, a spiral staircase gives access to the lookout points high above the tall pointed vaulting, and the watch-path.

★★**Mont Gargan** – Altitude 731m/2.398ft. The road climbs steeply at first, leading to the summit which is crowned by the ruins of a chapel. As you go round the chapel, you see a vast **panorama★★**, southeast over the Monédières Massif, north over the hills of Marche and west to the Limousin Mountains.

MEHUN-SUR-YÈVRE★

Population 7 227
Michelin map 64 fold 20 or 238 fold 18

This charming old town on the banks of the river Yèvre and the Berry canal is a centre of porcelain manufacture.

Mehun's Golden Age – The third son of King John the Good, **Duke Jean de Berry** (1340-1416) was a lavish patron of the arts and admirer of the art of manuscript illumination. He rebuilt Mehun Castle in 1386 and it was here amid a brilliant court that he welcomed writers such as Froissart, miniaturists like the Limbourg brothers and André Beauneveu. The latter, who was also a sculptor and architect, worked for a lengthy period at the castle. The Duke was on friendly terms, with them all and often invited them to visit his menagerie or his luxurious bath pavilion. Duke Jean de Berry left the castle to his grand-nephew Charles VII, who received Joan of Arc here in the winter of 1429 and 1430. The Dauphin, the future Louis XI, spent his childhood at the castle and conspired against his father, Charles VII, who died here in 1461.

SIGHTS

Porte de l'Horloge – A 14C gateway (restored) at the top of rue Jeanne d'Arc.

Rue Jeanne d'Arc – This street leads down towards the Yèvre between old houses which sometimes have wells in front of them. Number 87, the house where Joan of Arc stayed, has elegant bays with trilobed arches; to the left is the esplanade leading to the castle. Further on the street crosses the Yèvre, giving fine views of the public washing boards and a 12C watermill. The mill houses the **Centre régional des métiers d'art "Les grands moulins"**, exhibits on the miller's trade. A shaded promenade running alongside the Berry canal affords views of the castle and church.

Château-musée Charles VII ⊙ – Of this marvellous fairy tale castle, visited and admired by Claus Sluter and Holbein, sculptor and painter respectively, there remain two round towers, one of which is named after Charles VII (extensively restored).Vaulting springers and some of the chimney pieces can still be seen. The original plan of the castle is still visible – note the position of the bastion jutting out like a spur towards the river. A miniature of the duke of Berry's *Très Riches Heures* (The Rich Hours) now in the Condé museum of Chantilly (north of Paris), executed by the Limbourg brothers, shows the castle as it existed in the 15C. Dismantled in the 17C the castle slowly fell into ruins. Excavations have revealed a Gallo-Roman foundation.

Collégiale Notre-Dame – The construction of this church, Romanesque in style with the exception of the chapel added in the 15C, started with the chancel (11C) which has a horse-shoe shape. The façade is preceded by a belfry-porch ornamented on the north side by a cross interlacing, in the centre of which is the Holy Lamb. At the entrance to the nave, on the left beside the baptismal font, is a 15C relics cupboard, which was fitted in the 17C with a carved wooden door representing the Education of the Virgin. In the south aisle is a Crucifixion painted by Jean Boucher from Bourges, the master of Mignard. There are also modern ceramic stations of the cross.

ALLOGNY FOREST *Round trip of 40km/25mi – 1 hr*

Leave Mehun by D 79 north in the direction of Neuvy-sur-Barangeon.

Centre émetteur d'Allouis (Allouis Transmitting Station) – Note *La Pierre de Lu*, a great conglomerate made up of flint nodules, to the right of the road. Situated on an open plateau, the Allouis Transmitting Station for Radio France, broadcasts the programmes of "France Inter", with its 308m/1 010ft–high radio mast.

Forêt d'Allogny – This wooded massif, a dark mass on the plateau which acts as a watershed, dominates the Cher and Barageon valleys. This densely forested area is mainly composed of oaks with isolated clumps of Norwegian pines, hornbeams, birch and beech.

D 56 between Allogny and St-Martin d'Auxigny traverses the forest. From the slope reaching down to St-Martin there is a fine view of the smiling and fertile Moulon valley, a striking contrast to the dark and mysterious forest.

MEILLANT Château★★

Michelin map 69 fold 1 or 238 fold 3
Local map see ST-AMAND DE MONTROND

Meillant Château, half-hidden by trees in its park, reveals the beauties of its architecture only a little at a time; the plain front seems, by contrast, to enhance the elegance and rich decoration of the east façade which is adorned with all the beauty of line of the late Gothic period graced by Italian influence *(illustration page 36)*.

The Amboise Family – Charles I of Amboise obtained the Meillant lands by his marriage in 1464 and wished, immediately, to modernise the castle which was a massive structure flanked by high towers. But death came and to his son, Charles II, fell the honour of completing the work on the château. Charles II was to become grandmaster, marshal and admiral of France. As governor of Milan, Charles II made such gains in Italy that he was able to complete the work planned for Meillant and also that for Chaumont in the Loire valley.

Louis XII wrote to Charles II: "I came to see you in your château of Meillant, but you were not home. I got bogged down in the mud, and the devil take me if I ever return." Fortunately, the roads in these wetlands have been upgraded since then!

In the 18C, the property passed onto the Béthune-Charost family, and in the 19C to the Mortemarts. Among the famous Mortemart ancestors in the 17C were Marie-Madeleine, abbess of Fontevrault and Françoise Athénaïs, marquise de Montespan and the mother of eight children by Louis XIV. The château was entirely restored in 1842.

TOUR ⊘

Exterior – The feudal character of the château can now only be seen in the southern front. The towers, though stripped of their watch-paths, still stand guard with narrow loop-holes.

The east façade is very different and approaches the château of the Loire in the richness of its decoration: two staircase turrets jut out from the main building and seem to have concentrated in them all the exuberance of the last blaze of the "flowering Gothic style": the pierced balustrade running at the base of the eaves, the carved dormer windows, the chimneys ornamented with flamboyantly decorated balustrades are all overshadowed by the incredibly intricate decoration of the Lion's Tower.

This tower, which owes its name to the lion, cast in lead, on its topmost lantern

Château de Meillant – Tour du Lion

J. D. Sudres/DIAF

205

turret, strikes the onlooker by the close juxtaposition of contrasting carvings: twisted small columns, hearts entwined, monograms and crests with interlaced C's – the initials of Charles of Amboise – mountains on fire, the emblem of the château of Chaumont (*chaud mont* = hot mountain), and figures looking out of false windows as at Jacques Cœur's Palace in Bourges. A pretty 16C well and an elegant chapel of the same period, with buttresses topped by pinnacles, complete this harmonious group of buildings.

Interior – Among the rooms containing remarkable furniture and furnishings are: the main dining hall (*Grand Salle à manger*), where the walls are covered in Cordoba leather; the great salon (*Grand Salon*), where a beautiful chimney piece is surmounted by a balcony once used as a musician's gallery. Note the 16C tapestries brought from Bruges and a portrait of Charles VII, long attributed to Clouet, hanging next to one of *La Montespan*, Louis XIV's favourite, and the Smyrna carpet. Beyond the library, replete with rare books and overlooking the chapel, is the so-called Cardinal d'Amboise Bed Chamber, perhaps the loveliest room in the château. Note the splendid 17C Flemish furnishings, tortoise shell encrusted with ivory; a wooden **statue** from Germany dated 1568, representing God the Father welcoming His Son. The Protestant origins of the statue recall the visit of Calvin in 1529. The final rooms on the tour are the Louis XII room with its chimney piece and Aubusson tapestry and the armoury, also hung with tapestries (17C Flemish) and arms. The recumbent figure is a funerary statue of François de Rochechouart-Mortemart.

In the courtyard, visit the chapel: interesting 16C stained glass; above the altar is a 15C altarpiece of the Rhenish School on painted and gilded wood, depicting scenes from the Passion.

Book well in advance
as vacant hotel rooms are often scarce in high season.

Tours de MERLE★★

Michelin map 75 fold 10 or 239 fold 28
Local map see ARGENTAT

The remains of this feudal fortress stand on a spur surrounded by the waters of the river Maronne flowing in a narrow bend. Approaching from the north, via D 13, admire the splendid panorama. There is a parking area on the side of a bend in the road: from here there is a striking bird's-eye **view★★** of the ruins (access by a path), tangled in lush vegetation.

An Impregnable lair – At the juncture of Auvergne and Limousin, the site was an obvious choice for defensive purposes. The promontory (200m/656ft by 40m/131ft) rises 30m/98ft above the river, and sits 150m/492ft below the high plateau. This type of border fortress takes best advantage of the lay of the land; it is, in theory, inaccessible, and commands a vast area around itself.

The lords of Merle were the most feared in the region in the Middle Ages and the family jealously guarded this the surest of strongholds.

Les tours de Merle

Alongside the 11C castle rose the castles of the younger sons until by the 14C the Merle domain was divided into seven. During the Hundred Years War the hill proved impregnable to the English who had made themselves master of all the strongholds of Auvergne and Bas-Limousin. Only the advent of artillery changed the fortune of this fortress which could be bombarded from neighbouring heights –made vulnerable, the old fortresses were one by one abandoned.

Tower tour ⊘ – Merle is made up of a series of seven castles, like pearls on a rope, strung from north to south. On two terraces, three distinct units in various states of disrepair can be distinguished, made up of keeps, towers, and main buildings dating from the 12C through the 15C.

The entrance is on the northern side. After passing through the vestiges of the St-Léger chapel, visitors enter the "old castle" of Hugues and Fulcon de Merle, which occupies the highest point of the site: Romanesque keep (terrace access) and main buildings. The second section is made up of two square towers with castellated crowns, on the far end of the platform: the Noailles and Pestellis towers. From the top of the second tower, there is a good view over the whole site. A mysterious and magical air floats around the impressive façades broken into bits, fireplaces suspended in mid-air, stairways to nowhere.

MEYMAC★

Michelin map 73 fold 11 or 239 fold 16
Local map see Plateau de MILLEVACHES

Perched on the edge of the Millevaches Plateau (see below), Meymac is one of the prettiest villages in Corrèze, its streets and old houses clustered around the old St-André Abbey.

In bygone days, the mountain folk came to town to trade their wool, cheese and chestnuts for products manufactured on the plains. Today, forestry is at the forefront of the local economy; a technical school trains future foresters.

Rural and rustic, Meymac is an attractive tourist site, in lovely surroundings. The road to Tulle goes to the **Sechemaille Lake**, where a large wooded shoreline and various amenities attract vacationers.

SIGHTS

Église abbatiale – In 1805, Archambaud III, viscount of Comborn, founded a Benedictine abbey on the site of a church his forefathers had built.

The church was under construction in the 12C, and was finished in the 13C after modifications to the initial plans were made. There are some unusual aspects to the plans: a deviation of the transept arms, an irregular alignment of the apse and its chapels. The belfry-porch has a multifoil doorway in the Limousin style, an arch on either side. The porch is adorned with Romanesque capitals carved in the archaic style. The nave has ogive vaulting and continues into a chancel which is equally wide. Note a 12C black Virgin on the pillar to the left of the chancel. Except for the turban on her head, the statue is typical of Auvergne in the posture and position of the long, protective hands.

Fondation Marius-Vazeilles ⊘ – Established in a building beside the abbey, the foundation owns an interesting collection of artefacts from prehistoric times (stone tools), the Gallo-Roman period (funerary items, vestiges from habitations) and the Middle Ages. In the ethnology section, displays include a farmhouse room, ploughing tools, clothing and other objects recalling traditional life styles in Haute-Corrèze.

Centre d'Art contemporain ⊘ – In the southern wing of the old cloisters of St-André's Abbey, the art museum is open to the public from March to December, presenting one-person shows devoted to young artists as well as retrospectives (Markus Lüpertz, 1989; François Bouillon, 1990, Jesus Rafaël Soto, 1992) and thematic exhibits on trends in contemporary art. Catalogues are published for each exhibit. The monumental sculpture in front of the centre is by Robert Jakobsen.

Vielle ville – The old town is a charming place for a stroll. To the left of the church, an early 19C covered market, its framework resting on granite pillars, is set in a square formed by the buildings of the Hôtel-Dieu, erected in 1681.

Follow the street up towards the clock tower, which once guarded the castle gate, and discover the sculpted doorways (15-16C), stair towers with pepper pot caps, granite houses with steeply sloping slate roofs. Past the clock tower, a fountain embellishes a pretty little square.

The town is busiest during the annual *Fête du mouton (see Calendar of Events in Practical information)*, giving honour to sheep, especially served up hot from one of the many stalls that set up for business, alongside booths where craftsmen demonstrate their trades and offer their wares for sale.

Plateau de MILLEVACHES★

Michelin maps 73 fold 11, 72 fold 20 or 239 folds 15,16

With the Gentioux plateau and the Monédières hills, the Millevaches plateau marks the borders of the area known as the *montagne limousine*. The origins of its name ("a thousand cows") remain mysterious: perhaps a combination of the Gallic *melo*, meaning high place, and the Latin *vacua*, empty. Other scholars cite the Celtic *batz*, springs, which are indeed numerous on the plateau. A more fanciful explanation is pure legend: a shepherdess was caught in a storm with her thousand head of cattle, all too agitated to be driven back to the barn. She sold them to the devil, and thereupon watched them turn to stone, one by one.

The Rooftop of Limousin – The climate on this high tableland is marked by rugged winters and plentiful precipitation, turning it into a veritable reservoir feeding the many rivers that run from it: to the north, the rivers Creuse, Taurion and Maulde; to the south the Vienne, Vézère, Corrèze, Diège. Waters running off the Millevaches plateau head either for the Loire or the Dordogne and the Gironde.

One of the oldest outcrops in Limousin, the site impresses by its very monotony. Bracken and heather serve only to increase the impression of solitude and poverty.

Such life as there is, is sparse and widely scattered, grouped in the hollows where pasture and crops can be grown; the density of the population, in fact, does not exceed 10 per km² (one km² = 0.38 mi²) and the traditional poverty of the plateau has led to its gradual abandonment.

Initially, agriculture was limited to modest substance gardens which gave way to sheep and some cattle breeding. The open spaces are well-suited to sheep grazing. Considerable efforts have been made to improve this vast area where the rigors of the climate exclude the growing of fruit trees and even chestnut trees. Reclamation began in about 1860 with the development of the railway. The indigenous forest, burnt down in 1575 during the Wars of Religion, had never been replanted; today thousands of acres have been planted with conifers which can resist the cold and whose cultivation provides an economic resource for the area (note the many saw-mills), while posing problems for the few farmers left. More recently, tourism has brought new opportunities and recreation areas (lakes, parks, trails, sports facilities) have been developed to take advantage of city-dwellers' quest for fresh air and open space. Now fires are burning again in old farms newly renovated as vacation homes.

The dark patches of the forests alternate with the lighter heaths with their occasional granite outcrops. On the plateau itself the low granite crests seem as though they would roll on forever, though the outline of the Auvergne Mountains stands out on the horizon. Here and there a herd of cattle or a flock of sheep graze, serving as a reminder of what the inhabitants once had to depend on for their livelihood.

FROM FELLETIN TO MEYMAC

130km/78mi – 5 hr

Felletin – *See AUBUSSON.*

The road winds pleasantly along the Gourbillon valley, amid prairies and woodlands.

St-Quentin-la-Chabane – Surrounded by hilltops, this hamlet takes its name from one of them, the Puy de Cabanne. The 13C **church** has a Limousin-style door and bell gable. The nave is vaulted with diagonal ribs. Beneath the chancel, an 11C crypt, Notre-Dame-de-Sousterre, harbours a Black Virgin.

Continue along D 955 for 5km/3m, then take D 59⁴ to the right, towards la Nouaille.

Domaine de Banizette ⊘ – This 17C lordly manor, which has been partially transformed into a museum of rural life, shows what a big farm must have been like at the beginning of the 20C, the dawn of the mechanical age. The vaulted sheep barn, the mill, the wash house, the big oven with its special chambers for pastries and patés, the stables with the original cobblestones, the dovecot, the woodshed, sharecroppers' land and immense grain storage barn, characteristically gathered around a closed courtyard, are all remarkable, and it is encouraging to witness their progressive restoration.

Leave the manor and turn right on D 59. At St-Marc-à-Loubaud, turn left and take D 16 towards Gentioux.

Pont de Senoueix – This ancient Roman bridge over the Taurion has only one original arch left. The carefully mounted stones defy time, while the trickle of water at the river's source seems to mark it.

Gentioux – As of the 11C, Gentioux attracted stone masons from around the Creuse. The 13C **church**, rebuilt in the 15C by the Knights of Malta is adorned with curious 16C sculptures; in the chancel, note the bas-reliefs and grimacing faces.
In the cemetery, the most remarkable tomb stands in homage to local sculptor Jean Cacaud.
The town's monument to the fallen of the First World War is unique and moving in its pacifist expression: a child in wooden shoes and a school smock, beret in hand, raises a clenched fist in front of the inscription *Maudite soit la guerre*, ("Cursed be war").

Leave Gentioux on D 8 towards Pigerolles. After 3km/1.8m, turn left on D 35.

Chapelle de Pallier ⊘ – Built in the 12C by the Knights Templar, the chapel's façade is admirable, and the belfry gable stands out clearly against the sky. The doorway is flanked by two buttresses and crowned with a pointed arch and 14C sculpted tympanum. Inside, a single nave and a rectangular shape; to the right of the stone altar, there is a small Templar's cross on the floor.

In the cemetery, there is a double-sided cross dating from the 16C, and an intriguing, loaf-shaped stone carved with three symbols: a square (for the Holy Scriptures), a circle (religion), and eight loops (eternity).

The chapel is atop a hill just above the 18C home of the Jabouille family of Royal Notaries, an example of the master craftsmanship of Gentioux stone masons. Several displays relate the history of the Templars in the Creuse region.

1km/0.6mi before the town of le Rat, take a small lane on the right, marked "Chapelle". Park your car just beyond the turn-off and continue on foot (1.2km/0.7mi round trip).

S. Sauvignier/MICHELIN

Chapelle de Pallier

Le Rat – The short walk leads to one of the loveliest **sites** on the plateau. A magnificent row of ancient trees shades the path to the 17C granite chapel. Some of the boulders may have been placed there in Celtic times, for purposes which remain enigmatic to us today. Beyond the moss-covered chapel, a path through the pine and heather leads to a group of massive boulders which invite the visitor to climb their broad backs and admire the wide open view over the hushed moorlands.

Peyrelevade – This attractive town with its slate-roofed houses welcomes tourists. The church and the Templar's Cross date from the 13C.

Plateau d'Adouze – The streams that run down from the western and northern slopes of the Plateau of the Audouze provide the waters for the river Vienne; the streams from the eastern and southern slopes those for the Diège, a tributary of the Dordogne. The Ardouze Beacon (Signal d'Ardouze) which is out of bounds (military area) towers over the plateau.

Millevaches – This little village (alt. 912m/2992ft) sits in the middle of the plateau of the same name, and is indeed characteristic of the region. The church, rebuilt in 1871 after a fire, is the only monument in town.

Just 3km/1.8mi south of Millevaches *(take D 36 and stay right)* **Chavanac** has a small 13C-14C **church**. Inside, a stone polychrome statue, known as la Dansarelle, is said to represent Salomé, the bewitching Biblical figure who charmed Herod into bringing her the head of John the Baptist on a platter.

Tarnac – The **church** in this village is party Romanesque and partly Gothic. The northern doorway is adorned with sculpted covings and medallions; Saint George appears on the right, Saint Gilles on the left.
In front of the church, two ancient oaks, and a fountain with another Saint George.

Les Cars – In the middle of nowhere, **Gallo-Roman vestiges** emerge from the greenery. The ashlar stone blocks now in a pile were once part of a temple and mausoleum. The temple was rectangular, with a semi-circular apse; visitors can still see the foundations, the podium and the monumental staircase.
The mausoleum was certainly very large , with a funeral urn in its centre.
A small path bordered with larch trees leads to another site about 300m/984ft away. The impressive tank above (it weighs about 8 metric tons) was a reservoir which supplied water to the building.
This was probably not a public bath, but more likely a luxurious private residence built in the mid-2C and abandoned at the end of the 3C. Elements found on the site demonstrate the penetration of Roman civilisation in this hidden corner of the world: an underfire heating system, a mosaic, marble panelling and fragments of painted walls.

Mont Bessou – With the Puy Pendu, just across the way, this is the highest point on the plateau (977m/3205ft). Above the forest, a television transmitter rises; the 67ha/165 acres are now a municipal park. An artificial lake offers a shady resting area. A road goes all the way round the mount.

Château de Rochefort – Built on a rock above a picturesque valley, this old fortress had a wing added in the 17C.
The road to Meymac on D 172 and D 36 is lovely, with a perspective of the Luzège valley.

★Meymac – *See MEYMAC.*

MONBAZILLAC CHÂTEAU

Michelin map 75 folds 14 and 15 or 234 fold 8 – Local map see BERGERAC.

Emerging from the undulating vineyards, this **château** rises proudly on the edge of a limestone plateau overlooking the Dordogne valley. It is owned by the Monbazillac Wine Co-operative, which restored and refurbished it.

TOUR ⊙

This relatively small château was built in 1550 and is surrounded by a dry moat.

Its elegant silhouette is eye-catching, the architectural style half-way between a defensive castle and a Renaissance château. There are machicolations and a crenellated watch-path around the main building, which is flanked at each corner by a massive round tower.

The façade is pierced by a double row of mullioned windows and a doorway with Renaissance-style ornamentation. Two tiers of dormer windows can be seen above the machicolations. The grey patina of the stone tones in well with the brown tiled roofs of the turrets and pavilions.

Château and vineyards at Monbazillac

Delderfield/IMAGES PHOTOTHÈQUE

From the north terrace there is a good view of the vineyard and of Bergerac in the distance.

Interior – The **Great Hall**, its painted ceiling decorated with gilt foliated scrolls, has a monumental Renaissance chimney piece, 17C furnishings and two beautiful Flemish tapestries of the same period. In an adjoining room rustic furniture from the Périgord region is on display. There are also interesting documents tracing the history of Protestantism in France in another room.

Several rooms are open on the first floor; note in particular the viscountess of Monbazillac's **bedchamber** furnished in Louis XIII style.

The castle cellars house a small **wine museum** displaying harvesting and wine-making equipment used in the past.

Les MONÉDIÈRES★

Michelin map 72 south of fold 19 or 239 folds 15 and 27

Adjoining the Millevaches Plateau, the Monédières Massif stretching between the upper valley of the Vézère and the river Corrèze, forms the southern bastion of the area known as the *montagne limousine*. This relatively low massif (the tallest peak is the Puy de la Monédière with an altitude of 919m/3015ft) is a highly eroded mass of crystalline rocks. Although the region is open to considerable oceanic influences, brought by the Westerlies, the climate is essentially a mountainous one with arduous snowy winters and short hot summers.

The Forest in Flames – At the time of the Roman conquest, the massif was covered by a forest which provided refuge for the Druids who organised resistance to the invaders. Caesar became irritated and ordered the forest to be burned, the fire lasted for many months.

Patiently the medieval monks of Treignac set about replanting the Monédières. In the 16C, while his powerful neighbours sided with the Protestants, **Louis de Pompadour**, baron of Treignac, remained a Catholic. His enemies sacked his domains. Returning to the tactics used by Caesar, Pompadour set fire to the forest; the fire spread over an area of 80km²/31sq mi, destroying castles, villages and crops. Louis was ruined, but the Huguenots fled.

In spite of many subsequent attempts, reforestation has never been completed. Recently replanting has increased and thousands of conifers cover hillsides already crossed by a network of forest roads.

Heather and Bilberries – In late summer the slopes are covered with a carpet of pink heather. Slowly but gradually bilberries (known as blueberries in North America) are replacing the heather above 700m/2 300ft, creating a new source of income and activity especially at harvest time. Picked with an adroit movement of the hand, the fragile berries are dispatched to markets, canning factories and pharmaceutical laboratories.

TOUR STARTING FROM CHAUMEIL *30km/18mi – 1 hr*

Chaumeil – This attractive village, capital of the Monédières, with its sturdy granite houses roofed with slates or stones, is clustered round the church adorned with a fine 16C porch. Inside the church, on the left of the chancel, there are a polychrome naive *Pietà* (16C) in wood, a Madonna and child, and a reliquary.

An artificial lake has been created just north of the village.

Take D 121, a narrow road which descends gently.

Freysselines – This small hamlet lies huddled into an amphitheatre of the same name. The road winds along the south facing slope where arable crops alternate with rough grazing and chestnut groves.

At Chauzeix, take the road which climbs to the right, then right again onto D 128 which rises amid meadows and conifers. Note to the left the long ridge of the Puy Pantout (770m/2 526ft).

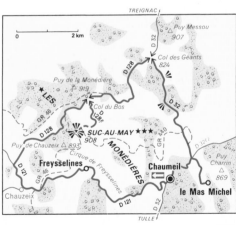

Les MONÉDIÈRES

The road skirts the Puy de Chauzeix with its wooded slopes and leaves the Puy de la Monédière to the left. At the pass, Col du Bos, take D 128ᴱ to the right which leads to Suc-au-May.

★★★ **Suc-au-May** – *15min round trip on foot.* Altitude 908m/2 979ft.

From the viewing table there is a **panorama** of the Limousin countryside and the Millevaches Plateau to the northeast; the Monts Dore and Monts Dômes to the east and the Cantal Mountains to the southeast. The Monédières Massif in the foreground has an undulating severely eroded surface.

Return to D 128 and at the pass, Col des Géants, take D 32 to the right, which goes downhill amid conifers. There are fine glimpses of the Puy Messou (907m/2 976ft) to the left and the Suc-au-May to the right.

Le Mas Michel – At the crossroads take the narrow road leading to this hamlet, which lies at the foot of the Puy Charrin. Old cottages built of dry stone make it worth a visit.

Return to D 32 which leads backs to Chaumeil.

MONPAZIER★

Population 531 Michelin map 75 fold 16 or 235 fold 9

Monpazier was one of the bastides built to command the roads going from the Agenais region to the banks of the Dordogne. The square, surrounded by arcades, the *carreyrous* (alleyways), the old houses, the church and the ruined fortifications make it the best preserved of all the Périgord bastides *(illustration page 37)*.

A difficult start – The bastide of Monpazier was founded on 7 January 1285 by Edward I, king of England and duke of Aquitaine. This bastide was designed to complete the process of defence and colonisation of Périgord begun in 1267 with the founding of Lalinde, Beaumont, Molières and Roquépine. To this end Edward I allied himself with Pierre de Gontaut, lord of Biron. Many difficulties soon arose: delays in the building, disagreements between the lord of Biron and the people of Monpazier and renewed hostilities between the king of England and Philip the Fair.

The situation grew even more complicated during the Hundred Years War; the bastide was assaulted and pillaged as often by the English as by the French.

Monpazier receives royalty – The Reformation, in which the marshal of Biron played a prominent part, marked the beginning of a violent era. On 21 June 1574, the town was betrayed and fell into the hands of the well-known Huguenot leader, Geoffroi de Vivans, who later won fame with the capture of Domme.

Jeanne d'Albret, who was going to the wedding of her son Henri IV de Navarre to Marguerite de Valois, stayed at Monpazier. In her honour "the streets and squares were scrubbed and the dunghills were taken away". Despite this homage to the militant Calvinist Jeanne, the town did not hesitate to lay on an equally grand display soon afterwards, when receiving the Catholic leader the Duc d'Anjou – the future Henry III of France.

Buffarot the Croquant – After the Wars of Religion were over, the peasants rose again in revolt. The rebels, known as *croquants*, held a great gathering at Monpazier in 1594. The revolt flared up again in 1637. Led by a man named Buffarot, a local weaver from Capdrot, 8 000 peasants rampaged through the countryside plundering the castles.

The soldiers of the duke of Épernon pursued them and, after some difficulty, captured Buffarot. He was brought back to Monpazier, tortured and broken on the wheel in the main square.

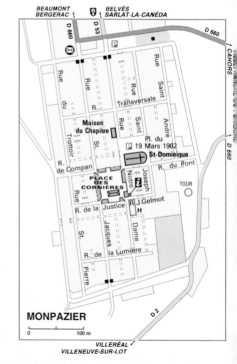

MONPAZIER

0   100 m

VILLERÉAL
VILLENEUVE-SUR-LOT

SIGHTS

The general layout of the **bastide** ⊘ is still in evidence, as are three of its original six fortified gateways. Several houses still have their original appearance.

The town is in the shape of a quadrilateral 400m x 220m (1312ft x 722ft), the main axis running north-south. Streets are laid out from one end to the other, parallel with the longer sides, and four transverse roads run east to west, dividing the town into rectangular blocks. Originally all the houses had the unique characteristic of being of equal size and separated from each other by narrow spaces or *androbes*, to prevent the spread of fire.

★**Place des Cornières** – The main square's rectangular shape echoes the bastide itself. On the south side stands a covered market housing the antique weights and measures. Round the edge, the arcades or covered galleries are supported on arches, some of which are pointed, and have angle irons (*cornières*).

Église St-Dominique – The church façade has been restored at various times; the doorway decorated with archivolts, the rose window and the gable were all rebuilt in c1550. The wide aisle has pointed vaulting and extends into a polygonal east end.

Chapter-house – This 13C house stands near the church and place du 19-mars-1962. It was used as a tithe barn. Paired windows light the upper floor.

Château de MONTAIGNE

Michelin map 75, fold 13 or 234 fold 4 (9km/5.4mi northeast of Castillon-la-Bataille)

Lovers of literary history will find the spirit of the great essayist Montaigne in the tower library of this château, where he was able to meditate and write in peace.

A Renaissance man – The essayist **Michel Eyquem de Montaigne** (1533-1592) was born and died in this château; in his lifetime he served as a member of the Parliament of Bordeaux, was twice elected mayor of that city, and participated in high-level diplomatic negotiations during the Wars of Religion.

In 1571, at the age of 38, Michel de Montaigne took refuge in his family home in Périgord to reflect and write, as well as to care for his property. He continued to perform civic duties when called upon, and travelled throughout Europe (his travel journal was published posthumously in 1774). His personal life was saddened by the loss of his one great friend (Étienne de la Boétie, to whom the essay *On Friendship* is dedicated), an uninspiring marriage, and the death in infancy of five of the six daughters he fathered.

> ### "...I myself am the matter of my book."
>
> Montaigne's *Essays* have been widely read and highly influential in the world of letters. Among his Anglophone readers were John Webster, William Shakespeare, Lord Byron, Ralph Waldo Emerson, Virginia Woolf, T.S. Eliot and Aldous Huxley. He is recognised as the inventor of the essay form. The original title of the works, *Essais*, signifies "attempts", which reveals his penchant for exploration of the mind: *...to follow a movement so wandering... to penetrate the opaque depths of its innermost folds, to pick out and immobilise the innumerable flutterings that agitate it.*
>
> Many readers have been charmed by Montaigne's unassuming self-portrait of a doddering country gentleman *(I want death to find me planting my cabbages)*, full of contradiction. In fact, he was active in public life, following a tradition begun by his grandfather, and viewed public service as a noble duty. Today's readers will find him remarkably timely in his defence of cultural relativism and tolerance, personal dignity and fidelity to nature.

Château – The main building was rebuilt after fire ravaged it in 1885; the **Library tower** ⊘, Montaigne's domain, was saved. From his room above the chapel, the philosopher attended services by means of an opening in the wall (he died while hearing Mass thus). On the top floor, his famous **library**, is lined with books and decorated with Greek and Latin inscriptions.

Outside, visitors can admire a landscape little changed since the author's day: wooded hillsides, vineyards which produce a popular white wine, the outline of the feudal keep of Gurson on the horizon.

Travel with Michelin Maps (scale 1 : 200 000) which are revised regularly.

Château de MONTAL★★

Montal Castle is a harmonious group of buildings with pepper-pot roofs on a wooded knoll on a hillside near the charming Bave valley.

The wonder of a mother's love – In 1523 Jeanne de Balsac d'Entraygues, widow of Amaury de Montal, governor of Haute-Auvergne, had a country mansion built on the site of a feudal stronghold for her eldest son, Robert, who was away fighting in Italy for François I. The chatelaine had the best artists and workmen brought from the banks of the Loire to Quercy, and by 1534 the masterpiece begotten of a mother's loving pride was there for all to see.

"Hope is no more" – Everything was ready to welcome home the proud knight. But days, then years passed; Marignano, Pavia, Madrid are far away; the mother waited day after day for her eldest son's arrival. Alas, Robert's body was all that returned to the castle. The beautiful dream crumbled. Jeanne had the high window from which she had watched for her son blocked up and she had carved beneath it the despairing lament "Hope is No More" *(plus d'espoir)*.

Jeanne's second son, Dordé de Montal, a church dignitary, was absolved from his ecclesiastical duties by the pope in order that he might continue the family line; he subsequently married and had nine children.

Death and resurrection – Montal was declared a national asset but became uninhabitable as a result of the spoliation it suffered during the Revolution; finally in 1879 it fell into the hands of a certain Macaire. This adventurer, permanently short of cash, made a bargain with a demolition group and divided the palace into lots; 120 tons of carved stone were parcelled up and sent to Paris. The masterpieces of Montal were then auctioned and dispersed throughout the museums and private collections of Europe and the United States. In 1908 Montal rose from its ruins; a new and devoted owner set about finding and buying back at ransom prices all the Montal treasures, until he had refurbished the castle. He donated it to the state in 1913.

Château de Montal – Detail of the façade

TOUR ⊘

Exterior – Steeply pitched *lauzes* roofs and massive round towers with loopholes give the castle its fortress-like appearance. But this forbidding exterior accentuates the contrast with the inner courtyard, designed with all the graceful charm of the Renaissance.

Montal consists of two main wings set at right angles and linked at the corner by a square tower containing the staircase. A two-storey gallery, also set at a right angle to complete the square, was planned for the other two sides of the courtyard but was never built. The façade of the main building with all its rich decoration is one of the castle's most glorious features.

The frieze – Above the ground floor windows and doors, runs a 32m/105ft long frieze. It is a marvel of ornamental diversity: cupids, birds and dream-like figures appear beside shields and a huge human head. There are also the initials of the founder and her sons: I (Jeanne), R (Robert) and D (Dordé).

The busts – On the first floor mullioned windows alternate with false bays with intricately carved pediments, which contain seven busts in haut-relief, all masterpieces of realism and taste. Each statue is a likeness of a member of the Montal family; from left to right they are: Amaury with a haughty air, wearing a hat; Jeanne, his wife and the founder of the castle, with the air of a holy woman transfixed in eternal sorrow; Robert, the eldest son killed in Italy, wearing a plumed hat in the style of François I; Dordé, the second son, is shown as a young page; Jeanne's parents, Robert de Balsac with a Louis XII-style hat and Antoinette de Castelnau, and, as the last descendant of the line, Dordé de Béduer who was abbot of Vézelay.

The dormers – There are four, and their decoration brings to mind those of Chambord; the dormer gables have small supporting figures on either side and the niches contain statues.

Interior – The entrance is at the corner, where the wings meet, through a door flanked by pilasters and topped with a lintel supporting several niches.

★★ **Renaissance staircase** – The staircase is built in the fine gold-coloured stone from Carennac, beautifully proportioned and magnificently decorated. Admire the fine carving beneath the stairs: ornamented foliage, shells, imaginary birds, initials and little figures form a ceiling, with decoration which completes that of the lierne and tierceron vaulting of the vestibules. This masterpiece of sculpture combines elegance with fantasy.

The apartments – The guard room, vaulted with basket-handled arches, and containing a lovely chimney piece, the Stag Room (Salle du Cerf) and the other rooms which contain fine pieces of furniture (mainly in the Renaissance and Louis XIII styles), altarpieces, paintings and plates attributed to Bernard Palissy, as well as tapestries from Flanders and Tours constitute a marvellous collection.

MONTPEZAT-DE-QUERCY★

Population 1 411
Michelin map 79 fold 18 or 235 fold 18

On the edge of Limogne Causse, this picturesque small Lower Quercy town with its covered arcades and old half-timbered or stone houses owes its fame and its artistic treasures to the munificence of the Des Prés family.

The Des Prés family – Five members of this family from Montpezat became eminent prelates.
Pierre Des Prés, cardinal of Préneste (now Palestrina in Italy), founded the Collegiate Church of St Martin, which he consecrated in 1344; his nephew, Jean Des Prés, who died in 1351, was bishop of Coïmbra in Portugal and then of Castres in France. Three other members of the family were consecrated bishops of Montauban: Jean Des Prés (1517-39), who gave his famous Flemish tapestries to the collegiate church at Montpezat, Jean de Lettes (1539-56) and Jacques Des Prés (1556-89). Jacques was a warrior-bishop, and committed persecutor of the Huguenots. He fought on for 25 years, his diocese being one of the most ardent Protestant strongholds, and was killed in an ambush at Lalbenque, some 15km/10mi from Montpezat.

COLLÉGIALE ST-MARTIN

This church, dedicated to St Martin of Tours, was built in 1337 by an architect from the papal court at Avignon. It is comparatively small in size and has many of the characteristics of a Languedoc building: a single nave with no side aisles and chapels separated by the nave's interior buttresses.

R. Lanaud/EXPLORER

Tapestry representing St-Martin dividing his cloak

Nave – Unity, simplicity and harmony make a striking impression as visitors enter the nave. Its pointed vaulting has hanging keystones painted with the founder's coat of arms. The side chapels contain several notable religious objects: a 15C Virgin of Mercy in multicoloured sandstone (first chapel on the south side), three 15-16C Nottingham alabaster altarpiece panels depicting the Nativity, the Resurrection and the Ascension (second chapel on the south side), a 14C alabaster Virgin and Doves (second chapel on the north side), and 15C wooden caskets with gold inlay work (fourth chapel on the north side).

★★**Tapestries** – These 16C tapestries, which were specially made to fit the sanctuary, are nearly 25m, 82ft in length and 3m, 6ft in height. They were woven in workshops in the north of France and consist of five panels, each divided into three scenes. The excellent condition of these tapestries, the vividness and richness of their colouring and the fact that they are still hanging in the exact spot for which they were designed all contribute to their outstanding interest.

Sixteen scenes depict the best-known historic and legendary events in the life of St Martin, including the dividing of his cloak, many of the various cures performed by the saint and his victorious struggle with the devil.

Each scene is accompanied by a quatrain in old French woven at the top of the panel.

★**Recumbent figures** – Although the body of Cardinal Pierre Des Prés lies beneath the paving before the chancel, his statue and tomb carved in Carrara marble were placed on the right of the chancel entrance in 1778. Opposite, making a pair, lies the recumbent figure of his nephew Jean Des Prés, which is a masterpiece of funerary statuary.

MOUTIER-D'AHUN★

Population 195
Michelin map 72 fold 10 or 239 fold 4

The village of Moutier-d'Ahun lies between Guéret and Aubusson, near the upper valley of the Creuse which is spanned by an old bridge bristling with cutwaters. The village clusters round the church which contains remarkable 17C woodwork.

An abbey's Fortunes and Misfortunes – Shortly before the year 1000 Boson, count of Marche, gave a church consecrated to Our Lady, which he owned on the banks of the Creuse, to Uzerche Abbey as a first step towards founding a Benedictine monastery. The monastery became independent of its mother house and took the name Moutier d'Ahun; in the 12C the monks replaced Boson's church by a larger building.

But the Hundred Years War put an end to this long period of prosperity; the abbey church was first destroyed by the English, it had scarcely been resurrected from the ruins, when, during the Wars of Religion, the nave was pillaged and set on fire.

It was in 1610 that the woodwork to ornament the chancel was made. When the monks fled at the time of the Revolution, the woodwork was whitewashed; patient restoration by the Abbé Malapert, priest of Moutier-d'Ahun, has restored its glory.

Église ⊘ – The church is now partly Romanesque (transept crossing, belfry and chancel), and partly Gothic (15C west door). The western doorway, built in granite, is adorned with six covings embellished with little figures – prophets and angels jostle jugglers, musicians and dancers. The arms of the transept have been destroyed.

Moutier d'Ahun – Western doorway of the church

S. Sauvignier/MICHELIN

The space where the nave and the chancel were crossed by the transept is surmounted by a square Romanesque belfry, pierced by three double bays on each side, supported by slender columns with smooth capitals.

A Gallo-Roman funerary plaque is set into the façade, a figure and inscription carved upon it.

Pass below the grand cupola supported by squinches to reach the chancel under the arch made of three arcades in juxtaposition. The chancel's eastern end is flattened, and the two chapels were embellished with ribbed vaulting in the 15C.

Outside; traces of the 14C fortifications can still be seen on the chevet.

★★ The Woodwork – The woodwork and the stalls entirely occupy the walls of the apse and chancel. All the carving was commissioned by the monks of Moutier-d'Ahun and was done between 1673 and 1681 by the master-craftsman of Auvergne, Simon Baüer.

On either side of the high altar, whose base was covered with 17C Cordoba leather, are the two parts of a huge altar screen. These consist of ornately carved twisted columns bearing a broken pediment. The part of the chancel next to the altar screen is panelled with decorated woodwork which forms a monumental door which in turn gives access to a 15C chapel. The 26 stalls are magnificently sculptured portraying animals, flowers and fantastic scenes. The screen enclosing the chancel is surmounted by a double figure of Christ carved from the trunk of an oak tree. The lectern is made up of two lions back to back with the pulpit resting on their paws. Items from the old monastery may be seen in the sacristy. They include 12C statues in multicoloured granite of St. Benedict and St. Antony the hermit, 15C and 17C reliquaries and, above all, a wonderful Christ skilfully carved in boxwood (17C).

NANÇAY
Population 784
Michelin map 64 fold 20 or 238 fold 18

This village in the Sologne region is home to many artists' studios, as well as one of Europe's most modern astronomical observatories.

Grenier de Villâtre ⊘ (Gallerie Capazza) – Established in the nicely restored stables of the château is an exhibit of sculptures, pottery, drawing, etc, created by 65 different artists. One of the rooms, the **musée imaginaire du Grand Meaulnes**, is full of memories of Alain-Fournier, evoked by the family memorabilia on display: photographs, model of a scene from the novel, small furnishings.

Espace Ciel Ouvert – Station de radioastronomie ⊘ – Created in 1953 by the École Normale Supérieure, the station came under the authority of the Paris Observatory in 1956. The main field of study involves radio waves from around the universe, which provide useful information on the solar system, distant galaxies and interstellar matter. Three of the instruments used in the research are the radio telescope (one of the largest in the world in terms of its sensitive surface), the radioheliograph (for studies of the solar corona and other measurements of the sun), and the network of 144 antennae for capting decametric radio waves (mainly emitted by the planet Jupiter).

NOHANT★
Population 481
Michelin map 68 fold 19 (6 km/4mi north of La Châtre)

Near the Indre valley, this quaint Berry village is clustered round a little square where century-old elms shade the church and its rustic porch.

The Passionate Life of George Sand (1804-1876) – Amandine-Aurore-Lucile Dupin was born to scandal. Her father was an army officer, grandson of the celebrated Marshal General of France, Maurice de Saxe (albeit through an illegitimate branch of the family tree). Her mother, Sophie, was a camp follower, wed to the Lieutenant just before their daughter's appearance. The accidental death of her father did nothing to calm the stormy family atmosphere created by the circumstances of Aurore's birth. Her wealthy grandmother agreed to raise her, on the condition that Sophie stay out of sight. Thus, in her early childhood, Aurore developed a sense of rebellion, a sensitivity to injustice and social charade (indeed, the famous Marshal himself was an illegitimate son of the monarch), but also a deep attachment to nature and the Berry countryside which would later mark her work. She was married at 18 to Baron Casimir Dudevant and had two children, Solonge and Maurice. Profoundly unhappy, she left her husband, established herself in Paris with Jules Sandeau in 1831, and out of financial necessity began writing for the satirical review *Figaro*. Her first independently written novel, *Indiana* (1832, English translation 1978), the story of a wife who struggles to free herself from the bonds of an unhappy marriage – which she did not hesitate to compare to slavery – was an immediate popular success. She thereafter kept up a prolific pace of literary production to support herself and her children.

Her encounter with the poetic author Alfred de Musset and their trip to Venice fueled her romantic works, most notably, *Lélia* (1833, English translation 1978), which amazed readers with its frank discussion of women's sensual feelings and a passionate call for the right to emotional satisfaction.

Sand's reputation for iconoclasm sprang from such themes and also from exaggerated reports of her unconventional behaviour: she smoked regularly and in public, occasionally dressed like a man (initially she did so to gain entrance to the cheap, standing room section of theatres, where women were forbidden) and carried on love affairs with Musset, Prosper Mérimée and Frédéric Chopin. Yet she remained an idealist, convinced of the virtues of marriage between equals, and enraged at the prevalent social system which made

Nohant – Portrait of George Sand by Blaize

such marriages impossible. Her own marriage to the aged Baron, a disreputable skirt-chaser who physically abused her, ended in notorious separation proceedings, which added to her reputation for scandal.

An uncommon woman – And yet, Sand was truly inhabited by the great ideas of moral progress that animated her times. France's leading woman author produced what are sometimes called "socialist" novels, including *Horace* (1841) and the *Consuelo* cycle (1842-44, English translation 1870), perhaps her finest work. Dedicated to the advance of democracy, she put her pen to political pamphlets, created a local newspaper, and rejoiced when the French monarchy fell and the Second Republic was established. The return of Napoleon III so disappointed Sand that she withdrew to the estate at Nohant. She continued to write successful plays and the ever-popular "pastoral" or "rustic" novels with their tender descriptions of the Berry countryside: *The Haunted Pool* (1846, English translation 1976), *The Country Waif* (1847, English translation 1976), and *Fanchon the Cricket* (1848, English translation 1977). Many readers enjoy her letters and journals, as well as her masterful autobiography, *Histoire de ma vie* (*My Life*, English translation 1979) and the travel essays collected under the title *Lettres d'un voyageur* (Letters of a Traveler, 1834-36). In her final years, she undertook charitable works which earned her the affectionate title *la bonne dame de Nohant* (the good lady of Nohant).

With seventy novels, fifty volumes of other writing and twenty-five plays to her credit, George Sand has been an inspiration to many women writers, including Elizabeth Barrett Browning and George Eliot; her work has been praised by the likes of Turgenev and Flaubert.

★CHÂTEAU ⊘

This country estate was built around 1760 on the site of an old château, and became the property of Mme Dupin de Francueil in 1793. Now a museum, it is devoted to the memory of George Sand and her many guests, composers Chopin and Liszt, novelists Balzac and Flaubert, painters Delacroix and Fromentin among them. The old-fashioned charm of Sand's home has remained unchanged since the 19C, and the visitor almost expects to find the author herself sitting at her desk.

The ground floor has eight rooms: the vesitbule, the kitchen, the dining room, Aurore de Saxe's room and boudoir with its painted woodwork, where Sand's career began and *Indiana* took shape. "I was living in my grandmother's old boudoir ... It was so small that with my books, my herbarium, and my rock collection, there was no room for a bed. I had a hammock installed instead. My table was made of a wardrobe which could fold out like a writing desk."

The theatre was built in 1849, for family entertainment. The puppet theatre, set up in 1854 still has many marionettes carved by young Maurice; Sand's son left other traces of his artistic temperament in the paintings hanging in the vestibule, the salon, and Aurore Lauth-Sand's room.

The salon, an "inner sanctum", is the expression of family harmony, as suggested by the portraits on the walls.

On the upper floor, a vestibule, antechamber and George Sand's room, where she passed away on 8 June 1876. Also, her writing room, which was Chopin's room untill 1846, the library, Aurore Lauth-Sand's room (the château's last resident, she died in 1961), was once occupied by George Sand and her mother.

The grounds of the house are lovely as well, and a visit to the family cemetery reveals George Sand's tomb in the centre of the plot, carved in Volvic stone.

Abbaye de NOIRLAC★★

Michelin map 69 south of fold 1 or 238 fold 31
Local map see ST-AMAND-MONTROND

Between the river Cher and the Meillant forest, this beautiful abbey is well worth a visit.

The foundation – This abbey was founded around 1136 by Robert of Clairvaux, St. Bernard's cousin, on the right bank of the Cher, on the site known as Maison-Dieu on the edge of the wood, and later came to be known as Noilac.

The first years were trying, and the monks knew hardship and hunger. In 1149, Bernard himself went begging for a royal grant of wheat. But the situation finally improved: Ebbes V of Charenton made a significant gift which ensured the perennity of the community. The hard-working monks went to work on the land, clearing and building, and prosperity was just around the corner. By its fiftieth year, the abbey had a vast domain and was receiving revenues (indirectly, because in theory the order's rule forbade it).

From destruction to restoration – After the surge of recruits in the 12C and 13C, fewer monks inhabited Noirlac in the 14C, and commercial activities there slowly came to a halt. After the Hundred Years War, a stoke of bad luck befell the community in 1510: the abbot would be appointed by the king, and was to manage the place *in absentia*. Shortly thereafter, the Wars of Religion brought about further destruction. As the French Revolution drew near, only six monks were left at Noirlac.

Declared national property, the abbey was sold. Sold again in 1820, it became a pro-celain manufactory. Prosper Mérimée discovered it in 1838, but not until 1909 did the Cher *département* acquire it for 46 000 francs. Restoration began slowly; the buildings were still in use for humanitarian purposes until 1949. In 1950, a vast restoration programme got underway, and the extraordinary results captivate visitors today.

TOUR ⊘

The buildings are set up in a typical Cistercian pattern. They are one of the best standing examples in France of such a monastery, made of fine white stone from the region. The magnificent paving stones have been restored to their original appearance. The stained-glass windows were executed in grisaille by Jean-Pierre Raynaud in a style which coincides with the Cistercian sobriety. In this exceptional setting, Gregorian chants, concerts and other cultural events take place.

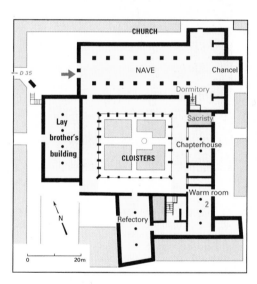

Church – Work started in 1150 and lasted for 100 years, thus illustrating the passage from Romanesque to Gothic style. The sanctuary was built first, followed by the nave and the side aisles. The simplicity of line and the lovely pale stone add to the beauty of the architecture and to the sense of peace. In accordance with the rule of the order, sculpted ornamentation was barred: the capitals are plain and the windows uniformly grey in tone.

The nave with its ribbed vaulting is linked to the side aisles which have ogive vaulting with great pointed arches and rests on square pillars; the rectangular transverse ribs are supported by engaged columns with a simple tapered pedestal just above floor level.

The chancel, lower than the transept, is the oldest part of the building; it is roofed with broken barrel vaulting and ends in a flat chevet lit by a row of triplet windows topped with a six-lobed oculus.

Abbey buildings – The other buildings were erected at various times: late 12C (east wing and lay brothers' building); first part of the 13C (refectory); second part of the 13C and early 14C (cloister galleries). Other works were carried out in the 18C (staircase with wrought iron bannister (1), dormitory rooms).

The Cloisters and Adjacent Buildings – The buildings form a rectangle which is 38m/125ft by 33m/108ft, probably built above an earlier construction built at the same time as the church. At the heart of the abbey, it provides access to all the other areas. The east and south galleries have the most ornate carvings and all have fine ogive

Noirlac Abbey – The refectory

vaulting and rich ornamentation which contrasts with the simplicity of the church: corbels decorate the springing of the arches and capitals with different plant motifs crown the small pillars.

The chapterhouse has a rounded doorway flanked by twin windows; the six square bays are divided by polygonal columns. There is a great chimney piece (2) in a corner of the heated common room which is roofed with flattened pointed vaulting. The refectory, a tall room crowned with eight ogive domes and palm leaf mouldings adorning the capitals of the three columns, is lit by four large windows surmounted by two multilobed rose windows.

Only a portion of the **lay brothers' building** still stands. It was the economic centre of the monastery. The vast cellar is divided in two by a row of four pillars which support the vaults of the bays. On the upper floor, the lay brothers had their dormitory: it was used as attic storage space in the 18C and today serves as an exhibit area.

ORADOUR-SUR-GLANE

Population 1 998
Michelin map 72 south of fold 6 and 7 or 233 fold 22 – Local map see LIMOGES

Ruined, fire-scarred walls and a cemetery stand in memory of 642 victims of a brutal attack by a detachment of SS troops, one of the cruellest events of the Second World War. An oddly peaceful impression seizes the visitor to this commemorative site, despite the fact that part of the horror of the massacre was that Oradour had been chosen for its very innocence and insignificance, the better to terrorise the French. The atrocity took place just four days after the announcement of the allied landing in Normandy.

10 June 1944 – The people of Oradour, a large Limousin village, were going about their daily affairs on a busy Saturday morning. There were visitors from the city out for a day in the country, and visitors from the outlying farms had come to town for the day; a party of teen-age cyclists was passing through. At 2 pm, as a cordon of German soldiers closed all the exits, a column of lorries and armoured cars entered the village.

Curiosity soon gave way to fear. On Nazi orders everyone gathered on the fairground: men, women and 247 schoolchildren brought there by their teachers. The women and children were locked in the church, the men in the barns and garages. Grenade explosions and machine-gun bursts killed a great many; fire and dynamite completed the massacre. One woman managed to get out of the burning church through a window in the east end; a young boy and a few men were the only others to escape death.

The Ruins ⊙ – Go through the outer walls and along the streets of the ruined village. For a guide apply to the old church, where 500 women and children died. A visit to the **Maison du Souvenir** which contains objects which did not perish in the flames, and to the cemetery where the remains of the victims lie, is a moving experience.

Oradour-sur-Glane – The ruins stand to commemorate the victims

The New Oradour – Nearby, a new Oradour has been built. The modern church with its luminous stained glass windows and square belfry may surprise at first, but it has been designed to blend harmoniously with the neighbouring buildings and surrounding countryside.

Jardins du Prieuré N.-D. d'ORSAN★

10km/6mi southeast of Lignières
Michelin map 68 fold 20 or 238 fold 30 – Local map see ST-AMAND-MONTROND

On the border of the Cher and Indre *départements*, between St-Amand-Montrond and la Châtre, a former priory is home to a medieval garden; its design is loosely based on illuminations and minatures created by monks of the time.

Founded in the 12C by Robert d'Abrissel, the priory is said to possess a relic (the heart) of the founder, who died here in 1116. Pillaged and destroyed in 1569, the priory was rebuilt in the 16C and 17C, before the French Revolution brought about the end of its religious vocation for all time.

TOUR ⊙

In medieval times, religious communities tended gardens planted to correspond to biblical themes. Generally, the plots were encompassed by buildings and a row of oaks. Gardeners provided for both earthly and spiritual nourishment in the choice of vegetables and the planning of green spaces appropriate for meditation.

The garden in the middle of the monastery, was a natural cloister, a place of prayer and spiritual renewal. Marked out by four squares of grapevine, two grassy paths intersect; at the central point, a fountain symbolises the source of the waters of earthly paradise.

Jardins du Prieuré N.-D. d'ORSAN

Jardins du Prieuré N.-D. d'Orsan

Jardins du Prieuré N.-D. d'Orsan

Eight gazebos provide access to the many adjacent gardens: herbs, small fruits, orchards, the **vegetable labyrinth**, the aromatic garden (near the kitchens), the **rose garden** (a harbour of peace dedicated to the Virgin), the pergola and the olive garden (symbol of mercy), the flowerbeds and the secret gardens.
To the north of the gardens, a path (1.2km/0.7mi) passes through the gate and invites walkers to discover the typical landscape of the Boischaut-Sud region.

EXCURSION

★**Lignières** – In the heart of a landscape of well-kept family farms and meadows neatly bordered by hedgerows, this small town was a centre of Calvinism when the famous protestant reformer was a student in Bourges. The classical **château** ⊙ was designed by François Le Vau (exhibit in the orangerie), brother of the more famous Louis, who designed the Louvre, Vaux-le-Vicomte and Versailles. Near the bank of the river Arnon, there is a pretty 12C **church**.

Gouffre de PADIRAC★★

Michelin map 75 fold 19 or 235 fold 7 or 239 folds 38 and 39

The Padirac Chasm provides access to wonderful galleries hollowed out of the limestone mass of Gramat Causse by a subterranean river. A visit into the vertiginous well and a tour of the mysterious river and the vast caves adorned with limestone concretions leave visitors with a striking impression of this fascinating underground world.

From legend to scientific exploration – The Padirac Chasm was a source of superstitious terror to the local inhabitants right up to the 19C, as people believed that the origin of this great hole was connected with the devil.
St Martin, so the tale went, was returning from an expedition on the *causse* where he had been looking unsuccessfully for souls to save. All at once his mule refused to go on; Satan, bearing a great sack full of souls which he was taking to hell, stood in the saint's path. Jeering at the poor saint Satan made the following proposition: he would give St Martin the souls he had in his sack on condition that St Martin make his mule cross an obstacle that he, Satan, would create on the spot. Whereupon he hit the ground hard with his foot, and a gaping chasm opened up. The saint coaxed his mule forward and the beast jumped clear with such force that its hoofprints are still visible. Satan, defeated, retreated to hell by way of the hole he had created.
The chasm served as a refuge for the people living on the causse during the Hundred Years War and the Wars of Religion, but it would appear that it was towards the end of the 19C, following a violent flooding of the river, that a practicable line of communication opened between the bottom of the well and the underground galleries. The speleologist, **Édouard A. Martel**, was the first to discover the passage in 1889. Between 1889 and 1900 he undertook nine expeditions and in 1890 reached the Hall of the Great Dome.
Padirac was opened for the first time to tourists in 1898. Since then, numerous speleological expeditions have uncovered 22km/13.5mi of underground galleries.

222

The 1947 expedition proved by fluorescein colouring of the water that the Padirac river reappears above ground 11km/7mi away where the Lombard rises and at St George's spring in the **Montvalent Amphitheatre** near the Dordogne.

During the expeditions of 1984 and 1985, a team of speleologists, paleontologists, prehistorians and geologists discovered a prehistoric site, 9km/5.5mi from the mouth of the hole, on an affluent of the Joly, with bones of mammoths, rhinoceroses, bison, bears, cave-dwelling lions and deer, all of which were found to date from between 150 000 and 200 000 years ago. Amid the bones found were chipped flints dating from between 30 000 and 50 000 years ago. Copies of some of the bones are exhibited in the entrance hall.

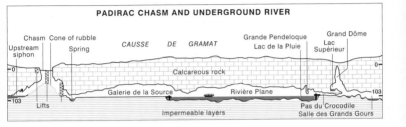

TOUR ⏱ *1hr30min*

Two lifts and some staircases lead into the chasm, which is 99m/325ft in circumference, and to the pyramid of rubble, debris of the original caving-in of the roof. From the bottom of the lift (75m/247ft), there is a striking view of walls covered by the overflow from stalagmites and by vegetation and of a little corner of the sky at the mouth of the hole. Stairs lead down to the underground river, 103m/338ft below ground level. At the bottom, the 2 000m/1.25mi underground journey begins, 700m/0.5mi of which is by boat.

Galerie de la Source – This chamber is at the end of an underground canyon, the roof of which gets gradually higher and higher; it is 300m/984ft long and follows the upper course of the river that hollowed it out. At the far end is the landing-stage.

Rivière Plane – A flotilla of flat-bottomed boats offers an enchanting journey over the astonishingly translucent waters of this "smooth river". The depth of the river varies from 50cm to 4m (20in to 13ft), but the water temperature remains constant at 10.5°C (51 °F). The height of the roof increases progressively to reach a maximum of 78m/256ft; the different levels of erosion corresponding to the successive courses of the river can be seen from the boat. At the end of the boat trip admire the **Grande Pendeloque** ("Great Pendant") of **Lac de la Pluie** ("Rainfall Lake"). This giant stalactite, the point of which nearly touches the water, is simply the final pendant in a string of concretions 78m/256ft in height.

Pas du Crocodile – A narrow passage between high walls links the underground lake and the chambers to be visited next. Look to the left at the magnificent column known as the Grand Pilier, 40m/131ft high.

Salle des Grands Gours – A series of pools separated by gours, natural limestone dams, divides the river and the lake into basins; beyond them cascades a 6m/20ft waterfall. This is the end of the area open to tourists.

Lac Supérieur – This lake is fed only by water infiltrating the soil and falling from the roof; its level is 20m/66ft above that of the Rivière Plane. *Gours* ring the lake's emerald waters.

Salle du Grand Dôme – The great height of the roof (91m/295ft) is most impressive in this, the largest and most beautiful of the Padirac caverns. The viewpoint, built half-way up, enables visitors to appreciate the rock formations and the flows of calcite decorating certain parts of the walls. The return trip (to the landing-stage) offers interesting views of the great pillar and the great pendant. From the end of the Galerie de la Source, four lifts (to avoid the walk up 455 steps) lead back to the entrance.

*The annual **Michelin Red Guide France** gives the addresses and telephone numbers of main car dealers, tyre specialists,*
and garages which do general repairs and offer a 24-hour breakdown service.
It is well worth buying the current edition.

Grotte du PECH MERLE★★★

Michelin map 79 fold 9 or 235 east of folds 10, 14

Prehistoric people performed religious rites in this cave, which was only rediscovered thousands of years later in 1922. Not only is its natural decoration interesting, there are also wall paintings and carvings which are of great documentary value to prehistorians.

The underground explorers – Two boys of 14 were the heroes of the Pech Merle Cave rediscovery. Inspired by the expeditions and discoveries made throughout the region by **Abbé Lemozi**, the priest from Cabrerets who was a prehistorian and speleologist, the boys explored a small fault known only to have served as a refuge during the Revolution. The two friends ventured forward, creeping along a narrow, slimy trench pitted with wells and blocked by limestone concretions. After several hours their efforts were rewarded by the sight of wonderful paintings.

Abbé Lemozi, who soon afterwards explored the cave scientifically, recognised the importance of the underground sanctuary. It was decided to open it to tourists. In 1949 the discovery of a new chamber led to the finding of the original opening through which men had entered the cave about 10 000 to 20 000 years ago.

TOUR ⓥ *1hr45min*

In addition to the interest it offers lovers of speleology who can marvel at the caverns of vast size communicating with each other through wide openings and decorated with beautiful concretions, the Pech Merle Cave offers prehistorians the sight of highly advanced paintings and engravings and material traces of prehistoric man's sojourn there.

Visitors may, at present, walk through 1 200m/1mi of chambers and galleries. The upper level of the Salle Préhistorique is called the **Chapelle des Mammouths** (Chapel of Mammoths) or the black frieze; it is decorated with drawings of bison and mammoths outlined in black and forming a frieze 7m/23ft long by 3m/10ft high.

The Salle des Disques is patterned with many strange concretions that look like discs; the origin of their formation remains a mystery. The footprints made by a prehistoric individual can be seen, petrified forever in the once wet clay of a *gour* (natural dam). Further on are huge, impressive columns, eccentrics with delicate protuberances that defy the laws of gravity and cave pearls, with colours ranging from the shining white of pure calcite to red-ochre caused by the presence of clay and iron oxide in the limestone.

Go down a narrow passageway, which contains an engraving of a bear's head, to the lower level of the prehistoric gallery, where one wall is decorated with the **silhouettes of two horses**, with dots patterning them and the surface around them, mysterious symbols and outlined hand prints, known as "negative hands" *(see illustration in Introduction, Prehistoric Art)*. These prints were made by stencilling in different pigments around the hands placed flat against the rock. The horses are depicted with distorted silhouettes (similar to those at Lascaux): a huge body and

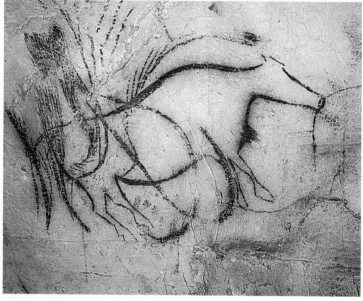

Prehistoric painting

R. Delon/CASTELET

a tiny head. These prints and the roof of hieroglyphics once decorated a sanctuary older than that of the Chapel of Mammoths.

In the last cave to be visited, Salle de Combel, are the bones of cave bears and the roots of an oak tree that bored down into the cave in search of moisture.

Musée Amédée-Lémozi ⊙ – This is a research and information centre on prehistory in Quercy. On the lower floor, which is open to the public, there is an attractive and informative display of bones, tools, weapons, utensils and works of art from 160 different prehistoric sites, dating from the Lower Paleolithic to the Iron Age. In an adjoining room photographs of the decorated caves in the region (in particular Pech Merle and Cougnac) are exhibited. The museum visit ends with a film on Paleolithic art in Quercy.

PÉRIGORD NOIR★

Michelin map 75 folds 7 and 17 or 235 folds 2 and 6

Périgord Noir, a vast Cretaceous plateau carved by the Vézère river to the west and the Dordogne river to the south, overruns into the Sarladais region.

Périgord Noir means Black Périgord and the word "black" refers to the dark colour of the forest cover consisting mainly of oaks, chestnut and sea pines.

The houses, castles, châteaux, manor-houses and churches have walls of golden-coloured local limestone and steeply-pitched roofs covered with *lauzes* or small flat tiles in a warm brown hue. These architectural elements, combined with the rolling, wooded countryside, make a harmonious picture.

Part of Périgord Noir is described in the itinerary of the Dordogne Valley from Souillac to Limeuil *(see Vallée de la DORDOGNE)*, the other part in the Vézère Valley itinerary from Montignac to Limeuil *(see Vallée de la VÉZÈRE)*, while the itinerary described below completes the third side of the triangle formed by the Vézère and Dordogne rivers.

La Grande Filolie

FROM MONTIGNAC TO SARLAT *56km/35mi – 3hr*

Montignac – Lying along the banks of the river Vézère, this town consists of a group of houses around a tower, a last reminder of the fortress which once belonged to the counts of Périgord. In only a few years, this pleasant hamlet has become a busy tourist centre, thanks to the nearby Lascaux Cave. In the tourist information centre, there is a **museum** ⊙ devoted in part to local writer Eugène Le Roy; other rooms include exhibits on age-old crafts and regional history, and prehistory.

La Grande Filolie – Set in the hollow of a small valley, this charming castle dating from the 14C and 15C consists of a group of overlapping buildings and towers linked together. This building, part-castle, part-farm, is built in golden-coloured limestone and covered with a superb roof of *lauzes*. The castle includes the nobles' residence, a 15C quadrangular building flanked at each end by a square machicolated tower, a Renaissance wing, a gatehouse with a bartizan, and a chapel, which has at one end a round tower with a very pointed roof.

★**St-Amand-de-Coly** – See ST-AMAND-DE-COLY

★**St-Geniès** – This is one good example of the Périgord Noir's many beautiful villages with its golden limestone houses covered in *lauzes*, the ruins of a Romanesque keep and the 15C castle next to the church. Access to the church is through a fortified belfry-porch, which was added in the 16C. Above the pentagonal east end there is an arched cornice supported on brackets carved with faces.

Located at the top of a mound behind the Post Office, the **Chapelle du Cheylard**, a small Gothic chapel, is decorated with lovely 14C **frescoes★** depicting the Life of Christ and lives of popular saints.

The road, on the left after a wayside cross, leads down through a cool valley to St-Crépin-et-Carlucet.

St-Crépin-et-Carlucet – St-Crépin and Carlucet form one *commune*, (that is, an administrative area under the direction of a mayor and a town council). The charming **Château de Lacypierre** ⊙ at St-Crépin was built at the end of the 16C on the spot where a fortified building had once stood. The square main building is entirely roofed in *lauzes* and framed by turrets.

The Romanesque **church**, further down, was altered during the Gothic period.

Continue winding along this narrow country road through the valley to Carlucet.

Carlucet – The church of Carlucet has an unusual 17C cemetery. Some of the tombs have been set in carved recesses in the curtain wall.

Salignac-Eyvigues – *See SALIGNAC-EYVIGUES.*

Manoir d'Eyrignac – *See SALIGNAC-EYVIGUES.*

Ste-Nathalène – *Leave the village, taking the road to Proissans for 1.5km/1mi.* The 16C **la Tour watermill** ⊙, driven by the flow of the river Enea, continues the traditional manufacture of walnut and hazelnut oils. There used to be many grain mills in Périgord which were also adaptable for the production of walnut oil during the winter. The mechanism of this mill is 150 years old. The tour of the mill explains the different stages of the production process.

Temniac – The chapel of Notre-Dame, set on a hill overlooking Sarlat, offers a good **view★** of that city. Once a pilgrimage centre, this 12C structure has certain Romanesque Périgord School characteristics: a nave vaulted with two domes and a pentagonal chancel. A black Virgin, the object of pilgrimages, is to be found in the crypt, which has archaic-style ogive vaulting.

Near the chapel stands the curtain wall of a castle (now in ruins), which was once a commandery of the Knights Templar before it became the residence of the bishops of Sarlat.

★★★Sarlat – *See SARLAT-LA-CANÉDA.*

Michelin on the Net: www.michelin-travel.com

Our route planning service covers all of Europe – twenty-one countries and one million kilometres of highways and byways – enabling you to plot many different itineraries from wherever you are.

The itinerary options allow you to choose a preferred route – for example, quickest, shortest, or Michelin recommended.

The network is updated three times weekly, integrating ongoing road works, detours, new motorways, and snowbound mountain passes.

The description of the itinerary includes the distances and travelling times between towns, selected hotels and restaurants.

PÉRIGUEUX★★

Population 51 450
Michelin map 75 fold 5 or 233 folds 42, 43

Built in the fertile valley of the river Isle, Périgueux is an ancient town. Its long history can be traced in its urban architecture and its two distinctive districts, each of which is marked by the domes of its sanctuary: the Cité District, overlooked by St Stephen's tiled roof, and Puy St-Front District, with the Byzantine silhouette of the present cathedral bristling with pinnacles.

There is a good overall view of the town from the bridge beyond Cours Fénelon to the southeast.

The wonderful Vésone – The town of Périgueux derives from the sacred spring known as the Vésone. It was near the stream, on the Isle's south bank, that the Gaulish Petrocorii (Petrocorii, which meant the "four tribes" in Celtic, gave its name both to Périgueux and Périgord) built their main oppidum (defensive town). After siding with Vercingetorix against Caesar, the Petrocorii finally had to accept Roman domination but in fact benefited greatly from the Pax Romana, which enabled the city to become one of the finest in all Aquitaine. Vesunna, as the town was then called, spread beyond the bend in the Isle; temples, a forum, basilicas and an arena were built and an aqueduct over 7km/4mi long was constructed to carry water to the baths. But in 3C AD the city's prosperity was destroyed by the Alemanni, who sacked this town as well as seventy other towns and villages throughout Gaul.

The unfortunate town – To avoid further disaster the Vesunnians shut themselves up in a narrow fortified enclosure; stones from the temples were used to build powerful ramparts, the arena was transformed into a keep.

In spite of all these precautions, the town suffered the alternate depredations of fire and pillaging by barbaric invaders such as the Visigoths, Franks and Norsemen. Such misfortune reduced Vesunna to the status of a humble village and finally even its name died; it was known as the "town of the Petrocorii" or more simply still as *la Cité*. St Front later established the town as an Episcopal seat and, in the 10C, it became the unassuming capital of the county of Périgord.

The ambition of Puy St-Front – A little sanctuary containing the tomb of St Front, apostle of Périgord, was built not far from the Cité. Initially the object of a pilgrimage, the sanctuary became a monastic centre. A busy market town, Puy St-Front, grew up round the monastery, soon eclipsing the Cité in size.

The townspeople of Puy St-Front joined the feudal alliances against the English kings, established an emancipated consular regime and then sided with Philip Augustus against King John of England.

Little by little, the expanding Puy St-Front annexed the Cité's prerogatives; there were more and more squabbles between the rivals. The Cité, unable to win against its neighbour who was under the protection of the king of France, was forced to accept union. On 16 September 1240, an act of union established that the Cité and Puy St-Front would now form one community governed by a mayor and 12 consuls.

The municipal constitution was established in 1251 and the two towns united under the name of Périgueux. Nevertheless, each town kept its distinctive characteristics; the Cité belonged to the clerics and aristocrats while Puy St-Front belonged to the merchants and artisans.

Loyal Périgueux – "My strength lies in my faithful citizens" is Périgueux's proud motto. The town, independent of France under the Treaty of Brétigny in 1360, was the first to answer the call of Charles V to take up arms against the English. It was in Périgueux that Du Guesclin planned the famous campaigns which enabled him to drive the English from the land.

Soon afterwards, bribed by the English, Count Archambaud V openly committed treason against the king and rode roughshod over the consuls. Hostilities broke out in earnest against the loyal townsfolk and their wicked overlord. When eventually royal troops arrived, Archambaud V fled and the parliament claimed Périgord on behalf of the crown. During the Fronde (1648-52) the loyalty of Périgueux was unexpectedly put to the test by Condé. The Fronde supporters laid siege to the town; the churches of St Front and St Stephen were badly damaged. The leaders, their patience exhausted, forced the people to revolt; the garrison was rendered useless and soon afterwards the king's men entered the town in triumph.

Périgueux becomes Préfecture – In 1790, when the Dordogne *département* was created, Périgueux was chosen over Bergerac as Préfecture. The town, which had slowly become dormant, having encountered no upheavals in the 18C but the construction of the Allées de Tourny (by the administrator of the same name), suddenly found itself the object of a building boom. The old quarters were enhanced by the addition of avenues and new squares.

Périgueux today – A small regional capital in the centre of an agricultural region, Périgueux is first and foremost a market town. Its gastronomic specialities, with truffle and foie gras occupying prize position, have become famous around the world.

PÉRIGUEUX

B	Tour Mataguerre	**F**	Maison Tenant ou maison du Pâtissier
D	Maison natale de Daumesnil	**H**	Hôtel de Lagrange-Chancel (Hôtel de ville)
E	Hôtel de Lestrade	**K**	Maison Lambert

Its functions are essentially administrative and commercial, however there is some industry, mainly repair workshops for railway equipment and a stamp printing plant. The transfer of the latter activity from Paris to Périgueux in 1970 was one of the earliest implementations of the government's policies of decentralisation and national development. It includes the production of postal stamps (more than 3.5 billion per year!) for France and a dozen or so other countries, as well as tax stamps, vehicle road tax discs and other types of supplementary taxes, postal cheques and money orders.

★DOMED CHURCHES

★**Église St-Étienne-de-la-Cité** ⊘ (**BZ**) – Built in the 12C on the site of the ancient temple of Mars, this church, the town's first Christian sanctuary, was consecrated by St Front to the martyr Stephen and was the cathedral church until 1669.
It included a row of four domed bays, one after the other, preceded by an imposing belfry porch. When the town was occupied in 1577, the Huguenots demolished all but the two east bays. The Episcopal palace, nearby, was also destroyed. Restored in the 17C, ravaged again during the Fronde, secularised during the Revolution, St Stephen's was consecrated anew at the time of the First Empire.

L	Maison Cayla	**N**	Maison du Lur
M¹	Musée du Périgord	**R**	Maison romane
M²	Musée militaire du Périgord	**S**	Domus du Bouquet

The church as it now stands is a good example of the pure Périgord-Romanesque style. Still visible outside are the beginnings of a ruined bay and the vestigial foundations of a dome.

Inside, it is interesting to compare the architecture of the two bays built within a 50-year interval. The first is archaic, primitive, short and dark. The arches serve as wall ribs and the 11C dome, the largest in Périgord, being 15m/49ft in diameter, is illuminated by small windows which open onto the top of the dome. The second bay is more elongated. Its dome rests on pointed arches held up by square pillars, made less heavy in appearance by twinned columns. Moulded windows with small columns throw light onto an elegant blind arcade with columns which supports an open passage.

This part was greatly damaged by the Huguenots; when it was rebuilt in the 17C, scrupulous attention was paid to reproducing the original.

Against the south wall of the first bay is an impressive 17C **altarpiece** in oak and walnut built for the seminary. Facing it is a carved arcade, part of the tomb of Jean d'Astide, bishop of Périgueux (1160-69), which now frames the 12C baptismal font.

A modern Stations of the Cross is the work of the painter J-J Giraud.

AROUND TOWN

Parking – The two largest car parks (first hour free) among those around the city centre: place Montaigne (**CY**) and place Francheville (**CZ**).

Metered parking rates are based on a sliding scale, the cost identified by the colour-coded signs.

Add hours onto your **Parking card** at the automatic machines on avenue d'Aquitaine (near the theatre), place Montaigne (**CY**); place de la Clautre (**DZ 26**). Some shops give customers vouchers for buying more time on the card.

An evening out – The pedestrian streets in the old town boast many friendly bars. Place St-Louis (**DY**), have a seat at *La Grenouille, Le Goûter de Charlotte* or *le St-Louis* for a cocktail. Near St-Front Cathedral, *le Minos* on place Daumesnil (**DZ 32**) and *le Kristal* in rue Taillefer (**CZ**) are popular. Behind the town hall, *le Centurion* (rue du Serment) offers a wide choice of beers.

Le Montaigne is the town's only cinema (six screens), located on the boulevard of the same name (**CY**). After the show, join the conversation at *la Rotonde* or the *Café de Paris*.

If it's music you're after, head for the *Gordon-pub* near the tourist office, for a bit of Britain abroad, or *le Pub* near the Cours de Tourny (**DY**), for the weekly *apéritif-concert*.

★**Cathédrale St-Front** (**DZ**) – This cathedral, dedicated to St Front, first bishop of Périgueux, is one of the largest in southwest France and one of the most curious. Built in the purest Périgord style, it was largely reconstructed by Abadie from 1852 onwards in the style of Second Empire pastiche. He was to use this restoration later as the inspiration for the design of the Sacré Cœur Basilica in Paris.

A chapel was first built on the site of the saint's tomb in the 6C. The origin of the abbey established around the sanctuary is either Augustinian or Benedictine. In 1047 a larger church was consecrated. This second building was almost completely destroyed by fire in 1120, whereupon it was decided to construct an even bigger church.

This third basilica, completed about 1173, was Byzantine in style, with a dome and with a ground plan in the form of a Greek cross. This architecture, which is uncommon in France, brings to mind St Mark's in Venice and the Church of the Apostles in Constantinople. This was the first domed church to be built on the Roman road, which was still used in the Middle Ages by those travelling from Rodez to Cahors and on to Saintes.

In 1575, during the Wars of Religion, St Front's was pillaged by the Huguenots, the treasure was scattered and the saint's tomb destroyed. Restoration was carried out with little regard for the original design. From 1852-1901, under the supervision of architects Abadie and Boeswillwald, a reconstruction project demolished the buildings used by the resident clergy. Only the cloisters remain standing.

Exterior – Stand in place de la Clautre to have an overall view. Before the restoration, the domes, covered in stones and tiles, had small end ornaments. The façade overlooking place de la Clautre and the open bays were part of the 11C church.

Périgueux – Cathédrale St-Front

The beautiful tiered belltower is all that remains of the 12C church, and is preserved more or less as it was originally. Abadie drew on its lantern as inspiration for the tall pinnacles which adorn the new domes.

Interior – Enter the cathedral by the north door. In order to respect the chronological order of the building's construction, visitors should first of all see, near the base of the belltower, the remains of the 11C church; two bays covered with domes perched on tall column drums.

From its prestigious Romanesque model, the church redesigned by Abadie appropriated its dimensions, the boldness of its domes on pendentives and the strength of its odd-looking pillars carved in places in the shape of a cross.

Adorning the back of the apse is a monumental **altarpiece★★** in walnut; this masterpiece of baroque sculpture, from the Jesuit College, depicts the Dormition and the Assumption of the Virgin. The 17C stalls are from the old Benedictine abbey of Ligueux.

Admire the **pulpit★**, a fine example of 17C craftsmanship, where Hercules is holding up the stand while two atlantes carry the sounding board. The five monumental brass candelabra, hanging at each of the bays, were designed by Abadie.

Cloisters – The cloisters date from the 12C, 13C and 16C and are of a half-Romanesque, half-Gothic architectural style. The chapter-house is covered with groined vaulting resting on columns. The enormous pine-cone-like mass in the centre of the cloisters once crowned the belltower; during the Revolution it was replaced by a weathercock which was later replaced by Abadie's angel. On display in the cloisters' galleries are architectural elements of St Front's before its restoration.

★1 PUY ST-FRONT DISTRICT

The old artisans' and merchants' district has been given a face-lift. A conservation program for safeguarding this historic area was set up, and the area has been undergoing major restoration. Its Renaissance façades, courtyards, staircases, elegant town houses and shops have been brought back to life; the pedestrian streets have rediscovered their role as commercial thoroughfares.

Place du Coderc and Place de l'Hôtel de Ville are colourful and animated every morning with their fruit and vegetable market, while Place de la Clautre is where the larger Wednesday and Saturday market is held. During the winter, the prestigious truffle and foie gras markets attract hordes of connoisseurs. In the summer, the restaurants, overflowing onto the pavements, serve high quality Périgord cuisine in an atmosphere of days past...

Start at Tour Mataguerre (tower) opposite the syndicat d'initiative (tourist office).

Tour Mataguerre ⊙ (**CZ B**) – This round tower (late 15C) is crowned by a machicolated parapet and pierced by arrow-slits. It was part of the defensive system which protected Puy St-Front in the Middle Ages. On the side of rue de la Bride part of the ramparts can be seen. The name Mataguerre is believed to have come from an Englishman who was imprisoned in the tower.

From the top is a view of the old district with its tiled roofs, the towers of the noblemen's town houses, the domes of St-Front's and the neighbouring hills, one of which is the well-known Écornebœuf Hill (*écorner*: to break the horns of an animal; *bœuf*: ox) so named because the hill was so steep that the oxen broke their necks... and lost their horns.

Rue des Farges (**CZ**) – At nos 4 and 6 stands the **Maison des Dames de la Foi** ("House of the Women of Faith"). The medieval (13C) layout of its façade is still visible in spite of its damaged state: pointed arches on the ground floor, rounded arches on the upper storey and a loggia beneath the eaves. A small bell turret set in one corner brings to mind the fact that in the 17C the building was a convent, whose congregation gave the house its name.

It is said that the building housed Du Guesclin during the Hundred Years War.

Rue Aubergerie (**CZ 9**) – At no 16, the **Hôtel d'Abzac de Ladouze** consists of a main building, preceded by a great round arch, an octagonal tower and a corbelled turret, all characteristics of 15C architecture.

At nos 4 and 8 the **Hôtel de Sallegourde**, also 15C, has a polygonal tower surmounted by a machicolated watchpath.

Rue St-Roch (**CDZ 48**) – At no 4 a small arcaded loggia is decorated with diamond-work.

Rue de Sully (**DZ 53**) – The houses in this attractively restored street are half-timbered.

Rue du Calvaire (**DZ 16**) – The condemned, on their way to be executed on place de la Clautre, came up this street, their "road to Calvary". At no 3 there is a lovely door ornamented with nailheads beneath a Renaissance porch.

Place de la Clautre (**DZ 26**) – There is an interesting view of the imposing St Front's Cathedral from here. Tombs are concealed underneath the square.

Périgueux – Market day, place de la Clautre

Place du Thouin (DZ **54**) – The two bronze cannon with the inscription "Périgueux 1588" were excavated at place du Coderc in 1979 on the site of the armoury in the old consulate.

Maison Natale de Daumesnil (DYZ **D**) – *7 rue de la Clarté*
This house has an 18C façade. **General Pierre Daumesnil** was born here on 27 July 1776. This soldier followed Napoleon to Arcola, to Egypt and to Wagram, where he lost a leg. In 1814, while governor of the Vincennes fortress, he gave the enemy, who were laying siege and urging him to give up, the response: "I'll surrender Vincennes when you give me back my leg."

Place de l'Hôtel-de-Ville (CZ **37**) – The town hall is located in the 17C and 18C **Hôtel de Lagrange-Chancel** (**H**). The 15C house at no 7 has a polygonal staircase tower characteristic of the period. Its machicolations, as well as the small shop opening directly onto the street, are neo-Gothic.

Place du Coderc (DY **28**) – Originally a field for keeping pigs, this square has become the geographic and administrative centre of the Puy St-Front District. In the early 19C the old consulate, the heart of municipal and legislative life, still had its old square belfry, some 600 years old. The covered market was built on this site in c1830.

Rue de la Sagesse (CDY **51**) – At no 1, the **Hôtel de Lestrade** ⊘ (**E**) contains an elegant **Renaissance staircase★**, of a square design and decorated with a coffered ceiling depicting mythological scenes, one of which recounts Venus putting down her weapons, symbolising the young wife entering the household. The intertwined H and S represent the initials of the Hauteforts and Solminihacs.

Place St-Louis (CDY) – This square is known locally as Foie Gras Square, as it is here that the foies gras are sold in late autumn.
It features a modern fountain, decorated with a bronze sculpture by Ramon.
The Maison Tenant or **Maison du Pâtissier** (**F**), opposite, used to be the Talleyrands' town house; it consists of a square residential part with an adjoining corbelled turret. The corner door, oddly enough, has a double squinch above it. A machicolated parapet runs around the small inner courtyard. The façade on rue Eguillerie has a marvellous Gothic window.

Rue Lammary (DY **38**) – No 9 has an unusual superposition of mullioned corner windows.

★**Rue Limogeanne** (DY) – In the past, this street led to Limogeanne Gate (Porte Limogeanne), which opened onto the Limoges road. The large pedestrian street is lined with numerous stores and several elegant Renaissance town houses.
In the courtyard of the **Hôtel de Méredieu** (no 12) there is a 15C carved doorway decorated with a coat of arms, which was added in the 17C.
At no 7, note the initials A C in the centre of the wrought-iron impost; these denote Antoine Courtois, the famous 18C caterer, whose partridge pâtés were the talk even of the Court of Prussia. His headquarters were in the cellars of this town house.

The elegant Renaissance façade of the **Maison Estignard** (no 5) is embellished with highly ornate dormers, mullioned windows and pilaster capitals decorated with heads of men, animals and other motifs.

The Regional Department of Architecture is to be found at no 3. Behind the heavy balustrade above the doorway, the inner courtyard has a lovely door decorated with grotesques on the lintel and François I salamanders on the tympanum. The huge staircase leads into a permanent exhibition on the restoration of the buildings in Périgueux.

Lapeyre House (no 1), which is at the corner of place du Coderc, has a corbelled corner turret.

★**Galerie Daumesnil** (DYZ 30) – This leads off rue Limogeanne, opposite no 3. It consists of a network of courtyards and small squares linked together by alley-ways. The buildings, which were grafted onto each other over the centuries, have been demolished, creating open spaces and revealing the fine 15C, 16C and 17C façades. The arcade ends on rue de la Miséricorde, beneath an attractive doorway with a broken pediment.

Walking along rue St-Front, made in the 19C, notice on the left the unusual Masonic Lodge (Loge Maçonnique) perforated by openings like arrow-slits. The sculptures on the façade represent masonic emblems.

Rue de la Constitution (DY 29) – At no 3 is the **doorway of the Hôtel de Crémoux** with a crocketed arch between tall pinnacles.

At no 7, the **Hôtel de Gamanson** consists of two 15C wings set at right angles, linked by a staircase tower, flanked by a corbelled turret and perforated by mullioned windows. A 17C well is sheltered by a Moorish dome.

Rue du Plantier (DY) – Beyond the crossroads with rue Barbecane is the Mint (no 24) with its very steep crocketed gable, which dates the building to the 16C.

Rue du Port-de-Graule (DY 45) and rue Ste-Marthe (DZ 50) – These two roads still have a medieval air about them with their large uneven paving stones, their low doors and the little staircase-alleyways that lead off them. In 1967, several scenes from the film of Jacquou le Croquant (based on local author Eugene le Roy's novel) were shot here.

The quays (Boulevard Georges-Saumande) (DYZ) – Along the river there are several fine houses standing side by side.

The Maison Lambert (DZ K) called the House with Columns because of its gallery, is a fine Renaissance town house with two wings set at a right angle and lit by mullioned windows. Next to it, the **Maison Cayla** (DZ L), also called the Consul's

Périgueux – Maisons de Lur, Cayla, Lambert

House, was built on the ramparts in the 15C. The roof is decorated with Flamboyant-style dormers. At the corner of avenue Daumesnil, the **Maison du Lur (DZ N)** dates from the 16C.

Continue along the quays; on the other side of avenue Daumesnil the half-timbered building, corbelled over the fortress wall, is a remainder of the **barn** attached to the cathedral, called the old mill, which once jutted out over the river.

② CITÉ DISTRICT: TOUR OF LOCAL ANTIQUITY

On the site of ancient Vesunna, this district contains numerous Gallo-Roman ruins.

Arènes (BZ) – A pleasant public garden occupies the space where the arena once stood. Built in the 1C, this elliptical amphitheatre, one of the largest in Gaul, (153m x 125m/502ft x 410ft) had a capacity for 20 000 people. Great blocks of stone still mark the stairwells, the passages between banks of seating and the vaulting, but all of the lower part of the building is still buried below ground. Demolition of the arena began in 3C, when the amphitheatre was turned into a bastion and became part of the city ramparts. In the 11C a count of Périgord built a fortress in the arena, which was then dismantled after Archambaud V's betrayal in 1391. The arena was next transformed into a quarry, its stone being used to build houses in the town.

Gallo-Roman wall – Several buildings have been put up on the old elliptical defence works of the 3C, which were destroyed once and for all during the Wars of Religion.

Porte normande (BZ) – This is the most interesting monument in this group. There is some disagreement over whether it was built in the 3C or the 10C. The story behind the name is that the gate is supposed to have played a part in the defence of the city against the Vikings who came up the river Isle in the 9C.

Maison Romane (BZ R) – This 12C (Romanesque) rectangular building is neighbour to the vestiges of a tower from the Gallo-Roman defence wall, jumbled up with bits of capitals, column drums and other architectural elements. An altar on which bulls were sacrificed was discovered here; it is now on display in the Périgord Museum *(see Additional Sights below)*.

Château Barrière (BZ) – This castle has a 12C keep rising above one of the towers on its ramparts. It was altered during the Renaissance period but kept the lovely main entrance door in the staircase tower. Its Flamboyant style and decoration with pinnacles and crockets bring to mind l'Herm Castle *(See Grottes de ROUFFIGNAC)*.

Turn right on rue de Turenne, towards the railway bridge which leads into rue des Vieux-Cimetières.

From the bridge there is an interesting view of the ancient wall.

Turn left into rue des Vieux-Cimetières.

Domus du Bouquet, "VilladePompeius" (BZ S) – The ruins of this *domus* (detached town house) were discovered in 1959 during the early stages of a building project. The excavations uncovered the base of this luxurious Gallo-Roman residence. Its rooms overlook a square court enclosed by a peristyle. The domus had every comfort with a hypocaust (a heating system: hot air circulated through brick pipes), baths, a cold plunge (piscina) and individual baths. There were also workshops for the smith and potter. There are plans to develop the site for tourists.

Tour de Vésone ☉ **(BZ)** – This tower, 20m/65.5ft high and 17m/56ft in diameter, is all that remains of the temple dedicated to the titular goddess of the city. The temple, which was built in the heart of the forum in the old Cité when the Antonines were in power in the 2C AD, originally had a peristyle, and was surrounded by porticoes and framed by two basilicas. The tower is still impressive despite being damaged.

Périgueux – Tour de Vésone

ADDITIONAL SIGHTS

★**Musée du Périgord** ⊘ (DY **M¹**) – The Perigord museum, located in the Allées de Tourny, on the site of what was an Augustinian convent, was created to house the Gallo-Roman finds of ancient Vesunna, including also the wealth of objects uncovered in the numerous prehistoric sites in the region. It is today one of the most important museums of prehistory in France. An ethnography collection completes the museum's display. The collections are described in order of the tour.

Terracotta figures (16C) used as finials on roof cresting from the Château de la Borde at Festalemps

Prehistoric Section – The Maurice Féaux Gallery is devoted to the Lower Paleolithic Era and displays mainly flint bifaces and stone tools. On display in a special case is the Neanderthaloid skeleton from Régourdou (c 70 000 BC) found near Montignac.

The Michel Hardy Gallery is concerned with the Upper Paleolithic and Mesolithic Ages as shown by the massive carved blocks from Castel-Merle, the painted flat stones from Mas d'Azil and in particular the skeleton of the Chancelade man (15 000 years old) which was found in the Raymonden shelter, among his belongings. The skeleton of the Combe-Capelle man discovered at St-Avit-Sénieur (designated burial place from the Lower Gravettian era, 25 000 BC) is a casting.

The Henri Breuil Gallery illustrates evolution from the Neolithic Era to the Iron Age, using as examples the sandstone used to polish the flint, polished axes, earthenware, bronze axes and jewellery, as well as some relics of the "Barbarian Years". The hall before the "Vesunna Petrucorum" display room is decorated with a reproduction of a fresco in Pompeian style and contains two exceptional exhibits; a perfectly preserved wooden **water pump** found in Périgueux, and a **funerary tiara**★ in very delicately worked gold, made in Magna Graecia in the 3C.

"Vesunna Petrucorum" room: Gallo-Roman Archeology – For the most part, this collection (mosaics, steles, gravestones, glassware and earthenware) has been formed with the finds from the excavations of the ancient town of Vesunna.

Note the **altar**, found near the Viking Gate (*see Porte Normande above*), dedicated to Cybele (a goddess who personified Earth), which was used for the sacrifice of animals. Carved on one of its sides note a bull's head wreathed with a narrow band from which the sacrificial knife, hook (to rip out the animal's entrails), pitcher and cup are hung.

The altar dedicated to Apollo also comes from Vesunna; the **floor mosaic** with a central motif depicting a stag and a doe has been transferred here from a 4C villa near Terrasson.

Room L – The magnificent enamelled terracotta **roof finial** from Thiviers once adorned the roof of the Château de la Borde. It depicts its maker, Christophe Joumard, in the costume of a 16C foot soldier. On the walls are caricatures by the satirical illustrator of Parisian high society Sem (Georges Goursat, 1863-1934), born in Périgueux.

Octagonal Room – This contains a collection of medieval exhibits, in particular the **Rabastens diptych** – 13C illuminated manuscripts on large pieces of parchment, a small, beautifully detailed 15C stone *Pietà* and a Christ giving Blessing in polychrome wood, a 15C German work of art.

Painting Department – Note among the pictures the portrait of Fénelon by F Bailleul. Beautifully carved furniture is also on display, including a 15C liturgical cupboard which used to belong to Chancelade Abbey.

Cloisters – These galleries house the lapidary collection which covers all periods: Gallo-Roman inscriptions, funerary steles, Renaissance sculptures, architectural elements from St Front's including an altarpiece representing the Death of the Virgin (12C).

Musée Militaire du Périgord ⊘ (CZ **M²**) – Arms and weapons of all sorts, standards and uniforms evoke the military history of Périgord from the Middle Ages to today. The great military men of the region are also honoured: Bugeaud, deputy of the Dordogne, and General Daumesnil. Particularly honoured is the 50th Infantry Regiment stationed in Périgueux since 1876; note one of the regiment's flags, which Colonel Ardouin wrapped around his body to prevent it from falling into enemy hands after the surrender of Sedan.

VALLÉE DE LA BEAURONNE

Round trip 45km/28mi – 2hr

★★ **Périgueux** – *See above.*

Leave Périgueux by ⑤ on the plan.

★ **Abbaye de Chancelade** – *See Abbaye de CHANCELADE.*

Leave Chancelade on D 2 travelling northwest.

Merlande Priory – *See Abbaye de CHANCELADE: Excursion.*

Return to D 2, turning left.

Château-l'Évêque – The town took its name from the Episcopal castle. This has been altered several times since the 14C. It consists of an asymmetrical main building. The façades facing the Beauronne valley have mullioned windows, and a machicolated watchpath runs around the line of the roof.

The parish church is where St Vincent de Paul, founder of missionary organisations to help the poor, was ordained by Monsignor François de Bourdeille in September 1600 at the early age of twenty.

Agonac – In a pleasant setting in the wooded hills of the area known as Périgord Blanc, the **Église St-Martin** gives this town its character. The interior (late 11C and 12C) is typical of Romanesque churches in Périgord. The system of two-storey high defensive chambers encircling the dome recalls the troubled times when churches were turned into fortresses. The square belfry and the buttresses (16C) were added to repair damage incurred during the Wars of Religion.

Standing in a clearing of the Lanmary forest, the **Château de Caussade,** a noble fortress, represents on a small scale all the characteristics of a 15C stronghold. Its polygonal curtain wall, surrounded by a moat (half-filled), is flanked by square towers.

Le QUERCY BLANC★

Michelin map 79 folds 17 and 18 or 235 between folds 17 and 18

Between the Lot and Tarn valleys, the region known as Quercy Blanc, so-called because of the white colour of the chalky soil, is characterised by low, long plateaux, arranged in rows *(serres)* with narrow, fertile valleys between them. The landscape and architecture are similar to that of the neighbouring Garonne region: red brick constructions, nearly flat roofs covered in pale pink Roman tile. Agriculture centres around vineyards (the highly appreciated Chasselas variety is grown in Moissac), plum trees, peach trees and melons are grown on the sunny hillsides; tobacco, sunflower and corn are grown on the valley floors.

BASTIDES, CHURCHES AND MILLS

Round trip of 65km/39mi – 3 hr

Lauzerte – This bastide was built in 1241 by the count of Toulouse and was occupied at one time by the English.

Upper Town – The pale grey stone houses with their almost flat roofs are clustered round the church of St Bartholomew and a square, place des Cornières.

This square, named after its covered arcades *(cornières)*, still has one half-timbered house. There are several old houses in rue du Château, some half-timbered, some Gothic in style with twin windows and some Renaissance with mullioned windows. There are extensive views of the gentle, rolling countryside of hills and small valleys.

Leave Lauzerte travelling eastward on D 34, towards Cazes-Mondenard.

The road rises quickly to the top of a plateau, where fields roll out behind the rows of fruit trees.

Take D 31.

In a valley south of Molières, the Malivert lake is a good place for a refreshing break.

★ **Montpezat-de-Quercy** – *See MONTPEZAT-DE-QUERCY.*

Continue along D 20 towards Cahors. After 2km, take a little road on the left.

Église de Saux ⊙ – Once the centre of a large parish, this church now stands isolated in the middle of the woods. The plain interior consists of three domed bays decorated with beautiful 14C and 15C **frescoes**. The best preserved are in the chancel and show Christ in Majesty with the symbols of the four Evangelists, the Crucifixion and scenes from the Childhood of Jesus. In the south chapel the legend of Saint Catherine is depicted; in the north chapel, the legend of Saint George.

At the crossroads, turn right to take D 38.

Castelnau-Montratier – This hilltop bastide was founded in the 13C by Ratier, lord of Castelnau, who gave it his name. It replaced a small village, Castelnau-de-Vaux, which was destroyed by Simon de Montfort in 1214 at the time of the Albigensian Crusade. The town "square" is in the form of a triangle, surrounded by covered arcades and old houses. North of the promontory are three windmills, one of which still works. Such mills with rotating caps were once common in Quercy.

Return to D 74. Cross the Lendou and turn left on D 55.

Montcuq – Main town of a castellany to which Raymond VI, count of Toulouse, granted a charter of customary law in the 12C. Montcuq was the centre of many a bloody battle during the Albigensian Crusade, the Hundred Years War and the Wars of Religion. All that remains of this once fortified village is a tall castle keep (12C), on a hillock over-looking the Barguelonnette river. The view stretches over the surrounding hills and valleys.

South of town, D 28 is a picturesque road winding towards the Lendou valley. D 7 returns to Lauzerte along the river.

One of three mills at Castelnau-Montrabier

MICHELIN TRAVEL PUBLICATIONS

The Red Guide (hotels and restaurants)
Benelux – Deutschland – España Portugal – Europe – France – Great Britain and Ireland – Italia – Switzerland

The Green Guide includes fine art, historical monuments, scenic routes:

EUROPE: Austria – Belgium and Luxembourg – Berlin – Brussels – Europe – France – Germany – Great Britain – Greece – Hungary and Budapest – Ireland – Italy – London – Netherlands – Portugal – Rome – Scandinavia and Finland – Scotland – Sicily – Spain – Switzerland – Tuscany – Venice – Vienna – Wales – The West Country of England

North America: California – Canada – Chicago – Florida – New England – New York City – New York, New Jersey, Pennsylvania – Quebec – San Francisco – USA East – USA West – Washington DC

And Mexico, Guatemala, Belize – Thailand and the complete collection of regional guides for France

ROCAMADOUR★★★

Population 627
Michelin map 75 folds 18 and 19 or 235 fold 6 or 239 fold 38
Local map see GRAMAT CAUSSE

Rocamadour, with its slender castle keep towering above it, comprises a mass of old dwellings, oratories, towers and precipitous rocks on the rugged face of a causse cliff rising 150m/492ft above the Alzou Canyon. This unique site is one of the most extraordinary places in France.

★★★**The site** – The best way to arrive in Rocamadour is on the L'Hospitalet road (*see below*). From a terrace there is a marvellous **view**★★ of Rocamadour: the Alzou winds its way between fields at the bottom of a gorge, while some 500m/1 640ft above, clinging to the cliff face, can be seen the extraordinary profile of this village; such an incredibly daring construction appears to defy the force of gravity. The ecclesiastical city rises above the village, and the whole scene is crowned by the castle ramparts. Morning, when the sun shines full upon the rock, is the best time of all to admire the view. There is another striking view of Rocamadour from the D 32, the Couzou road, going down from the plateau past a road off to the left.

ROC AMADOUR, CENTRE OF MEDIEVAL CHRISTIANITY

The enigmatic St Amadour – The identity of St Amadour, who gave his name to the sanctuary village, has never been firmly established. A 12C chronicler reported that in 1166 "as a local inhabitant had expressed the wish to be buried beneath the threshold of the Chapel of the Virgin, men began to dig a grave only to find the body of a man already buried there. This body was placed near the altar so that it might be venerated by the faithful and from that time onwards miracles occurred". Who was this mysterious person whose tomb appeared to be so old? Conflicting theories have been put forward: some contend that he was an Egyptian hermit, others that it was St Silvanus.

The most widely accepted theory, since the 15C, is that the body was that of the publican Zaccheus, a disciple of Jesus and husband of St Veronica, who, when she saw Christ on His way to Calvary, wiped the blood and sweat from His face with her veil. Both Zaccheus and Veronica were obliged to flee Palestine. They took a boat and were guided on their journey by an angel. They set up home in Limousin. On the death of Veronica, Zaccheus retired to the deserted and wild Alzou valley to preach. All this is hearsay, but one thing is certain: there was a hermit, and he knew the rock well as it often sheltered him.

The Langue d'Oc expression – *roc amator* (he who likes the rock) – was adopted as the name of this village sanctuary, later becoming Roc Amadour and finally Rocamadour.

The fame of Rocamadour – From the time that the miracles began until the Reformation, the pilgrimage to Rocamadour was one of the most famous in Christendom. Great crowds would gather there. Thirty thousand people would come on days of major pardon and plenary indulgence. Since the village was too small to house all the pilgrims, the Alzou valley was transformed into a vast camp. Henry Plantagenet, king of England, was miraculously cured and among the first to kneel before the Virgin; his example was followed during the Middle Ages by the most illustrious people including St Dominic, St Bernard, St Louis and Blanche of Castille, Philip IV the Fair, Philip VI and Louis XI. Veneration of Our Lady of Rocamadour was established at Lisbon, Oporto, Seville and even in Sicily; the Rocamadour standard, flown at the Battle of Las Navas at Tolosa, put the Muhammadans to flight and gave victory to the Catholic kings of Spain.

Pilgrimage and penitents – Ecclesiastical, and in some cases, lay tribunals used to impose the pilgrimage on sinners. It was a considerable penance, inflicted especially on Albigensian heretics, who were said to hate the Mother of God. On the day of their departure, penitents attended mass and then set forth dressed in clothes covered with large crosses, a big hat upon their head, a staff in their hand and a knapsack on their back. On reaching the end of their journey, pilgrims stripped off their clothes, climbing the famous steps on their knees in only a shirt, with chains bound round their arms and neck. Before the altar to the Black Virgin in this humiliating condition they pronounced their *amende honorable*. A priest recited prayers of purification and removed the chains from the penitents, who, now forgiven, received from the priest a certificate and a kind of medal in lead bearing the image of the miraculous Virgin, called a *sportelle*.

But the pilgrimages were not always motivated by piety; lords and town consuls sought the protection of Our Lady when making a treaty or signing a charter. Others came to Rocamadour to see the crowds or even to do a little business.

Decline and renaissance – Rocamadour reached its zenith in the 13C. Favours not even granted to Jerusalem were granted to it; money poured in, but wealth brought covetousness with it.

For 100 years the abbeys of Marcilhac and Tulle disputed who should own the church at Rocamadour; Tulle was finally awarded the honour after arbitration. During the Middle Ages, the town was sacked several times: Henry Short Coat, in revolt against his father Henry Plantagenet, pillaged the oratory in 1183; during the Hundred Years War, bands of English and the local soldiery plundered the treasure in turn; during the Wars of Religion the Protestant Captain Bessonies seized Rocamadour to desecrate it and lay it to waste; only the Virgin and the miraculous bell escaped. The body of St Amadour, still intact, was thrown to the flames, but it would not burn! Furious, Bessonies hacked it to pieces with his axe. Rocamadour did not rise from its ruins; the abbey remained idle until it was dealt its final blow by the Revolution. In the 19C, the bishops of Cahors tried to revive the pilgrimage, and the churches were rebuilt. Though much of its splendour has vanished, Rocamadour has found again the fervour of its former pilgrims and is today a very respected pilgrimage centre.

THE VILLAGE

The village and the ecclesiastical city are pedestrian zones. They can be accessed from the plateau (car park) on foot or by **lift** *⊙, or from the Alzou valley (car parks) on foot or by a small train (there is a charge) which runs to the village, and then from here to the ecclesiastical city either by the flights of stairs up the Via Sancta or by lift. A* **tourist train** *⊙ offers visitors a view of the village by night, with commentary.*

Musée du jouet ancien automobile ⊙ (**AZ M¹**)
– *Place Ventadour.*
At the entrance to the town, this museum houses a collection of **pedal cars★**, exact replicas of legendary models (Bugatti, Cadillac, De Dion Bouton, Delage) race cars (Ferrari, Maserati), and family automobiles (Citroën, Peugeot, Renault), dating from 1910 to 1960. A plane, pedal boats, scooters and even a **flying saucer** round out the exhibit.

Rocamadour – Toy car museum

S. Sauvignier/MICHELIN

A display case of Dinky Toys is sure to excite the nostalgia of a generation of boys who collected these prized items, and make adult fingers itch to run the perfect little cars across the floor (while humming "vroom vroom")!

Once a fortified town, Rocamadour still retains many features which bear witness to its past. Go through **Porte du Figuier** (**AZ**), which was a gateway to the town as early as the 13C, and enter the main street which is now cluttered with souvenir shops. The narrow street, clinging to the living rock, is overlooked by a towering tiered arrangement of houses, churches and the castle.

Beyond the Porte Salmon, which is crowned by a two-storey tower, the town hall (*Hôtel de Ville*) can be seen to the right.

Hôtel de Ville ⊙ (**BZ H**) – The town hall is located in a 15C house (restored), known as the Couronnerie or the House of the Brothers. In the council chamber there are two fine **tapestries★** by Jean Lurçat which portray the flora and fauna of the *causse*.

Rue de la Couronnerie passes under the 13C Porte Hugon and, as far as the Porte Basse (Lower Gate), it goes through a picturesque quarter where small houses descend the slope to the banks of the Alzou.

Nearby stands the old fortified mill, known as the Moulin de Roquefrège.

THE ECCLESIASTICAL CITY

Climb the 223 steps of the Great Stairway (Via Sancta). Pilgrims often make this ascent, kneeling at every step.

The first 141 steps lead, in five flights, to terraces on which buildings for the canons to live in once stood. These have now been converted into shops and hotels.

The fort (**BZ B**) – This vast building of military appearance, which used to be the palace of the bishops of Tulle, stands at the base of the huge cliff face. It was here that important pilgrims were lodged. Built in the 14C, it was extensively restored in the 19C.

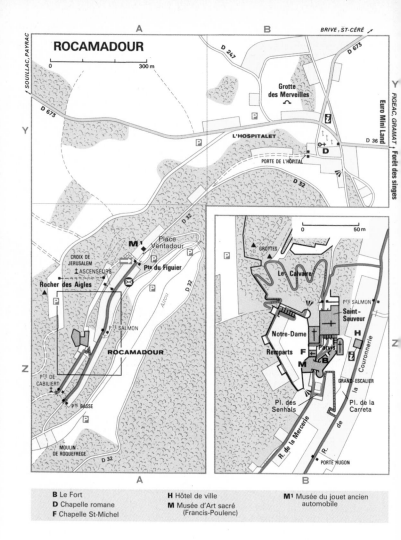

ROCAMADOUR

0   300 m

BRIVE, ST-CÉRÉ

↑ SOUILLAC, PAYRAC

FIGEAC, GRAMAT • Forêt des singes

Euro Mini Land

Grotte des Merveilles

L'HOSPITALET

PORTE DE L'HÔPITAL

D 247

D 673

D 36

D 32

D 32

Place Ventadour

CROIX DE JERUSALEM
ASCENSEURS

Pte du Figuier

Rocher des Aigles

M¹

Alzou

D 32

Pte SALMON

ROCAMADOUR

Pte DE CABILIERT

Pte BASSE

MOULIN DE ROQUEFREGE

D 32

0   50 m

GROTTES

Le Calvaire

Pte SALMON

Saint-Sauveur

Notre-Dame

Parvis

H

Remparts

F

M   B

Couronnerie

de la

GRAND-ESCALIER

Pl. des Senhals

Pl. de la Carreta

R. de la Mercerie

de

R.

PORTE HUGON

B Le Fort	**H** Hôtel de ville	**M¹** Musée du jouet ancien
D Chapelle romane	**M** Musée d'Art sacré	automobile
F Chapelle St-Michel	(Francis-Poulenc)	

This terrace is called Place des Senhals because of the pilgrims' insignia called *senhals* or *sportelles* that were made there; coming out onto the square is the small rue de la Mercerie.

Rue de la Mercerie (BZ) – There are terraced gardens all along this, the oldest street in Rocamadour. The street ends at the 13C Porte de Cabiliert; the gate was once flanked by a defensive tower.

The **Porte du Fort**, which opens under the palace perimeter wall, is an old entrance way leading to the sacred perimeter wall. Seventy-five steps lead up to the parvis surrounded by its churches.

Parvis (BZ) – The parvis (open space in front of the churches), which is also known as place St-Amadour, is fairly small and has seven churches: St Saviour's Basilica opposite the stairway, St Amadour's Crypt below the basilica, the Chapel of Our Lady or Miraculous Chapel on the left, the three chapels of St John the Baptist, St Blaise and St Anne on the right and the Chapel of St Michael standing on a terrace to the left.

Basilique St-Sauveur – This 11-13C Romanesque-Gothic sanctuary has three naves of equal size, divided into two bays each by two massive columns. One of the basilica walls is made out of the cliff's living rock, upon which the arches of the end bay are supported. The mezzanine was added in the last century to enlarge the basilica during the great pilgrimages.

Above the altar stands a fine **16C Christ**, in polychrome wood, with a cross which resembles a tree.

Crypte St-Amadour ⊘ – It is a sanctuary which lies below the basilica. It consists of a flat chevet and two bays with quadripartite vaulting. It used to be a place of worship: the body of St Amadour was venerated here.

Chapelle Notre-Dame

(BZ) – From the parvis, 25 steps lead to the Miraculous Chapel or Chapel of Our Lady, considered the "Holy of Holies" of Rocamadour. It is here that the hermit is believed to have hollowed out an oratory in the rock.

In 1476 the chapel was crushed by a rock-fall; it was rebuilt in the Flamboyant Gothic style. This new chapel, sacked during the Wars of Religion and the Revolution, was restored last century.

On the exterior façade, to the right of the Flamboyant doorway, part of the 13C fresco remains, illustrating the dance of death of the "three living and three dead men": three menacing skeletons are ready to bury or kill their victims.

On the altar, in the semi-darkness of the chapel blackened by candle smoke, is the miraculous Virgin, also called **Black Madonna★**.

Rocamadour – Porte du Fort

This rustic-style reliquary statue, carved in walnut, dates from the 12C. It is small in size (69cm/27in). The rigidly-seated Virgin holds the Infant Jesus, who has the face of an adult, on Her left knee, without touching Him. It was covered with silver plating of which several fragments, blackened by candle smoke and oxidation, remain.

The interior is adorned with many votive offerings: ex-votos and chains worn by the penitents during certain ceremonies of repentance.

Difficult to see in the darkness, the miraculous **bell**, made of jointed iron plates and most likely dating from the 9C, hangs from the roof. It rang out of its own accord to foretell miracles, for example when sailors lost at sea invoked Our Lady of Rocamadour.

As early as the 11C the pilgrimage to Rocamadour was very popular with Breton sailors, and a chapel dedicated to Our Lady of Rocamadour was built at Camaret-sur-Mer. This explains the presence of the small ship figures among the ex-votos. On leaving the chapel, stuck in the cliff face above the doorway, one can see a great iron sword, which legend identifies as **Durandal**, Roland's famous sword. The story goes that Roland, surrounded by the Saracens and unable to break his sword to prevent it falling into enemy hands, prayed to the Archangel Michael and threw him his sword, which in a single stroke implanted itself in the rock of Rocamadour, far from the Infidels.

Chapelle St-Michel ⊘ (BZ F)

This Romanesque chapel is sheltered by a rock overhang. The apse, which houses a small oratory, juts out towards the square. It was used for services by the monks of the priory, who had also installed a library there.

On the wall outside are two frescoes representing the Annunciation and the Visitation; the skill of the composition, the richness of colour – ochre, yellow, reddish-brown, and the royal blue background, protected from condensation and, therefore, well preserved – and the grace of movement all seem to point to the works having been painted in the 12C. They may well have been inspired both by Limousin reliquaries (note the figures in relief in the background) and Byzantine mosaics (note the swarthy complexions).

Below them, a 14C fresco depicts an immense St Christopher, patron saint of travellers and thus of pilgrims.

Inside, the chancel is adorned with paintings (not as well preserved as those outside): Christ in Majesty is surrounded by the Evangelists; further down a seraph and the Archangel Michael are weighing souls.

Musée d'Art Sacré (Francis-Poulenc) ⊘ (BZ M)

The museum of sacred art is dedicated to the famous composer Francis Poulenc (1899-1963), who, having received a revelation during a visit to Rocamadour in 1936, composed

Litanies à la Vierge Noire de Rocamadour. The museum displays an important collection of sacred art which came from the churches' treasuries, donations and from several churches in the Lot. In the hallway various documents recount the history of Rocamadour and its pilgrimage, with the help of maps and a statue of St James as a pilgrim (Rocamadour was a pilgrims' stop on the way to Santiago de Compostela). The vestibule displays objects from the sanctuary: 13C stained glass (the only remaining stained glass from the basilica), showing the death of St Martin, and the 17C reliquary casket of St Amadour, which once contained the relics of the saint's body (destroyed during the Wars of Religion).

The first gallery contains objects (ex-votos, paintings and items in carved wood) dating for the most part from the 17C. A naïve panel (1648) shows St Amadour hailing the Virgin with the Ave Maria; next to it, a baroque statue of Flemish origin represents the prophet Jonas as an old man writing.

The treasury contains fine items which came from the once fabulous treasure collection of the sanctuary. **Limoges reliquary caskets** from Lunegarde and Laverhne (both 12C) and Soulomès (13C), ornamented with enamelwork, demonstrate the craftsmanship of the Limousin artist. Among the other works displayed note the reliquary of St Agapit, in the form of a head, the silver reliquary monstrance surmounted by a Crucifixion with the Virgin and St John on either side, a 15C silver processional cross and a 12C seated Virgin in wood. The next gallery contains 17C, 18C and 19C religious paintings.

On leaving the museum take the gallery, known as "the tunnel", which passes beneath St Saviour's Basilica and comes out on a terrace overlooking Alzou Canyon.

THE PLATEAU

Calvary (BZ) – A shaded Stations of the Cross *(calvaire)* winds up towards the ramparts. After passing the caves *(grottes)* of the Nativity and the Holy Sepulchre, visitors will see the great Cross of Jerusalem, brought from the Holy Land by the Penitential Pilgrims.

Ramparts ⊘ (BZ) – These are the remains of a 14C fort which was built to block off the rocky spur and protect the sanctuary. Leaning against the fortress, the residence of the chaplains of Roc-Amadour was built in the 19C. From the ramparts, which tower above a sheer drop, there is an unforgettable **panorama★★★** of the *causse*, the site of Rocamadour and the rock amphitheatre surrounding it.

Rocher des Aigles ⊘ (AZ) – The "Eagles' Rock" is a breeding centre for birds of prey. Regular demonstrations showing the birds in flight and how they hunt are popular with visitors.

To return to the village, go back to an esplanade which is on the same level as the Ecclesiastical City and take the lift to the main street near Porte Salmon.

L'HOSPITALET *1.5km/1mi east of Rocamadour*

The name of this village, clinging to Rocamadour's cliff face, comes from the small hospital founded in the 11C by Hélène de Castelnau to nurse the pilgrims on the pilgrim road from Le Puy (Auvergne) to Santiago de Compostela. Only a few ruins of this hospital remain; the **Romanesque chapel** (BY D), which is set in the middle of the churchyard, was remodelled in the 15C.

L'Hospitalet is very popular with visitors for its **viewpoint★★** which overlooks the site of Rocamadour. There is a large tourist information centre *(syndicat d'initiative)*.

Grotte des Merveilles ⊘ (BY) – Discovered in 1920, the "Cave of Wonders" is small, only 8m/24ft deep, but has some lovely formations: stalactites, stalagmites and natural limestone dams reflecting the cave roof and its concretions.

On the walls are cave paintings dating back, most likely, to the Solutrean Period (*c*18 000 years ago), depicting outlined hands, black spots, a few horses, a cat and the outline of a deer.

Euro Mini Land ⊘ – *On the road to Figeac*

Visitors sit on bleacher seats which move, back and forth, alongside a giant scale model (85m²/915sq ft) including **animated miniatures**.

A fantastic **decor** represents city, country and mountainous landscapes, criss-crossed by a train network at 1:87. Light and sound effects accent groups of automata playing out realistic scenes (marriage ceremony, ski run). Some of the animation is extremely detailed (circus, fun fair) and unusual (hot air balloons taking off); these are also visible on a video monitor, for fuller appreciation.

Forêt des Singes ⊘ – *On the road to Figeac*

Living at liberty on 10ha/25 acres in this "Monkey Forest" woodland are 150 animals in an environment similar to the upper plateaux of North Africa, where they originated. The monkeys are Barbary apes and macaques, a species which is becoming extinct.

ROCHECHOUART

Population 3 991

Michelin map 72 north of fold 16

Rochechouart Castle rises above a rock promontory; the best view of it is from the D 3bis where it passes the foot of the cliff.

On the last day of the *ostensions (see Introduction)*, held once every seven years, a unique procession takes place; the participants wear special costumes and carry precious shrines.

A distinguished family tree – The Rochechouart family can be traced back beyond the year 1000; their first castle rose up near the monastic settlement governed by the Charroux abbey. A son of the viscount of Limoges became the lord upon his marriage to Ève d'Angoulême, whose dowry was the Rochechouart title and property. The dynasty was active in the crusades: in 1099, Aymeric IV accompanied Gouffier de Lastours, member of a powerful local family and hero of troubadours' ballads. Lastours, they recounted, saved a lion from death in the desert and the beast thereafter followed him like a faithful dog, only to drown in the sea trying to swim after his master's ship. In 1150, another Aymeric travelled to the Holy Land, while the troubadou Bertrand de Born celebrated the beauty of Agnès de Rochechouart. The château was compeltely rebuilt when Aquitaine shifted to the English crown.

Around 1205, another lion, another Amyeric and another Rochechouart beauty became the stuff of romatic legend. In that year, Viscount Aymeric de Rochechouart married the heartbreakingly beautiful Alix de Mortemart. The castle steward, mad with love for the viscountess, tried to seduce her, but she repulsed his advances. In revenge the steward told his master that the viscountess had solicited him. The jealous and impulsive Aymeric had his wife thrown to a lion in the east tower. Two days later, when he went to contemplate his act of justice, he found the lion crouched docilely at his wife's feet. The guiltless woman was brought back into favour, truth and virtue won out and the steward was dispatched to the lion, which, this time, proved to be hungry.

In the struggle facing off Capetians and Plantagenets, the Rochechouart family sided with the king of France. One family member was killed at the Battle of Poitiers (1356), protecting the life of his sovereign liege, another was imprisoned by the prince of Wales. In the centuries following, the Rochechouart family continued to serve France, while the family tree branched out. The Mortemart line *(see Château de MEILLANT)* is also replete with history-making figures. The château was buffeted by wars and often threatened with ruin, but always kept its head up – often with the help of Rochechouart wives who brought hefty dowries into their alliances. The French Revolution called for its destruction, but given the size of the buildings, the project was abandoned. In 1836, the State acquired the buildings and set up some offices within.

SIGHTS

★**Château** – The castle stands in a remarkable **setting**★ above the confluence of the Graine and the Vayres and is mostly late 15C. The 13C keep which flanks the northeast entrance fort, was razed level with the rooftops in the 16C.

The second tower at the left end of the façade bears a lion carved in granite in a niche, perhaps in hommage to the beautiful Alix, or more likely the crusading viscounts of Limoges. A drawbridge leads to the small fortified castle.

Rochechouart – Mural

J. D. Sudres/DIAF

243

Cour d'honneur – The buildings which line the court on three sides were restored in the 18C and now house the public services including the sub-prefecture. They are adorned with a gallery supported on elegant twisted columns. The fourth side is closed by a curtain wall.

Musée départemental d'Art contemporain ⊙ – The Haute-Vienne General Council began building up the collection in 1985; today it is a significant centre for contemporary art. It includes representative examples of "Arte Povera", "Land Art", the German school and unique artists such as François Bouillon and Raoul Hausman (1886-1971, co-founder of the Dada-Berlin group in 1918). The collection is one-of-a-kind in France. Some of the works (*Cercle du coucou*, Richard Long, 1987) were created especially for exhibit in the château. Three temporary exhibits are staged every year. A magnificent 15C timber framework can be seen in the attic space.

Besides the main focus on contemporary art, the museum gives over two rooms to a remarkable group of 16C **frescos★**. The **salle d'Hercule** is decorated with rare murals painted in grisaille. Created by several artists, they may have been inspired by the bas-reliefs in the Limoges Cathedral; almost like a comic strip, they illustrate the labours of Hercules. Nearby, the **salle des chasses** contains slightly older frescos, which depict scenes from a royal hunt: the cortege setting out, the sounding of the horn, the baying dogs and the banquet table. The attire, the setting – Rochechouart, the château and small town surrounded by ramparts, is easily recognizable – make these paintings an interesting study of the times of Louis XII.

Prehistoric and Gallo-Roman objects from the Chassenon site are also found in the historical section of the museum.

Promenade des Allées – Leaving the château, the promenade is on the left, a shady terrace fragrant with age-old lime trees. From the site of the cross standing at the end of the walk, there is a good view of the valleys of the Graine and the Vayres and the front of the castle, framed by round towers and set with elegant windows with their stone cross-pieces intact. The view also enfolds the terraced gardens, accessible by a double flight of stairs, hidden by the greenery in season.

Church – This is the former priory church, consacrated in 1076; only the western doorway, the nothern wall, and part of the transept and chancel have survived. The unusual belfry with its twisted spire was rebuilt in the 18C. Inside, there is a stone coffin sarcophagus dating from the 12C; modern paintings embellish the chancel.

Around town, note the 15C **maison des Consuls** *(rue Jean-Parvy)* and, further on, a corner town which stood within the medieval city wall. In the cemetery *(outside town on the road to Chabanais)*, there is a novel funerary monument shaped like a large cask. Closer inspection reveals that it honours the memory of one Léonce Chabernaud, profession... you guessed it, wine merchant.

EXCURSION

Biennac – *2km/1mi to the east by the D 10*
The church dating from the 12C and 13C is topped with a hexagonal belfry and supported at each corner by buttresses. To reach the church pass a covered well and then go up the semicircular flight of steps.

La ROQUE-GAGEAC★★

Population 407
Michelin map 75 fold 17 or 235 fold 6 – Local map see Vallée de la DORDOGNE

The village of La Roque-Gageac, huddled against a cliff which drops vertically to the river Dordogne, occupies a wonderful **site★★** – one of the finest in this part of the valley, in which Domme, Castelnaud and Beynac-et-Cazenac are all within a few miles of each other.

★★View – The best view of La Roque-Gageac is from the west: the late afternoon sun highlights the tall grey cliff face covered with holm-oaks, while the houses, with their stone slab (lauzes) or tile roofs, are reflected in the calm waters of the river below. **Tour boats** ⊙ carry visitors along its stream.
In the foreground the outline of the Château de la Malartrie can be seen; at the other end of the village, at the foot of the sheer rock-face, is the charming Tarde manor-house.

The village – Attractive little streets, in which the humble homes of peasants and craftsmen nestle side by side with the grander residences of the gentry, run tightly along the rocky bluff. One of them, leading off to the right of the Belle Étoile hotel, climbs through luxuriant plant life towards the small church (beautiful view of the Dordogne) and then to the Tarde manor-house.

La Roque-Gageac

Manoir de Tarde – Two pointed gabled buildings, with mullioned windows, stand next to a round tower. This charming manor-house is associated with the Tarde family, the most famous members of which are the canon Jean Tarde, a 16C local humanist, historian, cartographer, astronomer, mathematician, etc and Gabriel Tarde, a 19C sociologist.

At the top of the cliff there are clear traces to remind visitors of the tragic night in 1957 when a huge block of rock came away from the cliff-face, crushing the homes and their sleeping residents below.

Château de la Malartrie – A castle built in the early 20C, greatly influenced by the 15C style.

Grotte de ROUFFIGNAC★

Michelin map 75 fold 6 or 235 fold 1

This dry **cave** ⊘, also known as Cro de Granville, was already well-known in the 15C. The galleries are more than 8km/5mi long. An electric train carries visitors to the main galleries. It is worth noting that this is one of the few prehistoric sites in the area which is fully accessible to persons of limited mobility.

In 1956 Professor L. R. Nougier called attention to the remarkable group of paintings marked with black lines and **engravings**★ *(see illustration in Introduction, Prehistory)* produced during the Middle or Upper Magdalenian Period (some 10-13 000 years ago). These engravings are of horses, ibexes, rhinoceroses, bison and a great number of mammoths, among which may be seen the "Patriarch" and an amazing frieze depicting two herds locked in combat. There is an outstanding group of drawings on the ceiling of the last chamber.

Église de Rouffignac – *5km/3mi north on D 32*

The church is all that escaped when the Germans set about burning the town in March 1944 as a reprisal; the town has since been rebuilt.

The church entrance is through an interesting belfry-porch containing a doorway built in the style of the Early Renaissance. It was constructed in about 1530 and is decorated with Corinthian capitals and surmounted by a finely carved lintel; the somewhat irreverent decoration – mermaids, busts of women – seems surprising in a place of worship.

The church's main body has three aisles of equal height built in the Flamboyant style; the pointed vaulting is supported by round pillars reinforced by remarkable engaged twisted columns.

ST-AMAND-DE-COLY★

Population 312

Michelin map 75 fold 7 or 239 fold 25 – Local map see PÉRIGORD NOIR

Tucked away in the fold of a small valley off the Vézère valley is St-Amand-de-Coly, its old *lauze*-roofed houses clustering round the impressive abbey church.

★★**Church** – This church of fine yellow limestone is perhaps the most amazing of all Périgord's fortified churches. The Augustinian abbey of which it was once part saw its spiritual activity reduced during the Hundred Years War – by 1430 there were only two monks left. It transformed itself into a fortress, as documents of that period illustrate by their references to "St-Amand fort". The highly elaborate defence system was designed to keep enemies at a distance, but also to drive them away should any forays be made into the church. The Huguenots occupying the church in 1575 were able to hold out for six days against 20 000 soldiers of the Périgord seneschal, who had powerful artillery backup.

St-Amand-de-Coly – The Village and church

Exterior – An impression of tremendous strength is created by the tower-keep, indented by the enormous pointed arch of the doorway which supports a defence room intended to prevent anyone approaching. A wooden hoarding was added to the corbels, still visible, on its upper wall. A narrow, paved passageway, protected by a defence-work perforated with strong-rooms, runs around the east end. The harmony of the apsidal chapels is a contrast to the severity of the high walls of the nave and transept. These are made to seem even heavier by the defensive balconies resting on the gabled ends of the transept arms. A rampart walk runs around the building beneath the *lauze*-covered roof.

Interior – Purity of line and simplicity of decoration, both of which are usually to be found in Augustinian architecture, contribute to the beauty of the lofty space inside. There is an archaic-style dome on pendentives above the transept crossing. The chancel, raised by eight steps and roofed with ribbed vaulting, ends in a flat east end. The concern for protection also affected the interior design; remains of the defence system include a narrow passage enclosing the chancel and some of the transept arms, small lookout posts in the pillars of the transept area and the loopholes in the base of the dome.

Opposite the church, in the **former presbytery** ⊘, there is an audio-visual show on the church and its history.

ST-AMAND-MONTROND

Population 11 937
Michelin map 69 folds 1 and 11

Capital of the region known as Val de Germigny, where the fields are dotted with white Charollais cattle, the village developed around a monastery, founded in the 7C by Saint Amand, a disciple of Saint Colomban. Later, a castle rose above it, on the hill known as Mont-Rond, and served to protect the growing town. In 1621, Sully turned over the much-embellished château to the duke of Bourbon, father of the Grand Condé. Thus, the revolt known as the *Fronde*, in which Condé was famously involved, led to the ruin of the château, which was invaded in 1652 and then destroyed. On the hill top, a park (A) has since been created.

Since the Second World War, the town has undergone much change, its built-up area doubling in size. The basis of the economy is light industry (metalworks) and printing.

Church – The church stands in the southeast part of the town, south of D 951 which goes to Decize and Nevers.

This interesting 12C Romanesque building with a Benedictine floor plan opens with a beautiful round arched doorway framed by two multifoiled bays. The nave with its barrel-vaulting, is rather dark. The transept crossing has pointed arches which certainly replaced an earlier cupola. In the 15C, side chapels were added. The capitals in the nave are interesting for their traditional Romanesque design: birds with long, twining necks, monstrous faces and acanthus leaves. In the south aisle note the fine late 16C carving of Christ Reviled and opposite, the early 16C stone figure of St Rock.

Musée St-Vic ⊘ (**B M**) – The 16C St-Vic Mansion, set amid a pleasant garden, was the town residence of the commendatory abbots of Noirlac (*see NOIRLAC*). The exhibit area presents a wide panorama of this region, rich in history and vestiges.

A prehistoric room traces the first human settlements from the Paleolithic through the Bronze Age. Note the human figure attributed to Magdalanian artists.

Gallo-Roman settlements were dense along the Cher river valley (*see Drevant, below*), and displays illustrate daily life at that time through objects such as the rare set of shoe soles found at Allichamps. Information on Drevant completes the overview of this period.

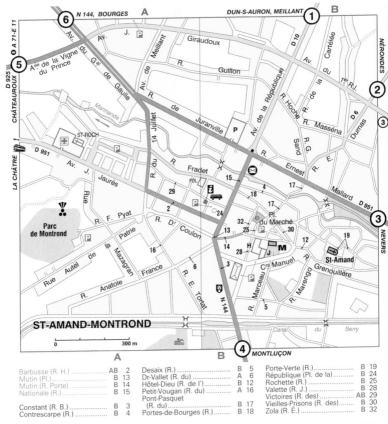

Barbusse (R. H.)	AB 2	Desaix (R.)	B 5	Porte-Verte (R.)	B 19
Mutin (Pl.)	B 13	Dr-Vallet (R. du)	A 6	République (Pl. de la)	B 24
Mutin (R. Porte)	B 14	Hôtel-Dieu (R. de l')	B 12	Rochette (R.)	B 25
Nationale (R.)	B 15	Petit-Vougan (R. du)	A 16	Valette (R. J.)	B 28
		Pont-Pasquet		Victoires (R. des)	AB 29
Constant (R. B.)	B 3	(R. du)	B 17	Vieilles-Prisons (R. des)	B 30
Contrescarpe (R.)	B 4	Portes-de-Bourges (R.)	B 18	Zola (R. É.)	B 32

247

The Middle Ages and the Renaissance are represented by archeological items (notably a Carolingian gold coin), and some fine pieces of furniture (credenza and inlaid travelling desk), as well as paintings by Hugo Van der Goes and Bernardino Conti.

The other rooms are devoted to excavations and materials related to the old castle; to local ethnography (furnishings, pottery, headdresses); the ceramic work of the potters of Borne. *The Clog Tree*, a sculpture by Louis Touzet, regional landscapes painted by Brielman, Cals, Delavaux, Detroy, Osterlind (the Crozant school), fill out the collection along with oddments from the Belle Epoque and some surprising local inventions and crafts.

EXCURSIONS

① Le Grand Bois de Meillant *25km/15mi – 1hr*

Leave St-Amand by ①, D 10.

The road goes through the forest, Grand Bois de Meillant.

★★Château de Meillant – *See Château de MEILLANT.*

La Celle – The church of St-Blaise, originally a dependency of Déols Abbey has an impressive square belfry and an east end adorned with modillions and Romanesque capitals. The nave is supported by stout flying buttresses. Inside, the apsidal chapels are separated from the chancel by massive columns with interesting capitals. The church contains the tomb of St Silvanus, the legendary apostle of Berry, whose relics were moved from Levroux to La Celle in the 15C.

Bruère-Allichamps – A Gallo-Roman milestone was found in the town in 1757. It was erected in its present site at the junction of N 144 and D 92 in 1799. Since 1865, this point has been popularly held to mark the geographical centre of France.

The D 35 now follows the course of the picturesque Cher valley rich in meadowland.

★★Abbaye de Noirlac – *See Abbaye de NOIRLAC.*

The N 144 follows the right bank of the Cher back to St-Amand-Montrond.

② Le Boischaut *Round trip of 105km/65mi – 4hr*

Leave St-Amand travelling south on D 97.

Drevant – This quiet village is infused with a feeling of timelessness. The ruins of a theatre and traces of a forum, baths and temples, were part of a Gallo-Roman rural sanctuary. The Berry canal runs through a park by the ruins, providing a lovely spot for a walk or picnic.

Take N 144 through the rolling countryside of the Cher valley.

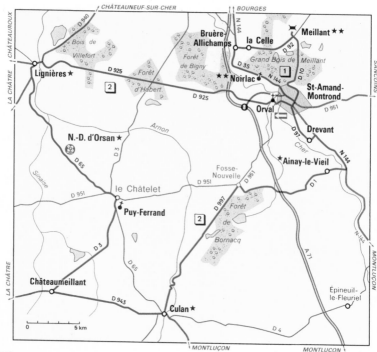

Château d'Ainay-le-Vieil

★**Ainay-le-Vieil** – The **castle**★ is the town's proudest feature, its severe **medieval walls** (12-14C) hiding a gracious Renaissance building within. The **hexagonal tower** (early 16C) is reminiscent of Meillant, and from the watchpath visitors can admire the moat and castellated ramparts. The interior is beautifully decorated and furnished, and the **rose garden** in bloom is fragrant with its many varieties (the oldest is a variety first named in 1420).

Southwest of Fosse-Nouvelle, the road winds through fields and meadows patterned with hedgerows and skirts Bornacq forest before entering the Arnon valley, bordered by heather-clad rocks.

★**Culan** – *See CULAN.*

West of Culan, the itinerary crosses hilly cattle country.

Puy-Ferrand – The former abbey church of Puy-Ferrand, south of Le Châtelet, is a fine Romanesque building. The façade is ornamented with bays, finely carved capitals and geometrical designs.

★**Jardins du prieuré Notre Dame d'Orsan** – *See Notre Dame d'ORSAN.*

★**Lignières** – *See Notre Dame d'ORSAN.*

The road goes through the Habert forest.

Orval – The church in town has a 13C reliquary cross in gold plated silver, its cross-pieces embellished with enamel.

ST-CÉRÉ★

Population 3 760
Michelin map 75 folds 19 and 20 or 235 fold 7 or 239 fold 39

The lovely old houses of St-Céré cluster in the cheerful Bave valley, at the foot of St Laurence's Towers. St-Céré stands at the junction of roads from Limousin, Auvergne and Quercy, but has become a good place to stay in its own right because of its pleasant site. It is also an excellent starting-point for walks and excursions in Upper Quercy.

A prosperous town – In the 13C the viscounts of Turenne, overlords of St-Céré, granted a charter with franchises and many advantages to the town. Other charters added to the wealth of the town by giving it the right to hold fairs and establish trading houses. Consuls and officials administered the town, which was protected by St Laurence's Castle and a formidable line of ramparts. Even the Hundred Years War left the town practically unscathed. With the 16C dawned a new period of prosperity.

An early Academician – St-Céré had the honour to be the birthplace of Marshal Canrobert, who won renown as a soldier in Algeria, was commander-in-chief in the Crimea and distinguished himself at St-Privat in the Franco-Prussian War of 1870.

The town can also count the poet **François Maynard** among its most famous citizens. The poet, son of a member of Parliament, was born in Toulouse in 1582, but spent many years of his life in St-Céré. While still young, he managed to obtain the post of secretary to Marguerite de Valois, wife of Henri IV.

He soon became known as one of the most skilful court poets of the period. Malherbe noticed him, as did Cardinal Richelieu, who honoured him by nominating him a member of the Academy he had just founded. The story goes that Maynard, who enjoyed receiving honours but was not above receiving money also, asked the Cardinal for a tangible expression of the latter's confidence. He sent a cheeky little poem, asking:

"But if I'm asked what you have asked me to do, and what I've received from you in return, what would you have me say?" "Nothing", the Cardinal is said to have replied dryly.

Dismissed by Parisian society, the poet came to live in St-Céré. He devoted himself to versification, frequented literary circles and society and went to the fabulous receptions given at Castelnau-Bretenoux. When he died in 1646, he was buried beneath the chancel of the Church of Ste-Spérie in St-Céré.

Jean Lurçat and St-Céré – Born in 1892 in the Vosges, Jean Lurçat, whose parents had planned that he would become a doctor, directed his talents instead to painting, decoration of theatrical scenery, mosaics and ceramics. He soon became interested in tapestry as a medium; it is for his work on tapestry design and technique that he achieved world renown (*see AUBUSSON*).

After a period spent in Aubusson, he participated in the Resistance movement and through this discovered the region of the Lot. He settled in St-Céré in 1945. It was in St Laurence's Towers that he set up his studio, and this is also where he lived until his death in 1966.

Lurçat had the Aubusson tapestry factory weave most of the tapestries for which he had painted the designs (cartoons).

OLD TOWN

The 15C, 16C and 17C houses give St-Céré a picturesque character all of its own. Some houses still have their half-timbered corbelled façades and fine roofs of brown tiles.

Place de l'Église – The church of Ste-Spérie was rebuilt in the 17C and 18C in the Gothic style. **The Hôtel de Puymule** (15C), in the square near the east end, is a turreted town house, with doors and windows decorated with ribbed arches.

Rue du Mazel (**15**) – This street and the surrounding area form one of the most charming districts in the old town, with old houses and fine doorways. At the corner of rue St-Cyr, note the 15C **Hôtel Ambert** (**B**) with its two corbelled turrets and Renaissance doorway.

Further along on the right, the narrow cobblestoned **Passage Lagarouste** (**12**), with a stream down the middle, is overshadowed by tall corbelled houses.

Place du Mercadial (**16**) – This was the market square where fishermen brought their catch to be displayed on the *taoulié*, a stone bench beside the 15C **Maison Jean de Séguirier** (**D**) at the corner of rue Pasteur. From this spot, there is a lovely view of the square surrounded by half-timbered houses against St Laurence's Towers. The **Maison des Consuls** (**E**) has an interesting Renaissance façade overlooking rue de l'Hôtel-de-Ville.

St-Céré – Maison Jean de Séguirier

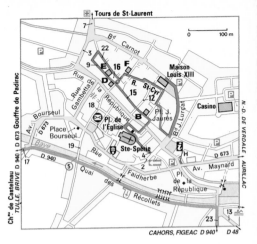

ST-CÉRÉ

B	Hôtel Ambert
D	Maison de Jean de Séguirier
E	Maison des Consuls
F	Hôtel de Miramon

Rue St-Cyr – At the beginning of the street stands a lovely medieval house with three corbelled façades. Further on, to the right, is the 15C **Hôtel de Miramon** (**F**) flanked with a corner turret. The street, which runs in a semicircle and has old houses all along it, ends in rue du Mazel.

Maison Louis XIII – This fine mansion has an elegant façade adorned with a loggia.

ADDITIONAL SIGHTS

Galerie du Casino ⊘ – In addition to temporary exhibitions, this gallery displays a large collection of **Jean Lurçat's tapestries**★. Hung on the walls, the tapestries combine a variety of forms and colours, depicting fantastic animals and cosmic visions.

Tours de St-Laurent – *2km/1mi to the north*
Perched on a steep hill which overlooks the town, the two tall medieval towers and curtain wall are a familiar local landmark.
Although the road to the right is private, the restriction is not strictly enforced. From a track *(1hr on foot round trip)* skirting the ramparts, admire the **view**★ of the town, the Bave and Dordogne valleys and the surrounding plateaux.

★**Atelier-musée Jean-Lurçat** ⊘ – In the artist's studio, now a museum, the ground floor rooms (studio, drawing room, dining room) exhibit Lurçat's works (tapestries, designs, paintings, ceramics, lithographs, gouaches, wall paper). Note the copies of the thrones ordered in 1956 by Haile Selassie, emperor of Ethiopia.

EXCURSIONS

★**1 Vallée de la Bave** *40km/24mi – 3hr*

The towers of Montal Castle soon come into view on the left, rising above fertile fields and meadows interspersed with lines of poplars.

★★**Château de Montal** – *See Château de MONTAL.*
The road towards Gramat climbs above the Bave valley, offering views of St Laurence's Towers.

★**Grotte de Presque** ⊘ – The cave consists of a series of chambers and galleries that go back 350m/380yd into the rocks. Concretions, especially strange-shaped stalagmite piles and thousand-faceted frozen falls along the walls, have built up in the different salles or chamber of the caves, named for the imagery evoked: Draperies, Salle Haute, Grande Cuve (basin), Marbre Rouge (red marble). Slender columns of astonishing whiteness stand at the entrance to the **Salle des Merveilles**★ (Hall of Wonders).

★**Cirque d'Autoire** – *Leave the car in a parking area. Take, on the left of the road, the path that overlooks the Autoire river, which here forms a series of waterfalls (viewpoint).*
Cross the little bridge and go up the steep stony path cut in the rocks. Very soon a wonderful **view**★★ of the natural amphitheatre, the valley and the village of Autoire unfolds.

★**Autoire** – Autoire in its picturesque **setting**★ is typical of the character of the Quercy region. Enchanting scenes are revealed at every street corner: a fountain at the centre of a group of half-timbered houses, old corbelled houses with brown-tiled roofs, elegant turreted manors and mansions.

From the terrace near the church, which has a fine Romanesque east end, there is a good view of the Limargue Mill and the rocky amphitheatre that lies to the southwest.

★**Loubressac** – This old fortified town stands on a rocky spur overlooking the south bank of the Bave river.

From near the church, there is a good view of the valley and of St-Céré, marked out by its towers. Walk through the enchanting narrow alleys as they wind between brown-tiled houses to the castle's postern.

This 15C manor-house, which was rebuilt in the 17C, stands on a remarkable **site**★ at the very end of the spur on which the village was built. The D 118 and then D 14 from the hamlet of La Poujade descend towards the Bave valley, giving fine **views**★ of the Dordogne valley dominated by the impressive outline of Castelnau-Bretenoux Castle.

★★**Château de Castelnau-Bretenoux** – *See Château de CASTELNAU-BRETENOUX.*

2 **Northwest of Ségala**
45km/27mi – 3hr

Leave St-Céré travelling eastward on D 673. After 2km/1mi, turn right on D 30.

The road passes wooded hills and meadows at it goes up the Bave valley.

1km/0.5mi beyond Latouille-Lentillac a narrow road branches off to the left and runs along the river. Park the car in the area provided and continue on foot.

★**Notre-Dame de Verdale** – *1hr round trip on foot*
Walk up a path, which runs beside the Tolerme, as it falls in cascades over the rocks. After crossing the stream twice on primitive wooden bridges the path climbs steeply, in a hilly setting.

Shortly, the pilgrimage chapel of Our Lady of Verdale appears perched on a rocky crag. From the site, there is an extensive **view**★ of the Tolerme gorges and the chestnut-covered hills.

The site can also be reached by an easier path leading from the village of Verdale. Return to D 30.

The road twists along a few more miles, then leaves the upper Bave valley to follow a stream (La Buste). From the cool green waterside route, the village of Salers can be seen beyond the far fields; the town is in the Cantal region.

Latronquière – Lac du Tolerme

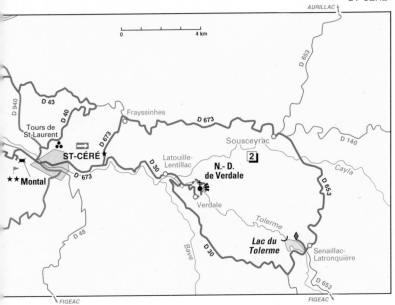

3km/2mi beyond the intersection with D 25, take a left turn off D 30.

The road rises then dips into the Tolerme valley, providing a broad view of a man-made lake.

Lac du Tolerme – At 530m/1 739ft, the lake is surrounded by greenery and covers 38ha/94 acres, including a **recreation centre** ⊙. A lakeside footpath (4km/2.4mi) is a pleasant place to stretch your legs.

At Senaillac-Latronquière, take D 653 north towards Aurillac. At Sousceyrac, turn west on D 673.

This pretty road leads back to St-Céré, with the St-Laurent Towers guiding the way at the last.

ST-CIRQ-LAPOPIE★★

Population 187
Michelin map 79 fold 9 or 235 fold 14
Local map see Vallée du LOT: Cliffs and Promontories

St-Cirq-Lapopie ("Cirq" pronounced "Sear"), faces a semicircle of white cliffs and is itself perched (80m/262ft) on a rocky escarpment that drops vertically to the left bank of the Lot; it is a remarkable **setting**★.

A contested stronghold – This rock commanding the valley has probably tempted would-be occupiers since Gallo-Roman times. The present name of the site commemorates the martyrdom of the young St Cyr, killed with his mother in Asia Minor during the reign of Diocletian; his relics were brought back, it is said, by St Amadour. The La Popies, local lords in the Middle Ages, gave their name to the castle built on the cliff's highest point and, by extension, to the village that grew up at its foot.

The history of the fortress is a long series of sieges. In the struggle against Pepin the Short in the 8C, Waïfre, duke of Aquitaine, pinned his last hopes on this bastion. In 1198 Richard the Lion Heart tried in vain to seize the stronghold.

During the Hundred Years War, the English fought bitterly to take St-Cirq from the garrison, commanded by the lord of Cardaillac, who remained loyal to the king of France. In 1471, Louis XI ordered the castle to be demolished but the ruins were still of sufficient strategic importance for the Huguenots to fight for them during the Wars of Religion. In 1580 Henri de Navarre, the future Henri IV, ordered that those walls of the valiant fortress which were still standing be knocked down.

The end of a craft – St-Cirq-Lapopie had a strong guild of wood-turners dating back to the Middle Ages. Until the late 19C, there were a considerable number of craftsmen still to be seen working their primitive lathes; their industry added a colourful note to the old-fashioned village alleyways. The "tap-makers" made taps for the casks, the bushel-makers candlesticks, rosary beads and crossbars for chairs. Their shop fronts set small and large arched openings side by side. Nowadays, other businesses take advantage of the distinctive architecture; there is only one woodworker left in St-Cirq.

St-Cirq-Lapopie rises above the Lot

SIGHTS

It is a perennial pleasure to wander along narrow, steeply sloping streets lined with houses with lovely brown-tiled roofs. The corbelled façades and exposed beams of some of the houses are further ornamented with Gothic windows, or bays with mullioned windows in the Renaissance style. Most of the houses have been carefully restored by artists, particularly painters and craftsmen who have been attracted by the beauty of St-Cirq-Lapopie and the Lot valley. Among the most famous are the writer André Breton, who lived on place du Carol in the old sailors' inn, and the painters Henri Martin and Pierre Daura, the latter of whom lived in the house with carved beams (his own work) in Ruelle de la Fourdonne.

Church – This 15C sanctuary stands on a rock terrace overlooking the Lot. A squat belfry-tower, flanked by a round turret, stands at the front end.
Inside, the main body of the church has pointed vaulting and contains several baroque statues. There is a good view from the terrace to the right of the church.

Château de la Gardette – The two main buildings, each flanked by a battlemented turret, house the **musée Rignault** ⊘, so named as the painter and collector left his works in legacy to the *département* of the Lot.
Exhibited are old furniture (Renaissance cabinet and sideboard, 14C dowry chest), 14C and 15C statues, lacquered items from China and frescoes dating from the Ming Dynasty.

La Popie – Take the path that starts on the right of the town hall *(mairie)*, to reach the castle ruins and the highest part of the cliff. From the cliff top (telescope), on which once stood the keep of La Popie fortress, there is a remarkable **view★★** right over the village of St-Cirq, with the church clinging to the cliff face, to a bend in the Lot river, encircling a patchwork of arable fields and meadows delineated by poplars, and to the north, the wooded foothills that border the Gramat Causse.

Le Bancourel – Follow D 40 towards Bouziès for 300m/30yd to reach this rock promontory overlooking the Lot. A lay-by esplanade (car park) has been built where D 8 branches off to the left from the tourist road that has been cut corniche-fashion into the cliff *(see Basse Vallée du LOT)*.
There is a **view★** from Le Bancourel of the Lot valley and St-Cirq, with the rock of La Popie rising up out of the village.

ST-GENOU

Population 1 065
Michelin map 68 fold 7 or 238 fold 27

St-Genou is worth visiting for its abbey church. The town also has two porcelain manufactories.

Church – The church was once part of a Benedictine abbey, founded in 828 by Wilfred, the count of Bourges. The place was then known as "Strata" (currently Estrées), on the Roman road from Déols to Tours. The relics of Saint Genou held within gave the church its name. Genou was sent to evangelise Gaul by Pope Sixtus II, was made bishop of Cahors, and died near Estrées.

Begun in 994, the church was consecrated in 1066. The regular abbots were elected by the monks and blessed by the archbishop of Bourges; but the final decision was approved by the archbishop of Tours, and this double patronage was at the root of many conflicts in the community.

The abbey went into decline in the early 16C, gradually falling into ruin. The archives were destroyed in 1580, the nave knocked down in 1676. One hundred years later, only a few monks were left and the monastery was closed. Registered as a historic building in 1882, restoration works were undertaken soon thereafter.

Exterior – Only the transept and the choir, in the Berry Romanesque style, give a clue to the church's past. Around the apse, a row of blind vaulting and a ledge punctuated by modillions; stately supporting columns are set on pedestals and surmounted by acanthus-leaf capitals, framing high windows and completing the architectural composition.

Interior – Beyond the triumphal arc, the vast choir has an oven-shaped vault. The monumental columns have remarkable capitals with fantastic animal figures, biblical scenes (Adam and Eve, Daniel in the lion's den) and episodes from the life of Saint Genou.

ST-JUNIEN

Population 10 604
Michelin map 72 fold 6 – Local map see LIMOGES

St-Junien is a busy town, known for its paper-mills, taweries (leather dressing works) and particularly its glove factories. The collegiate church is Romanesque-Limousin in style.

The "Ostensions" of St-Junien – In the early 6C, in a forest along the banks of the river Vienne, at Comodoliac, lived a saintly hermit named Amand. Drawn to the hermit and his reputation for holiness, a young man from Cambrai, Junien, joined him in his solitude. For some 40 years, Junien lived in this place, using waters from a sacred spring to cure those who came to see him, often from afar. His own reputation was so great that when he died, in 540, the bishop of Limoges, Rorice II, personally presided over his funeral ceremonies and ordered the construction of a sanctuary above his tomb. A monastery grew up and a settlement around it: the town of St-Junien was born.

Ostensions (see Introduction, Folklore and traditions) commemorate, every seven years, the memory of St Junien. When the ceremony is held the relics are shown and a picturesque spectacle unfolds: rich costumes are brought out, the main street is decorated with foliage and caged birds as a reminder of the forest in which the saint lived. The main events of the saint's life are evoked; music and ringing bells add an air of celebration.

The Development of Glove-making – St-Junien lies in the centre of a livestock rearing region and therefore had on hand the necessary raw materials – kid and lambskin. In addition the waters of the Vienne possess exceptional properties for tanning.

Glove-making began here in the Middle Ages and by the 15C had made the town famous. It is even said that Louis XI, on his return from Bayonne, was received in great style at St-Junien and permitted the master-glovers to present him with pairs of gloves.

Expansion of the industry has brought about many changes, but mechanisation is excluded as handwork alone can ensure a good finish. Today, 300 workers in seven workshops produce over 480 000 pairs of gloves each year, 45% of all French production.

SIGHTS

★**Collégiale St-Junien** – The nave and transept of this remarkable Romanesque-Limousin building are late 11C; the main part of the building was completed when the façade was added at the end of the 12C; the plain, square chevet is 13C. The central bell-tower was rebuilt after it had fallen down in 1922.

The west doorway is divided into two bays and is framed by small columns. It is surmounted by a massive belfry-porch two storeys high, flanked by two stone bell-turrets.

Inside, the nave and the chancel are of equal length. The transept crossing is punctuated by bays, one of which is quite narrow and extends the side aisle, the chapels have primitive pointed arches. In the second bay on the northern side of the chancel is the **Chapelle St-Martial**. Of Gothic design, it once harboured the relics of the saint, whose life is depicted in the 13C frescoes which are only partly visible. A polychrome wall niche holds an early 16C Entombment; Christ is shown surrounded by seven figures (only Saint John has kept his head). At the crossing, an octagonal cupola with flat pendants, pierced by four Limousin-style bays and a multifoil occulus. The capitals in the chancel are ornamented with common motifs: palmettos, animals, figures. The two last bays and the rose window in the east end were added in the 13C.

St-Junien – Tomb

Behind the main altar is **Saint Junien's tomb★**, a masterpiece of 12C Limousin sculpture. Two-thirds of the tomb is of limestone adorned with sculpture; the remainder is only a plaster covering added last century when the high altar was moved and no longer formed part of the sarcophagus. On the east side, Christ is shown in glory surrounded by the symbols of the Evangelists; medallions depict the theological and moral virtues. On the north face the Virgin, within a glory, holds the Infant Jesus; seated on one side are the figures of twelve Old Men of the Apocalypse. On the opposite side the other twelve Old Men are portrayed together with a medallion of the Holy Lamb. Against the pillars stands an interesting collection of 14C, 15C and 16C multicoloured statues.

Chapel of Notre-Dame du Pont ⊘ – Standing on the right bank of the river Vienne beside a 13C bridge equipped with cutwaters is the elegant Chapel of Our Lady of the Bridge. There is a legend that the statue of the Virgin which now stands in the apse was originally found alongside the bridge on the river bank; the statue was immediately taken in solemn procession to the collegiate church, but the next day was found, once more, on the river bank. The people of St-Junien erected a chapel to the Virgin on the spot where the statue was found. The present church was built in the 15C on the site of the earlier sanctuary; it was enlarged and completed thanks to Louis XI, who came there twice on pilgrimage.

The overall architectural effect is of graceful flamboyance; a sculptured balustrade lines the base of the roof. The nave and two aisles of equal height are supported by elegant octagonal pillars; the vaulting is ornamented with finely carved keystones.

EXCURSIONS

Site Corot – *Take N 141. As you leave town, take a sharp right turn at the bend in the road, then turn left immediately on a small road. Follow this road as far as the porcelain manufactory and park at the entrance of the lane. 15min round trip on foot.*

Walk for a few minutes beside the river to reach the setting of the stream, flowing past rocks and trees, which inspired Corot and many other painters.

Château de Rochebrune ⊘ – *13km/8.4mi northwest*

In the 16C the château became the property of Marshal Blaise de Montluc, who, during the Wars of Religion, distinguished himself by his implacable pursuit of the Protestants.

After admiring the outbuildings with their round tiled roofs, cross the moat and enter the main courtyard. Three buildings link the four massive towers built in the 11C and 13C. Above the doors hang the arms of Marshal Blaise de Montluc. The apartments are furnished in the Empire and Renaissance style and contain many souvenirs of the Napoleonic period.

Use Michelin Maps with Michelin Guides.

ST-LÉON-SUR-VÉZÈRE★

Population 427
Michelin map 75 fold 17 or 233 fold 44 or 235 folds 1 and 2
Local map see LES-EYZIES-DE-TAYAC

Built in a picturesque loop of the Vézère river, this charming village, overrun by greenery, possesses two castles and one of the finest Romanesque churches of Périgord.

★**Church** – The church was part of a Benedictine priory which was founded in the 12C and depended upon the Sarlat abbey. It was built on the ruins of a Gallo-Roman villa. The remains of one of the villa's walls can be seen on the river side.

From the square, the apse, the perfectly smooth radiating chapels and the fine square 2-storey arcaded bell-tower form a harmonious unit. The church is roofed with the heavy limestone slabs *(lauzes)* of Périgord Noir.

Inside, the transept crossing is vaulted with a dome, while apsidal chapels are connected to the apse by narrow openings, known as *passages berrichons* as they are a feature of churches in the Berry region in particular.

D. Cauchois/PIX

St-Léon-sur-Vézère – Church

The apse and south radiating chapel are decorated with parts of Romanesque frescoes, in which red is predominant.

Château de la Salle – Standing on the square, this small castle built of dry-stone has a fine 14C square keep crowned with machicolations.

Château de Clérans – This elegant 15C and 16C palace, flanked with machicolated towers and turrets, stands on the banks of the river.

Chapelle du cimetière – This small 14C chapel in the cemetery is roofed, like the church, with lauzes. An inscription in the *langue d'oc* above the door harks back to an extraordinary event: in 1233, a servant who had let fly an arrow onto the crucifix guarding the entrance to the cemetery dropped dead on the spot, "with his head turned back-to-front". In 1890, the blasphemer's grave was excavated, and a skeleton with its skull back-to-front was unearthed. The cemetery still has a tall crucifix, and there are six tombs in the defence wall.

Le Conquil ⊘ – *Access by D 66. Cross the bridge, then take a small road on the left.*

Located on the banks of the Vézère, this site, built into the cliff, is best discovered on foot, amid the lush vegetation.

To reach the limestone cliff, follow the riverside; the approach provides a nice **view**★ of the church, Clérans Château *(see above)* and an old lock for raising barges.

The **dovecot**★ roof is held up with 148 putlogs (short pieces of timber extending horizontally), and just below these, a row of holes shows where a floor was once supported by beams. Farther on, steps carved out of the rock *(slippery when wet)* lead to a series of dwellings cut into the cliff: shelters for guards, storerooms, defensive areas. Marks on the floor show how these were set up to repel invaders. The return path climbs towards an overlook with a view of the valley, then continues on through the woods.

The site also offers some **prehistoric activities** ⊘: initiation to bow-and-arrow hunting and flint knapping; demonstrations of prehistoric rock painting techniques.

Michelin on-line gives motorists the freedom to create their own itineraries, to stop and discover tourist attractions. At any time, you can print out your complete route map, as well as the information from the Red Guide and the cost of tolls on the selected itinerary.

*Log in at **www.michelin-travel.com***

Bon voyage!

ST-LÉONARD-DE-NOBLAT★

Population 5 024

Michelin map 72 fold 18 or 239 fold 14

Perched on a hill top above a vast valley defined by the rivers Vienne, Maulde and Taurion, the bell tower of the old church in St-Léonard-de-Noblat is a remarkable example of Limousin-style Romanesque architecture.

The main industry in town is the manufacture of porcelain (four companies), and the valley is famed for its cattle. The distinctive, ruddy brown animals known as *vaches limousines* originate from the area around St-Léonard, which is an active export and breeding centre.

For visitors with a sweet tooth, St-Léonard is memorable for its *massepain*, a speciality found in local pastry shops, made with sugary crushed almonds.

A Hermit – Long before the Roman conquest, the road between Bourges and Bordeaux, crossing the Vienne near the village of Noblat, was well-travelled. The road, watched over by a castle belonging to the bishops of Limoges, was used by pilgrims on their way to Compostela in the 12C.

The town was named after the hermit **Léonard**, godson of Clovis, who early in the 6C chose Pauvain forest, which has since disappeared, as his place of retreat. He built a rustic sanctuary. His piety and the many miracles he performed made him one of the most popular saints in Limousin. A village was built alongside the retreat and took the name Noblat (derived from *nobiliacum*, meaning noble site). His help was invoked in protecting horses and seeking the release of prisoners. Because Léonard was the patron saint of prisoners, it is the tradition in St-Léonard, in the month of November to celebrate the *Quintaine*. A small wooden fortress (representing a prison) or *Quintaine* is trampled down by riders on horseback armed with clubs.

A Great Scholar – Joseph-Louis **Gay-Lussac** was born in St-Léonard in 1778 (died 1850). He distinguished himself in physics and chemistry: he discovered the law of expansion of gases and made ascents in a balloon to examine whether the earth's magnetic attraction decreased as the altitude increased. Later he devised the law of gaseous combination. In 1809 he demonstrated that chlorine was an element and discovered boron and fluoboric acid. In addition to his scientific achievements and awards, Gay-Lussac represented the Haute-Vienne in the French *Chambre des Deputés*.

SIGHTS

★**Church** –This 12C church (restored) remains a fine specimen of Romanesque architecture. The side walls and the chapel for the Holy Sepulchre go back to the 11C. It is said that Richard the Lion Heart contributed to the construction of the church on his release from prison in Austria.

Exterior – The **belfry**★★, built above a porch which is open on two sides and embellished with remarkable capitals, adjoins the third bay of the nave. The bell-tower consists of four storeys built square, surmounted by two recessed storeys which are octagonal in shape. The transition from the square plan to the octagonal is managed by devising a sharply pointed gable for each of the four walls of the top quadrilateral. Each tier is adorned with beautiful blind arcades. The final touch of elegance is given by the stone spire which was constructed in the 12C. The baptistery, between the belfry and the transept, now restored to its original appearance, was probably modelled on that of the Holy Sepulchre in Jerusalem.

The church's west façade, built in the 13C, has a wide door flanked by small columns decorated with finely carved crotcheted capitals supporting the covings. The east end rises harmoniously in tiers and the chapels are roofed with rounded tiles.

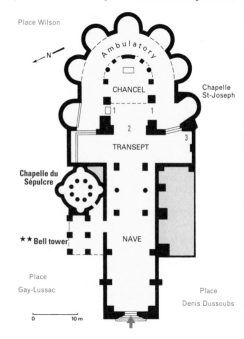

Interior – The church went through several different building stages *(see the scale model at the entrance)*, which are apparent in the disunity of style within.

The powerful nave has cradle vaulting, the transept crossing is roofed with a high dome placed atop a drum pierced by 8 windows and resting on pendentives and smaller and less ornate domes rise above the end of each transept arm. The chancel (late 12C) is wider than the nave, and rather awkwardly linked to the transept; its complex design involves arches, each divided down its centre by a pillar or column supporting a suspension arch. The ambulatory has asymmetrical groined vaulting resting on elegant small columns which stand between the seven apsidal chapels.

In the 17C, a new vault, higher than the cupola in the transept, was added on and the church had to be shored up. Two thin columns in the sanctuary were set into a chunky block, while another such supporting block was added beneath the central arcade. Outside, buttresses were used to hold up the new vaulting.

The 15C oak wood stalls (1) are sculpted with satirical motifs. On the gilded main altar (2), dating from the 18C, the relics of Saint Léonard are in a case below his statue. In the transept crossing (3), a wall niche holds the saint's tomb and a revered lock bolt; the bolt is symbolic of Léonard's power to intervene on prisoners' behalf (tradition also holds that it is effective in curing cases of sterility).

Old Houses – It is easy to imagine the lay-out of the medieval town: the ring of boulevards follows the path of the old defensive wall, whose vestiges can be seen on boulevard Carnot (south) and rue Jean-Jaurès (northwest). Some of the many old houses in this neighbourhood date back to the 13C.

In the days of the pilgrims, rue Georges-Perrin (then rue Aomônier), led from the Noblat bridge to the centre of town; a 13C hospital gate still stands in this main street.

Musée Gay-Lussac ⓥ – The museum devoted to this man of science is located in a former convent. His memory and accomplishments are recalled in documents, objects (a hot air balloon basket; the re-creation of a 19C chemistry laboratory) and instruments (barometer, oven etc).

Historail – *South of town on D 39*

The history of the iron horse is the subject of this museum's displays, which include genuine train parts as well as working models (six different scales; one of the models operates outdoors). Re-creations and simulations bring the heyday of rail back to life; in the yard, there are tracks, signals, a water tower, and engine motors.

VALLÉE DE LA MAULDE *40km/25mi – 1hr15min*

★**St-Léonard-de-Noblat** – *See above.*

Leave St-Léonard travelling south on N 141, towards Limoges.

Pont-de-Noblat – In the Vienne valley, on the outskirts of town, this area has developed on both sides of the river. A 13C bridge spans the water; old houses line the time-worn path known as the *Pavé*.

Promenade du chêne de Clovis – Between the bridge and the church, a steep path leads to a plateau where a castle once stood. The archeological site encompasses a feudal hillock and a view on the river below.

Leave Pont-de-Noblat on D 39A.

The road follows the Vienne valley. Where the Vienne and the Maulde meet, the château de Muraud rises up on the promontory; turn left.

The road runs up the Maulde valley through a rocky, wooded gorge. The river has been transformed by the French electric company into a giant, watery staircase, with remote-controlled dams.

Barrage de l'Artige – This last dam of the series serves to regulate the flow of water coming from the others upstream. The road overlooks the dam and affords a fine view of the valley and the ruins of the former Priory of Artige.

Ancien Prieuré de l'Artige – *A narrow road opposite the dam to the left leads to the entrance of the Priory.*

Founded in the 12C and secularised shortly before the Revolution, part of it was subsequently left to fall into ruin. From the road you can see the vast buildings with their round tiled roofs, the arcades between the chapterhouse and the cloisters, and the remains of emblazoned doors which create a romantic scene.

The road winds through wooded country before crossing the wooded farmland plateau.

Turn right on D 14.

After crossing the reservoir, behind the Villejoubert Dam the road rises to Bugaleuf affording fine views on the left of the stretch of water retained by the Langleret Dam.

Bujaleuf – Bear left to reach the bridge spanning the reservoir from which you can enjoy a good **view**★ of the two shores of the lake forming the recreation centre.

Beyond Bujaleuf, D 16 descends into the valley affording lovely views of the stretches of water and the mountains on the horizon.

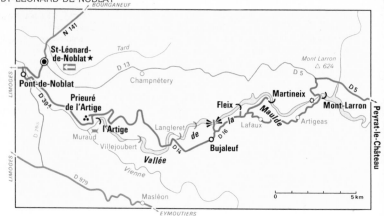

Barrage de Fleix – Set in a fine wooded site, the slim form of the dam (50m/164ft long and 16 m/53ft high) is supported by vertical buttresses.

Barrage de Martineix – A similar construction to the previous one, this dam stands in a wild but picturesque site.
After Artigeas the high road affords fine glimpses over the valley and the surrounding hills.

Usine et Barrage du Mont-Larron (**Power Station and Dam**) – This stark looking building is the control centre for the series of dams. To the right of it a path, tarred to begin with, leads to the foot of the massive dam which is of the vaulted type. A path to the right climbs to the crest of the dam which is 183m/600ft long.

Peyrat-le-Château – In this rolling landscape where broom and heather alternate with pine and beech, the remains of a castle stand by a lake; the square keep of this fortress was once the home of the Lusignan family. The church was destroyed by fire in 1184, and rebuilt in the Gothic style (keystones carved with symbolic ornamentation).

ST-MARCEL

Population 1 687
Michelin map 68 folds 17 and 18 or 238 fold 39

The medieval hamlet of St-Marcel stands on a hill overlooking the right bank of the Creuse, on the site of the Gallo-Roman town of **Argentomagus**, high above the river Creuse. An archeological dig is being carried out on the site and in the surrounding area and a large number of items have been excavated. Some of these are now part of the collections of the local museum.

SIGHTS

★**Church** – To the left of the nave, the massive 14C bell tower was used as a keep, once the inhabitants of St-Marcel had received permission from their *seigneur*, Guy de Chauvigny, to fortify the priory. The severe, shingled tower differs from others in the region in its defensive allure. The chevet dates from the 12C.
Except for the apse and its chapels, with oven vaulting, the interior of the church has been rebuilt (ribbed vaulting dating from the 13C and 14C).
The chancel is ornamented with 16C **stalls**, (restored), the work of Antoine Barbaud, prior of St-Marcel from 1484-1522, which are a good illustration of the transition from Gothic to Renaissance styles.
Some parts of the wall in the nave have been pierced with small, ceramic-lined holes, which serve to improve the acoustics, amplifying the resonance of religious chants.
At the end of the nave, to the left above the door, a 15C **Fresco of Our Lady** (Notre-Dame-de-Pitié) shows St Louis in a fur coat presenting a priest to the Virgin, who holds the Infant Jesus in her arms.
The **doorway** on the western façade has two rounded arches, topped by a band of mouldings with a diamond pattern. The narrow, almost rectangular stones are sculpted with Carolingian-style interlacing, geometric designs, and animal figures (lions, griffins, horses) standing alone or facing each other, inspired by Eastern tradition.

Treasure and Crypt – The treasure contains several processional crosses (13C), a 15C sculpted shrine representing the martyrdom of Saint Marcel and Saint Anastase (a scene which took place close by in the 3C, under the reign of Emperor

Declus), a gilded copper shrine from the 13C adorned with Limoges enamel, the arm of Saint Marcel and a 14C reliquary.

Outside the church, the visitor can walk around the **medieval streets of town:** vestiges of the 15C fortifications, many entranceways surmounted by lintels, some with a tympanum bearing the arms of the household. *At the town hall and in the museum, a map is available for an interesting self-guided tour.*

Archeological excavations ⓥ – The site is remarkable for the preservation of its vestiges, which long slumbered beneath a vineyard. Several roads passed through the town, a pivotal point between the upper valley of the Creuse and the low wet lands of the Brenne; the river runs a regular course here and is navigable. The development of trade, the abundant game, the presence of water and wood (which made metal work possible), explain why this land was occupied so long ago, and the diversity of the archeological discoveries. Magdalenian reindeer hunters dwelled in caves here (1400-8000 BC), while their Gallo-Roman successors built an *oppidum*, or fortified city, to live in.

Following the Roman conquest (50 BC), **Argentomagus** (perhaps from the Latin *argenteum*, silver, or from the Gaulish man's name *Argentos* and *magus*, meaning market) underwent spectacular demographic and economic growth, as trade, crafts and especially metal working – the Bituriges *(see BOURGES)* were specialists – developed. The site figures on a 15C reproduction of the road network of the lower Roman Empire known as the Peutinger Table *(see box)*, and is mentioned in a 4C text as the leading Gaulish arms manufactory. For two centuries, the town expanded well beyond the bounds of the original *oppidum*, although it never rated as a major city, covering no more than 70ha/173 acres with a population of 5000.

All roads lead to Rome

Probably the earliest important era in the development of cartography in Western civilisation can be traced to the ancient Greeks, who left a legacy of information for Western cartographers and geographers. The ancient Greek cartographer Ptolemy produced a mapping textbook, *Geographica*, which included map projections.

The Romans inherited the Greek knowledge of geography, but they were more interested in surveying and engineering. Provincial boundaries and towns, rivers, and roads of the Roman Empire were recorded in *Itineraria*, road manuals and route maps.

In the 13C, a monk in Colmar (Alsace) made a copy of a map of the Roman world on 12 sheets of parchment. This copy later came to be the property of Konrad Peutinger (1465-1547). The rectangular shape of the sheets resulted in the compression of the north-south axis, and the elongation of the east-west distances, distorting the world view considerably. The original of the six-colour map is long lost, and not all scholars are convinced that the "Peutinger Table" was strictly based on Roman maps and manuals.

A few of the manuals, which must have been precious to private and official travellers, have survived, including the 4C "Antonine Itinerary", which names several thousand geographic locations and the distances between them. A 7C document known as the "Ravenna Cosmography" names the islands in the Atlantic as well as places and rivers in Europe, Africa and Asia.

"Les Mersans" – This plateau (27ha/67 acres), protected by cliffs and a moat, was the first urban core. Excavations have been ongoing since 1962. The so-called "Sergius Macrinus" house is on the site, as well as a religious enclave made up of two temples *(Fanum)* and a square edifice. In the Celtic tradition, very different from Greek and Roman styles, the architecture of the **Fanum** consists of two square forms, one within the other, open to the east. The inner square *(cella)* held statues of gods; around, a gallery served as an ambulatory where, according to ancient documents, processions took place, following the path of the sun. A long covered gallery separated the large temple on the right from the smaller one. A large central stairway and two side doors provided access.

Along with most of the rest of the town, these temples were destroyed during a Barbarian invasion in 276.

During excavations, archeologists discovered some lovely bronze statuettes: a goat lying down, an eagle, and the famous Mercury. Some forty sacrificial pits have been found in the sanctuary. In one of them, the split skull of a trout and many pig bones were discovered along with a large cutlass. Near the big temple, a ring set in a slab was used for tying up animals.

To the east of the temple area, the forum and other ancient monuments are still buried. In 1967, a monumental fountain was discovered by chance. As the earth was removed, two large stairways appeared, leading down to a square pool 6m/20ft on each side. The water drained from here into a sewer, still in perfect condition, which has been uncovered along a 90m/295ft course. The exact purpose of this fountain (the largest of its kind from the period) is uncertain. It certainly played some cultural role, before it was filled in by metal workers, some time after 276.

★ **"Virou" theatre** – *Return down the hill towards Argenton; turn right just before the railway bridge, go along for about 200m/219yd, then take a steep path on the right which goes up to the theatre.*

Until 1966, only a part of the outside wall was visible (the rest was underground), and this gave the parcel of land its name: *Virou*, something which rotates or revolves. Now the building has been entirely uncovered, revealing the two successive stages of construction: the first, rustic period, from the early 1C, and a second 2C part. The way the works of two centuries have been superimposed creates an interesting study for archeologists. The first theatre, with poor acoustics, was typical of Gallo-Roman times in its horseshoe shape, small stage area, and wide orchestra section. Mime and dance were commonly performed in such theatres, where the Greek influence is strongly felt.

Simple in design, the theatre provided open-air seating, hewn out of the rock; spectators sat with their legs crossed in front of them.

The 2C improvements brought the theatre into line with Roman design: the circular seating (84m/275ft in diameter) could accommodate an audience of 6000. In addition to the sections known as "Mersans" and "Virou", other areas have been explored, including a necropolis, called "Champ de l'image" (200m/219yd northwest of the museum).

Musée archéologique d'Argentomagus ⊘ – This modest building was put up between 1983 and 1990. Inside, a wide ramp spirals down to the archeological crypt, where the collection includes items from the immediate area. Only the prehistoric section extends to cover the whole Creuse valley.

Visitors travel back in time to a million years BC, to the period known as the lower Paleolithic. A hut from the **Lavaud** site, in Éguzon-Chantôme has been re-created. The prehistoric displays continue in chronological order and include: tools from a Solutrean find (18000-16000 BC) from Fressignes and the Roches shelter, in Pouligny-St-Pierre; and many items found in the **Garenne cave** (hills around St Marcel). Among these exceptional pieces, note the "pendant with dancers", where six stylised female dancers hold hands in a prehistoric roundel; the "Baptist", a human face on a pierced rod; the collection of 20 lamps.

The Gallo-Roman section is organised around themes: the city and its monuments (scale models); work, daily life, and trade (an interesting display of pottery and household utensils); funerary rites (re-creation of part of the Roman cemetery at Champ de l'image).

The final room, devoted to religious practices, illustrates, with statuary, the co-existence of gods of many origins in Gaulish civilisation. Native, Greek and Eastern divinities are depicted; the small bronzes are most remarkable. Notice the masterly **Mercury**, made in the 1C, god of tradesmen and thieves, venerated in Argentomagus and throughout Gaul. Cast in wax and finished with a chisel, the anatomic perfection of the figure contrasts with the rustic stone upon which the god sits, creating an elegant effect. Also on view: a Gaulish god sitting cross-legged, many mother goddesses, the "Vergobret" urn (named for a magistrate in independent Gaul), and a plaque commemorating the dedication of a temple.

Finish the visit with a walk through the **crypte archéologique**, 150 m/492ft along the vestiges of the north moat (the wall measures 20m/66ft long by 5m/16ft high), and past an area devoted to crafts (leather and dye workers' tanks) and shelters, where a rare domestic altar has been left in place *(see photograph)*.

Gesell/MUSÉE D'ARGENTOMAGUS, St-Marcel

Musée d'Argentomagus – Domestic altar

ST-YRIEIX-LA-PERCHE

Population 7 558
Michelin map 72 fold 17

Bordering the Périgord vert region *(see Introduction, Landscapes)*, St-Yrieix (pronounced St-Irieh) stands at the centre of a rich stock rearing region (fairgrounds about
4km/2.4mi outside of town on the Limoges road); the local economy is diversified,
encompassing the food industry, manufacture of clothing, shoes, electric appliances,
and government print shops.

The origins – A Gallo-Roman settlement named Attanum was probably the first on
the site. Around 530, Aredius, a noble from the court of King Théodebert, friend of
Grégoire de Tours and Fortunat de Poitiers, inherited his father's house and came to
stay there. A pious man, he founded a sanctuary which welcomed monks and, in 572,
wrote his last will and testament (a document which tells us much about Merovingian
society), leaving most of his property to the abbey of St-Martin de Tours.
Near the monastery, a hamlet grew up, and took the name St-Yrieix, a transforma-
tion of Aredius, to which "la Perche" was added in the 15C.
From 1307, the town was partly subject to royal authority, but was dominated by
the powerful canons of the church at Moûtier. After the Hundred Years War, which
brought Du Guesclin to town, and the terrible plague of 1563, St-Yrieix became a
full-fledged municipality in 1565. Henri IV stayed here just before the Battle of
La Roche-l'Abeille, and visitors are still shown the room he slept in.

Darnet and Kaolin – Limoges owes its position as china capital of France to St-Yrieix,
where kaolin deposits were discovered in the 18C. Kaolin, already employed in China
in the 17C, was named after a hill called Kao-ling. It was first used in Europe in 1710,
in great secrecy, by the Meissen factory near Dresden. Experiments on this pure white
clay had been conducted by manufacturers of the translucent soft-paste porcelain *(see
LIMOGES)*. Searches were being made all over southwest France, when, quite by
chance, a surgeon by the name of Darnet who lived in St-Yrieix, came in touch with
a chemist who was taking samples of clay and analysing them for the manufacturers.
Darnet showed the chemist his wife's mixture for making her laundry snow-white.
Analysis revealed the pure kaolin content. In 1771 Darnet was charged by the king
to supervise the mining of the kaolin. Thanks to Turgot, the general intendant of Lim-
ousin, development was encouraged and St-Yrieix became the source of kaolin for
Limoges and the whole region. Since 1774, a manufactory has been operating in
Seynie, 1km/0.5mi from St-Yrieix.

SIGHTS

★**Collégiale du Moûtier** – The church stands on the site of the abbey founded by
Aredius.
This vast edifice is a curious hodgepodge of Romanesque and Gothic styles: the
Romanesque church, built in the 11C, was replaced by the larger building at the
end of the 12C.
All that remains of the Romanesque church is the belfry-porch with its town arrow
aisles. Massive, with stout buttresses capped with crenellations, it looks fortified. The
south door, however, is ornamented with fine covings and is surmounted by a Christ
in Majesty dating from the 12C set in delicate blind arcades.

The nave has ogive vaulting and
is very wide but the length is
limited to two bays. A huge
transept is followed by a long
chancel. The walls are decorated with elegant blind arcades. A gallery which circles
the nave, transepts and chancel
is supported by modillions ornamented with carved heads,
animals and floral motifs some
of which are very beautiful. In
the chancel the gallery is bordered by a fine wooden rail.

Trésor – In a niche in the chancel, rests the reliquary head of
St-Yrieix made of wood plated
with chased silver, the beard
and eyebrows are picked out in
gold. The bust dates from the
15C while the necklace is probably 13C.
There are also a small 13C reliquary of enamelled gilt copper,
adorned with 20 medallions

St-Yrieix-la-Perche –
Musée de la Porcelaine (biscuit by Thabard)

J. D. Sudres/DIAF

showing angels with outstretched wings; a Eucharistic dove in gilded copper, with wings which open to reveal the Host; a fabric banner adorned with pearls which was used to cover the dove.

Tour du Plô – Near the collegiate church stands this 13C keep with twinned windows; it once formed part of the monastery's fortified precincts.

Porcelain Museum – *Take the road to Limoges; after 2km/1mi, turn left towards the pond.*
There is a rich collection dating from the 18C to the present day. Next to the soft paste porcelain from Vincennes, Arras and Strasbourg, are fine specimens in soft and hard paste from the count of Artois' factory. Presented in a glass case are items from Germany and England and two other cases display French ceramics of the 19C, mainly from Limoges. The absence of local production may seem surprising but although St-Yrieix did and still does manufacture porcelain, it is decorated at other factories.

SALIGNAC-EYVIGUES

Population 1 035

Michelin map 75 folds 17 and 18 or 235 fold 2 – Local map see PÉRIGORD NOIR

In Artaban country – The small region dominated by Salignac has come to be called Artaban country, after a character created by Gauthier de Costes, known familiarly as La Calprenède (after the land he owned) and born at Toulgou Manor. The novelist was very successful during the 17C and was greatly admired by all the *précieuses* who ran literary salons, but his success was not long-lived. Although the author has fallen into obscurity, the expression "proud as Artaban" is still commonly used in France.

Salignac village – The market square, which is overlooked by the façade of the 13C convent (Couvent des Croisiers), and the neighbouring streets, in particular rue Sainte-Croix, are a charming sight, just a few yards away from the entrance to the castle.

Château ⊘ – There is a good overall view from D 60, east of the village, of this medieval fortress which still belongs to the family of the archbishop of Cambrai, François de Salignac de la Mothe-Fénelon *(see CARENNAC)*.
The castle, which was built between the 12C and 17C, is encircled by ramparts. Mullioned windows lighten the façade of the main building, which is flanked by round and square towers. The whole building is enhanced by the warm colour of the stone and the lovely stone slab *(lauzes)* roofs.
Go up a Renaissance spiral staircase to visit several rooms with interesting furnishings, mainly in the Renaissance and Louis XIII styles.

EXCURSION

Jardins d'Eyrignac ⊘ – *6km/3.6mi south on D 61*
Created in the 18C by the marquis de la Calprenède, an important treasury official, these gardens have been restored to their original aspect with patient and tender care. The result is a happy compromise between the French-style garden and Tuscan topiary art, rich in evergreens which make for year-round delight. The grassy paths are bordered with well-trimmed yew, creating little green chambers; there are pine hedges, shapely boxwood bowers, apple trees in quincuncial arrangements (four trees in the corners and a fifth in the middle); cypress groves, urns, pools and dainty pavilions ornament the grounds of the 17C mansion, built in pale Sarlat stone.

SANCERRE★

Population 2 059
Michelin map 65 fold 12 or 238 fold 20 – Local map below

High above the banks of the river Loire, Sancerre roosts above St-Satur and St-Thibault. From this **vantage point★**, a wide panorama embraces the river and the Nivernais to the east, Berry to the west. This little city, reigning over a land of trim vineyards and frisky goats, is renown for its delicious white wine, "flinty" in flavour, and its little round cheeses, especially those from Chavignol. This creamy and savoury goat's cheese is so well-loved in France, that no one is put off in the slightest by its amusing name, *Crottin* (roughly translated as something you'd rather not step in in the barnyard). The steep streets of the town are enticing for their tempting food shops, restaurants and wine merchants.

Le Sancerrois – Vineyards and hillside of Sancerre

A strategic location – Sancerre, already well-known in Roman times as the site of an *oppidum*, has long stood watch over the Loire. It may have been the 9C residence of Robert le Fort, an early member of the Capetian dynasty. Later, the city played an important role in the Hundred Years War, as the gateway to Berry, placed between the Burgundians and the English. Charles VII, the so-called "king of Bourges", assembled 20 000 warriors there, personally commanding them for a time.

Having embraced the Reformists as of 1534, Sancerre became a stronghold of Protestantism, withstanding the assault of royal forces. The Treaty of St-Germain (1570) and the Saint-Bartholomew's Day Massacre (1572) had no effect on those who held to their "reformed" views of religion, and refused to give in. Thus, on 3 January 1573, the Maréchal de La Châtre, accompanied by 7 000 men, laid siege to Sancerre. After an intense artillery preparation, an assault took place on three fronts, but the local resistance was strong. La Châtre decided to starve the people out by setting up a blockade. Inside the city walls, hungry people were eating ground slate, animal skins and leather. Capitulation came after seven long months of struggle. The population's surrender was accepted with honour, and they were allowed the freedom of their religion.

Sancerre wine – "Wine," wrote Balzac in 1844 in *La Muse du Département*, "is the main industry and the most important trading item of this land, which produces many generous vintages of rich bouquet, so similar to those of Burgundy that an untrained Parisian palate cannot taste the difference. Sancerre wines are therefore popular in Parisian cabarets where they flow steadily, which is a good thing, as they cannot be kept more than seven or eight years."

Vineyards are planted on every hill where the sun shines. The Sancerre label is only applied to white Sauvignon wines, and to red and rosé wines made from the Pinot grape.

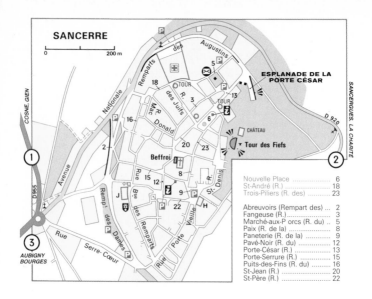

SANCERRE

0 ___ 200 m

COSNE, GIEN

SANCERGUES, LA CHARITÉ

ESPLANADE DE LA
PORTE CÉSAR

Nationale

R. Mac Donald

des Juifs

R. 3

TOUR

18

16

2

20 23

Beffroi

15 12

8

9

22

Rue des Remparts

Rue Porte Vieille

St-Denis

CHÂTEAU

Tour des Fiefs

D 920

Rue Serre-Cœur

AUBIGNY
BOURGES

Remp des Dames

D 955

Avenue

(1)

(2)

(3)

Nouvelle Place	6
St-André (R.)	18
Trois-Piliers (R. des)	23
Abreuvoirs (Rempart des)	2
Fangeuse (R.)	3
Marché-aux-Porcs (R. du)	5
Paix (R. de la)	8
Paneterie (R. de la)	9
Pavé-Noir (R. du)	12
Porte-César (R.)	13
Porte-Serrure (R.)	15
Puits-des-Fins (R. du)	16
St-Jean (R.)	20
St-Père (R.)	22

SIGHTS

★★ Esplanade de la porte César – From this terrace, there is a great **view★★** over the vineyards, St-Satur and the viaduct, St-Thibault and the Val de Loire, and even farther afield to the Puisaye region of woods and lakes, between the Loire and the Loing, northeast of Sancerre; the first hills of the Morvan region also can be seen on the horizon.

Tours des Fiefs ⊙ – This 14C cylindrical keep is the only vestige of the château of the counts of Sancerre, a Huguenot citadel bitterly defended during the 1573 siege. From the top, there is a wide **scenic view★** of the Loire valley and the hills of Sancerre.

Belfry – This old belfry, dating from 1509, serves the church of Notre-Dame de Sancerre.

Old town – Visitors will enjoy strolling in the old neighbourhoods, where many of the interesting houses and vestiges are marked with informative signs. There are many architectural details to attract the eye; around the Nouvelle Place, recently renovated, nice shops sell local crafts and pottery.

★① LE SANCERROIS *95km/59mi – 5hr*

★Sancerre – *See above.*

Leave Sancerre travelling southwest on D 955 towards Bourges. Shortly thereafter, turn right on D 923.

Sancerre wine and Chavignol cheese

J. D. Sudres/SCOPE

The road seems to part the waters of a sea of vineyards, then rises up into the so-called "white hills", where hearty wines are produced in the clay and limestone soil. At the intersection with D 7, there is a splendid **view★★** over Sancerre high atop its bluff, the vineyards, St-Satur and, beyond, the Loire valley.

Chavignol – This lovely little wine growers' village is nestled in a hollow with vineyards all around. The name is synonymous with one of France's tastiest and most popular cheeses, the little round goat's cheese known as "Crottin de Chavignol".

Just outside the village, take a little road on the right which leads to the hamlet of Amigny.

On the Sens-Beaujeu road, near the intersection with D 85, there is a nice **view★** of the village of Bué *(see BLANCAFORT and Calendar of Events for information on the annual festival honouring the limited local vintage)* and the rolling countryside.

Château de Boucard ⊘ – The castle, surrounded by a moat and well-kept outbuildings, was built between the 14C and the 16C. The furnished interior has several impressive chimneys (the one in the kitchen has a mechanical roasting spit) and a chapel which was specially redesigned to allow the Princesse de la Trémoille attend Mass without leaving her bedroom.

Continue along D 74.

Jars – Visitors to this charming town will notice the manor house with its round towers and the 15-16C church in pink and white stone. Walk round to the back of this building for a view over the countryside.

Leave Jars travelling northwest on D 923.

The road leads to **Vailly-sur-Sauldre**, on the riverside; from there on, views of the valley succeed each other all the way to Villegenon.

Henrichemont – In the early 17C, Sully, minister to Henri IV, decided to carve out a little territory in Berry, which would serve as a refuge for his fellow Protestants. As he already owned a château in Chapelle-d'Angillon, he decided to build a town nearby, in a sandy, deserted place, which he called Henrichemont in honour of the king.

Never completed, the design for the town includes eight streets like spokes of a wheel, converging on a central square. A few 17C houses with arched doorways and the old well with its decorative moulding are intact. The region's soil lends itself well to earthenware manufacture, and several potter's workshops operate in and around Henrichemont *(see La Borne, below)*.

Leave Henrichemont travelling eastward on D 22.

La Borne – Berry is a good place for potters because of the rich clay soil; the abundant timber was an important factor in the past, when wood-burning kilns were the rule. Gallo-Roman earthenware household objects are on display in the Berry Museum *(see BOURGES)*. Here in La Borne, visitors can see more recent items in the **Musée de la Poterie** ⊘, established in an old chapel; or purchase local ceramics in the **sales room** ⊘. **Workshops** ⊘ will also open their doors to the interested public.

Musée Vassil Ivanoff ⊘ – This Bulgarian ceramic artist came to Paris in 1922 where he worked in interior decoration, fabric painting and photography. When he was 48 years old, strolling by the booksellers' stalls along the river Seine, he discovered a book on the "Art of Pottery". He became interested in learning new techniques and was soon installed in La Borne, in a small house which doubled as his workshop. He built his own kiln and set to work, producing some 3 000 pieces before his death in 1973.

The museum houses a generous collection of the artist's work: vases, pots, cups, engraved plaques, pieces with tubular structures, some of them resembling figurative or abstract sculptures. The red enamels known as "bull's blood" are especially eye-catching. His workshop can be seen on request.

Leave La Borne travelling southeast on D 46.

Église de Morogues – This 13C Romanesque church, fronted by an octagonal belfry-porch in reddish stone has a wonderful wooden dais inside, which was originally in the Sainte-Chapelle in Bourges. Three finely worked pinnacles rise above the chairs where the priests sat. On each side of the chancel, two artfully crafted 14C polychrome statues: John the Baptist and Saint Symphorien; in the chapel to the left, a Virgin and Child.

Leave Morogues travelling westward on D 59.

Château de Maupas ⊘ – Set in the greenery of a forest, on the edge of a lake, parts of the castle date from the 13C (main building, two towers). It was rebuilt in the 15C, then transformed in the 17C and 18C, when it fell into the hands of the Maupas family. The furnishings are attractive, and pride of place is given to the **collection of plates★** dating from the 17-19C, 880 pieces in all. There are some fine old tapestries; the modern era is represented in the collection of toys; in the kitchen, copper pots gleam on their pegs.

Return to Morogues and take D 185 northeast.

The ridge road which goes to La Borne runs by the Motte d'Humbligny (alt 431m/1 414ft), the highest point in the Sancerrois region.

Leave Humbligny travelling northeast on D 74.

This is a lovely route along the Grande Sauldre valley, as far as Neuilly-en-Sancerre, where D 22 goes back to Sancerre by way of the vineyards beyond Crézancy.

② ALONG THE LATERAL CANAL, EAST OF THE "PAYS FORT" *60km/36mi – half a day*

★Sancerre – *See above.*

Leave Sancerre travelling southwest on D 955, then turn left on D 10 towards Baugy.

Cross the vintners' village of Vinon, and go on to St-Bouize to reach the road which runs along side the **Loire lateral canal**. The canal, which is parallel to the river, has many locks; since 1836 it has enabled navigation from Roanne to Briare.

St-Satur – This village was once called Château-Gordon, until the relics of the African martyr Satyrus were brought here and it was renamed St-Satur.

Église St-Guinefort ⊘ – The first church went up in the 12C, and was later completely destroyed by the English. A new abbey church was begun in 1362, but only the chancel and apse were finished. Their size, and the pure soaring lines of the design can only leave us to imagine the splendour of this unrealised project.

St-Satur – St-Thibault quais and the Loire

Continue on D 955.

Bannay – Tucked between the northern edge of the Charnes wood and the canal, this village in the vineyards has a curious church with two pepperpot roofs.

Jardin du Tisserand ⊘ – *Access from D 955 by the street to Cantin (left in front of the canal lock).* Born with the passion of a silk painter who loved his raw materials, this museum tells the story of the four steps to making that deliciously soft fabric. In a moderately heated room (20°C/70°F), visitors discover the enchanting world of **sericulture**, where the 600 eggs laid daily by the *bombyx mori* are coddled until they hatch into silk worms, which feed on mulberry leaves. The worms spend four days spinning their cocoons by secreting gelatinous protein, sericin, which hardens in contact with the air, eventuallly providing a continuous fibre between 900 and 1 500 meters long (3 000 to 5 000ft).

The history of the **filature** (the name given to a factory where silk is manufactured) is illustrated through the display a different types of machines used to draw the silk from the cocoon. To make raw silk thick enough for textile weaving, a process called **throwing** involves twisting the fibre, plying it with another yarn, and twisting it again. Machine **weaving** is also demonstrated.

Continue along D 955.

Facing the road which leads to Cosne-sur-Loire, the 15C château de Buranlure has a lovely natural setting; the road then follows the canal for about 5km/3mi as far as the lock in the Houards.

The vineyards are shown in green

Léré – On the border of the region known as the Pays Fort *(see below)* and the Val de Loire, this hamlet was once fortified, as the remaining round towers and curving rue des Remparts show.

Collégiale St-Martin ⊘ – Heavily restored after the 16C, this edifice has kept its Romanesque apse, adjoining a 15C chancel; above the Gothic doorway, note the tympanum where a few sculpted figures remain intact. Despite the damage, one can still recognise Saint Martin sharing his cloak. Beneath the sanctuary, there is a **crypt**; the central part, a half circle, is divided into three naves with ribbed vaulting.

Leave Léré travelling southwest on D 47.

Following the Judelle valley as far as Savigny, the road goes through the eastern part of the Pays Fort, a verdant landscape of meadows and hedgerows. The "villages", tucked in wooded groves, are often gatherings of houses occupied by members of an extended family (les Henriots, les Naudeaux, les Thibauts) and built of local materials (wood, stone, cob).

D 54 carries you back to the vineyard south of the typical village of Ste-Gemme. Return to Sancerre on D 86 (to Sury-en-Vaux) and D 57.

The current edition of The Red Guide France
offers a selection of pleasant and quiet hotels in convenient locations.

Their amenities are included (swimming pools, tennis courts, private beaches and gardens...) as well us their dates of annual closure.

The selection also includes establishments which offer excellent cuisine: carefully prepared meals at reasonable prices, Michelin stars for good cooking.

The current annual Michelin Camping Caravaning France lists the facilities offered by many campsites (shops, bars, restaurants, laundries, games rooms, tennis courts, miniature golf courses, playgrounds, swimming pools...)

SARLAT-LA-CANÉDA ★★★

Population 9 909
Michelin map 75 fold 17 or 235 fold 6
Local maps see Vallée de la DORDOGNE and PÉRIGORD NOIR

At the heart of Périgord Noir, Sarlat-la-Canéda (Sarlat for short) was built in a hollow surrounded by wooded hills. Its charm lies in its preservation of the past; it still gives the impression of a small market town – the home of merchants and clerks during the Ancien Régime (period before the Revolution) – with narrow medieval streets, restored Gothic and Renaissance town houses *(hôtels)* and its famous Saturday **market**.

HISTORICAL NOTES

From abbey to bishopric – Sarlat grew up around a Benedictine abbey founded in the 9C and to which the relics of St Sacerdos, bishop of Limoges, and of his mother, St Mondane, had been entrusted under Charlemagne.

The abbots were all powerful until the 13C when internal strife and corruption caused their downfall. In 1299 the Book of Peace, an act of emancipation signed by the community, the abbey and the king, stated that the abbot might continue in his role of lord but that the consuls should be given all administrative power concerning the town itself. In 1317, however, Pope John XXII divided the Périgueux diocese and proclaimed Sarlat the Episcopal see of an area which extended far beyond the Sarladais region. The abbey church therefore became a cathedral, and the monks formed a chapter.

Sarlat's golden age – The 13C and early 14C had been a prosperous time for this active market town, but the Hundred Years War left it weakened and depopulated. Therefore, when Charles VII bestowed numerous privileges (new revenues and certain tax exemptions) upon Sarlat and its population to thank them for their loyalty and strong resistance against the English (despite Sarlat having been ceded to the English with the Treaty of Brétigny in 1360), the people of Sarlat began reconstruction. Most of the town houses to be seen were built between 1450-1500. This has created an architectural unity which is appreciated by the townspeople and tourists alike.

The magistrates, clerks, bishops, canons and merchants formed a comfortable bourgeois class which included such men of letters as Étienne de La Boétie.

The true and faithful friend – **Étienne de La Boétie**, who was born in Sarlat in 1530 in a house that can still be seen *(see below)*, became famous on many counts. He proved himself to be a brilliant magistrate in the Bordeaux Parliament as well as an impassioned writer – he was only 18 when he wrote the compelling appeal for liberty, Discourse on Voluntary Subjection or *Contr'un* (Against One), which inspired Jean-Jacques Rousseau when he came to write the Social Contract. He formed a friendship with **Michel de Montaigne** that was to last until he died and which has been immortalised by posterity. Montaigne was at La Boétie's bedside when the young man died all too early in 1563; with his friend in mind, Montaigne wrote his famous Essay on Friendship in which he formulated the excellent sentiment: "If I am urged to explain why I loved him, I feel I can only reply: because he was himself and I am myself..."

Sarlat's secular architecture – Sarlat's old district was cut into two in the 19C by the "Traverse" (rue de la République), separating it into a more populated western section and a more sophisticated eastern section.

The town houses are quite unique: built with quality ashlar-work in a fine golden-hued limestone, with interior courtyards; the roofing, made of heavy limestone slabs *(lauzes)*, necessitated a steeply pitched framework so that the enormous weight (500kg per m^2 – about 102lb per sq ft) could be supported on thick walls. Over the years new floors were added: a medieval ground floor, a High Gothic or Renaissance upper floor and classical roof cresting and lantern turrets.

AROUND TOWN

Sarlat by night ⊘ – The talented lighting designer Jacques Rouveyrollis worked with the Gaz de France company to create a unique ambience in town. When the sun goes down, the lights come up: 36 natural gas street lamps and a system of electric spotlights under glass create a special charm. The effect is intimate, enhancing the soft lines of the architecture and the medieval atmosphere.

An excellent guided tour is offered by the tourist office *(see Practical information at the end of this guide)*; the later the hour, the greater the enchantment.

Regional products – At the beginning of rue des Armes, rue des Consuls, rue de la Liberté, and just about everywhere you go in Sarlat, there are shops galore selling locally preserved foods. Many have samples to taste, and all provide friendly service true to regional tradition. To boost your endurance, begin at the Maison des vins de Bergerac, place des Oies, for a tasting. The delicious foods and wines of this region are not the least of its proud heritage!

This architectural unit escaped modern building developments in the 19C and 20C because of its distance from the main communication routes. It was chosen in 1962 as one of the new experimental national restoration projects, the goal of which was to preserve the old quarters of France's towns and cities. The project, begun in 1964, has allowed the charm of this small medieval town to be recreated.

★★★ OLD SARLAT *Start from place du Peyrou.*

Cathédrale St-Sacerdos (Z) – St Sacerdos' Church was built here in the 12C. In 1504 the Bishop Armand de Gontaut-Biron had the church razed, in order to build a cathedral.

However, when the bishop left Sarlat in 1519, the construction work ceased for more than a century. Although the present church was built during the 16C and 17C, the base of the tower on the western front is Romanesque. Of its three storeys, the lowest is formed of blind arcades, the second has open bays, whereas the third is a 17C addition.

Inside, the most striking features are the elevation and harmonious proportions of the nave. Among the furnishings are an 18C organ loft and an organ by Lépine (a well-known 18C organ maker).

Ancien Évêché (Z T) – To the right of St Sacerdos' Cathedral, is the former bishopric. Its façade has windows in the Gothic style on the first floor, Renaissance on the second floor and an Italian Renaissance loggia above, added by the Italian bishop Nicolo Goddi, friend of Catherine de' Medici. The interior has been converted into a theatre.

★**Maison de la Boétie** (Z) – This house was built in 1525 by Antoine de La Boétie, a criminal magistrate in the seneschal's court at Sarlat, and is the birthplace of Étienne de La Boétie.

A large arch on the ground floor used to shelter small shops; the two upper floors of Italian Renaissance style have large mullioned windows, framed by pilasters carved with medallions and lozenges. The steeply pitched gabled roof is decorated with crockets, and on the left side there is a heavily ornamented dormer window.

On the left of the house is **Passage Henri-de-Ségogne** (Z 21), between Hôtel de Maleville and La Boétie's House. The alleyway leads visitors through an arch, a passageway and a covered passageway.

Picturesque half-timbered buildings have been restored and, in summer, craft shops do a swift business.

★**Hôtel de Maleville** (Y) – This town house is also known as the Hôtel de Vienne after the man who built it, Jean de Vienne. Born of humble parents in Sarlat in 1557, he successfully climbed the social ladder to become financial secretary under Henri IV.

Later, the town house was bought by the Maleville family; a member of this same family, Jacques de Maleville *(see DOMME)*, helped write the French *Code Civil*, the general rules of law. Three existing houses were combined in the mid-16C to form an imposing mansion. In front of the tall, narrow central pavilion, like a majestic tower, is a terrace under which opens the arched main doorway surmounted by medallions depicting Henri IV and Maria de' Medici. It is flanked by a corbelled turret which joins it to the left wing.

Sarlat – Maison de La Boétie

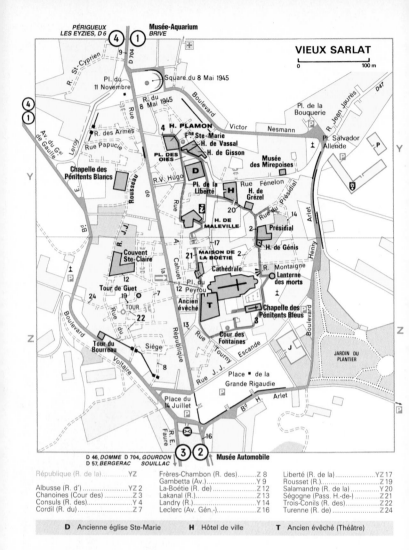

VIEUX SARLAT

D Ancienne église Ste-Marie	**H** Hôtel de ville	**T** Ancien évêché (Théâtre)

The right wing, overlooking place de la Liberté, has a gable which very much resembles one at La Boétie's House, although it is in a later Renaissance style with bays surrounded by small columns supporting entablature and pediment.

Take the covered passage to the left of the entrance, then take rue A.-Cahuet to rue des Consuls.

★**Rue des Consuls** (Y 4) – The town houses in this street are beautiful examples of Sarlat architecture from the 14-17C.

★**Hôtel Plamon** (Y) – As identified by the shield on the pediment above the doorway, this town house belonged to the Selves de Plamon family, members of the cloth merchants' guild. Because it is made up of a group of buildings built in different periods, it is a particularly interesting illustration of the evolution of the different architectural styles used in Sarlat construction.

The 14C ground floor opens through two large pointed arches. The first floor has three Gothic windows ornamented with High Gothic tracery, and the second floor has 15C mullioned windows.

Left of the town house is the very narrow Plamon Tower with windows which get smaller the higher up they are; this architectural ruse makes the tower seem much taller than it is.

On the corner of the street is a rounded overhanging balcony supported by a squinch. Go into the courtyard to admire the elegant 17C wooden **staircase**★.

Fontaine Ste-Marie (Y) – Opposite the Hôtel de Plamon, the fountain splashes in a cool grotto.

★**Place des Oies** (Y) – Appropriately called Goose Square, this is the place where on Saturdays from November to March people come from far and wide to haggle over the price of geese and, of course, of delicious goose liver *(foie gras)*.

The square is an elegant architectural collection of turrets, pinnacles and corner staircases.

Hôtel de Vassal (Y) – Located on a corner of place des Oies, this 15C town house consists of two buildings at right angles flanked by a twin battlemented turret. Beside it, the **hôtel de Gisson** (16C) is made of two buildings joined by a hexagonal staircase tower with a remarkable pointed roof.

Hôtel de Grézel (Y) – Built at the end of the 15C, the town house straight ahead has a half-timbered façade with a tower and a lovely Flamboyant Gothic ogee-arched doorway.

The skill and artistry of the carpenter and roof-layer can be admired by looking further down onto several of the roofs: the fine layout of the *lauzes*, following the line of the roof perfectly down to where the roof widens and levels out (this is achieved by furring: nailing thin strips of board under the line of the roof; a technique used to compensate for the thickness of the walls).

Continue on to rue Présidial, then rue de Génis, until you can see the tower of the **Présidial**, former seat of royal magistrates.

Retrace your steps.

At the corner of the dead end (where the old rest-stop for post-horses can be seen) and rue d'Albusse stands the **Hôtel de Génis**, a massive, plain 15C building with an overhanging upper storey supported by seven stone corbels.

Go down rue Sylvain Cavaillez and enter the garden.

Lanterne des Morts (Z) – Built at the end of the 12C, this mysterious cylindrical tower topped with a cone and split into tiers by four bands contains two rooms. The room on the ground floor has domed vaulting held up by six pointed arches; the other room is in the cone part of the tower and is not open to visitors.

A number of hypotheses have been put forward concerning the lantern's function: was it a tower built in honour of the visit of St Bernard in 1147 (he had blessed bread which miraculously cured the sick); or a lantern of the dead (but it is difficult to imagine how the lantern was lit because the top room was inaccessible); or a funerary chapel. *(See Introduction, Folklore and traditions, for more information on lanterns of the dead.)*

From the garden near the lantern, there is a fine **view**

Typical house in old Sarlat

of the cathedral's east end and its various courtyards.

Take the stairs next to the stage used for the theatre festival and walk around the **Chapelle des Pénitents bleus** (12C).

Go into the **Cour des Chanoines** then the **Cour des Fontaines**.

Rue Munz and rue Tourny lead back to place Peyrou.

★WEST SIDE

This part of town, on the opposite side of rue de la République (the so-called Traverse), is currently under renewal. Its steep and winding lanes are quieter, off the main tourist track, and offer another image of Sarlat.

Chapelle des Pénitents Blancs (Y) – Used by the order of Pénitents Blancs, the chapel was part of the religious establishment of the Pères Récollets. Construction began in 1622 and it was completed four years later. The intriguing doorway is composed of four fluted columns; the capitals and entablature are curiously designed.

Rue Jean-Jacques Rousseau (Y) – This is the main street in this part of town, and many attractive old houses grace it. At the corner of Côte de Toulouse, there is an admirable 18C façade (Hôtel Monméja); at the intersection with rue de la Boétie, you can see the castellated turret which marks the site of St Clare's Convent, a vast 17C building once occupied by the Poor Clares, and today providing low-rent housing. The garden is used during the theatre festival in the summer, and also hosts concerts and other cultural events.

Tour du Guet (Z) – Overlapping the buildings, the watch tower is crowned by 15C machicolations and flanked by a corbelled turret.

Rue des Trois-Conils (des Trois Lapins) (Z 22) – This street bends sharply left around the foot of a house flanked by a tower, which once belonged to consuls related to the Boétie family.

Tour du Bourreau (Z) – The "Executioner's Tower", which was part of the ramparts, was built in 1580.

Virtual Sarlat...

Looking for a house to rent? Want to place an ad? Maybe you'd like to pick up some useful tips from others who are reesiding or vacationing in the area... log in to www.sarlat.com. The site exists in an excellent English version and includes the option of subscribing to a newsletter which keeps you up-to-date about events in Sarlat year-round.

ADDITIONAL SIGHTS

Musée Automobile ⊘ – *Access by ③ on the plan*
Sixty vehicles are on display, shiny and ready to roll. A Panhard-Levassor is one of the more venerable cars, with its rudimentary body and wagon wheels; it was built sometime between 1891 and 1894. Visitors can admire a rare survivor of the fleet of "Marne Taxis"; 600 of these cars transported 6 000 infantrymen from Paris to the site of the First Battle of the Marne in 1914. Other prize models: Rolls Royce (1929), Hispano Suiza (1926), Dion-Bouton, Hotchkiss, Bentley, Amilcar, Bugatti and a futuristic red Ferrari. A bright yellow Citroën from the 20s has a nickname whose translation doesn't it do justice: the French called it "The Lemon".

Musée-Aquarium ⊘ – *Access via Avenue Gambetta, then follow the signposts.*
The objective of this museum is to describe the Dordogne river and everything related to it: fishing, fishing vessels, navigation, construction of dams, etc.
About 30 freshwater species from the region can be seen swimming about in vast aquariums. Anadromous fish (Atlantic salmon, lamprey, shad) and non-migratory species (pike, perch, barbel, bleak) live side by side.
Fishing techniques from prehistory to the present are explained on panels and illustrated with displays of primitive harpoons, more modern nets and the traditional, flat-bottomed *gabare*. The most original fishing technique used was the seine: an immense net was dropped, extending from one bank of the river to the other, which caught a large quantity of migrating fish swimming up river to spawn. This type of fishing has practically disappeared due to the damming up of rivers.
A film shows the large-scale management measures used to attract the migrating fish in spite of the dams: collecting the fish, fishing ladders. Other audio-visual displays supplement this presentation of river life.

Nimetz/IMAGES PHOTOTHÈQUE

Les Bories

EXCURSIONS

Temniac – *3km/mi north. See PÉRIGORD NOIR.*

Château de Puymartin ⊘ – *9km/5mi northwest on D 47.*
Constructed in the 15C and 16C, the several buildings linked by towers stand atop a steep hill, protected by a curtain wall. The **decoration★** is impressive: period furnishings, Aubusson tapestries, decorative panelling and paintings.

Cabanes de Breuil ⊘ – *Travelling from Sarlat on D 47, 2km/1mi after the Allas cemetery, turn right and follow the signs.*
The hamlet of Breuil has the richest collection of the dry stone buildings known as *bories* in Périgord *(see Introduction: Traditional rural architecture, for more details).* There are a dozen or so huts, forming an architectural grouping unique in the region. Members of the family now resident on the farm show visitors around.

SÉGUR-LE-CHÂTEAU★

Population 269
Michelin map 75 northeast of fold 7 or 239 fold 25

Nestled in a deep gorge carved out by the river Auvézère, the charming village of Ségur is pretty for its old houses perched atop steep hills. One of these hills bears the ruins of a 12-13C castle with double curtain walls. Ségur may go back as far as Gallo-Roman times; it certainly played an important role in the Middle Ages and under the Ancien Régime. Cradle of the first viscounts of Limoges, when feudalism was at its peak, this prosperous settlement was the birthplace, in 1470, of Jean d'Albret, first king of Navarre and grandfather of Jeanne d'Albret, herself mother of Henri IV. But Ségur's fame derives from the three centuries (15C to 1750) during which it served as the seat of the high court of appeals for hundreds of feudal jurisdictions in Limousin and Périgord.

Ségur owes its allure to the many court officials who lived here and built beautiful residences, including the **maison Febrer** (15C), with its Renaissance chimneys and turrets, and the **maison Henri IV**, named in honour of the d'Albret family. Today the long robes and powdered wigs of magistrates are not seen in streets, but painters are commonly at work capturing the half-timbered houses and turrets of the old houses (15C-17C), the characteristic pointed brown tiled roofs, the gothic doorways opening onto narrow, winding lanes.

SOLIGNAC★

Population 1 345
Michelin map 72 fold 17 (13 km/8mi south of Limoges)
Local map see LIMOGES

Solignac lies near the green valley of the Briance and has an interesting Romanesque church, once part of the famous abbey founded in 632 by St Eligius.

The Great Saint Eligius – The legendary figure of St Eligius dominated the Merovingian Age. This wise and saintly man was not only Dagobert's chief minister, but is also remembered as a goldsmith and loved as a man of inexhaustible charity.
He was born at Chaptelat in 588 and learned his skill as a goldsmith in the workshops at Limoges. He went to work in Paris; but it was due to the confidence in him of good King Dagobert – who is famous to all French school children thanks to a nursery rhyme on the theme of his knickers – that St Eligius was able to use his talents as a minister. St Eligius, though titular bishop of Noyon, felt the call of his native countryside and asked the king for land at Solignac on which to found a monastery where he could die in peace. "My king and master", the holy man said, "may you grant me this out of your bounty so that I may build a ladder, for by this ladder we shall climb to heaven, you and I." The king replied favourably to Eligius' request.
The abbey was built on a grand scale from the start, but in spite of its fortifications it did not escape the depredations of the Normans, the Saracens, the English and the Huguenots, each of whom plundered it in turn during its long history.

★ABBEY CHURCH

The present church dates from the first half on the 12C and is the Limousin church which is most influenced by the Périgord style of architecture.

Exterior – The big bell-tower built at the same time as the abbey was replaced in the 19C by a bell-gable. As you walk around the northern side of the church, admire the harmony of the construction: large buttresses and recessed columns reaching up to the ledge around the roof; on the lower part, groups of four arches

ABBEY CHURCH

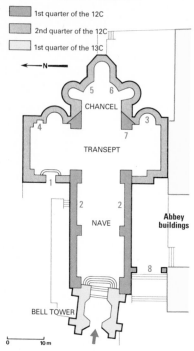

1st quarter of the 12C

2nd quarter of the 12C

1st quarter of the 13C

← N ——

CHANCEL

5 6

4

3

7

TRANSEPT

1

2   2

NAVE

Abbey buildings

8

BELL TOWER

0   10 m

falling alternately on plain pilasters and bases embellished with scrolling designs, crouching figures and monsters. Just above, the succession of windows and blind trefoils illustrates the influence of Mozarabic tradition (which qualifies styles originating with Christians who lived in the Iberian Peninsula after the Arab invasion of 711, and who were thus exposed to Islamic culture and art forms). A bas-relief of Christ in Majesty (1) rises above the northern transept doorway. Step back to embrace the view of the transept and the apse, a frieze of blind arcades circles the upper part of the building adding further elegance to the lovely building.

Interior – Go in through the door in the porch. From the top of the steps looking down into the nave you will be struck by the harmony of proportion, the purity of line, the strength of the architectural design and the warm colour of the granite of this church whose plan, with neither side aisles nor ambulatory, is that of a plain Latin cross. The main body of the church is covered over with vast semicircular domes. An elevated passageway runs down both sides of the nave and is supported by blind arcading which in turn is carried by engaged columns and pilasters. Note also the carved archaic capitals and modillions which become more intricate towards the chancel.

The stalls (2), on each side of the nave, mostly date from the 15C, the carved "misericords" – a small ledge which a worshiper could use to rest on while standing up – and arm rests depict foliage, animals and grimacing faces.

The transept is asymmetrical. The south arm is roofed with cradle vaulting; note the 18C polychrome Virgin carved in wood (3). In the north transept which is covered with an ovoid cupola pierced by a round window, a glass case (4) contains works of art including the 12C reliquary-bust of St Théau in gilded copper and silver.

The chancel, covered with an imperfectly shaped cupola, is punctuated by seven arcades and three chapels. The capitals bear a variety of embellishments: palmettos, figures struggling with griffins, twining serpents etc. Two 17C frescoes represent the Temptation of Christ (5) and the Olive Garden (6). Some of the windows date from the 15C. On the right pillar, note the restored "distemper" painting (powdered colours and size mixed with water) of St Christopher (7), which probably dates from the 15C.

Monastery Buildings – The buildings which were reconstructed in the 18C and ravaged during the Revolution, have been occupied since 1945 by student missionaries of the Oblate of Mary Immaculate.

The courtyard faces the south side of the church, which was connected to the cloisters by an archway leading from the second bay. The pointed arch (8) under which you pass as you go around towards the front of the building may have been another entrance to the cloisters, or else the entrance to a chapel.

SOUILLAC★

Population 3 459
Michelin map 75 fold 18 or 235 fold 6
Local maps see Vallée de la DORDOGNE and Causse de GRAMAT

At the confluence of the Corrèze and the Dordogne, in the centre of a fertile region, of an abundance greatly in contrast with the poverty of the *causses* (limestone plateaux) of Martel and Gramat, Souillac is a small town bustling with trade and tourists. It developed in the 13C, growing up around the abbey which was a dependency of the Benedictine Monastery at Aurillac; today, the town is bisected by national highway 20.

When the Benedictines settled in the plain of Souillès – so-called after the local word *souilh*, meaning bog or marshland where wild boar wallow – story has it that they replaced the community established there previously by St Eligius. The monks drained the land continuously, transforming the marsh into a rich estate. Souillac Abbey was plundered and sacked several times by the English during the Hundred Years War, but rose from its ruins each time thanks to the tenacity of its abbots. Greater disasters, however, befell it during the Wars of Religion: in 1562 Huguenot bands pillaged the monastery; ten years later the monastery buildings were set ablaze and only the abbey church, protected by its domes, escaped the flames. The abbey was rebuilt in the 17C and attached to the Maurist Congregation, but it then ceased to exist during the Revolution. Its buildings are now used for storing tobacco.

Abbey Church – Dedicated to Mary, Mother of Christ, this church became a parish church to replace the church of St Martin, which was destroyed during the Wars of Religion. The disfigured bell-tower, which is all that remains of St Martin's, is now the town hall belfry.

Built in the 12C, the church is related to the Romanesque cathedrals of Angoulême, Périgueux and Cahors with their Byzantine inspiration, but it is more advanced in the lightness of its columns and the height of its great arcades than the others. From place de l'Abbaye it is possible to admire the attractive east end with its five pentagonal apsidal chapels, three of which radiate out from the apse, whereas the other two are in line. At the front of the interior is a tower decorated on its lowest tier with carved brackets, which was part of a previous building and dates from the 10C or perhaps the beginning of the 11C. It is the equivalent of the tower-porches which usually formed the narthex of Romanesque churches. Inside, the pure lines of the nave are covered with a row of three tall domes on pendentives. In the first bay on the left there is a 16C polyptych painted on wood, depicting The Mysteries of the Rosary.

★**The back of the doorway** – This composition consists of the remains of the old doorway, which was badly damaged by the Protestants and had been placed inside the nave of the new church, when it was erected in the 17C.

Above the door, framed by the statues of St Peter on the right and St Benedict on the left, is a low relief relating episodes in the life of the monk Theophilus, deacon of Adana in Cilicia: a new abbot, misled by false reports, removes Theophilus from his office of treasurer of the monastery of Adana; Theophilus, out of resentment, signs a pact with the devil to regain his office (left). Repenting of his sins, Theophilus implores forgiveness and prays to the Virgin Mary (right) who appears before him in his sleep, accompanied by St Michael and two angels who guard her; they bring him the pact he has made with the devil, and she shows how she has had his signature annulled and has obtained his pardon. The engaged pillar on the right, which was originally the central pillar of the doorway, is richly decorated. The right side depicts concupiscence during the various stages of life; on the main facet monstrous animals grip and devour one another. The left side proclaims the remission of sin through the sacrifice of Isaac. The hand of Abraham is stayed by the messenger of God.

On either side of the door are fine low reliefs, in boldly decorative attitudes, of the prophet **Isaiah**★★ (right), striking in its expression, and the patriarch Joseph (left). Beneath the narthex is a crypt containing primitive sarcophagi.

★**Musée national de l'automate et de la robotique** ⊙ – *Enter by the parvis of the abbey church* (*abbatiale St-Pierre*).

The museum contains some 3 000 objects, including 1 000 automata donated by the **Roullet-Decamps** family, who for four generations were leaders in the field. In 1865 Jean Roullet created his first mechanical toy: a small gardener pushing a wheel barrow. In 1909 he created the first Christmas window display for the Bon Marché department store.

Prophet Isaiah

The collection illustrates the evolution of automata from Antiquity to the present-day. These mechanical objects were considered precious enough to offer to nobility; they were also offered as sophisticated toys and even used as publicity items.

Note especially the **Jazzband** (1920), a group of electric automata with black musicians performing a concert; or the lovely fairy-like **Snow Queen** (1956), based on the tale by Hans-Christian Andersen. The impressive electronic brain which controls the movements of the automata and the new collection of "robots of the year 2000" both reflect the extent of the amazing developments that have been made in this field on the eve of the 21C.

Musée des attelages de la Belle Époque ⊘ – *Rue Chambert*

This large museum has room for 50 horse-drawn carriages from the 19C and a tack room with harnesses and stable gear. Many different models, whether luxurious, spacious, or simply utilitarian, are to be admired.

EXCURSION

Lanzac viewpoint – *5km/3mi south, parking*

There is a wide view to the left of N 20, revealing the Dordogne valley, where Château de la Treyne can be seen standing out to the east and the dovecot of Le Bastit Castle to the southeast.

Le THOT, ESPACE CRO-MAGNON★

Michelin map 75 fold 7 or 235 fold 2 (7km/mi south of Montignac)
Local map see Vallée de la VÉZÈRE

Created in 1972, the Cro-Magnon centre offers and initiation to prehistoric art and is a good place to start a tour, before venturing out to visit the many prehistoric sites for which the region is renown, especially Lascaux II, the reproduction of the Lascaux Cave *(see Grottes de LASCAUX)*.

TOUR ⊘

The **museum** displays a large overview of the expression of prehistoric people through painting, sculpture, graffiti etc; prehistoric cultures are placed in the historical context of civilisation, its evolution and driving forces. These topics are developed with the aid of modern technology: re-creations, enormous slide shows, film and so on.

The **park** is especially well-designed, and is home to a number of species which inhabited the area in prehistoric times, such as the aurochs, European bison, Prjewalski's horses. Species which no longer roam the planet, the mammoth and the woolly rhinoceros, are represented by animatronics.

Dramatic re-creations of campsites from the upper Paleolithic period make the visit both exciting and instructive.

TULLE

Population 17 164
Michelin map 75 fold 9 or 239 fold 27

Tulle extends over a couple of miles, its main street following the course of the narrow and winding valley of the Corrèze and its old houses rising in terraces on the hillsides overlooking the river. From the centre of the city rises the elegant stone steeple of the Cathedral of Notre-Dame. The administrative seat of the *département* of Corrèze, although it is not the largest city, Tulle is well-known in France as a centre for the manufacture of armaments.

A Litigious Abbey – Tulle Abbey, founded on what is believed to be the site of a temple dedicated to the Roman Goddess Tutela, became powerful very early in its history. The monks frequently showed an aggressive zeal for affairs, as in the Rocamadour quarrel, in which for more than a century, the abbeys of Tulle and Marcilhac disputed possession of this wealthy sanctuary.

One of the abbots of Tulle, Élie de Ventadour, found an unusual method of replenishing his treasury which was all too often empty: he borrowed large sums at exorbitant rates of interest from the Jewish bankers of Brive; once the money was safely stowed in the abbey, the abbot, who controlled the court, charged the lenders with usury, condemned them and confiscated their property. Another abbot, Arnaud de St-Astier, obtained for himself in 1317 the title of bishop of Tulle. This encroachment deprived Limoges of one the most flourishing dependencies of its diocese: lawsuits dragged on endlessly bringing a bitterness that lasted for a long time between the two Limousin cities.

A Heavy Toll – During the Hundred Years War the town fell twice, in 1346 and 1369, to the English. Each time the invaders were driven away by the local militia.

During the Wars of Religion, Tulle sided with the "papists", the Protestant army under the viscount of Turenne failed to take the city in 1577, but in 1585 Turenne came back and with bloody vengeance sacked the city after first assaulting it.

On 8 June 1944 Tulle was liberated by the men of the *maquis*, but the next day the Germans retook the town. Several hundred townspeople were arrested: 99 were hanged in the streets, the others were deported: 101 never came back. South of town *(N 89, the road to Brive)*, a monument has been erected to the memory of the victims of hanging.

SIGHTS

Cathedral of Notre-Dame – In 1103, Abbot Guillaume wished his abbey, which was then very prosperous, to have a worthy setting, so he undertook the reconstruction of the church and the cloistral buildings. The 12C saw the building of the nave, the porch and the first of the belfry. The original plan was like that of many Benedictine churches, namely a nave and side-aisles, transept with dependent chapels, an apse and an ambulatory with apsidal chapels. The delays in construction explain why the columns and side walls are Romanesque but the vaulting is pure Gothic in style. In 1796 the dome above the transept and a part of the chancel collapsed. This caused the east part of the building to be taken down and the nave closed by a plain wall.

The **belfry**★ is 73m/240ft high; the three storeys are surmounted by an elegant octagonal spire surrounded by bell turrets. This spire, which dated from the 14C, was struck by lightning in 1645, but has been restored to its original form. The ogive-vaulted porch contains a tiers-point doorway, adorned with moulding and small columns in the Limousin style.

The interior decoration is plain, although the colours of the modern windows (1979) in the chancel are vivid. In the centre, Our Lady of Tulle; above, John the Baptist bearing the Lamb of God. The border shows (right) Bishop Dumoulin-Borie, a local missionary who suffered martyrdom in Tonkin; (top) Saint Sebastien; (left) Saint Jacques; above, a hanged man commemorating the terrible events of 1944. A much venerated 16C wooden statue of St John the Baptist stands in the north aisle. Since the 14C, the inhabitants of Tulle have celebrated his birth with a procession known as *la lunade (see Practical information at the end of this guide)*.

Cloisters – Built in the early 13C, the building has been greatly damaged over time. Still standing are the west gallery, two bays in the north and east galleries. The south gallery was destroyed in the 19C for the purposes of a municipal theatre project.

The two restored galleries have fine ribbed vaulting; admire the elegant sculptures on the capitals and keystones.

The east gallery (the farthest back) is the most elaborately decorated (note the angels on the keystones, capitals with human heads); the entrance to the chapterhouse is guarded by two recumbent figures. The vaulted ceiling rests on two central pillars. On the wall to the left, two early 14C paintings depict Christ entering Jerusalem and the Last Supper.

Many vestiges are displayed along the galleries: a collection of 16-18C firebacks, statues, copies of recumbent figures representing popes from Limousin, various stone fragments (capitals, ribs).

Tulle – Maison de Loyac

J. D. Sudres/DIAF

Musée du cloître ⊘ – The museum adjoins the west gallery of the cloisters. The **ground floor** is used for temporary exhibits of contemporary art. The spiral staircase dates from the Middle Ages (note the engravings); it leads to the **first floor** rooms, which display a collection illustrating the history, the popular arts and traditions of Tulle and its region. The collection includes water-colours by Gaston Vuillier, which depict the landscapes of Corrèze, and drawings showing the practice of witchcraft as well as the religious practices in the countryside in the late 19C. Local lacemakers are credited with having created the distinctive pattern which bears the name of the town. The last room devotes pride of place to the **accordion**, for Corrèze was once well known for the manufacture of these instruments. Those on display date from 1835 to 1950, and include the work of a local craftsman still in business.

Old Town – This area, known as the "Englos" (the Enclosure) retains a medieval atmosphere with alleys, stairways and old houses.

★ **Maison de Loyac** – This is the most outstanding secular building in Tulle. Built in the 15C it has an attractive façade: the windows and door are framed by small columns and are topped by accolades adorned with sculptured foliage, roses and animals. Take rue de la Tour-de-Maïsse, to the left of the building; the street is a narrow stairway, where the roofs of corbelled houses almost meet above the alley. Bear left again into rue de la Baylie and yet again into the sloping rue des Portes-Chanac, where, among a group of old houses, you will notice on the left, at no 9, a fine sculptured doorway belonging to a late Renaissance mansion.

Rue Riche – carved façade at no 13 – leads back to the cathedral.

TURENNE★

Population 740

Michelin map 75 fold 8 or 239 fold 26 – Local map see BRIVE-LA-GAILLARDE: Excursions

Pompadour pompe. Ventadour vente. Turenne règne. This old French pun defies translation, but can be loosely construed as crediting Turenne with noble dignity, while the other cities mentioned are just full of hot air. Today the ruins of the proud castle, stronghold of viscounts, rise above the picturesque town.

HISTORICAL NOTES

The small town with a great past – The incapability of the last Carolingians to govern the whole of their territories and the aptitude of the lords of Turenne for resisting Viking invasion seems to have been the root of the fief's emancipation from royal power. As early as the 11C, a fortress was set on the outlines of the Martel Causse. In the 15C, Turenne held sway over a third of Lower Limousin, Upper Quercy and the Sarladais region or 1 200 villages and a number of abbeys.

Turenne – Aerial view

The viscounty, in its heyday, enjoyed enviable privileges; like the king of France, the viscounts ruled absolutely, ennobling subjects, creating offices and consulates, minting money and levying taxes.

The La Tour d'Auvergne-Turenne families – The name Turenne became famous through the family of La Tour d'Auvergne. In the 16C, Henri de la Tour d'Auvergne was leader of the Limousin Huguenots and the most valiant supporter of the Reformation. As a reward for his zeal, Henri IV allowed him to marry the heiress to the duchy of Bouillon, Charlotte de la Marck; the Turennes then went to live in Sedan and administered their viscounty, which remained sovereign, at a distance. Charlotte died three years after her marriage, leaving the titles of duke de Bouillon and prince of Sedan to her husband Henri, who remarried Elizabeth of Nassau. His youngest son, also a Henri, was to become the great Turenne. His eldest son, who inherited the viscounty and title of duke de Bouillon, participated in the Fronde (an aristocratic rebellion against Mazarin with which Turenne had associated himself in its early days – 1648). In 1650 he welcomed two supporters of the Fronde, the princess of Condé and her son the duke of Enghien. The meeting was celebrated with such pomp and magnificence that it was baptised "Turenne's wild week" and in consequence the people of Turenne were taxed for two years to refill the impoverished coffers.

Happy as a viscount – The fortunate inhabitants living in the reflected glory of their lord's prowess in battle passed their days quietly within their small state and were envied since they were exempt from the tithes which fell so heavily on French peasants at the time. But this golden age had to end. In 1738, the last member of the La Tour d'Auvergne dynasty, the ninth viscount, who no longer had two coins to rub together, sold the viscounty to Louis XV for 4 200 000 *livres*, ending the state of virtual independence of Turenne. Once united to the French kingdom, the taxes of the once-proud viscounty were multiplied by ten!

TOUR

Lower town – At the foot of the hill is the Barri-bas Quarter, the old part of town. On **place du Foirail** (**6**), the Hôtel Sclafer (**B**), with a loggia, was a residence for notaries in the 17C. Opposite, there is a small shop (15C) (**D**) with a large arcade. rue du Commandant-Charollais goes into place de la Halle. The town houses around this square reflect the wealth of its inhabitants, especially the **Maison Vachon**, the residence of the consuls of Turenne in the 16C and 17C.

Between two town houses, the narrow **rue Droite** climbs towards the castle.

The street is lined with old houses with overhanging upper storeys and small shops. Turn right onto rue Joseph-Rouveyrol and note the **Maison de l'Ancien Chapitre** (Old Chapter-house), the tower of which is decorated with a lovely Flamboyant-Gothic-style doorway.

Church – The construction of the church was decided upon by Charlotte de La Marck in 1593, the year Henri IV converted to Catholicism. After Charlotte's death, Elizabeth of Nassau took over the project; and yet it was not consecrated until 1668. The church is in the form of a Greek cross, and has an unusual ornamentation – a yellow and white mosaic forming a network of prismatic ribbing.

The 17C and 18C furnishings include stalls and a high altar surmounted by a carved and gilded wooden altarpiece depicting the Passion of Christ. The trompe l'œil decoration between the twisted columns was added later on.

Just above the church, a vast building, the **Maison Tournadour** was once the town's salt storehouse.

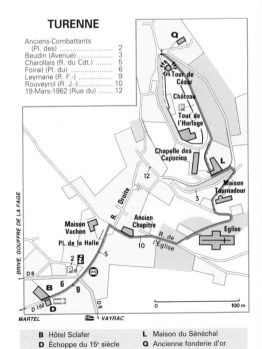

TURENNE

B Hôtel Sclafer	**L** Maison du Sénéchal
D Échoppe du 15ᵉ siècle	**Q** Ancienne fonderie d'or

281

Upper town – Access is through the **fortified gateway** of the second of the three curtain walls which protected the castle. On the right the Seneschal's House (**L**) has an elegant tower. On the left the **Chapelle des Capucins** (1644) houses exhibitions.

Go round the castle from the right. A series of manor-houses, roofed with slate and flanked by squat towers have names which evoke their past purpose – the Gold Foundry (**Q**), for example.

Le château ⊙ – The castle was demolished by the king once the viscounty was sold to the crown. Only the Clock and Caesar's towers, at each end of the promontory, were spared. The **site★** is remarkable. Once the fortified buildings and chapel (behind the clock tower) occupied the entire promontory.

Tour de l'Horloge – The clock tower was the castle keep, dating from the 13C. Only the guards' room with pointed barrel vaulting is open to visitors. Above it is the *salle du trésor* – the counting room or treasury.

Tour de César – This round tower with irregular stone bonding seems to date from the 11C. A staircase goes up to the top, from where there is a vast **panorama★★** of the region. In the foreground below are the village's slate roofs, in the distance, beyond a green valley landscape, appear the Monts du Cantal to the east and the Dordogne valley directly southwards *(viewing table)*.

Return to place du Foirail via the fortified gateway and rue Droite.

USSEL

Population 11 448
Michelin map 73 fold 11 or 239 fold 17

Built 631m/2 067ft above sea level on the edge of the Millevaches plateau, between the Diège and Sarsonne valleys, Ussel has kept a raiment of 15-17C monuments, souvenirs of a prosperous past.

SIGHTS

The old town – Follow rue de la Liberté, behind the church, to place Joffre, where a fountain flows, and wander around the narrow streets surrounding. Many of the old houses have been restored; admire the turrets and decorative doorways.

Behind place de la République, the **Hôtel de Ventadour** is an elegant Renaissance residence built by the dukes of Ventadour at the end of the 16C, to replace the austere feudal castle (now in ruins).

Only the chancel and flat east end of the **église St-Martin** date from the late 12C; the nave and side aisles were redone in Gothic style; the façade and bell-tower (19C) are modern. Inside: the woodwork and stalls are 18C; there is a 16C polychrome *Pietà* carved in wood.

Hôtel Bonnot de Bay – This unadorned residence from the early 18C houses a museum devoted to local crafts and traditional trades which are slowly dying out.

Musée du pays d'Ussel ⊙ – Old-fashioned workshops have been faithfully recreated, illustrating tradtional crafts practiced by the village smithy, the weaver (rare 18C loom), the clog-maker, the *galochier* (who made leather shoes with wooden soles, typically in Bort-les-Orgues), the milliner, the caner and basketweaver, the woodworker. Several rooms are devoted to *la bugeade* (washing linens and clothes), music, cooking, and local furniture. One small room is set up like an old countryside café. On the floor above, a display case is given over to a presentation of selected local writers.

Chapelle des Pénitents – The religious life of the region is addressed by themes, including the historical context, parish services, processions and brotherhoods, popular devotions and religion as practised "cradle to tomb".

There are some remarkable pieces of local art, a gilded wood altar screen made in 1711; a painting (1664) by the Cibille brothers, *Pentecost*; several painted wooden statues (the 17C praying angel is especialy lovely).

In the ethnology section, there is a surprising 19C hearse, complete with a stuffed and mounted horse to draw it.

Aigle romain – The "Roman eagle" monument, craved in granite, was discovered in the Peuch mill on the banks of the river Sarsonne. Nearby, at 18 rue Michelet (17C house), an old lithographic printing press and related items are on display.

Chapelle N-D-de-la-Chanbanne – *South of town, access by rue Pasteur.* From the esplanade near this pilgrims' chapel, there is an extensive **view**, reaching the Plateau des Millevaches (northwest), the Monts Dore (east), and the hills of Cantal (southeast).

UZERCHE★★

Population 2 813

Michelin map 75 northeast of fold 8

"He who has a house in Uzerche, has a castle in Limousin"; the number of attractive mansions and old houses to be seen in the city confirms this popular old saying. Uzerche, a charming small Limousin town, stands on a promontory encircled by a bend in the river Vézère. On this picturesque site a surprising number of buildings are crowned with bell-turrets, watch-towers and pepper-pot roofs.

The Trick which Always Succeeded – In 732 the Saracens, after being beaten back by **Charles Martel** at Poitiers, attacked Uzerche. The town was protected by solid walls and eighteen fortified towers and held out for seven years, but the population became decimated by famine and surrender seemed near until the besieged hit on a trick: they presented the emir of the Saracens with their last fatted calf, and with their last ration of corn. Amazed at such prodigality, the infidels raised the siege.

The Uzerche arms – tow bulls – recall this trick. The old town was never taken by force during any of the many sieges of the Middle Ages. Charles V, when he authorised the town to add three gold lilies to its arms, also gave it the appellation "Uzerche the maid", and its crest *non polluta* (never sullied) confirms the glorious epithet.

★★**View** – At the Turgot Bridge, take D 3, the Eymoutiers road, which climbs steeply and goes through the Ste-Eulalie suburb. Half a mile from the bridge, before a turning on the left you get a good **view** of the site with the town perched on top of the rock and the Vézère running below. The church (St-Pierre) overlooks the many pinnacles atop the slate-covered turrets; below stand the many towers of Pontier château.

Uzerche – View of the town

SIGHTS *Leave from place Marie-Colein.*

Rue Gaby-Furnestin – On the left, you will see the 16C timbered house in which Alexis Boyer, surgeon to Napoleon I, was born. In this street which extends into rue Jean-Gentet, note a group of renovated old houses with fine carved doorways.

Porte Bécharie – This fortified gateway is the only one of the old city gates still intact: a modern statue of the Virgin stands in a niche above the arched passageway. Adjoining the gateway is a building known as the Château Bécharie, which is flanked by a square tower and a pendant turret; in the left wall is a great stone emblazoned with the Uzerche arms.

Turn right immediately beyond the Bécharie Gateway, into rue Escalier-Notre-Dame.

Place des Vignerons – This little square, the Wine-Grower's Square, was formerly the fruit market. It is surrounded by old houses and the Chapel of Notre-Dame, the oldest church in Uzerche. The covered, La Perception, passageway leads to a small terrace which affords a bird's-eye view of the Vézère and of part of the town. Leave the Tour du Prince Noir (Black Prince's Tower) on your left and walk along rue-St-Nicolas which brings you out onto place de la Libération. This square is dominated by the impressive mass of the church of St-Pierre.

★**Église St-Pierre** – This is an interesting Romanesque building dating from the 12C and 13C, built in several phases: the chancel and north arm of the transept date from the 11C; the nave is from the 12C and was extended in the 13C. Fortified during the Hundred Years War, repaired in the 17C, the church was restored in the beginning of the 20C.

The nave has broken barrel vaulting and is flanked by narrow aisles. An octagonal dome rises above the transept crossing. In the chancel with its ambulatory and the side chapels, the capitals are ornamented with tracery, foliage and animals. Three of them have been converted into holy-water fonts; on one, monsters with lions' bodies and men's heads cavort.

The 12C belfry is Limousin in style. Three square tiers with paired windows and gables are surmounted by a fourth, octagonal in shape; this, in turn, is topped with a short roof covered in shingles which replaced the original stone pyramid roof.

To the southwest stands a massive round tower, erected as the defence point for the main door, built of rough-hewn stone with loopholes. Since restoration work on the church was undertaken last century, this tower is all that remains of the ancient defence system. The perimeter wall included 18 towers and five fortified gateways.

Crypt – *Access through the chevet*. Beneath the chancel is an 11C crypt, (believed to be the oldest in the Limousin region), in the shape of a rotunda with three apsidal chapels supported by massive pillars. Traces on the wall and vaulting indicate that the ceiling was once coffered. The central room, with its single pier on a rectangular base, communicates with the ambulatory.

The 14C tomb in the north chapel is of unknown origin.

In the past, two stairways connected the crypt to the church.

La Lunade Esplanade – From this esplanade, built on the site ofn the former monastic buildings, there is a **view** immediately below of the La Pomme quarter which rises in terraces along the N 20 roadway, of the Vézère meander, and beyond, of the hills encircling the town.

Rue Pierre-Chalaud – It is lined with old houses where you may see a Gothic or Renaissance door and timbered houses. At the end of the street the Château Tayac (12-14C) is a fine house with turrets and a door surmounted by a shield.

Centre régional de documentation sur l'archéologie du paysage ⊙ – Set up in a 17C residence, the regional centre documents recent archeological research in the area, covering the period from the Iron Age to the late Middle Ages.

Return to place de la Libération.

Walk along rue Jean-Gentet, where you will notice carved doorways, to the Bécharie Gateway and place Marie-Colein.

EXCURSION

Vigeois – *25km/15mi southwest. See Vallée de la VÉZÈRE.*

Château de VALENÇAY★★

Michelin map 64 fold 18 or 238 fold 16

Geographically, Valençay is part of the Berry region, but the château can be included with others of its kind which grace the Loire valley, by virtue of the time of its construction as well as its enormous size.

A Financier's Château – Valençay was built c1540 by Jacques d'Estampes, the owner of the castle then existing. He had married the daughter of a financier, who brought him a large dowry, and he wanted a residence worthy of his new fortune. The 12C castle was demolished and in its place rose the present sumptuous building.

Finance has often been involved in the history of Valençay; among its owners were several Farmers-General and even the famous **John Law**, whose dizzy banking career was an early and instructive example of inflationary practices.

Charles-Maurice de Talleyrand-Périgord, who had begun his career under Louis XVI as bishop of Autun, was foreign minister when he bought Valençay in 1803 at the request of Napoleon, who was seeking a place to receive important foreign visitors. Talleyrand managed his career so skilfully that he did not finally retire until 1834.

Son et Lumière – *See the Calendar of Events at the end of this guide.*

TOUR ⊙

The entrance pavilion is a huge building, designed like a keep only for show not defence, with many windows, harmless turrets and fancy machicolations. The steep roof is pierced with high dormer windows and surmounted by monumental chimneys.

Château de Valençay – Entrance pavilion

Such architecture is also found in the Renaissance châteaux of the Loire valley, but here we see the first signs of the classical style: superimposed pilasters with Doric (ground floor), Ionic (first floor) and Corinthian (second floor) capitals.

The classical style is even more evident in the huge corner towers: domes take the place of the pepperpot roofs which were the rule on the banks of the Loire in the 16C.

West wing – The west wing was added in the 17C and altered in the 18C. At roof level the mansard windows alternate with bulls' eyes (round apertures). The tour of the ground floor includes the great Louis XVI vestibule; the gallery devoted to the Talleyrand-Périgord family; the Grand Salon and the Blue Salon which contain many works of art and pieces of Empire furniture, including the so-called "Congress of Vienna" table; the apartments of the duchess of Dino.

On the first floor, the bedroom of Prince Talleyrand is followed by the room occupied by Napoleon from 1808 to 1814; the apartments of the duke of Dino and those of Madame de Bénévent (portrait of the princess by Elisabeth Vigée-Lebrun); the great gallery (with a *Diana* by Houdon) and the great staircase. Something of the spirit of the festivities organised by Talleyrand and his master chef, Marie-Antoine de Carème, still lingers in the great dining room and the kitchens beneath.

Park ☉ – Black swans, ducks and peacocks strut freely in the formal gardens near the château. Under the great trees in the park, deer, llamas, camels and kangaroos roam in vast enclosures.

Musée de l'Automobile du Centre ☉ – The car museum, concealed in the park, contains the collection of the Guignard brothers, the grandsons of a coach-builder from Vatan *(Indre)*. There are over 60 vintage cars (the earliest dating from 1898), perfectly maintained in working order, including the 1908 Renault limousine used by Presidents Poincaré and Millerand; there are also road documents from the early days of motoring, old Michelin maps and guides from before 1914.

Lac de VASSIVIÈRE

Michelin map 72 folds 19, 20 or 239 fold 15

The lake covers 970ha/2 397 acres, behind the Vassivière dam over the river Maulde. It is set in dark green hills and the site of many regular sporting and cultural events (sailing, motorcycle endurance trials, Tour de France bicycle race, contemporary art exhibits and more).

The lakeside road *(route circumlacustre)* goes around the 45km/28mi shoreline, offering beaches and coves for swimmers, fishing enthusiasts, sailors, and many footpaths for avid ramblers *(see Practical information for details)*.

★★Centre d'art contemporain ☉ – In 1991, a graceful new building (visible from the dam) rose up on the island in the middle of the lake, a centre for contemporary art which has since gained an international reputation.

Take the lakeside road southward, towards Beaumont-du-Lac. The road goes around Vassivière Island and the smaller Île aux Serpents. After 4km/2mi, turn left towards Pierefitte and park the car in the lot. Take the little train or cross the bridge on foot to reach the island. **Boat tours** ☉ *are also available.*

The **views★** from the bridge are wide open on the water and surrounding hills.

Île de Vassivière

The path from the bridge leads to "the castle", once the home of Mme de Vassivière, who owned most of the land which was submerged when the lake was created to supply hydro-electric power. Now the tourist centre and temporary exhibits have taken the place of footmen and chambermaids. Beyond, stands the art musuem, and the surrounding woodland is home to the scultpure park, botany trails, a deer park and a farm with animals.

The distinctive structure housing the collection was designed by the Italian architect Aldo Rossi, in cooperation with French architect Xavier Fabre. The design inspires an image of a ship (**galerie**) flanked by a lighthouse (**phare**) 27m/89ft tall, and is well-integrated in the landscape, pointing its prow up the hillside as though into a wave. The red brick, grey granite, and green paint on the metallic parts of the structure also bring it into harmony with the environment.

Inside the lighthouse, a spiral stair leads past a monumental sculpture to the viewing platform above. From here, the visitor can appreciate the length and breadth of the gallery (80m/262ft by 10m/33ft). Inside the long gallery, wooden beams on a high, keel-shaped ceiling again recall the nautical theme.

Contemporary artists, both French and foreign, are often invited to exhibit their works in the musuem and the **sculpture park** ⟳. Along the path laid out for exploration of this outdoor extension of the musuem are works by David Nash (*Descending Vessel*, hollowed out of a standing tree), Kimio Tsuchiya *(Ever, Eternity)*, Dominique Bailly *(Sans Titre)* and Jean-Pierre Uhlen *(Steinland)*. Beyond the artistic interest of the promenade, the woodland walk is enjoyable and offers views over the lake and forest. There is also a good view from the cafeteria in the musuem, ground floor.

AROUND THE CAMPFIRE

Vassivière attracts nature lovers as well as fans of contemporary art. There is a wide range of accommodation available, from a patch of shade for pitching your tent through *hameaux de gîtes* – little villages of three to eight houses, modern or traditional. Water sports and rambling are popular, of course, and many activities and events are organised in season. In August, tellers of tall tales arrive for the *Festival du Conte*. Legends come to life in the deep woods or around the traditional bread oven. If your idea of a holiday includes trout fishing, blueberry picking, silent starry nights, and the crackle of the campfire, consider a stop in this remote corner of Limousin. *See Practical information for details.*

Ruines de VENTADOUR

Michelin map 75 fold 10 or 239 fold 28 (7km/13mi southeast of Égletons)

On a rocky spur high above the Luzège gorges, the ruins of Ventadour castle rise in an untamed natural site★.

Bernard de Ventadour – Ventadour was a literary hotbed in the 12C. Generations of lords and ladies composed poetry there. In this rarefied atmosphere, Bernard was born (1125), son of a castle servant. As a youth, he revealed an extraordinary talent for versifying, and became a tender and passionate bard of courtly love. The viscountess willingly lent her ear to the clever young man's ardent words. Indeed, her jealous husband had the handsome but humble bard sent packing, and thereafter kept a close eye on his lady.

Bernard de Ventadour was welcomed into the household of Eleanor of Aquitaine, duchess of Normandy, then married to Henry II Plantagenet. Eleanor, credited as an inspiration for the ideals of courtly love, liked Bernard's verses so well that when she became queen of England, she took him with her court to London. Later, Bernard followed her to Poitiers, and when the Queen was carried back to England as a prisoner of her husband, Bernard retired to the home of the count of Niort for the next ten years. Drawn to the monastic life, the ageing poet returned to his homeland and the Abbey at Dalon, near Hautefort château *(see Château de HAUTEFORT)*. There he met another famous troubadour, Bernard de Born, and passed away at the end of the century.

The fortress – Its location and formidable defences made Ventadour seem impregnable. But the stronghold was vulnerable on one point – treason – and for 13 years was held by the English as the Hundred Years War raged. During the Renaissance period, the viscounts left the cold fortress for the cosier rooms of an elegant manor in Ussel *(see USSEL)*. Speaking with pride of his castle, the duke of Ventadour told Louis XIV: "All the straw in the kingdom would not be enough to fill the moats of Ventadour".

TOUR

Around the ruins – The ruins can be admired from the narrow road leading out of Moustier-Ventadour.
To reach the ruins, take the footpath, 30min round trip.

Two tours, high walls, old inner courtyards, vestiges of the main building and a barbican give an idea of what the medieval fortress must have been like. From the platform on the southern side, there is a dizzying **view** over ravines of the Luzège valley.

Tour des fossés – *A tour of 7km/43mi starting from the base of the castle; continue turning to the right as you go along.*
Take the access road which turns into a narrow, but paved lane and dips sharply (hairpin curves) down into the *fossés* (natural moats) surrounding Ventadour castle. Half-way down, the road passes by the lowest part of the ruins, before leading to N 961. From that road, admire the picturesque **views**★ of the ruins and the bends in the river Luzège.

Vallée de la VÉZÈRE★★

Michelin map 75 folds 7 and 8 and 16 and 17
or 239 folds 25 and 26 and 235 folds 1, 2 and 5

This valley, classified as part of the world's heritage by UNESCO, is a tourist route remarkable both for the beauty of the countryside it passes through and for its fascinating prehistoric sites, particularly around Montignac and Les Eyzies-de-Tayac, a region inhabited for approximately the past 100 000 years *(see Introduction, Prehistory)*.

THE UPPER VALLEY *125km/78mi – about 5hr*

The Vézère begins its upper course on the Millevaches Plateau, northwest of Meymac, its rocky bed twisting through the granite hills and heather of this corner of Limousin. Most of the river's length is now tamed and controlled by dams; two broad lakes spread out from the dams at Monceaux-la-Virole and Treignac, bottle-necks in the water course where cascades once fell. Upstream from Saillant, the railway alone follows the path of the gorges dug out by the Vézère between Uzerche and the Brive basin, yet there are some nice **views** of the upper valley from the towns settled along the riverside.

Bugeat – Near the source of the river, this sizeable town sits between the Millevaches plateau and the Monédières hills. The Gallo-Roman vestiges reveal that people have lived here for a long time, despite the rugged climate. The proximity of the forest and rivers make Bugeat a centre for sports and recreation.

Leave Bugeat on D 979 towards Treignac.

Barrage de Monceaux-la-Virole – The first of the dams on the Vézère straddles Lake Viam, where waterfalls once tumbled down. The view reveals the contrasts of the surrounding landscape.

Return to the spot where the road crosses D 160 and take that road to the left.

Lac des Bariousse – The road goes along the shoreline of this lake and provides a lovely drive. The wooded site (chestnuts, oaks and evergreens) is the setting for a recreation centre.

Treignac – This town fits snugly between the river and the hills, picturesque for its Gothic bridge over the rapidly flowing water, the ruined castle, slate-roofed church and the 15C granite market place in the upper town. There is a nice waymarked ramble *(45min round trip – the path starts at the southwestern end of town)* up to the Rocher des Folles – "Crazy Women's Rock"!

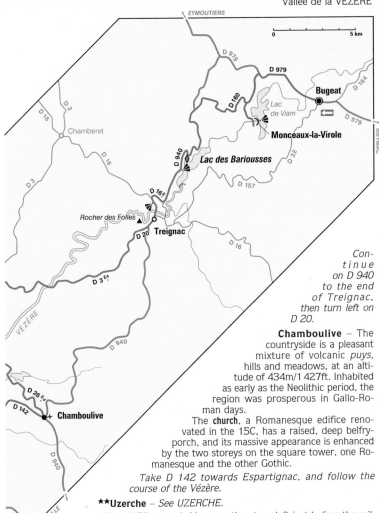

Vallée de la VÉZÈRE

EYMOUTIERS

0   5 km

D 979

D 979

Bugeat

D 164

D 160

Lac
de Viam

Monceaux-la-Virole

MEYMAC

Chamberet

D 16

D 3

D 16

D 940

Lac des Bariousses

D 32

D 157

D 16 E

Rocher des Folles

Treignac

D 20

D 16

D 3 E4

VÉZÈRE

D 940

D 26 E4

D 142

Chamboulive

D 940

TULLE

*Con-
tinue
on D 940
to the end
of Treignac,
then turn left on
D 20.*

Chamboulive – The
countryside is a pleasant
mixture of volcanic *puys*,
hills and meadows, at an altitude of 434m/1 427ft. Inhabited
as early as the Neolithic period, the
region was prosperous in Gallo-Roman days.
    The **church**, a Romanesque edifice reno-
vated in the 15C, has a raised, deep belfry-
porch, and its massive appearance is enhanced
by the two storeys on the square tower, one Romanesque and the other Gothic.
    *Take D 142 towards Espartignac, and follow the
course of the Vézère.*

★★**Uzerche** – *See UZERCHE.*
    *Take N 20 towards Limoges, then turn left just before the rail-
way bridge.*

    Cascades de Bialet – A footpath starts at the wooden bridge across
the stream; other wooden bridges criss-cross the water which froths
and tumbles its way down to the Vézère.
Continue on the road to Baby, which goes down to the river's level.

Vigeois – An abbey was founded in the 6C; time an again it was ruined in wars
until it was finally abolished in the wake of the French Revolution. The present
church dates from the 12C, although it has been much restored and renovated. A
street leads down to the **old bridge**, also 12C, which runs a quiet course here.
Nearby, the **Poncharal Lake** and recreation centre is spacious and welcoming.

★**Site de la Roche** – A pretty little road leads to the edge of a precipice overlooking
the Vézère gorges. To the right, a rocky trail under the chestnut trees leads to an
orientation table (391m/1 283ft) which is well situated.
The view extends over the wooded **gorges du Saillant** in the foreground, and farther
out to the village of St-Robert.
To the left, a path leads to the **panorama**, where there is another spectacular view
over the gorges.
Return to D 9.

Allassac – The distinctive houses of this town are built in black schist and roofed
with slate; some have red sandstone corner pieces (rue L.-Boucharel).
The **church**, commemorating the beheading of John the Baptist, is also built of black
schist, except for the lovely **southern door★**, where various colours of sandstone are
set in contrast. The nearby Caesar's Tower (30m/98ft) is all that remains of the
old Medieval fortifications.
Before the First World War, the processing of slate for roofing brought prosperity
to Allassac and Donzenac, as thatched roofs were replaced in the countryside all
around. The last slate quarry closed in 1982.

Leave Allassac travelling northeast on D 134.

Le Saillant – This hamlet is on a pleasant site at the mouth of the gorges. From the **old bridge** spanning the river, admire the Lasteyrie du Saillant manor, where the revolutionary orator Mirabeau (brother of the Marquis du Saillant) regularly came to visit.

Continue on D 134.

Vertougit – This charming village is beautifully located – overlooking the **gorges de la Vézère** and just across from the Site de la Roche. It is a good place to stop and stretch your legs, admire the typical houses, the orchards and vineyards, or study the view from the orientation table.

Take D 3.

Voutezac – Built into the hillside, this agreeable village has a fortified church with a 15C square tower. At the corner of the street leading to Objat (wayside cross), there is an ox yoke surrounded by old farm tools.

THE LOWER VALLEY

From Brive to Limeuil *108km/7mi – allow 1 day*

Swollen by the waters of the Corrèze, the Vézère, flowing from the north, suddenly changes course and flows westwards to run through a typically Périgord countryside where willows, poplars and roughly hewn cliffs make up a harmonious landscape.

Brive-la-Gaillarde – *See BRIVE-LA-GAILLARDE.*

Leave Brive westwards.

N 89 crosses the Brive basin, the centre of market gardening and fruit growing, and joins the Vézère near St-Pantaléon.

Between Larche and Terrasson the road leaves the valley on D 60, which climbs onto the plateau.

Chavagnac – At the limit of the limestone plateau of Corrèze and Périgord, this village is dominated by a powerful keep topped with corbels, the remains of a 13C castle. The 12C church has kept its dome.

The picturesque D 63 winds through walnut tree plantations. On the way down to Terrasson, notice slopes thick with vineyards.

Terrasson-la-Villedieu – Terrasson, built beside the Vézère, has old districts stretching in tiers up the side of a hill overlooking the left bank of the river, across from La Villedieu. It is a busy little town with a prosperous trade in truffles and walnuts.

The **church** was built in the upper part of the old town in the 15C and has undergone many bouts of restoration. The single aisle, transept and chancel have pointed vaulting.

From the terrace, on the north side of the church, there is a view of the site of Terrasson: on the left, the slate roofs of the houses of the upper town spill down the hillside to the Vézère, spanned by two bridges; in the distance beyond the part

Terrasson-la-Villedieu – Market on the old bridge

Roulland/IMAGES TOULOUSE

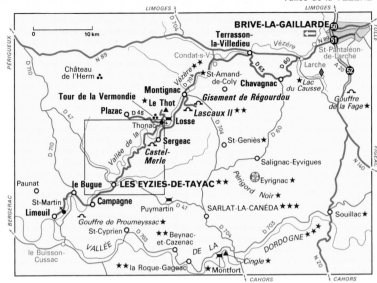

of the town built on the right bank is the Périgord countryside with its characteristic lines of poplars, walnut plantations and rich arable land, slowly making
room for houses.
The old bridge, Pont Vieux, was built in the 12C and is complete with cutwaters.
Between Terrasson-la-Villedieu and Condat, the road follows the valley floor before
crossing to the right bank of the river. 3km/mi after Condat, the river cuts through
wooded slopes.

Montignac – *See PÉRIGORD NOIR.*

★★**Lascaux II; Régourdou** – *See Grotte de LASCAUX.*

From Montignac to Les Eyzies the road closely follows the course of the river, which
is lined with magnificent poplars. This is the most attractive part of the valley.
From D 65, shortly after Montignac, the elegant outline of the Château de Losse
can be seen towering above the Vézère between the trees.

Château de Losse ⊘ – This elegant 16C building set amid greenery is perched
high on a rock above the right bank of the river Vézère. A terrace adorned with
a balustrade, supported by a fine basket-handled arch, projects in front of the main
building, which is flanked by a round tower at one corner. Inside, there are splendid
furnishings (16C Italian cupboards and coffers, Louis XIII furniture) and in particular **tapestries**. Note the fresh colours of the Flemish tapestry in the tower room
and the Florentine tapestry depicting the Return of the Courtesan in the main
chamber; both are 17C.

Sergeac – This village is pleasantly situated beside the Vézère at a spot where tall
cliffs follow the line of the valley.
The village of Sergeac, which has an interesting and delicately carved 15C cross
standing at its entrance, also contains old houses roofed with *lauzes* and a turreted manor-house, the remains of a commandery, which once belonged to the
Order of St John of Jerusalem. The restored Romanesque **church**, despite its porch
of fine ochre-coloured stone and recessed arches, still retains a fortified appearance with its loopholes, machicolations and belltower. A rounded triumphal arch
supported by twinned columns opens onto the chancel, which has a flat east end,
and is adorned with carved capitals.

Castel-Merle – This site, which is well-known to the specialists, was for a long
time closed to the public. Some of the finds – bones, flints, head-dresses –
discovered are exhibited in the museums of Les Eyzies, Périgueux and St-Germain-
en-Laye *(west of Paris)*.
Near the site, a small local **museum** ⊘ exhibits a number of interesting artefacts
from the Mousterian Age to the Gallo-Roman era. Note the handsome necklaces,
found during the excavations, made of stone and bone beads, teeth and shells.
Several shelters **(abris)** ⊘ can be visited, one of which contains wall sculptures (bison,
horses) from the Magdalenian Age. In the Souquette shelter a section of strata is
shown with the different levels from the Aurignacian Age to the modern era.
The so-called Fort of the English, upstream, is a fine shelter under rock, rearranged
in the Middle Ages, entered by a staircase carved into the rock. This is an astounding
example of a troglodyte dwelling with living quarters and stables. Its location enabled
its inhabitants, who occupied it during troubled times, to watch the Vézère.

★Le Thot – *See Le THOT.*

Thonac – In the church there is an emotive **Virgin in Majesty★**, made locally from polychrome wood.

Tour de la Vermondie – This curious leaning tower, which, it is said, was demolished by the Saracens in 732, stands near a 15C manor-house on a hillside overlooking the Vézère. A delightful legend tells how, long ago, a young prince was held prisoner in the tower; every day his fiancée passed below; moved by the young people's misfortune, the tower leaned so low one day that the lovers were able to exchange kisses.

Plazac – The Romanesque church, in the centre of a churchyard planted with cypress trees, stands on a hillock overlooking the village. The 12C belfry-keep is roofed with *lauzes* and embellished with blind arcades resting on Lombard bands.
Return to Thonac. For this section of the itinerary between Thonac and Les Eyzies-de-Tayac see local map and text under Les EYZIES-DE-TAYAC.

After Thonac, the road gives a succession of very pleasant views of typical Périgord landscapes: a background of meadows, a line of poplars or willows mirrored in smooth waters and tall, eroded white and grey cliffs, scattered with scrub and evergreen oaks. These caves, in some cases hanging over the road, served as shelters for prehistoric man. Such scenery is often to be found south of St-Léon-sur-Vézère, as for instance at St-Christopher's Rock, at Rusac and near Les-Eyzies-de-Tayac, with castles and manor-houses adding a touch of elegance.

★St-Léon-sur-Vézère – *See ST-LÉON-SUR-VÉZÈRE.*

★La Roque St-Christophe – *See Les-EYZIES-DE-TAYAC: Sights: Along the Vézère river.*

Le Moustier – *See Les-EYZIES-DE-TAYAC: Sights: Along the Vézère river.*

Tursac – *See Les-EYZIES-DE-TAYAC: Sights: Along the Vézère river.*

★★Les Eyzies-de-Tayac – *See Les-EYZIES-DE-TAYAC.*

Beyond Les Eyzies, the valley widens, the slopes become more gentle, and crops interspersed with plantations of walnut trees become more widespread.

Campagne – *See Le BUGUE*

Le Bugue – *See Le BUGUE*

The D 703 in the direction of Bergerac and D 31 towards Trémolat lead to the delightful country chapel, **Chapelle St-Martin,** *built at the end of the 12C.*

Limeuil – *See Vallée de la DORDOGNE*

VIC

Michelin map 68 fold 19 or 239 fold 41 (8 km/5mi northwest of La Châtre)
Local map see La CHÂTRE

This village was built along the Roman road, thus its Latin name *Vicus* meaning village; it contains a small Romanesque church with interesting frescoes.

Église St-Martin – The church was presented by the bishop of Bourges to the monks of Déols Abbey at the end of the 11C. It was decorated with frescoes the following century. The paintings were brought to light in 1849.

The **frescoes★** adorn both sides of a wall that divides the chancel from the nave, as well as the walls of the chancel itself and the wall and vaulting of the apse. Redemption is shown as the main theme throughout the life of Christ from birth to death. Six colours are used in the paintings: carmine, red-ochre, yellow-ochre, ceruse white, black and grey-blue. Though the faces lack expression, the composition is so skilled, the movement of the figures so

Vic – Fresco in the apse

Arthaud/PIX

alive and the detail so accurate, these paintings form a group whose technique was later copied in the pictorial and sculptural art of Limousin and the southwest. Note on the wall facing the main door, Christ in Majesty with the Lamb of God in a medallion; on the right, a Descent from the Cross (representations of the sun and moon); on the vaulting of the apse, the four Evangelists and a Christ in Majesty; on the north wall of the chancel, the Washing of the Feet, Judas' Kiss, Simon Carrying the Cross and episodes in the life of St-Martin; on the south wall, Jesus entering Jerusalem; facing the altar, the Last Supper.

VIERZON

Population 32 235
Michelin map 64 fold 19, 20 or 238 fold 17

Vierzon came to be in 1937, as four local administrative districts were joined (Vierzon-Ville, Village, Bourneuf, Forges). Its location is strategic, at the confluence of the rivers Yèvre and Cher, the intersection of highways, and the railway junction for the Paris-Toulouse and Nantes-Lyon lines; it is the gateway between the Champagne Berrichonne region and Sologne (whose forests begin just northwest of town).

Industrial heritage – The comte d'Artois, brother of Louis XVI opened a forge in Vierzon in 1779, and in short order a number of industries began work, in particular ceramics and later, mechanical construction.

The first porcelain manufactory went into operation in 1816. At the turn of the century, there were a dozen such enterprises in town, making it second only to Limoges (it is still the biggest manufacturer of porcelain in Berry). The second field of production began in the mid-19C with the establishment of the "Société française de matériel agricole" (making farm machinery, today the company is called La Case-Poclain). The first mobile threshing machine in France was made there. Other companies included Brouhot (1860 – they went so far as to build automobiles) and Merlin (1879). This period is recalled by the iron architecture of the Grand Magasin de la Société française, and by the presence of the canal, created in 1835 to link Vierzon to Montluçon. No traffic troubles its waters today, but strollers enjoy walking beneath the poplars on its banks.

Old town – This pedestrian area has been artfully developed around the winding streets and old, half-timbered houses up against a slope watched over by a Gothic **belfry**, formerly the gate to the city.

Notre Dame church (B), built in the 12C, enlarged and renovated in the 15C (side aisles), is fronted by a belfry-porch and a basket arch above the doorway. Inside, admire the restored barrel-vaulting and the Renaissance windows representing the Crucifixion (south wall of the Ste-Perpétue chapel). The stone marked with a seal at the entrance to the chancel bears a long inscription in Gothic letters, noting the date of the church's foundation, 1409. In the transept, a painting by Jean Boucher depicts John the Baptist.

To the left of the church, a stairway leads to a garden which is a good place from which to look at the building.

Square Lucien-Beaufrère (B) – This garden, designed in 1929 in the Art Deco style, replaced an abbey whose remaining buildings are now attached to the town hall. At the entrance, the 1935 Auditorium, by Albert Collet, and, from the same period, a monument to fallen heroes embellished with bas-reliefs representing the trades practised in Vierzon. From the banks of the Yèvre, a pretty view over the old town.

CHAMPAGNE BERRICHONNE *75km/46.5mi – 2hr*

Leave Vierzon by ④ on the map, then take D 27.

Brinay – This village is tranquil on the banks of the Cher upstream from Vierzon. The Romanesque church is worth visiting for its 12C **frescoes★**.

Take D 18ᴱ towards Méreau.

Massay – The **church**, rebuilt between the 14C and the 16C, was once part of a Benedictine abbey founded in the 8C. Destroyed during the Hundred Years War and the Wars of Religion, it became the parish church in the 18C, replacing its dilapidated predecessor of the same name. The vestiges of the abbey which remain include the chapterhouse, parts of the dormitory (13C), cellars (12C) and the tithing barns. The 12C abbot's Chapel (also known as St-Loup) is well preserved; it stood in the centre of the cloisters. The abbot's lodging dates from the 17C.

Leave the village travelling southwest, towards Châteauroux.

Vatan – The **église St-Laurian**, restored, has a 16C chancel with windows from the same period, recounting the life of the saint. There are some interesting 8C paintings and sculpted door leaves dated 1498.

VIERZON

Brunet (R. A.)	B	Ponts (R. des)	B	Caucherie (R. de la)	A 4
Foch (Pl. du Mar.)	B 7	République (Av. de la)	A 16	Dr-P.-Roux (R. du)	B 6
Joffre (R. du Mar.)	B 12	Voltaire (R.)	B 20	Gaulle (R. Gén.-de)	A 19
Péri (Pl. Gabriel)	A 15			Larchevêque (R. M.)	A 10
		Baron (R. Bl.)	A 2	Nation (Bd de la)	A 13
		Briand (Pl. Aristide)	B 3	Roosevelt (R. Th.)	B 18
				11 Novembre 1918 (R. du)..	A 22

North of town, take D 922.

Graçay – This medieval town has kept its ramparts and a few old houses.

St-Outrille – Separated from Graçay by the river Pozon, this village has an interesting **collegiate church**. Romanesque and Gothic styles are both present: the nave is 15C, the chancel, side chapels (except one) and the transept from the 12C. The east end (note the intertwining pattern on the pilasters of the blind vaulting) is surmounted by a curious twisted bell tower covered with shingles. In the chancel, the capitals have a simple design of acanthus leaves, and sit atop slightly curved monolithic columns. The western doorway dates from the 14C.

Leave the village travelling east on D 68.

Nohant-en-Graçay – Inside the charming **église St-Martin**, the columns supporting the vaulting of the central tower bear remarkable 12C capitals. The unusual bell tower with its spiral spire is similar to the one in St-Outrille.

Genouilly – At the far end of town stands the **église St-Symphorien**. This 12C edifice, with a handsome porch, has stained-glass windows made in 1536. The chancel is covered by a 13C vault, exceptional in Berry because it is in the *angevin* style typical of the region of Anjou. The slender columns support Romanesque capitals of acanthus leaves, interlacing patterns, foliated scrolls, faces and animals. On the capital of the pillar to the right, at the entrance to the chancel, there is an acrobat standing on his hands, accompanied by two imaginary animals who hold his feet. In the southern chapel, the mausoleum of the La Châtre family is from the turn of the 16-17C.

Return to Vierzon on D 19 and D 90.

World Heritage List

In 1972, The United Nations Educational, Scientific and Cultural Organization (UNESCO) adopted a Convention for the preservation of cultural and natural sites "of outstanding universal value". To date, more than 150 States Parties have signed this international agreement, which has listed over 500 sites "of outstanding universal value" on the World Heritage List. Each year, a committee of representatives from 21 countries, assisted by technical organizations (ICOMOS – International Council on Monuments and Sites; IUCN-International Union for Conservation of Nature and Natural Resources; ICCROM – International Centre for the Study of the Preservation and Restoration of Cultural Property, the Rome Centre), evaluates the proposals for new sites to be included on the list, which grows longer as new nominations are accepted and more countries sign the Convention. To be considered, a site must be nominated by the country in which it is located.

The protected cultural heritage may be monuments (buildings, sculptures, archaeological structures, etc.) with unique historical, artistic or scientific features, groups of buildings (such as religious communities, ancient cities); or sites (human settlements, examples of exceptional landscapes, cultural landscapes) which are the combined works of man and nature of exceptional beauty. Natural sites may be a testimony to the stages of the earth's geological history or to the development of human cultures and creative genius or represent significant ongoing ecological processes, contain superlative natural phenomena or provide a habitat for threatened species.

Signatories of the Convention pledge to co-operate to preserve and protect these sites around the world as a common heritage to be shared by all humanity.

Some of the most well-known places which the World Heritage Committee has inscribed include: Australia's Great Barrier Reef (1981), the Canadian Rocky Mountain Parks (1984), The Great Wall of China (1987), the Statue of Liberty (1984), the Kremlin (1990), Mont-Saint-Michel and its Bay (France – 1979), Durham Castle and Cathedral (1986).

UNESCO World Heritage sites included in this guide are:

The Decorated Grottoes of the Vézère Valley (Vallée de la VÉZÈRE)
Bourges Cathedral (Cathédrale de BOURGES)

Down the River Lot by canoe

Practical
information

Planning your trip

Climate and seasons

This inland region is open to oceanic influences from the Atlantic. The climate on the whole is mild, winter frosts are limited, spring is early and warm and summer is hot. Rainfall is evenly distributed throughout the year. In Berry, however, several "micro-climates" make for small, distinct weather systems within the region. For example, the Champagne Berrichonne, with its vast fields of grain crops, is often dry and gets very hot in the summer, while the humidity keeps things cooler in the Boischaut, the Brenne wetlands and the high forests of the Motte d'Humbligny.

The climate in Limousin is also variable, in particular with regard to altitude. The prevailing southwest winds blow hard against the foothills of the Massif Central mountain range, provoking significant rainfall (1200-1700mm/47-67in per year) – although summer droughts are not unusual. Winter on the high plateaux (Millevaches, Gentioux, Monédières, Combraille) is long and harsh, with low temperatures and chill, stiff winds. Elsewhere in the region, winters are milder, with less rain, but crops are often damaged by freezing temperatures in the spring and fall.

The Dordogne is more clement on the whole, beginning with the Brive basin. While the climate is nearly Mediterranean, there is enough water to keep the landscape green and crops prosperous throughout the summer. In that season, rain often falls in torrential storms, in the wake of a hot wind blowing steadily from the west. In the winter, snow is infrequent; frosty nights and foggy mornings come with the spring. A blanket of flowers soon covers the countryside, as the region quickly warms to the new season. The summer holidays bring many tourists to enjoy the delights of the beautiful natural settings, towns and monuments and the many festivals and activities organised for visitors. Autumn is quieter and a lovely time to appreciate the flowering heather, the browns and golds of the changing leaves, the colourful markets with an abundance of harvest produce, or the delights of wild mushrooms served with game from the forest.

French Tourist Offices

For information, brochures, maps and assistance in planning a trip to France travellers should apply to the official tourist office in their own country:

Australia – New Zealand

Sydney – BNP Building, 12 Castlereagh Street
Sydney, New South Wales 2000
☎ (61) 2 231 52 44 – Fax: (61) 2 221 86 82.

Canada

Montreal – 1981 Ave McGill College, Suite 490
Montreal, PQ H3A 2W9
☎ (514) 288-4264 – Fax: (514) 845 48 68.

Summer in Dordogne

J. P. Clabarn/MICHELIN

Eire

Dublin – 10 Suffolk Street, Dublin 2.
☎ 00353 1 679 0813 – Fax: 00353 1 679 0814.

United Kingdom

London – 178 Piccadilly, London WIV OAL.
☎ (0891) 244 123 – Fax: (0171) 493 6594.

United States

For general information ☎ 202-659-7779
or Internet: www.francetourism.com

East Coast: New York – 444 Madison Avenue
NY 10022. ☎ 212-838-7800 – Fax: (212) 838 7855.

Mid West: Chicago – 676 North Michigan Avenue, Suite 3360
Chicago, IL 60611
☎ (312) 751 7800 – Fax: (312) 337 6339.

West Coast: Los Angeles – 9454 Wilshire Boulevard, Suite 715
Beverly Hills, CA 90212.
☎ (310) 271 2693 – Fax: (310) 276 2835.

Cyberspace

http://www.info.france-usa.org

The French Embassy's Web site provides basic information (geography, demographics, history), a news digest and business-related information. It offers special pages for children, and pages devoted to culture, language study and travel, and you can reach other selected French sites (regions, cities, ministries) with a hypertext link.

Other sites include: www.franceguide.com (UK);
www.visiteurope.com (European Travel Commission)
www.fr-holidaystore.co.uk (French Tourist Office)

Local tourist offices

In addition to the French tourist offices abroad listed above, visitors may wish to contact local offices for more precise information, to receive brochures and maps. Below, the addresses are given for each local tourist office by *département*. The index lists the *département* after each town; the *Introduction* at the beginning of this guide also gives information on the administrative divisions of France.

Address inquires to the
*Comité départemental de tourisme
(C.D.T.):*

Tourist Offices

Cher

5, rue de Séraucourt
18000 BOURGES
☎ 02 48 67 00 18
Fax: 02 48 67 01 44

Corrèze

Maison du tourisme
Quai Baluze, 19000 Tulle
☎ 05 55 29 98 78
Fax: 05 55 29 98 79

Creuse

43, place Bonnyaud
23000 Guéret
☎ 05 55 51 93 23
Fax: 05 55 51 05 20

Dordogne

25, rue du Président Wilson
24000 Périgueux
☎ 05 53 35 50 24
Fax: 05 53 06 30 94

Haute-Vienne

Maison du Tourisme
4, place Denis-Dussoubs, 87000 Limoges
☎ 05 55 79 04 04
Fax: 05 55 79 57 81

Indre

1, rue Saint-Martin
BP 141, 36003 Châteauroux Cedex
☎ 02 54 22 91 20
Fax: 02 54 22 31 21

Lot

107, quai Eugène-Cavaignac
46000 Cahors
☎ 05 65 35 07 09
Fax: 05 65 23 92 76

Further information can be obtained from
the *Syndicats d'Initiative*, as the tourist offices in most large towns are called. The addresses and telephone numbers are listed after the symbol 🗓, in the *Admission times and charges* following.

Travellers with special needs – The sights described in this guide which are easily accessible to people of reduced mobility are indicated in the *Admission times and charges* by the symbol ♿.
Useful information on transportation, holidaymaking and sports associations for the disabled is available from the *Comité National Français de Liaison pour la Réadaptation des Handicapés* (CNRH), 236 bis, rue de Tolbiac, 75013 Paris. Call their international information number ☎ 01 53 80 66 44, or write to request a catalogue of

publications. Web-surfers can find information for slow walkers, mature travellers and others with special needs at www.access-able.com. If you are a member of a sports club and would like to practice your sport in France, or meet others who do, ask the CNRH (236bis rue de Tolbiac, 75013 Paris) for information on clubs in the *Fédération Française du Sport Adapté* (FFSA – ☎ Paris 01 48 72 80 72). For information on museum access for the disabled contact *La Direction, Les Musées de France, Service Accueil des Publics Spécifiques*, 6 rue des Pyramides, 75041 Paris Cedex 1. ☎ Paris 01 40 15 35 88.

The **Michelin Red Guide France** and the **Michelin Camping Caravaning France** indicate hotels and campsites with facilities suitable for physically handicapped people.

Formalities

Passport – Visitors entering France must be in possession of a valid national passport (or in the case of British nationals, a Visitor's Passport). In case of loss or theft report to the embassy or consulate and the local police.

Visa – No entry visa is required for Canadian and US citizens staying less than 3 months; it is required of Australian citizens in accordance with French security measures. If you need a visa, apply to the French Consulate (visa issued same day; longer if submitted by mail).

US citizens should obtain the booklet *Safe Trip Abroad* ($ 1.25) which provides useful information on visa requirements, customs regulations, medical care etc for international travellers. Order by phone (Government Printing Office, ☎ 1 202 512 1800) or consult on Internet at www.access.gpo.gov. Passport information is available at ☎ 800 688 9889; download applications from http://travel.state.gov.

Customs – Apply to the Customs Office in your country for a leaflet on customs regulations and the full range of duty-free allowances. The US Customs Service www.customs.ustreas.gov offers a publication *Know Before You Go* for US citizens. There are no customs formalities for holiday-makers bringing their caravans or pleasure boats into France for a stay of less than 6 months.

Americans can bring home, tax-free, up to US$400 worth of goods; Canadians up to CND$300; Australians up to AUS$400 and New Zealanders up to NZ$700. Persons living in a Member state of the European Union are not restricted in regard to purchasing goods for private use, but the recommended allowances for alcoholic beverages and tobacco are as follows:

Spirits (whisky, gin, vodka, etc) .... 10 litres	Cigarettes.................... 800
Fortified wines (vermouth, ports, etc).............. 20 litres	Cigarillos 400
Wine .... 90 litres (not more than 60 sparkling)	Cigars 200
Beer... 110 litres	Smoking tobacco......... 1 kg

Embassies and Consulates

Australia	Embassy	4 avenue Jean-Rey, 75015 Paris, ☎ 01 40 59 33 00, Fax: 01 40 59 33 10.
Canada	Embassy	35 avenue Montaigne, 75008 Paris, ☎ 01 44 43 29 00, Fax: 01 44 43 29 99.
Eire	Embassy	4 rue Rude, 75016 Paris, ☎ 01 44 17 67 00, Fax: 01 45 00 84 17.
New Zealand	Embassy	7 ter rue Léonard-de-Vinci, 75016 Paris, ☎ 01 45 00 24 11, Fax: 01 45 26 39.
UK	Embassy	35 rue du Faubourg St-Honoré, 75008 Paris, ☎ 01 42 66 91 42, Fax: 01 42 66 95 90.
	Consulate	16 rue d'Anjou, 75008 Paris, ☎ 01 42 66 06 68 (visas).
USA	Embassy	2 avenue Gabriel, 75008 Paris, ☎ 01 43 12 22 22, Fax: 01 42 66 97 83
	Consulate	2 rue St-Florentin, 75001 Paris ☎ 01 42 96 14 88.

Getting there

By air – Choose between scheduled flights on national airlines (Air France, TAT) or commercial and package-tour flights with rail or coach link-ups or Fly-Drive schemes. Contact airlines and travel agents for information. There are daily flights from Paris Orly to Périgueux and Bergerac (Air Littoral) and Brive (TAT); private planes can land at the Bourges airfield; the airfield outside Limoges is Limoges-Bellegarde.

By rail – French Railways (SNCF) and British companies operate a daily service via the Channel Tunnel on Eurostar taking 3 hours between London (Waterloo International Station, ☎ 0345 881 881) and Paris (Gare du Nord).

The French National Railway (SNCF) operates an extensive network of lines including many high speed passenger trains (TGV) and rail services throughout France. The main connecting stations from Paris (Gare d'Austerlitz) to the region are Bourges, Limoges, Brive and Cahors. There are connections for Périgueux in Bordeaux and Angoulême (TGV from Gare Montparnasse + express train). The Paris-Rodez line provides service to Martel, Rocamadour, Gramat, Figeac and Capdenac.

Rail passes offering unlimited travel, and group travel tickets offering savings for parties are available under certain conditions. **Eurailpass, Flexipass** and **Saver Pass** are options available in the US for travel in Europe and must be purchased in the US – ☎ 1 800 4 EURAIL or write Rail Europe, 2100 Central Avenue, Boulder, CO 80301. Consult Internet www.eurail.on.com, or your travel agent.

In the UK, information and bookings can be obtained from French Railways, 179 Piccadilly, London W1V 0BA, ☎ 0891 515 477, in main line stations, or from travel agencies.

The SNCF operates a telephone information, reservation and pre-payment service in English, from 7am to 10pm (French time). In France, call: 08 36 35 35 39. From abroad: 33 8 36 35 35 39. Ask about discount rates if you are over 60, a student, or travelling with your family.

A rail ticket used within France must be validated *(composter)* by using the orange automatic date-stamping machines at the platform entrance.

For information on schedules, consult the SNCF Web site: www.sncf.fr.

Baggage trolleys (10 F coin required – refundable) are available at main line stations.

By coach (bus) – Regular coach services are operated from London to Paris. For further information, contact Eurolines:

London: 52 Grosvenor Gardens, Victoria, London SW1W 0AU. ☎ 0171 730 8235.

Paris: 28 avenue du Général de Gaulle, 93541 Bagnolet. ☎ 01 49 72 51 51.

By sea – There are numerous **cross-Channel services** (passenger and car ferries, hovercraft, SeaCat) from the United Kingdom and Eire. For details contact travel agencies or:

P&O Stena Lines, Channel House, Channel View Road, Dover CT17 9TJ; ☎ 0990 980 980.

Hoverspeed, International Hoverport, Marine Parade, Dover, Kent CT17 9TG; ☎ 01304 240 241.

Brittany Ferries, Millbay Docks, Plymouth, Devon PLl 3ᴱW; ☎ 0990 360360.
The Brittany Centre, Wharf Road, Portsmouth, Hampshire PO2 8RU; ☎ 01705 827 701.

Sally Direct, Ferry Terminal, Ramsgate, Kent CTII 8 RP; ☎ 0845 600 2626, Fax 01843 853 536.

To choose the most suitable route between your point of arrival and your destination, use the **Michelin Motoring Atlas France** or Michelin maps from the 1:200 000 series with yellow covers.

Join us in our constant task of keeping up-to-date.
Please send us your comments and suggestions.

Michelin Travel Publications
38 Clarendon Road
WATFORD – Herts WD1 1SX
Fax: 01923 415250 or
TheGreenGuide-uk@uk.michelin.com

Motoring in France

Documents – Nationals of European Union countries require a valid national **driving licence**; nationals of non-EU countries require an **international driving licence** ($ 10 – obtainable in the US from the American Automobile Club; cost for members US$10, for non-members US$22). For the vehicle it is necessary to have the registration papers (log-book) and a nationality plate of the approved size.

Insurance – Certain UK motoring organisations (AA, RAC) offer accident insurance and breakdown service schemes for members. Members of the American Automobile Club should obtain the brochure *Offices to Serve You Abroad*. Check with your current company in regard to coverage while abroad. If you plan to hire a car using your credit card, check with the company, which may provide liability insurance automatically (and thus save you having to pay the optional fee for optimum coverage).

Highway Code – The minimum driving age is 18 years old. Traffic drives on the right. It is compulsory for the front-seat passengers to wear **seat belts** and it is also compulsory for the back-seat passengers when the car is fitted with them. Children under the age of ten must travel on the back seat of the vehicle. Full or dipped headlights must be switched on in poor visibility and at night; use side-lights only when the vehicle is stationary.

In the case of a **breakdown** a red warning triangle or hazard warning lights are obligatory. Drivers should watch out for unfamiliar road signs and take great care on the road. In built-up areas where no other indications are given, vehicles joining the road from the right have **right of way**. However, traffic on main roads outside built-up areas (indicated by a yellow diamond sign) and on roundabouts has right of way. Vehicles must stop when the lights turn red at road junctions and may filter to the right only where indicated by an amber arrow.

The regulations on **drinking and driving** (limited to 0.50 g/litre) and **speeding** are strictly enforced – usually by an on-the-spot fine and/or confiscation of the vehicle.

Speed limits – Although liable to modification, these are as follows:
– toll motorways *(péage)* 130kph/80mph (110kph/68mph when raining);
– dual carriageways and motorways without tolls 110kph/68mph (100kph/62mph when raining);
– other roads 90kph/56mph (80kph/50mph when raining) and in towns 50kph/31mph;
– outside lane on motorways during daylight, on level ground and with good visibility – minimum speed limit of 80kph/50mph.

Parking Regulations – In town there are zones where parking is either restricted or subject to a fee; tickets should be obtained from the ticket machines (*horodateurs* – small change necessary) and displayed on the inside of the windscreen on the driver's side; failure to display may result in a heavy fine or even the offending vehicle being towed away. In some towns you may find blue parking zones *(zone bleue)* marked by a blue line on the pavement or road and a blue signpost with a **P** and a small square underneath. In this case you have to display a cardboard disc with various times indicated on it. This will enable you to stay for 1hr 30min (2hr 30 min over lunch time) free. Discs are available in supermarkets or petrol stations (ask for a *disque de stationnement*); they are sometimes given away free.

Route Planning – For 24-hour road traffic information in France: dial 01 56 96 33 33 or consult Minitel 3615 Code Route (1.29F/min).

www.michelin-travel.com is the Michelin Web page, with a service for plotting an itinerary and finding a hotel or restaurant on the route.

The road network is excellent and includes many motorways. The roads are very busy during the holiday period (particularly weekends in July and August) and to avoid traffic congestion it is advisable to follow the recommended secondary routes (*Bison Futé-itinéraires bis*).

Tolls – In France, most motorway sections are subject to a toll *(péage)*. This can be expensive, especially if you drive south (e.g. Calais to Tours, around 190F for a car). You can pay in cash or with a credit card (Visa, Mastercard).

Car Rental – There are car rental agencies at airports, railway stations and in all large towns throughout France. European cars have manual transmission; automatic cars are available in larger cities only if an advance reservation is made. Drivers must be over 21; between ages 21 and 25, drivers are required to pay an extra daily fee of 50-100F; some companies allow drivers under 23 only if the reservation has been made through a travel agent. It is relatively expensive to hire a car in France; Americans in particular will notice the difference and should make arrangements before leaving, take advantage of Fly-Drive offers, or seek advice from a travel agent, specifying requirements. Central Reservation in France:

Avis: 01 46 10 60 60
Budget: 01 46 86 65 65
Baron's Limousine and Driver 01 45 30 21 21

Europcar: 01 30 43 82 82
Hertz: 01 47 88 51 51

Petrol – In France you will find 4 different types of petrol (US: gas):
super (super leaded)   *sans plomb 98* (super unleaded 98)
sans plomb 95 (super unleaded 95)   *diesel/gazole* (diesel)
Petrol is more expensive in France than in the USA and the UK.

General information

Electricity – The electric current is 220 volts. Circular two pin plugs are the rule. Adapters should be bought before your leave home; they are on sale in most airports.

Medical treatment – First aid, medical advice and chemists' night service rota are available from chemists/drugstores (*pharmacie* identified by the green cross sign).
It is advisable to take out comprehensive insurance cover as the recipient of medical treatment in French hospitals or clinics must pay the bill. Nationals of non-EU countries should check with their insurance companies about policy limitations. Reimbursement can then be negotiated with the insurance company according to the policy held.
All prescription drugs should be clearly labelled; it is recommended that you carry a copy of the prescription. American Express offers its members a service, "Global Assist", for any medical, legal or personal emergency – call collect from anywhere ☎ 01 47 16 25 29.

British and Irish citizens should apply to the Department of Health and Social Security for Form E 111, which entitles the holder to urgent treatment for accident or unexpected illness in EU countries. A refund of part of the cost of treatment can be obtained on application in person or by post to the local Social Security Offices *(Caisse Primaire d'Assurance Maladie)*.

The American Hospital of Paris is open 24hrs for emergencies as well as consultations, with English-speaking staff, at 63 bd. Victor Hugo, 92200 Neuilly sur Seine, ☎ 01 46 41 25 25. Accredited by major insurance companies.

The British Hospital is just outside Paris in Levallois-Perret, 3 rue Barbès, ☎ 01 46 39 22 22.

Tipping – Since a service charge is automatically included in the price of meals and accommodation in France, it is not necessary to tip in restaurants and hotels. However taxi drivers, bellboys, doormen, filling station attendants or anybody who has been of assistance are usually tipped at the customer's discretion. Most French people give an extra tip in restaurants and cafés (at least 50 centimes for a drink and several francs for a meal).

Currency – There are no restrictions on the amount of currency visitors can take into France. Visitors carrying a lot of cash are advised to complete a currency declaration form on arrival, because there are restrictions on currency export.

Coins and notes – *See illustration following.* The unit of currency in France is the French franc (F) subdivided into 100 centimes.

Banks – Banks are open from 9am to noon and 2pm to 4pm and branches are closed either on Monday or Saturday. Banks close early on the day before a bank holiday. A passport is necessary as identification when cashing travellers or ordinary cheques in banks. Commission charges vary and hotels usually charge more than banks for cashing cheques for non-residents. Most banks have **cash dispensers** (ATM) which accept international credit cards (have your PIN number handy). These are easily recognisable by the CB logo. Visa and Mastercard are accepted almost everywhere; American Express cards can only be used in dispensers at 11 rue Scribe (Amex office), and inside the Gare de Lyon and the Gare Montparnasse train stations.

Credit Cards – American Express, Visa, Mastercard- Eurocard and Diners Club are widely accepted in shops, hotels and restaurants and petrol stations. If your card is lost or stolen, call the following 24-hour hotlines:

American Express	01 47 77 72 00	Visa	01 42 77 11 90
Mastercard/Eurocard	01 45 67 84 84	Diners Club	01 47 62 75 00

You must report any loss or theft to the local police who will issue you with a certificate (useful proof to show the credit card company).

Post – Main Post Offices open Monday to Friday 8am to 6pm, Saturday 8am to noon. Smaller branch post offices generally close at lunch time between noon and 2pm and at 4pm.
Postage via air mail:
   UK letter (20 g) 3.00 F
   North America: letter (20 g) 4.40 F
   Australia and NZ: letter (20 g) 5.20F
Stamps are also available from newsagents and *bureaux de tabac*. Stamp collectors should ask for *timbres de collection* in any post office.

News – Dordogne is a very popular destination for British travellers, and several local papers are published in English; the most widely available is *The News*. Two monthly papers are *The New Recorder* and *The South-western*. In the large towns, and in particular in the summer months, British dailies and the *International Herald Tribune* are available.

Conversion tables

Weights and measures

1 kilogram (kg)	2.2 pounds (lb)	2.2 pounds
1 metric ton (tn)	1.1 tons	1.1 tons

to convert kilograms to pounds, multiply by 2.2

1 litre (l)	2.1 pints (pt)	1.8 pints
1 litre	0.3 gallon (gal)	0.2 gallon

to convert litres to gallons, multiply by 0.26 (US) or 0.22 (UK)

1 hectare (ha)	2.5 acres	2.5 acres
1 square kilometre (km²)	0.4 square miles (sq mi)	0.4 square miles

to convert hectares to acres, multiply by 2.4

1 centimetre (cm)	0.4 inches (in)	0.4 inches
1 metre (m)	3.3 feet (ft) - 39.4 inches - 1.1 yards (yd)	
1 kilometre (km)	0.6 miles (mi)	0.6 miles

to convert metres to feet, multiply by 3.28. kilometres to miles, multiply by 0.6

Clothing

Women							Men
	35	4	2½	40	7½	7	
	36	5	3½	41	8½	8	
	37	6	4½	42	9½	9	
Shoes	38	7	5½	43	10½	10	Shoes
	39	8	6½	44	11½	11	
	40	9	7½	45	12½	12	
	41	10	8½	46	13½	13	
	36	4	8	46	36	36	
	38	6	10	48	38	38	
Dresses &	40	8	12	50	40	40	Suits
Suits	42	12	14	52	42	42	
	44	14	16	54	44	44	
	46	16	18	56	46	48	
	36	08	30	37	14½	14,5	
	38	10	32	38	15	15	
Blouses &	40	12	14	39	15½	15½	Shirts
sweaters	42	14	36	40	15¾	15¾	
	44	16	38	41	16	16	
	46	18	40	42	16½	16½	

Sizes often vary depending on the designer. These equivalents are given for guidance only.

Speed

kph	10	30	50	70	80	90	100	110	120	130
mph	6	19	31	43	50	56	62	68	75	81

Temperature

Celsius (°C)	0°	5°	10°	15°	20°	25°	30°	40°	60°	80°	100°
Fahrenheit (°F)	32°	41°	50°	59°	68°	77°	86°	104°	140°	176°	212°

To convert Celsius into Fahrenheit, multiply °C by 9, divide by 5, and add 32.
To convert Fahrenheit into Celsius, subtract 32 from °F, multiply by 5, and divide by 9.

Notes and coins

500 Francs featuring
scientists
Pierre and Marie Curie
(1858-1906), (1867-1934)

200 Francs featuring
engineer Gustave Eiffel
(1832-1923)

100 Francs featuring
Post-Impressionist painter
Paul Cézanne
(1839-1906)

50 Francs featuring
pilot and writer
Antoine de Saint-Exupéry
(1900-1944)

20 Francs

10 Francs

5 Francs

2 Francs

1 Franc

50 Centimes

20 Centimes

10 Centimes

5 Centimes

Time – France is one hour ahead of Greenwich Mean Time (GMT).
When it is **noon in France**, it is

        3am in Los Angeles
        6am in New York
        11am in Dublin
        11am in London
        7pm in Perth
        9pm in Sydney
        11pm in Auckland

In France "am" and "pm" are not used but the 24-hour clock is widely applied.

Public holidays – Museums and other monuments may be closed or may vary their hours of admission on the following public holidays:

1 January	New Year's Day *(Jour de l'An)*
	Easter Day and Easter Monday *(Pâques)*
1 May	May Day
8 May	VE Day
	Whit Sunday and Monday *(Pentecôte)*
	Ascension Day *(Ascension)*
14 July	France's National Day (Bastille Day)
15 August	Assumption *(Assomption)*
1 November	All Saint's Day *(Toussaint)*
11 November	Armistice Day
25 December	Christmas Day *(Noël)*

Telephoning

Public Telephones – Most public phones in France use pre-paid phone cards *(télécarte)*. Some telephone booths accept credit cards (Visa, Mastercard/Eurocard: minimum monthly charge 20F). *Télécartes* (50 or 120 units) can be bought in post offices, branches of France Télécom, *bureaux de tabac* (cafés that sell cigarettes) and newsagents and can be used to make calls in France and abroad. Calls can be received at phone boxes where the blue bell sign is shown; the phone will not ring, so keep your eye on the little message screen.

National calls – French telephone numbers have 10 digits. Paris and Paris region numbers begin with 01; 02 in northwest France; 03 in northeast France; 04 in southeast France and Corsica; 05 in southwest France.

International calls – To call France from abroad, dial the country code (33) + 9-digit number (omit the initial 0). When calling abroad from France dial 00, then dial the country code followed by the area code and number of your correspondent.
To use your personal calling card dial:

	AT&T:	0-800 99 00 11
	MCI:	0-800 99 00 19
	Sprint:	0-800 99 00 87
	Canada Direct:	0-800 99 00 16

International Information, US/Canada	00 33 12 11
International operator	00 33 12 + country code
Local directory assistance	12
Toll-free numbers in France begin with	0 800

International dialling codes:

Australia: 61	New Zealand: 64
Canada: 1	United Kingdom: 44
Eire: 353	United States: 1

Emergency numbers: Police: 17
Fire (Pompiers): 18
"SAMU" (Paramedics): 15

Minitel – France Télécom operates a system offering directory enquiries (free of charge up to 3 min), travel and entertainment reservations, and other services (cost varies between 0.37F – 5.57F/min). These small computer-like terminals can be found in some post offices, hotels and France Télécom agencies and in many French homes. **3614 PAGES E** is the code for Directory assistance in English (Turn on the unit, dial 3614, hit the "connexion" button when you get the tone, type in "PAGES E", and follow the instructions on the screen). For route planning, use Michelin services **3615 MICHELIN** (tourist and route information) and **3617 MICHELIN** (information sent by fax).

Cellular phones in France have numbers which begin with 06. Two-watt (lighter, shorter reach) and eight-watt models are on the market, using the Itinéris (France Télécom) or SFR network. "Mobicartes" are pre-paid phone cards that fit into mobile units. Cell phone rentals (delivery or airport pickup provided):

Ellinas Phone Rental	01 47 20 70 00
Euro Exaphone	01 44 09 77 78
Rent a Cell Express	01 53 93 78 00

Accommodation

The Places to Stay map in the Introduction indicates recommended places for overnight stops, spas, winter and seaside resorts; it can be used in conjunction with the **Michelin Red Guide France** which lists a selection of hotels and restaurants.

Loisirs-Accueil is a booking service which has offices in most French *départements*. For information contact Réservation Loisirs Accueil, 280 boulevard St-Germain, 75007 Paris; ☎ 01 44 11 10 44.

The Accueil de France Tourist Offices which are open all year make hotel bookings for a small fee, for personal (non-business) callers only. The head office is in Paris (127 avenue des Champs-Élysée; ☎ 01 49 52 53 54 for information only) and there are offices in many large towns and resorts.

The Logis et Auberges de France brochure (a selection of inns) is available from the French Government Tourist Office.

Relais et Châteaux, 9 avenue Marceau, 75016 Paris ☎ 01 47 42 20 92: Hotel accommodation in châteaux and manor houses around France.

The Maison des Gîtes de France has a list of self-catering (often rural) accommodation where you can stay in this region (and all over France). This usually takes the form of a cottage or apartment decorated in the local style where you will be able to make yourself at home. Gîtes de France have offices in Paris: 59 rue St-Lazare, 75009 Paris, ☎ 01 49 70 75 75.

You must purchase the list (a small guide book with details and ratings) for the area that interests you and make reservations directly through the proprietor.

Bed and Breakfast – Gîtes de France *(see above)* publishes a booklet on bed and breakfast accommodation *(chambres d'hôte)* which includes a room and breakfast at a reasonable price.

You can also contact **Bed & Breakfast (France)**, International Reservations Centre, PO Box 66, Henley-on-Thames, Oxon RG9 1XS. ☎ 01491 578 803 – Fax: 01491 410 806; e-mail: bookings@bedbreak.demon.co.uk.

Youth Hostels – There are two main youth hostel associations *(auberges de jeunesse)* in France: **Ligue Française pour les Auberges de Jeunesse**, 38 boulevard Raspail, 75007 Paris, ☎ 01 45 48 69 84 – Fax: 01 45 44 57 47 and **Fédération Unie des Auberges de Jeunesse** 27 rue Pajol, 75018 Paris, ☎ 01 44 89 87 27, Fax: 01 44 89 87 10. FUAJ publishes a booklet, also available on Internet (www.fuaj.org).

The international Youth Hostel Federation (www.iyhf.org) is establishing a computerised booking network (IBN), which allows hostellers to view bed availability and to reserve as much as six months in advance. The annual guide *Hostelling International Europe* is on sale in book shops and can be ordered from your national association. US: American Hostels Inc, 733 15th Street NW, Suite 840, Washington DC 20005; UK: Youth Hostels Assocation, Trevelyan House, 8 St Stephen's Hill, St Albans, Hertfordshire AL1 2DY.

Camping – There are numerous officially graded sites with varying standards of facilities along the coast, inland, and in the mountains. The **Michelin Guide Camping Caravaning France** lists a selection of campsites. An International Camping Carnet for caravans is useful but not compulsory; it may be obtained from the motoring organizations or the Camping and Caravaning Club (Greenfields House, Westwook Way, Coventry CV4 8JH; ☎ 01203 694 995).

The Fédération française des Stations Vertes de Vacances publishes an annual list of **rural localities** selected for their tranquillity and the outdoor activities available. Information from the Federation, 16 rue Nodot, 21000 Dijon ☎ 03 80 43 49 47.

Ramblers can consult the guide entitled *Gîtes et refuges France et Frontières* by A. and S. Mouraret (Editions La Cadole, 74 rue Albert-Perdreaux, 78140 Vélizy. ☎ 01 34 65 10 40).

The guide has been written mainly for those who enjoy rambling, riding and cycling holidays.

The national guide *Bienvenue à la ferme* (Editions Solar) includes the addresses of farmers who have signed a charter drawn up by the Chambers of Agriculture. *Bienvenue à la ferme* farms, vetted for quality and meeting official standards, can be identified by the yellow flower which serves as their logo.

Eating out

Guide Rouge Michelin France

This guide book provides a very wide selection of restaurants, for all tastes and pocket-books, serving the finest specialities in Dordogne, Berry and Limousin as well as the rest of France.

When the word *repas* ("meal") is printed in red, it refers to a high-quality but reasonably-priced meal. Pictograms indicate places with charming décor, a beautiful view, or a quiet setting. This a gourmet guide you can trust.

Fermes-auberges (Farm-inns) may or may not offer overnight accommodation, but they do serve farm produce and local speciality dishes. They are open at weekends; advanced booking is required. Contact local tourist offices.

Menu reader – Regional specialities

Ballottine	Turkey and foie gras moulded in aspic	Jambon	Ham
Bréjaude	Cabbage and pork soup with rye bread	Langue de bœuf	Beef tongue
Cabecou	Quercy goats' cheese	Lapin	Rabbit
Canard	Duck	Lièvre	Hare
Cèpes	King bolete mushrooms (Boletus edulis)	Magret	Filet (cutlet) of duck or goose
Chabrol	Broth with wine	Marcassin	Young wild boar
Champignons des bois	Wild mushrooms	Noix	Walnut
Châtaigne	Chestnut	Œufs au vin	Eggs in wine sauce
Clafoutis	Cherry pie/flan	Oie	Goose
Confit	Duck or goose preserved in its own fat	Petit salé	Salt pork
Crottin	Small, round goats' milk cheese	Picard	Potato pâté
Dinde	Turkey	Pommes de terre	Potatoes
Écrevisse	Crayfish	Potée	Boiled dinner with cabbage, potatoes, meat, sausage, and the cook's secret
En conserve	Preserved	Poulet en barbouille	Chicken in thick wine sauce
Enchaud or Anchaud	Pork confit	Pounti	Pork and prune loaf, served sliced
Farcidures	Potato dumplings	Pruneaux	Prunes
Foie de veau	Calf's liver	Rognons	Kidneys
Foie gras	Fattened liver	Sanciaux	Honey doughnuts
Fraise	Strawberry	Tourain blanchi	Garlic soup
Galantine	Cold cuts in jelly	Truffe	Truffle
Gibier	Game	Truffiat	Potatoes in pastry crust
Girole	Chanterelle mushroom (cantharellus cibarius)	Truite	Trout

well-done, medium, rare, raw = **bien cuit, à point, saignant, cru**

Shopping

Opening hours – Department stores are open Monday to Saturday, 9am to 6.30 or 7.30 pm. Smaller shops may close during the lunch hour. Grocers, wine merchants, bakeries and other food shops are open from 7am to 6.30 or 7.30pm. Some open on Sunday mornings, and may close on Monday. Bakery and pastry shops sometimes close on Wednesday.

VAT refunds – The French Value Added Tax *(TVA)* of 20.6% is included in the price of most of the goods (clothing, luxury items) you purchase. Travellers from outside the European Union can seek a refund. In practice, the system works when you buy more than 2 000F of goods in the same shop at the same time and pay with a credit card.

The paperwork is time-consuming, and only the main department stores, or luxury stores catering to tourists, are actually able to provide the service without hassle. Inquire before you pay.

To market, to market, to buy a fat ... goose liver – The souvenir of choice is edible, but remember that *foie gras* and truffles are expensive, even here at the source! Dordogne is also famous for its red fruit and nut liquors (especially in Villamblard and Brive), pork and duck preserves, and wines from Cahors and Bergerac. The wines of Sancerre in Berry deserve their fine reputation. Many of the specialities can be purchased directly from the producer – look out for signs along the road side (*dégustation – vente* for wines, *produits de la ferme* for preserves).

Fresh food and plants may not be carried home, and for Americans this includes non-pasteurised cheeses, nuts and fruit.

Cracking walnuts at the market

The main markets in the region are:

Périgueux (Wednesday and Saturday), livestock and flowers.

Brive-la-Gaillarde (November to March) local farm products, preserves and *confits*, etc.

Sarlat (Saturday in October and November), chestnuts, walnuts, *foie gras* and truffles.

Brantôme (Friday in the winter months), chestnuts, walnuts and *foie gras*.

Porcelain – Limoges is synonymous with fine china, and there is no dearth of shops selling it, including factory outlets *(vente directe d'usines)* just outside of town. Many workshops *(manufactures)* and showrooms *(magasins)* are also open on the road between Vierzon and Bourges. The larger outlets often have interesting museums, video presentations and demonstrations.

Limoges is also a historical and contemporary centre for the production of **enamelware** *(émaux)*. Look for shops around the place Wilson in town, or stop in one of the many workshops scattered around the region.

Porcelaine à pâte dure	**True porcelain** (hard-paste) or **china:** Resonant when struck, translucent, made from ground feldspathic rock and kaolin clay.
Porcelaine tendre	**Artificial porcelain** (soft-paste): Softer than true porcelain, it can be cut with a file, while true porcelain cannot. Dirt accumulated on an unglazed base can only be removed with difficulty; on true porcelain it comes off easily.
Porcelaine phosphatique or *Porcelaine hybride*	**Bone china:** A translucent ware, neither hard-paste nor soft-paste porcelain, that contains kaolin, petuntse and bone ash.
Faience fine	**White earthenware, opaque porcelain** or **creamware:** A generic term for a fine, hard earthenware of high strength and durability.
Grès or *Grès céramique*	**Stoneware:** Glassy in appearance, or semivitreous, with a fine texture, stoneware is always hard and is always fired in a high temperature kiln; the non-porous clay does not require a glaze.
Terre Cuite	**Terra Cotta, redware:** This clay is fired at a low temperature to a rather soft and porous body ranging in colour from pinkish-buff to brick-reds and reddish browns. As a rule it is covered with a soft lead glaze.

Sports and recreation

WATER SPORTS

This inland region is awash with man-made lakes, many well-equipped for swimming and boating, and the rivers and streams are inviting, too. The region's leading water sports centre is the **Lac de Vassivière** (970ha/2 397 acres), which offers beaches suitable for youngsters as well as opportunities for sailing and wind-surfing. Contact the **SYMIVA** (development authority) at BP 1, 23460 Royère-de-Vassivière or the *Maison du Tourisme (see Admission times and charges)*.

Canoeing is a popular family pastime on the peaceful waters of the region. In fact, on some weekends, in Dordogne, there seem to be more people on the water than on the road! **Kayaking** is practised on the lakes and, for more experienced paddlers, rapid sections of the rivers. For an initiation, the Dordogne and the Lot rivers are not only ideally calm, but also offer splendid views. The Corrèze, Elle, Auvezère, Céou and the upper parts of the Dronne, Isle and Célé rivers are more of a challenge. In all cases, be sure to wear the buoyant life jacket the rental agent must provide.

J. Damase/MICHELIN

La Roque-Gageac

For detailed information on these sports, contact the **Fédération française de canoë-kayak,** 87 quai de la Marne, BP 58 – 94340 Joinville-le-Pont, ☎ 01 45 11 08 50, which publishes a map. The bases listed below welcome all comers, experienced or not, renting boats and in some cases providing guides; a pick-up point downstream carries boaters and boats back to the base. Off-road bikes are sometimes available at the same sites. The average price for renting a canoe is 110 to 120F, a kayak 80 to 100F.

Canoës des Courrèges (Dordogne and Vézère) – Route du Buisson, 24260 Le Bugue, ☎ 05 53 08 75 37.

Canoës du Port d'Enveaux (Dordogne) – 24220 St—Vincent-de-Cosse, ☎ 05 53 29 54 20.

Canoë Raid (Céou, Dordogne and Vezère) – Campeyral, 24170 Siorac-en-Périgord, ☎ 05 53 31 64 11.

Copeyre Canoë (Dordogne) – Quercy Land, 46200 Souillac, ☎ 05 65 37 33 51.

Jean Rivière Loisirs (Dordogne and Vezère) – 24510 Limeuil, 05 53 63 38 73.

Kalapca (Lot and Célé) – Halte nautique, la Plage, 46330 St-Cirq-Lapopie, ☎ 05 65 30 29 51.

Safaraid (Dordogne, Lot and Célé) – 46140 Albas, ☎ 05 65 30 74 47. Bases at Vayrac, Vitrac, Bouziès.

LAKES AND PONDS	Dép.	Acreage	Swimming	Water sports	Fishing
Angoisse (Plan de Rouffiac)	24	99	🏊	💧	🐟
Aubazine (Plan d'eau du Coiroux)	19	59	🏊	–	Cat. 1
Bessais (Étang de Goule)	18	334	🏊	💧	🐟
Bort-les-Orgues (Lac de Val)	19	3459	🏊	💧	Cat. 2
Bourges (Lac du Val d'Auron)	18	203	🏊	💧	Cat. 2
Carsac-de-Gurson (Lac de Gurson)	24	44	🏊	–	–
Cazal (Plan d'eau de)	46	7	🏊	–	–
Compreignac (Lac de St-Pardoux)	87	815	🏊	💧	Cat. 2
Coursac (Lac du Rosier)	24	22	🏊	💧	Cat. 2
Dégagnac (Plan d'eau de)	46	6	🏊	💧	Cat. 1
Egleton (Lac du Deiro)	19	32	🏊	–	Cat. 1
Éguson (Lac de Chambon)	36	778	🏊	💧	🐟
Gimel (Étang de Ruffaud)	19	49	🏊	💧	🐟
Gourdon (Lac de)	46	10	🏊	–	–
Guéret (Étang de Courtille)	23	30	🏊	💧	–
Laval-de-Cère (Lac de Brugale)	46	61	🏊	💧	🐟
Lissac-sur-Couze (Lac du Causse)	19	222	🏊	💧	Cat. 2
Luzèche (Base de Caix)	46	371	🏊	–	🐟
Marcillac (Barrage de la Valette)	19	568	🏊	–	Cat. 2
Meymac (Lac de Sechemailles)	19	104	🏊	–	Cat. 2
Mézière (Étang de Bellebouche)	36	247	🏊	💧	🐟
Montcuq (Lac de St-Sernin)	46	12	🏊	💧	Cat. 2
Neuvic (Lac de Triousoune)	19	1013	🏊	💧	–
Seilhac (Lac de Burnazel)	19	79	🏊	–	–
Sénaillac-Latronquière (Lac du Tolerme)	46	17	🏊	💧	Cat. 1
Sidailles (Lac de)	18	222	🏊	💧	🐟
St-Estèphe (Étang de)	24	74	🏊	–	🐟
Trémolat (Barrage de Mauzac)	24	247	🏊	💧	🐟
Trignac (Lac de Bariousses)	19	247	🏊	💧	Cat. 2
Vassivière (Lac de)	23	2471	🏊	💧	Cat. 2
Viam (Lac de)	19	467	🏊	–	Cat. 2
Videix (Plan d'eau de Lavaud)	87	99	🏊	–	Cat. 1
Vigeois (Lac de Pontcharral)	19	35	🏊	–	–

Dep = *Département:* 18 Cher; 19 Corrèze; 23 Creuse; 24 Dordogne; 36 Indre; 46 Lot; 87 Haute-Vienne.

Lac = Lake; *Étang* = Pond or small lake; *Barrage* = Dam; *Plan d'eau* = a flat body of water.

Category 1 fish from the Salmonidae family (trout), usually the upper portion of major rivers.

Category 2 Cyprinidae (carps, barbels, tenches, breams, chubs, dace, shiners).

Fishing

The rivers, lakes and streams are a joy for those who love to fish. *A Carte de Pêche* (fishing permit) is required; it may be purchased for a day or for the year in sports clubs, tourist information centres, and cafés where a sign so signifies. Local regulations are enforced; crayfish are protected in most areas, and anglers should seek information on which fish are in season. Frogs are a speciality of the Brenne wetlands. For further details, contact the **Conseil supérieur de la pêche**, 134, avenue de Malakoff, 75016 Paris, ☎ 01 45 02 20 20, which publishes a map and brochure on fishing in France (15F).

Carp

Trout

Pike

House-boats

For a weekend or a week, enjoy the pleasant pace of life as you cruise the river Lot, where new sections of locks have recently been opened for pleasure craft. No license is required; the captain must be an adult, and go through a brief course given on board before departure. The rental agent explains, in particular, the methods for going through a lock and for docking, which is about all you need to know to operate these holiday barges. The average price varies according to the season, but plan on at least 8 000F for a week for a family of four.

Babour Marine – Rivière de St-Mary, 46000 Cahors, ☎ 05 65 30 08 99.

Bateaux Safaraid – Le Bourg, 46330 Bouziès, ☎ 05 65 30 22 84.

Crown Blue Line – Le Moulinat, 46140 Douelle, ☎ 05 65 20 08 79.

Locaboat Plaisance – Cévenne de Caix, 46140 Luzech, ☎ 05 65 30 71 11.

Lot Navigation Nicols – Le Bourg, 46330 Bouziès, ☎ 05 65 30 24 41.

Tourist cruises

For a shorter trip, and without the responsibility of the helm, take a cruise on the Lac de Vassivière, on the Lac de Val at Bort-les-Orgues, or enjoy a ride in a traditional gabare on the Dordogne at Spontour *(see the Admission times and charges for these places).*

RAMBLING

There is an extensive network of well-marked footpaths in France which make rambling *(la randonnée)* a breeze. Several **Grande Randonnée (GR)** trails, recognisable by the red and white horizontal marks on trees, rocks and in town on walls, signposts, etc, go through the region. Along with the GR exist the **Petite Randonnée (PR)** paths, which are usually blazed with blue (2hr walk), yellow (2hr15mi – 3hr45min) or green (4-6hr) marks. Of course, with appropriate maps, you can combine walks to suit your desires.

To use these trails, obtain the "Topo-Guide" for the area published by the *Fédération Française de la Randonnée Pédestre*, 9, rue Geoffroy-Marie, 75009 Paris, ☎ 01 48 01 80 80. Some English-language editions are available. An annual guide ("Rando Guide") which includes ideas for overnight itineraries and places to stay as well as information on the difficulty and accessibility of trails, is published by the *Comité national des sentiers de Grande Randonnée*, 64, rue de Gergovie, 75014 Paris, ☎ 01 45 45 31 02. Another source of maps and guides for excursions on foot is the *Institut National Géographique (IGN)*, which has a boutique in Paris at 107, rue de La Boétie (off the Champs-Elysées), ☎ 01 43 98 85 12) or you can order by mail from IGN-Sologne, 41200 Villefranche sur Cher, ☎ 02 54 96 54 42. Among their publications, France 903 is a map showing all of the GR and PR in France (27F); the "Série Bleue" and "Top 25" maps, at a scale of 1:25 000 (1cm=250m), show all paths, whether blazed or not, as well as refuges, campsites, beaches, etc (46-57F) for a precise area. In the region, you can find many of the publications cited above in bookstores, at sports centres or equipment shops, and in some of the country inns and hotels which cater to the sporting crowd. Some guides can be ordered from McCarta *(Footpaths of Europe series)*, 15 Highbury Place, London N 5 1QP, ☎ 017 354 16 16.

Local tourist organisations also provide maps of itineraries. In Sarlat the tourist office publishes **Chemins de petites and moyennes randonnées en Périgord Noir**, a series of 25 itineraries ranging from 3 to 42km/2 to 25mi. The **Brenne nature reserve** is a choice spot for quiet rambles; contact the *Reserve naturelle de Chérine (address in Admission times and charges)*, which publishes documents and conducts guided tours. For a truly French walk in the woods, take along a publication from the **Limousin Mushroom Society**, *Société mycologique du Limousin* (2, rue du Dr-Marcland, 87000 Limoges, ☎ 05 55 01 51 62 ext. 1163, Fax: 05 55 50 11 84) which will help you identify the edible delights of the underbrush: "Les Champignons du Limousin".

Spontour – Gabare on the Dordogne

G. Guittot/DIAF

A little help from a friend

To be relieved of the weight of a pack on your back, take along a friendly donkey to carry your provisions. Able to carry up to 40kg/88lb, he steps right along with the family and can be an inspiring companion for children. The animals can be hired for a day or a week and guides are also available to accompany a group and help you discover the countryside.

Fédération Nationale Ânes et Randonnées (FNAR) – Ladevèze, 46090 Cours, ☎ 05 65 31 42 79.

Picotin et Constant – St-Avit Vialard, 24260 Le Bugue, ☎ 05 53 07 15 40.

Stepping smart

Choosing the right equipment for a rambling expedition is essential: flexible hiking shoes with non-slip soles, a rain jacket or poncho, an extra sweater, sun protection (hat, glasses, lotion), drinking water (1-2l per person), high energy snacks (chocolate, cereal bars, banana ...), and a first aid kit. Of course, you'll need a good map (and a compass if you plan to leave the main trails). Plan your itinerary well, keeping in mind that while the average walking speed for an adult is 4kph/2.5mph, you will need time to eat and rest, and children will not keep up the same pace. Leave your itinerary with someone before setting out (innkeeper or fellow camper).

Respect for nature is a cardinal rule and includes the following precautions: don't smoke or light fires in the forest, which are particularly susceptible in the dry summer months; always carry your rubbish out; leave wild flowers as they are; walk around, not through, farmers' fields; close gates behind you.

If you are caught in an electrical storm, avoid high ground, and do not move along a ridge top; do not seek shelter under overhanging rocks, isolated trees in otherwise open areas, at the entrance to caves or other openings in the rocks, or in the proximity of metal fences or gates. Do not use a metallic survival blanket. If possible, position yourself at least 15m/15yd from the highest point around you (rock or tree); crouch with your knees up and without touching the rock face with your hands or any exposed part of your body. An automobile is a good refuge as its rubber tires ground it and provide protection for those inside.

CYCLING

For general information concerning France, write or call the **Fédération Française de Cyclotourisme** (8 rue Jean-Marie-Jégo, 75013 Paris, ☎ 01 44 16 88 88). Off-road enthusiasts, contact the **Fédération Française de Cyclisme** (5 rue de Rome, 93561 Rosny-sous-Bois) and request the "Guide des centres VTT". The *IGN (see address above, under rambling)* offers Map 906, "Mountain bike and cycle touring in France" (27F). Local tourist offices have a list of cycle hire firms, which include SNCF train stations in St-Amand-de-Montrond, Uzerche, Bergerac, Le Bugue, Cahors, Gourdon, Gramat, Rocamadour-Padirac, Sarlat and Souillac. Maps and suggested itineraries are provided.

> *From the top of the hills, plunge downward deep into the*
> *hollows of the landscape; discover, as if in flight, the distant*
> *road which widens and blooms with your approach; cross a*
> *village in a heartbeat and see it all in a glance … Only in dreams*
> *had I experienced such a charming ride, such lightness of being.*
>
> Alain-Fournier, *Le Grand Meaulnes*

EQUINE ADVENTURES

Savour the countryside at a gentle pace aboard a **horse-drawn caravan**. At 4kph/2.5mph, you will have ample time to look around the back roads and lanes you are travelling. This nomadic life can last for 2-7 days, according to the itinerary.
To travel the Dordogne in gypsy style (equipped with sleeping berths and a kitchen), at a rate of 15 to 20km/9 to 12mi a day, will cost about 4 500F for the rental.

Roulottes du Périgord – Métairie du roc, 24560 Faux, ☎ 05 53 24 32 57.

Tourisme Attelé Diffusion – Château d'Aynac, ☎ 05 65 10 23 30.

Les Roulottes du Quercy – Sérignac, 46700 Puy-l'Évêque, ☎ 05 65 31 96 44.

If you prefer to sit right down on the horse, the *Délégation Nationale du Tourisme Équestre* (30 avenue d'Iéna, 75116 Paris, ☎ 01 53 67 44 44) publishes an annual review called *Tourisme et Loisirs Équestres en France*. It lists all the possibilities for riding by region and *département*. It is also possible to contact regional associations directly, by writing to the following *Associations Régionales du Tourisme Équestre*:

Aquitaine – Serge Mercadié, Écuries des Sables, 47200 Montpouillan.

Limousin – Jean-Charles Sanconie, Romanet, 19470 Le Lonzac, ☎ 05 55 98 20 23.

Val-de-Loire-Centre – Maison des Sports, 32, rue Alain-Gerbault, 41000 Blois, ☎ 02 54 42 95 60.

Riding in the Monédières

EXPLORING CAVES

Dordogne attracts many speleologists; its limestone relief is pitted with caves and caverns. A few addresses for spelunkers:

Fédération française de Spéléologie – 130, rue de St-Maur, 75011 Paris, ☎ 04 43 57 56 54.

École française de spéléologie – 23 rue de Nuits, 69004 Lyon, ☎ 04 78 39 43 30. The school publishes a yearly calendar of training sessions for all levels of cavers.

Comité régional de spéléologie – Aquitaine – avenue d'Espérance, 40140 Soustons, ☎ 05 58 41 55 10.

Comité départemental de spéléologie – Dordogne – La Vergne, 242000 St-André-d'Allas, ☎ 05 53 31 27 30.

Comité départemental de spéléologie – Lot – La Marchade, 46000 Cahors, ☎ 05 65 35 73 53.

COURSES IN LOCAL COOKERY

If your favourite recreation takes place with pots and pans for equipment, why not spend 2 or 3 days in a French kitchen for a holiday? In Dordogne, the season for preparing *foie gras* is generally from October to mid-December and from mid-January to April. A number of farmhouse-inns offer sessions which include lessons on preparing *foie gras*, *confits*, *cou farci* and other delights, as well as lodging and board (about 1 400F per person). Generally, you must buy your own duck or goose, which adds 600-700F to the total price. For information, contact:

Loisirs-Accueil Dordogne – 25, rue du Président Wilson, 24000 Périgueux, ☎ 05 53 35 50 24.

Loisirs-Accueil Lot – 53, rue Bourseul, BP 162, 46003 Cahors Cedex, ☎ 05 65 22 19 20 Two family-run operations, specialising in goose and duck, respectively, are more than learning experiences, but take the visitor right into the heart of local matters. Excellent cooking and facilities and a warm welcome await at:

Fort de la Rhonie – Coustaty Family, Boyers, 24220 Meyras, ☎ 05 53 29 24 83, Fax: 05 53 29 62 58.

La Maurinie – Alard Family, Eyliac, 24330 St-Pierre-de-Chignac, ☎ 04 53 29 24 83. Sessions open when enough participants have enrolled. You are also welcome to stay and eat as a regular guest, without cooking, and just enjoy the food, the company, and life on the farm.

Thematic itineraries

HISTORY

Travel itineraries on specific themes have been mapped out by the *Caisse Nationale des Monuments Historiques et des Sites* (CNMHS – 62 rue St-Antoine, 75004 Paris). You can write to obtain brochures on:

Berry – *La route des Dames de Touraine, la route François I, la route George Sand, la route Jacques Cœur, la route des Parcs et Jardins Beauce-Val de Loire-Berry.*

Limousin – *La route des Lémovices, la route des Marches du Quercy, la route Richard Cœur de Lion, la route de St-Jacques, la route de Ventadour.*

Dordogne – *Circuit des églises à coupole du Ribéracois* (domed churches), *Circuit Jacquou le Croquant, la route des métiers d'art en Périgord, la route du Tabac de Bergerac à Sarlat, la route historique des mille et un châteaux en Périgord, la route historique des Marches du Quercy.*

Signs posted along the roads help you follow these itineraries as well as other thematic routes which have been created by regional associations: *Chemin des Lavoirs dans le Cher* (15 waterside wash houses to discover in the Germigny Valley, maintained by the association *Nos villages en Berry*); *La Ronde des Champs d'Amour* ("fields of love" in the Champagne Berrichonne region and Issoudun); De Moulins en Barrages (Mills and dams along the valleys of the Maulne, the Vienne and the Combade); Circuit du Châtaignier (A day trip in chestnut country, where the crafting of hoop-wood strips for barrel-making is traditional). Contact the local tourist offices for details and maps.

Limousin in the autumn

315

ANOTHER POINT OF VIEW

There are still other ways to get around and enjoy the region, for example, aboard a **train**.

In Limousin, four different routes are travelled by vintage railroad 1930s cars, with a steam engine leading the way. Visit the Haute Vallée de la Vienne (Limoges-Eymoutiers-Limoges); the Millevaches Plateau (Limoges-Meymac-Limoges); the Vienne Gorges (Eymoutiers-Châteauneuf-Bujaleuf-Eymoutiers); the Realm of Ventadour (Meymac-Ussel-Meymac). Contact local tourist offices or the association **Vienne Vézère Vapeur** (Mairie d'Eymoutiers, 87120 Eymoutiers, ☎ 05 55 69 10 21).

In Dordogne, **Autorail Espérance** offers a guided tour and a taste of regional cooking, travelling from Sarlat to Bergerac in one hour (☎ 08 36 35 35 35). *Quercyrail* runs trains from the 1950s along the old Cahors-Capdenac line, where passengers get a good look at the Lot valley (☎ 05 65 35 09 56 – reservations recommended).

From above

For those who prefer a speedier tour, try a **helicopter**. A trip with *Creuse Hélicoptère Services* (Château du St-Maixant, 23200 Aubusson, ☎ 05 55 66 12 62) will reveal the crazy-quilt patchwork of fields and groves that make **Berry** so mysterious. Two options for a bird's-eye view of **Périgord**: *Héli Périgord* (route d'Agen, 24100 Bergerac, ☎ 05 53 27 01 55 or 05 53 57 70 46) flies helicopters on four different routes; 2 people minimum, starting from 590F; or float in a **hot air balloon** operated by *Montgolfière du Périgord* (24250 La Roque Gageac, ☎ 05 53 28 18 58). The balloon goes up every morning and afternoon in season, and the rest of the year by request (1 100F/hr or 700F/30min).

Regional wines

French wines are classified according to a system which provides a rough guide to price and quality, although there is plenty of room for overlapping, especially where small growers are concerned. The lowest category is simply labelled **Vin de table**. Such wines may have been "elaborated" using any variety of grape from any country in the EU (although this must be stated on the label). While generally to be avoided in shops and restaurants, you may buy satisfactory "table wine" from a local producer or co-operative (bring your own container). Next comes the **Vin de Pays**, which bears a label identifying the place of origin and possibly the grape variety (if not a blend) and the year. The category following is the **VDQS**, *Vin Délimité de Qualité Supérieur*, which also shows place of origin and may show variety and year. The superiority comes from the fact that the grape varieties are approved and the district of production clearly defined; in addition, these wines pass a yearly taste test to confirm their quality.

The top 20% of French wines are labelled **Appellation d'Origine Contrôlée** (abbreviated AOC or simply AC). These wines come from designated vineyards, use approved grape varieties and are vinified in a manner specific to each one. The system is controlled by the *Institut National des Appellations d'Origine*, and it is a serious business indeed. The AOC label is a reward for years of continuous merit and lobbying. Similar systems are now being put into use for other products, notably meats and cheeses.

SANCERRE

The wines of Sancerre are commonly classified as Eastern Loire Valley wines. The upper reaches of the Loire are mostly planted with the Sauvignon Blanc grape, which produces two of the finest wines in France: **Sancerre** and **Pouilly-Fumé**. These wines are produced within 8km/5mi of each other, on different sides of the river, and yet their taste is, to the connoisseur, leagues apart. Mostly white wines are produced; the term *fumé* is in reference to the "smoky" bloom that forms on the skin of the fruit rather than to the resulting flavour. Sancerre is reputed for its full, round finish, while Pouilly-Fumé is considered a more complex, flowery wine.

In addition to these famous labels, some of the other wines in the region are delightful discoveries for the traveller. Certain wines, produced in small quantity and difficult to find outside the region, make for a memorable and unique experience. It is worth a visit to the wine-growers of **Bué**, **Chavignol**, **Ménétréol** and **Fontenay** to savour the regional *savoir-faire*.

Mostly white, but also some rosé and red AOC wines are produced in the villages of **Ménétou-Salon**, **Quincy**, and **Reuilly**. Reds and rosés are drawn from Sauvignon Blanc, Pinot Noir, Pinot Gris and Meunier grapes.

Sancerre is a beautiful wine town, surrounded by hillside vineyards which sweep away from the town like striped skirts on a lovely lady. The signposted wine route meanders around back roads and through the village of Chavignol, famous for its *crottin de Chavignol* goats' milk cheese. The Sancerrois is not a very big region, but visitors will have plenty of temptation to stop and sample local wines and cheese and to enjoy a slower pace of life.

Wine cellar – Château de Chambert

BERGERAC

Another leading wine-producing centre in the region covered in this guide is Bergerac, which has 12 different types of AOC wines. There is a well-marked wine route around the vineyards *(information at the Maison des Vins, Cloître de Récollets, in Bergerac)*. The varieties grown are Cabernet Franc, Cabernet Sauvignon, Merlot, Cot, Semillon and Sauvignon Blanc. **Bergerac, Côtes de Bergerac** and **Pécharmant** are strong red wines; the rosés are less enticing, and the white wines are sweet *(moëlleux)* or if dry, bottled under a separate AOC, **Bergerac Sec.** Ambrosial **Monbazillac** white wines, very sweet, are often served with *foie gras*. The flavour is similar to Sauternes, and the wine keeps for about four years, although a good year may age better. **Rosette** is a less sweet white wine produced in small quantity and not found elsewhere; enjoy it as an apéritif wine. **Montravel** vineyards are in the Dordogne, but also on the far edge of Bordeaux territory. The white wines (from dry to sweet) are bottled as Montravel, whereas the reds are sold as Bergerac.

CAHORS

The deep red wines of Cahors are made from Malbec, Merlot and Jurançon grapes, grown in ruddy soil scattered with limestone pebbles. Start a tour of the regional vineyard right at the famous Pont de Valentré, pictured on the cover of this book. From here you can go to Pradines and Douelle, where wine was once loaded onto flat-bottomed boats for transportation. The wine road is a beautiful route through the countryside and along the river; many of the vineyards have been producing wine for centuries. During the Roman occupation, the Emperor Dolmitian ordered the vines uprooted as punishment for an uprising, thus temporarily (for 200 years) halting production, which is now back in full swing. The AOC label was awarded to regional wines in 1971.

To earn the name **Cahors**, the hearty red wines must have at least 70% Malbec, and at most 20% Merlot and Tannot; the remaining 10% is Jurançon. While they are known for their dark colour bordering on black, robust and tannic flavour, Cahors wines are evolving to suit modern tastes and now more subtle vintages are coming to light. Labelled *vieux* (old), it has aged three years or more in a wooden cask.

Locally made **Coteaux de Quercy,** red and rosé wines from the Lot valley, are *Vins de Pays.*

To plan a special itinerary :
> *– consult the Map of touring programmes which indicates recommended routes, tourist regions, principal towns and main sights.*
> *– read the descriptions in the Sights section which include Excursions from the main tourist centres.*

Michelin Maps *indicate scenic routes, interesting sights, viewpoints, rivers, forests...*

Suggested reading

Eleanor of Aquitaine, queen of France and England, a 12C divorcée, patroness of poets, source of inspiration for chivalry and Courtly Love, ruler of a kingdom that spanned from Scotland to the Pyrenees, mother of ten children (including Richard the Lion Heart), lived her 82 years as few women in history before or since. The story of her life is a good introduction to regional history, and a fascinating tale:

Eleanor of Aquitaine: The Mother Queen, Desmond Seward, N.Y., Dorset Press, 1986.
Eleanor of Aquitaine and the Four Kings, Amy Kelly, Cambridge MA, Harvard University Press, 1950.
Beloved Enemy: the Passions of Eleanor of Aquitaine: a Novel, Ellen Jones, N.Y., Simon and Schuster, 1994.
For young readers:
A Proud Taste for Scarlet and Miniver, E.L. Konigsburg, N.Y., Atheneum, 1974 (illustrated).
Queen Eleanor: Independent Spirit of the Medieval World, Polly S. Brooks, N.Y., Lippincott, 1983 (illustrated).

George Sand was a prolific novelist and correspondent, and many of her works have been translated *(see her biography under NOHANT)*. Her rustic tales of country life are suitable for younger readers, too, in particular *The Story of My Life* and *Tales of a Grandmother*. Among the many biographies, the following are especially recommended:

Infamous Woman: the Life of George Sand, Joseph Barry, 1977.
The Double Life of George Sand, Woman and Writer, Renée Winegarten, 1978.
For an even closer view of the author's life:
The Intimate Journal of George Sand, Chicago, Cassandra Editions, 1988.
The George Sand – Gustave Flaubert Letters, Chicago, Academy Chicago LTD, 1979.

Alain-Fournier was the pen name of Henri-Alban Fournier *(see ÉPINEUIL-LE-FLEURIEL)*. His only completed novel has been published in English both under its French title, *Le Grand Meaulnes* and as *The Lost Domain*.

Josephine Baker's life of scantily-clad artistry, wartime heroism, social idealism, bankruptcy and triumphant stage returns makes for good reading. There was more to this woman than a banana skirt, as you will learn in these excellent biographies:

Jazz Cleopatra: Josephine Baker in Her Time, Phyllis Rose, N.Y., Doubleday, 1989.
Naked at the Feast: A Biography of Josephine Baker, Lynn Haney, N.Y., Dodd-Mead, 1981.
Josephine, Josephine Baker and Jo Bouillon (Transl. by Mariana Fitzpatrick), N.Y., Harper & Row, 1977.

To wet your appetite:

The Wines of France, Alexis Lichine, N.Y., Knopf, 1963. A classic that ages well.
Enjoying Wine, Don Hewitson, London, Elm Tree Books, 1985. Friendly, no-nonsense approach to one of life's great pleasures, with useful explanations and illustrations.
The Wine Lover's Guide to France, Michael Busselle, London, Pavilion Books, 1986.
At Home in France, Ann Barry, N.Y., Ballantine, 1996. An American journalist explores happiness in Carennac.
Goose Fat and Garlic, J. Strang, London, Kyle Cathie.

Calendar of events

These events may be held at different dates, depending on the year. It is best to inquire at the tourist office for precise details.

FESTIVALS

Late April

Bourges .... *Printemps de Bourges* – International festival of popular contemporary music and songs ☎ 02 48 24 30 50.

May-June

Limoges .... *Photographies sur un fil* – 5 photographers on a single theme ☎ 05 55 32 30 78.

June

Bourges .... *Synthèse* – international festival of experimental music ☎ 02 48 20 41 87.

Nohant .... *Fêtes romantiques* ☎ 02 54 48 22 64.

June-July

Bellac .... *Les Amis du Festival de Bellac* – Jean Giraudoux theatre and music fesitval ☎ 05 55 68 10 44.

Printemps de Bourges – On stage

Mid-June-mid-August

Noirlac .... *Été de Noirlac* – Chamber music and song in the abbey ☎ 02 48 67 00 18.

Bourges .... *Très Riches Heures de l'Orgue en Berry* – Organ festival (all summer and early fall) ☎ 02 48 20 25 24.

July

Cahors .... Blues Festival. ☎ 05 65 35 22 29.

Gourdon .... Summer festival (early June- end July), ☎ 05 65 41 20 06.

La Châtre .... *Rencontres internationales Frédéric-Chopin* – piano festival (third week of July) ☎ 02 54 48 22 64.

Montignac .... International Folklore festival (last week of July), ☎ 05 53 50 14 00.

Souillac .... Jazz festival (third week of July) ☎ 05 65 37 81 56.

July-August

Belaye .... Cello festival (late July to early August) ☎ 05 65 24 14 75.

Bergerac, Le Bugue, Les Eyzies .... *Musique en Périgord* ☎ 05 53 22 68 59.

Biron, Bergerac, Cadouin, Monpazier .. *Festival du Périgord Pourpre* ☎ 05 53 22 68 59.

Bonaguil	Music and theatre festival ☎ 05 53 71 17 17.
Bourges	*Ballades à Bourges* – classic, jazz, pop concerts around town ☎ 02 48 24 75 33.
Cahors, Lauzerte, Montcuq, Montpezat	*Festival du Quercy Blanc* (early July to mid-August) ☎ 05 53 90 28 67.
Sarlat	*Festival des jeux de théâtre* (last week of July to mid-August) ☎ 05 53 31 10 83.
St-Céré	*Festival de Musique* (late July to mid-August) ☎ 05 65 38 28 08.
St-Léon-de-Vézère and environs	*Festival musical du Périgord Noir* (last week of July and third week of August) ☎ 05 53 51 95 17.

August

Aubusson	*Musique au cœur de la tapisserie* – organ and chamber music concerts (last two weeks of August) ☎ 05 55 66 17 43.
Gargilesse	*Festival musical d'été* – harp workshops (last week of August) ☎ 04 54 47 85 06.
Périgueux	*Mimos* – International mime Festival 05 53 53 18 71.

August-September

Périgueux	French song festival (late August to early September) ☎ 05 53 53 22 72.

September-October

Bourdeille, Chancelade, Périgueux, St-Jean-de-Côle	*Sinfonia en Périgord* (second week of September) ☎ 05 53 53 19 70.
Solignac	*L'Œil Ecoute* – photography festival ☎ 05 55 32 30 78.
Tulle	*Festival des Nuits de Nacre* – "pearly nights" accordeon festival ☎ 05 55 26 99 10.

October-November

Brive	Book Fair (early November) ☎ 05 55 92 39 39.
Guéret	*Rendez-vous international du piano en Creuse* – piano from every point of view (late October-early November) ☎ 05 55 52 14 29.
Limoges	*Festival international du jazz en Limousin* ☎ 05 55 34 70 70.

November-December

Périgueux	*Salon international du livre gourmand* – cookbook show (Friday to Sunday) ☎ 05 53 53 18 71.

January

Limoges	*Danse Emoi* – dance festival (first two weeks of January in even-numbered years) ☎ 05 55 34 45 49 (Jean-Gagnant cultural centre).

SON ET LUMIÈRE

"Sound and light" shows are a great way to spend a summer night outdoors and give new perspectives on the monuments they highlight. There are a lot of variations on the theme, from "living history" plays through costumed pagentry and creative combinations of lighting effects and music which bring out the details of architecture. Check with the local tourist office for details: in some cases you may need to bring your own blanket and chairs; in others, visitors stand and walk around the site. These shows are held in July and August, and generally start at nightfall, which may mean after 10pm.

Château de Castelnaud	A different play takes place inside the château every year, using the various rooms as the setting. Candle light and intrigue create the backdrop for historical figures from the Castelnaud's past. Two shows (except weekends) at 8.30pm and 10.15pm. 50 people only, reservations recommended. ☎ 05 53 31 30 00.
Chénérailles	July. Light show. ☎ 05 55 62 34 34 or 05 55 62 37 22.
Tours de Merle	Medieval pagent. ☎ 05 55 28 22 31.
Nohant	Late July-early August, a show drawn from the works of George Sand. ☎ 02 54 31 02 62.
Solignac	*Les Lumières de la Briance.* ☎ 05 55 00 43 54.
Valençay	Late July-early August, *Escarmonde.* ☎ 02 54 00 04 42.
Rilhac-Lastours	Mid-July-mid-August.

FAIRS AND MARKETS

January

Brive.............................. Epiphany Fair (early January).

Périgueux...................... Epiphany Fair (first Wednesday after 6 January).

Sunday after Mardi Gras

Mézières-en-Brenne...... *Fête des Brandons* (torchlight procession).

Easter

Reuilly .... Wine Fair.

April

Aubazine .... Goat Fair.

May

Calès............................. Flower Fair.

Menetou-Salon .... *Frairie de Brangers* – Village festival, historical tableaux and craft demonstrations.

May -June

Rocamadour................. Cheese Fair (Whit Sunday – *Pentecôte*).

July

Martel .... Wool Fair.

Aubigny-sur-Nère .... France-Scotland Festival – historical tableaux, parades, folk dancing and music (first part of the month).

August

Bué-en-Sancerre........... *Foire au sorciers* – witchery at the village fair (early August).

St-Léonard-de-Noblat ... Mediaeval Festival (early in August).

Hautefort...................... Turkey Fair (first Monday of August).

Lalinde .... Wine Fair (early August).

Belfort-du-Quercy......... Melon Fair (15 August).

Duravel .... Wine Fair (15 August).

October

Limoges....................... *Frairies des petits ventres* (third Friday in October) – regional festival for hearty eaters and wine lovers.

J. Boyer/IMAGES TOULOUSE

Félibrée folklore

Admission times and charges

Every sight for which the times and charges are listed is indicated by the symbol ⊙ in the text in the main part of this guide.

Admission times and charges are liable to alteration without prior notice; the information below is given only as a general indication. Dates given are inclusive. The information was, as far as possible, correct at the time of going to press.

The admission charges quoted here are full price for one adult; there are usually reduced rates or free entry for children and often reductions for family groups, students or senior citizens; proof of age may be required. In some cases admission is free on certain days (Weds, Sundays or public holidays). Ticket offices often close 30-45 minutes before the actual closing time. Many sights are closed on public holidays (listed in the Practical Information section).

Churches and chapels are usually closed during the lunch period from noon to 2pm and do not admit visitors during services, except for worship; tourists should refrain from visits when services are being held. Visitors to chapels are often accompanied by the person who keeps the key; a donation is welcome.

Whenguided tour are indicated, the departure time of the last tour of the morning or afternoon will be up to an hour before closing time. Mostguided tour are conducted by French-speaking guides but in some cases the term "guided tour" may cover group visits with recorded commentaries. Some of the more popular sights may offerguided tour, audio tours, notes or pamphlets in other languages. The symbol ▲ indicates that a tour is given by a lecturer from the Historic Monuments Association. Enquire at the ticket office or book stall for information on tours and documents in English.

Enquire at the local tourist office or tourist information centre (Office de tourisme, Maison de tourisme or Syndicat d'Initiative) – the address of which is shown following the 🚹 below – for details of local religious holidays, market days, etc.

The symbol ⑤ indicates places which are accessible to persons of reduced mobility. Never leave valuables in unattended vehicles.

A

ARGENTAT

La Xantrie

Moulin de Malesse – ⑤ Guided tour (45min) July and Aug daily at 3pm, 4pm and 5pm; 20F; ☎ 05 55 28 21 01.

ARGENTON-SUR-CREUSE   🚹 place de la République – ☎ 02 54 24 05 30

Guided tour of the town – Contact the tourist office.

Musée de la Chemiserie – ⑤ Open daily except Mons from 9.30am-noon and from 2pm-6pm; closed Jan to mid-Feb and on 25 Dec; 20F; ☎ 02 54 24 34 69.

Chapelle Notre-Dame-des-Bancs – Open June to Sept daily from 9am-7pm; the rest of the year open weekends and public holidays.

ARNAC-POMPADOUR   🚹 ☎ 05 55 98 55 47

Château – ⑤ Guided tour (30min) Apr to Sept daily (but closed in afternoons on race days) from 10am-noon and from 2pm-6pm (last admission 11.30am and 5.30pm); Oct to mid-Nov and mid-Feb to March from 2pm-5pm (last admission 4.30pm); closed mid-Nov to mid-Feb; 10F; ☎ 05 55 98 55 47.

Haras national – ⑤ Guided tour (1hr) July to Sept from 10am-noon and from 2pm-6.30pm (last admission 11am and 5.30pm); fewer tours on race and competition days; Oct to June from 2.30pm-5.30pm (last admission 4.30pm); closed 1 Jan and 25 Dec; 25F; ☎ 05 55 98 55 47.

Excursions

Jumenterie nationale de Beyssac – ⑤ July to Sept: guided tour (45min, last admission 45min before closing) 3pm-5.45pm; race days 3pm-5pm; April to June: 2pm-5.45pm; early Feb to March: 2pm-5pm. Closed Oct to early Feb. 20F. ☎ 05 55 98 55 47.

Chartreuse de Glandier – Guided tour (1hr) June to Oct 3pm-7pm; Oct to June by prior arrangement; 10F; ☎ 05 55 73 81 00 or 05 55 98 55 47 (tourist office).

Les ARQUES

Musée Zadkine – Open June to Sept and school holidays 10am-1pm, 2pm-7pm; weekends and holidays 10am-1pm, 2pm-7pm. Closed 1 Jan, 1 May, 1 Nov, 25 Dec. 15F; ☎ 05 65 22 83 37.

Chapelle St-André-des-Arques – Key at Musée Zadkine (see above).

AUBAZINE

Conventual buildings – ♿ Guided tour (1hr) daily except Monday: June to Sept Tues to Sun at 11am and 4pm; July and Aug at 11am, 3.30pm, 4.30pm; Oct to May at 4pm. Closed Jan and 26-31 Aug. 20F. ☎ 05 55 84 61 12.

AUBETERRE-SUR-DRONNE

Église monolithe St-Jean – Open 9.30am-12.30pm and 2pm-7pm (mid-Oct to mid-June closes at 6pm.°20F. ☎ 05 45 98 57 18.

AUBIGNY-SUR-NÈRE 🅘 Ilôt Sainte-Anne – ☎ 02 48 58 40 20

Guided tour of the town – Apply to the tourist office.

Église St-Martin – Open Easter to All Saints' Day daily from 2pm-6pm. ☎ 02 48 81 50 00 (town hall).

Ancien château des Stuart (Musée Marguerite-Audoux) – Easter to Oct : weekends and public holidays 2.30pm-6pm (July to mid-Sept : daily 2.30pm-7pm) ; Nov to Easter : Sundays and holidays 2.30pm-6pm. Admission free. ☎ 02 48 81 50 07.

Excursion

Château de la Verrerie – ♿ Guided tour (45min) 10am-1pm, 2pm-6m (June-Sept : 10am7pm). 40F (children : 30F). ☎ 02 48 81 51 60.

AUBUSSON 🅘 rue Vieille – ☎ 05 55 66 32 12

Musée départemental de la Tapisserie (Centre Jean-Lurçat) – ♿ Open (1hr guided tour available by prior arrangement) July and Aug daily (except Tues mornings) from 10am-6pm; the rest of the year daily (except Tuess) from 9.30am-noon and from 2pm-6pm; closed 1 Jan and 25 Dec; 20F. ☎ 05 55 66 33 06.

École nationale d'Art Décoratif – ♿ Open daily except Sundays and public holidays from 9am-noon and from 2pm-5pm. Admission free. ☎ 05 55 83 05 43.

Forum de la tapisserie – Open mid-June to Sept daily from 10am-7pm; Sun and holidays 10am-1pm, 2pm 7pm. 15F. ☎ 05 55 66 32 12.

Manufacture de Tapis et Tapisseries St-Jean – Guided tour (1hr) April to Oct, Mon to Fri, 9am-noon and 2pm-5.30pm and weekends 2pm-5.30pm; the rest of the year Mon to Fri only. 35F (children : 20F); ☎ 05 55 66 10 08.

Maison du Tapissier – July and Aug : 10am-7pm (last admission 45min before closing) ; Sun and holidays 10am-12.30pm, 2.30pm-5.30pm ; Sept to June : 9.30am-12.30pm, 2.30pm-5.30pm ; Sun and holidays 10am-noon, 2pm-4pm. Closed 1 Jan, 1 May, 25 Dec. 17F. ☎ 05 55 66 32 12.

Haute Vallée de la Creuse

Château de Villemonteix – Easter to Oct : guided tour (1hr15min), 10am-noon, 2pm-7pm ; Nov to Easter : by request. 23F (children :12F). ☎ 05 55 62 33 92.

Masgot village – Information available from the association "Les Amis de la Pierre de Masgot". ☎ 05 55 66 98 88.

Aubusson – High-warp loom

B

BEAULIEU-SUR-DORDOGNE

🚹 6, place Marbot – 19120 – ☎ 05 55 91 09 94

Trésor de l'Église St-Pierre – Mid-July to Aug: guided tour (1hr30min) Mon to Fri, 5pm-6.30pm; Sat by request. 20F. Apply to M Sapin. ☎ 05 55 91 18 78.

Chapelle des Pénitents – July and Aug: 10am-noon, 3pm-6pm. 10F. ☎ 05 55 91 11 31 (town hall).

BELLAC

🚹 rue Louis Jouvet – ☎ 055 55 68 12 79

Birthplace of Jean Giraudoux – Guided tour (30min) Mon to Fri 2.30pm-6.30pm (June to Aug daily except Tues). Closed firts two week in Sept, 1 Jan, 25 Dec. 10F. ☎ 05 55 68 03 77.

La Basse Marche

Châteauponsac: Musée René Baubérot – June to Sept and school holidays: 2pm-6pm; Oct to May: Wed, Sat, Sun and holidays 2pm-6pm. 30F. ☎ 05 55 76 56 72.

BERGERAC

🚹 97, rue Neuve d'Argenta – ☎ 05 53 57 03 11

Guided tour of the town – Apply to the tourist office.

Boat trips on the Dordogne – One hour trips with commentary, Easter to Oct daily; depart from the Ancien Port every 30min during the tourist season and every hour outside the season; 35F (children:25F). ☎ 05 53 24 58 80.

Cloître des Récollets and Maison des vins – ♿ May to Dec: 10am-1pm, 2pm-6pm (mid-June to mid-Sept: closes at 7pm); last two weeks in April; daily except Sun and Mon 10am-1pm, 2pm-6pm. Free admission. ☎ 05 53 63 57 55.

Musée du Tabac – ♿ Tues to Fri: 10am-noon, 2pm-6pm; Sat: 2pm-5pm; Sun: 2.30pm-6.30pm. Closed holidays. 17F. ☎ 05 53 63 04 13.

Musée d'Histoire urbaine – ♿ Same admission times and charges as for Tobacco Museum above (included in ticket).

Exhibitions in temple – July to early Sept: 10am-noon, 4pm-6pm. Free admission.

Musée du Vin, de la Batellerie et de la Tonnellerie – Mid-March to mid-Nov: Tues to Fri 10am-noon, 2pm-5.30pm (Sat: morning only; Sun: afternoons only, to 6.30pm); mid-Oct to mid-March: Tues to Fri (Sat morning only) 6F. ☎ 05 53 57 80 92.

Église St-Jacques – Mon to Sat: 2pm-7pm; Sun: 8.30am-10am, 5.30pm-7.30pm.

Musée d'Art sacré – July and Aug: Tues to Sat, 3pm-6pm; Sept to June: Sun and holidays by request. M Delage. 15F. ☎ 05 53 57 33 21.

BESSE

Excursion

Villefranche-du-Périgord

Maison du châtaignier, marrons et champignons – ♿ June to Oct: Tues to Sat, 9am-noon, 3pm-6pm; Sun and Mon: 9am-noon; Nov to May: Sat 10am-noon, 3pm-6pm; Tues and Sun: 10am-noon. 20F. ☎ 05 53 29 98 37.

BEYNAC-ET-CAZENAC

🚹 La Balme – ☎ 05 53 29 43 08

Château – Guided tour (1hr) 10am-noon, 2pm-6.30pm. 30F (children: 15F). ☎ 05 53 29 50 40.

Barge trips on the Dordogne – ♿ May to Sept: leave from the car park (1hr, every 30min) 10.30am-1pm, 2pm-6pm; July and Aug: 10am-1pm, 2pm-6pm; mid-March to April and in Oct: by request. 35F (children: 15F). ☎ 05 53 28 51 15.

Musée de la protohistoire – July and Aug: Sun to Fri, 10am-7pm; Sept to June: Sat, Sun and holidays, 8.30-5.30; Mon to Fri by request. 10F.

Parc archéologique – July to mid-Sept: Sun to Fri: 10am-7pm. 30F (children: 20F) ☎ 05 53 29 51 28.

BIRON

Château – April to Oct: guided tour (45min) Tues to Sun, 10am-12.30pm, 1.30pm-7pm; July and Aug: 10am-7pm; Nov to March: Tues to Sun 10am-12.30pm, 1.30pm-5.30pm. Closed in Jan and 25 Dec. 30F (children: 15F). ☎ 05 53 35 50 10.

BLANCAFORT

Château – Mid-March to mid-Nov: guided tour (45min) daily except Tues, 10h-noon, 2pm-6.30pm); June to Sept, every day 10am-7pm. Closed mid-Nov to mid-March. 35F. ☎ 02 48 58 60 56.

Excursion

Musée de la Sorcellerie – &. Easter to end Oct: 10am-6pm; June to Sept: 10am-7pm. 34F. ☎ 02 48 73 86 11.

BONAGUIL

Château – July and Aug: 10am-5.45pm; June 10am-noon, 2pm-5pm; Sept to May: 10.30am-noon, 2.30pm-4.30pm; year-end school holidays: 2.30pm-4.30pm. Closed Dec and Jan. 30F. ☎ 05 53 49 59 76.

BORT-LES-ORGUES
🛈 place Marmontel – ☎ 05 55 96 02 49

Boat excursions – Tour No 1: Bort dam/Château de Val: July and Aug: 2.15pm-5pm, every 30min; May to Sept: hours vary. 30F (children: 20F). Tour No 2: château de Vals/ Dordogne Valley and Gorges: May to Sept. 30F (children: 20F). ☎ 04 71 40 30 14.

"Circuit-visiteurs" – 9am-6pm. Free admission. Tourist office.

BOUGES

Château – April to Oct: guided tour (45min) daily except Tues, 10am-noon, 2pm-6pm; June: closes at 7pm; July and Aug: every day 10am-1pm, 2pm, 7pm; March and Nov: weekends 10am-noon, 2pm-5pm. Closed 1 May. 35F. ☎ 02 54 35 88 26.

BOURDEILLES

Château – April to Oct: guided tour (1hr) daily except Tues, 10am-12.30pm, 1.30pm-7pm; July and August: every day 10am-7pm; Nov to March: daily except Tues 10am-12.30pm; 1.30pm-5.30pm. Closed in Jan and Dec. 30F (children: 15F). ☎ 05 53 35 50 10.

BOURGES
🛈 21, rue Victor-Hugo (near the cathedral) – ☎ 02 48 23 02 60

Guided tour of the city ⬛ – Apply to the tourist office.

Themed tour – Apply to the tourist office (see above) or to the *Service de Patrimoine* (Heritage Department).

Cathédrale St-Étienne:
Crypt – April to Oct: guided tour (1hr) 9am-noon, 2pm-6pm, Sun 2pm-6pm; July and August: 9am-1pm, 2pm-7pm, Sun 2pm-9pm; Nov to March: 9am-noon, 2pm-5pm, Sun 2pm-5pm. Closed 1 Jan, 1 May, 1 and 11 Nov, 25 Dec. 32F (crypt and tower). ☎ 02 48 65 49 44.
North tower – Same times and charges as for crypt (included in ticket).

Palais Jacques-Coeur – July and Aug: guided tour (1hr) 9am-1pm, 2pm-7pm; Sept to Jun: 9am-noon, 2pm-6pm; Nov to March closes at 5pm. Closed 1 Jan, 1 May, 1 and 11 Nov, 25 Dec. 32F. ☎ 02 48 24 06 87.

Musée du Berry (Hôtel Cujas) – Daily except Tues 10am-noon, 2pm-6pm, Sun: 2pm to 6pm. Closed 1 Jan, 1 May, 1 and 11 Nov, 25 Dec. Free admission. ☎ 02 48 57 81 15.

Musée des Arts décoratifs (Hôtel Lallemant) – Tues to Sat 10am-noon, 2pm-6pm; Sun: 2pm-6pm. Closed 1 Jan, 1 May, 1 and 11 Nov, 25 Dec. Free admission. ☎ 02 48 57 81 17.

Musée de l'École – Weds, 2pm-5pm; Tues and Thurs, 10am-noon by request. Closed 1 Jan, 1 May, 1 Nov, 25 Dec. Free admission. ☎ 02 48 57 81 15.

Musée Estève (Hôtel des Échevins) – &. Daily except Tues, 10am-noon, 2pm-6pm, Sun: 2pm-6pm. Closed 1 Jan, 1 May, 1 and 11 Nov, 25 Dec. Free admission. ☎ 02 48 24 75 38.

Église Saint-Bonnet – Closed Sun afternoon and holidays.

Musée d'Histoire naturelle – &. Daily 2pm-6pm; school holidays, 10am-noon, 2pm-6pm; Closed 1 Jan, 1 May, 1 Nov, 25 Dec; 20F (children: 10F); ☎ 02 48 65 37 34.

BRANTÔME
🛈 Pavillon Renaissance – ☎ 05 53 05 80 52

Guided tour of the town – Contact the tourist office.

Boat trips on the Dronne – May to Sept: tour (45min) on the river leaves from quai du Pavillon Renaissance (Near the tourist office). 35F (children: 20F).

BRANTÔME

Bell tower – Mid-June to mid-Sept: guided tour (1hr) daily except Tues, 10am-12.30pm, 2pm-6pm; July and August daily except Tues 10am-7pm. 25F. ☎ 05 53 05 80 63.

Musée Fernand-Desmoulin et de la Préhistoire – Under renovation.

Rêve et miniatures – ♿ July and Aug: 10.30am-6.30pm; Apr to June Sat to Thurs (and Fri when holiday) 2pm-5pm. Closed 11 Nov to end March. *Current rates not known, last rate 28F (children 18F)*. ☎ 05 53 35 29 00.

"Du Creusé au Construit" cave tour – ♿ April to Sept: daily except Tues, 10am-12.30pm, 2pm-6pm; July and Aug: every day 10am-7pm; Oct to March: daily except Tues 10am-noon, 2pm-5pm. Closed Jan. 20F. ☎ 05 53 05 80 63.

Excursions

Thiviers: Musée du foie gras – ♿ April to Sept: Tues to Sat, 9am-12.15pm, 3pm-6pm (last admission 11.30am and 5.30pm); Oct to March: Tues to Sat 10am-noon, 3pm-6pm. 10F. ☎ 05 53 55 12 50.

Grottes de Villars – July and Aug: guided tour (45min) 10am-7pm; June and Sept: 10am-noon, 2pm-7pm; April, May and Oct: 2pm-6.30pm. 38F (children 25F). ☎ 05 53 54 82 36.

La BRENNE

Réserve naturelle de Chérine – July and Aug: guided tour (2hr) by request Tues and Thurs 6pm; Sat and Sun 8pm; April to June: Tues, Thurs, Sat 4pm. 35F (children: 15F). Easter to Aug: 10am, a presentation is made free of charge, no reservation required. ☎ 02 54 38 12 24.

Château du Bouchet – July, Aug and holidays: guided tour daily except Tues, 2pm-6.30pm (last admission 6pm). 25F (children: 12F)

Mézières-en-Brenne: Maison de la Pisciculture – March to Oct: daily except Tues, 2pm-6pm (5pm the rest of the year). Closed 1 Jan, 1 May and 25 Dec. 12F. ☎ 02 54 38 12 99.

BRIVE-LA-GAILLARDE

🆑 place du 14-Juillet – 19100 ☎ 05 55 24 08 80

Musée d'Art et d'Histoire Labenche – ♿ April to Oct: daily except Tues, 10am-6.30pm; Nov to March: daily except Tues 1.30pm-6pm. Closed 1 Jan, 1 May, 1 Nov and 25 Dec. 27F. (free admission the last Sun of the month); ☎ 05 55 24 19 05.

Musée de la Résistance et de la Déportation Edmond-Michelet – Mon to Sat, 10am-noon, 2pm-6pm. Closed holidays. Free admission. ☎ 05 55 74 06 08.

Excursions

Église de Noailles – Guided tour available; enquire at the town hall. ☎ 05 55 85 80 88.

Gouffre de la Fage – Mis-June to mid-Sept: guided tour (1hr) 9.30am-7pm; April to mid-June: unaccompanied visit 2pm-6.30pm; mid-Sept to mid-Oct: unaccompanied visit 2pm-5.30pm. 30F (children: 20F). ☎ 05 55 85 80 62 or 05 55 87 12 21.

Lac du Causse leisure park – July and Aug: 10am-7pm. 35F ☎ 05 55 85 18 11.

Le BUGUE

Le Village du Bournat – ♿ May to Sept: 10am-7pm; Oct to April: 10am-5pm. Closed in Jan. 50F (children: 30F). ☎ 05 53 08 41 99.

Aquarium du Périgord Noir – ♿ April to Sept: 10am-6pm (June to Aug: 9am-7pm); mid-Feb to March and Oct to mid-Nov: 10am-noon, 2pm-5pm. 43F (children: 33F). ☎ 05 53 07 16 38.

Musée de Paléontologie – Same times and charges as the Maison de la Vie Sauvage (below).

Maison de la Vie Sauvage – ♿ July to Sept: 10am-1pm, 3pm-7pm; Easter to June and school holidays: 2pm-6pm; Oct to Easter: Sun 2pm-6pm. Closed 1 Jan and 25 Dec. 25F (children: 18F). ☎ 05 53 08 28 10.

Excursions

Caverne de Bara-Bahau – July and Aug: guided tour (30min, last admission 30min before closing), 9am-7pm; Feb-June: 10am-noon, 2pm-5.30pm; Sept to Dec: 10am-noon, 2pm-5pm. Closed Jan. 29F (children: 18F). ☎ 05 53 07 44 58.

Gouffre de Proumeyssac – June to Aug: guided tour (45min), 9am-7pm; March to May, Sept and Oct: 9.30am-noon, 2pm-5.30pm; Feb, Nov and Dec: 2pm-5pm. Closed Jan and 25 Dec. 41 F children: 24F). ☎ 05 53 07 27 47.

C

CADOUIN

Cloisters and Musée du Suaire – ♿ April to Oct: guided tour (45min) daily except Tues, 10am-12.30pm, 1.30pm-7pm (July and Aug: every day 10am-7pm); Nov to March: daily except Tues 10am-12.30pm, 1.30pm-5.30pm. Closed Jan and 25 Dec. 30F (children: 15F). ☎ 05 53 35 50 10.

Musée du Vélocipède – ♿ Daily 10am-6pm. 30F (children: 20F). ☎ 05 53 63 46 60.

CAHORS
🛈 place François-Mitterrand, BP 207 – 46004 – ☎ 05 65 53 20 65

Guided tour of the medieval city M – Contact the tourist office.

Boat trips on the Lot – April to Nov: tour (1hr30min) including passage through a lock, leaving from Port de Bouzies at 11am, 3pm, 4.30pm, 6pm. 50F (children: 25F). July and Aug: "Alliance du rail et de l'eau", tour of Cahors Valley and St Cirq Lapopie by boat and train, Tues and Wed, departure 9am, return 5.30pm. 150F (children: 75F). ☎ 05 65 35 98 88.

Pont Valentré – Closed.

Millboat – No longer open to the public.

Chapelle St-Gausbert – Guided tour daily except Tues, 10am-12.30pm, 3pm-6pm, Sun and holidays 3pm-6pm. Contact the tourist office.

Maison de Roaldès – Easter to mid-Sept and 1 week at All Saints' Day: guided tour (45min) 10am-noon, 2pm-4pm, Sun and holidays 2pm-4pm (mid-June to Aug: 10am-noon, 2pm-6pm). 20F (children: 5F). ☎ 05 65 35 04 35.

Église St-Barthélemy – Sun 9am-noon, by advance request. ☎ 05 65 35 06 80.

CARENNAC

Maison de la Dordogne Quercynoise – July to mid-Sept: 10am-7pm, Sat 2pm-7pm; April to June, 10am-1pm, 2pm-7pm, Sat 2pm-7pm; mid-Sept to Oct: 10am-1pm, 2pm-6pm, Sat 2pm-6pm. Closed Nov to March. 30F (children: 15F). ☎ 05 65 10 91 56.

Cloisters – July and Aug: 10am-7pm; March to June: 10am-noon, 1.30pm-6pm; Sept and Oct: 10am-noon, 1.30pm-5.30pm. 10F. ☎ 05 65 10 97 01.

CASTELNAU-BRETENOUX

Château fort – April to Sept: guided tour (30min, last admission 45min before closing), 9.30am-12.15pm, 2pm-6.15pm (July and Aug: 9.30am-6.45pm); Oct to March: daily except Tues 10am-12.15pm, 2pm-5.15pm. Closed holidays. 32F (children: 21F). ☎ 05 65 10 98 00.

CASTELNAUD

Château – May to Sept: 10am-7pm (July and Aug: 9am-8pm); March to April, Oct to mid-Nov and school holidays: 10am-6pm; mid-Nov to Feb, daily except Sat: 2pm 5pm. 35F (children: 18F). ☎ 05 53 31 30 00.

Vallée du CÉLÉ

Cuzals: Musée du plein air de Quercy – ♿ April to Oct, daily except Sat (unless holiday): 2pm-6pm (June to Aug: daily excpet Sat (unless holiday) 10am-7pm). 50F (off season: 40F). ☎ 05 65 22 58 63.

CÉNEVIÈRES

Château – ♿ Mid-April to Sept: guided tour (1hr) 10am-noon, 2pm-6pm; Oct: 2pm-5pm. 27F (children: 14F). ☎ 05 65 31 27 33.

CHÂLUS

Excursions

Château des Cars – July and Aug: daily except Tues 10am-6pm. 10F. ☎ 05 55 36 90 22 (town hall).

Ph. Clair/Éd. La Clé des Champs, Cahors

Quercy museum – Steam tractor

Chateau de Lastours – March to Nov: Sat, Sun and holidays 10am-7pm (mid-July to lid-August: daily except Mon 10am-7pm). 10F (by night with entertainment July and Aug: 25F). ☎ 05 55 58 38 47 or 05 55 58 34 78.

Château de Brie – April to Oct: guided tour (45min) Sun and holidays 2pm-7pm; 25F (children: 15F). ☎ 05 55 78 17 52.

Abbaye de CHANCELADE

Conventual buildings – ♿ July and Aug: 2pm-7pm? 25F (children: 10F). ☎ 05 53 04 86 87.

La CHÂTRE
🚩 square Georges Sand – 36400 ☎ 02 54 48 22 64

Musée George-Sand et de la Vallée Noire – July and Aug: 9am-7pm; Sept:June: 9am-noon, 2pm-7pm (Oct to March closes at 5pm). Closed Jan; 20F. ☎ 02 54 48 36 79.

George Sand Tour

La Berthenoux church – Daily except Tues, 9am-noon, 2pm-6pm.

Abbaye de Varennes – From Ascension Day (40 days after Easter) for two weeks. July and Aug: guided tour (15min) 1pm-7pm; Sun and holidays 10am-noon, 1pm-6pm. Free admission free.

Haute Vallée de l'Indre

Château de Sarzay – Daily 10am to nightfall. 30F (children: 15F). ☎ 02 54 31 32 25.

COUSSAC-BONNEVAL
🚩 Town hall – 87390 – ☎ 05 55 75 20 29

Château – Mid-March-Oct: guided tour (45min, last admission 30min before closing) 2.30pm-6pm (July-Sept closes 7pm). 35F (children: 15F). ☎ 05 55 75 24 15.

Vallée de la CREUSE

Ceaulmont: Château de Prune-au-Pot – Closed to visitors.

Gargilesse: church and crypt – Daily 10am-noon, 3pm-6pm.

Gargilesse: George-Sand's retreat, Aligra – April to Sept: guided tour (45min) 9.30am-12.30pm, 2.30pm-7pm. 25F. ☎ 02 54 47 84 14.

Éguzon: musée de la vallée de la Creuse – May-Sept: guided tour (45min) 10am-noon, 2pm-6.30pm; April: daily except Sun and holidays 2pm-6pm; Oct: Mon to Fri except holidays 2pm-6pm. Closed Jan and Feb. 20F. ☎ 02 54 47 47 75.

CROCQ
🚩 Town hall – 23600 – ☎ 05 55 67 49 02

Guided tour of the town – Contact the tourist office.

Towers of the former château – Mid-June to Sept: daily except Tues 11am-noon, 3pm-7pm. 10F

Ruines de CROZANT

April to mid-Nov: 10am-noon, 2pm-6pm; Sat, Sun and holidays 10am-noon, 2pm-7pm (July and Aug: 10am-noon, 2pm-7pm, Sat, Sun and holidays 10am-7pm). 10F. ☎ 05 55 89 80 12 (town hall).

Boat trips – April to Oct: guided tour (1hr15min), departure 2.45pm, 4pm (July and Aug: 2.45pm, 4pm, 5.30pm). Minimum 20 people required; 45F. Information at the Hotel du Lac, ☎ 05 55 89 81 96.

CULAN

Château – Mid-March to Nov: 10am-noon, 2pm-6pm (July and Aug: 10am-7pm). 40F (children: 23F). ☎ 02 48 56 64 18.

Church – Open Sundays from 4pm-7pm, or during the week contact the priest at the presbytery (2, rue Jeanne d'Arc).

D

DOMME
🚩 place de la Halle – 24250 – ☎ 05 53 28 37 09

Caves – April to Oct: guided tour (30min) 10am-noon, 2pm-6pm (July and Aug: 10am-7pm); Nov to March: 11.30am-noon, 2pm-5pm. Closed Jan. 33F (children: 18F) ☎ 05 53 31 71 00.

Musée d'Art et de Traditions populaires – April to Sept: daily except Sat 10am-12.30pm, 2.30pm-6pm (July and Aug: every day 10.30am-7pm). 17F; ☎ 05 53 31 71 00.

🅱 17, place de la Collégiale -87210- ☎ 05 55 60 76 81

Collégiale St-Pierre:

Crypt – July to mid-Sept: guided tour 2pm-6pm; mid-Sept to June: by request (at the toursit office).

Vallée de la DORDOGNE

The Great Dams

Spontour:

The Dordogne river by barge – July and Aug: daily; April to June and Sept to Oct, ask for information; five boarding points at Chastang, Pont de Chambon, Spontour, Chalvignac and Bort-les-Orgues. ☎ 05 55 27 68 05

The Quercy Stretch of the Dordogne

Grottes de Lacave – July and Aug: guided tour (1hr15min) 9.30am-6pm; March to June: 10am-noon, 2pm-6pm; Sept to 11 Nov: 10am-noon, 2pm-5pm. Closed 12 Nov to Feb. 42F children: 32F). ☎ 05 65 37 87 03.

Château de la Treyne – June to Sept: daily except Mon 9am-noon, 2pm-6pm. 20F children: 7F). ☎ 05 65 27 60 60.

The Périgord Stretch of the Dordogne

Château de Fénelon – June to Sept: guided tour (1hr) 9.30am-7pm; Oct to May: 10am-noon, 2pm-6pm. 35F children: 20F). ☎ 05 53 29 81 45.

Cénac: church – June to Sept: 9am-7pm; Oct to May: by prior request to parish priest *(M. le Curé)*. ☎ 05 53 28 32 73.

Château des Milandes – April to Sept: 10am-6pm (June to Aug: 9am-7pm); mid-Feb to March and Oct to Dec: 10am-noon, 2pm-5pm. 43F (children: 33F). ☎ 05 53 59 31 21.

Couze-et-St-Front: Moulin de la Rouzique – April to mid-Oct: guided tour (1hr30min) 2pm-6.30pm, mornings by request (one week in advance). 25F. ☎ 05 53 24 36 16.

Moulin de Larroque – Workshop: Mon to Fri 9am-noon, 2pm-5pm; shop: Mon to Sat 9am-noon, 2pm-6pm (Sat: closes 5pm). Closed holidays and between Christmas and New Year's. Workshop: 15F. ☎ 05 53 61 01 75.

Château de Lanquais – May to Sept: guided tour (45min) daily except Tues 10.30am-noon, 2.30pm-6pm (July and Aug: every day 10am-7pm); March, April and Oct: daily except Tues 2.30pm-6pm. 35F (children: 17F). ☎ 05 53 61 24 24.

La DOUBLE

Mussidan: Musée des Arts et Traditions populaires du Périgord André-Voulgre – Marc to Nov: guided tour (1hr30min) Sat, Sun and holidays 2pm-6pm (June to mid-Sept: every day 9.30am-noon, 2pm-6pm). Closed last 2 weeks of Sept, 1 May and Dec to Feb. 15F. ☎ 05 53 81 23 55.

Château de Neuvic – ♿ Guided tour (45min) 1.30pm-6.30pm. Closed 1 Jan and 25 Dec. Château and botanical gardend: 30F (children: 15F). ☎ 05 53 80 86 65.

Botanical garden – 10am-noon, 1.30pm-6.30pm (Oct to May: 10am-noon, 1.30pm-6.30pm, Sat, Sun and holidays 1.30pm-6.30pm). Closed 1 Jan and 25 Dec. 20F. ☎ 05 53 80 86 65.

E

ÉPINEUL-LE-FLEURIEL

L'École du Grand Meaunes – April to mid-Sept: 10am-noon, 2pm-6pm (July and Aug: daily except Tues 10am-7pm); mid-Sept to mid-Nov: 10am-noon, 2pm-(pm. 35F (children: 20F). ☎ 02 48 63 04 82.

EYMET

Museum – Mid-June to mid-Sept: by prior request daily except Sun, 3pm-6.30pm. 10F. ☎ 05 53 23 74 95.

Les EYZIES-DE-TAYAC
🅱 place de la Mairie – ☎ 05 53 06 97 05

Musée national de Préhistoire – Mid-March to mid-Nov: daily except Tues 9.30am-noon, 2pm-6pm (July and Aug: daily except Tues 9.30am-7pm); mid-Nov to mid-March: daily except Tues 9.30am-noon, 2pm-5pm. Closed 1 Jan and 25 Dec. 22F (children: 15F). ☎ 05 53 06 45 45.

Grotte de Font-de-Gaume – Same times and charges as the Grotte de Combarelles (see below).

Abri Pataud – April to Oct: daily except Mon 10am-12.30pm, 1.30pm-7pm (July and Aug: every day 10am-7pm); Nov to March: daily except Mon 10am-12.30pm, 1.30pm-5.30pm. Closed Jan and 25 Dec. 30F (children: 15F). ☎ 05 53 35 50 10.

Église de Tayac – Tour by request, Sun 11am-noon. Contact the town hall. ☎ 05 53 06 97 15.

Musée de la Spéléologie – Mid-June to mid-Sept: daily except Sat 11am-6pm. 20F (children: 10F); Open July and Aug daily from 11am-6pm; 20F (adults); 10F (children); Contact the town hall. ☎ 05 53 06 97 15.

Grotte de Carpe Diem – April to Oct: guided tour (30min) 10am-6pm (July and Aug: 9.30am-7pm); Nov to March: school holidays (daily except Mon) and Sun 10am-6pm. Closed 1 Jan and 25 Dec. 30F. ☎ 05 53 06 91 07.

Abri du Poisson – Same times and charges as Grotee de Laugerie Haute (below)

Grotte du Grand Roc – April to Oct: guided tour (30min) 9.30am-6pm (July and Aug: 9.30am-7pm); Nov to March: 10am-5pm (except Sat in Feb and Dec not during school holidays). Closed Jan. 38F (children: 20F). Entrance to Grand Roc and Laugerie-Basse: 48F (children: 25F). ☎ 05 53 06 92 70.

Habitats préhistoriques de Laugerie-Basse – ♿ April to Oct: 9.30am-6pm (July and Aug: 9.30am-7pm); Nov to March: 10am-5pm (except Sat in D+Feb and Dec). Closed Jan. 28F (children: 15F). Entrance to Grand Roc and Laugerie-Basse: 48F (children: 25F). ☎ 05 53 06 92 70.

Gisement de Laugerie Haute – ♿ April to Sept: guided tour by reservation (45min, last admission 1hr before closing) daily except Wed 9am-noon, 2pm-6pm; March and Oct: daily except Wed 9.30am-noon, 2pm-5.30pm; Nov to Feb: daily except Wed 10am-noon, 2pm-5pm. Closed 1 Jan, 1 May, 1 and 11 Nov, 25 Dec. 15F. Inquire at the Grotte de Font-de-Gaume. ☎ 05 53 06 90 80.

La Roque-St-Christophe – July and Aug: guided tour (45min) 10am-7pm; Sept to June: without guide 10am-6pm. 34F (children: 17F). ☎ 05 53 50 70 45.

Préhistoparc de Tursac – ♿ March to 11 Nov: 10am-6pm (July to Sept: 9.30am-7pm). 30F (children: 15F). ☎ 05 53 50 73 19.

Grotte des Combarelles – ♿ April to Sept: guided tour by reservation (45min, last admission 1hr before closing) daily except Wed 9am-noon, 2pm-6pm; mArch and Oct: daily except Wed 9.30am-noon, 2pm-7.30pm; Nov to Feb: daily except Wed 10am-noon, 2pm-5pm. Closed 1 Jan, 1 May, 1 and 11 Nov, 25 Dec. 35F (children: 23F) Inquire at the Grotte de Font-de-Gaume. ☎ 05 53 06 90 80.

Grotte de Bernifal – July and Aug: guided tour (1hr) 9am-7pm; June and Sept: 9am-noon, 2pm-6pm; Oct to May: By request. 30F. ☎ 05 53 29 66 39.

Abri du Cap-Blanc – April to Oct: guided tour (30min) April to Oct: guided tour (30min) 10am-noon, 2pm-6pm (July and Aug: 9.30am-7pm). 30F (children: 16F). ☎ 05 53 59 21 74.

F – G

Guided tours of the old town 🅰 – Contact the tourist office.

Musée de l'Hôtel de la Monnaie – July to mid-Sept: 10am-1pm, 2pm-7pm; May and Jun: 10am-noon, 2.30pm-6pm, Sun and holidays 10am-1pm; mid-Sept and Oct: 10am-12.30pm, 2pm-6.30pm, Sun and holidays 10am-1pm; Oct to April: Mon-Fri except holidays 11am-nonn, 2.30pm-5.30pm. Closed 1 Jan and 1 May. 10F. ☎ 05 65 34 06 25.

Musée Champollion – March to Oct: daily except Mon (unless holiday) 10am-noon, 2.30pm-6.30pm (July and Aug: every day); Nove to Feb: daily except Mon 2pm-6pm. Closed 1 Jan, 1 May, 25 Dec. 20F (children: 12F). ☎ 05 65 50 31 08.

Commanderie des Templiers – July to Sept: guided tour (1hr) 11am-noon, 3pm-7pm. 26F (children: free admission). ☎ 05 65 50 15 4734 48 11.

Excursions

Domaine de loisirs du Surgié – April to Sept: 9am-11pm. *Current rates not known, last rate 20F.* ☎ 05 65 34 59 00.

Cardaillac: Musée Éclaté – July and Aug: guided tour by request (2hr) Tues to Fri 3pm-6pm; Sept to June: by request. ☎ 05 65 40 10 63 (Annie Mage) or 05 65 40 15 65 (Roger Mazembert).

FOISSAC

Caves – July and Aug: guided tour (1hr, last admission 1hr before closing) 10am-7pm; June and Sept: 10am-12.30pm, 2pm-7pm; April, May and Oct: daily except Sat 2pm-7pm; Nov to March: by request. Closed 1 Jan, 1 and 11 Nov, 25 Dec. 34F (children: 22F). ☎ 05 65 64 77 04.

Excursion

Château de Larroque-Toirac – July to early Sept: guided tour (45min) 10am-noon, 2pm-6pm. 22F (children: 10F). ☎ 05 65 34 78 12.

GIMEL-LES CASACADES

Cascades – March to Oct: sunrise to sunset 20F. ☎ 05 55 21 26 49.

Excursion

Château de Sédières – July and Aug: guided tour (30min) 10am-noon, 2pm-7pm. 20F (children: 10F). ☎ 05 55 27 76 40.

GOURDON
🛈 24, rue du Majou – 46300 – ☎ 05 65 41 06 40

Guided tours of the town – Contact the tourist office.

Église des Cordeliers – July and Aug: by request. Contact the tourist office.

Excursions

Grottes de Cougnac – East to Nov 1: guided tour (1hr15min) 9.30am-11am, 2pm-5pm (July and Aug: 9.30am-6pm). 33F (children: 20F). ☎ 05 65 41 47 54.

Chapelle Notre-Dame-des-Neiges – Open by prior arrangement with the tourist office in Gourdon.

Le Vigan: Church – July and Aug: 10am-noon, 2pm-6pm; Sept to June: by request at the town hall. ☎ 05 65 41 12 90.

Musée Henri-Giron – ♿ May to Oct: daily except Mon 10am-noon, 3pm-6pm (July and Aug: daily except Mon 10am-6pm); Nov to April: by request. 15F. ☎ 05 65 41 33 78 (Mr. Hoving).

Causse de GRAMAT

Outing on the Causse

Parc animalier de Gramat – ♿ Easter to Sept: 9am-7pm; Oct to Easter: 2pm-6pm; 43F (children: 30F). ☎ 05 65 38 81 22.

Moulin de Cougnaguet – April to mid-Oct: guided tour 10am-noon, 2pm-6pm (July and Aug: 9.30am-noon, 2pm-7pm). *Current rates not known, last rate 16F.* ☎ 05 65 32 63 09.

GUÉRET
🛈 avenue Charles de Gaulle – 23000 – ☎ 05 55 52 14 29

Musée de la Sénatorerie – Mid-Jun to Oct: 9am-noon, 2pm-6pm; Nov to mid-June: 2pm-6pm. Closed holidays. 15F. ☎ 05 55 52 07 20.

Musée du présidial Louis-Lacrocq – ♿ Mid-June to Oct: 9am-noon, 2pm-6pm. Closed holidays. 15F. ☎ 05 55 52 07 20.

H

HAUTEFORT

Château – April to mid-Oct: guided tour (1hr, last admission 45min before closing) 10am-noon, 2pm-6pm (mid-July to Aug: 9.30am-7pm); school holidays: 2pm-6pm; mid-Nov to mid-Jan: Sun 2pm-6pm. Closed mid-Dec to mid-Jan. 32 F (gardens and grounds only: 25F). ☎ 05 53 50 51 23.

ISSOUDUN
🛈 place St-Cyr – 36100 – ☎ 02 54 21 74 02

Musée de l'Hospice St-Roch – ♿ April to Oct: 10am-noon, 2pm-7pm, Mon and Tues 2pm-7pm; Nov to March: daily except Tues 2pm-6pm, Sat, Sun and holidays 10am-noon, 2pm-6pm. Closed Christams to end Jan, 1 May, 1 and 11 Nov. Free admission. ☎ 02 54 21 01 76.

L

LABASTIDE-MURAT

Musée Murat – July to Sept: guided tour (1hr) 10am-noon, 3pm-6pm. 20F.

LASCAUX

Lascaux II – &. April to Sept: guided tour (45min) 9am-7pm; Oct: daily except Mon 9am-7pm; Feb, March, Nov and Dec: 10am-12.30pm, 1.30pm-5.30pm. Closed 1 Jan and 25 Dec. NB: In summer, the ticket office in in Montignac, at the toursit office. Ticket sales begin at 9am and stop when 2 000 have been sold (which can happen quickly in season). 50F (children: 25F); ticket with entrance to Thot museum included: 57F (children: 30F). ☎ 05 53 35 50 10.

Régourdou: prehistoric site – *Last known times and charges: March to Oct: guided tour 15min) by request (a week in advance) 9am-noon, 2pm-6pm (June to Aug: 9am-6.30pm); Nov to Feb: 10am-noon, 2pm-5pm. Site Préhistorique de Régourdou, 24290 Montignac-sur-Vézère. 25F (children: 15F). b 05 53 51 81 23.*

LEVROUX
🗎 rue Gambetta – 36110 – ☎ 02 54 35 70 54

Musée du Cuir et du Parchemin – Mid-June to mid-Sept: 10am-12.30pm, 2pm-6pm. 15F. ☎ 02 54 35 83 58.

Excursion

Château d'Argy – Easter to 1 Nov: guided tour ˈ=(1hr) 10am-noon, 2pm-6pm. 25F.

LIMOGES
🗎 boulevard de Fleurus – 8700 – ☎ 05 55 34 46 87

Guided tours of the town – Mid-June to mid-Sept: enquire at the tourist office.

Musée de l'Évêché – Musée de l'Émail – June to Sept: 10am11.45am, 2pm-6pm; Oct to May: daily except Tues 10am-11h45am, 2pm-5pm. Closed 1 Jan, 1 May, 1 and 11 Nov, 25 Dec. Free admission. ☎ 05 55 34 44 09.

Musée de la Résistance – &. Mid-June to mid-Sept: daily except Tues 10am-11.45am; 2pm-6pm; mid-Sept to mid-June: daily except Tues 2pm-5pm. Closed 1 Jan, 1 May, 1 and 11 Nov, 25 Dec. Free admission.

Remains of the Abbaye St-Martial – July to Sept: 9am-noon, 2pm-7pm. Free admission. ☎ 05 55 34 46 87 (Musée Municipal) or tourist office.

Maison de la Boucherie – July to Sept: guided tour (1hr) 9.30am-noon, 2.30pm-7pm. Free admission.

Musée National Adrien-Dubouché – Daily except Tues 10am-12.30pm, 2pm-5.45pm (July and August: 10am-5.45pm). Closed 1 Jan, 1 May, 25 Dec. 22F (children: free admission). ☎ 05 55 33 08 50.

Aquarium du Limousin – &. Mid-June to mid-Sept: 9.30am-7pm; mid-Sept to mid-June: 9.30am-noon, 2pm-7pm. 35F (children: 25F; under age 4: free admission). ☎ 05 55 33 57 33.

Musée des distilleries Limougeaudes – &. Tues to Sat: 8am-noon, 2pm-6pm. Closed hoidays. Fre admission. ☎ 05 55 77 23 57.

Basse vallée du LOT

Cliffs and Promontories

Capdenac: Musée du donjon – Mid-June to mid-Sept: 10am-noon, 2.30pm-7pm. 15F. ☎ 05 65 34 17 23 (town hall).

Meanders of Lower Reaches

Grézels: Château de la Coste – Guided tour (1hr) July and Aug: 4.30pm. 25F (children: 15F); ☎ 05 65 21 34 18.

Puy l'Évêque: Church – July and Aug: Mon to Fri 10am-noon, 3pm-6pm. ☎ 05 65 21 37 63.

LUZECH

Boat trips on the Lot – &. April to Sept: from the Caix marina, tours (1hr30min) 4.15pm-6.30pm. 45F (children: 25F). ☎ 05 65 20 18 19.

Musée archéologique Armand-Viré – May to Sept: 10am-12.30pm, 4.30pm-6.30pm. Free admission. ☎ 05 65 20 17 27.

Site de la MADELEINE

Village troglodytique – July and Aug: guided tour (45min) 9.30am-7pm; Sept to Jun: 10am-6pm. 30F (children: 17F). ☎ 05 53 06 92 49.

MARCILHAC-SUR-CÉLÉ

Grotte de Bellevue – *Current times and charges not known; last information: July and Aug: guided tour (45min) 10am-7pm; June and Sept: by request. 28F (children: 20F).* ☎ 05 65 40 63 92.

Carving on antler found at La Madeleine Site

Musée national des Eyzies

MASSERET

Le Mont Gargan

St-Germain-les-Belles: Church July and Aug: guided tour 9am-5pm. Information from the tourist office; ☎ 05 55 71 88 65.

MEHUN-SUR-YÈVRE

🚩 place du 14 Juillet -18500 – ☎ 02 48 57 35 51

Château-Musée Charles VII – Same times and charges as for Pôle de la Porcelaine (see above).

Château de MEILLANT

March to Oct: guided tour (45min) 9am-11.45am, 2pm-6.45pm; Feb and Nov: 9am-11.45am, 2pm-5.30pm. Closed Dec and Jan. 45F (children: 20F). 05 48 63 32 05.

Tours de MERLE

May to Sept an school holidays: 2pm-6pm (July and Aug: 10am-6pm); Feb to April, Oct and Nov: Sun and holidays 2pm-6pm. 23F Mid-July to mid-Aug: medieval pageant: 2.30pm-6.30pm. 40F. Soudn and light show: mid-July and Aug: 10pm; June: Sat 10.30pm; Sept: Sat at 9pm. ☎ 05 55 28 22 31.

MEYMAC

🚩 place de la Fontaine – 19250 – ☎ 05 55 95 18 43

Guided tours of the town – Contact the tourist office.

Fondation Marius-Vazeilles – Mid-April to mid-October: daily except Tues 10am-noon, 2.30pm-6.30pm. 15F.

Centre d'Art contemporain – July and Aug: daily except Tues 10am-noon, 2pm-7pm; Sept to June: daily except Tues 2pm-6pm (mornings by request). Closed during Christmas holidays. 25F. ☎ 05 55 95 23 30.

Plateau de MILLEVACHES

Domaine de Banizette – July and Aug, last 2 weekends in June and 1st 3 weekends in Sept: guided tour (1hr15min) 3pm, 4.15pm, 5.30pm; May, June and Sept to mid-Nov: Sun and holidays and 3pm. 30F (children: free admission). ☎ 05 55 83 28 55.

MONBAZILLAC

Château – June to Sept: 10am-12.30pm, 2pm-7.30pm (July and Aug: 10am-7.30pm); May and Oct: 10am-12.30pm, 2pm-7pm; April: 10am-noon, 2pm-6pm; Nov to March: daily except Mon 10am-noon, 2pm-5pm. Closed mid-Jan to mif Feb. 35F (children: 16F). ☎ 05 53 61 52 52.

Wine cellars – July and Aug: daily except Sun 10am-7pm; Sept to June: daily except Sun 10am-12.30pm, 1.30pm-7pm. Closed holidays. Free admission. ☎ 05 53 63 65 00.

MONPAZIER

🚩 rue Jean Galmot – 24540 – ☎ 05 53 22 68 59

Guided tours of the bastide – Contact the tourist office.

Château de MONTAIGNE

Mid-Feb to early Jan: guided tour (30min) Wed to Sun 9am-noon, 2pm-7pm. 18F. ☎ 05 53 58 60 56.

Plateau de Millevaches

Château de MONTAL

April to Oct: guided tour Sun to Fri 9.30am-noon, 2.30pm-6pm. 30F (children: 15F). ☎ 05 65 38 13 72.

MOUTIER-D'AHUN

Church – ♿ 10am-noon, 2pm-6pm. 12F. ☎ 05 55 62 57 55.

N

NANÇAY

Grenier de Villâtre – **Musée imaginaire du Grand Meaulnes** – Mid-March to mid-Dec: Sat, Sun and holidays 9.30am-12.30pm, 2.30pm-7.30pm, Mon-Fri by request (2 weeks in advance). 25F (children: free admission). ☎ 02 48 51 80 22.

Espace Ciel Ouvert – daily except Tues 9.30am-noon, 2pm-6pm. Closed last Mon before Christmas through Jan. 35F (children: 25F); with radio observatory admission: 50F.

Radio observatory – ♿ July and Aug: guided tour (1hr15min) at 10am, 11am, 3pm, 4pm; Feb to June and Sept to Mon before Christmas: daily except Tues at 10am and 4pm, Sat, Sun and holidays at 10am, 11am, 3pm, 4pm. Closed last Mon before Christmas through Jan. 25F (children: 20F); with planetarium: 50F. ☎ 02 48 51 18 18.

Plantarium – ♿ July and Aug: guided tour (1hr) at 10.30am, 11.30am, 2.30pm, 3.30pm, 4.30pm, 5.30pm; Feb to June and Sept to Mon before Christmas daily except Tues 11.30am, 2.30pm, 3.30pm, 5.30pm (additional tour Sat, Sun and holidays at 10.30am and 4.30pm).

NOHANT

Château – July and Aug and 3rd weekedn of Sept: guided tour (1hr) 9am-7.30pm (last admission 1hr before closing); April to June and Sept to mid-Oct: 9am-12.15pm, 2pm-6.30pm; mid-Oct to March: 10am-12.15pm, 2pm-4.30pm. Closed 1 Jan, 1 May, 1 and 11 Nov, 25 Dec. 35F. ☎ 02 54 31 06 04.

Abbaye de NOIRLAC

April to Sept: 9.45am-noon, 1.45pm-6.30pm (July and Aug: 9.45am-6.30pm); Oct to Jan: daily except Tues 9.45-noon, 1.45pm-5pm. Feb to March: 9.45am-noon, 1.45pm-5pm; Closed 1 Jan and 25 Dec. 35F (children: 20F). ☎ 02 48 62 01 01.

ORADOUR-SUR-GLANE
🅱 place du Champ-de-foire – 87520 – ☎ 05 55 03 13 73

Ruins – ♿ April to Sept: 9am-noon, 2pm-7pm (July and Aug: 9am-7pm); Oct to March: 9am-noon, 2pm-5pm. Closed 1 Jan, 1 May, 25 Dec. Free admission. ☎ 05 55 03 13 73 (tourist office).

Jardins du prieuré de Notre-Dame-d'ORSAN

Lat May to Nov: 10am-7pm. 48F (children: 24F). ☎ 02 48 56 27 50.

Excursion

Lignières: Château – ♿ July to Sept: 10am-12.15pm, 2pm-7pm; April to June and Oct: Sat, Sun and holidays 2pm-6pm. Closed Nov to March. 25F. ☎ 02 48 60 16 13.

P

Gouffre de PADIRAC

Aug: guided tour (1hr30min) 8am-7pm; July: 8.30am-6.30pm; April to June and Sept to Oct: 9am-noon, 2pm-6pm. *Rates not given.* ☎ 05 65 33 64 56.

PECH MERLE

Cave – Easter to Oct: guided tour (1hr) 9.30am-noon, 1.30pm-5pm. Maximul of 700 visitors admitted daily (reserve ina davnce in season). 44F (children: 30F). Off season: 44F (children: 25F). ☎ 05 65 31 27 05.

Musée Amédée-Lemozi – Same times and charges as Peche Merle, one ticket for both. ☎ 05 65 31 23 33.

PÉRIGORD NOIR

St-Crépin-et-Carlucet: Château de Lacypierre – ♿ Easter to Oct: guided tour by request (7 days in advance). ☎ 05 53 59 29 41.

Ste-Nathalène: Moulin de La Tour – ♿ July and Aug: guided tour (15min) Mon, Wed, Fri 9am-noon, 2pm-7pm, Sat 2pm-7pm (last admission 1+6.30pm); April to June and Sept: Wed et Fri 9am-noon, 2pm-7pm; Oct to March: Fri 9am-noon, 2pm-7pm. Closed Feb school holidays, 1 Jan, 1 Nov, 25 Dec. 25F. ☎ 05 53 59 22 08.

PÉRIGUEUX
🅱 Rond-Point Mataguerre, 26 place Francheville – 24000 – ☎ 05 53 53 10 63

Guided tours of the medieval and renaissance town 🅰 – Contact the tourist office.

Guided tours of the Gallo-Roman site – Contact the tourist office.

Église St-Étienne-de-la-Cité – daily except Sun and holidays 8am-7pm.Open daily (except Sundays and public holidays) from 8.30am-6.30pm; ☎ 05 53 53 21 35.

Tour Mataguerre – guided tour: contact the tourist office.

Hôtel de Lestrade – guided tour: contact the tourist office.

Domus du Bouquet – guided tour: contact the tourist office.

Tour de Vésone – guided tour: contact the tourist office.

Musée du Périgord – April to Sept: daily except Tues 11am-6pm, Sat and Sun: 1pm-6pm; Oct to March: daily except Tues 10am-5pm, Sat and Sun: 1pm-6pm. Closed holidays. 20F. ☎ 05 53 06 40 70.

Musée militaire du Périgord – April to Sept: daily except Sun 10am-noon, 2pm-6pm (last admission 30min before closing); Jan to March: Wed and Sat 2pm-6pm; Oct to Dec: daily except Sun 2pm-6pm. Closed holidays. 20F. ☎ 05 53 53 47 36.

Q – R

QUERCY BLANC
Saux: Church – Contact Montpezat town hall or presbytery. ☎ 05 63 02 08 31.

ROCAMADOUR
🅱 Hôtel de Ville – 46500 – ☎ 05 65 33 62 59

Guided tours of the Ecclesiastical City (Chapelle Notre Dame) Contact Pélerinage de Rocamadour, le château, 46500 Rocamadour; ☎ 05 65 33 23 23.

ROCAMADOUR

Lifts – ♿ July to Aug: 8am-10pm: May and June: 8am-8pm; Sept to mid-Nov: 8am-6pm; Feb school holidays to April and during Christams holidays: 9am-8pm. Closed mid-Nov to mid-Dec and Jan. 15F both ways, 11F one-way (children: free admission). ☎ 05 65 33 62 44.

Evening train ride – Mid-May to Aug: guided tour (30min) 9.45pm and 10.15pm (mid-June to mid-July: 10pm and 10.30pm); Easter to mid-May and late Aug to Sept: 9.30pm and 10pm. Departure porte du Figuier. 30F (children: 15F). ☎ 05 65 33 67 84 or ☎ 05 65 33 65 99.

Musée du Jouet ancien automobile – April to Sept: 10am-noon, 2pm-6pm; Oct to March, by request. 20F (children: 10F). ☎ 05 65 33 60 75.

Jean Lurçat tapestries (Hôtel de ville) – April to Sept: 10.30am-12.30pm, 1.30pm-6pm (mid-July Aug: 9.30am-7.30pm); Oct to March: 2.30pm-5.30pm. Closed 1 Jan and 25 Dec. 10F. ☎ 05 65 33 22 00.

Crypte St-Amadour – Included in the guided tour of the Ecclesiastical City (see above).

Chapelle-St-Michel – Included in the guided tour of the Ecclesiastical City (see above).

Musée d'Art sacré Francis-Poulenc – ♿ July and Aug: 10am-7pm; Sept to June: 10am-noon, 2pm-6pm. 28F (children: 15F). ☎ 05 65 33 23 30.

Ramparts – 8am-8pm. 13F. ☎ 05 65 33 23 23.

Rocher des Aigles – ♿ Easter to 1 Nov: 10am-noon, 2pm-6pm. 40F (children: 25F). ☎ 05 65 33 65 45.

L'Hospitalet

Grotte des Merveilles – April to 11 Nov: guided tour (30min) 10am-noon, 2pm-6pm (July and Aug: 9am-7pm). 30F (children: 15F). ☎ 05 65 33 67 92.

Féerie du rail (Euro-mini-land) – ♿ Mid-July to 3rd week of Aug: show (45min) at 10.45am, 11.30am, 1.45pm, 2.40pm, 3.30pm, 4.15pm, 5pm; mid June to mid-July: 11.15am, 2.40pm, 3.30pm, 4.15pm, 5pm; April to mid-June and Sept: 11.15am, 2.45pm, 4.30pm; Oct: 2.45pm, 4.15pm. Closed Nov to March. 35F (children: 23F). ☎ 05 65 33 71 06.

Forêt des Singes – ♿ April to Sept: 10am-noon, 1pm-6pm (July and Aug: 10am-7pm); Oct to 11 Nov: 1pm-5pm, Sat and Sun 10am-noon, 1pm-5pm. Closed 11 Nov. 35F (children: 20F). ☎ 05 65 33 62 72.

ROCHECHOUART   🖪 6, rue Victor Hugo – 87600 – ☎ 05 55 03 72 73

Musée départemental d'Art contemporain – Closed for renovations. Opening scheduled for autumn 2000.

La ROQUE-GAGEAC

Barge trips on the Dordogne: Les Caminades – ♿ Easter to 1 Nov: guided tour (1hr) 10am-6pm 45F (children: 25F). ☎ 05 53 29 40 95.

Rochechouart – Le château

Barge trips on the Dordogne: Les Norberts – April to Oct: guided tour (1hr). 45F (children: 25F). Reservations and information ☎ 05 53 29 40 44.

ROUFFIGNAC

Excursion

Grotte de Rouffignac – 🚹 NB: Number of admissions is limited. Easter to Oct: guided tour (1hr) 10am-11.30am, 2pm-5pm, Sun and holidays 11.30am-5pm (July and Aug: 9am-11.30am, 2pm-6pm, Sun and holidays 11.30am-6pm) 31F (children: 10F) ☎ 05 53 05 41 71.

S

ST-AMAND-DE-COLY

Former presbytery: Diaporama – July and Aug: 5pm-6.30pm. 15F. ☎ 05 53 51 83 49.

ST-AMAND-MONTROND ◼ place de la République – 18200 – ☎ 02 48 96 16 86

Musée St-Vic – Daily except Tues 10am-noon, 2pm-6pm, Sun and holidays 2pm-6pm. Closed 1 Jan, 1 May, 25 Dec. 12F. ☎ 02 48 96 55 20.

ST-CÉRÉ ◼ place de la République – 46400 – ☎ 05 65 38 11 85

Galerie du Casino – Mayto Sept: 9.30am-noon, 4pm-6.30pm, Sun 11am-7pm (May and June daily except Tues); Oct to April: daily except Tues and Sun 9.30am-noon, 4pm-6;30pm. Closed 1 Jan, 1 and 11 Nov, 25 Dec. Free admission. ☎ 05 65 38 19 60.

Atelier-musée Jean-Lurçat – Easter week and mid-July to Sept: 9.30am-noon, 2.30pm-6.30pm. 15F

Excursion

Grotte de Presque – March to Sept: guided tour (45min) 9am-noon, 2pm-6pm (July and Aug: 9am-7pm); Oct to mid-Nov: 10am-noon, 2pm-5pm. 33F (children: 16F50). ☎ 05 65 38 07 44.

ST-CIRQ-LAPOPIE

Musée Rignault (Château de la Gardette) – April to Oct: daily except Tues 10am-12.30pm, 2.30pm-6pm (July and Aug: closes 7pm). 15F. ☎ 05 65 31 23 22.

ST-JUNIEN ◼ place du Champ de Foire – 87200 – ☎ 05 55 02 17 93

Chapelle Notre-Dame-du-Pont – Mayto Sept: 2pm-6pm. ☎ 05 55 02 12 52.

ST-LÉON-SUR-VÉZÈRE

Le conquil – Easter to Oct: 10am-6pm (May to Sept: 10am-7pm). 28F (children: 17F). ☎ 05 53 51 29 03.

ST-LÉONARD-DE-NOBLAT ◼ rue Roger Salengros – 87400 – ☎ 05 55 56 25 06

Guided tours of the town – Contact the tourist office.

Musée Gay-Lussac – 🚹 Easter to 1 Nov: Sun 2pm-6pm (July and Aug: every day 10am-12.30pm, 2pm-6pm). Closed 14 July and 15 Aug. 10F ☎ 05 55 56 25 06 (tourist office) or ☎ 05 55 56 00 13 (town hall).

Historail – July and Aug: Mon to Fri 2pm-6pm. Closed holidays. 25F (children: 15F). ☎ 05 55 56 11 12.

ST-MARCEL

Archeological excavations – 🚹 Admission free; ☎ 02 54 24 47 31 (Musée d'Argentomagus).

Musée archéologique d'Argentomagus – 🚹 Daily except Tues: 9.30-noon, 2pm-6pm. Closed 1 Jan and 25 Dec. 20F (children: 10F). Tactile area for the visually impaired, and some labelling in braille. ☎ 02 54 24 47 31;

ST-YRIEIX-LA-PERCHE ◼ Town hall – ☎ 05 55 75 00 04

Musée de la Porcelaine – July and Aug: daily except Mon 9am-noon; Sept-June: Tues to Sat: 9am-noon, 3pm-7pm. Closed holidays. Free admission. ☎ 05 55 75 10 38.

SALIGNAC-EYVIGUES

Château – July and Aug: guided tour (30min) daily except Tues 10am-noon, 2pm-6pm. 25F (children: 15F). ☎ 05 53 28 81 70.

Excursion

Jardins d' Eyrignac – ♿ June to Sept: guided tour (45min) 9.30am-7pm; Oct to May: 10.30am-12.30pm, 2.30pm to nightfall. 35F (children: 20F) ☎ 05 53 28 99 71.

SANCERRE   🛈 avenue de Verdun – 18300 – ☎ 02 48 54 00 26

Tour des Fiefs – March to Oct: Sat, Sun and holidays 2pm-6pm. Free admission.

Le Sancerrois

Château de Maupas – July to early Sept: guided tour (45min) 2pm-7pm, Sun and holidays 10am-noon; Easter to June and mid- Sept to mid-Oct: 2pm-7pm. Closed mid-Oct to Easter. 40F (children: 25F). ☎ 02 48 64 41 71.

Along the canal

La Borne: Musée de la Poterie – School holidays periods and Sat, Sun and holidays all year: 3pm-7pm. Free admission. ☎ 02 48 26 96 21.

La Borne: Craft workshops – Same opening times as museum.

La Borne: Exhibition centre – Same opening times as museum.

La Borne: Musée Vassil Ivanoff – ♿ May to Sept: daily except Tues 2pm-6.30pm. 15F. ☎ 02 48 26 95 99.

Bannay: Jardin du Tisserand – ♿ July and Aug: 10.30am-7pm; mid-April to June, Sept and Oct: 2pm-6pm. Closed Nov to mid-April. 35F (children: 20F). ☎ 02 48 72 32 10.

SARLAT-LA-CANÉDA 🛈 Hôtel de Vienne, place de la Liberté – 24203 – ☎ 05 53 59 27 67

Guided tours of the town 🅰 – Contact the tourist office.

Musée Automobiles – ♿ July and Aug: 10.30am-7pm; May, June and Sept: daily except Mon 2.30pm-6.30pm; April: daily except Mon and Tues 2.30pm-6.30pm. 35F (children: 25F). ☎ 05 53 31 62 81.

Excursions

Château de Puymartin – April to early Nov: guided tour (45min) 10am-noon, 2pm-6pm (July and Aug: 10am-noon, 2pm-6.30pm). 30F (children: 16F). ☎ 05 53 59 29 97.

Cabanes du Breuil – ♿ Mid-March to mid-Nov: 10am-noon, 2pm-6pm (June to Sept: 10am-7.30); mid-Nov to mid-March: by request. 15F. ☎ 05 53 29 67 15.

SÉGUR-LE-CHÂTEAU

🛈 19230 – ☎ 05 55 98 72 45

Guided tours of the town – Contact the tourist office.

SOUILLAC

🛈 boulevard Louis-Jean-Malvy – 46200 – ☎ 05 65 37 81 56

Guided tours of the town – Contact the tourist office.

Musée national de l'Automate et de la Robotique – ♿ June to Sept: 10am-noon, 3pm-6pm (July to Aug 10am-7pm); April to May and Oct: daily except Mon 10am-noon, 3pm-6pm; Nov to March: daily except Mon and Tues 2pm-5pm. 30F (children: 15F). ☎ 05 65 37 07 07.

Musée des Attelages de la Belle Époque – ♿ July and Aug: 10.30am-1pm, 2pm-6.30pm; April to June, Sept and Oct: daily except Mon 10.30am-noon, 2.30pm-5pm (June and Sept: every day). 25F. ☎ 05 65 32 72 31.

Association Vassil Ivanoff

Stoneware vase – Ivanoff museum

T

LE THOT

Espace Cro-Magnon – April to Sept: 10am-7pm; Oct: daily except Mon 10am-7pm; Nov to March: daily except Mon 10am-12.30pm, 1.30pm-5.30pm. Closed Jan, 25 Dec. 30F (children: 15F). Le Thot and Lascaux II: 57F (children: 30F). July and Aug: tickets must be bought from the Point-Information arches in Montignac, (on the site during the rest of the year). ☎ 05 53 35 50 10.

TULLE

🛈 2, place Émile-Zola – 19000 – ☎ 05 55 26 59 61

Musée du Cloître – 9am-noon, 2pm-5pm; Wed and Sat 2pm-5pm only (April to Sept: closes at 6pm). Closed 1 Jan, 1 May, 1 Nov, 25 Dec. 15F. ☎ 05 55 26 22 05.

TURENNE

Excursion

Gouffre de la Fage – Mid-June to mid-Sept: guided tour (1hr) 9.30am-7pm: April to mid-June: unaccompanied visit 2pm-6.30pm; mid Sept to mid Oct: unaccopanied visit 2pm-5.30pm. 30F (children: 20F). ☎ 05 55 85 80 62 or 05 55 87 12 21.

U

USSEL

🛈 19200 – ☎ 05 55 72 11 50

Musée du Pays d'Ussel (Hôtel Bonnot de Bay) – July and Aug: 10am-noon, 2pm-7pm; Sept to June: by request 5 days in advance. Free admission free. ☎ 05 55 46 54 00 (town hall).

UZERCHE

🛈 Town hall – 19140 – ☎ 05 55 73 15 71

Centre régional de documentation sur l'archéologie du paysage – Mid-June to mid-Sept: 10.30am-12.30pm, 2.30pm-6.30pm; Mon 2.30pm-6.30pm only. 10F. ☎ 05 55 73 26 07.

V

Château de VALENÇAY

Château – April to Oct: 9.30am-6pm (July and Aug: 9.30am-7.30pm); March: 2pm-5pm (Sat and Sun 10am-5pm); Jan and Feb: Sat and Sun 2pm-5pm. Closed 1 Jan and 25 Dec. 52F château, grounds and automobile museum (children: 42F). ☎ 02 54 00 10 66.

Grounds – Same times and charges as château.

Musée de l'Automobile du Centre – Same times and charges as château.

CENTRE D'ART CONTEMPORAIN DE VASSIVIÈRE, Beaumont-du-Lac

Vassivière – Centre d'art contemporain

Lac de VASSIVIÈRE ▪ Maison du tourisme – Île de Vassivière – 87120 – ☎ 05 55 69 76 70

Guided tours of the Île de Vassivière – July and Aug: guided tour (1hr15min) at 4pm. 10F. ☎ 05 55 69 76 70.

Boat trips on the lake – Easter to 1 Nov: on board the Escale IV (1hr). 38F. Lunch and dinner cruises (3hr). Capacity 180 people. 150F-200F, depending on menu. Off-season, inquire first, as a minimum number of passengers is required for departure. ☎ 05 55 69 41 35.

Centre d'Art contemporain – April to Sept: 11am-7pm; Oct to March: 11am-6pm. Closed early Jan to mid-Jan and 25 Dec. 15F. ☎ 05 55 69 27 27.

Parc de sculpture – Maybe visited independently at any time of year; also included in guided tour of Centre d'Art contemporain (see above).

Vallée de la VÉZÈRE

Château de Losse – June to Aug: unaccompanied visit of grounds and ramparts; guided tour (45min) of the main part of interior 10am-7pm; Easter to May and Sept: 10am-12.30pm, 1.30pm-6pm. 32F (children: 16F). ☎ 05 53 50 80 08.

Castel-Merle: Museum – ♿ Guided tour (1hr) by request (1 day in advance). Contact the curator, René Castanet, le Bourg, 24290 Sergeac. *Price not given, last price: 10F.* ☎ 05 53 50 77 45.

Castel-Merle: Prehistoric site – Guided tour (1hr) by prior request (same number as the museum).

Index

Notes